Fish, Fur & Feathers

Fish and Wildlife
Conservation in Alberta
1905 - 2005

THE
FISH AND WILDLIFE
HISTORICAL SOCIETY

The Federation
of Alberta Naturalists

PRINTED NOVEMBER 2005

Published by The Fish and Wildlife Historical Society and the Federation of Alberta Naturalists

Additional copies of this book may be obtained by contacting the Federation of Alberta Naturalists at:

11759 Groat Road
Edmonton, Alberta
T5M 3K6
(780) 427-8124 www.fanweb.ca

Printed and bound at Friesens Printers
Altona, Manitoba, Canada

COVER PHOTOGRAPHS:

Enjoying Alberta's Fisheries Resource. COURTESY ALBERTA SUSTAINABLE RESOURCE DEVELOPMENT (FOREST PROTECTION IMAGE LIBRARY)

A Fish and Wildlife Officer Checking a Hunter. COURTESY B. STEVENSON

A Biologist Instructing Fish and Wildlife Officers at Training School. COURTESY B. STEVENSON

A Family Fishing, ca. 1930. COURTESY M. SULLIVAN

Two Youngsters Learning About Burrowing Owl Conservation. CREDIT: G. ERICKSON

Bob McClymont Working in the Provincial Wildlife Forensics Lab. COURTESY ALBERTA FISH AND WILDLIFE DIVISION

Biologist Gerry Kuzyk Collecting Information for Wolf Population Studies. COURTESY G. KUZYK

Biologist John Stelfox Conducting an Inventory of Large Ungulates in the Coalbranch Region. CREDIT: E. KELLERMAN

CANADIAN CATALOGUING IN PUBLICATION DATA

    Fish, fur & feathers : fish and wildlife conservation in Alberta
1905-2005 / the Fish and Wildlife Historical Society.

Includes index.
Co-published by the Fish and Wildlife Historical Society.
ISBN 0-9696134-7-4

    1. Wildlife censervation--Alberta--History. 2. Fishes-
Conservation--Alberta--History. I. Federation of Alberta Naturalists
II. Fish and Wildlife Historical Society III. Title: Fish, fur and
feathers.

QL84.26.A4F57 2005   333.95'4'160971230904   C2005-906563-X

DEDICATED TO

We dedicate this book to the many Albertans who devoted their lives to the management and conservation of fish and wildlife over the past century.

Within government, this includes Fish and Wildlife Managers, Biologists, Technologists and Technicians; Game Guardians, Fish and Wildlife Officers, and Conservation Officers; Forest Officers and Rangers; Park Wardens, Rangers, and Interpreters; and technical and administrative support staff. Outside of government, it includes consultants, naturalists, conservationists, hunters, anglers, trappers, guides and outfitters, professors, graduate students, and other fish and wildlife enthusiasts. And finally, it includes the many landowners, landholders, and land managers who retained fish and wildlife on the landscape by successfully integrating habitat needs with other land-use priorities. Through the combined interest and commitment of all of these forces, Alberta has retained in large part, a healthy and diverse fish and wildlife heritage throughout the 20th century.

Equally important, we also dedicate this book to those who are just beginning their careers in fisheries, wildlife, biodiversity, and habitat management and conservation, yet will make significant contributions to maintaining this provincial legacy throughout the 21st century and beyond. By providing this archive of historical events, we hope new managers will be better able to meet the challenges of the future. Herein we recall the good and the bad, the successful, and the not-so-successful programs. We leave it to those who come after us to build on the successes and to avoid repeating the mistakes of the past. To them, we recall the words of retired Wildlife Research Biologist Bill Wishart addressing the attendees of the May 26, 1999 Fisheries and Wildlife Management Workshop:

"First of all, you are in one of the best professions there is and you are doing a great job with the resources at hand. Your best attribute is your passion and dedication to the fish and wildlife resources…enjoy what you do!"

Table of Contents

Foreword

Kevin Van Tighem, Jasper, Alberta

The young Earl of Southesk may have been Alberta's first tourist when he made his swing through the wind-swept ranges at the head of the Brazeau River drainage back in the late 1850s. The shots he and his party fired along the ridges above the Cairn River may have been the first gunshots ever to echo down from those heights, if the rumour he reported was true, that aboriginal people in the area did not hunt so far up that drainage.

i

Over the course of a week, the English lord and his party of Mètis and Iroquois guides killed more than thirty bighorn sheep, a smaller number of marmots and porcupines and, much to his chagrin, no grizzly bears. "I did not look back on the previous day's slaughter with unmingled pleasure," the Earl wrote in his day-log after the biggest kill of their trip, but then qualified his regrets with the excuse that "… a man who travels thousands of miles for such trophies may be excused for taking part in one day's rather reckless slaughter. After all, there were not more than twelve killed, and a few wounded, out of a very large herd, which perhaps may never again be alarmed by the sight of man."

Southesk left, but others remained, and our numbers grew. In 1905, when Alberta became a province in the young land of Canada, gunshots were no longer a novelty to the wild things that lived among the high peaks, forests, plains, and valleys of this sprawling landscape that spills east from the Continental Divide. Nor was the self-indulgent young Englishman the last game-hog to excuse his greed with the comfortable rationalization that the frontier's wealth of fur, fish, and game would go on forever.

On the wall behind my desk at work is a framed photograph of my grandfather, taken in 1929. On a line stretched between two pine trees he and his fishing partner have hung thirty-six huge trout. Three are monster bull trout; the rest are rainbows caught off their spawning beds between Upper and Lower Kananaskis Lakes. I remember my grandfather's voice from the childhood afternoons I spent listening to him weave Alberta's wild places into tales of wilderness exploration, giant bull trout, grizzly bears, and flocks of ducks so vast that you could not shoot without bringing down three or four at one shot. It seemed unbelievable that fate would have put me down on a part of the earth that could produce such stories, such opportunity. But when I was old enough to venture out into the places he told me about, the big fish were gone and there were no grizzly tracks along the streams. Something had gone missing; Alberta was not what I had been promised.

I was born when Alberta was already close to fifty years old, a century after Southesk's tour of destruction, and the year that the Alberta government hired its first professional wildlife biologist. I have an old copy of Alberta's hunting ii

regulations for that year which prohibit the shooting of any deer southeast of Calgary—because there were so very few. That same year, a major poisoning campaign was underway to eradicate wolves, coyotes, and the risk of rabies from as much of the province as possible. I grew up knowing that if I wanted to see a wolf, I would need to head north of Nordegg, and that grizzly bears survived almost exclusively in the big mountain national parks of Banff, Jasper and Waterton. It was not until I was well into my teens that I saw my first deer east of Calgary. The contradiction between the Alberta I imagined and the one I actually lived in was never so clear as the day I learned that the Sheep River downstream from Turner Valley was polluted with petroleum residues; it just didn't seem possible that a place of such natural wealth and beauty could also be polluted. Surely those things only happened in other, lesser places where people didn't care?

Others less naïve than me had recognized years earlier that frontier myths, growing human populations, and expanding access into Alberta's wild lands were all conspiring to make this place far less than it had been, and what it ought to be. Conservationists were already hard at work protecting and restoring Alberta's natural wealth— from progressive-minded farmers and ranchers, to organizations like local fish and game clubs, and Ducks Unlimited, to the many professionals working in provincial and federal resource agencies. And so, among my earliest memories of hunting pheasants in the Western Irrigation District, fishing for trout along the East Slopes, and hiking into the breathless high country of Banff National Park, are scattered encounters with Fish and Wildlife officers, biologists, and national park wardens. Handing over a fishing or hunting licence to be examined by a uniformed officer always engendered in me a sense of pride that I was living up to my part of the conservation equation, and confidence that others were watching out for those who weren't.

My father, uncle, brother and I hunted Camp Wainwright the first year that it was opened for deer hunting, back in 1967. I was newly turned

fourteen, licensed to carry my own gun for the first time, and wild with excitement about my first big game hunt. Late one afternoon, having managed to ditch my Dad, I spotted a big mule deer buck standing beside a clump of wolf willow. The camp commander had instructed us to shoot only antlerless deer until he and the Fish and Wildlife staff supervising the hunt could clarify some contradictions in the information they had received. Fortunately, there was another deer bedded in front of the buck and in my naïveté I assumed that that deer, which I couldn't see as well, must logically be a doe. So I shot it. Much to my horror and my father's wrath, it proved to be a large four-by-four buck.

Years later, I still remember the combination of professional rigour and human compassion that I encountered when we arrived at the check station to turn my first deer over to Al Boggs, the fish and wildlife officer in charge. The deer was seized, I received a stern talking-to, and my annoyed father treated me to a further lecture as we drove home through the mid-winter darkness. Everyone made it clear to me that I was lucky not to have been charged with a poaching offence.

Then, two weeks later, officer Al Boggs arrived on our doorstep with my deer—head, hide and butchered meat. When the clarification on the hunt rules had arrived from head office in Edmonton the day after our hunt, the biologists and conservation officers supervising the hunt learned that it was intended to be an either-sex season. Feeling sorry for the young kid whose first deer he'd had to seize, Mr. Boggs went well above-and-beyond the call of duty to return it to me. And I've never forgotten, nor ceased to be grateful. These are the kinds of people who take care of Alberta's fish and wildlife, and it is little wonder that they are held in such high esteem by so many of us who benefit from their work.

Originally, conservation work in Alberta was focussed on inventorying game populations and protecting dwindling stocks from poachers and predators. As the Province's population and economy grew, the challenges facing fish and wildlife became more complex, and programs were added or adapted to deal with habitat protection, wildlife disease, problem wildlife and land-use planning. It has doubtless been daunting for biologists, technicians, and officers to have to deal repeatedly with priority changes, re-organizations, budget cuts, and new conservation problems, but there can be no doubt that during my half of Alberta's first century their efforts have continued to pay off.

Where a century ago, the settled parts of Alberta were running out of deer and elk, today there are so many that the big challenges are reducing crop damage and road collisions. Where over-fishing and wanton destruction of native fish like the bull trout were once the biggest challenge along Front Range streams, today there are so many anglers eager to release their catch alive that the Province has brought in barbless-hook rules to reduce handling injuries. In recent years, grizzly bears have been appearing as far east as Milk River and Claresholm, and wolves have re-populated the southern foothills; now instead of trying to stave off extinction for our native predators, the challenge is finding ways for people to coexist safely with them.

A few years ago, I was at the University of Montana in Missoula to do research for a book I was writing on deer and elk. Jack Ward Thomas, recently retired as head of the U.S. Forest Service and newly appointed to the Boone and Crockett Chair at the university, was kind enough to agree to an interview. A soft-spoken and courtly Texan with a lifetime of experience in practical conservation, he summarized his views on the challenge for fish and wildlife professionals as Alberta enters her second century. "Conservation in the twentieth century," he said, "was about dealing with the consequences of failure. Conservation in the twenty-first century will be about dealing with the consequences of success."

That may be so, but other challenges will test the mettle of the men and women who work to conserve our shared heritage of fish, wildlife and habitat. Perhaps the most daunting of those

challenges is to conserve nature in a changing society where fewer and fewer modern Albertans have any day-to-day contact with nature or understanding of their own history. A society that lacks memory and connectedness is a society only partly conscious—and at risk of repeating old mistakes or making new ones.

The spawning beds where my grandfather and his friend slaughtered so many huge trout three-quarters of a century ago are flooded now beneath a hydroelectric reservoir. While the scene of his bighorn slaughter is now protected in a national park, much of the terrain through which the Earl of Southesk travelled fifty years earlier on his way there is being stripped for coal. New diseases fester behind game farm fences or in the mud caked on visiting anglers' boots. The three million modern Albertans whose day-to-day choices will decide the fate of fish and game—and the agencies and groups that work to conserve them—are addicted to energy royalties that come at the expense of habitat fragmentation by roads and pipelines, and are ideologically resistant to the idea of having their activities regulated. The future of fish and wildlife depends, increasingly, on the decisions of an urban, industrialized society so distracted by digital information and entertainments that people seldom even think about the fact that they live embedded in nature.

But most of those people also love this place called Alberta. And books like this can help them to understand its history and the history of the people who serve, on their behalf, to keep it the rich and wonderful place it was meant to be. Conservation faces many challenges today, but it faced no fewer a generation, two generations, or three generations ago. And the professionalism, creativity, collegiality and determination of Alberta's many professional and volunteer conservationists has, each step of the way, risen to overcome the challenges unique to each stage of our shared journey through time. That's a source of pride, and of promise, for the fish, wildlife and people of one of the world's great places—the province of Alberta.

Editors' Note

Through the tremendous efforts of countless volunteers, this book presents an overview of the conservation of Alberta's fish and wildlife over the past century. At times, it dips into finite detail and personal insights; however, the book is not, nor was it ever intended to be, an exhaustive look at the topic at hand. Instead, limited by time and space, we scratch the surface of one hundred years of history in the hopes that others will be spurred on to dig deeper, provide spin-off publications, or simply think long and hard about from whence we came. If nothing else, we trust the publication will pique the reader's interest, as it has our own.

This is not an academic work, although we believe academics will certainly find it useful. Regardless of training and background, students and professors of natural resources will find much here. We hope both researchers and professionals alike will learn and absorb from those who went before. For those who want to delve more deeply into a subject, we have, wherever possible, referred the reader to more specific works. We also strongly encourage students, academics, historians, and others to consider more detailed study in this area. We welcome and encourage any inquiries where we may be able to offer guidance, advice, or materials to support such endeavours. Over the life of the project, a number of archival materials were gathered and can be made available to researchers through the Society. You will find that the history of fish and wildlife management in Alberta is a deep, deep pool, rich in stories and personalities and fully worthy of more in-depth research and understanding.

While it is also worthy of telling, this book does not include in any detail the aboriginal experience with fish and wildlife stretching back over the eons before European arrival. The topic is beyond the scope of this book and other than brief mention, we leave that history to someone more qualified than us to tell.

And finally, as with any historical work, it is unlikely that this book is free of error. We often found ourselves working from faded memories, differing interpretations, or incomplete written work. The editors ask forgiveness for any incorrect names, dates, or omissions. We also encourage readers to submit any such corrections, comments and clarifications to the Society for future publication efforts.

PLEASE SEND YOUR COMMENTS TO:
The Fish and Wildlife Historical Society
c/o Federation of Alberta Naturalists
11759 Groat Road, Edmonton, Alberta
T5M 3K6

The mission of the Fish and Wildlife Historical Society is "to encourage and participate in projects that promote and document the history of fish and wildlife management and conservation in Alberta and elsewhere". The three animals in the Society logo are the provincial symbols for fish, mammal, and bird. These animals also reflect the title of our book (fish, fur and feathers), the three primary components of wildlife habitat (water, land and air), and the three eras of fish and wildlife management. Bull trout are at risk in Alberta and symbolize the need for **preservation** of our native species. Bighorn sheep are rugged emblems of our game species and reflect successful **conservation.** Great-horned owls are a popular and conspicuous predator species, once maligned, but now used in many education programs promoting the need for **shared stewardship** of the landscape.

Acknowledgements

"Nothing great was ever achieved without enthusiasm."
RALPH WALDO EMERSON (1803 - 1882)

This book is the result of an enthusiastic volunteer effort to compile more than a century of details on the history of fish and wildlife conservation in Alberta. The Fish and Wildlife Historical Society is particularly indebted to Linda Westwood[1] and Eric Holmgren[2] whose earlier works provided the foundation for this effort. As well, the periodical *Alberta Lands-Forests-Wildlife* (later *Alberta Lands-Forests-Parks-Wildlife*), published at intervals by the Government of Alberta between 1958 and 1970, provided an excellent source of articles reflecting the people, problems and solutions during this exciting period of research and growth. This body of work continues to provide the foundation of many of today's wildlife management policies. As a profession, fisheries and wildlife managers in Alberta should lament the loss of such a treasure and focus their energies on bringing about its resurrection. The book was also greatly enhanced by the addition of photographic material from several sources including Alberta Sustainable Resource Development (Forest Protection Image Library and Fish and Wildlife Division), Ducks Unlimited Canada Archives, Glenbow Archives, Provincial Archives of Alberta, Royal Alberta Museum, University of Alberta Archives, Bob Stevenson personal collection and numerous individual contributors.

The ability of Alberta's fish and wildlife community to rise to any challenge put before them has been a continuous thread throughout the century. This project has been no different and we are extremely pleased to have had the financial and in-kind support of the following agencies, conservation organizations, and individuals:

vii

SPONSORING ORGANIZATIONS:

Alberta Conservation Association
Funded by Alberta Anglers, Hunters, and Other Conservationists

SUSTAINABLE RESOURCE DEVELOPMENT

Alberta NAWMP Partnership

SUPPORTERS:

ALBERTA LOTTERY FUND

ASPB

ALBERTA SPORT, RECREATION PARKS & WILDLIFE FOUNDATION
Enhancing Alberta's Communities

APOS

Ken Crutchfield

DELTA Helicopters Ltd.

Brad Stelfox, FOREM TECHNOLOGIES

Karvonen Films

Northwest Section of the Wildlife Society

Shell Environmental Fund

Strathcona County

IN-KIND SUPPORT:

A work of this magnitude can neither be achieved alone nor in isolation. With much appreciation, we acknowledge the following individuals for their tremendous contributions of time and energy:

MANAGING COMMITTEE

Ernie Ewaschuk, Gordon Kerr, Don Meredith, the late Dr. Martin Paetz, Margo Pybus, Blair Rippin, Petra Rowell, Bob Stevenson, Jim Struthers, and Bill Wishart

EDITORIAL AND PUBLICATION SUPPORT

Jim Burns, Kim Dacyk, Dave Ealey, Robin Leech, Cheryl Lund, Martin McNicholl, Karen Rimney and Glen Semenchuk

CONTRIBUTORS (OF RECORDS, STORIES, INSIGHTS, PHOTOGRAPHS, COMMENTS, REVIEWS, ETC.)

Tom Bateman, Ron Bjorge, Dave Boag, John Bourne, Mark Boyce, Jim Burns, Gary Byrtus, Brett Calverley, Grant Campbell, Lu Carbyn, Sue Clarke, Glen Clements, Norm Cool, Sue Cotterill, Gordon Court, Cheryl Croucher, Ken Crutchfield, Dawn Dickinson, Pat Dunford, Lionel Dunn, Dave Ealey, Deryl Empson, Gary Erickson, Ernie Ewaschuk, Dave Fairless, Jan Ficht, Cam Finlay, Joy Finlay, Randy Flath, Lee Foote, Bill Fuller, Vic Gillman, John Girvan, Bill Glasgow, Chuck Gordon, Jan Hall, Brian Hammond, Gordon Haugen, Len Hill, Michelle Hiltz, Craig Hockley, Carl Hunt, Martin Jalkotzy, John Kenny, Gordon Kerr, Marilyn Kerr, Floyd Kunnas, Gerry Kuzyk, Archie Landals, Glen Lawrence, Robin Leech, Guy L'Heureux, Ken Lungle, Diane Markham, Bob McClymont, Dennis McDonald, Don Meredith, Beth Michener, George Mitchell, Dave Moyles, Fred Neuman, Carol Paetz, Ernie Psikla, Margo Pybus, Lew Ramstead, Blair Rippin, Grace Rippin, Martin Robillard, Petra Rowell, Bill Samuel, Kelly Semple, Nyree Sharp, Chris Shank, Joyce Shaw, Brad Stelfox, Harry Stelfox, John Stelfox, George Sterling, Bob Stevenson, Nadine Stiller, Jim Struthers, Michael Sullivan, Dennis Surrendi, Arlen Todd, Bruce Turner, Pat Valastin, Kevin Van Tighem,

George Walker, Bob Webb, Rhonda Weir, Heather Wheeliker, Francine Wieliczko, Jay Wieliczko, Daryl Wig, Kevin Wingert, Bill Wishart, Pat Wishart, Ken Wright, Ken Zelt, Wendy Zelt and everyone else who took the time to discuss this project with us.

RESEARCH ASSISTANCE

Sue Clarke, Coral Grove, Beth Michener, Nyree Sharp, Mona Southron, and Francine Wieliczko

INTERVIEWERS

Margo Pybus, Petra Rowell, Jim Struthers, Pat Valastin, Francine Wieliczko, and Bill Wishart

INTERVIEWEES

Ken Ambrock, Morley Barrett, Eldon Bruns, Harold Carr, Buck Cunningham, David dePape, Gary Erickson, Bert Freeman, Jacki Gerwing, Jan Hall, Gordon Kerr, Marilyn Kerr, Diane Markham, Terry McFadden, Gerry McKeating, George Mitchell, Carol Paetz, Gerry Pelchat, Grace Rippin, Winfried Schenk, Joyce Shaw, John Stelfox, Bruce Turner, Bob Webb, Dennis Weisser, Pat Wishart, Bill Wishart, and Wendy Zelt

ARCHIVE, DATABASE, PHOTOGRAPHIC AND LIBRARY SUPPORT

Peter J. Murphy and Robert E. Stevenson: Historical Forestry Photograph Collection, Forest Protection Division, Alberta Sustainable Resource Development, Edmonton • Raymond Frogner, University of Alberta Archives, Edmonton • Staff of the Alberta Agriculture, Food and Rural Development Library, Edmonton • Staff of the Alberta Environment Library, Edmonton • Staff of the Canadian Wildlife Service Library, Edmonton • Staff of the Glenbow Archives, Calgary • Staff of the Provincial Archives of Alberta, Edmonton • Staff of the Royal Alberta Museum, Edmonton • Staff of the Whyte Museum of the Canadian Rockies, Banff • Stuart Nadeau, Fish and Wildlife Division, Alberta Sustainable Resources Development, Edmonton • Sarah Primeau, Land Stewardship Centre of Canada, Edmonton • Ted Sheard, Saskatchewan Archives, Regina

COVER/BOOK DESIGN/LAYOUT

Judy Fushtey, Broken Arrow Solutions Inc.

PRINTER

Friesens Printers

References

[1] Westwood, Linda. 1977. Background Report on History of Government Administration of Fish and Wildlife Resources in Alberta. Unpublished report prepared for the Department of Recreation, Parks and Wildlife, Fish and Wildlife Division, Edmonton.

[2] Holmgren, Eric J. 1986. Fish and Wildlife Management in Alberta: A History. Unpublished report prepared for the Department of Forestry, Lands and Wildlife, Fish and Wildlife Division, Edmonton.

Prologue

In the Beginning

I killed a fisher today. There are many of this animal about the woody hills, as also of wolverines. Buffalo, red deer [elk], moose, and small deer are also plentiful and grizzled bears but too many.[1]

DAVID THOMPSON NEAR ROCKY MOUNTAIN HOUSE, OCTOBER 12, 1800

■ ■ ■

When Europeans first arrived in the territory that would become Alberta, they couldn't help but notice the amazing array of flora and fauna spread throughout the vast landscape.

Fur traders and explorers marvelled at the variety of species, writing at length in journals and letters, describing wildlife conditions in detail for posterity. At the turn of the 19th century, David Thompson, one of the premier surveyors and traders in the West, was particularly impressed and noted deer, moose, and "reindeer" [caribou] in seemingly endless numbers. These written observations, added to the wealth of information in aboriginal oral history and traditions, give a picture of immense diversity and abundance.

To all those who beheld this spectacle, there was no doubt that the plentiful fish and game would last forever. Unfortunately, the myth of superabundance was soon to be proven false. By 1870, what was once everlasting was now showing signs of depletion. In a few short years, huge tracts of land across the West were largely emptied of game—a situation that extended into the settlement era and beyond. The principal cause of this decline was excessive hunting: first to feed the fur traders who in turn were feeding the insatiable commercial fur markets in faraway lands, then to feed the rail crews laying the foundations of a new nation. And finally, the new settlers moved in and took their toll. The final blow in the settlement era was—and continues to be—the destruction of wildlife habitat. Humans do not share the landscape well. Increasing demand for urban and agricultural lands, mineral and fibre supplies, and recreational and scenic terrains was a dominant theme throughout the last century and will continue to be so into the next.

2

BISON AT WAINWRIGHT BUFFALO NATIONAL PARK, ca. 1920s.
COURTESY OF: B. STEVENSON

A HERD OF ELK AT THE WAINWRIGHT BUFFALO NATIONAL PARK, ca. 1920s.
COURTESY OF: B. STEVENSON

3

Fortunately, a number of individuals not only noticed the significant declines in wildlife populations, they also took the initiative to do something about it. During treaty negotiations between the government and the Plains Cree in 1876, Chief Sweetgrass pleaded (unsuccessfully) for the protection of the few remaining buffalo.[2] But the time was not yet right for such enlightened thought. Trading companies also tried to introduce measures to reduce the destruction of game populations during the fur trade, mainly limiting hunting to certain times of the year. Although these restrictions went largely unheeded, the continuing devastation of wild populations could not be ignored. With time and persistence, a new philosophy towards fish and wildlife slowly entered the social conscience.

By 1883, the governing body of the Northwest Territories (then including the area of the future Alberta) implemented and, later, strengthened modest game regulations with the first *Ordinance for the Protection of Game*. Then, shortly after becoming a province in 1905 and 25 years before receiving full legal responsibility for it, a young Alberta put into legislation a system of game laws and game guardians to protect and conserve its fish and wildlife resource. These early actions provided the foundation for many of the management programs we have today. Thus, the history of fish and wildlife conservation in Alberta stretches back over more than a century, and is a rich and colourful tapestry waiting to be explored.

So, as we let the journey begin, prepare to enjoy…and to learn!

In a mere hundred years, the responsibility for fish and wildlife management has grown from a handful of volunteer game guardians to a diverse array of federal and provincial government biologists, technicians, and enforcement officers, with strong proponents within the professional, academic, and conservation communities throughout the province. This diversity is necessary in today's complex world, where a growing number of users place an increasing number of stresses on all wild species and the habitats on which they depend.

To make some sense out of this complexity, in the following chapters we review a number of historical subject areas. We introduce the province's prehistory in Chapter One (*Pre-1905: Setting the Stage*) and government mandate towards fish and wildlife in Chapter Two (*A Provincial Mandate: the Alberta Fish and Wildlife Division*). We then follow with three general "eras" of wildlife management as it played out over the century including

preservation (protecting game species by establishing parks and reserves), *conservation* (using science to better manage a renewable resource), and *shared stewardship* (integrating wildlife and their habitat needs with other resource and environmental management at the landscape or ecosystem level). While not everyone will agree with the use of this framework, we remind the reader it is only that—a framework—and a starting place from which to begin our explorations.

Our study deals with Alberta, but it is hoped that those who read it will realize the necessity of preserving what is a precious resource and that they will perhaps look further afield at what else is happening worldwide. For only with awareness, can fish and wildlife be preserved for posterity.[3]

ERIC J. HOLMGREN

References • PROLOGUE

[1] Hopwood, Victor G. (ed.). 1971. David Thompson: Travels in Western North America, 1784 – 1812. The Macmillan Company of Canada Limited, Toronto.

[2] MacEwan, Grant. 1995. Buffalo: Sacred & Sacrificed. Alberta Sport, Recreation, Parks and Wildlife Foundation, Edmonton.

[3] Holmgren, Eric J. 1986. Fish and Wildlife Management in Alberta: A History. Unpublished report prepared for the Department of Forestry, Lands and Wildlife, Fish and Wildlife Division, Edmonton.

Chapter 1

PRE-1905:
SETTING THE STAGE

Jim Burns and Petra Rowell with contributions from Sue Clarke and Don Meredith

Wilderness is a necessity…They will see what I meant in time. There must be places for human beings to satisfy their souls. Food and drink is not all. There is the spiritual. In some it is only a germ, of course, but the germ will grow.
JOHN MUIR, 1838-1914[1]

Alberta's Changing Landscapes

In its history exceeding the last two and a half billion years, the geographical area that was to become Alberta underwent numerous physical changes including four mountain-building episodes. During the dinosaur-dominated Cretaceous, the land supported rich tropical forests that were later submerged by periodic incursions of both the Pacific and Arctic oceans. Climatic changes brought an ebb and flow of warming and cooling periods and, subject to climatic and other physical forces, Alberta was "created, moulded, shaped and reshaped, and borne from distant latitudes and far meridians to its present dwelling place".[2]

These forces created the mountain, foothills, forest, parkland, and prairie landscapes Albertans are so familiar with today. Wildlife that occupied these changing landscapes also changed over time from strange aquatic fauna dwelling on the rich Devonian-aged coral reefs near Leduc about 375 million years ago; to thundering herds of Cretaceous dinosaurs near Drumheller about 75 million years ago; to majestic mammoths, lions, and camels around Edmonton late in the Ice Age about 30,000 years ago; and to periods almost devoid of species as wildlife retreated south when glaciers reigned dominion over the land. Alberta's wild fauna has a long and diverse history.

ALBERTA'S OLDEST ROCKS
Alberta's oldest rocks, just over two billion years old, are found in the Canadian Shield area of Wood Buffalo National Park. Just to the north of this area, rocks near Yellowknife, Northwest Territories, are dated at around 3.8 billion years old. The oldest rocks in Canada are from northern Quebec, dating from 3.825 billion years before present.

In the more recent past, wildlife occupying Alberta was relatively new to the area when humans first arrived. The province remained ice-free throughout much of the glaciation period (Pleistocene Epoch) that began approximately 1.8 million years ago. About 21,000 years ago, it finally succumbed to the ravages of advancing ice, from both the mountains in the west and the arctic barrens in the northeast. Ice engulfed 95 percent of Alberta's landscape. The Ice Age megafauna of Alberta, including mammoths, mastodonts, horses, muskoxen, camels, lions, giant bears, giant bison, bighorn sheep, caribou, and wolves—animals formerly distributed widely in North America, were pushed south to warmer pastures. Some of these animals recolonized Alberta soon after the glaciers began their retreat 14,000 years ago. However, many of the large Ice Age species, like mammoths, were going extinct by then, and the fresh new landscape was impoverished by their loss.

The First Wildlife Watchers

Early findings led researchers to believe that Clovis people were the first humans to walk the continent, entering North America relatively shortly after game returned to the once frozen barrens. These people are believed to have first expanded north on the Asian continent reaching the western shores of the Arctic Ocean between 15,500 and 12,500 years ago. They then pushed east across the Beringian plains into Alaska, eventually heading south as the ice sheet that separated Alaska from the rest of North America

began to melt. Tim Flannery imagines what may have been the first walk into North America: "After threading their way past freezing mires, under louring walls of ice and through dense fogs of a hundred miles or more, those early explorers emerged somewhere near present-day Edmonton."[3]

While dramatic and evocative, there may not be many who agree with Flannery's imagery now. Several other sources, including a popularized account in Elaine Dewar's book *Bones: Discovering the First Americans*, draw a slightly different picture from the one above.[4] There are suggestions—based more on theory than on new findings—that there were several earlier waves of peoples into North America, and perhaps not all of them used the Mackenzie Valley route, as previously thought. Instead, migrating bands may have travelled down the west coast on foot (there is no evidence yet for use of watercraft) and crossed into the interior at a more southerly point. There are strong suggestions that the recolonizing fauna of the future Alberta—including humans—came first from south of the ice, and only later from the north.

There is also mounting evidence that humans were already in America (Monte Verde, Chile) 12,000 years ago or even as early as 50,000 years ago if archaeological sites like Topper, South Carolina are verified.[5] However, there is no direct connection between the occupation of these early sites and the use of western coastal or inland routes to the mid-continent. Presently,

MOOSE IN ALBERTA – RELATIVE NEWCOMERS?
While there is still much speculation about their genetic relationships, the earlier Stag Moose (*Cervalces scotti*) may have split off from its Eurasian relatives and spread to the Arctic and the rest of North America about 800,000-200,000 years ago. This species looked like a cross between an elk and a moose, and ranged from Saskatchewan to Arkansas, and east to New Jersey. However, no fossils of this species have been found in Alberta—yet! Never common, the Stag Moose went extinct about 12,000 years ago for reasons unknown. This made way for the postglacial dispersal of today's modern moose (*Alces alces*), which may have evolved from a Eurasian relative about 100,000 years before spreading from Alaska to suitable habitat throughout Canada and the northern United States. Perhaps the important point to make is that wildlife is never static, and changes in species composition and range are ongoing.

there appear to be more questions than answers, and the story of North America's first humans may never be completely known.

Whether they were descendants of the first people to wander across Beringia, or one of a wave of peoples to follow the melting glaciers northward, we know Alberta was inhabited by groups of nomadic hunters by 11,000 years ago. These first inhabitants may have been descendants of spectacular big game hunters. Although the mighty mammoths may not have paid much attention to the newly arrived humans, these "mammoth hunters" quickly proved their adeptness at attacking these animals when they were in a poorly defendable area such as a bog. Their stone-tipped spears seem to have been effective, judging from the remains of mammoth, mastodont, and giant bison carcasses found at a few North American kill sites. While it was once believed that hunters hunted the megafauna to extinction, most researchers now believe that a combination of hunting pressure and rapid climate change was responsible for these species' demise.[6]

Regardless of the cause of the megafauna's downfall, this loss, in turn, may have triggered its own changes to the environment. As any student of range management knows, removal of a primary browser can affect the composition of vegetation remaining for smaller grazers, with larger, woody plant material free to invade grassy areas. As well, the entire nutrient cycle may have been disrupted with the removal of these rather large walking fertilizer factories. (A similar historical example would be the removal of the bison from the prairie grassland ecosystem.[7]) Although probably unaware of it at the time, the Clovis people, and those who came after them, may have had an effect on the remaining wildlife, which tended to smaller body-size through time, perhaps in part owing to hunting pressure as well as changes in climate and available nutrition. Hunting pressure can also significantly alter faunal diversity and richness.

Fire can also be an efficient agent of change. Historical evidence suggests aboriginal people used fire as a tool to alter wildlife habitat.[8] "People appear to have frequently burned the mountain valleys for numerous purposes, ranging from improving wildlife habitat to regenerating vigorous berry crops."[9] Initially, fires set in wetter springtime conditions created meadows for medicinal and food plants, and berries for making pemmican. If these meadows were left undisturbed and conditions were right, young willow and aspen might colonize them, in turn, attracting deer,

ALBERTA'S FIRST HUNTERS

What animals did Alberta's first human hunters hunt? The gradual retreat of glaciers about 14,000 years ago would have allowed much of North America's flora and fauna to expand their range north once again. Humans likely followed, arriving in the province about 11,000 years ago. The first humans *could* have encountered late-surviving woolly mammoths and camels, and large herds of horses and bison, as well as the carnivores that dogged their tracks, like bears and wolves. While a checklist of wildlife from 11,000 years ago would not fill a Peterson's field guide, the complement of large-mammals in early postglacial Alberta was significant.[10]

One of the few Clovis sites in the province, Lake Minnewanka, has produced fossils of an ancient long-horned bison and an extinct species of mountain sheep that were both much larger than today's. However, we do not know if Clovis people hunted these species.[11] At least as far north as Edmonton, small postglacial-age horses appear to have been abundant. At an 11,000-year-old site on the St. Mary Reservoir, near Cardston, Alberta, archaeologists found evidence suggesting that early inhabitants butchered horses.[12] Unfortunately, we have yet to learn what other plants and animals early people used, what effect the arrival of a new predator (humans) had on the local wildlife, and what changes in wildlife occurred through time.

moose, elk, and bison to the advantage of human hunters.

Although they used wildlife for food, clothing, and shelter, aboriginal people were widely dispersed in low numbers. They likely did not have more than a local impact on game populations and their habitat, most of which were sustained over the last 11 millennia. By the 18th century, wild game, including moose, elk, and deer, was still the main source of aboriginal food. Waterfowl, fish, berries, and other edible plant material supplemented their diet.

AN 1820 SKETCH OF A CREE BUFFALO POUND BY LIEUTENANT GEORGE BACK.
COURTESY GLENBOW ARCHIVES (NA-1344-2)

For many southern tribes, bison [or buffalo] were the main source not only of food but also of hides for clothing and tents. With an estimated 30-60 million bison spread across the Great Plains and an estimated 200,000-400,000 aboriginal people hunting them, a balance appeared to be maintained for several millennia. However, the relationship between man and beast likely changed through time as both species evolved. The early postglacial bison, a moderately long-horned form travelling in loose herds, evolved into a herding mass of modern shorthorns out on the open plains. Similarly, human hunters progressed from spear-wielding individualists to herd-driving cooperatives who carried out massive kills at sites such as Head-Smashed-In Buffalo Jump as long as 6,000 years ago.[13]

European Inventions, Explorations, and the Fur Trade

Any balance that existed between early hunters and wildlife was definitely tipped by a quick succession of events. The first major event occurred when the horse was brought back to North America. Several smaller horse species had occupied the New World but disappeared along with other fauna approximately 11,000 years ago. In modern times, the Spaniards introduced a newer and larger breed of horse to North America, its distribution spreading from Mexico north. Once tamed, the horse contributed to the hunters' increased mobility and hunting success. In Alberta, the Peigan are believed to have been the first tribe to acquire the "big dog" during a battle with the American Shoshoni in 1730.[14]

The second major event was the introduction of firearms and later, repeating firearms. These were also brought by the Europeans. More effective than snares, deadfalls, or the bow and arrow, firearms further increased the odds against wildlife in favour of human hunting ability.

European explorers, searching for the Northwest Passage, reached Hudson Bay, and eventually extended their way west to what is now Alberta. In 1754, Anthony Henday, sent out by the Hudson's Bay Company to promote trade with Indian trappers of the unexplored interior, is credited as the first European to travel as far as Alberta.

Henday is believed to have entered the province on the 11th of September, at a point on Ribstone Creek, east of present day Wainwright. On the 13th, he recorded the following:

> *Here is Great plenty of Buffalo, I went a hunting and in one plain I saw 60 Buffalo feeding, my companion and I singled one out; when we both fired he Ran directly towards us, his Breath fail'd him, before he Could Come up with us, this day killed 7 Buffalo, and 3 Moose.* [15]

On the 15th, Henday again commented on the abundant wildlife:

> *Sunday fine weather, wind SW. took my Departure from sporting plain and traveled 14 miles WNW fine level land, no woods to be seen, passed by a Lake, the Buffalo so plenty, obliged to make them sheer out of our way; also Wolves without number; lurking about after the Buffalo, Indians killed a great many taking only what they chused to carry, I am now stocked with tongues, we also see Moose and Waskesus [elk] but as the Natives seldom kills them with the Bow And Arrow, they will not shoot them with the gun while the Buffalo are so numerous...* [16]

For 80 years prior to Henday's explorations, fur traders had tried to induce the Natives to travel from the surrounding countryside to Hudson Bay to trade furs. Some bands travelled by canoe from the prairies to York Factory on the Hudson Bay coast, trading primarily beaver, as well as muskrat, otter, fox, and mink in return for domestic goods and guns. Henday was not successful in convincing more Natives to bring their trade goods east. However, he was followed by a number of explorers, eager to map the uncharted west. This land came to be known as Rupert's Land (named after Prince Rupert of the Rhine), and was governed by a royal charter extended to the Governor and Company of Adventurers trading into Hudson Bay (the Hudson's Bay Company).

With the Natives unwilling to travel east, the Company decided it would have to build trading posts inland. This decision was accelerated by the appearance of French traders from Montreal (in the employ of the North West Company), who started to build their posts at sites convenient to the Natives. After the Hudson's Bay Company sent Henday to Alberta in 1754, the North West Company sent Peter Pond to explore the banks of Lake Athabasca. There he built Alberta's first trading post southwest of present-day Fort Chipewyan in 1778. In order to improve their knowledge and their maps of the interior, trading companies commissioned a number of expeditions by explorers Philip Turnor, Peter Fidler, David Thompson, and Alexander Mackenzie. By 1814, through the combined efforts of these and other explorers, an accurate map of the prairies could be drawn.

An Era of Exploitation

Exploration of the West, with the subsequent establishment of a string of trading posts, was a period of excitement and challenge. It led the way for fur traders, surveyors, naturalists, and eventually settlers to infiltrate this unknown land. Nevertheless, like progress anywhere, it came at a cost—particularly to local game. In addition to obtaining furs for the trading posts, hunters were employed in supplying meat to feed the staff of these establishments. This hunting pressure affected local populations of bison, moose, deer, wildfowl, and fish so that game became scarce in some localities, leaving trading forts to be abandoned or re-located elsewhere.

Rivalry between the Hudson's Bay and North West companies only compounded the problem. From the 1790s until they merged in 1821, the two companies were embroiled in a "struggle for the fur forest".[17] They competed with each other to open up new areas for exploration and exploitation. Each aimed at keeping the other out and all methods of trickery and, at times, violence were employed. One such technique to keep rivals at bay was to "trap out" an area whereby all fur-bearing animals were trapped to local extinction (extirpation). As a result, many areas were devoid of fur-bearing wildlife for a number of years.

9

By 1821, both the Hudson's Bay and North West companies were exhausted by their efforts to out-compete one another and both were facing bankruptcy. To avoid complete ruin, they merged under the Hudson's Bay Company name. An attempt was made to prevent excessive trapping and killing of game but, in spite of good intentions, this was generally unsuccessful. The fort hunters, supplying the trading posts, continued their ways despite pleas to do otherwise. Colin Campbell, Chief Trader at Dunvegan, noted in the Post Journal of February 16, 1830:

Our two Fort Hunters arrived and report of having killed 53 buffaloes—a great many more than we want and they are not fat enough to make dried provisions, so that the meat will be lost. The snow is so very deep that all large animals cannot run from their pursuers and there will be no doubt a great number wantonly killed. Although I do my best by persuasion to prevent it.[18]

As the 19th century progressed, the game supply dwindled to the point that hunters needed to travel some distance for meat. By the mid-1850s, a few cattle had been brought in as a meat source, but not nearly enough. Observers travelling in the area noted the variety of game and its subsequent decline. By 1858, James Hector, second in command of the Palliser Expedition, wrote that near Fort Edmonton: "At one time, they [moose] were very common in this district and formed a sure source of food for the traders, but for many years they have almost disappeared."[19]

Any pleas from company officials fell on deaf ears: indiscriminate hunting went on not only with bison and moose, but also with wildfowl and other wildlife. By the 1860s, it was apparent that bison, critical to the Natives and trading post staff, were disappearing rapidly. Paul Kane commented on the destruction of a herd near Fort Pitt, Saskatchewan (on the North Saskatchewan River just east of the Alberta

10

A DEER HUNTING PARTY NEAR ROCKY MOUNTAIN HOUSE, ca. 1880.
COURTESY GLENBOW ARCHIVES (NA-782-18)

THE EARLY NATURALISTS
[SUE CLARKE]

"We are now entered Muscuty plains, and soon shall see plenty of Buffalo, and the Archthinue Indians hunting them on Horse-back…"[20] So wrote Anthony Henday on that day in September 1754 when he became the first European to enter Alberta. In that moment, Henday's journal provided the first written information on the flora and fauna of these uncharted wilds. Over the next 60 years, much of the European knowledge about Alberta's natural history was the result of such anecdotal observations made by Henday and those who followed him. These early travellers passed on their observations to each other by word of mouth, or through accounts of their travels written in their journals and reports.

As early as 1744, the Hudson's Bay Company realized that more accurate maps of that vast land to the west were needed. However, "untrained traders could not be expected to produce reliable maps of the interior…"[21] It took until 1778 for a new era in scientific exploration to begin. That's when Phillip Turnor arrived, a trained surveyor and the first scientific observer to work in the Canadian West. Of equal significance, Turnor trained young David Thompson and Peter Fidler in survey techniques, thus enabling accurate collection of cartographic and natural history data.

While David Thompson the explorer is well known, David Thompson the early naturalist is not. His contributions to the knowledge of flora, fauna, and meteorological data of the western interior, so clearly and meticulously detailed in his journals, are no less significant than his maps. Thompson made some of the first detailed descriptions of several plants and noted which species were indigenous to an area. He noted the number of animals seen, their preferred habitats, mating seasons, and number of offspring each typically produced. Locations of minerals, such as coal on the Red Deer River, and regular astronomical observations likewise found places in his journal. Thompson's habit of measuring the air temperature three to four times a day justly earned him credit as the first man to make regular recorded meteorological observations in the interior, sixty years prior to Palliser's well-mounted scientific expedition.

At approximately the same time as David Thompson was making his way west, Alexander Mackenzie was actively seeking a route to the Pacific Ocean, travelling from Fort Chipewyan on Lake Athabasca to the Arctic Ocean via the Slave and Mackenzie rivers. Four years later, he accomplished his Pacific Ocean quest by ascending the Peace River into British Columbia. Mackenzie's itinerary-style journals, though not as comprehensive or detailed as Thompson's, provided descriptive reports of the Peace River area.

From 1788-1822, fur trader and map maker Peter Fidler surveyed more than 4700 miles (7562 km) of river and lakeshore. In 1792, Fidler surveyed the Battle, Bow, and Red Deer rivers. In 1799, he built Greenwich House on Lac La Biche. He is also credited as being the "first to write a description of the tar sands" near Fort McMurray.[22] Fidler was the first naturalist to describe the synchronous eight- to ten-year cycles in snowshoe hare and lynx, the vast numbers of passenger pigeons, and the already declining numbers of swans.

The 1800s ushered in an era of more scientifically oriented investigation and exploration. While the quest for commercially viable trading routes continued to be the motivation for exploring Canada's interior, the need for scientifically accurate information was also on the rise. Trained scientists, Dr. John Richardson and Robert Hood, accompanied Captain John Franklin on his 1819-22 quest to find an overland trade route to Asia. Richardson and Hood spent the spring of 1820 in the Fort Chipewyan area making natural history notes. Hood also painted a number of bird species then unknown to science.[23]

In 1826-27, Thomas Drummond, assistant naturalist to the second Land Arctic Expedition under Franklin, left the expedition for an inland journey to the vicinity of Jasper's House enroute to the Columbia River. Drummond's account in *Sketch of a Journey to the Rocky Mountains and to the Columbia River in North America* is a botanical taxonomy of Alberta.[24] Along the way, he discovered several new varieties of mosses and some previously unknown plant species, and recognized that certain endemic plants in mountain valleys were found nowhere else. Numerous samples that Drummond preserved were brought back with him to Cumberland House.

Following his election to the Royal Geographical Society in London, Captain John Palliser proposed an expedition to the Rocky Mountains. He left London in 1857 accompanied by James Hector, geologist and naturalist, Eugène Bourgeau, botanist, Lt. Thomas Blakiston, magnetic observer and ornithologist, and John Sullivan, secretary and astronomer. Palliser was instructed to "make an impartial assessment of the region—gathering information on soils, climate, flora and fauna, farming potential, general geography, and possible transportation routes."[25] The expedition travelled extensively over modern Saskatchewan and Alberta between the 49th and 54th parallels. Palliser's journals provided detailed accounts of his journeys and vivid descriptions of plants and animals and drew attention to the rich soil on the banks of the Saskatchewan River. He also identified the drought regions of southern Alberta, today known as "Palliser's Triangle".

In 1872, Sanford Fleming, engineer-in-chief to the Canadian Pacific Railway, invited John Macoun to be the official botanist on an expedition to assess the proposed Yellowhead Pass route for the new transcontinental railway. The expedition crossed the Prairie Provinces, into the Peace River country, and terminated at the Pacific Ocean. Macoun believed that a natural scientist should be a "jack-of-all trades whose role was to assemble an inventory of God's wondrous bounty".[26] In a letter to his wife, Macoun reported: "I can only say that I was astonished for as far as the eye could reach stretched a grassy plain without a fence and nothing to be seen but grass and flowers. In less than an hour I found 32 new plants."[27] Visiting the then wetter prairies, Macoun assessed and reported upon the agriculture potential of the interior, viewing it in a more favourable light than Palliser had 15 years earlier. He was convinced that conditions were ideal for large-scale settlement. [By this time, the plains bison had been largely eradicated and ranches and cattle were still few and far between: it was virtually an ungrazed prairie.]

Macoun returned home to Belleville, Ontario, in 1873 after a journey of 3000 miles (4827 km) to the Pacific Ocean and back. Reviewing his specimens, he found a regional uniformity in the vegetation of the western interior. "The hill-top, the plain, the marsh, the aspen copse, the willow thicket, he reported, each had its own flora throughout the region, never varying and scarcely ever becoming intermixed."[28]

Macoun's vast number of specimens became the core of natural history collections at Ottawa, Montreal, and Banff.

Macoun continued to traverse the Canadian West until 1897, documenting its climate and cataloguing its flora and fauna. Like many early naturalists, he kept meticulously detailed journals that included botanical, historical, and political information. Because of his work, Macoun emerged as the country's leading expert on Western Canada.

Following the more optimistic reports of Fleming and Macoun, the carving up of the prairies began. In 1872-1875, George Dawson led the British North America Boundary Commission Canada Survey. Joseph Burr Tyrrell assisted Dawson in 1883 with a survey of the Rocky Mountains and, between 1884 and 1887, explored north of Calgary between the Bow and Saskatchewan rivers. In 1884, Tyrrell found the dinosaur bones that would lead to the naming of the present-day Royal Tyrrell Museum of Palaeontology in his honour. Tyrrell made many contributions as an early naturalist and provided new information on geography, geology, botany, mammalogy, and palaeontology.[29]

Surveys were continued between the 1880s and the early 20th century by Robert Bell and, later, Charles Camsell. Many of the specimens collected on these surveys were shipped to Ottawa for National Museum of Canada collections. The specimens that did not go east generally went south. As early as 1859, the young naturalist Robert Kennicott spent three years in Rupertsland collecting (and encouraging Hudson's Bay Company traders to do the same) birds, eggs, mammals, plants, and ethnographic artifacts for the research collections of the Smithsonian Institution.[30] Other collectors came to collect specimens for the American Museum of Natural History. Thus, a number of botanists, biologists, and geologists, many affiliated with museums or universities, advanced Henday's work started more than 250 years earlier of documenting and collecting specimens representative of Alberta's natural history.

It is a cliché—but a true one—that in the field of knowledge the present stands on the shoulders of the past to reach into the future.[31]

EARLY TRAPPERS WITH THEIR CATCH IN THE EUREKA DISTRICT OF ALBERTA, ca. 1900.
COURTESY GLENBOW ARCHIVES (NA-4292-1)

border): "This is the third herd that had been driven into this pound within the last ten or twelve days, and the putrefying carcasses tainted the air all round. There are thousands of them annually killed in this manner..."[32]

The idea of managing a limited resource obviously had not yet entered the social consciousness, for Kane recounts that in another instance, when his party required food, they "selected the fattest of the calves taking only the tongues and boss, or hump, and not burdening ourselves unnecessarily with more".[33]

DID YOU KNOW?
Woodpecker Lake in Central Alberta was renamed Pigeon Lake for the passenger pigeon—once so common it could be counted in the tens of thousands nesting in the woods surrounding the area.[34] Passenger pigeons were considered a great delicacy and trapped by the thousands until there were no more. The very last passenger pigeon died in a Cincinnati zoo in 1914.

SETTLERS COMING TO ALBERTA, ca. 1920.
COURTESY ALBERTA SUSTAINABLE RESOURCE DEVELOPMENT
(FOREST PROTECTION IMAGE LIBRARY)

The Taming of the West

In 1867, eastern Canada joined in Confederation with a vision towards westward expansion that would see the country stretch from coast to coast. Rupertsland, that great preserve of the Hudson's Bay Company, passed to the young Dominion of Canada becoming the Northwest Territories. Later, the provinces of Alberta and Saskatchewan would be carved out of the territory. The plains were to be surveyed and opened for settlement.

Law and order were to be provided by the newly formed North West Mounted Police.[35] By the time the first detachments were established at Edmonton and Fort Macleod in 1874, the once thriving bison herds of the plains and the parklands were nearly gone. Only in more northerly areas would they survive to any notable extent. As well, moose and

other large animals were found only in relatively inaccessible areas and other game and wildfowl had declined in numbers.

While the fur trade and the establishment of trading posts exerted heavy local pressure on fur-bearers and big game, the settlement of Alberta took an even heavier toll on game animals that provided fresh meat to the newly arrived pioneers. That which remained of the wilderness changed rapidly in the 1880s as railroads pushed across the prairies bringing new European settlers with them. Regional representation and a local government were required to build the infrastructure demanded by this new society. Although the Northwest Territorial government was first appointed in 1875 (later becoming an elected council, then an elected Legislative Assembly), regulation of game remained under the Federal Department of Agriculture. At the time, there was virtually no game control or protection across the prairies.

Early in its existence, the Territorial government attempted to address game concerns within its jurisdiction. Lieutenant-Governor Laird, in his address to the Territorial Council on Thursday, March 8, 1877, said:

You will also be invited to consider what steps ought to be taken to protect the Buffalo from wanton destruction. The extinction of this animal on which many Indians and others largely rely for support, should, if possible, be prevented, at least until stock raising and agriculture can be introduced to take the place which the Buffalo has supplied for generations.[36]

WOLFERS

The Cypress Hills Massacre in 1873 precipitated the creation of the North West Mounted Police (NWMP). Unrestricted whiskey- and fur-trading contributed to this massacre, where wolf hunters killed several Natives. Although wolf pelts provided fashionable and warm winter coats and blankets, society generally despised "wolfers" because of the method they used. A well-baited strychnine-laced deer or bison carcass could net as many as 100 wolves. However, the poisoned bait also killed other species, including many local dogs, thus precipitating the hard feelings between wolfers and many Native bands. Kootenai Brown, a noted conservationist and Park Warden involved in the creation of Waterton Lakes National Park, spent a short period of his career as a wolfer, but after one winter of profit-making, turned his attention to guiding in the area that he would spend the rest of his life protecting.[37]

BUFFALO BONES STACKED UP WAITING FOR TRANSPORT BY TRAIN TO FERTILIZER FACTORIES.
COURTESY PROVINCIAL ARCHIVES OF ALBERTA (B10101)

Early Legislation for the Protection of Buffalo and Other Game

Unfortunately, there is no record of the debate that occurred for *An Ordinance for the Protection of the Buffalo*, introduced on March 20, 1877. It was, however, read the required three times and passed on March 22, 1877.[38] The Ordinance called for a closed season on female buffalo and year-round protection of young until two years of age. This was the Northwest Territories' first piece of legislation to preserve any kind of game animal and it would be satisfying to report that it was enforced. However, this was not the case.

At the direction of the Federal Government, the ordinance was repealed on the grounds that the Indians, who depended upon buffalo, would starve if the buffalo were protected. The truth was, of course, that buffalo were already quickly disappearing under pressure of market hunters and a voracious demand for hides. Laird made it explicit in his speech that the extinction of the buffalo should be prevented. The Federal Government, as it is prone to do from time to time, also noted that enactment of such legislation was beyond the powers of the Territorial Administration.

So the bison continued to decline. The Council encouraged the Métis to abandon their annual buffalo hunts and take up agriculture to avoid the destitution that would result from the extinction of buffalo.[39] Many did, and a good account of the attempts of one Métis family, the Callihoo, to farm in central Alberta is outlined by Elizabeth Macpherson in *Sun Traveler*.[40]

For the next three years, nothing was done for the disappearing buffalo. Finally, on October 4, 1883, Council passed *An Ordinance for the Protection of Game*.[41] On July 29, 1884, Journals for the Council noted that Game Guardians were to be appointed to enforce provisions of the *1883 Ordinance*. This was the first large scale recognition of the need to limit the harvest of wildlife by enforcing game laws and the first reference to an enforcement body. As well, the *1883 Ordinance* stated which big game and game birds could—and could not—be hunted and when. In addition, narcotics, nightlights, nets, and similar devices for capturing game, were now outlawed.

The *1883 Ordinance* was deemed too general. Accordingly, the more comprehensive *An Ordinance*

for the Protection of Game was passed in 1888.[42] The new legislation outlined more clearly closed seasons (when hunting was not allowed) on elk, moose, caribou, antelope, deer, mountain sheep, and mountain goat. Buffalo hunting was not allowed. The annual big game season opened for hunting from September 1 to February 1 with the remaining months closed to allow for the species' natural increase through reproduction. Similarly, open season for ducks was September 1 to May 1. For other game birds, such as grouse, open season was from September 1 to February 1. Except for bona fide scientific purposes, the taking of eggs of any game bird was prohibited. Nets, narcotics, and nightlights were again prohibited.

Provisions were made for licences and special permits for scientific collectors, as well as for the appointment of Game Guardians. These men had the power of constables, with the ability to arrest and seize. Their task was not easy. These volunteers, in addition to their farming and trapping, watched to see if there were any violations of the Game Ordinance. If a guardian arrested his neighbour for an infraction of the law, reprisals

1883 GAME ORDINANCE PASSED BY THE NORTHWEST TERRITORIAL GOVERNMENT BUT LATER REPEALED.
IMAGE COURTESY ALBERTA FISH AND WILDLIFE DIVISION

could result. Many Game Guardians sincerely believed that what they were doing was the best course of action, and that their actions would keep game from sliding into extinction. However, North West Mounted Police, as ex-officio guardians, were invariably more successful in securing convictions.

The *1888 Ordinance* was passed into law by the Territorial government in February of that year.

A SMALL HERD OF PLAINS BISON WAS KEPT AT BANFF BUT THEY NEVER THRIVED IN THIS LOCATION.
COURTESY ALBERTA SUSTAINABLE RESOURCE DEVELOPMENT (FOREST PROTECTION IMAGE LIBRARY)

17

Reaction from Ottawa was predictable: disallowance, which came in 1890. Again, aboriginal interests were claimed as the reason in spite of a clause in the Ordinance that explicitly excluded Indians from any provisions of the law. Ottawa still controlled the natural resources of the Territories, a situation that would last until 1930. However the Territorial government eventually won this round for, in 1890, the Ordinance was amended, and the Federal Government had to be content with what was done. By then, the Northwest Territorial Assembly had come into being and was flexing its muscle. The Federal Government had other more pressing problems with Territorial Administration, including the continual request for more money to look after a burgeoning western population.

Unfortunately, and despite best intentions, by the time the political wrangling was over, the plains bison were, for all practical purposes, extirpated in

Canada. Only a few remained in private reserves. In northern Alberta, small numbers of wood bison still roamed, but these survived only because their habitat was remote and inaccessible.

The *1888 Ordinance* was thoroughly revised as a new act in 1893 and appeared in the *Consolidated Ordinances of 1898*.[43] Changes included a shorter open season for big game (October 1 to February 1) and no hunting on Sunday. Bounties set on wolves at $5.00 and coyotes at $0.50 yielded $2,005.00 for 401 wolf pelts and $531.50 for 1063 coyote pelts as reported by the Chief Game Guardian in 1899. At this time, it was believed that placing a bounty on a species for a significant period would slow its increase in numbers.[44] To the early settlers, particularly farmers with livestock, wolves and coyotes were pests—a nuisance to be exterminated.

THE *REGINA HEADER*
On September 23, 1890, it was reported on page eight of the evening edition of the "Regina Header", that the following, all from Edmonton, had been appointed by the Lieutenant-Governor of the Northwest Territories as Game Guardians: Robert Bailey, Fred Ellett, R.G. Bardisty, T. Hutchings, J. Inkster, A.A. Johnstone, W. Mackay, James Nonne, and W.S. Robertson.[45]

By 1901, 127 Game Guardians had been appointed to ensure compliance to the new legislation. Responsibility for the Game Ordinance now rested with the Commissioner for Agriculture. The annual reports of the Chief Game Guardian appeared within the main report of that Department. These reports provide a wealth of information and insight into the early days of game management. For example, the Chief Game Guardian noted in his 1897 report that, in response to a questionnaire filled out by hunters, there were many opinions about how game should be managed. Some hunters desired an open season on prairie chicken. Other respondents requested a closed season for partridge [grouse] in the northern areas since these birds, like the prairie chicken, had been rather heavily hunted. Still others wanted spring shooting of birds prohibited outright; they prudently pointed out that this would provide the opportunity for the birds to increase through their natural reproduction. Based on these and other observations, changes were made to the legislation as required. For example, in 1903, the Ordinance was amended to set out in greater detail provisions for hunting.[46] That year, it was recommended that spring shooting of birds be prohibited; the following year brought a closed season on geese

and ducks as well as a ban on semi-automatic shotguns. After amendments made in 1904, this was the last Game Ordinance enacted by the old Territorial Administration before the new province of Alberta assumed such duties in 1905.

The Close of Territorial Administration

At the close of the Territorial Administration in 1905, fish and wildlife policy consisted simply of imposing bag (harvest) limits and closed seasons in areas where the numbers of a species had declined. A small but dedicated body of people had limited success enforcing fish and game laws, and pest species were managed with bounties. Yet the beginnings were all there—a government mandate to ensure the viability of fish and wildlife in perpetuity; legislation and a force to back up those game laws agreed upon for the general good; and a body of individuals willing to tackle problems that would arise, learning the intricacies of resource management as they went. All provided a solid beginning for the challenges that were to come to fish and wildlife managers in the next century—a century that would see this new frontier settled, put to the plough, and developed into an industrial economy that today is widely touted as the "Alberta Advantage".

THE HISTORY OF HUNTER FEEDBACK QUESTIONNAIRES
Starting as early as the 1890s, the practice of consulting fish and wildlife users (the hunters, trappers, fishermen, and eventually, naturalists and conservationists) about how this resource should be managed became a tradition that provincial wildlife managers maintained throughout much of the last century. Who better to know about wildlife than the people who used the resource?

The questionnaire referred to in the 1897 report of the Chief Game Guardian was probably the first attempt in Alberta to set game regulations through the use of hunter feedback. Later on, during the 1940s, William Rowan, professor at the University of Alberta, used hunter surveys to determine game bird populations and to document the highs and lows of game cycles.

Eventually, hunter questionnaires became a standard practice of the Game Branch and, later, the Fish and Wildlife Division. Even now, a sample of big game hunters is asked each year where and when they hunted; for how many days; and the date, location, age and sex of any animal harvested. Similarly, a sample of game bird hunters is asked how many days they hunted and the number of birds taken in each Wildlife Management Unit. Trapper questionnaires have also been used for a number of years. Data from questionnaires, compulsory registrations, and animal population surveys are compiled and used to determine the status of game populations. These in turn provide the foundation for setting harvest limits and hunting seasons for the following year.

MAJOR EVENTS IN FISH AND WILDLIFE CONSERVATION PRIOR TO 1905

11,000 B.P.	Clovis people are present in Alberta. The megafauna die out.
1730	Peigan Indians of southern Alberta acquire the modern horse.
1754	Anthony Henday is the first European to enter Alberta.
1778	Peter Pond builds the first trading post in Alberta at Fort Chipewyan.
1792	Peter Fidler surveys the Battle, Bow, and Red Deer rivers.
1799	Peter Fidler builds Greenwich House on Lac La Biche.
1819-1822	Scientists Dr. John Richardson and Robert Hood accompany Captain John Franklin on his quest to find an overland trade route to Asia.
1821	The Hudson's Bay and North West companies merge after their "struggle for the fur forest".
1826-27	Thomas Drummond, assistant naturalist to the second Land Arctic Expedition under Franklin, journeys to Jasper's House en route to the Columbia River describing many new plants along the way.
1857-1860	Palliser and several scientists explore western Canada during a dry cycle.
1867	Rupertsland is added to the Dominion of Canada (a confederation under the British North America Act) as the Northwest Territories.
1872	John Macoun assesses the suitability of the interior for agriculture, viewing the prairies in a more favourable light than Palliser had 15 years earlier
1872-1875	George Dawson leads the British North America Boundary Commission Canada Survey.
1874	The first NWMP outposts are established at Edmonton and Fort Macleod.
1875	The first Northwest Territorial government is appointed.
1877	Lieutenant-Governor Laird introduces the *Ordinance for the Protection of Buffalo*.
1883	*An Ordinance for the Protection of Game* is introduced.
1884	Game Guardians are deputized to enforce provisions of the *1883 Game Ordinance*.
1888	*1888 Game Ordinance* passed into law by the Territorial Government but Ottawa disallows it.
1890	The *1888 Ordinance* is revised and, finally, accepted by Ottawa.
1893	The *1888 Ordinance* is revised with changes including a shorter open season for big game (October 1 to February 1) and no hunting on Sunday. Bounties are set on wolves and coyotes.
1897	The Chief Game Guardian uses a hunter survey to assess game conditions.
1901	127 Game Guardians now ensure compliance to the Game Ordinance.
1903	The 1903 *Game Ordinance* is introduced setting out greater details for hunting, including a number of closed seasons and bag limits. Spring shooting of birds is prohibited, the following year sees a closed season on geese and ducks as well as a ban on semi-automatic shotguns.
1905	Sept. 1, Alberta becomes the eighth province in Confederation.

References • CHAPTER 1

[1] John Muir, 1838-1914, was a well-known conservationist as well as the founder of The Sierra Club in the U.S.

[2] Stelck, C.R. 1967. The record of the rocks. Pp. 21–51 *in* Hardy, W.G. 1967. Alberta – A Natural History. Mismat Corporation, Edmonton.

[3] Flannery, Tim. 2001. The Eternal Frontier – An Ecological History of North America and its Peoples. Text Publishing, Melbourne.

[4] Dewar, Elaine. 2001. Bones: Discovering the First Americans. Random House, Toronto.

5   Walton, Marsha and Michael Coren. 2004. Man in Americas earlier than thought: Archaeologists put humans in North America 50,000 years ago. Edition.cnn.com/2004/TECH/science/11/17/Carolina.dig/index.html.

6   Grayson, Donald and David Meltzer. 2002. Clovis Hunting and Large Mammal Extinction: A Critical Review of the Evidence. Journal of World Prehistory, 16(4) (Provides a review of the evidence against the "overkill" theory.) See also Shapiro *et al.* 2004 (Science 306:1561-1565) in which the authors infer a decline in genetic diversity approximately 37,000 years ago which precedes the onset of the last ice advance by about 15,000 years.

7   England, Raymond E. and Anton DeVos. 1968. Influence of Animals on Pristine Conditions on the Canadian Grasslands. Journal of Range Management 22:87-94.

8   Murphy, Peter J. 1985. History of Forest and Prairie Fire Control Policy in Alberta. Alberta Energy and Natural Resources, Edmonton.

9   Remington, Robert. 2002. Research shows native fires shaped Banff. Interview of Cliff White, Parks Canada conservation biologist, National Post, March 23, 2002. Also, for an in-depth review of the use of fire in northern Alberta see Lewis, Henry T. 1977. Maskuta: the ecology of Indian fires in northern Alberta. The Western Canadian Journal of Anthropology, 7(1).

10 J. Burns, unpublished data.

11 See the Heritage Community Foundation website at www.collections.ic.gc.ca/alberta/archaeology/site_profiles_lake_minnewanka.html for a profile of Archaeologist Alison Landals' work at Lake Minnewanka.

12 Kooyman, Brian, Margaret E. Newman, Christine Cluney, Murray Lobb, Shayne Tolman, Paul McNeil, and L.V. Hills. 2001. Identification of horse exploitation by Clovis hunters based on protein analysis. American Antiquity 66(4):686-691.

13 Reid, Gordon. 2002. Head-Smashed-In Buffalo Jump. Fifth House Ltd., Calgary.

14 Holt, Faye. 1996. Alberta – A History in Photographs. Altitude Publishing, Canmore.

15 Belyea, Barbara (ed.). 2000. A Year Inland, the Journal of a Hudson's Bay Company Winterer. Sir Wilfred Laurier University Press, Waterloo, Ontario. Also see McGregor, John G. 1954. Behold the Shining Mountains, The Travels of Anthony Henday, 1754-1755. Applied Art Products, Edmonton.

16 Ibid.

17 Morton, A.S. 1971. A History of the Canadian West to 1870-71. Thomas Nelson & Sons, Toronto.

18 Provincial Archives of Alberta (PAA). Accession 74.1 Journals of Fort Dunvegan (manuscript), 1829-1830. Entry for February 6, 1830.

19 Spry, Irene. 1963. The Palliser Expedition. Macmillan Company of Canada Ltd., Toronto. The Palliser Expedition or officially, the British North American Exploring Expedition, was sent out to report upon the southern half of what are now the prairie provinces; its farthest north exploration was the Athabasca River from Fort Assiniboine to Jasper. (See also Erasmus, Peter. 1999. Buffalo Days and Nights. Fifth House Ltd., Calgary. The original manuscript is at the Glenbow Alberta Institute, Calgary. This manuscript was dictated by Erasmus, a keen observer and a guide for the Palliser Expedition.)

20 Belyea, B., op. cit., p. 87.

21 Warkentin, John. 1962. The Western Interior of Canada. McClelland and Stewart, Toronto.

22 Houston, C. Stuart. 1997. Fidler, Peter. Pp. 268-269 *in* Sterling, K.B., R. P. Harmond, G. A. Cevasco and L.F. Hammond (eds.). Biographical Dictionary of American and Canadian Naturalists and Environmentalists. Greenwood Press, Westport, Connecticut.

23 Houston, C.S. (ed.). 1974. To the Arctic by Canoe 1819-1821. The journal and paintings of Robert Hood, midshipman with Franklin. McGill-Queen's University Press, Montreal.

24 Drummond, Thomas. 1830. Sketch of a Journey to the Rocky Mountains and to the Columbia River in North America. Microfiche, FC 51 C3496 #16840, University of Calgary Library, Calgary (original manuscript is held by the Library Division, Provincial Archives of British Columbia.

25 Spry, Irene. 1963. op. cit.

26 Waiser, W.A. 1989. The Field Naturalist: John Macoun, the Geological Survey, and Natural Science. University of Toronto Press, Toronto.

27 Ibid.

28 Ibid.

29 See Tyrrell biographies by Loudon, W.J. 1930. A Canadian Geologist. Macmillan Company of Canada, Toronto; and Inglis, A. 1978. Northern Vagabond: The Life and Career of J.B. Tyrrell. McClelland and Stewart, Toronto.

30 Lindsay, D. 1991. The modern beginnings of subarctic ornithology: correspondence to the Smithsonian Institutions 1856-1868. The Manitoba Record Society Publications (Has considerable detail on Robert Kennicott; brief notes on Thomas W. Blakiston, Eugène Bourgeau, James Hector, John Palliser, Sir Alexander Mackenzie and Sir John Richardson).

31 Hardy, W.G. 1967. Alberta – A Natural History. Mismat Corporation, Edmonton.

32 Kane, Paul. 1925. Wanderings of an Artist among the Indians of North America from Canada to Vancouver's island and Oregon through the Hudson's Bay Company's territory and back again, 1846-1848. Radisson Society Canada Ltd., Toronto. (An account by the artist of the west before settlement commenced.)

33 Ibid., p. 89.

34 Nyland, Edo. 1970. Miquelon Lake. Alberta Lands Forests Parks Wildlife 13(1):18-25. Department of Lands and Forests, Edmonton.

35 Cruise, David and Alison Griffiths. 1996. The Great Adventure: How the Mounties Conquered the West. Penguin Books, Toronto.

36 Northwest Territories. Council Journals. Thursday, March 8, 1877. See also North-West Territories. *Journals.* 1877 – 1883. Regina (A compilation of documents showing the beginnings of enactment of legislation concerning wildlife) North-West Territories. *Ordinances.* 1881 – 1905 (These have the Game Ordinances and amendments; they illustrate the improvements in legislation in this period); and North-West Territories. Department of Agriculture. *Annual Reports of the Chief Game Guardian, 1891 – 1905.*

37 Hollihan, Tony. 2001. Kootenai Brown. Folklore Publishing, Canada.

38 Northwest Territories. Council Journals. Thursday, March 22, 1877.

39 Ibid., July 10 and 11, 1878. Also, see Journals of July 30, 1877.

40 Macpherson, Elizabeth. 1998. The Sun Traveler. Musée Héritage Museum, St. Albert, Alberta.

41 Northwest Territories. Council Journals. September 9, 1883 and October 4, 1883.

42 Northwest Territories. Ordinances. 1888. Chapter 25.

43 Northwest Territories. Consolidated Ordinances. Chapter 85. Regina, Saskatchewan, 1898.

44 Courtesy of Ted Sheard, Saskatchewan Archives.

45 Northwest Territories. Department of Agriculture. Annual Report, 1898. Regina, P. 84 (found in Provincial Archives of Alberta 72.214 Microfilm, Roll 11)

46 Northwest Territories. Ordinances. Second Session, 1903. Chapter 29. Regina, 1903.

Chapter 2

A PROVINCIAL MANDATE: THE ALBERTA FISH AND WILDLIFE DIVISION

Petra Rowell and Bill Wishart with contributions from
Sue Clarke, Jan Hall, Marilyn Kerr, Diane Markham, Beth Michener, George Mitchell,
Carol Paetz, Margo Pybus, Grace Rippin, Nyree Sharp, Pat Valastin,
Pat Wishart, Francine Wieliczko and Wendy Zelt

To Manage the Fish and Wildlife Resources of the Province of Alberta for the Benefit and Enjoyment of the People. 1988-89 Alberta Fish and Wildlife Division Mission Statement

Provincehood

Prior to 1905, the Northwest Territories, administered by the Territorial Civil Service based in Regina, stretched the full expanse from Manitoba to the Rocky Mountains and from the U.S. border to the Arctic Ocean. The federal government had begun to recognize, however, the need for autonomous regional governments that could develop the infrastructure required to support the growing settler population in the west. Thus the great territory was carved up. On September 1, 1905, Alberta became the eighth province in Confederation. The Northwest Territories remained, as such, north of the 60th parallel; the remaining lands were established as the Province of Saskatchewan or added to an expanded Province of Manitoba. The former territorial administration in Regina formed a nucleus for the Saskatchewan Public Service. Alberta's provincial government had to start afresh.

Despite obtaining provincehood, Alberta was not granted official control over its own resources including its fish, game, forests, minerals, petroleum, water, and lands. With the *British North America Act* of 1867 and the formation of the Government of Canada, the British Government had granted the originating provinces ownership of their resources, with the Federal Government receiving the remaining resources throughout what was then the "Territories". With the formation of the new provinces of Alberta, Saskatchewan, and an enlarged Manitoba in 1905, it was logical that ownership of resources would also be transferred, and thus all provinces would be equal. However, this did not occur immediately. In spite of arguments for change, based on the fact that Ontario and British Columbia controlled their own resources, the reply from Ottawa was negative. It took another 25 years for resource ownership to be devolved to the prairie provinces.

Prior to 1930, the federal government maintained direct control and a high profile in Alberta, particularly where forestry, mines, and lands were concerned. The control of game was vested in the federal Department of the Interior through its Department of Agriculture. Similarly, control of fisheries was under the federal Department of Fisheries, although federal Forestry Officers frequently acted as Fishery Control Officers for commercial and sport fisheries. Alberta was, however, allowed to administer wildlife outside federal forest reserves and national parks, particularly where licensing and enforcement of provincial game laws were concerned. Thus, the provincial government enacted and enforced game laws to control hunting on its crown lands, an arrangement that originated in the territorial times, and which remained convenient for both governments.

This is not to say that everyone had a clear understanding of jurisdiction at the time. In 1916, provincial Game Guardian Henri Rivière queried the Chief Game Guardian: "Is a person hunting in Alberta on a game preserve created by the Dominion without the consent of Alberta authorities, liable to a prosecution, fine, etc. and if such person got his outfit outside of the game preserve limits, would he still be subject to Dominion legislation, as regards confiscation, etc.?" Rivière complained about the Dominion Parks Commissioner J.B. Harkin who, in no uncertain terms, let Rivière know the Dominion had the power to legislate as it saw fit in regards to Alberta's game without consulting the province. Harkin felt that the province had no right that the Dominion could not override![1]

Establishment of Alberta's First Game Branch

Despite the confusion, the province moved forward as best it could with managing its wildlife. In its first year, Alberta continued to use the 1903 *Northwest Territories Game Ordinance*. This ordinance set out a number of provisions for hunting and trapping, including bag limits (the number of animals that could be legally harvested) and closed seasons (when hunting was not allowed). In 1906, the province established its first provincial Game Branch under the Department of Agriculture Administration. Benjamin J. Lawton was appointed the first Chief Game Guardian. Lawton inherited 218 volunteer Game Guardians who had been appointed under the previous Territorial Government.

AN EARLY GAME GUARDIAN ISSUING A SUMMONS TO A POACHER NEAR HARDISTY.
COURTESY GLENBOW ARCHIVES (NA-2284-13)

EARLY HISTORY OF THE DEPARTMENT OF AGRICULTURE

Prior to provincehood, agriculture across the prairies was governed under the federal government's Department of the Interior. However, as the Northwest Territorial Government gained a footing, agriculture came under the control of its Department of Agriculture. *An Ordinance Respecting the Department of Agriculture* gave the department the powers to administer agriculture, wildlife, statistics and public health across the Territories.

The *Alberta Act* establishing the Province on September 1, 1905 also established a provincial authority for agriculture. W.T. Finlay was appointed the province's first Minister of Agriculture. In 1906, the provincial *Agriculture Department Act* remained consistent with older legislation in that the new provincial department continued to administer agriculture, wildlife, statistics and public health, with colonization added to its list of duties.

The new province also installed its own legislation: Alberta's first *Game Act (1907)* superseded the 1903 territorial game ordinance.[2] This Act generally followed the old ordinance with a few changes including the requirements for hunting licences for General Game, Resident Big Game, Guiding, Trapping, as well as Game Dealers, and permits to Collect and Export. Where a species was scarce, a closed season could be imposed in the hope that natural productivity would bolster population numbers. North of latitude 55°, hunting regulations were non-existent. People there hunted for food and were entitled to take whatever they needed for their own consumption. Trapping was uncontrolled throughout the province.

With a Game Branch established and legislation in place, the primary concern of provincial wildlife managers during the first three decades of the 20th century was to maintain a supply of game. However, there were also several very early efforts at wildlife conservation beyond matters of consumption. The disappearance and eventual resurrection of bison was a case in point.[3] As well, the founding of the Calgary Fish and Game Preservation Association in 1906 was promising. This volunteer association (which evolved into the Alberta Fish and Game Association) assisted Game Guardians with their duties, lobbied governments, and educated hunters and anglers that fish and wildlife resources needed to be managed carefully rather than wasted through misguided sport. In a pioneer community where hunting and fishing were regarded as a necessity of life, and where closed seasons were often viewed with disgust, this was a major undertaking.

On a federal level, the Commission of Conservation was established to advise the government on the management of its natural resources.[4] Created in 1909, it survived until after the First World War. For ten of its twelve years, Sir Clifford Sifton, former Minister of the Interior in the Laurier government, chaired the Commission. Sifton and many others worked to increase public awareness, and to shape public opinion to accept that natural resources were not inexhaustible, but rather were a limited resource requiring proper management.

23

BENJAMIN J. LAWTON, ALBERTA'S FIRST CHIEF GAME GUARDIAN

Appointed on June 30, 1906, Benjamin J. Lawton remained in the office of the Chief Game Guardian for a quarter of a century until his death in November 1931. Lawton took his schooling and clerked in a general store in Ontario before trying his hand at farming, first in Kansas, and later in Alberta on the Blindman River just south of Lacombe. In December 1905, he was again clerking, this time in the accounting office of Alberta's Department of Agriculture. Six months later, he was promoted to Chief Game Guardian. Little evidence remains of his qualifications that led him to this position. The only paper he appears to have written, aside from annual reports, was *The Destruction of Gophers* for the Department of Agriculture in Edmonton, sometime between 1909 and 1921.[5] Regardless, he must have been well suited, as he was a strong influence in defining the Game Branch and its actions as the first provincial authority over the wildlife resource.

From a historical standpoint, Lawton is credited for his conviction in using game preserves as a method of reviving declining game stocks. In hindsight, his participation in establishing a national antelope preserve at Nemiskam, and his own initiatives to establish elk and other big game preserves throughout the province, are a contributing factor to the presence of these species in Alberta today. Lawton also was no stranger to international conservation efforts. He praised the Migratory Bird Treaty as "the greatest move towards game conservation that has ever been made on the North America continent", and actively voiced his opinions at the first Federal-Provincial Wildlife meeting, a national conference on wildlife protection held in Ottawa in 1919.[6]

Lawton "gained a reputation for impartiality and fairness when it came to enforcement and otherwise pursued the implementation of the [Game] Act both with conviction and diligence in spite of having a very small force of salaried guardians who had to cover the entire province".[7] With solemn respect, H.A. Craig, Deputy Minister of Agriculture, gave his "sincere regret at the removal by death [of Ben Lawton] who served the Province with a high degree of devotion and efficiency".[8]

SIR CLIFFORD SIFTON: CHAMPION OF CANADIAN CONSERVATION
[SUE CLARKE]

Canada's vast natural resources were regarded as unlimited by the Canadian public in 1909. In the minds of most, these resources existed solely for the purpose of development and financial gain. Therefore, it was remarkable that Prime Minister Sir Wilfred Laurier created a Commission mandated to examine conservation issues. He also appointed an equally remarkable individual, Sir Clifford Sifton, as its first Chairman.

Sifton, former Minister of the Interior, was a prominent politician with a great interest in conservation matters. As early as 1905, he had established the forestry branch within the Department of the Interior and encouraged other "conservation measures in areas under federal jurisdiction".[9] Sifton recognized with great clarity that Canada's natural resources were finite, and were in grave need of protection for future generations. In his inaugural address to the Commission in 1910, he articulated these views:

Our population is spare, our resources only in an initial state of development. So much so is this the case that I have heard the view expressed that what Canada wants is development and exploitation, not conservation. This view, however, is founded upon an erroneous conception, which it must be our work to remove. If we attempt to stand in the way of development, our efforts will assuredly be of no avail either to stop development or to promote conservation. It will not, however, be hard to show that the best and most highly economic development and exploitation in the interests of the people can only take place by having regard to the principles of conservation.[10]

The Commission was designed to consider a variety of subjects regarding the conservation of natural resources with a goal towards collecting scientifically accurate information. This information would then be used to advise the government on proper management of the same. Towards that end, Sifton had a mandate to administer the Commission as he saw fit, and to explore or make inquiry into any and every aspect of conservation utilizing the best and brightest scientific minds available. Scientists and technical experts were given the freedom to pursue diverse areas of interest and concern.

The work of the Commission had significant implications for wildlife conservation in Alberta in two ways. First, work done through the Committee on Forests led to the establishment of the Rocky Mountains Forest Reserve in 1911. All the land above 4000 feet (1219 m) along the eastern slopes of the Rockies was set aside as a forest reserve, some 18,000 square miles (46,166 sq. km) stretching from the international boundary to a point over 100 miles (161 km) northwest of Jasper. This farsighted measure not only ensured the protection of the East Slopes watersheds, it also preserved a vast tract of valuable wildlife habitat throughout much of the 20th century.

Second, the Committee on Game and Furbearing Animals recognized the need for wildlife conservation, and the development of conservation policies nationally and provincially. Such policies called for the establishment of game preserves, reservations, and sanctuaries. In Alberta, the Wainwright Buffalo Park, the Foremost Antelope Reserve, and Elk Island Park were created and "maintained solely for the conservation of native mammals that would otherwise have been exterminated".[11]

Sifton was also a strong advocate of cooperation among governments and departments on conservation issues, something that at the time, and still today, is sometimes uncommon.[12] He was a strong promoter of the *Migratory Bird Treaty* (1916) between the U.S. and Great Britain (on behalf of Canada), perhaps one of the greatest examples of such cooperation.[13] However, while Sifton was one of the first government officials to promote conservation in Canada, it is important to remember that he did so primarily from the perspective of utilizing resources, and not preservation for its own sake.[14] Furthermore, he was "aggressive in promoting settlement of the prairies and promoting expansion of mining, thus contributing substantially to an early stage of the habitat loss we continue to experience today".[15] He was, nevertheless, a pioneer in government application of conservation principles and well ahead of most of his contemporaries.

24

In 1914, the Commission heard submissions from various groups concerning the conservation of wildlife. In particular, it noted the value of fur-farming, which was becoming a thriving industry in Alberta. It also discussed the need to extend the boundaries of Waterton Lakes National Park. In 1917, the Commission's Committee on Fisheries pointed out the need for fisheries preservation. The Commission also regarded the 1916 *Migratory Bird Treaty* and *Migratory Birds Convention Act* (the federal legislation that enacted the treaty in Canada) as vital to the protection of migratory waterfowl.[16] The object of this treaty was to protect migratory birds at their nesting and wintering grounds. Alberta, along with the other provinces, endorsed the Act.[17] Also in 1917, a special branch of the Commission was organized to look into town planning and its effect on the environment—perhaps one of the earliest attempts at integrated land-use planning. A number of committees, including those for lands, forests, waterpower, minerals, fisheries, game, and fur-bearing animals, carried out the work of the Commission. Much of this work was presented in a series of short reports or in individual monographs. These and the annual reports of the Commission reveal many of its accomplishments.

As the Commission of Conservation did much of its major work in the years of the First World War, it was only too well aware that a lack of enforcement arose from the lack of available manpower. Many men who had been Game Guardians, Park Wardens, or Fire Rangers had enlisted in the war effort and conservation staff was at a premium. When the Commission was dissolved in 1921, it was considered unnecessary as public opinion had changed for the better. As well, the newly elected Conservative government may no longer have seen the need for a Liberal initiative.

Early Reports of the Chief Game Guardian

For the first three decades of the 20th century, the annual reports of the Chief Game Guardian dealt mainly with the enforcement of game laws and the payment of bounties for predators. By 1914, Ben Lawton was able to report that game was doing fairly well. Elk were scarce, whereas moose and deer were reasonably plentiful. Antelope were increasing in numbers following establishment of a game preserve at Nemiskam. Wild geese and ducks were less numerous than before.

There were complaints concerning the market hunters. During the settlement era, professional market hunters filled a niche in society as the middlemen between the resource and those who could not reach it. Unchecked, market hunters took a heavy toll on wildlife, easily switching from one species to the next as plundered populations quickly dwindled. Although permitted in Alberta, many hunters felt that market hunters took far more than their fair share of game. By 1916, market hunting was becoming less common and, by 1922, it was declared illegal.

Of course, there were, as there are today, ups and downs in wildlife numbers. In 1918, Lawton reported that the year had not been good for game in general. Moose were not as plentiful in some areas that year. The summers of 1917 and 1918 had been very dry with wetlands shrinking or drying completely to the detriment of waterfowl. Fur-bearing animals were scarce. Beaver were an exception, having increased in the southern areas of the province as a result of their protection since 1902. In contrast, 1920 was a good year for both big game and waterfowl.

WORKING FOR WILDLIFE
Janet Foster's *Working for Wildlife: The Beginning of Preservation in Canada* (1978) provides an excellent overview of the Federal Government's early involvement in wildlife conservation.[18] It includes events such as the creation of the national parks and forest reserves, the Commission of Conservation, and promotion of the Migratory Bird Treaty. Foster also described the far-seeing individuals who promoted these events. As many of these federal activities took place concurrently with and affected Alberta's own efforts at conservation, this book is highly recommended reading.

THE MARKET HUNTERS

While the vast herds of bison and elk (or "wapiti") that roamed the prairie grasslands astounded early explorers and settlers, this picture would not last long. Market hunters slaughtered thousands upon thousands of bison for nothing more than their hides and tongues. As the bison harvest dwindled, eastern tanners, finding elk hides more pliable than bison, began paying more for them.

The Manitoba elk was once found throughout the midwestern states and north into the Canadian prairie provinces. This elk had smaller antlers and a larger body mass than today's Rocky Mountain elk. Uncontrolled market hunting sent this subspecies into near extinction by 1900. Some researchers believe the Manitoba elk may have interbred with Rocky Mountain elk, also known as the Yellowstone elk, inhabiting the mountainous regions of the west. The rugged mountain terrain probably saved this species from extinction. These elk eventually became the seed crop used to reintroduce the elk into many of its former haunts. Market hunters also took their toll on other big game species including bighorn sheep which they were commissioned to shoot "by the flatcar" to feed labourers in the rail crews and mining towns.

Between the late 1800s and early 1900s, market hunters overharvested many bird species including shorebirds like the piping plover. Waterfowl, such as the canvasback, were particularly craved by city folk. Market hunters often fired their guns at rafts of birds, killing dozens with one shot. (The name "canvasback" may have originated from the early method of shipping the birds to market in canvas bags labelled "canvas back" to indicate return of the bags for reuse.)

The trumpeter swan occupied a breeding range over much of northern North America until intense exploitation by market hunters led to its decline. The species was considered endangered by the early 1900s. Swans were desired for their feathers and their meat. Hunting was stopped but, by 1932, biologists knew of only 69 trumpeters in the wild (those in Alaska were not yet known). Although never as scarce as trumpeters, tundra swans were also subjected to market hunting, but numbers rebounded after market hunting was outlawed.

As society became aware that wildlife was not inexhaustible, certain activities were no longer viewed in a positive light. Undue exploitation would no longer be tolerated. Market hunting, and the uncontrolled sale of wildlife, was prohibited. Activities such as night hunting became illegal. Wasting carcasses while taking only the most desirable or valuable parts (such as the tongue) was also banned.

One of the pleasant features in so far as the Game conditions of this Province are concerned is the lack of market hunters. True it is that instances occur where game and game birds have been sold in various cafes, and again, big game meat has been used, and still is in isolated districts by small logging concerns. However, it has been my endeavour and that of the field officers to deal drastically with reported cases.

W.H. WALLACE, 1938-1939 ANNUAL REPORT OF THE GAME BRANCH

In 1923, Lawton's official title changed from Chief Game Guardian to Game Commissioner. Lawton believed it was essential that a breeding stock of big game be maintained through adequate protection, and that the protection of game lands was necessary for the benefit of an increasing human population. He argued that an organization for the protection of wild animals was needed. The concept of wildlife management was just beginning to appear. Unfortunately, Alberta along with the rest of Canada and the world was entering the depression and money was scarce. For the time being, wildlife management continued to revolve around game preservation where local populations were protected within established game preserves; bounties were used for predator control; and transplanting or introducing species in areas where they no longer occurred, rounded out management options.

Alberta Takes Control: the 1930 Resources Transfer Act

Prior to 1930, the federal control of provincial resources was a source of irritation to most residents of the west. What rankled even more was the continued refusal of Ottawa even to discuss the matter. Prime Minister Sir Wilfred Laurier, while introducing the Alberta Bill in the House of Commons in February 1905, noted that Alberta and Saskatchewan never owned their lands and, therefore, should not have any ownership of such.[19] Although this satisfied no one, the matter was put aside. While it was raised from time to time, other things, such as the Alberta Great Waterways Railway affair (a scandal that led to the downfall of Premier Rutherford) and the First World War, intervened and the natural resources question went unresolved.

27

ELK BEING RELEASED OUT OF THE BACK OF A ONE-TON TRUCK AND TRANSPLANTED INTO AN AREA WHERE ELK WERE SCARCE.
COURTESY ALBERTA FISH AND WILDLIFE DIVISION

In the late 1920s, the three prairie governments again raised the topic, this time lobbying hard for a transfer of ownership. John E. Brownlee, Premier of Alberta, spearheaded the negotiations. His counterparts, James Gardiner of Saskatchewan and John Bracken of Manitoba, soon followed his example. Negotiations with Ottawa were sporadic, and it was not until December 14, 1929, that the transfer agreement was finally settled.[20] Ottawa enacted legislation transferring to provincial ownership all Crown lands, forest resources, mines, minerals, and royalties thereof, as well as fisheries and wildlife. The Alberta Legislature enacted complementary legislation confirming the transfer, which became law on April 3, 1930.[21] The provincial *Administration of Natural Resources Act* outlined the methods for control of these resources.[22] A short while later, the *Lands and Mines Act* was passed for the control of mines and minerals, petroleum, forest reserves, and later, fisheries and wildlife.[23] The Game Branch remained within the Department of Agriculture. Fisheries were placed under the Department of Lands and Mines; however, the Federal Government maintained a measure of control in fisheries as it does today across the country through its Department of Fisheries and Oceans.

The transfer of natural resources presented the Alberta government with an enormous challenge. At first, there was confusion as the transfer progressed. Most staff from the federal Department of the Interior were displaced, but some simply transferred to the relevant provincial departments. Initially, the province had no money to pay its natural resources

staff; so the Federal Government assumed this obligation for one year. The province later repaid the debt.[24] The depression began its long course, and governments across Canada began some unpleasant long-term financial belt-tightening. In Alberta, the United Farmers Administration formed the government of the day and considered farmers as its first obligation. As a result, little money was available for natural resources budgets and certainly not for staff. In 1931, the Game Branch consisted of the Game Commissioner and twelve salaried, seasonal Game Guardians responsible for enforcing game laws throughout the province. This figure would change little over the next decade.

The Start of many Departmental Transfers and Reorganizations

In November of 1931, after a 25-year career with the Game Branch, Benjamin Lawton, Game Commissioner, died. Stanley H. Clark filled the position for the next five years, during which time the Game Branch remained within the Department of Agriculture. During the same period, fisheries remained within the Department of Lands and Mines established in 1930, under Director R.T. Todd.

In time, however, the responsibilities of the Department of Agriculture evolved from being extensive in scope to being more specialized. Many of its functions, including wildlife management, were transferred to other departments. Thus, the Office of the Chief Game Guardian was transferred to the Department of Lands and Mines in 1936 in the first of numerous reorganizations. In the same

THE NATURAL RESOURCES (BOWKER) BUILDING
After the Depression and throughout the Second World War, money in the province and the rest of Canada was in short supply. Despite poor economic conditions, the Alberta Government was able to complete the Natural Resources Building in Edmonton. Built in 1931, the Natural Resources Building at 9833-109 Street was one of the first office buildings owned by the province, marking the 1930 transfer of the natural resource wealth from federal to provincial jurisdiction. Constructed within Government Centre, it was designed by Cecil Burgess, then a professor of architecture at the University of Alberta. Burgess used a grand style similar to that of the Legislature Building, including a Manitoba Tyndalstone finish. This building became the headquarters for the Department of Lands and Mines, and later served the Department of Lands and Forests. After being renovated in 1981, it housed the Department of the Attorney General (as it does today) and was renamed after Wilbur Bowker, a long time Dean of Law at the University of Alberta and director of the Institute of Law Research and Reform.

THE OFFICIAL SIGNING OF THE 1930 *NATURAL RESOURCES TRANSFER ACT,* GIVING ALBERTA AUTHORITY OVER ITS NATURAL RESOURCES INCLUDING FISH AND WILDLIFE. COURTESY ALBERTA FISH AND WILDLIFE DIVISION

year, the Assistant Director of Forestry, J.A. Hutchison, was for a short time given additional duties, replacing Clark as Game Commissioner. Forest Rangers assumed some of the game administration duties. The following year, W.H. Wallace was appointed Commissioner of a newly combined Fish and Game Branch, which was then moved back to the Department of Agriculture Administration in 1938.

Despite the departmental reorganizations, changes were underway for the provincial Fish and Game

GAME COMMISSIONER STANLEY H. CLARK

Although wildlife management was a relatively new term in 1936 (Aldo Leopold wrote the first major text on the subject in 1933), and the term sustainable development was not yet in use, it is obvious that Stanley Clark of Entrance, Alberta, had a firm grasp of both concepts. In the annual report of 1936, he wrote:

There is encouraging evidence that our rich natural endowment of wildlife is receiving increasing support for its conservation and restoration. Through various programmes of education the public is becoming more conscious of the fact that our big game, game birds, and fur-producing animals are an asset, which we hold in trust with the obligation that future generations should inherit their share of this valuable resource. Conservation is best applied by making wise use of wildlife and to so regulate the taking of animals and birds to assure a sufficient supply of breeding stock for propagation.[25]

Branch. In 1939, separate Fisheries and Game sections were created, recognizing the first major shift away from exclusive enforcement of fish and game laws, and towards responsibility for management of these resources. Sections were headed up by Game Superintendent, Don E. Forsland, and Fisheries Superintendent, H.B. Boney Watkins. The change in approach took place in conjunction with a number of conferences and meetings to gauge public opinion on matters relating to fish and wildlife.

In 1941, the Fish and Game Branch was returned to the Department of Lands and Mines where Forestry was located. Eric Huestis, Director of Forestry, was given additional duties as Fish and Game Commissioner (replacing Wallace). At this time, there were three employees in the Fish and Game Branch, along with six fishery and four game officers who were seasonal (laid off for the winter and re-employed each spring) and paid $90.00 a month. Throughout the Second World War, manpower was again in short supply—a particular problem for enforcement although game appeared to show a net increase (in part because there were fewer hunters, ammunition supplies were severely restricted, and gasoline rationing made long hunting trips virtually impossible). However, fish and game work was expanded with the assistance of Forestry personnel as directed by Commissioner Huestis.

ERIC HUESTIS, THEN DIRECTOR OF FORESTRY AND FORMER COMMISSIONER OF FISH AND GAME, WITH BERTIE BEAVER, MASCOT FOR THE ALBERTA FOREST SERVICE, 1960.
COURTESY ALBERTA SUSTAINABLE RESOURCE DEVELOPMENT (FOREST PROTECTION IMAGE LIBRARY)

PROVINCIAL DEPARTMENTAL AUTHORITIES FOR FISH AND WILDLIFE (1906 TO 2005)

1906 – 1936	Department of Agriculture Administration	Game Branch
1930 – 1936	Department of Lands and Mines	Fisheries Branch
1936 – 1938	Department of Lands and Mines	Fish and Game Branch
1938 – 1939	Department of Agriculture Administration	Fish and Game Branch
1939 – 1941	Department of Agriculture	Fish and Game Division
1941 – 1949	Department of Lands and Mines	Fish and Game Division
1949 – 1975	Department of Lands and Forests	Fish and Game Division (Fish and Wildlife Division in 1959)
1975 – 1979	Department of Recreation, Parks and Wildlife	Fish and Wildlife Division
1979 – 1986	Department of Energy and Natural Resources	Fish and Wildlife Division
1986	Department of Forestry	Fish and Wildlife Division
1986 – 1992	Department of Forestry, Lands and Wildlife	Fish and Wildlife Division
1992 – 1999	Department of Environmental Protection	Fish and Wildlife Service
1999 – 2001	Department of Environment	Natural Resources Service
2001 –	Department of Sustainable Resource Development	Fish and Wildlife Division

Huestis also favoured efforts to educate the public and change attitudes towards the wildlife resource. In 1946 he wrote:

> *Past experience clearly indicates that law enforcement is not enough to solve the problem of game conservation. It is necessary that the public realize the value of game as a natural resource and that it must be conserved and used with intelligence and discretion. It is impossible for the Game Branch with its limited number of enforcement officers to preserve this natural resource for posterity unless the public as a whole is willing to cooperate, and unless the public will come to realize that game laws are made to protect a natural resource belonging to them and not for the purpose of interfering with or retarding their hunting pleasures.*[26]

Working Together: Foresters and Fish and Wildlife Management

Early Dominion foresters and rangers, patrolling a system of horse trails from the U.S. border to Hinton, were in constant contact with fish and wildlife resources. However, assistance from forestry personnel in fish and game matters was not always a given and, at times, federal Forest Officers were not anxious to assist provincial Fish and Game Officers. The phrase "the pine curtain" was coined in reference to the Green Area Boundary, delineating Alberta's productive forests from the White Area agricultural lands. As well, the phrase was sometimes used to describe the lack of cooperation between the two sectors. With the 1930 *Natural Resources Transfer Act* a new provincial Forest Service was born.

31

ERIC HUESTIS: A COOPERATIVE APPROACH

Born in Sydney, Nova Scotia, Eric Stephen Huestis moved with his family to Alberta in 1903. He graduated from high school and worked as a teacher in Castor before completing two years of pre-medicine at the University of Alberta. He also spent six summers working on the John Day farm near Red Deer. He entered the Faculty of Forestry at the University of British Columbia in 1922, and in 1923 he began his career while a summer student on a survey crew in the Slave Lake Forest Reserve. Before completing his degree, he spent time surveying the Brazeau and Cypress Hills forests.

In 1925, Huestis began working full-time for the Dominion, starting on a survey crew in the Clearwater Forest. With the 1930 transfer of resources to the province, Huestis, like many others, moved to the newly formed Alberta Forest Service and was promoted to Forest Supervisor at Rocky Mountain House the same year. The early days were not easy: "…we took the department over in 1930 and it took us ten years to really get going."[27]

Huestis then moved through several positions including Assistant Superintendent of the newly combined Crowsnest-Bow River Forest in 1934, Superintendent of the Brazeau/Athabasca Forest, and Acting Assistant Director of Forestry in 1940. The next year he was also named Fish and Game Commissioner, a position he held until 1959. Under his direction, the first scientifically trained fisheries and wildlife biologists were hired.

During his time as Fish and Game Commissioner, Huestis continued to advance in Forestry. He was appointed Assistant Director in 1947, Acting Director in 1948, Director of Forestry in 1949, and finally, Deputy Minister of the Alberta Department of Lands and Forests in 1963—a position he held until his retirement in 1966. Over the span of his career, Eric Huestis was involved in several major developments including the establishment of the Green Area, *Forest Act*, *Forest Protection Act*, Forest Management Area program, Quota Timber Disposition system, extended forest fire control, Land Use Planning, as well as the Hinton Forest Technology School and the Junior Forest Warden program. He proudly stated in 1983: "I have been on and worked on every forest reserve in the province."[28]

Eric Huestis showed foresight and commitment throughout more than 40 years of public service. His career spanned the period of the federal-provincial resources transfer, an era of dynamic change and development within Alberta's natural resources sector. He passed away on November 14, 1988. However, his contributions continue to serve the natural resources of Alberta well.

FORESTER AND JACK-OF-ALL-TRADES—THE STORY OF JACK MORDEN, 1884-1974

[ADAPTED FROM AN ARTICLE BY JAMES R. KERR[29]]

John Augustus (Jack) Morden was born in Michigan in 1884. When he was a small boy, the family moved to Lacombe, Alberta. At the age of thirteen, he left home with his most valuable possession, his axe, which he used with proficiency. In 1903, Jack arrived at Blairmore to work at McLaren's Mill where he advanced to millwright. Except for a trip to Idaho and Washington in 1910, he spent the rest of his life in southwestern Alberta.

Jack had much to do with the early days of forestry, having worked for the Dominion Forestry during the period of Ted Blefgen, George Ritchie and Harry Boulton. He worked at Kelly's Camp, Lynx Creek, West Porcupine and The Gap. He also worked stringing early telephone lines in the Porcupine Hills and as a forest ranger for the Canadian Pacific Railroad in the Castle-Carbondale country.

In those days, forestry work was seasonal. Another job had to be found in winter. Trapping took up the slack and Jack became an expert at it. In 1914, he trapped on Racehorse Creek. In the same year, he shot a tremendous bighorn sheep in the vicinity of the Seven Sisters. This majestic ram reportedly graced the wall of the Alberta Legislative Building for many years.

In 1930, Alberta took over the management of its natural resources from the Dominion and forestry became a year-round job. Winter jobs were always available for axe-man Morden. Samples of Jack's work can still be found on bridges built near Snake Creek on the Livingstone River in the Gap and on Racehorse Creek. He also helped build a log cabin in the replica of the original North West Mounted Police barracks at Fort Macleod. The two-storey log house standing near the old railway crossing at Lundbreck is also a monument to Jack's art.

At some point, Jack branched out into guiding and outfitting. He made much of the required equipment himself including rawhide pack boxes, harness for the dogs, hackamores and bridles for the horses. When he needed clothes, he often turned to buckskin even though he always said buckskin was wet two days before a rain and it took two days after a rain to dry it out.

When beaver became a problem in certain spots, Jack was hired to live-trap the animals and transport them to areas where they were scarce. On many occasions, they were moved several hundred miles. Other times, they were moved only a short distance where Jack could pick them up again when their pelts were prime. When Forestry needed young men trained in the art of blacksmithing, Jack was called in to instruct. When Fish and Wildlife required live-trapped ring-necked pheasants for their propagation and study at Brooks, Jack Morden was the man of the hour. When there were no squirrels in the Cypress Hills area, Jack was the man to live-trap them and plant them there.

Pretending not to know when he was born, Jack stayed on with Forestry longer than the sixty-five year milepost of his life. When he eventually retired, he could not stay idle. He went to work for Johnson Brothers' Sawmill where his expert ability was appreciated. Jack kept up with the affairs of the world until his last few days with us. He was well known and well liked. He passed away quietly in the Pincher Creek Hospital on December 18, 1974, at the age of 90. If there is a Happy Hunting Ground, Jack has already reached it, axe in hand.

EARLY DOMINION FOREST RANGERS ON PATROL, 1909.
COURTESY ALBERTA SUSTAINABLE RESOURCE DEVELOPMENT (FOREST PROTECTION IMAGE LIBRARY)

Watch over the Forest (1999).[30] Gilliat joined the Alberta Forest Service in the 1940s, and worked in many of Alberta's forest districts. Along with his forestry duties, he issued hunting licences and trappers' permits, responded to problem wildlife complaints, dealt with rabies concerns, and carried out other aspects of fish and wildlife management.

33

The Dominion Forestry Branch did not completely disappear, but evolved into today's Canadian Forest Service that continues to fulfill the role of a national forest research agency. Though somewhat modified, the federal agency celebrated its centennial year in 1999.

The provincial Forest Service struggled with its own beginnings until 1949 when it successfully evolved into the Forestry Division under the newly created Department of Lands and Forests. The Fish and Game Branch also moved into this department the same year. Between 1953 and 1960, forestry actually absorbed Fish and Wildlife, becoming the Forests and Wildlife Division with Branches of Forest Protection, Forest Surveys, Fish and Wildlife, and Radio Communications. In 1959, the Forests and Wildlife Division became the Alberta Forest Service. At the same time, Fish and *Game* became Fish and *Wildlife*, maintaining its own Division status within the same department.

For a look at how provincial forestry personnel assisted in fish and wildlife management, see Neil Gilliat's books *If Moose Could Only Talk* (1989) and

The Science of Game Management

As early as 1916, C. Gordon Hewitt, Dominion Entomologist, started writing about conservation and the need to preserve and carefully manage wildlife.[31] However, a generation ahead of their time, these ground-breaking works received scant notice except from a few serious-minded scientists. Game management would receive little study until after the First World War.

Hewitt, originally of Macclesfield, England, graduated from Manchester University as a Doctor in Zoology and Entomology. He came to Canada in 1909 as the newly appointed Dominion Entomologist. During his 11-year tenure in this position, Hewitt is credited with the successful development of the Canadian Entomological Service from a small unit of the Experimental Farms Service to an important, separate Entomology Branch of the federal Department of Agriculture.

Under Hewitt's leadership, several important initiatives were undertaken by the Service, starting with the development of the *Destructive*

Insect and Pest Act passed in 1910. This legislation was designed to prevent the introduction and spread of noxious insects, plant diseases, and other agricultural pests. Resident agricultural pests were a problem for livestock and plants alike. Thus, a series of 12 field laboratories was established across Canada including one at Lethbridge, Alberta "for the purpose of watching, combatting, and forestalling insect injury to forests and crops".[32] Insects included the voracious hordes of grasshoppers and biting flies, as well as field crop pests such as the pale western cutworm and wheat stem sawfly.

As well as being an avid entomologist and able administrator, Hewitt showed a broad range of interests for all of Canada's wildlife. His role was enlarged in 1916 when he became Consulting Zoologist to the Dominion Government. He accepted the position of Canadian representative on the International Commission for the Protection of Nature from which he commenced work on drafting the *Northwest Game Act*. After this, he was involved in the *Migratory Bird Treaty* of 1916 and its 1917 ratification via the *Migratory Birds Convention Act*. Hewitt also was a strong believer in the use of game preserves. His influence was soon felt in Alberta

with the establishment of the Cooking Lake Forest and Game Reserve (1918) adjoining the southern boundary of the Dominion Elk Island Park (1906), and the Cypress Hills Forest and Game Reserve (1918) southeast of Medicine Hat. Hewitt's love of wildlife was demonstrated in his book, *The Conservation of the Wild Life of Canada* (1921). Unfortunately, he did not live to see his work published, dying suddenly of pleural pneumonia on February 29, 1920 at only 35 years of age.

It was during the inter-war years that the need to apply scientific principles to wildlife populations became apparent. People began asking why some species were still declining in spite of closed seasons. They wondered if disease was the cause. It appeared that some species recovered quickly from over-hunting, while others did not. These questions and others had triggered research in Europe where game was often found on private reserves and was relatively easy to study.

In North America, with wildlife roaming free, often in relatively inaccessible areas, other research methods had to be applied. Aldo Leopold's 1933 treatise *Game Management* was then, and still is, the major text on the subject of wildlife management.[33]

WILDLIFE MANAGEMENT – ALDO LEOPOLD-STYLE

To gain an understanding of Aldo Leopold, the student of wildlife management should start with Leopold's *A Sand County Almanac*. Then, once fully immersed in the land ethic and an understanding of living in harmony with our surroundings, they are ready to tackle the mechanics of this science as outlined in Leopold's *Game Management*.

Aldo Leopold grew up in Iowa where he first gained an appreciation for the outdoors. He graduated a Master of Forestry from Yale in 1909. He then joined the U.S. Forest Service (est. 1905) and worked there until 1928. Leopold spent several years conducting game surveys for various states before accepting the first Chair of Game Management, Department of Agriculture Economics, at the University of Wisconsin in 1933. There he was a founding member of The Wildlife Society in 1936.

In 1948, Leopold's manuscript for *A Sand County Almanac* was accepted for publication; however, he died of a heart attack before seeing its publication. In 1949, the Almanac was published, an insightful treatise that became the century's literary landmark in conservation.

Acts of creation are ordinarily reserved for gods and poets, but humbler folk may circumvent this restriction if they know how. To plant a pine, for example, one need be neither god nor poet; one need only own a good shovel. By virtue of this curious loophole in the rules, any clodhopper may say: Let there be a tree—and there will be one.[34]

In it, Leopold identified three major steps for game management. First, an inventory of the game species is made. Second, the productivity (fecundity) of the species is determined. And third, any factors limiting fecundity are identified and quantified. Once population numbers, productivity and limiting factors are known, wildlife can be managed more effectively. Historical yield can be determined and compared with present regimes so that active steps are taken to manage future harvests successfully.

When the Second World War finally ended, taking with it the economic difficulties and manpower shortages of the past three decades, the philosophies of Hewitt and Leopold would finally have an opportunity to be implemented in Alberta. Prospects for the future appeared hopeful. In 1945, the Department of Lands and Mines celebrated its 15th anniversary. In 1947, the major oil field discoveries at Leduc would lead to a new source of provincial income from oil and gas royalties. Among other things, increased revenues would provide more money for wildlife management and research.

Throughout the 1950s, Fish and Game Commissioner Huestis sought outside advice on fish and wildlife management through the Fish and Game Advisory Council. This Council was composed of three members of the Alberta Fish and Game Association, and two representatives of the University of Alberta. The Council was soon enlarged to include representation from farmers (Western Stock Growers Association), natives, fur dealers, and later, trappers and outfitters. It also included three staff members of the Fish and Game Division who played a major role in providing biological data to keep the Council well informed. Advisory Council members wrestled with the multitude of problems that plagued wildlife management of the times. They aided in the design of new legislation and hunting regulations, recommended bag limits and open seasons, and kept the government advised of fish and game conditions. The Council also recommended that the government hire more professional scientific staff to implement fish and game management techniques as described by

35

THE FISH AND GAME ADVISORY COUNCIL WAS CREATED IN 1943 BY COMMISSIONER HUESTIS AS A MEANS OF CONSULTATION WITH PUBLIC STAKEHOLDERS.
COURTESY ALBERTA SUSTAINABLE RESOURCE DEVELOPMENT (FOREST PROTECTION IMAGE LIBRARY)

Leopold. Soon, trained wildlife biologists would be hired to undertake scientific studies of fish and wildlife populations. Trained and uniformed enforcement officers would ensure compliance with legislation reflecting these new methods.

Much of this new science was emphasized at the 1952 staff training school held at the abandoned German prisoner-of-war camp, which today is the Kananaskis Field Station. This field school provided specialized instruction in conservation and forestry. Lectures were provided by Commissioner Huestis as well as several university professors, including William Rowan, who had conducted migration experiments on crows; Robert G.H. Cormack, one of the founding fathers of botanical study in Alberta; and Richard B. Miller, who was conducting inventories and studies on many of Alberta's lakes and fish populations. Later, provincial fisheries and wildlife biologists including Martin Paetz and George Mitchell would also give lectures on wildlife biology, management, and techniques at this camp, and later at the new training school at Hinton.

COMMISSIONER HUESTIS LECTURING AT KANANASKIS FIELD STATION.
COURTESY ALBERTA SUSTAINABLE RESOURCE DEVELOPMENT (FOREST PROTECTION IMAGE LIBRARY)

A New Breed of Men, a New Approach to Management

Following the advice of the Fish and Wildlife Advisory Council, Huestis hired a number of professionally trained forestry and fish and wildlife people. Martin J. Paetz, a student of Richard B. Miller at the University of Alberta, was the first full-time Fisheries Biologist hired by the province (see more on Paetz and other fisheries staff in

ROBERT G.H. CORMACK AND THE *WILD FLOWERS OF ALBERTA*

After receiving his education in Ontario, Robert George Hall Cormack joined the Botany Department of the University of Alberta in 1936 as a plant anatomist and conservationist. He quickly rose to the level of Professor and was known as a popular and enthusiastic teacher. His research established him as an authority on plant root hairs, with a number of papers appearing in botanical journals in North America and Europe. In 1957, Cormack was elected Fellow of the Royal Society of Canada.

Encouraged by Eric Huestis, Acting Assistant Director of Forestry, Cormack began a study in 1944 on the flora of the eastern slopes of the Rockies and the effects of fire, logging, strip mining, and overgrazing by cattle. In 1945, he made a two-month study of overgrazing in undisturbed forest areas of the Cypress Hills and its effects on natural regeneration, forest soils, springs and trout streams, soil erosion, and water conservation.[35] [One might surmise that Dr. Cormack would approve of today's Cows and Fish Program!] In 1955, Cormack assisted wildlife biologist George Mitchell in an in-depth study of range conditions in the Crowsnest Forest, and in 1965 Mitchell briefly accompanied Cormack in his quest for additional floral photographs for his 1967 book *Wild Flowers of Alberta*.[36] This guide to common flowering plants of the province joined the ranks of Salt and Wilk's *The Birds of Alberta* (1958) and Soper's *The Mammals of Alberta* (1964) thereby "arming the layman with a trilogy of references to go forth and inventory Alberta's natural history". [Note that E.H. Moss preceded Cormack's work with the *Flora of Alberta* published in 1932.] Robert G.H. Cormack died in Edmonton on October 24, 1995 at the age of 91 years.

THE RENOWNED WILLIAM ROWAN (1891-1957)
[BETH MICHENER]

A conservationist, artist, public speaker, writer, and teacher, William Rowan remains one of Alberta's pre-eminent biologists. Despite international renown for his pioneering research concerning photoperiodism (the role of day-length in migration), Rowan remained a local figure, contributing to many aspects of Alberta's wildlife and natural history.

For a detailed examination of Rowan's life, one should start with Ainley's biography—*Restless Energy: a Biography of William Rowan, 1891 - 1957.*[37] According to Ainley, Rowan spent his early childhood growing up in mainland Europe. Fascinated by nature, his first migration experiment may have been at the age of ten when he trapped a dozen flies, placed them in a cage in his pocket, and transported them from France to England for release. At an early age, Rowan was sketching and photographing the landscape while studying eggs, snakes, bugs, and bird nests. In his quest for "adventure and escape", seventeen-year-old Rowan left England for the Wild West. He arrived in Crawling Valley, Alberta and took up as a cowpuncher. Here, he evidently developed his life-long love affair with the wilderness and the prairies.

Rowan returned to England for his formal education, a BSc (Honours) in Zoology. After graduation, he married and moved to Winnipeg, Manitoba. For a short period, he lectured in the University of Manitoba's Zoology Department, before moving to Alberta. In 1920, Rowan was hired to build a Department of Zoology in Edmonton under University of Alberta President Henry Marshall Tory. As head of the Zoology Department, Rowan was able to assemble a scientific library and taxidermy collection of vertebrates and invertebrates, often in exchange with other researchers. Rowan lectured to medical, arts, and zoology students developing a reputation as a zoologist while pursuing his immense interests in ornithological work in his spare time. He developed a wide range of contacts throughout Canada, the United States, and England. At home, Rowan was acquainted with Benjamin Lawton, Alberta's Chief Game Guardian, who among other things granted provincial collecting permits to shoot birds and mammals. Rowan joined the Alberta Fish and Game Association in 1921 and was elected chairman of the songbird committee. He was also a member of the predator committee of the Edmonton Bird Club. Farther afield, he was a scientific advisor to the Delta Research Station in Manitoba and, in 1927, was elected a member of the American Ornithologists Union.

Rowan was exceptionally talented in art—a field he occasionally considered pursuing full-time. He drew with pen and pencil, painted, and eventually learned to sculpt. In 1955, a five-cent postage stamp with Rowan's drawing of Whooping Cranes was issued. His exceptional paintings, photographs, and drawings can be seen in several of his published materials, including his articles from *British Birds* which were collated in *Alberta Waders.*[38] Many of these materials reside in the archives of the University of Alberta.

Shorebirds were of great interest to Rowan and he studied them for a number of years. He was interested in migration and once asked all reputable Alberta naturalists to send their migration records to the University to be filed and collated. But his groundbreaking work began at Beaverhill Lake, where he noticed the differences in gonad size in birds migrating north and south.[39] After eliminating temperature and barometric pressure, Rowan postulated that day length, which changes at the same rate every year, was the factor that induced migration. His migration experiments began in 1924. He used a sparrow trap beside his house to catch dark-eyed juncos. These he put in to two large aviaries he built at the far end of his garden, away from artificial heat and from H.M. Tory, who disapproved of ornithology. One aviary was the control and the other was the experimental, with a light fixture to control daylight. Rowan used juncos because of their hardiness and because they are one of the first migrants to reach Canada. By Christmas, the experimental juncos exposed to artificial dark/light regimes had gonads equal to their breeding condition and were singing as if it were spring.[40] Rowan's work on migration introduced experimental science into the field of ornithology and stimulated worldwide experimentation.

Concurrently, Tory recommended that in order to secure his position as Chair of Zoology, Rowan should pursue a doctorate. His thesis dealt with photoperiodism and migration and was completed under the direction of J.P. Hill of University College.[41] Rowan moved from juncos to crows to pursue induced reverse migration. His research on crows made him a public figure in Edmonton as his experimental aviaries were located west of the High Level Bridge along the North Saskatchewan River—in full view of the street cars and trains that used the top deck and the pedestrians and other traffic on the lower deck. He involved the whole community, with crow food supplied by animals from the city pound, scraps from fish stores, and stale bread from the bakery. Rowan released press bulletins asking people to "join in the crow hunt" and offered a bounty for every five U.S. Government bird bands returned with carcasses.[42] As well as light, Rowan manipulated the star patterns in his artificial pens to prove that birds also used such patterns to initiate migration. After their reverse treatment, birds tried to go south in the spring and north in the fall!

Rowan often worked with J.B. Collip, a biochemist at the university who was renowned for his insulin research. While Collip analyzed blood for hormones, Rowan dissected and stained testes. He found that while the control testes remained the same size, those from birds subjected to artificial light regimes to increase day length grew larger. Through forced exercise of his crows, he found that activity levels also played a role in the reproductive cycle.

Rowan's interests went far beyond migration. In 1925, he became a vocal opponent of the federal government's proposal to mix diseased plains bison herds from Wainwright with the wood bison in Wood Buffalo Park.[43] To further his personal knowledge of the area, he funded a trip to the park through the sale of two wood buffalo

skeletons to colleagues at Harvard. He also studied population cycles, an interest that was born out of his hunting and conservation pursuits. Rowan became a household name through his book *The Riddle of Migration*.[44] He also wrote several articles for newspapers including the *Edmonton Journal* and *Calgary Herald*, and many radio talks. His thesis was mentioned in the *Saturday Evening Post* and the *New York Times*. He wrote several unpublished manuscripts such as *Beloved Wilderness, As the Crow Flies,* and *The Last Chapter,* as well as a novel *This Great Advertisement* based on the superficiality of American life.

Rowan received an exceptional response from radio talks on the Canadian Broadcasting Corporation. He gave a talk for the Royal Society on *Intellect and Human Survival* and was a guest lecturer for the Fourth International Photobiology Congress in Amsterdam. Before his research in 1924, there were fewer than six papers published on photoperiodism; at the 1954 conference on this topic there were 150 papers presented. In 1956, Rowan retired with a party in his honour at the Men's Faculty Club. During his short retirement, he focussed on drawing and fieldwork and spent time at his favourite locations including Francis Point (Beaverhill Lake), the muskegs around Edmonton, the marshes near Delta, Manitoba, and what is now Cypress Hills Interprovincial Park. He passed away in 1957.

Rowan was a staunch supporter of public education and conservation measures. He was a hunter, humanitarian, artist, teacher, prominent biologist, and a stubborn and independent thinker when it came to research. He was a pioneer who left a lasting imprint on the science of ornithology.

...the final criterion of human success is not the material output of science...It is the sum-total of moral and spiritual values expressed in one simple word— integrity—that matters most, and of integrity, science is at least one of the world's outstanding exponents.[45]

Chapter 6). George J. Mitchell, a graduate of the University of British Columbia, arrived in 1952 as the province's first game biologist. The primary duties of both men were to compile an inventory of species, determine population characteristics, and discover factors that affected their numbers.

When George Mitchell began his career with Fish and Wildlife, his office consisted of "a small space on a laboratory bench with a stool to sit on" in the Zoology Department housed in the University of Alberta Medical Building. In 1953, he was assigned to room 65A—a small ground-floor office that he shared with the Human Embryo Morgue. He was joined by Bob Webb in an adjacent office in 1954.

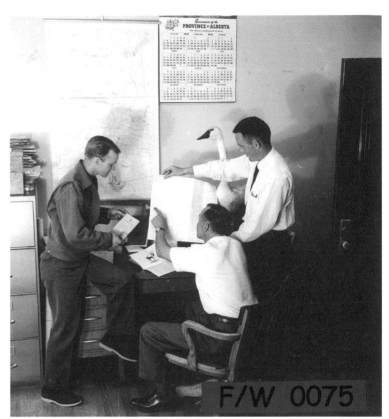

BIOLOGISTS JOHN STELFOX, GEORGE MITCHELL AND BOB WEBB, HIRED BY THE PROVINCE IN THE EARLY 1950s, IN THEIR EDMONTON OFFICE IN 1958.
COURTESY B. STEVENSON

39

THE KANANASKIS FIELD STATIONS
[FRANCINE WIELICZKO]

During the depression of the 1930s, a government relief camp was built at Barrier Lake in the Kananaskis River valley west of Calgary to supply employment for people without work. Workers cleared fire roads, erected picnic shelters, and thinned forests. When the relief program ended in 1936, the site became the federal Kananaskis Forest Experiment Station. During the Second World War, it was used as a federal internment camp. German and Italian nationals living in Canada, whose loyalties were suspect were detained here until the summer of 1940. Later, German commissioned officers captured in battle were imprisoned in the camp. Prisoners of war cleared trees for the construction of the Barrier Lake Reservoir. Finally, in 1948 the site was once again used as a federally operated forestry experimental station.

In 1966, the federal government granted a lease to the University of Calgary to operate the Kananaskis Field Station on a small section of the site. From 1966 to 1973, the Barrier Lake Station was built in stages. The federal forest station was transferred to the Government of Alberta in 1979 and then to the University of Calgary in 1993. The University of Calgary currently has a lease with the provincial government to operate the Kananaskis Field Station. The province provides logistic support to field researchers and manages adjacent land use so that a suitable land base is maintained for research.

The University of Calgary also operates the R.B. Miller Field Station nestled in the Sheep River Wildlife Sanctuary, 110 km southwest of Calgary, one of Canada's oldest fish and wildlife research stations.[46] Together, the Kananaskis Field Stations provide a suitable environment for local and international researchers to carry out studies that assist with managing fish and wildlife resources and advancing the understanding of the Canadian Rockies and foothills ecosystems. In 2005, the Kananaskis Field Stations celebrated 55 years of research.

EARLY PROVINCIAL STAFF DON BARWISE, MARTIN PAETZ AND JOHN STELFOX
WORKING AT THE UNIVERSITY OF ALBERTA LABORATORY.
COURTESY ALBERTA FISH AND WILDLIFE DIVISION

40

Big Island Lake (east of Edmonton) to document the causes of fluctuations in this species. Schmitke was awarded his Master's degree on the subject posthumously following a fatal boating accident in 1965 while surveying waterfowl on the North Saskatchewan River. In 1963, following the completion of his dissertation on Rocky Mountain goats, Gordon Kerr joined the wildlife team and started surveying game birds and big game in southern Alberta and the foothills.

Martin Paetz was joined by fisheries biologist Ron Thomas that same year and a third fisheries biologist, Gord Hartman, in 1956. John Stelfox began working with the Alberta Government in 1955, undertaking work similar to Mitchell's. Bill Wishart, a former student of Rowan's, came on staff in 1957, first replacing Hartman (who returned to work in British Columbia) but soon becoming a wildlife biologist. By 1959, Wishart was using Leopold's game management methods to survey bighorn sheep and to determine why their numbers had fluctuated over the years.

In 1959, Game Branch staff of the Fish and Wildlife Division were assigned to particular parts of the province: Bill Wishart to Edmonton North and the Peace River Block; Bob Webb to the Parkland between Edmonton and Calgary including the central foothills and northern prairies; George Mitchell to the Eastern and Western Irrigation Districts, southern prairie, foothills, and other southern sectors; and John Stelfox to the Northern Foothills. About the same time, the Fisheries Branch was doubled in size by the addition of Rod Paterson and Buck Cunningham to assist Martin Paetz and Ron Thomas.

In 1961, Roger Schmitke joined the wildlife team and began his studies of a muskrat population at

BIOLOGIST ROGER SCHMITKE
COLLECTING INFORMATION ON MUSKRATS.
COURTESY ALBERTA FISH AND WILDLIFE DIVISION

ALBERTA'S FIRST GAME BIOLOGIST
[GEORGE MITCHELL]

I was fortunate to spend my early summers on the Sunshine Coast in B.C., swimming, hiking, hunting, catching saltwater fish, and participating in other wildlife and outdoor activities. A high school science teacher encouraged me in the areas of biology and the environment. I joined the RCAF in 1943 and was in the first ex-servicemen's class at the University of British Columbia (UBC) in 1945. I graduated with a Bachelor's degree in 1950 and a Master's in 1952. My thesis was titled "Wintering Distribution of Diving Ducks on the Coastal Waters of Southern B.C.".

In 1952, I was hired by Eric Huestis as Alberta's first Game Biologist. I arrived in Edmonton on May 13. It was a banner year for disease. Tularaemia was discovered in beaver in the southwest corner of the province and in Waterton Lakes National Park. Tularaemia, also known as rabbit fever, is a plague-like disease of rodents caused by the bacterium *Francisella tularensis*. It is primarily transmitted in contaminated water and mortality will occur in high-density populations. Colonies of beavers in the headwaters of Pincher Creek and in adjacent Waterton Lakes National Park were decimated in 1952. Along with Game Officer Jim Stewart and rancher Andy Russell, we located and retrieved dead beaver from several ponds. Each beaver had white spots in the spleen, diagnosed as tularaemia by veterinarians in Kamloops, B.C. Because beaver were dying on the watershed flowing north through Pincher Creek, the ranchers in the region were very concerned about the possibility of tularaemia spreading to their livestock. They were assured there would be no problem. Interestingly, we found no evidence of tularaemia in trapped muskrats [a common host for the bacteria].

That same year, there was an outbreak of foot and mouth disease in cattle in southern Alberta and movement of livestock between Alberta and Montana was stopped. Further, there was an outbreak of rabies in dogs, coyotes, and wolves in northern Alberta. The first case in Alberta was reported at Fitzgerald in June 1952 when a wild red fox bit a trapper's dog, which later developed the disease. To counter its spread south, the authorities set up a temporary east-west barrier in the Peace River and north area, using trappers to eliminate rabid animals. Finally, it was a year of polio epidemic in people, which was countered by the closure of all outdoor swimming pools in Alberta for the summer.

My initial tasks as game biologist were game species inventories, distribution, and habitat evaluation—a combination that can aid in setting harvest dates, season lengths, and bag limits. Fieldwork commenced at the

R.B. Miller Station at Sheep River where I observed bighorn sheep, mule deer, moose, elk, cougar, and coyotes, and also identified local trees, shrubs, grasses, and weeds. Graduate student John Stelfox from Rocky Mountain House joined me and we began an upland game bird census in the irrigation districts in southern Alberta. These habitats were prime areas for ring-necked pheasant and gray (Hungarian) partridge. We got involved in an eclectic array of additional projects such as assessing waterfowl damage to field crops; teaming up with mammalogist A.W.F. Banfield to examine the parasite loads in elk and bison at Elk Island National Park; helping David Stelfox collect snowshoe hares in the Athabasca area for Dr. Rowan's study; and discussing new wildlife management principles, objectives, and techniques with sportsmen as well as fish and game and forestry officers.

From 1952 through 1956, I expanded the format and content of the annual big game and bird game hunter questionnaires, and analyzed the responses in order to document hunter effort and success, as well as regional game harvests. In 1953, the first hands-on organized assessment and tally of hunter game bird harvests, hunter effort, and success in Alberta was achieved through early hunter check stations. That year, the Brooks and Tilley stations were manned by three Game Officers, three RCMP Officers, two assistants, and me. Check stations operated each year and in different irrigation districts throughout the 1950s and 1960s.

Other activities over the years included study of upland ungulate range conditions, parasites and diseases in avian and mammalian species, recommendations of annual seasons and limits, development of census techniques and research programs for summer assistants, presentation of training courses for conservation officers and foresters, collaboration with other management agencies and the general public (especially members of sportsmen's groups) as well as a number of administrative duties. Research and management emphasis was placed on ring-necked pheasant, Hungarian partridge, sharp-tailed grouse, blue grouse, bighorn sheep, elk, mule deer, moose, pronghorn antelope, and avian parasites and diseases.

[In his interview, Officer Gerry Pelchat recalls: "George had me collecting antelope for him. In fact, one year I shot fifty-two bucks, one buck every week of the year and I shot eighty-seven does, if I remember correctly, during the gestation period. I did all the measurements, collected the eyeballs, pituitary glands, the live weight and the dressed weight and the stomach samples and you name it, and I collected it. I smelt like antelope for six months!"]

The basic tools in the early 1950s were cameras, spotting scopes, binoculars, pack horses, snowmobiles, succinylchloride darts, throw-nets, live-traps, ear tags with markers, coloured neck collars, and drive traps. Fixed-wing aircraft were used for surveys in prairie, boreal, and mountain habitats. Because of a lack of budget, antelope aerial surveys in the late 1950s were done by hitching a ride with the U.S. Fish and Wildlife Service crew. They were counting waterfowl and ponds while I was counting pronghorns. In the early 1960s, I made deer, elk, and moose surveys in the foothills using aircraft out of the Lethbridge Flying Club as a "student" and getting a "student rate". This arrangement was soon squelched by the Department of Transport in Ottawa! Ground transects were established in some irrigation districts to obtain pheasant and gray partridge trend data via annual crowing counts and brood observations. Initially, my Labrador retriever flushed pheasants adjacent to the transects but eventually more sophisticated tools, such as radio collars, became available and the numbers of wildlife biologists and assistants increased considerably.

Two main issues were convincing sportsmen, government officials, and fish and wildlife officers of the validity of management and game research techniques, and establishing the need for inventory data that could be translated into hunting limits for game animals. In the early 1950s, wildlife research was almost non-existent and on the back burner. One year, an enforcement official in the Game Branch told me to put my vehicle on blocks in the fall because there's nothing important to do concerning wildlife management in the winter months. Winter is, of course, a crucial season for animal welfare, survivorship, and the collection of biological and management information. Initially, many people, unaware of wildlife research and management techniques, were skeptical of methods for determining animal abundance and distribution. Many of these issues were resolved by inviting sportsmen and officers to accompany me on one or more surveys.

I received a two-year educational leave from the Alberta Government to attend Washington State University (WSU) from 1960 to 1962. My doctoral thesis on antelope was published in 1980 as a book.[47] Throughout these years, my primary influence and guidance came from Ian McTaggart-Cowan and George Spencer at UBC, and Irvin Buss and Hal Buechner at WSU. In 1962, I was promoted to Chief Wildlife Biologist in charge of planning, developing, and regulating wildlife research, management, and policies; supervising the work of eight experienced and capable wildlife biologists, numerous summer assistants, and game hatchery personnel; attending national and international wildlife and land classification meetings; and preparing annual reports and other literature designed to develop understanding and acceptance of the Division's programs.

WILDLIFE BIOLOGIST GEORGE MITCHELL AND HIS DOG, BRANT, 1956.
CREDIT: J. STELFOX

AL JOLITZ AND GEORGE MITCHELL COLLECT BIOLOGICAL INFORMATION FOR AN ANTELOPE STUDY, 1958.
COURTESY ALBERTA FISH AND WILDLIFE DIVISION

[George Mitchell resigned from the Alberta Government in 1966 and moved his family to Regina to accept a position as Associate Professor in Biology at the University of Saskatchewan. He continued to espouse sound biological research and management in his lectures and field trips and at national and international conferences. Today, George and his wife Connie still live in Regina where he is Professor Emeritus at the University of Regina. He is actively engaged in preparing several reports on research he did as a wildlife biologist. He also sits on the Fish and Wildlife Development Fund Steering Committee for the Government of Saskatchewan.]

ROBERT (BOB) WEBB, PROVINCIAL WILDLIFE BIOLOGIST
[INTERVIEWED BY PAT VALASTIN[48]]

Robert (Bob) Webb was born in the small town of Davidson, Saskatchewan in 1931 where he spent his early years drawing and birdwatching. He completed a B.Sc. at the University of British Columbia where he was particularly impressed with Ian McTaggart-Cowan. "He was the wildlife management man at the time and graduate students came from all around just because of him. He was a mesmerizing speaker. People would come and sit in the aisles to listen to him. Fascinating man."

Webb graduated from UBC in 1952 and took a summer job conducting range studies at Banff National Park. He returned to Alberta the following summer to start a graduate study of pintail duck behaviour at Tilley under the supervision of McTaggart-Cowan. In 1954, Webb was offered a position with Alberta Fish and Wildlife. "Jobs were scarce, so I dropped the Master's project and never got back to it. George [Mitchell] and I shared the province. I had the northern half. As each biologist came on, we re-divided the province. In 1963, I moved to Calgary to start up a new region stretching from Red Deer south. Those were perfect jobs. The resources were there—from antelope and sage grouse, through mountain goats and bighorn sheep. We had the diversity and the responsibility. Eric Huestis wasn't a hands-on kind of guy so we were very independent. He left it to us: with the strong influence and advice of the University professors."

"We had a little group called the Alberta wing of the Canadian Society of Fish and Wildlife Biologists [later renamed the Canadian Society of Environmental Biologists]. We got together quite often and hashed out environmental issues like the introduction of Merriam's wild turkey into Cypress Hills. Merriam's turkey, a western sub-species, occurs naturally in the Dakotas, New Mexico, and Colorado. I'm convinced the only reason they weren't in southern Alberta is the isolated habitat and no opportunity to get here. I later trapped some of the birds from Cypress Hills and brought them up to the Porcupine Hills.

"When we first came, we tried to bring in some scientific principles of wildlife management. We started surveys and liberalized the hunting opportunities: that meant antlerless seasons and opening up hunting seasons on new species and in new areas. We all believed there was an opportunity to use wildlife consumptively without putting populations in jeopardy. We did it with elk and moose, and then deer and antelope.

"We tried to monitor the harvest, so we collected reproductive data and lower jaws for age determination. We then built rather basic population models, something never done before. We established surveys to gauge trends in numbers and sometimes, absolute numbers. Our antelope survey was pretty good, so we started a series of aerial surveys. We also counted sharp-tails dancing, ruffed grouse drumming, and pheasants crowing. It was pretty well geared towards hunting. We were all interested in non-consumptive uses of wildlife, but you couldn't do much promotion of that.

"Public attitudes were a little different then. It was essentially a rural province. All farmers hunted and even city people were only a generation away from the farm. They knew about carrying capacity and knew it wasn't an infinite number; that there was a limit to the carrying capacity of the land; and that you could actually control populations. Their experience was cattle, but it was quite easy for them to transfer it to wild ungulates. The intrinsic support was there, but we still had to sell the idea to people because they were reluctant to see hunting seasons open where there hadn't been any and were reluctant to see females being shot. We spent a lot of time talking at dinners, cultivating outdoor newspaper columnists, and appearing on television and radio shows."

[Elmer Kure, a former member of the Fish and Game Advisory Council, recalled considerable scepticism concerning these management issues as presented to them at the 1948 convention of the Alberta Fish and Game Association in Calgary.[49]]

"A high point of my career with Fish and Wildlife was my positive working relationship with the officers. We tried to enlist them in the gathering of data. We gave them forms and taught them how to interview hunters while they were checking them. We tried to make them into "conservation" officers, but we didn't have the

43

authority. So we used personal influence by talking to officers at the annual service training schools. Enforcement is a very important part of resource management."

In 1967, Webb left Alberta to become Chief of Wildlife Management in Manitoba. In 1971, he left government and returned to Vancouver where he established a consulting career. One of his first contracts brought him back to Alberta to draft the Alberta Assessment Regulations and help set up the Environmental Impact Assessment process. "I've done Environmental Impact Assessments of major projects ever since, many of them in Alberta. Coal mines, pipelines, gas plants. As for the future of wildlife management, I think it's beset with problems. A lot of major policies that affect wildlife are made by quasi-judicial bodies that adjudicate through public hearings and recommend whether permits be issued or not. That's all good and it's better than it was. But you get so many interests represented that the hearings have lives of their own. And the wildlife resources tend not to be valued highly at these things. I've spent the last thirty years representing wildlife at these hearings, and finding my ability to influence lessening over the years. I sincerely believe I had the best of times by being able to initiate things as we were able to do."

Even though it was challenging, it was very rewarding.

Throughout the 1950s and 1960s, government staff and university academics continued to expand their research of fish and wildlife management. Much of the fieldwork and analysis was documented in publications such as the *Canadian Field-Naturalist* and the *Journal of Wildlife Management*. The result was a valuable exchange of knowledge between fish and wildlife scientists not only in Alberta, but also across Canada and on the international scene. This enhanced the reputations of the Alberta biologists and researchers and established high standards for subsequent staff.

In addition to their surveys and research, the new biologists contributed to staff and public education. Detailed information on the biology, ecology, and distribution of fish and wildlife in the province was provided at three Forestry Training School semesters attended by Forestry and Fish and Wildlife Officers. The last of these semesters was designed to give first hand experience in fish and wildlife management and census techniques to enforcement staff. Officers then began assisting biologists with pheasant crowing counts, crop damage assessments, collecting diseased specimens and other fish and wildlife activities.

Other Players on the Scene

Throughout this period of growth and research, the provincial government was not the only player on the fish and wildlife scene and in fact, it benefitted from several partnerships. The Calgary Fish and Game Association had worked throughout the First World War to keep the concept of conservation alive at a time when attention was devoted to fighting the war. Starting in the 1940s, the Division started working more closely with several local fish and game clubs.

A strong relationship continued to exist between Division staff and several University of Alberta academics (and later the universities of Calgary and Lethbridge) from the departments of botany, physiology, medicine, zoology, and entomology. Many researchers, such as Richard B. Miller, Professor of Zoology, worked closely with the Division on particular matters of interest to both.

A BRIEF HISTORY OF THE ALBERTA FISH AND GAME ASSOCIATION
[SUE CLARKE]

Of the many stakeholder groups that presently exist, one that had a great deal of influence on government attitudes toward the fish and wildlife resource is the Alberta Fish and Game Association (AFGA). The AFGA played a significant role in the provincial Fish and Wildlife Division's creation and struggle for recognition at the political level. No other agency went to bat for fish and wildlife in the 1950s and 1960s like the AFGA did.

ERNIE PSIKLA, RETIRED FISH AND WILDLIFE OFFICER.

Following Alberta's creation as a province in 1905, expansion, development, and population were viewed as the keys to economic prosperity. Conservation was not a primary concern of Albertans. Yet, as early as 1908, a few individuals, including sportsmen Fred J. Green, George I. Wood, and Austin de B. Winter, were in fact beginning to recognize the need for fish and wildlife protection. Together, they and other like-minded sportsmen formed the Calgary Fish and Game Protective Association, one of several local groups that would become the precursor of today's Alberta Fish and Game Association. From its inception, the AFGA and its local clubs have played a significant role in developing and influencing fish and wildlife conservation practices and policies in Alberta.

As early as 1910, the Calgary Association provided input to the Alberta government's proposed amendments to the *Game Act* by making suggested changes to hunting regulations in a variety of areas such as licensing, bag limits, the length of hunting seasons, and licensing of market hunters. [50] Ben Lawton, Chief Game Guardian, actively solicited suggestions from several local Fish and Game clubs. Since sportsmen were actively and more frequently involved in the field, Lawton relied upon their input concerning the status of game and game numbers.

On July 11, 1928, Austin de B. Winter and delegates of twenty-two local groups, rural clubs and city associations, came together in Calgary to form the Alberta Fish and Game Association (AFGA). "Local Fish and Game Associations knew that what was needed most of all was a united voice made up of their composites to act as a clearing house for recommendations to be presented to the government on wildlife, habitat, and hunter management policies, a voice that would be seriously listened to and respected by the members of the Legislature."[51] The newly formed Alberta Fish and Game Association did just that.

From the 1920s through to the 1940s, the AFGA actively participated in a variety of conservation initiatives. The association lobbied for freshwater game fish hatcheries, especially north of Red Deer; participated in transplanting fingerlings and fry to local streams; and began to recognize the impact of pollutants and contaminants on fish habitat.[52] Other efforts included the transplant of large wild game species, such as elk, into areas where they'd been extirpated. In one such example, several elk were captured in the Bow Valley corridor, outside Canmore, and transplanted to the Elbow Valley.

The Association's lobbying and political pressure was a strong impetus for legislation to create the Alberta Fish and Wildlife Division in the latter half of the 1950s. Prior to that time, fish and wildlife had virtually no profile within the government. Although legislation was a sign of progress, the fact that the Social Credit government did not consider the resource to merit ministry status is, in retrospect, an indicator of the prevailing attitude of the day. Curt P. Smith, the Division's first Director under the new legislation, was a previous President of the Alberta Fish and Game Association.

Throughout the remainder of the century, the AFGA continued to be not only a strong voice for hunters and fishermen, but also a voice for the protection and appreciation of fish and wildlife and their habitat. They were instrumental in implementing many of the programs that benefit the resource today.

AN EARLY ALBERTA FISH AND GAME ASSOCIATION MEETING.
COURTESY ALBERTA FISH AND WILDLIFE DIVISION

As well, several university students undertook graduate programs in cooperation with the Fish and Wildlife Division, providing their labour in return for the opportunity to address provincial research issues.

Cooperation with the Veterinary Branch of Alberta Agriculture was on-going from early times, but became much easier in 1969 when Fish and Wildlife staff and the Veterinary Services Branch shared quarters in the newly erected O.S. Longman Provincial Laboratory Building in Edmonton. Research scientists from the two departments occupied this facility, named for a former Deputy Minister of Agriculture, and cooperation between personnel was greatly facilitated. The close working relationship continues to this day, benefitting both disciplines.

Provincial game agencies across the three prairie provinces cooperated in matters of mutual interest such as commercial fisheries and fur marketing. Federal and provincial governments cooperated in a number of fish and wildlife matters (for example, a joint fisheries school was held in 1945). Numerous meetings and conferences were also held between the Division and various provincial, federal, and state (Montana) jurisdictions and with a number of diverse agencies including the International Association of Game, Fish and Conservation Commissioners; the Western Canada-Yukon Council; and the Western Stock Growers Association.

Provincial fish and wildlife staff also established new working arrangements and cooperative programs for gathering and sharing data and knowledge. A good example is the large coordinated effort to survey and manage waterfowl and their wetland habitat shared between the province, the federal Canadian Wildlife Service and the U.S. Fish and Wildlife Service. Non-government organizations like Ducks Unlimited Canada added strength to these partnerships and programs.

A New Fish and Wildlife Division

With the infusion of new staff, new ideas, and strong partnerships, the provincial authority for fisheries and wildlife continued to grow. On January 1, 1959, the Fish and Game Branch officially became the Fish and Wildlife Division with Curt P. Smith as Director. Smith came to the job with a background of experience in agriculture and wildlife. Formerly a farmer in the Wetaskiwin area, he was also Past-president of the Alberta Fish and Game Association and the Western Canada Fish and Game Council. Prior to his appointment as Director, Smith was Superintendent of Elk Island National Park.

Between 1958 and 1963, total staff numbers in the Division grew from 78 to 121 including a Director, three Section Chiefs, ten Biologists, two Hatchery Superintendents, seven Conservation Officer IIs, 56 Conservation Officer Is, and 42 other staff. Branches included Commercial Fisheries, Sport Fisheries Management, Game Management and Research, and Law Enforcement. Emphasis was placed on a cooperative approach where biological programs were integrated with Fish and Wildlife Officer activities. As well, better public awareness of fish and wildlife management issues was sought through public education and outreach programs.

In 1964, the province was divided into five physiographic regions: mixed forest, sub-alpine [including alpine], foothills, parkland, and grasslands. Within these five regions, 134 wildlife management units were further delineated to provide a more detailed framework for fish and wildlife management. Wildlife management zones were first utilized in the late 1940s for hunting migratory birds, with three bird zones established in 1948, and a fourth zone added in the south in 1949. About the same time, three zones were established for upland game birds. More management zones were developed in the late 1950s as the new cadre of wildlife biologists generated new population statistics for various populations. For example, in 1956, multiple zones were established for antelope, moose, elk, and deer.

FEDERAL-PROVINCIAL CONFERENCES AND COOPERATION
[NYREE SHARP]

Interactions between the federal and provincial governments were the rule rather than the exception in the early years as the young province established itself. The Dominion continued to manage the National Parks and Forest Reserves throughout much of the 20th century. The first official meeting of the two levels of government concerning wildlife occurred in 1919 when representatives from the provinces, the Advisory Board on Wildlife Management, the Conservation Commission, the United States, and a variety of nongovernmental organizations attended the first *Conservation Conference on the Protection of Wildlife.*[53] This was a precursor to Federal-Provincial Conferences held every two years from 1922-1932, every two to three years between 1937-1947, and annually thereafter. These conferences initially dealt with administration of the *Migratory Bird Convention Act*. This legislation was to be enforced by both the provinces and a new federal agency, the Dominion Wildlife Service. In 1950, this agency became the Canadian Wildlife Service.

In addition to cooperatively managing waterfowl, the two governments would soon look at other issues. Barren-ground caribou declined significantly after the turn of the century and concerns were raised as to the potential implications for Inuit communities dependent on this species for food. The issue was discussed at the Federal-Provincial Wildlife Conference in 1953, where it was agreed that a policy would be coordinated among federal, provincial, and territorial jurisdictions through which the northern caribou herds migrated. A multi-year study of the status, range, and general ecology of barren-ground caribou led researchers to believe the 1955 population estimates were significantly smaller than those of only a few years previous. The governments of Canada, Northwest Territories, Manitoba, Saskatchewan, and Alberta soon agreed to finance and organize an extensive research program to find out why. The Beverly caribou herd became the focus of a field program from April 1957 to September 1958. A wealth of data indicated that the largest single cause of mortality contributing to the ongoing caribou decline was humans with high-powered rifles. Several other studies on barren-ground caribou followed, but this single study seems to be the extent of Alberta's involvement. Barren-ground caribou is listed as *Accidental/Vagrant* in Alberta, and migrating populations pass only through the very northeast corner of the province, although they have been known to winter as far south as Fort McMurray in years past.

By the 1960s, the Federal-Provincial Wildlife Conferences were dealing with several emerging conservation issues. At the 24th Federal-Provincial Conference in 1960, increasing concern culminated in a resolution to investigate and control pesticides. The issue of exotic species imports was also discussed. The following year, the important position of wildlife in the economy was the issue of the day. In 1962, the topics included law enforcement, land use, research, and public information. In the following years, the Canadian Wildlife Service (CWS) was reorganized partly to address these specific topics. In 1963, the Canadian Council of Ministers of the Environment was established to deal with many of the same issues, but now discussions took place at a ministerial level.

In 1976, the recommendation to strike a standing committee to establish the status of endangered and threatened species and habitats in Canada was made and the Committee on the Status of Endangered Wildlife in Canada (COSEWIC) was born. The following year, COSEWIC asked delegates to provide advice on the addition of invertebrates and plants to the groups it might consider. Later federal-provincial conferences often focussed on a theme: "Habitat is the key" (1979), "CWS is for the birds" (1980), and "Teamwork in wildlife management" (1984).

While the 1970s and 1980s were the heydays of federal-provincial conferences, they continued at a diminished scale after 1989. A closed meeting of wildlife directors or a modest get-together to exchange information with a few nongovernmental organizations was preferred.

The need for a uniform law to protect endangered species across Canada was raised periodically at conferences for more than 20 years. By the 1990s, the deteriorating quality of communication between jurisdictions and the level of participation in federal-provincial meetings may have been factors in the resulting lack of progress made on this issue at the end of the century. However, with persistence and resolve all-round, the federal *Species at Risk Act* was finally adopted in 2003. Today, an annual national meeting of federal/provincial/territorial wildlife directors, deputy ministers, and ministers continues to provide a platform for fish and wildlife issues of a national concern.

The expansion of wildlife management units was a significant improvement designed to produce more precise control and increased opportunity for hunting wildlife. If wildlife was reported by biologists, fish and wildlife officers, or hunters as being scarce in a given management unit, a closed season or reduction in the number of entry permits could be declared followed by intensive study of the population in question. New hunting seasons, permit numbers, and closures were then determined. This new management system incorporated seasons on pronghorn antelope, mule deer and white-tailed deer, moose, elk, caribou, bighorn sheep, and Rocky Mountain goat.[54]

In 1965, Curt Smith resigned as Director of the Fish and Wildlife Division to take a position at the Northern Alberta Institute of Technology. Under Smith's direction, the Division had increased its field officer staff by one-third its former strength. More emphasis had been placed on research and management of the fish and wildlife resource. As well, the Hunter Training and Wildlife Damage Insurance programs were organized under his guidance. Stuart B. Smith assumed directorship of the Division. Stu Smith continued with a program of decentralization in an attempt to provide better area management of fish and wildlife resources.

To match biologists to this new system of ecological regions and wildlife management units, in 1966, staff from Edmonton Headquarters were transferred to six subdivision headquarters at Peace River, St. Paul, Edson, Red Deer, Calgary, and Lethbridge. In addition, new positions were established in Edmonton to aid in much needed fish and wildlife research programs. Bill Wishart was appointed Section Head of Wildlife Research reporting to Gordon Kerr, Acting Chief Wildlife Biologist (made Chief Wildlife Biologist in 1967). Bill Hall was also appointed to this section. The Research Section was given an annual budget of approximately $100,000 to conduct projects and fund the work of a number of graduate students, many of whom were later employed by the province.

On the fisheries side, Bryant Bidgood was appointed Section Head of Fisheries Research Section, which included Dave Berry. Bryant reported to Martin Paetz, Chief Fishery Biologist until 1967 when Paetz left on educational leave and Rod Paterson, previously Senior Fisheries Management Biologist assumed the position of Acting Chief Fishery Biologist. C.W. Scott was appointed to the new position of Commercial Fishery Coordinator in 1967.

Along with enforcement, fisheries, and wildlife, a fourth unit evolved to administer a number of programs that didn't fit easily elsewhere. The Administration Branch was established in 1966 and later became Program Support Services, then Policy and Business Management. This branch was initially involved with licensing, regulation development, trap-line administration, and other services. As well, the Hunter Training Branch, established in 1963, grew into the Conservation Education Branch in 1975 and Extension Services in 1977. Regardless of its name, the unit was responsible for conservation education and public information including the Alberta Hunter Training Program initiated in 1959, which became the most extensive per-capita program of its kind in Canada.

Logistical improvements were also made to operations through time. As access to wilderness increased for the general public, so too did the need for mobility and communication of officers and biologists. Within enforcement, privately owned vehicles were used for patrols and other Division activities until 20 new green and white trucks were introduced into enforcement field operations. Aircraft were incorporated into patrols, sting operations, and surveys. Similarly, radio equipment supplied to remote districts helped to coordinate Division efforts.

If we promote a better understanding of the value of fish and wildlife, and of conservation principles generally, we will be amply rewarded.
STUART B. SMITH, DIRECTOR OF FISH AND WILDLIFE, 1966.

A SPOUSES' PERSPECTIVE

[JAN HALL, MARILYN KERR, DIANE MARKHAM, CAROL PAETZ, GRACE RIPPIN, PAT WISHART AND WENDY ZELT]

Hesitation and uncertainty lingered in the air as we gathered around Pat Wishart's luncheon table on a cold snowy Saturday in January 2003. As the spouses of retired fisheries and wildlife biologists, we were brought together to share our unique perspective on the history of fish and wildlife management in Alberta. For the first few minutes, we seemed to doubt our contribution to the story. But as old friendships were renewed over hot soup and warm bread, the chatter got louder and soon the stories started to emerge…"Today, biologists are more likely to be found at a computer than in hip waders. But in the past, people were envious of biologists—they got to go out there and have a great time!" (Pat Wishart)

We all agreed that one of the perks of being married to a biologist was that our husbands were, for the most part, happy. They loved their work! And they often shared this love of wildlife and wild places with us, their wives, who sometimes joined them in the field. "I remember getting up very early to help Bill [a provincial wildlife biologist], with pheasant crowing counts" (Jan Hall). "I remember assisting Martin [first provincial fisheries biologist] take depth soundings on several Alberta lakes, despite my increasing discomfort with increasing distance from shore" (Carol Paetz). Others remembered recording waterfowl brood surveys, grouse counts, helping at hunter check stations, and involvement in various field surveys. All of us felt privileged to participate in this type of work, to see so much wildlife, to work alongside our spouse, and to increase our own observational skills and ability.

When the children were small, getting away for the weekend to do duck counts was seen as a bit of a holiday! Later on, when the kids were big enough to travel, we shared this love of the outdoors with them, too. Family vacations often revolved around hunting, fishing, and camping with lots of opportunities to see wildlife and different parts of Alberta. These early experiences, in some instances, influenced sons and daughters into carrying on the tradition—choosing professions as wildlife biologists or in similar fields. In other cases, it pointed the kids in quite a different direction!

We were often close to wildlife in other ways. In the days before wildlife rehabilitation centres, orphaned or injured wildlife often were brought home from work for care and attention. In addition, friends and neighbours all seemed to think fish and wildlife families could fix any critter. Over lunch, we heard stories of "Bandit" the ferret, a pet goose, and others. We laughed about the dead wildlife that found their way into our freezers and backyards, most of which ended up as museum skins at the local nature centre or museum. "One time, Martin brought home a rather large sturgeon from the North Saskatchewan and the whole neighbourhood came over to the backyard to see it!" (Carol Paetz). "Neighbours brought us orphan rabbits and lost ducks or some folks simply left wildlife on our doorstep!" (Pat Wishart).

A good biologist's wife had to know a lot about cooking (but not cleaning!) fish and game. Another perk of the profession was the great camaraderie amongst biologists. In an era of low budgets and few commercial accommodations, our homes often had an open door for visiting biologists in town to help out with various projects. This led to much socializing (and some great parties) amongst the families. Together, we became a tight-knit group, helping one another when needed, sharing experiences, trials and tribulations, and stories in later years.

Accommodation often was a laughing matter. The work was usually located far away from any amenities. Frequently, we ended up sleeping in tents, vans, or trailers but that was better than some of the hotels the husbands took us to. A rare stay in a hotel, even a cheap hotel, was quite a special event and often quite an adventure. Anyone in the vicinity of the Brooks Pheasant Hatchery could find cheap accommodation—but you had to compete with the ever-expanding mouse population!

Of course, there were downsides to being married to a biologist. Like travel budgets, the pay was low. Biologists in the 1950s and 1960s were at the bottom of the payscale, making less than a schoolteacher. And they were away from home a lot. And when they were home, they were often still working—sorting slides, preparing talks, and writing papers in the evenings. Though sometimes lonely, by necessity we learned to be independent, raising the kids on our own, keeping the house up and running, changing flat tires, fixing leaky taps, getting out of snow banks, and in our spare time, growing our own lives and careers. Social events through such groups as Brownies, Guides, and community meetings became important ways to fill in the gaps in human contact.

Concern for our husband's safety was a stressful issue whenever they were away. In an era before cell phones, there was very little communication between biologists in the field and their families at home. The nearest ranger station was often the only way to make a phone call, weather permitting. When due dates weren't met, or when check-in calls failed to materialize, we automatically worried. Sometimes the guys were so wrapped up in work that they just plain forgot to call. Boy, did they hear about that when they got home! When they finally walked in the door you were so angry and happy all at the same time. And vice versa, when there was a family emergency, there was often no way to tell a husband out in the field ... and where were they when the kids were born?

Despite hundreds of hours of accident-free flying, aerial surveys were always of particular concern. Habitat biologists spent a lot of time classifying habitat by air and wildlife biologists just kept counting whatever was out there. The biologist community, and we wives in particular, anguished when planes went down and staff were injured (e.g., Stan Clements) or lost. We remember Des Smith, Barry Young, and Cal Bohmer—all three lost in a plane crash in Edson in 1978; Orval Pall and several rescue workers and pilots in 1986; and more recently, Ian Ross in 2003. Accidents weren't limited to airplanes and we all still remember the tragedy of Roger Schmitke drowning in a boating incident in 1965.

And last but not least, a downside to the fish and wildlife profession was a growing feeling of frustration and inability to protect fish and wildlife resources as the trappings of human development outstripped wildlife habitat. This frustration was often brought home to sympathetic ears. We felt for our husbands' profession! We wives shared the heartache over loss of wildlife and wildlife habitat, and the lack of support for wildlife on the political and public agenda. We felt a constant need to embed these feelings into the family philosophy and to inform others of basic biological information.

When asked what we thought the future of fish and wildlife management needs to be, there was a quick and unanimous answer: *education!* We, as a society and particularly as a profession, need to do a better job of educating the public, especially children and their teachers, about fisheries and wildlife resources. The future is in the hands of our children and our teachers, but teachers can't teach what they don't know. Maybe biologists should be working more closely with teachers. Bring back projects like Project WILD and make use of resources like Knee High Nature. And we need to make sure that the public maintains some kind of contact with the natural world and therefore gains an appreciation of wildlife. We all need to take time to smell the flowers, listen to the birds, talk to a tree, watch hares hop or chipmunks scamper, and just enjoy being outdoors!

BIOLOGIST GEORGE MITCHELL AND OFFICERS BOB ADAMS AND GERRY PELCHAT WITH PILOT GAVIN BRECKENRIDGE AT GRANDE CACHE AIRSTRIP AFTER CONDUCTING AN AERIAL CARIBOU SURVEY, 1966.
CREDIT: J. STELFOX

50

Expansion and Decline

Throughout the 1970s, managers recognized that to protect fish and wildlife populations, they had to be involved in the provinces land-use planning processes. Hence, the Fish and Wildlife Division became more involved with the disposition of Crown lands. In 1970, a new Director, Gordon Kerr, placed the emphasis on habitat protection and development, with harvest management a secondary motive—a new concept that sounded less complicated than it proved to be. In his 1971 annual report, Kerr wrote:

Whereas fish and wildlife resources are entirely dependent on the condition of the land and vegetation growing upon it, the growing complexity of land-use development will necessitate a much increased emphasis on land-use management. Also, the growing intensity of the conflict between landowners and resource users prompts the Division to take a meaningful leadership role in the future. If one can generalize the three basic steps of fish and wildlife management as being sustained harvest, habitat protection, and habitat development, then one could say that during the past twelve months there has been a conscious shift in emphasis from step one to step two and partially in the area of habitat development.

Biologists specializing in land-use issues represented the Fish and Wildlife Division on various intergovernmental committees and task forces dealing with renewable resources and land management. Participation in programs for land leases and grazing reserves allowed the Division to make headway in the protection and retention of wildlife habitat and populations on Crown lands, primarily in northern areas. In addition, recommendations were made regarding the disposition of Crown lands surrounding waterbodies, and thus influenced the retention and protection of some waterfowl and furbearer habitat. The disposition of road allowance leases (rights-of-way) was important in supplying cover for birds in the prairies and foothills.

Much of this new habitat and land-use planning focus was placed under the Habitat Protection and Management Branch which made a brief appearance in 1980 before being reorganized into the Habitat Protection Branch and an associated Ecological Assessments Branch in 1982. Unfortunately, both of these Branches quickly became mired down in the difficulties of linking fish and wildlife management to land-use planning and decision-making. Both quietly disappeared during the 1990s, though not before leaving a legacy in the Buck for Wildlife Program.[55]

As significant as the recognition of the need for habitat management was the change in focus from game to wildlife. This change was reflected in changes to both the Division's name in 1959 and its enabling legislation, the *Wildlife Act* in 1970. While a game/harvest focus was appropriate at the dawn of a new Alberta, seven decades later, a broader, more comprehensive approach was better suited to a maturing province. The first non-game biologist position was offered to Gary Erickson in 1986. His early efforts focussed on reintroducing endangered peregrine falcons to the skies over Alberta. Soon after, Steve Brechtel was added to the non-game unit and, despite limited manpower, the efforts of this unit grew in accordance with the public interests in threatened and endangered species. Alberta non-game staff also made significant contributions to the national activities of the Committee on the Status of Endangered Wildlife in Canada (COSEWIC) and its corresponding endangered species recovery programs. Soon to follow were Alberta's Watchable Wildlife and Natural Areas programs, which would truly expand the Division's mandate to non-consumptive uses such as bird watching, nature hikes, and other naturalist activities.

In fisheries, a similar broadening of public interest and concern for the environment resulted in programs and policies directed towards habitat protection, access management, and pollution control. Ken Crutchfield, Dave Buckwald, Daryl Watters, Glen Clements, Cam Wallman, Vic Gillman, and Ray Makowecki were key staff

51

brought into these programs. Additional staff increases occurred throughout the 1970s and early 1980s.

While a core of highly trained and skilled wildlife and fisheries biologists, technicians, and enforcement officers became the solid foundation of the Fish and Wildlife Division, the growth in numbers slowed, peaking about 1981 with approximately 407 staff located across the province. Both staff numbers and budgets declined throughout the 1990s. Despite several departmental moves and name changes, the Division itself evolved along similar paths initiated in its first seven decades. Whether identified as "Sections", "Branches", or "Services", the enforcement, wildlife, fisheries, and administration units, for the most part, remained cohesive entities and continued to fulfill their roles as required.

The Division's administrative regions and central offices remained for the most part the same, falling into geographical boundaries of the east slopes (Edson), central (Edmonton), southern (Lethbridge), northwest boreal (Peace River) and northeast boreal (St. Paul), generally reflecting the prairie, parkland, boreal, and foothills/mountain natural regions of the province. Today, approximately 375 staff carry out their duties in four regions—northwest, northeast, southwest, and southeast.[56]

Unfortunately, while the complexity of fish and wildlife issues was expanding, the heyday of research and science-based decision-making was diminishing as the 20th century came to a close. Through the economic downturn of the late 1980s, budgets for research and surveys declined drastically, with a corresponding loss of morale and enthusiasm. Hiring freezes through the 1980s eventually created a knowledge gap ultimately realized with the retirement of several key managers, biologists, technicians, officers, and administrative staff at the beginning of the new millennium. There was little or no opportunity to pass on the wealth of corporate and biological information locked in the minds and philosophies

of those leaving to those who remained to continue on in the best interests of wise management of fisheries and wildlife resources in Alberta.

Perhaps the most difficult change to come for fish and wildlife was the shift to political decision-making rather than science-based management. In Lawton's day, the head of game management had the power to make decisions concerning all wild species, including setting aside large areas of habitat for population regeneration. As the 20th century was winding down, this authority shifted almost exclusively to the Minister responsible for fish and wildlife, and thus became subject to the political pressures facing an elected representative from individuals, constituency, and special-interest groups.

The Mission of the Fish and Wildlife Division

Although a great deal more could be written about the Fish and Wildlife Division, including its successes and failures over the last century, we leave this to a more academic and lengthier work. Instead, we conclude this chapter with a brief look at the Division's mission during its lifetime.

In 1975, the Fish and Wildlife Division came under the administration of the Department of Recreation, Parks and Wildlife with a goal "to manage the fish and wildlife resources of the Province of Alberta in order to maintain an optimum level and distribution of such resources for the benefit, reward, gain, and enjoyment of the people and to promote legislation, knowledge, attitudes, and resource information". To achieve this goal, the Division planned to continue conducting population inventories and identifying limiting factors. As well, objectives included habitat preservation and development, reducing conflicts with other land uses, and promoting public education.

In 1982, the *Fish and Wildlife Policy for Alberta* became the first formal, comprehensive position on fisheries and wildlife resources for the province. This policy included sections on

JOYCE [BARTON] SHAW: JANE OF ALL TRADES!
[INTERVIEWED BY MARGO PYBUS, MAY 2005, BARRHEAD]

My father, Pete Barton, was born in Lethbridge and moved with his mother in the 1920s to homestead a parcel of land near Naples, Alberta, not far from Barrhead. My mother came from Poland, married my Dad in 1937, and they lived on the old homestead. I was the oldest of six kids and money was pretty scarce on the farm. But I fought to stay in school so I could complete grade ten. I worked at odd jobs—at the Barrhead General Hospital, the Naples general store, and on a local farm where I pitched hay and did housework. I much preferred the housework! In 1955, Dad sent me to Edmonton as a live-in babysitter. My employer promised to make sure I took typing classes. She paid me, and I paid the night school fees at McTavish's in Edmonton.

In April 1956, my employer encouraged me to apply for a job with the provincial government. I wasn't sure, but she insisted. So I walked into the Legislature personnel office and handed a man my application. He read it and said: "Report to the Natural Resources Building on Monday morning". That was it. I hadn't even finished my typing course! On May 1, 1956 I started as a secretary in the steno-pool for the Grazing Lease Section of the Public Lands Division.

There was an advertisement for a new position as secretary to the first Fish and Wildlife Director. One of the other stenos said I should apply. On January 1, 1959, I started as secretary to Curt Smith in the newly named Fish and Wildlife Division. Lola Cameron, secretary to Eric Huestis, Director of Forestry, helped me organize the office, set up files, as well as figure out what duties I had and how to do them. She was great.

In those days, we had manual typewriters, the ones with the old black and red ribbons. And carbon paper for making copies of correspondence. Still, we typed slowly to avoid making mistakes! We had the old black rotary phones, although we did have separate phone lines. Our work dealt largely with correspondence, tracking staff annual leave, mailing monthly salary cheques, and sorting mail. The correspondence was mainly typing up hand-written notes—Rocky Hales and Curt Smith were always writing memos! There was no government courier then, so

everything went into the Queen's Royal Mail system. I also took a lot of dictation and short-hand minutes at a lot of meetings. I was in charge of a steno-pool of five or six secretaries assigned to various staff members.

In 1964, the girl in the Barrhead Fish and Wildlife office left and I requested a transfer from Edmonton to Barrhead. I was hired part time there in April 1964. My husband, Harvey Shaw, and I decided to try farming. We bought a quarter section of the old homestead from my Dad. The early days on the farm were the hardest time in my life. We needed money for equipment, stock, grain bins, feed bunkers and just about everything else, but of course we had no revenue coming in from the farm yet. Things got better when I became full-time later that year. There are some pretty deep ruts between the office and home. I remember the hard winters in the 1960s. It got to 50 below, and the steering wheel wouldn't turn on the car. But I made it in—I had to go to work. I was afraid to lose my job. We just don't get winters like that anymore.

District work was very different from the work at headquarters. It was, and still is, largely complaint-driven. But I also used to sell licences, explain the fishing and hunting regulations, and provide lots of public information on just about any topic. I assigned traps for problem wildlife occurrences and often had to help people figure out what animal was causing the problem, what trap to use, and show them how to set it. I was a regular "Jane of all trades". I also did the routine office correspondence and ordered supplies. Two or three years we put a Fish and Wildlife float into the parade for Blue Heron Days in Barrhead. That was with Milt McKee. He is so full of fun and games, along with lots of hard work.

I saw a lot of changes over the years. From manual typewriters, to electric, to word processors, to the computer: from carbon paper, to photocopiers, to machines that now collate, staple, and make colour copies. And even colour printers. We went from using regular mail, to government courier some time in the 1980s. And then came fax machines, and satellite and cell phones. Taking shorthand stopped some time

53

after Deryl Empson was in Barrhead (it's easier for me to track things by who was here, rather than by calendar year!). We used Dictaphones but only for a short time. I also got a lot of hand-written notes to type. Now, of course, the District Officer drafts correspondence on his computer and sends it out directly. Sometimes I review it, print it, and send it out. The changes generally brought improvements and efficiency. Life got much easier, once you learned the new system, procedure, or equipment. Including those darned computers. Now that was the hardest, the very toughest. I didn't know a thing about computers. I would go home in tears, and my husband would say: "Stick with it. You can do anything." So I decided to take the bull by the horns and just learn to do it. And now, I couldn't do without the computers!

Barrhead has always been a one-woman show. I would get STEP [Summer Temporary Employment Program] and ESP [Employment Services Program] girls from May to August, largely to help with licence sales. I remember in the late 1960s there were line-ups at the counter that stretched well out into the hall. It was the first seasons open to U.S. hunters and they flooded the District Offices. There was no need for a guide and licence fees were much lower than in the U.S. I was called in to work on Saturdays just to accommodate the demand. Also, in June 1981 during draw times, there were again long lines into the hall and over to the next offices. But Barrhead has always been a busy district. The mix of agriculture and being close to the city makes for a variety of issues: big deer, big farms, and big problems. But I don't give up my holidays! When I go on holiday, the office goes on auto-pilot until I get back.

On May 1, 2006 I will have been in government service for 50 years. I love my job. There were lots of great people to work with.

For example Curt Smith, Rocky Hales, Don Clark, Fred Neumann, Milt McKee, and a bunch of good junior officers like Sam Bundt, Jim Mitchell, Chuck Shipley, Jason Hanson, Chris Watson, and Owen Sabiston to name just a few. And the biologists, too, like Bill Wishart, Martin Paetz, George Mitchell, and Hugh Wollis. They all worked hard and had good fun—just a great combination. Also Annette Hendricks [Evansburg], Helen Walker [Athabasca], and Brenda Wood [Stony Plain] are great. We help each other out.

I didn't see any real change in basic administration approach over the years. Our job is to serve the public on a wide range of topics, or direct them to other government services. We did that before, and we still do it now. We have better ways now of providing the service, but it is still a matter of giving good information and education. Salary certainly changed. I started in 1956 at $130 a month, and that was a windfall. It paid the rent and board, and I thought I was rich. I bought my first summer coat and a pair of earrings. The monies gradually increased and reasonably matched the cost of living in the country. There are far more demands now, than there used to be. There are new issues, more issues. We don't see the public as much anymore, with licence sales now privatized. But there is still a steady stream of people looking for basic information and an explanation of the regulations.

I enjoy the district work. There is more variety, more people, and a better lifestyle (for me) than in the city. In the district, you are basically your own boss, with guidance, of course, from the District or junior officer. It's very satisfying, particularly when there is good mutual trust and respect. I thank my blessings to be here. Why would I leave?

54

Recreation, Wildlife, Fisheries, and Regulatory activities. In response to this policy, a draft *Fish and Wildlife Status* was prepared for public review. The two documents formed the basis for Divisional planning and programming throughout the late 1980s and a slightly revised mission statement and principles developed in 1988.

1988-1989 FISH AND WILDLIFE DIVISION MISSION STATEMENT
(1988-1989 ANNUAL REPORT)

To Manage the Fish and Wildlife Resources of the Province of Alberta for the Benefit and Enjoyment of the People

PRINCIPLES:

1. Our priority is for the long-term interest of fish and wildlife.
2. We undertake management within the context of the Natural Resources Transfer Agreement and the Canadian Constitution.
3. Management is based on fundamental ecological principles.
4. We manage for self-sustaining populations as a priority over stocking programs.
5. We undertake management addressing resource, human, and land factors.
6. We establish and obtain acceptance for population and habitat objectives for major wildlife groupings.

OBJECTIVES:

1. To maintain and protect scarce species;
2. To restore threatened populations;
3. To re-introduce extirpated species;
4. To establish and obtain acceptance for population objectives for major wildlife groupings;
5. To provide a variety of types and amounts of outdoor recreational opportunities;
6. To maximize economic returns from the commercial use of fish and wildlife resources;
7. To strive for no net loss of quality of fish and wildlife habitat;
8. To ensure that fish and wildlife populations are compatible with community interests;
9. To develop and administer legislation in a manner which is beneficial to the fish and

THE *FISH AND WILDLIFE POLICY FOR ALBERTA* PROVIDED GUIDANCE AND DIRECTION FOR THE MANAGEMENT OF THIS RESOURCE.
COURTESY ALBERTA FISH AND WILDLIFE DIVISION

55

wildlife resource, sensitive to public needs, and fosters socially acceptable behaviour;
10. To minimize the negative impacts of wildlife resources on people and property;
11. To deliver a public education program designed to enhance public sensitivity and understanding of the fish and wildlife resource;
12. To encourage the participation of other government agencies, the private sector, and the public in the enhancement and development of fish and wildlife habitat;
13. To retain, enhance, acquire and develop habitat for public benefit where species supply/demand shortfalls exist that are directly related to habitat quality/quantity;
14. To promote and encourage scientific and educational activities that will enhance knowledge of the fish and wildlife resource.

While the terms have varied since 1988, the intent of subsequent mission statements altered little over the next decade and a half as the Division continued to stay its course. Whether or not the

Alberta Fish and Wildlife Division has been successful in achieving its mission and delivering its mandate to the people of Alberta is not for these authors to determine. Certainly, countless hours could be spent documenting the wins, the losses, the challenges, and the frustrations that a hundred years of effort, carried out by hundreds of staff from across the diverse regions of this province, would have encountered. But such debate is not new and perhaps more vigorous debate is desirable. Albertans from every generation and from every walk of life have been discussing fish and wildlife matters for more than a century...and hopefully, will continue doing so well into the next.

MAJOR EVENTS OF THE PROVINCIAL FISH AND WILDLFE AUTHORITY, 1905-2005

1905	Sept. 1, Alberta becomes the eighth province in Confederation.
1906	The Game Branch is established in the Department of Agriculture. Ben Lawton is appointed the first Chief Game Guardian.
1907	The first provincial *Game Act* is adopted.
1909	The Canadian Commission of Conservation is established.
1916	The *Migratory Bird Treaty* is signed between Great Britain and the United States.
1921	C. Gordon Hewitt publishes a book on the need for conservation of wildlife resources.
1922	Market hunting is declared illegal.
1930	Jurisdiction over natural resources is transferred from the federal to provincial government. The first provincial fisheries unit is established in the Department of Lands and Mines.
1931	Game Commissioner Ben Lawton dies November 20, 1931 at the age of 64.
1936-1937	Fisheries and game management is combined in the Fish and Game Branch of the Department of Lands and Mines.
1939-1941	The Fish and Game Division is established and moved under Eric Huestis, Director of Forestry.
1943	A Fish and Game Advisory Council is established.
1947	The Dominion Wildlife Service is founded and becomes the Canadian Wildlife Service in 1950.
1949	The Fish and Game Division is moved from the Department of Lands and Mines to Lands and Forests.
1952	A staff training school is held with lectures from W. Rowan, R.B. Miller and R.G.H. Cormack.
1952-55	The first provincial fish and wildlife biologists including Martin Paetz, George Mitchell, Bob Webb, John Stelfox, and Ron Thomas are hired.
1959	The Fish and Game Branch officially becomes the Fish and Wildlife Division; the First Director is C.P. Smith.
1959-60	The provincial fish and wildlife research programs are expanded significantly.
1960-61	The *Game Act* is amended to include hunter safety.
1961-62	H.B. Watkins, Superintendent of Commercial Fisheries, retires.
1965-66	Stu Smith replaces retiring Fish and Wildlife Director Curt Smith.
1966-67	Six regional headquarters are established.
1970	Alberta's first *Wildlife Act* is proclaimed.
1970-71	Policy shifts from "harvest management" to "habitat management".
1973	The Buck For Wildlife Program is created to maintain, create, and enhance wildlife habitat.
1982	The *Fish and Wildlife Policy for Alberta* is published.
1986	The first non-game biologist position is created and Gary Erickson is hired to fill it.
2001-05	The Fish and Wildlife Division is moved to the new Sustainable Resource and Development Department where it, along with the province, celebrates its Centennial anniversary in 2005.

KEN AMBROCK, ASSISTANT DEPUTY MINISTER, FISH AND WILDLIFE DIVISION
[INTERVIEWED BY PAT VALASTIN SEPT. 8, 2004, EDMONTON]

I was born in Edmonton in 1949. Hunting and fishing was a big part of my family. It added to the larder! By high school, I had decided to go into some aspect of fish and wildlife work. After Bonnie Doon High School in Edmonton, I completed a B.Sc. (Honours) at the University of Alberta, where Bill Samuel, John Holmes, and Vic Lewin were my favourite professors; they taught courses that I was really interested in.
When I graduated in 1971, interest in the environment was starting to grow and a number of jobs came open. The Canadian Wildlife Service (CWS) offered me a position as a wildlife technician, part of a team working on migratory birds, moose, and bison on the Peace-Athabasca Delta. My job was to study the effects of the Bennett Dam on muskrat populations, so I spent a winter, two full summers, and a fall on the Delta trapping muskrats. When that was done I worked on migratory birds making recommendations to mitigate the effects of the dam. Ed Hennan from Ducks Unlimited was working on this, but he left to take a job in Kamloops. So I finished summarizing and writing it up. After that, I spent a bit of time in the north. The Mackenzie Valley pipeline studies were underway and the Canada Land Inventory was still going pretty strong. The northern part of Alberta hadn't been assessed, so I worked on that for about two years. From there, I became a habitat biologist with CWS in Edmonton around 1975 or 1976. A lot of the work was associated with referrals that came from the Department of Indian and Northern Affairs, for example, mining developments in the north. I also worked on a Wetland Committee chaired by the Alberta Fish and Wildlife Division.

In 1980, I joined the Northern Pipeline Agency as their senior environmental scientist. The Agency was the federal regulator monitoring the pre-built sections of the Alaska Highway Pipeline running from Alberta into Saskatchewan and B.C. We also reviewed the development plans for the northern end of the line through northern Alberta, B.C., and the Yukon. However, the pipeline project folded when there was a glut of gas on the market and the cost of the pipeline skyrocketed. In 1982, the oil and gas industry took a dive. People were losing jobs left and right. The market dropped. By chance, I heard about a job as

Executive Assistant to Dennis Surrendi, then Assistant Deputy Minister (ADM) of Fish and Wildlife. I applied for the job and got it.

In 1984, I became Director of the Habitat Branch after Dave Neave left. Issues of the day included forestry, oil and gas extraction, and other competing uses on the landscape. Access management was becoming a problem. I spent a lot of time in the 1980s on committees like the Resource Integration Committee. The Habitat Branch was a referral agency to the regulators, the forest managers and the public lands managers. Fish and Wildlife received a referral on a pipeline or a well-site application, and we developed conditions to mitigate the impacts on fish and wildlife. There were probably more strides made in the 1980s to recognize fish and wildlife in land-use decision-making than ever before. And there were lots of planning exercises as land-use picked up in the East Slopes.

The Habitat Branch grew rapidly until around 1986, when we were absorbed into the Operations Branch. I became Director of the Operations Branch, which also included Enforcement. But that didn't last very long. I think it was a couple of years. When Bob Adams, Director of Enforcement, retired in 1988, I moved into that job until 1991. So I've had a bit of background both on the enforcement and biological side.

The Enforcement Branch was growing. There was quite an issue as to whether officers should have firearms to perform their duties. We also worked pretty hard on what was called the "compliance model". We wanted our officers to be more than enforcement people, and to achieve compliance through things like prevention and education. The first time the public sees an Enforcement Officer shouldn't be when he's writing a ticket: he should be out on the lake, saying "Look, we have a problem. Here are the management implications." I wanted officers to meet with appropriate groups, whether it was a local Fish and Game Club, or whomever, to talk about the issues.

When Morley Barrett became the ADM, he combined the fisheries and wildlife units, and I became the Director of Fisheries and Wildlife

Management. I stayed with it until Morley left in 2000. With Morley's leaving, I became the ADM of Fish and Wildlife, where I am today. I believe a major issue facing the Fish and Wildlife Division is changing attitudes, combined with changing human population and demographics. We don't have the numbers of hunters we had back in the 1980s. At one time we had about 160,000 hunters, now we're down to less than 100,000. So we face a whole new set of issues: an over-abundance of deer and elk, for example. Right now we are trying to increase harvests, and our Problem Wildlife program is busier than ever. Tolerance of landowners to wildlife is less than it was twenty years ago. When you get elk or deer eating a farmer's haystack, and that farmer is stressed by things like BSE and failing markets, it's understandable that he wants something done.

Certainly our budgets are flat-lined and there are staff capacity issues. I'll use the East Slopes as an example. With the increased access for industry, trapping, hunting, fishing, outfitting, and ATV use, there's tremendous pressure on our staff to meet with various groups and be visible. So, that begs the question of how do we deliver all of these responsibilities? How can we become more efficient and effective within our current budgets? We are trying to look at options of building more partnerships.

The other challenge is the need to have good science that holds itself up to peer review. We have good research people, but by and large, we are not a research organization. Getting good applied research depends on our relationships with the universities and with the Alberta Conservation Association Wildlife Chair.

One of my biggest regrets is that we have not been successful in building an education extension program. I think the success of what we do is based on support from the public, and knowledge about fish and wildlife management generally. We always talk about it, but I don't think we take the action that it deserves. We're doing bits and pieces of it. Two prime examples are the Fish in Schools Program run out of the Sam Livingston Fish Hatchery, and the Cows and Fish Program that Lorne Fitch does. We had some really keen, smart, enthusiastic staff that went out there and started these programs. I would like to see something like a Cows and Fish program expanded to a fish and wildlife education extension program.

Fish and wildlife management is such a fascinating subject matter. Combined with the fact that I have such excellent staff, this has been the best career ever.

I have to tell you that our Fish and Wildlife management staff does fantastic work. I feel proud to be a leader of this outfit.

58

References • CHAPTER 2

1   Struthers, J.B. 1993. Lookin' Back. P. 4 *in* Alberta Game Warden. The original letter is in the government Archives in the 1916 Annual Report of the Chief Game Guardian, Department of Agriculture Administration, Edmonton.

2   Alberta. *Statutes. Game Act. 1907.* Chapter 14. Edmonton, 1907. The first piece of provincial legislation concerning game.

3   See more on this topic in Chapter 3.

4   Canada. Commission of Conservation. Reports, 1909 – 1921. This organization, established in 1909, addressed itself to many aspects of conservation: fish, wildlife, water power, forests, minerals and much more. Its publications are scarce but they show that the work of the Commission was an important milestone in the drive to conserve resources.

5   Lawton, Benjamin. Undated. The Destruction of Gophers. Department of Agriculture, Edmonton.

6   Foster, J. 1978. Working for Wildlife: The Beginning of Preservation in Canada. University of Toronto Press, Toronto.

7   Holmgren, Eric J. 1986. Fish and Wildlife Management in Alberta: A History. Unpublished report prepared for the Department of Forestry, Lands and Wildlife, Edmonton.

8   Alberta Department of Agriculture. 1931. Annual Report of the Chief Game Guardian. Unpublished report prepared for the Department of Agriculture, Edmonton. See also:
    Alberta Department of Agriculture. Annual Reports of the Chief Game Guardian, 1907 – 1940. These reports can be found at the Provincial Archives and illustrate the problems faced by the Chief Game Guardian (after 1923, Game Commissioner) in his efforts to preserve game and enforce laws. As much original material, such as correspondence of this period, was destroyed, these form the only governmental source of information. All of them up to 1931 were written by Benjamin J. Lawton, who occupied this office.
    Alberta Department of Lands and Mines. Annual Reports of the Fish and Game Commissioner, 1941 – 1948. These reports give a good picture of the work of the Commissioner in a transitional period.
    Alberta Department of Lands and Forests. Annual Reports of the Fish and Game Commissioner, 1949 – 1973. These reports in 1962 became the reports of the Director of Fish and Wildlife.

9   Hall, D.J. 1985. Clifford Sifton. Vol. 2. University of British Columbia Press, Vancouver, pp. 236-263. See also: Dafoe, John W. 1931. Clifford Sifton in Relation to His Times. Macmillan Company of Canada, Toronto.

10 The Commission of Conservation. 1910. Inaugural Address by Chairman, Honourable Clifford Sifton before the First Annual Meeting of the Commission of Conservation, 1910. University of Calgary Library. Microform. Call #FC51.C3496#82415.

11 Hewitt, C. Gordon. 1919. The Need of Nation-Wide Effort in Wild Life Conservation. National Conference on Game and Wildlife Conservation, Ottawa, 1919, p. 8. Reprinted from Report of National Conference on Conservation of Game, Fur-Bearing Animals and Other Wildlife sponsored by the Commission of Conservation in co-operating with the Advisory Board on Wildlife Protection, pp. 1-11, University of Calgary Library, Microfiche-Call #FC51.C3496.

12 Sifton, C. 1916. Brief remarks on the work and aims of the Commission of Conservation, pp. 8-9 *in* White, J.
    Conservation of fish, birds and game. Methodist Book and Publishing House, Toronto.

13 Phillips, J.C. 1934. Migratory bird protection in North America: The history of control by the United States federal government and a sketch of the treaty with Great Britain. Special Publication of the American Committee for International Wild Life Protection 1(4).

14 Foster, J., op. cit., p. 42.

15 As assessed by Martin K. McNicholl from the following references: Hall, D.J. 1985. Sifton, Sir Clifford, p. 1695 *in* Marsh, J.H. (ed.), The Canadian Encyclopaedia. Hurtig, Edmonton; pp. 1999-2000 in 2nd edition, (1988); and Waiser, W. A. 1989. The field naturalist: John Macoun, the Geological Survey, and natural science. University of Toronto Press, Toronto, pp. 116-117 and 143.

16 Lothian, W.F. 1976. A History of Canada's National Parks. Indian and Northern Affairs, Parks Canada. p. 52. Also Commission of Conservation, Annual Report, 1911, Committee on Fisheries, p. 6.

17 See Chapter 8 for further information.

18 Foster, J., op. cit.

19 Canada. House of Commons Debates. Ottawa, February 21, 1905. *In* Holmgren, Eric J. 1986. Fish and Wildlife Management in Alberta: A History. Unpublished report prepared for the Department of Forestry, Lands and Wildlife, Edmonton.

20 Memorandum of Agreement of Transfer of Natural Resources from Federal to Provincial Control. Ottawa, December 14, 1929.

21 Alberta. An Act Respecting the Transfer of the Natural Resources of Alberta. 1930. Chapter 31.

22 Alberta. An Act to Provide for the Administration of the Provincial Natural Resources. 1930. Chapter 22.

23 Alberta. An Act Respecting the Department of Lands and Mines. 1931. Chapter 42.

24 Huestis, E.S. Interviewed by Eric Holmgren, Edmonton. July 11, 1985.

25 Department of Lands and Mines. 1936. Annual Report. Game Branch.

26 Department of Lands and Mines. 1946. Annual Report. Fish and Wildlife Branch.

27 Ibid.

28 Murphy, Peter J. 1983. Interview with Eric S. Huestis. Edmonton, Alberta. September 26, 1983. See also Murphy, Peter J. 1985. A History of Forest and Prairie Fire Control Policy in Alberta. Edmonton. This work is relevant for its information on fire control in regards to habitat protection.

29 Originally appeared in *Crowsnest and its People*. 1979. Crowsnest Pass Historical Society. Adapted here with permission.

30 Gilliat, Neil. 1998. If Moose Could Only Talk. Brightest Pebble Publishing Co. Ltd., Edmonton. See also Gilliat, N. 1999. Watch over the Forest. Brightest Pebble Publishing Co. Ltd., Edmonton.

31 Hewitt, C. Gordon. 1921. The Conservation of the Wild Life of Canada. Charles Scribner's Sons. New York.

32 Ibid.

33 Leopold, Aldo. 1933. Game Management. C. Scribner, New York.

34 Leopold, Aldo. 1948. A Sand County Almanac and Sketches Here and There. Reprinted by Oxford University Press, New York, 1987.

35 Documented in the 100-page preliminary report entitled Botanical Survey—Cypress Hills Forest 1945 by R.G.H. Cormack.

36 Cormack, R.G.H. 1967. Wildflowers of Alberta. Department of Industry and Development, Government of Alberta, Edmonton.

37 Ainley, M.G. 1993. Restless Energy: a Biography of William Rowan, 1891-1957. Vèhicule Press, Montrèal, Quèbec.

59

[38] Rowan, W. Notes on Alberta waders included in the British list. British Birds 20:1-10; 20:34-42; 20:82-90; 20:138-145; 20:186-192; 20:210-222; 23:2-17.

[39] Lister, R. 1979. The Birds and Birders of Beaverhills Lake. Edmonton Bird Club, Edmonton.

[40] Rowan, W. 1925. Relation of light to bird migration and developmental changes. Nature 115:494-495.

[41] Rowan, W. 1929. Experiments in bird migration I: manipulation of the reproductive cycle: seasonal histological changes in the gonads. Proceedings of the Boston Society of Natural History 39:151-208.

[42] Rowan, W. 1930. Experiments in bird migration II: reversed migration. Proceedings of the National Academy of Sciences 16:520-525; and Rowan W. 1932. Experiments in bird migration III: the effects of artificial light, castration and certain extracts on the autumn movement of the American Crow (*Corvus brachyrhynchos*). Proceedings of the National Academy of Sciences 18:639-654.

[43] See Chapter 3 for more information.

[44] Rowan, W. 1931. The Riddle of Migration. The Williams and Wilkins Company, Baltimore, USA.

[45] Ainley, M.G., op. cit., p. 293.

[46] See more on this in Chapter 6.

[47] Mitchell, George J. 1980. The Pronghorn Antelope in Alberta. Department of Biology, University of Regina, Regina, Saskatchewan.

[48] Highlights from an interview, August 16th, 2002, at the 14th Annual Fish and Wildlife Reunion, west of Sundre, Alberta.

[49] Holmgren, E.J., op. cit.

[50] Lewis, Margaret. 1979. To Conserve a Heritage. Alberta Fish and Game Association, Calgary.

[51] Ibid., p.6

[52] Ibid., p.6

[53] Burnett, J.A. 2003. A Passion for Wildlife: a history of the Canadian Wildlife Service, 1947-1997. UBC Press, Vancouver.

[54] Alberta Department of Lands and Forests. 1965 Annual Report, pp. 67-69.

[55] For more on this program, see Chapter 11.

[56] Ken Ambrock, Assistant Deputy Minister, Fish and Wildlife Division, December 7, 2004. Pers. comm.

Preservation

It is assumed that the subject of wildlife sanctuaries was assigned to the Dominion Parks Branch because the Dominion parks in the west, which aggregate about 10,000 square miles [25,898 sq. km] in area, are maintained as game sanctuaries. They have been maintained as such for about ten years and if an exceedingly great increase in wildlife is the test of their success then there can be no doubt that sanctuaries properly and fearlessly administered will inevitably result not only in the preservation but in the very great increase of all forms of wildlife. In the parks today, the casual visitor does not need to be told that wildlife is abundant. He constantly has the best evidence of this fact, because wherever he goes his own eyes show him it is so. Perhaps the greatest results have been obtained in Rocky Mountains Park, of which Banff is the centre. Even in Banff, the evidence of the results can be seen from day to day. Deer may be seen at the most unexpected moments walking along the streets and paths of the town.[1]

J.B. Harkin, COMMISSIONER OF DOMINION PARKS,
1919 NATIONAL CONFERENCE ON GAME AND WILDLIFE CONSERVATION

■ ■ ■

THE *first* ERA

OF FISH AND WILDLIFE WILDLIFE MANAGEMENT IN ALBERTA:
Preservation of a Dwindling Resource

Armed with a brief overview of events leading up to provincehood and establishment of Alberta's first fish and wildlife authority, the Alberta Fish and Wildlife Division, we can now delve more deeply into several more specific areas of interest.

We place these roughly into the context of three eras of fish and wildlife management. The next three chapters examine the province's first era of wildlife management—preservation. Preservation—establishing protected areas that removed limiting factors such as hunting, and sometimes, natural predators—allowed a population to rebound through its natural increase. The era of preservation arose as a reaction to the overexploitation of game in the 19th century which drove many big game species into decline by the turn of the 20th century.

In response to this decline in big game, particularly elk, several national parks and provincial game preserves were created under the direction of a handful of far-sighted individuals (Chapter Three *Big Game and Big Parks: Preservation through National Parks and Game Preserves*). In some parts of the continent, the effort to protect all nature arose from an altruistic romanticism of the early naturalists including Emerson and Thoreau. In Alberta, early settlers were likely more utilitarian in their concern for a sustained food supply.

At the same time, attempts were made to sustain the consumption of game species by enforcing hunting and fishing restrictions through regulations (Chapter Four *The Enforcers: Game Laws and Those Who Upheld Them*). Of course, not everyone agreed with harvest limits and closed seasons. Many only begrudgingly went along with the rules in order to maintain the resource for future use by all. As the complexity of rules including seasons, bag limits, and other regulations grew, so did the need for a body of enforcers. Although it began with volunteer Game Guardians, the provincial enforcement branch eventually became a highly mobile, paid, uniformed and trained body of Fish and Wildlife Officers that to this day, is involved in many aspects of fish and wildlife management throughout the province.

By the 1930s, some of the driving force behind fish and wildlife management was economic in nature—using government initiatives to stimulate the economy in a young province trying to survive a decade of drought and depression. Oddly enough, after surviving years of exploitation during the fur trade, furbearers were now faring better than many big game species (Chapter Five *Furbearers: Trapping, Bounties and Fur Farms*). Trapping was still a viable industry and fur farms were encouraged as a way to diversify the depressed economy. The ever-increasing number of settlers harbouring a pest eradication mentality bode poorly for some furbearers. Bounties were placed on wolves and coyotes in the hopes of eradicating them or at least keeping them away from settled areas and livestock. Even in forested areas, carnivores like grizzly bears and cougars were often targeted as competitors for big game. Eradicating predators to benefit wild ungulate populations and thereby provide more surpluses for the human hunter was a strongly held concept. Both Forestry and Fish and Wildlife Officers were often the ones to deal with the administration of the fur harvest and farming of furbearers, as well as with bounties and problem wildlife.

While many of the issues discussed in the next section arose before the science of wildlife management was widely understood, the people involved persevered, learning what they needed as they needed it. They had an inherent desire to protect what they saw as a valuable and valued resource and they did so to the lasting benefit of all Albertans.

1 Harkin, J.B. 1919. Wildlife Sanctuaries: Proceedings of the National Conference on Conservation of Game, Fur-Bearing Animals and Other Wildlife under the Direction of the Canadian Commission of Conservation in Co-Operation with the Advisory Board on Wildlife Protection. February 18-19, 1919, Ottawa. (Available on microfiche at the University of Calgary Library call # FC51.C3496#82935)

Chapter 3

BIG GAME AND BIG PARKS:
PRESERVATION THROUGH NATIONAL
PARKS AND GAME PRESERVES

Margo Pybus with contributions from Sue Clarke, George Mitchell,
Bob Stevenson, Pat Valastin and Bill Wishart

"The main axiom of wild-life protection is this: a species of animal must not be destroyed at a greater rate than it can increase. Further, the preservation of any part of our native fauna depends upon the maintenance of sufficient of its normal range to permit unmolested feeding and breeding. In other words, killing for recreation or food must be wisely regulated, and the provision of refuges is indispensable."[1]

C. GORDON HEWITT, DOMINION ENTOMOLOGIST AND CONSULTING BIOLOGIST, 1921

A New Attitude

Provincial involvement in wildlife management began at a critical time for many of Alberta's big game species. A prolonged cold spell from 1875 to 1900 was capped with a series of severe winters in the 1880s.[2] As well, a peak in precipitation in 1900 was equal to or greater than any in the previous 300 years.[3] Local and regional ungulate (hoofed mammal) populations had been substantially reduced in a mere 30 to 40 years and were in decline across the continent at the turn of the 20th century. Human demands and activities exceeded the capability of wildlife populations to survive, let alone increase. Predators exacted their toll on the few remaining deer, moose, elk, and caribou. The combined effects of these factors pushed ecosystems, and ungulate populations, to near-collapse.

Fortunately, a small group of visionaries interested in the preservation of wildlife and wild spaces managed to stave off extermination of big game populations and even reversed some of the downward trends. Society was awakened to the fact that they had a responsibility to ensure big game species did not disappear and that lands were set aside for free-ranging populations needing sanctuary from insatiable human pressure to eat them, sell their parts, or plough their critical habitats. This new attitude set the stage for the development of the National Parks system, a highlight of wildlife management in Alberta, with specific programs for the conservation of elk, bison, and pronghorn antelope woven throughout. Lothian presents a detailed yet very readable history of Canada's national parks.[4] See also Janet

Foster's *Working for Wildlife* for a national perspective on these early efforts.[5]

The persistence, expansion, and success of Canada's National Parks program, beginning in the West in 1885 and greatly expanded in the first two decades of the 20th century, was a notable achievement at a time when governments and the people of Canada were focussed on pushing forward with plans to extend the human sphere rather than limit it. Contrary to previous examples in Europe, national parks in North America were designed to be inclusive rather than exclusive: that is, they were established for the benefit and lasting legacy of the public rather than the private use of privileged gentry. Preservation of natural resources, including wilderness and its components, were foremost in the minds of those far-sighted citizens and civil servants who laid the foundations of the parks system. This was a major step towards building a concept of wildlife conservation in western Canada.

National Parks: Sanctuaries for Big Game

The early national parks, located at Banff, Waterton, and Jasper, were set aside primarily for their magnificent mountain scenery—scenery that would draw tourists and provide an income to subsidize the expensive railways being built to connect Canada from coast to coast. Many tourists came on the Canadian Pacific Railway through Banff, and later, on the Grand Trunk Pacific Railway through Jasper. The corporate approach was encapsulated as: "…if you can't export the scenery, import the tourists." At first, the parks attracted only those visitors with the means to get

there, or those guides and adventurers driven by an internal need to scale the peaks and walk among the clouds. A steady parade of day-trippers from Calgary eventually added to the numbers. Sight-seers increased steadily as the stories of glorious encounters with wilderness and wildlife circulated in written and oral accounts.

However, the scenic grandeur was not the sole *raison d'être* for Canada's National Parks. The guiding regulations for early parks included a mandate for the preservation of scenery and the environment, as well as all forms of organic (plant and animal) and inorganic (mineral) resources. It then followed that park administrators would take steps to achieve such objectives. Thus began the first serious efforts of fish and wildlife management in Canada, a new discipline with many unknowns.

Rocky Mountains Park (established 1887)

It was 1883 when railway construction workers Frank McCabe and William McCardell took a day off and rafted across the Bow River at the foot of Terrace (now Sulphur) Mountain. They stumbled across what was to become the national treasure now known as the Cave and Basin Hot Springs. Word spread quickly and other workers came to shed the grime and misery of railway construction in the late 1800s. Various claims of ownership of the springs were lodged and the subsequent legal dispute and uproar was heard all the way to Ottawa.

In 1885, the Department of the Interior gave serious consideration to preserving the hot

THE BANFF CONUNDRUM

An icon of Banff National Park, the Banff Springs Hotel was opened in 1888. Offering 250 rooms, it was the largest hotel on earth and rooms went for $3.50 a night. It soon became the destination of choice for travellers around the world. Today, the park attracts over four million tourists each year. The Banff Springs Hotel remains the premier accommodation amongst a variety of commercial activities in the Banff townsite.

Since the beginning, park administrators have struggled to balance the needs of wildlife and park ecosystems with those of human visitors. Land-use and development decisions within Parks Canada continue to top the list of issues facing local and national park administrators.

65

BOW RAPIDS AND THE CANADIAN PACIFIC BANFF SPRINGS HOTEL.
COURTESY PROVINCIAL ARCHIVES OF ALBERTA (B9624)

springs. They issued an *Order in Council* specifying that: "...whereas near the station of Banff on the Canadian Pacific Railway, in the Provisional District of Alberta, North West Territories, there have been discovered several hot mineral springs which ... are hereby reserved from sale or settlement or squatting ..." summarily cutting off all claims to private ownership.[6] The public reserve was placed on ten sq. mi. (26 sq. km) around the hot springs, preventing private ownership of what soon became a significant tourist attraction for railway travellers.

EARLY PHOTO OF THE CAVE AND BASIN HOT SPRINGS, BANFF, 1885.
COURTESY PROVINCIAL ARCHIVES OF ALBERTA (B9622)

In 1886, W.F. Whitcher, a former federal Commissioner of Fisheries, recommended that wild game, birds, and fish be protected in the national mountain park being proposed by several individuals and interests. Such action would hopefully increase those species depleted by indiscriminate hunting during the railway construction years. Whitcher also called for the strict control of hunting and fishing within such a protected area. Building on this novel perspective, an Act establishing Hot Springs Reserve as Rocky Mountains Park, the first national park in Canada, was brought into being in 1887. Park regulations, finalized in 1889, provided for the protection of forests and game, control of private development, and preservation of natural phenomena within the new protected area. Firearms were prohibited except by permit from the superintendent.

The big picture value of preserved lands was recognized in 1902, when the hot springs reserve was expanded to include Lake Louise and a considerable portion of the eastern slopes of the Rocky Mountains: 4400 sq. mi. (11,440 sq. km) of spectacular mountains and valleys, rivers and lakes, and all the species contained therein. Although the actual size of Rocky Mountains Park expanded and contracted a few times over the next 20 years, the pattern to set aside large tracts of land for scenic and natural heritage values was entrenched in the *Dominion Forest Reserves and Parks Act* of 1911.[7]

Building on the popularity of Rocky Mountains Park, other lands already set aside as park reserves were soon given full protection as national parks. In Alberta, these included Waterton Lakes (forest park established in 1895) and Jasper (park reserve established in 1907). The system of conserving lands and wildlife in a series of national parks now had a solid foundation and set the stage for its expansion across the country. Big parks were here to stay. Big game populations would undoubtedly benefit from big parks, at least initially.

Early Park Management

Early park managers were faced with a multitude of issues. As was fitting for the times, fire was considered a primary menace to all things natural. Although lightning fires occurred, railway operations constituted a far greater risk. Engines with defective spark arresters and engineers who kept the ash pan doors open to obtain a better draft for the fire-box resulted in sparks and live embers regularly scattered over the rail right-of-way. With little or no manpower to locate and suppress them, wildfires often raged across protected areas. Managers also wrestled with the continued defacement of natural formations as well as illegal hunting and fishing inside the parks. Wildlife populations were in decline in some areas. Howard Douglas, Superintendent of Rocky Mountains Park, reported in 1902-1903:

Twenty years ago, the eastern slope of the Rocky Mountains from the Kicking Horse Pass to the [international] boundary line was filled with game. Moose were frequently seen, elk and black tail [mule] deer, white tail deer, bighorns, and goats were plentiful; now some of these have totally disappeared and the remainder have been so thinned out as to make this hunting ground practically useless.[8]

There is no doubt that systematic hunting throughout the foothills contributed to diminished game populations over large tracts of land. At first, effective enforcement proved impossible as budgets were limited, staff were seasonal, and few and far between. The establishment of a year-round Park Warden Service in 1909 gave rise to new energies and opportunities to enforce the regulations. The many stories of park wardens like Bo Holroyd and later, Hubert Green, show a picture of devotion and dedication to protecting the national parks, as well as the fish and wildlife found within them. Public education was added to the management matrix with the establishment of the Banff Museum in 1907. A herd of bison established near the Banff townsite about the same time was yet another component of the visitor experience.

NATIONAL PARK WARDENS AT PARK WARDEN SCHOOL IN BANFF, 1949.
COURTESY ALBERTA SUSTAINABLE RESOURCE DEVELOPMENT
[FOREST PROTECTION IMAGE LIBRARY]

67

JOHN CHARLES (BO) HOLROYD - NATIONAL PARK WARDEN

Born in 1889, John Charles (Bo) Holroyd was a rancher near Pincher Creek before becoming a soldier in the First World War and travelling to France and Belgium between 1914 and 1920. Upon his return, he was appointed a Park Warden in Waterton Lakes National Park, starting 27 years of civil service. In 1933, he became Supervising Warden of the park and moved to Lower Waterton Lake where he remained until his retirement in 1947. During his period of park employment, Holroyd was involved in horseback patrols, fire control, trail building and maintenance, search and rescue, fish and wildlife duties, law enforcement, supervision, and administration—the wildlife equivalent of a jack-of-all-trades. After his retirement, Holroyd ranched for another 27 years before passing away in 1974.[9]

PARK WARDEN, HUBERT UNSWORTH GREEN
[SUE CLARKE]

Hubert Unsworth Green was born in Paris, France, in 1886 but grew up on the English coast. His love of nature came from his father—an ardent naturalist with a bent for research. Young Hubert and his father visited the ancient remains of beaver dams in the once marshy country around Alderton and worked together to study hibernating dormice. The dormice were kept in cages in the barn and it was Hubert's job to feed them. He also took dictation from his father regarding detailed records of the dormouse's mating habits, gestation period, and number of young. These experiences proved of enormous benefit in later years when Green conducted his own wildlife research.

Green intended to enter the medical profession as his father had done. In 1905, he passed his matriculation exams and took a post-graduate tour to Moose Jaw, Saskatchewan, to visit family friends. He never returned either to England or to his medical studies. Instead, he joined the Royal North West Mounted Police in 1907 at Lethbridge, Alberta. During his tenure with the force, he served as a constable, corporal, sergeant, sergeant major, and again as sergeant until 1932, at which time he was discharged to pension after twenty-five years of service.

From 1932-1937, Green devoted his "…entire interests to original wildlife research…using Riding Mountain National Park as a fertile field of endeavour".[10] With the assistance of local authorities, he studied the ecology of elk and beaver in the park, and developed a checklist of mammals through collections and observation. His work was published in the *Canadian Field-Naturalist*. He was awarded the medal of the Manitoba Natural History Society for outstanding original research for his work on elk. He also authored a book on mammals in Manitoba that was subsequently distributed to schools.

In 1937, Green moved to Banff, Alberta, where he continued to study and write about wildlife. He undertook one of the first long-term studies of bighorn sheep in Banff National Park, on a private interest basis from 1938-1943 and then as a warden of the National Parks Service from 1944-1949. Green scientifically documented all aspects of this species including its habitat, distribution, and relationships with other park species. The results

were published by the National Parks and Historic Sites Service.[11] They also appear in the *Canadian Field-Naturalist*.[12]

Hubert Green also conducted extensive research on the elk (1947) and wolves (1951) of Banff National Park. He co-authored a report on fishes, published by the National Parks Bureau. Green believed that a major failing within park policy was the lack of promotion of wildlife as a major park attraction. He believed that park visitors were thirsting for wildlife information and leaving the park with this curiosity unsatisfied. In characteristic fashion, Green lobbied the federal government to provide park visitors with interpretive educational pamphlets about wildlife in Banff National Park. During the war years, he entertained troops stationed in the park with educational films on his favourite topic—wildlife.

While Hubert "the warden" passionately conducted wildlife research, under the pen name "Tony Lascelle" he also became nationally known as a writer. His works appeared in every leading naturalist and game-related magazine in Canada and the United States. Tony sold his first story to *Forest and Stream* in 1924. Thereafter, he wrote numerous articles on "natural history subjects, including many on the subject of conservation and the need for the scientific management of wildlife, and the application of science to wildlife problems".[13]

In later years, Hubert Green engaged himself in the study of western Canadian history, particularly ranching. After his death in 1962, his family donated his papers to the Whyte Museum of the Canadian Rockies. These files contain a wealth of information, including several manuscripts on conservation and wildlife, notes from national park studies, published copies of his papers, as well as much of his correspondence. These items are accompanied by photographs of ducks, beavers, cougars, elk, fish, horses, moose, mountain sheep, wolverine, wolves, Cypress Hills, and Riding Mountain National Park, as well as hunting and ranching.

Game Preservation in the Forest Reserves

Not all early conservation efforts were focussed in the mountains and not all reserves were created solely for the protection of scenery and wildlife. Forests were also disappearing across Alberta. An 1884 amendment to the *Dominion Lands Act* (1872) allowed the government to reserve lands on, adjacent to, or in the vicinity of the Rocky Mountains for the protection of forest trees and the maintenance of watersheds.

W. Millar, Dominion Forest Supervisor, spent a fair amount of time patrolling the forest reserves. In a 1915 report, he made it clear that wildlife in the forest reserves was being severely exploited by various groups, particularly in critical wintering areas.[14] Some of these areas were adjacent to the national mountain parks. According to Millar, the annual revenue from big-game hunting in 1912 was at least $100,000 in Alberta, including

$25,000 for supplies and the hiring of packhorses, guides, and camp assistants. Despite the economic gain, the need for special protection for elk, bighorn sheep, mule deer, and moose, as well as a general provision for "no hunting" within the early forest reserves in Alberta, was readily apparent.

The first *Game Act* of Alberta provided that all Dominion parks existing when the act was passed (1907) also be made into game preserves under provincial legislation, prohibiting hunting and the carrying of firearms inside the parks. However, Millar felt the Act was inadequate with no appropriate penalties for violators and no ability to create game preserves outside of the Dominion parks. He highlighted his report with a detailed map showing several proposed game preserves within the forest reserve system. He pointed out that the forest reserves were important areas for water conservation, timber and grazing utilization,

69

1915 MAP OF THE ROCKY MOUNTAIN FOREST RESERVE AND PROPOSED GAME PRESERVES.
COURTESY B. STEVENSON

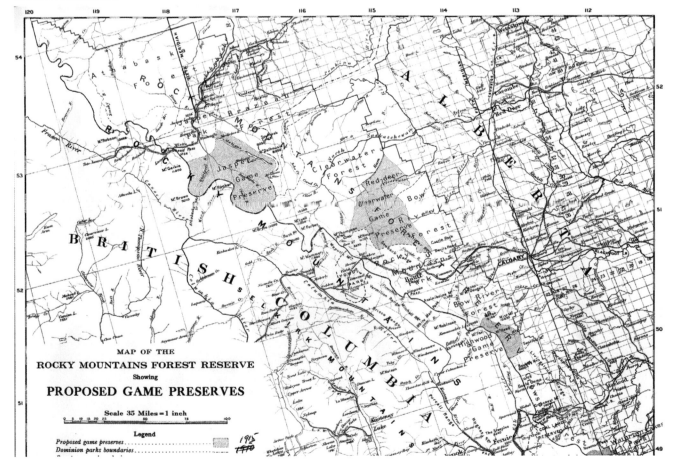

and wildlife. Forestry personnel had a good knowledge of their reserves and wanted to see them used for the protection and propagation of wild animals. In addition, rangers and patrolmen could keep an eye on the activities of those thought to be responsible for the overexploitation of big game within these areas.

A number of the proposed game preserves were soon incorporated into the federal parks, or later were established as distinct game preserves within the forest reserves [such as Kananaskis and Castle River game preserves] under the protection of ranger staff. Many of these remained until the mid-1950s when wild populations increased to the point where a surplus could be harvested, with regulations and hunting protocols in place to prevent overexploitation.

The Cooking Lake Timber Reserve was created in 1899 on the Cooking Lake Moraine some 30 mi. (50 km) east of Edmonton in the Beaver Hills of central Alberta. The thin soils and knob-and-kettle terrain remaining after the last glaciers retreated were unsuitable for homesteading. A few settlers tried in the 1880s and 1890s but soon abandoned such futility. However, the area supported magnificent stands of spruce and tamarack that were quickly disappearing. In conjunction with the numerous pothole lakes and sloughs, there was abundant habitat for a wide range of wildlife. This attracted hunters and soon the early concern for forests was extended to various plants and animals. In 1895, fires destroyed the forest cover over a huge expanse of land east of Edmonton. Balsam and aspen poplar and their associated understorey provided rapid regrowth and ground cover. By 1900, virtually all of the original timber, particularly the conifer species, had been burned by a combination of wildfire and intentional land clearing.

Following a request by 70 residents of Edmonton and district who were concerned about rumoured elk shoots in the Beaver Hills, the federal government created Island Park Game Reserve in 1904. With an estimated 75 elk in the area, it was "the largest existing herd in Canada outside the unexplored forests of the north".[15] Frank Oliver, Member of Parliament for Edmonton, had passed the request on to the Honourable Clifford Sifton, Minister of the Interior. Sifton's Deputy Minister, James A. Smart, promptly issued an order setting aside 16 sq. mi. (41 sq. km) around Island (now Astotin) Lake in the Cooking Lake Timber Reserve. In 1906, Island Park Game Reserve became Elk Island National Park. During the next two years, an industrious group of Fort Saskatchewan residents voluntarily built a game fence enclosing at least 35 elk and 24 mule deer in the new federal sanctuary. This park was to play a pivotal role in the conservation of elk and bison in the coming years.

The Fall and Rise of Elk in Alberta

Once numerous throughout Alberta on suitable range extending from the international border to within sight of the subarctic zone, elk populations had declined by the early 1900s to no more than 365 individuals in residual herds in the vicinity of the Brazeau valley, Highwood Pass, and Oldman River drainage. The Brazeau herd was the only remnant of the original populations in the east slopes of the Rockies; elk in the two southern populations had moved in from southeastern British Columbia after Alberta closed the hunting season on elk in 1910.[17] In addition, a small group of captive elk owned by a few private citizens in Manitoba was collected between 1900 and 1902 and housed at Banff.

"I enjoyed a scene, of which I do not presume to give an adequate description; and as it was the rutting season of the elk, the whistling of that animal was heard in all the variety which the echoes could afford it."
ALEXANDER MACKENZIE IN THE VICINITY OF THE CLEARWATER RIVER[16]

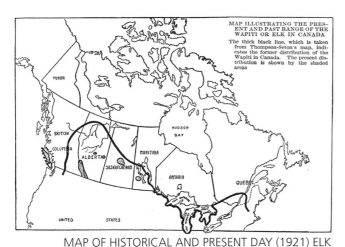

MAP OF HISTORICAL AND PRESENT DAY (1921) ELK
DISTRIBUTION IN CANADA.
SOURCE: HEWITT, C.G. 1921. THE CONSERVATION OF THE WILD LIFE
OF CANADA. CHARLES SCRIBNER'S SONS, NEW YORK.

By 1919, elk protected within the boundaries of
Yellowstone National Park (established in 1872) in
Wyoming exceeded carrying capacity and were
starving. To alleviate the pressures in Yellowstone
and to bolster sagging populations in Alberta, elk
were shipped between 1917 and 1920 to the
national parks at Banff (268 shipped, 244 survived),
Jasper (98 shipped, 88 survived), and Waterton (58
arrived).[18] These elk were the founding generation
of today's current park populations. As well, six elk
from Banff plus seven from Montana (in with the
bison from Michel Pablo—see next section)
founded the population in Buffalo National Park at
Wainwright; however, these were extirpated by the
late-1930s during disease control efforts. Elk in Elk
Island National Park originated from the
individuals enclosed within the perimeter fence in
1907.

In 1923, Game Commissioner Ben Lawton noted
that there was only one band of elk remaining in a
wild state on provincial lands in Alberta. He

realized that something must be done to protect
this small wild herd that ranged the rugged
country south of Edson between the upper reaches
of the Brazeau and Pembina rivers. These elk
persisted simply because the area was inaccessible
and few hunters managed to find their way in and
out. Also, it was close to the eastern boundary of
Jasper National Park and the elk could easily take
refuge there. In 1923, and again in 1926, Lawton
recommended that the area be proclaimed a game
preserve. A year later, he was able to report that
the area was finally closed and proclaimed the
Pembina-Brazeau Elk Preserve. By 1928 and
1929, Lawton noted that big game were increasing
in this area and doing well. In 1932-1933, there

CARL RUNGIUS, THE FAMOUS WILDLIFE ARTIST
AND BIG GAME HUNTER, WITH ELK.
COURTESY GLENBOW ARCHIVES (NA-3466-15)

71

RECIPROCITY WITH YELLOWSTONE: ELK FOR WOLVES
Between 1917 and 1920, approximately 400 elk went from Yellowstone National Park to Waterton, Banff, and
Jasper national parks. Most of the 4000 to 5000 elk found in these parks today are descendants from the
Yellowstone relocations. In the late 1990s, the tables were turned and Alberta cooperated with the U.S. Fish and
Wildlife Service in a program to reintroduce gray wolves to Yellowstone National Park and central Idaho. In total,
29 wolves were successfully captured from the central foothills region of Alberta and relocated. Additional wolves
were collected in British Columbia. Though the last of the original Canadian wolves died in 2003, their many
offspring are now an integral component of predator/prey relationships in Yellowstone.

was an open season on elk in the preserve. Although the preserve no longer exists, occasional relocations of elk to the Brazeau area from local federal and provincial populations have occurred.

Today, elk are consistently found throughout the mountains and foothills of western Alberta and along the Athabasca River as far east as Calling Lake. Isolated populations are also scattered throughout boreal and parkland areas, the Cypress Hills, and Canadian Forces Base Suffield. Populations are managed by a variety of hunting regimens including limited entry draws and trophy size (number of antler points) restrictions, as well as by occasional transplants from Elk Island National Park. In addition, significant management effort is expended to resolve conflicts associated with grazing elk attracted to hay crops produced by ranchers for domestic animals.

Restoration of the Buffalo/Bison

Bison or buffalo? It matters not what you call them; the story of North America's largest native land mammal is remarkable. They survived the Ice Age, but nearly succumbed to human greed and mismanagement. In a few horrific years, they were reduced from countless millions washing across the prairies like an endless tide to one or two remnant bands of a few stragglers that somehow managed not to be slaughtered. Their story is one of the most outstanding conservation achievements on the North American continent. Dr. Grant MacEwan, in his book *Buffalo: Sacred and Sacrificed*, wrote with eloquence and passion for this species.[19] The current chapter provides only a brief account of the

history of bison conservation. It also does not discuss the validity of the two bison subspecies.[20] Keeping within a historical context, plains and wood bison have been recognized and managed as separate races in the past and thus are reflected as such here.

Samuel Walking Coyote is now recognized as the unwitting saviour of the plains bison. In 1874, he came upon a small group of wild bison calves along the Canada/U.S. border, rounded them up, and drove them onto the Flathead Valley Indian Reservation in central Montana. Here they roamed free and relatively undisturbed. By 1890, wild bison were virtually non-existent on the western plains. A few individuals remained in private collections. The largest by far was the Montana herd, now belonging to Michel Pablo and Charles Allard. By 1896, it had grown to 300 head. In 1906, grazing privileges for the bison were cancelled by the U.S. Government as the land in the valley was thrown open for settlement. The bison had to go.

Michel Pablo (Charles Allard had died) approached the U.S. Government with a reasonable proposal for federal administrators to purchase the herd. Congress vetoed the deal as too expensive. In 1905, Alex Ayotte, Assistant Immigration Agent for Canada at Great Falls, Montana offered to find out if the Canadian Government might provide a grazing lease. He set in motion a series of letters and reports that went all the way to the top in Ottawa. It was determined that Pablo was an honest and shrewd vendor, but would accept a reasonable figure for sale. The herd, then some 350 animals,

MICHEL PABLO AND HIS COWBOYS HERDING BUFFALO IN MONTANA FOR SHIPMENT TO CANADA.
COURTESY GLENBOW ARCHIVES (NA-3581-3A)

MICHEL PABLO AND HIS COWBOYS, NUMBERING TWENTY,
AFTER TWO WEEKS ROUND UP, RIDING FIFTY MILES A DAY, CORRALLED EIGHTY ODD HEAD OF BUFFALO.

COPYRIGHTED 1906

BUFFALO TRAVELLING DOWN THE FENCED CORRIDOR AT LAMONT AND INTO ELK ISLAND NATIONAL PARK, 1907.
COURTESY GLENBOW ARCHIVES (NA-3581-12)

was considered in satisfactory condition and fully worthy of purchase. In January 1906, a deal was struck by Frank Oliver, federal Minister of the Interior, and approved by Prime Minister Sir Wilfred Laurier.

The Dominion of Canada agreed to purchase the entire herd at $245 for each head delivered to Alberta as soon as possible. However, this was no easy task and required all the skills, knowledge, and persistence that Pablo could muster. The bison were herded down the Flathead valley to the closest railhead and, once loaded (in itself, no small feat) took a 52-hour train trip to Lamont, Alberta, at the north end of Elk Island Park. In 1907 alone, 410 bison were shipped in boxcars via five railways. Their final destination was to be a new park at Wainwright, Alberta, created specifically to hold the bison from Montana. However, it was not yet ready when the first bison were shipped in 1907. Fortunately, the perimeter fence had just been completed at Elk Island Park, so the bison were sent there until the fence at Wainwright could be completed. From the train

station in Lamont, the animals were directed along a two and three-quarter mile fenced corridor to Elk Island Park. From 1907 to 1912, 716 bison were rounded up and shipped to Alberta at a total cost of approximately $200,000.

73

By 1909, the fence at Wainwright was completed and 325 bison were moved from Elk Island to the new Buffalo National Park. Additional bison were shipped directly from Montana to Wainwright. After fencing Buffalo National Park, it was noted that a number of elk—descendants from a few elk received along with the bison from Montana—as well as some resident moose and deer, had been enclosed as well. Of the 410 bison originally shipped to Elk Island, 48 escaped subsequent roundups for Wainwright. These became the foundation of the current herds of plains bison in the northern portion of Elk Island Park.

The bison thrived in their new location at Wainwright.[21] Fires had raged over the landscape in the previous decade and the nutrient-enriched soils were carpeted with lush grasses. The full

CHARLES M. RUSSELL IN MONTANA

In November 1908 and again the next spring, renowned western artist Charles M. Russell was invited by the Government of Canada to participate in and to help document the bison roundup in Montana. Russell, a worthy cowboy as well as artist, jumped at the chance for close observation of large numbers of bison. His personal experiences are reflected in the details of bison behaviour, gait, and body shape seen in his subsequent artworks. The realistic portrayal of animals and activities common to life on the western plains contributed to the international success Russell enjoyed, and the appreciation that his work continues to receive.

THE FIRST BUFFALO ARRIVING AT WAINWRIGHT BUFFALO NATIONAL PARK, 1909.
COURTESY GLENBOW ARCHIVES (NA-1792-3)

(TB) and brucellosis were common infections in domestic cattle. Bovine TB was identified in the Wainwright bison as early as 1917.[22] The close contact with experimental cattle and the local cattle ranging in and around the park provided ample opportunity for diseases to transfer to the bison. In addition, some of the early rearing of orphan bison had included the use of nurse cows probably infected with bovine tuberculosis.[23] By March 1923, there were more than 6600 bison at Wainwright.[24] This rapidly expanding herd provided ideal conditions for disease to spread.

reproductive potential of grass-fed bison with no predators is quite remarkable and was easily achieved in the new bison haven. With the increase in numbers, interests moved beyond simply conservation of bison. Agricultural managers saw bison as a potential commercial commodity, but only if they had more meat on their frame. The Dominion, eager to expand agricultural opportunities, began an extensive research program in 1916 to develop new hybrids, including cattle-bison crosses and bison-yak crosses. These studies were finally abandoned in 1964, as most male offspring produced were sterile.

Unfortunately, this was also a time when bovine tuberculosis

CATTALO AND YAKALO CROSS-BREEDS
AT WAINWRIGHT BUFFALO NATIONAL PARK.
COURTESY GLENBOW ARCHIVES (NA-537-10)

EDWIN JOHN "BUD" COTTON: PARK RIDER AND GAME WARDEN

A number of hired hands were employed by the new Buffalo National Park. One of these was Edwin John "Bud" Cotton. Bud was born in 1890 in Sherbrooke, Quebec, and came to Calgary, Alberta, in 1906. He worked as a cowboy until 1913, when he became a rider at the new buffalo park in Wainwright. During the First World War, he served with the 49th Battalion of the Canadian Mounted Rifles, but then went back to the park until it closed in 1940, rising to the position of Chief Warden. Not ready to call it quits, Cotton worked at Elk Island National Park until he retired to Calgary in 1947. Bud loved to tell tales and many of these were written down in books such as *Buffalo Bud: Adventures of a Cowboy*.[25] Bud Cotton took up woodcarving during his retirement, and became well known for his western-theme sculptures. He passed away in 1987.

74

Something had to be done. Proposals to slaughter the diseased herd were met with public outcry. After all, the images of massive bison carcasses rotting on the western plains were still fresh in the public conscience, and Buffalo National Park had been created specifically to preserve bison, not kill them. Yet proposals to ship the herd to a remote area in northern Alberta, an area where wood bison were known to occur, were vigorously opposed by biologists and veterinarians. Whatever the decision, politicians in Ottawa would be set upon by someone. Unfortunately, the politicians chose relocation as the path forward (see more on this later in this chapter).

Wood Buffalo National Park (established 1922)

Early explorers documented a northern form of bison that was larger, heavier, and darker-coloured than the bison on the plains. Samuel Hearne described them as plentiful in the region of the lower Peace River and Slave River lowlands in 1771-1772. Alexander Mackenzie reported large herds of bison along the Slave River in 1779. However, by 1870, wood bison were increasingly scarce and indeed were gone from large portions of their former range.

The ruminations over legislation and responsibility to protect northern bison were as convoluted as the ancient bison trails crossing the northern landscapes. The territorial government initially responded with the *Ordinance for the Protection of the Buffalo* (1877) but this was repealed under pressure from the federal government in 1878. Long-term protection finally came in 1890 when the territorial *Ordinance for the Protection of Game* (1888) was amended to include bison, and hunting of northern bison was prohibited. This was reaffirmed in the *Unorganized Territories Game Protection Act* (1894) and subsequent legislation. Although these efforts were put in place to try to stem the slaughter, enforcement was minimal and populations continued to decline. It was all too little and far too late. From their former range extending from Lesser Slave Lake northward, bison numbers were reduced to a small population in the northeastern corner of Alberta and the southern

75

BOVINE TUBERCULOSIS

Bovine tuberculosis (TB) is a bacterial disease of cattle, which can spill over into other ungulates—for example, bison in northern Alberta, white-tailed deer in Michigan, and elk in southwestern Manitoba. Infection generally occurs when animals breathe air contaminated with bacteria from an infected individual. Bovine TB is not native to North America, and was imported with the cattle that came with European settlement. In Canada, it is a federal reportable disease with serious implications for agricultural economics and, on occasion, human health. With a national TB control and eradication program, our domestic cattle and captive bison populations are considered TB-free (less than 1% of the national herd is infected). Recent cases involve captive elk, captive bison, wild elk and white-tailed deer near Riding Mountain National Park, and a few cattle herds in southwestern Manitoba. Bovine TB persists in free-ranging bison in and around Wood Buffalo National Park (WBNP) at a rate of approximately 50% of the remaining bison. Bovine TB has not been found in free-ranging elk, moose, or deer in Alberta except for a few individuals within WBNP.

The presence of infected bison in northeastern Alberta is considered a growing risk for wild wood bison in the Northwest Territories and northwestern Alberta. In addition, there is a concern that TB will spread to farmed bison and cattle in the Peace River-Fort Vermilion areas, with subsequent implications for domestic cattle and bison populations throughout Canada. Spread of the infection would jeopardize the national TB-free status and result in significant impacts on international trade in cattle and bison.

Although bovine TB does not readily transfer to humans, infected bison are a human health risk. The number of documented human cases in northeastern Alberta is low; however, there is a risk to First Nations people and other hunters who handle and consume bison killed in areas adjacent to WBNP.

Northwest Territories. In 1897, the remnants were designated *Bison bison athabascae*, a subspecies distinct from their southern cousins.

Even with protective legislation in place, it was apparent that the Royal North West Mounted Police force was spread too thinly to enforce legislation in the north. Calls for a national park to protect the remnant northern bison came as early as 1907.[26] In 1911, the Federal Superintendent of Forestry was given the responsibility for preserving the bison, and resident Game Guardians were appointed. Over the next two years, an estimated 200-300 individual bison were counted. The animals were reported to be in good condition and predicted to remain so if properly protected.

In 1916, the Forestry Branch noted that two herds of bison were present between Peace River and Great Slave Lake, and that it was possible to protect them by means of a small patrol. The larger southern herd occurred directly north of the Peace River, and the smaller herd was centred

farther north and east along a portion of the Little Buffalo River near Fort Smith—all in an area now included in Wood Buffalo National Park (WBNP). In 1922, a further reconnaissance was made of the wood bison ranges but no additional populations were found. Apart from these measures, little else was done as the area was still relatively inaccessible to most people and thus the bison were considered to be safe.

The *Northwest Territories Game Act* of 1917 finally brought the bison under the control of the Commissioner of National Parks. In December 1922, Wood Buffalo National Park, containing 10,500 sq. mi. (27,200 sq. km) was created and finally offered long-term protection to the free-ranging wood bison on the Peace-Athabasca delta and the Slave River lowlands.

So the stage was set: there were huge open spaces in Wood Buffalo, and far too many bison in Wainwright Buffalo National Park. And both parks were created for the preservation of bison. In 1923, the over-crowded range in Wainwright

BOVINE BRUCELLOSIS

Bovine brucellosis is a highly contagious bacterial disease associated with abortions in cattle. It raises global economic concerns related to production losses and occasional risk to human health. In North America, this disease spilled over from cattle and is established in bison in and around Wood Buffalo National Park (WBNP), as well as bison and elk in and around Yellowstone National Park. Bacteria are passed to new individuals when they eat contaminated tissue, particularly fluids and tissues from an aborted foetus. Predators and scavengers are at risk if they eat infected tissues; however, carnivores are poor habitat for the bacteria. Subsequent transmission from carnivores is limited.

Domestic cattle and captive bison in Alberta are considered brucellosis-free. Populations of free-ranging bison in and around WBNP are infected, but infection rates differ among local herds. Overall, 30% to 35% of the bison within the park are infected. The role of brucellosis in limiting bison populations remains controversial. Infected females abort or produce weak calves for the first year or two after infection and then appear to sustain normal reproductive success. There are no reports of reduced male fertility. Disease in northern bison populations continues to pose significant wildlife management concerns. Re-establishment of viable populations of wood bison (listed as an endangered animal in Alberta) currently is hampered by the presence of brucellosis (and bovine tuberculosis) in animals associated with WBNP.

Brucellosis in humans occurs as a relatively mild recurrent fever. Most human infections were associated with drinking milk or handling infected dairy cattle; however, as a result of pasteurization of milk and concerted eradication efforts, this is no longer a concern in Canada. There is limited risk associated with handling or consuming infected bison. The bacteria can enter through small cuts or scratches in the skin or through the eyes, nose, or mouth.

76

was facing disaster. At least 6600 excess bison and 1200 deer, elk, and moose lived and ate in the park.[27] Attempts to cull the herd were not popular and fell short of the productivity of the bison. A plan was devised to ship selected bison to the north. This plan met with immediate protests from conservationists and from Park veterinarians who pointed out that the two bison subspecies would interbreed with resulting hybridization. Charles Camsell, Geological Survey of Canada, assessed WBNP in 1916 and felt that wood bison populations in the southern part of the park did not overlap in range with those in the northern portions; thus, he surmised that hybridization would be limited. Disease specialists also warned that it was impossible to identify disease-free bison and this too would put the northern bison at risk. The National Supervisor of Wildlife Protection, Hoyes Lloyd, warned the Commissioner of Parks that it was "…very bad epidemiology to ship buffalo from a herd known to be diseased and place them in contact with the buffalo…which are not known to be diseased".[28] However, the public

outcry against a generalized cull program carried the day and the government in Ottawa proceeded with its plan.

From 1925 to 1928, 6673 plains bison were shipped by rail from Buffalo National Park to Fort McMurray and then by scow (river barge) along the Athabasca River to the new park in the north. The descendants of Walking Coyote's bison were again on the move. Again they went north. And again there were glowing forecasts that this would be their ultimate salvation. Upon their arrival, about 900 bison rapidly migrated to the Sweetgrass area and WBNP was enlarged to protect them. Its present size is 17,360 sq. mi. (44,980 sq. km).

Unfortunately, the bison from the south did indeed interbreed with those in the north. The cattle diseases also survived the journey and flourished in these remote herds. Foreign genetic material and disease agents readily spilled over into the remnant wood bison. In addition, in 1962

77

BUFFALO WERE UNLOADED FROM THE TRAIN AND INTO CORRALS AT FORT McMURRAY BEFORE BEING LOADED ONTO BARGES.
COURTESY B. STEVENSON

at least 265 bison on the west side of the Slave River died of naturally occurring anthrax.[29] An extensive program to try to eradicate bovine TB and brucellosis began in the 1970s. Huge corrals and chutes were built and the bison were rounded up with helicopters. Each animal was injected with a little vaccine and a lot of hope. However, the vaccination program was costly, labour-intensive, and extremely hard on the bison. The old adage that you can move a bison anywhere it wants to go held true and it was soon apparent that many of the bison simply would not move or could not be caught. The program was eventually abandoned.

To this day, bison management issues are front and centre for Wood Buffalo National Park, neighbouring First Nations, all levels of government, as well as a wide range of commercial and conservation interests. Indeed, moving the problem did not solve the problem. However, in spite of ongoing issues, there is no denying that the programs at Elk Island and Buffalo national parks, and later Wood Buffalo National Park, were instrumental in the ultimate salvation of plains and wood bison in western Canada.

Three further programs were undertaken as a result of events in Wood Buffalo National Park. In 1960, a small herd of bison along the Nyarling River in the northwest part of the park seemed to have little if any overlap with the hybrid bison in the southern regions. Morphometric studies by the National Museum indicated that these bison were indeed consistent with the early wood bison specimens.[30] This herd was then used as the basis for subsequent wood bison conservation efforts.

In 1963, 18 bison from the northwest herd were relocated to the north shores of Great Slave Lake, NWT, into what became the Mackenzie Bison Sanctuary. This population flourished, expanded its range, and is apparently disease-free. It is currently [2004] considered an increasing population of more than 2200 bison.[31]

From 1965 to 1968, 23 bison from the northwest herd were relocated to the isolation area south of Highway 16 in Elk Island National Park. Two eight-foot high game fences and a four-lane highway separate these bison from the plains bison in the park area north of Highway 16. Bovine tuberculosis was identified early in the bison moved from Wood Buffalo; however, by following an intensive eradication program, the disease was eliminated and has not recurred in Elk Island since 1979. This population, managed by park

ANTHRAX

Anthrax is an acute, highly infectious, bacterial disease that causes sudden death in many ungulate species. This disease has likely been in North America for centuries. Recent outbreaks in wildlife are limited to the bison in northeastern Alberta (Wood Buffalo National Park) and the Northwest Territories (Mackenzie Bison Sanctuary), with spill-over into a few moose. Sporadic cases in cattle occur in central Alberta. Human infection is extremely rare; however, anyone who finds dead bison should not touch them and should notify appropriate wildlife management officials.

Death comes quickly to animals infected with anthrax, usually in a matter of hours or days. Bacteria rapidly spread and multiply in the blood, producing potent toxins that poison the animal from within. As a result, carcasses bloat very quickly and black tarry blood or bloodstained fluids readily ooze from natural body openings. Clinical signs in live animals are minimal and carcasses are usually the first indication of a problem.

Anthrax spores can survive in soil for extremely long periods. Outbreaks often are associated with rainy spring weather followed by a hot dry summer. Localized floods or periodic flooding of low-lying areas also may expose and concentrate spores, particularly in bison wallows. Transmission generally involves taking in spores via contaminated food, water, or air. Rolling in their wallows or kicking dust onto themselves may be a common mechanism for air-borne transmission to bison. Fortunately outbreaks tend to occur in small pockets. As such, mortality is low and unlikely to affect overall population levels. There are no methods of prevention or treatment.

wardens, is maintained at 350 to 400 animals, and has been used as a source to establish a number of wood bison populations back into their former range.

In 1984, the Alberta Fish and Wildlife Division, in cooperation with the Government of Canada and the Dene Tha First Nations, initiated a project to return endangered wood bison to their former range in the Hay-Zama region northwest of High Level, Alberta. In 1985, 34 bison from the isolated southern population in Elk Island National Park were translocated to a fenced enclosure near the Hay-Zama Lakes. Successful reproduction and subsequent removal of the fences allowed these bison to become a free-ranging population along portions of the Hay and Chinchaga rivers.

Wainwright: The Continuing Story

After the transfers of bison to the north in the 1920s, the remaining bison herd at Wainwright was maintained at about 6000 to 7000 animals. This large herd soon overgrazed its range. As well, TB and brucellosis were common, and maintenance costs continued to rise. As bison were thriving in Wood Buffalo National Park, there seemed to be no further reason to keep sickly bison on the impoverished range at Wainwright. In addition, the Canadian Army was looking for a place to train in western Canada and the large fenced area at Wainwright looked inviting. Beginning in the winter of 1939-40, the majority of ungulates (except some elk and deer) in the park were slaughtered in an all-out attempt to eradicate bovine tuberculosis and bovine brucellosis as well as to make room for the incoming soldiers. The area was assigned to the Department of National Defence in 1940, used as a prisoner-of-war camp from 1944 to 1946, and continues to this day as Camp Wainwright, the Western Area Training Centre for the Canadian Armed Forces.

Bison have not completely disappeared from Wainwright. To reflect its historic role in bison conservation, a small display herd of bison is maintained south of the main road just inside the

entry gate to the Camp. In addition, the Town of Wainwright adopted the bison as its symbol and, from its place of prominence in the municipal park south of Highway 14, a full-sized bull bison statue guards the townsite.

Buffalo National Park, and its subsequent life as Canadian Forces Base Camp Wainwright, continued to play an integral role in many aspects of wildlife conservation. The area provided a rich source of biological data from a wide range of projects involving ungulates, upland game birds, and habitat changes. Early attempts at pronghorn antelope captive-breeding were carried out here. Later, big game programs included more than 20 years of study of deer population dynamics and the impact of hunter harvest on free-ranging white-tailed and mule deer. Upland game bird studies included long-term population monitoring and the collection of over 35 years of sharp-tailed grouse population data. As well, the site was used as one of the early provincial put-and-take pheasant hunting release sites.

Camp Wainwright has been a lasting example of federal-provincial co-operation in integrating wildlife management and national defence objectives. It also saw the integration of many aspects of wildlife management and agriculture, becoming the site of early parasite and disease eradication programs involving bovine tuberculosis, bovine brucellosis, and giant liver fluke. Early research studies also involved genetics, parasitology, and range management of wild and domestic species.

In its later years, Camp Wainwright was home to the Canadian Wildlife Service national peregrine falcon breeding facility—the primary source of peregrine chicks used in the successful reintroduction of a formerly endangered species across large areas of abandoned range. Public education was a critical component of the program and was supported by guided tours of the facilities. In recent years, spring tours to see dancing sharp-tailed grouse continue to contribute to on-going wildlife public education at the Camp.

GIANT LIVER FLUKE

Giant liver fluke (GLF) is a trematode (flatworm) that occurs in the liver of cervids (members of the deer family).[32] Although usually benign, large numbers of flukes can interfere with liver function and, in extreme cases, cause death, particularly in moose. GLF is an increasing concern on game farms in Alberta.

As their name implies, these flukes are giants in their world. Adults may grow to 70-80 mm long and 30 mm wide, but they are thin, as if flattened by a rolling pin. They are often found in pairs within walled capsules in the liver. The lesions in the liver vary markedly depending on the host species, the number of flukes present, and the length of time flukes are in the liver. In white-tailed deer, liver damage is usually limited. In elk, damage ranges from mild to extensive, involving changes in size, colour, and architecture of the liver. Large capsules and accumulations of eggs and detritus can occur throughout the liver making it appear swollen, pale, and irregular in shape. Often there are fibrous adhesions (small tufts of connective tissue) attached to the outer surface of the liver. On cut surfaces, you may see white fibrous capsules containing mature flukes, dark solid balls of eggs, haemorrhagic tracks or tunnels, and thin lines of black pigment embedded in the liver tissue. Black inky fluid may leak from the cut surfaces. In infected moose, the liver damage is often extensive, similar to the worst cases in elk.

Liver flukes have an interesting life cycle. Adult flukes produce eggs that are carried in the bile into the small intestine and eventually leave the gut on or in faecal pellets. If the eggs land in water, they hatch into fringed larvae that actively look for and then burrow into aquatic snails. Within a snail, larvae multiply and mature until they eventually escape as tailed larvae that can swim freely in water. These larvae glue themselves onto vegetation in the water, form a resistant cyst, and then wait days, weeks, or even years to be eaten by a passing herbivore. Once inside the gut, the encysted larvae are activated, burrow into blood vessels, and are carried to the liver. The immature larvae tunnel through liver tissue until they find another fluke larva, at which time they stop tunnelling and mature into adults. The infected herbivore then builds a fibrous capsule around the adult flukes to keep them from further wandering, but many eggs produced by the flukes can pass through tiny holes in the capsule wall and escape into the bile ducts in the liver.

In Alberta, GLF occurs in wild white-tailed deer, elk, moose and, rarely, mule deer, in the foothills and mountains south of the North Saskatchewan River. Natural infections also can be found in cervids in Banff, Waterton Lakes, and Elk Island national parks, as well as a few cases in the Cypress Hills. The fluke is a significant management concern when it occurs in source populations used for re-introducing elk to abandoned range (for example, elk from Elk Island National Park). Fortunately, there is a treatment protocol that can be used prior to translocating potentially infected cervids.[33] Infections in game farm elk occur throughout central and western Alberta. Infected cattle have been reported in the Waterton area.

In the early 1900s, GLF was probably transferred to Wainwright Buffalo Park with the animals that came from Montana. It subsequently established a population within the park, particularly focussed around Mott Lake.[34] When the ungulates were removed in the late 1930s, park managers also burned the slough grass and treated Mott Lake with copper sulfate to get rid of GLF larvae and aquatic snails. These were extremely destructive means of dealing with liver flukes; however, the combined effects were indeed successful and GLF is no longer found in Camp Wainwright.

And finally, Wainwright provided a study site and training ground for a generation of young graduate students and wildlife biologists, many of whom later became wildlife managers in Alberta. Among them, Bill Hall, Gary Erickson, Blair Rippin, Dave Moyles, Bruce Treichel, Dave Moore, Daryl Cole, and Margo Pybus all had their eyes opened to wildlife and wildlife management on the hills and fields within Camp Wainwright. The tradition continues today with ongoing graduate student research programs.

Conservation Efforts for Antelope

At the dawn of the European era in the west, the prairies virtually vibrated with the galloping hooves of uncountable numbers of pronghorn antelope. This unique North American mammal is a remnant species of the lineage of antelope that evolved on the continent prior to the Ice Age. It has a hollow horn—a feature shared with members of the cattle family (Bovidae)—but sheds the horn sheath annually, similar to antlers of the deer family (Cervidae). Extending across the great central plain from the northern boreal fringe to the southern tropical forests of Mexico, the pronghorn antelope existed in numbers to rival the abundance of bison in western Canada.[35] As the wave of settlers washed across the Canadian prairies, they recorded pronghorn from southern Manitoba, north to Fort Saskatchewan, and west to the Rocky Mountains.

But this abundance was not to last. A difficult place to live at the best of times, the northern prairies are subject to random severe late winter storms, large-scale periodic prolonged droughts, and raging natural wildfires. Add the constant pressure from land-hungry settlers, market hunters, lack of terrain in which to hide, and a behavioural repertoire that had no natural response to deal with fences (pronghorns rarely jump fences), and the outcome was predictable. By the late 1870s, pronghorn carcasses were being stacked up by hunters like cordwood. By 1881,

81

ANTELOPE HUNT NEAR BASSANO, ca. 1907-1908. COURTESY GLENBOW ARCHIVES (NA-297-3)

CHIN COULEE, NEMISKAM NATIONAL PARK, 1941.
COURTESY UNIVERSITY OF ALBERTA ARCHIVES

82

and produce offspring that could be taken back to the prairies. However, they did not do well and these well-intentioned efforts failed.

In 1912, Benjamin Lawton, Chief Game Guardian for Alberta, noted that settlement was rapidly encroaching on pronghorn habitat and extinction was certain unless a game preserve were created. In 1914, Maxwell Graham of the Dominion Parks Branch and Ernest Thompson Seton, the famous nature writer, arrived at Medicine Hat to look for a suitable area for an antelope preserve. Eventually they, along with Lawton, Frank Sibbald (Chief Park Warden), and H.H. Fauquier examined two areas: one near Carlstadt (now Alderson) and one near Foremost. East of Foremost, two small bands of antelope were located by Chin and Forty-mile coulees some three miles (5 km) from Nemiskam. Graham quickly secured permission to purchase land there and a small herd of antelope was enclosed within 12 miles (20 km) of wire fence. This became Nemiskam National Park, which ultimately grew to an area of 54 sq. mi. (139 sq. km). In addition to the park, Charlie Blazier was given government approval in 1919 to raise neonatal pronghorn on

pronghorn were gone from Manitoba.[36] A severe winter with deep snow in 1906-1907 significantly reduced the population in Alberta. That year, winter began in earnest in October and extended well into May. The effect on pronghorn was devastating.

The population fell from an estimated 10,000 in 1900 to only 1000 in the spring of 1907.[37] In 1909, a few pronghorn were collected and shipped to Banff National Park and for the next year or two, a few to Wainwright Buffalo National Park. It was hoped that these animals would thrive in the parks

REMEMBERING ANTELOPE STUDIES...
[GEORGE MITCHELL]

My study of pronghorn antelope in Alberta began in 1952 with ground counts followed by annual aerial transect counts until 1963. An extensive pronghorn antelope range evaluation was made over a three-summer period with the assistance of Dr. Cormack in 1962, and Sylvester Smoliak, Agriculture Canada range specialist, in 1963 and 1964. My pronghorn study and hunter check stations from 1956 to 1966 provided many pronghorn physical characteristics as well as female reproductive tracts that provided a window to reproductive biology and pronghorn pregnancy rates and fetal growth.

In 1964, I divided the entire antelope range in the province into 18 easily defined units or hunting areas. The units were established for wildlife management purposes and were particularly effective with pronghorn antelope. The allowable number of permits per unit was based upon pronghorn densities and desired harvest in each unit. Hunters could hunt pronghorns in one unit only—usually the unit of his/her first choice.

ELDON BRUNS, REGIONAL WILDLIFE BIOLOGIST
[INTERVIEWED BY PAT VALASTIN, ROCKY MOUNTAIN HOUSE]

"I was born, in Maple Creek, Saskatchewan in 1940. When I was four, my mother was killed when the house burnt down, and I was put up for adoption. I went to Pincher Creek with a tag on me that said: 'Deliver to Pincher Creek'. My adoptive parents are still there. They had their seventieth wedding anniversary a couple of weekends ago. My grandfather had a farm at Twin Butte. They lived next door to Charlie and Andy Russell.

"I sort of wanted to be a biologist while I was in high school. I saw some antelope stuff George Mitchell and Bill Wishart were working on. I can still remember seeing a picture of Mitchell with a baby antelope he had caught. It got me interested but I didn't want to go to university for four or five years. My parents couldn't really afford it. So I took the middle ground and took two years at SAIT [Southern Alberta Institute of Technology] in Calgary to be a land surveyor. I graduated and got a job with the federal government working as a hydrographic surveyor for eight years. Then, after sailing all the navigable water around Canada and the Mackenzie River, I decided I wanted to spend more time at home in the summer, so I went to university. I'd saved up the money from working.

"I went to the University of Calgary and took a Bachelor's of Science in Zoology and then a Master's degree. I was Val Geist's first graduate student. My thesis was on the winter behaviour of pronghorn antelope and I got the winter: 1969 was the worst winter they'd had in thirty years! I wanted to do my fieldwork in the winter, and do the writing up and be done by next fall. There was a little discussion on my committee whether one year was cricket. For a long time, I was the only guy who got his Master's at Calgary in one year. Maybe I still am?

"The antelope moved with the blizzards south into Montana (not all of them, but a big portion of them). I followed them down to about Havre. I was living at Onefour, at the Manyberries Research Station. I ended up trotting back and forth across the border every day. The Canadian Customs agent got to where he wouldn't even come out. He'd be watching television when I'd go through at seven o'clock, and I'd say, 'Will you let me back into Canada?' And he'd say, 'No, let yourself in. The key's behind the door.' So I'd let myself back into the country.

"After I finished my Master's degree, there were no jobs with Fish and Wildlife. So I went to Australia. I'd

rather be unemployed in a warm place. I kind of liked it, but there were no jobs. Duane Radford and I were classmates at university. He had gotten a job as a Fisheries Biologist in Lethbridge, so he was watching for jobs for me, but nothing came up for two years.

"When I came back, Bill Wishart was in Edmonton doing pheasant research and wanted a pheasant expert, so they hired Morley Barrett out of Ontario, because he'd done his thesis on pheasants. They were having trouble with mercury poisoning in pheasants. Morley went to Lethbridge and got interested in antelope and I was hired to catch them.

"That was in the days of PEP [priority employment] and STEP [student employment] programs. I was hired temporarily in the winter and then again in the summer. Between Morley and Duane Radford (I actually worked for Fisheries a lot), they kept me PEPing and STEPing until an area biologist position came up in 1972. Actually, two positions came up. I took Red Deer. Dave Neave had been there previously. Blair Rippin went to St. Paul. Issues then included seismic, oil wells, things that are still going on. Wolves were a problem then and still are. We also tried setting up some of the first habitat projects. Mel Kraft, the Fisheries Biologist, started up the Stauffer Creek Program. I started up a habitat program. I went around Red Deer County trying to get people interested in saving habitat for wildlife. Then in 1980, they reorganized the regions. I went to Rocky Mountain House, as Regional Wildlife Biologist. I've been here ever since."

When discussing issues of today, Eldon talked about the state of wildlife habitat. "When you think of it, Alberta is probably the envy of the world right now with $55 per barrel of oil and being debt-free. But, we didn't get to that position without being fairly tough on wildlife and wildlife habitat. Wildlife has paid the price, because oil feeds our family. Fish and Wildlife budgets have been flatlined for the past two, going on three years. Inflation, the cost of fuel, all that can eat a budget up, so we're still in quite dire shape as far as being able to deal with habitat protection. We have more new things to deal with like West Nile virus. And the population of Alberta is going up.

"We basically have two million Albertans living in two big cities and they are quite isolated from wildlife. We are really different from the western States: Montana,

Idaho, Wyoming, and Washington. You go down to Montana tomorrow, turn on your radio, and you'll hear something to do with wildlife within an hour. Over fifty percent of Montanans are hunters. So for the Governor of Montana, if there's an issue regarding wildlife, whether it's wolves eating cattle, or getting wolves from Alberta, or bears in huckleberry patches, he perks up, because he knows half of his electorate is interested.

"We're bringing out a caribou recovery plan and grizzly recovery plan. To save those two species we've got to lessen our footprint in Alberta. I don't know whether that will fly or not. That's another difference that's been around for a long time. When I went to Montana in the 1980s, Montana State Fish and Wildlife Division had something like twenty communications people: information and education staff. In Alberta we never had more than three.

"We've got some companies that have been quite generous, but at the same time they've been quite hard on wildlife habitat, too. They've done a pile of wildlife and habitat research, but at the same time they've eaten up the forest. So is that an overall win, lose or draw? Spending over a million to recover habitat, when you're building a pipeline through the herd's winter range may not be good enough. If wildlife is going to survive it has to have value to somebody, either economically or sociologically or both.

"We did a lot of good mitigation stuff with seismic programs over the years. We've gone from bulldozing an arrow-straight path sixteen feet wide, to meandering lines you can hardly see. We've probably kept most species. We even have a fair number of grizzly bears. Some species numbers have even increased quite a bit over the last thirty years. When I started in Red Deer, there wasn't a moose hardly to be seen east of Highway #2, and now there are quite a few. Sending the wolves down to Yellowstone was quite an accomplishment.

"I'm sixty-four now. I actually planned my life to go to school for thirty years, work for thirty years and play for thirty years. But I'm still here! My wife can't tell most days if I'm going to work or out to play! I have my miserable days, but overall I've been very happy with my career."

an antelope farm at the headwaters of Lake Newell, near Brooks.[38] Pronghorn kids were captured locally, raised at the farm, and their offspring released back to the wild.

This active intervention in the early part of the century provided sanctuary and protection for pronghorn antelope. Without it, we may have lost a unique animal on the Canadian prairies for many years until wandering bands from U.S. populations could make their way north in sufficient numbers to repopulate Alberta range. By the late 1920s, survey data indicated a slow recovery of pronghorn populations in Canada, aided no doubt by a few mild winters. Population growth fluctuated in the 1930s, hampered by four years of drought, three of which also had severe winters. Many pronghorn either died or retreated to Montana. But populations came back strongly following a series of relatively wet summers and mild winters. A hunting season was re-established in 1933—the first since 1913. Through the late 1940s, there was abundant evidence of increased pronghorn populations in southern Alberta and Saskatchewan. Nemiskam Park was deemed to have fulfilled its purpose and was closed in 1947. Unfortunately, the hunting season was seriously mismanaged in 1949. An unlimited number of licences were sold at a time when population estimates were low and structured hunting zones were lacking.[39] With antelope numbers again on the decline, the hunting season was again closed, this time for six years, other than for a limited number of permits issued.

Since the mid-1950s, antelope populations have fluctuated in the range of 8000-32,000 animals.[40] In 1964, the pronghorn range was divided into 18 antelope management units. These units allowed wildlife managers to forecast the numbers of antelope in particular areas and to spread the hunter harvest accordingly. George Mitchell began an *affaire du coeur* with pronghorn in 1952, which reached its full expression in 1980 with the publication of *The Pronghorn of Alberta*. The information contained therein provided the basis for sound management of the species ever since. Today, antelope range over a wide area in

CHARLIE BLAZIER FEEDING PENNED ANTELOPE ON HIS FARM NEAR LAKE NEWELL, ca. 1920s.
COURTESY PROVINCIAL ARCHIVES OF ALBERTA (P4725)

85

southeastern Alberta and are readily seen by passing motorists and local residents. Once again, the flashing white rump patches can be seen when startled pronghorn fly low over the prairie landscape.

Moose over the Century

Parks and preserves were critical in re-establishing elk, bison, and pronghorn populations in Alberta. But through the century, big game management involved more than just the creation of parks and more than just these three species. Moose, deer, caribou, mountain goats and bighorn sheep, both inside and outside the protected areas, were also important wildlife species.

Moose used to occur in all forested areas of the province. Northern populations remained relatively abundant through the early years, largely as a result of their solitary nature and widespread occurrence. However, moose were gone from southwestern Alberta by 1900 and it took quite some time for them to wander back from the northern foothills. By 1920, moose reappeared south of the Clearwater River and

the population increased steadily through the 1930s, often with a lag time following severe fires.

Occasional local declines often involved the presence of winter ticks. One such decline involved major losses in Manitoba and Saskatchewan (and presumably Alberta) from 1916 to 1920.[41] Increased numbers of moose, a shortage of food, and an exploding tick population were considered responsible for the die-off. Similar die-offs occur at 15-20 year intervals throughout moose range in Alberta.

Some things have not changed in 100 years. In the winter of 1997-1998, moose died in record numbers across the southern fringe of the boreal forest and down along the eastern edge of the foothills.[42] Moose density was relatively high, vegetation was heavily browsed and mild spring and fall weather increased the survival and productivity of ticks. In some populations, up to 30% of the winter losses were attributed to tick-associated mortality.[43]

Moose do not thrive under dense mature forest cover, and the extensive fire suppression in the

GHOST MOOSE AND WINTER TICKS

Have you ever seen a ghost moose? Have you ever seen a winter tick? Chances are that, if you see one, the other is not far away. Winter ticks (*Dermacentor albipictus*) are common residents of the foothills and boreal forest areas of the province. They are increasingly seen in the parkland region. Within these areas, their preferred habitat is moose; however, they also use elk, white-tailed deer, and mule deer. Moose regularly accumulate thousands of ticks, while elk and deer rarely have many at all.

Winter ticks are unusual ticks that complete all life stages beyond the egg on the same individual. Eggs laid in leaf litter in late spring hatch during the summer and appear as larvae in the fall. The larvae climb up any available vegetation and, although they can climb to any height, they prefer to stay one to two metres above the ground—just about chest-height on a moose. In addition, peak larval activity coincides with the fall rut, when moose, elk, and deer wander extensively looking for potential mates. It is not just coincidence that the larvae find a host. Each larva can detect increased levels of heat and carbon dioxide in the air. So when a moose, for example, passes by a clump of larvae, its breath is warm and full of CO_2. The larvae detect this and immediately wake up, grab their neighbours, and wave their tiny front legs high in the air. On the end of each leg is a little hook exactly like the hooks on a Velcro© strip. If a moose or deer passes within reach, its hair acts as the fuzzy part of the Velcro© and the tiny little hooks get caught. This drags not only the larva whose leg was stuck but also a chain of other larvae that happen to have their legs linked together! Bill Samuel and his amazing observational skills are responsible for this interesting tidbit of knowledge.[44]

Once on a moose, larvae quickly move deep into the long protective hair and overwinter in comparative warmth and protection. Through winter, the larvae moult to nymphs and then to adults. Adult ticks appear any time after the New Year, but the majority occur in late winter. Each female tick mates and then must take a bloodmeal for her eggs to develop properly (just like mosquitoes). She takes enough blood to swell up as big as a grape then drops off the moose and eventually lays over 5000 eggs in the leaf litter. Most females die quickly if they have the misfortune to drop off onto snow.

Successful reproduction of winter ticks is largely driven by temperature and snow conditions. In winters when the snowpack is minimal, females are more likely to reach the leaf litter in spring and thus ensure greater production of eggs. Similarly, warm weather speeds egg development and increases hatching success. Thus mild winters and warm summers promote increased tick production and survival, and result in more ticks to be picked up by moose the following fall.

A MOOSE PREVIOUSLY INFESTED WITH WINTER TICKS.
CREDIT: M. PYBUS

Moose seem to be oblivious to newly arrived ticks but eventually the uninvited guests become a source of constant irritation. Infested moose use their teeth, antlers, hooves, and tongue to bite, chew, lick, rub, and scratch off the pesky ticks. They even rub up against trees, logs, and buildings. Moose hair is white at the base, so that areas where the hair has been roughed up or broken off are readily visible against the darker, undamaged hair. Moose with extensive hair damage have large white patches, sometimes over much of their body surface and end up looking like a ghost of their former self.

During hunting season, the tiny larvae (each one could dance on the head of a pin) are not conspicuous to hunters. Winter tick larvae are best seen in clumps on vegetation in October or as huge adult females on the ground or in moose beds in late winter. Bloodstains and chunks of moose hair in snow also are good indicators that winter ticks are in the area. They rarely live on non-cervid wildlife, and cannot live on domestic cats or dogs, but occasionally grab onto cattle and horses. Winter ticks very rarely bite humans (our blood does not have what they need) and are not known to transmit diseases.

But, are ticks good or bad? The number of ticks in the environment is related to the number of moose available to them as habitat, i.e., ticks need moose as a place to eat, take shelter, and reproduce. When moose die, massive numbers of ticks also die. On the contrary, as the number of moose in an area increases, so does the population of ticks. As the density of moose increases, so does their impact on vegetation. The role of ticks in reducing the density of moose through indirect mortality also helps to rejuvenate stressed vegetation, and perhaps, in the long run improves the survival of local moose populations. The southern boreal forest appears to be the battleground for this life and death interplay between moose and ticks. Although we may be stirred by sympathy for ticky moose, we need to look beyond the obvious effects on an individual to see the survival of the population of both moose and winter ticks as the greater underlying balance that nature strives for in all systems.

middle years of the 20th century did not favour moose in the foothills and mountain valleys. In contrast, open wooded conditions can lead to an overabundance of moose. Starting in 1957, antlerless hunting seasons (cows and calves) were used judiciously throughout the province to limit population growth and stabilize moose numbers.

Moose populations expanded into the central parklands in the late 1970s where they continue to show a steady increase in number and density.[45] This repopulated range no doubt contributed to the tremendous increase in moose numbers from approximately 45,000 in 1959 to the more than 100,000 that currently occur in the province. Moose remain a favourite target and critical part of the recreational and subsistence hunting experience in Alberta.

Bighorn Sheep and Mountain Goats

Mountain species of big game also persisted in the face of increasing human demands at the turn of the century. Fortunately, bighorn sheep and mountain goats are generally hard to find, hard to take home, and have an innate ability to climb more quickly than a hunter. Despite this, bighorn sheep, the defining species of western Canada, faced severe declines in the United States in the early 1900s. In many places, these populations have not returned; in other places they have been re-introduced, often starting with bighorns captured in Alberta.

Canadian populations fared somewhat better. The early establishment of Rocky Mountains Park (renamed Banff National Park), followed by parks at Waterton and Jasper, then Kootenay, Yoho, and Glacier-Mt. Revelstoke, sealed the security for protected populations of both bighorn sheep and mountain goats. In 1916, bighorn populations were rebounding within the parks, and mountain goats were the most abundant big game in the Canadian Rockies.[46]

Outside the national parks, accessible mountain goat herds on provincial lands in the southern foothills declined dramatically due to over-hunting through the 1960s when there were few restrictions and many hunters. The hunting season was closed in 1969 and then opened only in the Willmore Wilderness Park with restricted licence sales in 1972. There was a precipitous decline in the early 1980s and the hunting season was again closed in 1988. Long-term research studies at Caw Ridge, an area beside the Willmore Wilderness Park north of Jasper, indicate that low kid survival and relatively high predation by bears are two limiting factors on goat populations. Mountain goat populations steadily increased through the 1990s and limited goat-hunting opportunities were re-introduced in northern regions in 2001. Recent relocations of goats from Caw Ridge and British Columbia re-established small populations of goats in the mountains south of Calgary. Although not hunted, these populations provide excellent watchable wildlife opportunities in the Highwood valley and throughout Kananaskis Country. In addition, the goats in the national parks continue to maintain stable populations.

Bighorn sheep are emblematic of the rugged terrain and lifestyle of the Canadian Rockies. Specific programs to improve our management of

BIOLOGISTS CAPTURE, MARK AND COLLECT INFORMATION ON BIGHORN SHEEP.
CREDIT: B. WISHART AND J. JORGENSON

this keystone species were tried throughout the years. In 1950, a detailed study of bighorn sheep began in the Sheep River drainage. The program had its headquarters at the newly created University of Alberta research station at Gorge Creek. By 1954, fluctuations in bighorn numbers laid a foundation for a young Bill Wishart to undertake an extensive survey of the habits of bighorn sheep. Much of his later work involved capturing and tagging sheep so they could be followed on their daily and seasonal movements.

The work at Gorge Creek had two major consequences for bighorn management. In 1973, the Sheep River Wildlife Sanctuary was established with the primary goal of providing long-term protection to the bighorns ranging along the open hillsides and steep canyons of the upper Sheep River. The Gorge Creek station is within the sanctuary. Further to this,

MOUNTAIN GOAT KID WEIGHED DURING RESEARCH EFFORTS.
CREDIT: K. SMITH

BILL WISHART: 50 YEARS OF WILDLIFE MANAGEMENT IN ALBERTA
[INTERVIEWED BY PAT VALASTIN]

Bill Wishart was born at Alix, Alberta in 1932. According to his mother, there was a lake next to the hospital and during her stay she could hear geese coming in from the south. That, she said, is what influenced Bill to go into fish and wildlife. But the adventurous spirit of some of his ancestors perhaps also had something to do with it. Wishart's ancestry reaches a long way back into the fur trade, with great, great, great grandfather William Flett arriving near Edmonton with Peter Fidler in 1795. Another great, great, great grandfather was a *Nor'wester* back in the days of Alexander Mackenzie and David Thompson.

During his school days in Carstairs, Wishart's neighbour was Bill Weber, a future Fish and Wildlife Officer. "If we weren't in school, we were out in the fields shooting gophers and trapping for bounties and furs." Wishart was also influenced by his dad, a grain buyer who was quite the hunter ("I was his retriever.") and his older brother. The brothers would "traipse out to the hills to check traps. Weasels mostly. Then Weber and I combined to trap muskrats to increase our spending money."

A YOUNG(ER) WILLIAM (BILL) WISHART, THIRTY YEARS WITH THE ALBERTA FISH AND WILDLIFE DIVISION AND A LIFETIME OF WORKING FOR ALBERTA'S WILDLIFE.
COURTESY ALBERTA FISH AND WILDLIFE DIVISION

Wishart entered the University of Alberta in 1952, the first year the university offered a four-year degree in Conservation Biology. He soon became the first graduate of this course [Dave Boag was the second] under instruction from Drs. Rowan, Miller, Moss, and Cormack, the characters who wrote the books, quite literally, on early understanding of wildlife and botany in Alberta.

"My first summer was spent with Lloyd Keith working on the waterfowl portion of his Master's. I learned a lot from him. The rest of my summers, I spent at Gorge Creek working on fish with Dick Miller. I would see bighorns every day, and I asked Miller if I could do a Master's on sheep. In 1954, he said, 'Sure, go ahead.' It was a great summer. Boagy [Dave Boag], who was working on blue grouse, and I did a lot of our fieldwork together.

"In 1957, Bony Watkins, Commercial Fisheries Superintendent, asked if I was interested in a fisheries job, and I said yes. So I worked in fisheries for a year or so with Ron Thomas, who gave me the short course in seeing if potholes were suitable for trout. In the winter of 1957-58, I was out on commercial fisheries lakes, checking fish sizes, collecting scales, all that kind of stuff. I kind of got a taste of fisheries work."

In 1958, Bill married a schoolteacher, Pat, now well known for her own naturalist activities including the publication of a children's book series *Knee-High Nature*. When asked if his career affected his marriage, Bill replied: "Oh, I think so. I was away a lot. But I think what really ticked Pat off was my golf. I'd be away a lot, and when I was home, I'd go golfing!"

"In 1958, John Stelfox left to get another degree. So Bony asked if I wanted to transfer to Wildlife. I took over John's area in the north and northwest. A lot of the work involved big game and bird game hunter checking stations. It gave me an idea of what game was being taken out of an area, based on our hunting seasons. We collected lots of jaws and uteri. Old hat now, but we had no idea of pregnancy rates then. We found out antelope get pregnant in September and then have a very long gestation period. In the uteri, I saw as many as six embryos but only two survive: there's in utero competition whereby embryos kill the excess with a little spearing device. We found

89

out quite a few interesting things from uteri collections."

In 1969, Wishart started working as a wildlife research biologist out of the O.S. Longman Building in Edmonton. "Dr. Ed Ballantyne, Alberta Agriculture, wanted a collection of scientists, biologists, and agriculturists working in the same building. And it worked! The mercury scare we had in upland birds was one of the best examples. Mercury was showing up in raptors and they seemed to be getting it from the seed-eating birds they caught and ate. Richard Fyfe, Canadian Wildlife Service, came to me and asked if anyone looked at mercury levels in upland birds. So, right away we started collecting birds, and sure enough, Hungarian partridges and pheasants were feeding on mercury-treated seed grains (we could tell it was treated seed because it was dyed red)."

Throughout the period of his education and career, Wishart learned that the rudiments of wildlife management centred on four basic steps. "Inventory: get out there and see what you got. Productivity: are they producing, are they not producing? Limiting factors: why aren't they expanding? Then manage according to what you found out! A lot of our time in the early days was spent with inventory. We risked our necks flying aerial surveys. Despite some bad scares, we got a pretty good idea of what was out there. Probably the best species to inventory was antelope. They were so highly visible, particularly in early morning or evening when the light was reflecting off the white of their bellies when they were standing up, feeding. Usually about the end of July, kids were up and running with the adults. So there was an easy survey, with wide open transects and you could get numbers and productivity all in one fell swoop."

"One of my other favourite surveys was mountain goats. In August, they're up in the high alpine, white goats on a green background, just beautiful. The bighorns were always on the wind-swept ridges or bare south-facing slopes in winter. The winter ranges are like islands. So sheep are also fairly easy to survey. Of course, once you start getting into the forest, it's a little difficult to survey caribou and elk. Moose are more visible. Once we had an idea of numbers and production, we were able to establish our seasons and permits. I think one of the biggest steps that we made in wildlife management was setting up Wildlife Management Units. Smaller units were more manageable, and that made it much easier to set up antlerless or female seasons."

When asked if he would change anything, Wishart replied: "I've had a very good career and excellent staff. I was here during the good times. I became very discouraged just before I retired. You see, for many years I was in charge of research. I had about $100,000 I could distribute to students. Those were good years because there were all sorts of projects. I guess the ACA's doing that now, which is good. I must have been on 25 to 30 thesis committees in those years. I financed Bill Glasgow, Ernie Ewaschuk, and a lot of the biologists on staff now. Also, if you saw problems, you could do things. I retired early because there was a change of administration and focus. I got the impression that Fish and Wildlife was a pain in the ass for government, particularly the Habitat Section."

"Fish and game associations originally were our strong voice with the public, but there was a loss of interest in hunting. There are other organizations doing good things out there now. I think preservation of habitat is the ultimate goal. A lot of people, farmers and others, like to have wildlife around. And they have the ingredients, but they don't have the recipe. We do. Its habitat and good land management. Lorne Fitch's group, Cows and Fish, is a really good example. I have a little hope with the Endangered Species group; sage grouse are disappearing from the face of Alberta. It's absolutely terrible, and it could have been avoided if we'd had some control over the land. Not having any say on land-use has been a real problem."

[Bill enjoyed 30 years with the Fish and Wildlife Division and continues to work in the field after retirement. His accomplishments are many but perhaps most importantly, he has mentored and encouraged a new generation of biologists to follow in his footsteps. Today, Bill can usually be found in his office in the O.S. Longman Building, at any wildlife-related event, or out on the golf course.]

Bill Wishart, hooked on bighorns, began a long-term study of sheep biology on Ram Mountain (west of Rocky Mountain House). This study gave us some of our current sheep managers (for example, Jon Jorgenson and Kirby Smith) as well as the strong basis on which we still make sheep management decisions in Alberta. Bill Wishart recalls:

In 1966, we carried out an experiment on Ram Mountain to test orphan lamb survival. If you remove ewes, do the orphans survive? Yes, they do. That little experiment started one of the best long-term ungulate studies, I think, in North America, aside from the Isle Royale moose studies. I was intrigued by how the sheep herd responded to the reduction of ewes. Young ewes that normally never breed entered breeding mode. The result was a highly productive young sheep herd that we maintained at about a hundred sheep. Then we said: "Let's let it go, and see what happens." The result was predictable. With all those young productive ewes, the herd grew from 100 to over 200. Then, as the population aged, we saw the classic crash, and it went to less than 50 sheep. Now it is in a slow recovery phase.

In the early 1980s, bighorns in the area south of the Crowsnest Pass were seen hunched over and racked by violent coughing fits. Most of the sheep died. The problem appeared to start in British Columbia and spread to Alberta and into Montana by way of Waterton Lakes National Park. Wildlife biologists again joined forces with the Veterinary Services Branch of Alberta Agriculture to identify the cause and try to stem the spread. Examination of sick sheep revealed a virulent strain of bacterium. Bill Wishart summarized the work as follows:

We took the bacteria that domestic sheep harbour in their lungs, and we put them into bighorns. Within a few weeks, the bighorns died. We took pneumonia bacteria from bighorns and put them into domestic sheep and there was no response. It didn't affect them. So, it was a one-way street. Dr. Detlef Onderka,

Alberta Agriculture, designed the experiment that shed light on the whole story and is one of the best wildlife vets that we've had in Alberta.

Confounding factors in the die-off may have included pre-existing lungworm infection (most bighorns have roundworms in their lungs), social stress, and possible overlap with domestic sheep on bighorn ranges. Sporadic die-offs also occur in bighorn populations outside Alberta. While explanations are complicated and not yet complete, it is well established that if you mix bighorns and domestic sheep, bighorns are likely to die. There is not much that wildlife managers can or should do about the lungworms, but the province developed guidelines that recommended a buffer zone between wild and domestic sheep near critical bighorn ranges.

Today, bighorn sheep management focusses on hunting older rams (as defined by the curl of the horns), and setting ewe seasons to limit the nursery herds. Alberta is known for the biggest bighorn rams in North America and hunting interest remains high. Bighorn populations currently are stable across their range in Alberta, in the range of 6000 and 5500 sheep on provincial and federal lands, respectively.

Declining Caribou and Increasing Deer

There are two distinct types of woodland caribou in Alberta: a non-migratory flat-lander type that lives in the vast northern bogs and fens, and a mobile hilltop kind that migrates between high alpine areas and the adjacent mature forests in the western foothills. Neither type has fared particularly well. The flat-landers occur on ranges underlain with significant oil and gas deposits, the development of which brings increased linear access and travel lanes used extensively by humans and wolves. The hilltop type survived with reasonably good populations into the mid-1900s but faced significant habitat loss in more recent times from forest management practices that have a large appetite for old-growth timber.[47]

91

Unfortunately, old growth is the preferred habitat for caribou and is critical to over-winter success. When they migrate to lower altitudes, the hilltop caribou now find their preferred wintering areas have been cut to feed the demand for paper, pulp, and building supplies. Their only alternative is to not migrate and this, too, becomes a limiting factor on population growth.

The plight of caribou in Alberta has not gone unnoticed. Following an extensive study in the late 1970s, the caribou-hunting season in Alberta was closed indefinitely in 1980.[48] Since 1991, the northern Boreal Caribou Committee, a combined effort by governments, industries, and universities, has conducted extensive research at a cost of millions of dollars, to find a balance between caribou habitat needs and directly competing land and resource uses. While some promote the idea of more protected areas for caribou, the days of creating large preserves for big game appear to be well past.

Ironically, the human activity that has been detrimental to caribou and other species has been something of a boon to Alberta's deer populations. Early explorers recorded the presence of two deer species (using various names including: jumping deer, long-tailed deer, black-tailed deer, and Virginian deer) in the late 1700s and 1800s. However, in these accounts the deer were never as populous as moose, elk, and bison. Mule deer occurred in the foothills and montane regions near Calgary and Waterton. They were rare on the prairies.[49] White-tailed deer were limited to pockets in the central parklands and Cypress Hills, as well as along the lower Red Deer and upper Bow and Oldman rivers.

The two deer species fared comparatively well during the period of severe weather and maximum hunting pressure at the turn of the 20th century.[50] Although readily harvested by pot-hunters (settlers, miners, rail workers, and natives), they were able to maintain viable populations. Deer actually expanded their

geographic distribution in the face of reduced competition from elk, reduced predation with the demise of wolves and bears, and increased habitat and food as agricultural land-clearing went into full swing. Among other things, land-clearing opened travel lanes through the forests into the Peace country. Mule deer populations rapidly increased in the early 1900s and expanded into the Peace River area in 1910, reached Fort McMurray in 1914, and went as far north as Great Slave Lake in 1940. However, mulies have always been a curious deer. When disturbed, they trot or stot (a vertical bounce) a short distance and then turn and look to see what caused the disturbance—thus, providing an easy, often broad-side, target for hunters. This increased vulnerability tends to keep numbers in check whenever there is unrestricted hunting. Early hunting regimens were modified with time and knowledge from the Wainwright studies, and today, mule deer populations hold their own throughout the mountains, foothills, and major river valleys. Current provincial estimates are in the range of 200,000 mule deer.

White-tailed deer increased numerically and geographically in the wake of the settlers pouring in from the east. Settlers not only cleared land but also planted tame hay species. Whitetails took full advantage of the new open areas and gained a hearty appetite for alfalfa. They expanded into the Peace country in the 1940s and made spectacular population increases throughout the parkland and prairie regions in the 1940s and 1950s. Indeed, they remain the primary big game ungulate on the landscape throughout much of the non-boreal portions of the province. Current provincial population estimates are in the range of 250,000 white-tailed deer.

Commercial Wildlife
Until recently, ungulates in Alberta were exclusively a public resource. The importance of this long-standing relationship should not be understated, since many Albertans trace their origins to parts of Europe where average citizens neither owned nor had access to wildlife.

92

DEER STUDIES AT WAINWRIGHT

The military base at Camp Wainwright played a pivotal role in understanding the biology of deer and applying that understanding to deer management in the province. Large numbers of whitetails and mule deer died at Wainwright during the severe winter of 1964-65. Base commander, Colonel Gordon Donaldson, asked Alberta Fish and Wildlife to allow deer hunting as a means to reduce the potential for high losses of deer during severe winters. In March 1966, Fish and Wildlife staff did a preliminary survey of the camp and found an estimated density of approximately four deer per square mile. Approximately 90% of the deer observed were whitetails and the balance was mule deer. The Division agreed to introduce a hunting season under a limited-draw entry in the winter of 1966-1967. This first season was very restricted and unpopular. Through interviews and questionnaires with participating hunters, a more balanced, controlled hunt was developed that remains popular today with hunters from all over the province.

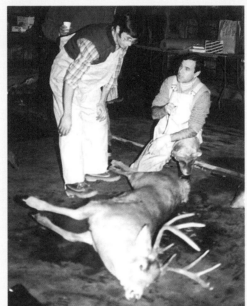

BOB McCLYMONT AND BRUCE TREICHEL EXAMINING A WHITE-TAILED DEER AT WAINWRIGHT ca. 1979.
CREDIT: B. WISHART

The camp provided a unique opportunity to manipulate deer management regimens and document the outcomes. Many discoveries from the Wainwright deer studies have been applied over the years to the present provincial deer management system. Some of the more significant findings included the high vulnerability of mule deer to hunting compared to whitetails; the high reproductive potential of whitetails; the most vulnerable periods of hunting for bucks versus does; the impact of bucks-only seasons versus both sex seasons; hunting success rates for primitive weapons (bows and muskets) versus rifles; the effects of winter severity on deer productivity; and the problems of hunters misidentifying the two deer species.

There was also a steady stream of deer carcasses for Bill Wishart and his crews to poke, prod, measure, and compare to their hearts' content. Considerable knowledge was gained from culled deer collected by government staff in the early years when hunter

harvests were low. This was supplemented later with carcasses provided by hunters returning the entire deer or parts thereof to hunter check stations. From 1966 to 1986, 2141 whitetails and 313 mulies were processed at Wainwright, reflecting the predominance of whitetails in the Camp during those years. Since then, there has been a reversal in the whitetail: mule deer ratio. Between 1995 and 2004, 2920 deer were harvested. In the last few years, there were three or four times more mule deer harvested than whitetails. The prevailing hypothesis is that the ongoing drought conditions along the eastern border had a greater effect on whitetail distribution and productivity than on mule deer.

Some other interesting findings include the fact that approximately one-half of the whitetail fawns breed during their first winter; mule deer fawns do not breed in their first year; whitetail does (females) over one year of age produce an average of two fawns per year; whitetails and mule deer are very similar in body size and weight but differ in the size of some internal organs; the two species generally occupy habitats with different topographic features but have similar food habits; there was no evidence of visible hybridization although blood tests indicated some hybridization does occur; there were no significant disease or parasite problems in this herd; some deer lived to 16 years of age; and the frequency of antlered whitetail does was one in 65.[51]

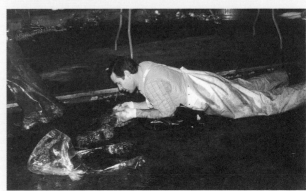

BRUCE TREICHEL CONDUCTING AN IN-DEPTH STUDY OF DEER ENTRAILS AT WAINWRIGHT.
CREDIT: B. WISHART

93

Similarly, the unfettered frontier attitude of early years often remains ingrained in many Alberta residents, many of whom hold dearly their right to experience and hunt public wildlife. While wildlife has remained a public good, there are presently two primary commercial uses of big game in Alberta: outfitter/guiding and game farming.

Many of Alberta's earliest guides and outfitters were contracted by the Canadian Pacific Railroad. These early packers carried supplies for surveyors and explorers looking for a suitable pass through the mountains and later, provisions for the legion of workers building the railway. Once built, the railway provided a steady stream of customers—adventurers, scientists, mountain climbers, missionaries, and tourists. They all wanted to see the mountains, to experience wild places, and to live to tell the tales. But many were pampered by title, social standing, or sheer accumulated wealth. They were ill-equipped to survive away from the railroad tracks. By 1897, the demand for outfitting services was growing. Tom Wilson, Bill Peyto, Ralph Edwards, Jim Simpson, and

Bill and Jim Brewster were all pioneers in setting the stage for the extensive use of outfitters to guide folks into the wilds and back out again. More and more sportsmen seeking adventure were lured to the Rocky Mountains for hunting and fishing expeditions and many a wealthy hunter sought the expertise of local guides and outfitters to partake in a hunt for the famed bighorn sheep of the Canadian Rockies. The Brewster legacy lives on, although most of the customers now tour the mountains in air-conditioned deluxe buses.

As access improved in the non-mountainous regions of Alberta, outfitting opportunities expanded beyond the mountains and railways. The abundance of trophy moose, black bear, white-tailed deer, and grizzly bear attracted hunters from outside the province and outside the country as Alberta developed a world-class reputation among sportsmen far and wide. Business for outfitters and guides waxed and waned depending on the ups and downs of stock markets and the impacts of various wars. However, the demand was always there to some extent and outfitters were there to supply the

OUTFITTING REQUIREMENTS IN ALBERTA
[ADAPTED FROM STELFOX (1993), *HOOFED MAMMALS OF ALBERTA*]

As professional outfitting gradually expanded, requirements also changed. Initially, passing a government exam and paying the required fees for a licence got you into the business. Once the licence was issued, the outfitter could ply the trade anywhere in the province. In 1972, the first significant regulation of outfitters and guides occurred. The overall number of bighorn sheep permits for Non-resident and Resident Alien clients of outfitters was limited to 80 rifle and 8 bowhunting permits. Shortly thereafter, outfitters were required to hold liability insurance, have a fidelity bond, and have enough outfitting equipment to provision up to four hunters in the field for two weeks. Each sheep outfitter was limited to a maximum of four non-Albertan clients per season.

In the absence of standards and operating guidelines, conflicts arose through the 1970s and 1980s, as more and more individuals got involved in the business. A new *Outfitter-Guide Policy* in 1989 created an allocation system for all hunted species. Following a three-year sealed bid period, individual operator allocations were re-issued in 1992. Allocations were good for five years, with an option for a further five years.

During the 1990s, the Professional Outfitters Society of Alberta was the voice of the outfitter-guide industry. In 1997, the Alberta Professional Outfitters Society (APOS) was created as a Delegated Administrative Organization of the provincial government. APOS is accountable to both the Minister responsible for wildlife and all Outfitter-Guide permit holders. As such, the Society is responsible for the delivery of all administrative services as well as disciplinary actions and further development.

need. More recently, Alberta's whitetails have become the mainstay of thriving outfitter-guide activities in the province. For a chance to bag bighorns, big bears, and big deer, some folks will pay big bucks to come to Alberta.

Interest in farming game as a means of generating economic benefits from marginal lands, as well as to diversify and expand agricultural prospects, began in earnest in the late 1970s. Entrepreneurs actively lobbied the government to modify the *Wildlife Act* to permit a game farm industry. The *Big Game Ranching Discussion Paper* was released in 1984 and became the basis for a political and public debate over the merits and structure of potential commercial big game farms. Numerous articles provided the pros and cons of game farming as perceived at the time.[52]

In 1984, a new *Wildlife Act* contained provisions to allow for private ownership of live wildlife, and thus laid the foundation for game farms in Alberta. The legislation and its associated regulations (finalized in 1987) contained strict controls, including individual animal identification, specified fencing and inventory requirements, and restriction of game farms to private property. In 1991, primary (but not exclusive) authority for administration of game-farming activities passed from the Fish and Wildlife Division to Alberta Agriculture under provisions of the *Livestock Industry Diversification Act*, where it remains today. This new Act limited game-farm activities to only four wildlife species: white-tailed deer, mule deer, elk, and moose. In current practice, elk are the predominant species on farms, with white-tailed deer a distant second. Bison on farms

95

GAME FARMING IN ALBERTA
[EXPANDED FROM STELFOX (1993) *HOOFED MAMMALS OF ALBERTA*, CHAPTER 11]

Although there was an initial phase of healthy growth associated with expanding breeding stocks and an increasing number of producers, markets for primary game farm products (meat and antler velvet) remained elusive or fluctuated widely. Disease concerns, initially bovine tuberculosis and more recently chronic wasting disease (CWD), had direct bearing on farm populations, market opportunities, and investor interest. The general downturn in agricultural economies associated with widespread drought conditions across much of the province and the finding of bovine spongiform encephalopathy (BSE) in one bovine cow in 2003 also had serious implications for game farm producers.

The Alberta Elk Commission (2002), formerly the Alberta Game Growers Association (1988) and Alberta Venison Council (1993), is "an association of individuals, farms, and corporations actively supporting and developing the elk-farming industry in Alberta".[53] As such, it provides a liaison between government and game farmers, and among its members. In October 2004, the commission had 450 members farming with more than 45,000 elk.

Opponents of game farming represent a vocal community in Alberta. This community continues to express concerns regarding the potential for increased opportunities for poaching and illegal trafficking of venison, contamination of genetic stock of free-ranging ungulate populations, and introduction of disease agents to Alberta when live game farm animals are imported. The latter concern was addressed through a moratorium on importation of game farm ungulates from October 1988 to June 2004. In the interim, the provincial departments associated with agriculture and wildlife, in consultation with the game farm associations, livestock associations, wildlife stakeholders, and potential trading partners, developed a set of restrictive protocols to govern the import of live farmed elk and deer from within Canada and the U.S. The protocols were adopted by the Government of Alberta midway through 2004.

In 2001, game farm associations presented government with a proposal to allow paid hunting on licensed game farms (cervid harvest preserves) as a supplemental source of income for producers. Following public consultation and extensive political debate, the proposal was denied in 2002.

were considered domestic and thus not included in the new legislation.

Advances in Big Game Management

Stelfox provided a comprehensive review of the biology and management of hoofed mammals in Alberta.[54] As well, Jack Ondrack's book is an excellent source of information and an interesting account of the philosophy of hunting.[55] Through trial and error, science and adaptation, managers of big game in Alberta modified, accepted, and/or rejected a variety of approaches to improve the management of big game populations. In particular, some key management aspects deserve mention.

One of the greatest obstacles to good management was the tremendous reluctance of hunters to kill females of any species. This aversion was deeply entrenched in a social context of protecting vulnerable individuals—save the women and children. There was also the bravado of trophy hunters who only saw the biggest and best and, of course, only the males. In the 1950s and early 1960s, the gang of four (Mitchell, Webb, Stelfox, and Wishart) took on the major hurdle of convincing the Alberta Fish and Game Association that shooting females would improve big game populations. These far-sighted biologists rose to the challenge and first proposed a short season on female elk. Fortunately, biology prevailed and eventually seasons on cows, does, and ewes were adopted. Wildlife managers now had another, very powerful, tool that could be applied with precision and discretion in managing big game populations.

In 1956-1957, multiple zoning for moose, elk, and deer management was expanded to increase the scope of detailed game management procedures. In 1964, this was permanently entrenched in a system of Wildlife Management Units (WMUs) that allowed managers to distribute the hunting pressure and manage specific local populations. This system is the basis on which current management practices succeed. It paved the way for current hunters to gain reasonable success and achieve satisfaction from their hunt.

In 1952, Mitchell introduced a standardized hunter questionnaire to garner feedback and help improve big game management. A variation of the original questionnaire continues to provide annual information regarding hunter success and effort. Today, big game managers combine the results with more modern methods of assessing populations and setting harvest targets.

Wildlife biologists continued to develop new techniques to better understand game populations. Noteworthy among these was radio tagging, which involved attaching disposable radio transmitters to an animal, usually an ungulate or a carnivore. The transmitter was attached to a collar around the animal's neck. Each transmitter emitted a distinct signal, which could be picked up by a directional aerial receiver. The biologist could dial in different animals like other folks dial in different radio stations. The wealth of new information was astounding. Managers now had direct information about where animals went, when they went there, what habitats they used, what they ate along the way, as well as how and how many individuals died. All of this information could be brought to bear on critical management decisions to improve big game populations. The technique continues to be improved with the recent downsizing of the radios as well as the introduction of satellite telemetry, mortality modes, remote-release mechanisms, and geographic positioning systems (GPS) to further refine the data collected.

Big Game Management Today

In time, the management of big game populations became routine across the province. Although bison and antelope were successfully returned from the brink of extirpation and their survival ensured for future generations, the spectre of thundering herds sweeping over a vast wind-blown prairie is gone forever. Wood bison, by their sheer isolation, survived the threat of overuse by hungry explorers and insatiable market hunters only to be threatened later with inadvertent contamination with bovine diseases and altered gene pools. Modern-day wood bison

96

HAROLD CARR: A REGIONAL PERSPECTIVE

[INTERVIEWED BY PAT VALASTIN]

Harold Carr was born in Winnipeg, in 1941. Like many prairie boys, he had a keen interest in hunting and fishing. "Rivers and lakes were pretty accessible, so hunting and fishing was a big part of my younger life." Harold became aware of career opportunities in biology through a family friend, a biologist with the government. "After my first year of university, I worked as a student biologist with the Manitoba Wildlife Branch out of Winnipeg. We worked on sharp-tailed grouse dancing ground counts, did some deer habitat work, and helped with the U.S. Fish and Wildlife Service annual waterfowl banding crew."

Carr became a Bachelor in Agriculture (University of Manitoba) and Master in Wildlife Biology (Colorado State), with his thesis involving the effects of herbicides on sage-grouse populations. After graduating in 1967, Harold and his new bride, Doreen, moved to Calgary where he worked as a District (soon to be Regional) Biologist for Alberta Fish and Wildlife. "I think it was Game Biologist in those days. Everybody felt this was too narrow—it wasn't what we wanted or what we were. I think Alberta was one of the first places to take up the term wildlife biologist."

"I didn't get there till August and my summer student was finished by the first week of September, so that didn't last very long. His name was Tom Sadler who went on to a successful career with Ducks Unlimited. The following year, I had the money for two people and we started a big inventory program. I think we hired the first girl in the Division that summer—Ruth Collins. At the time I came, there were six regions and they wanted one biologist per region. I was the only biologist in Calgary for a while (Bob Webb was there before me) and eventually they transferred a fisheries biologist (Dennis McDonald) down from Edmonton.

"In a lot of cases, your job was trying to find out what you had for wildlife resources in your region. What areas were important? That's a pretty big job in an area that extended from Saskatchewan to B.C. I had alpine, sub-alpine, foothills, prairie, and agriculture stuff thrown in. It was quite complex. I remember mapping cultivated land versus native prairie land: looking for islands of habitat that were really important and trying to get Fish and

Wildlife control over certain areas. The only piece of land that we ended up buying was at Millicent, north of Brooks. I guess in retrospect it was somewhat of an impossible goal for a number of reasons. The concept of acquiring enough land to have any real impact was pretty pie-in-the-sky. I didn't appreciate that in the beginning. At one time, I was advocating the purchase of the entire Red Deer River valley! This is a wonderful wildlife area—just fantastic—but there was no hope.

"The other impracticality was how to manage the area? One biologist couldn't handle it, even with summer assistants. I even used jailhouse crews. We'd take 25 people in a school bus, along with their guards, to hoe trees and irrigate habitat development stuff for us. We also did day-to-day things. I remember getting up at three in the morning to do pheasant crowing counts. Fairly early in the process, I got out of the waterfowl business, even though the reason I became a biologist more than anything else was duck hunting. I loved waterfowl, but it didn't seem to be a big issue in the Calgary region.

"Big game seemed to be a big issue in Alberta. More and more time was spent on winter surveys for big game and summer surveys for antelope. Problems involved the rather splintered and short focus that you could put on things, because of the wide variety of species. You can't be an elk biologist, a moose biologist, a mule deer and whitetail biologist, an antelope biologist, a sheep biologist, and a goat biologist, all in the same year. But that's essentially what we were trying to do. And I think we did a pretty good job of getting the basic feel of the countryside.

"I spent a fair bit of time working on elk—ten years or so, but with all the other things going on, I never felt I could do them justice. You never had time to write up the work you did in the field. The research we collected was well used over the years, but there is an immense amount that probably should be published. In some cases, it's not rigorous enough for the scientific journals because it's too scattered. It needs the focus of a university time-span and help from students and specialists and statisticians and so on. I've always felt guilty about the amount in our heads, as opposed to what is on paper. That's also one of

97

the disjoints that happened with cutbacks in staff. All of a sudden people were gone. For twenty year, there was very little in the way of new people coming on to absorb the information. Even if somebody new came in, the connection was not made and information was lost forever.

"Coal mining was one of the major issues of the day. Geologically, coal-producing areas underlie important wintering areas for bighorn sheep—the two are like hand and glove. We'd go to do a winter survey and there'd be somebody up there digging trenches in the middle of the winter range. The Forest Service was the controlling body in those days. Alberta was a booming province and development ruled the day. If somebody wanted to build a dam, they'd dam up the river. A lot of our early activities were trying to bring some order to that sort of thing: to create referral systems and methods of making people aware of it. It took a long time before we had a whole lot of impact, and it probably didn't happen until the public began to say they were not sure they wanted our beautiful mountainsides torn apart by coal mining.

"In 1987, I moved to Edmonton, to the O.S. Longman Building. Bruce Treichel and I were there. Bob McClymont was there, working on enforcement issues. Margo Pybus was there, but she wasn't yet permanent staff. That was it. It was like a morgue in there! Plus they had all those old bones and skulls lying around! Then

they transferred a bunch of the Species Management planning people from downtown (Bill Glasgow, John Gunson, and Arlen Todd). I can't really remember when, but at some point, someone put me into the Big Game Management position downtown, and that's where I ended my career.

For me, I'm enough of a wildlife guy that my whole career was a high point. There were lots of problems, but what better career could you have?

"The average person couldn't begin to see what we saw and understand the countryside to the same extent. The godfather of wildlife management for me is still Aldo Leopold. His textbook had a profound influence on me and my thinking. In the Alberta scene, we had a lot of good people. In the formative years, Gordon Kerr drove a lot of the wildlife business. He gave us a lot of freedom to do what we thought was important and to try and fight for wildlife principles. Bill Wishart is one of the more significant individuals in my mind, in terms of being a person whom I admire quite deeply, his philosophies, his ideas, his personality in general, and his dedication to wildlife."

[In 2001, Harold Carr retired from the government with 35 years of service—two years in Manitoba and 33 years in Alberta.]

numbers remain low and the risks remain unresolved.

Decimated elk populations had to be supplemented with translocated animals from outside the region. Deer and moose fared somewhat better but local populations waxed and waned over time in the face of continued pressure from competing uses of the landscape. Today, elk, deer, and moose generally abound and hunting seasons, based firmly in the system of Wildlife Management Units across the province, remain the primary instrument for management.

Bighorn sheep and mountain goats were immediate beneficiaries of the decisions to create big parks in the mountains, and their populations remained relatively stable. Bighorns are locally abundant and can withstand limited amounts of harvest; fortunately, populations remain relatively disease-free. Mountain goats rebounded in the northern mountains to levels considered safe for limited hunting pressure beginning in 2002; southern populations are still below preferred management levels.

Caribou, both within and outside protected areas, are still threatened with local extirpation, particularly in the northern foothills and southern boreal forest areas where industrial activity makes daily changes to the landscape. However, there is an air of optimism that wildlife values can and will be incorporated into commercial goals and market values. Generally, there is growing public support for managing big game populations at a landscape level in conjunction with other land uses. This is a tremendous improvement from the not-so-good old days when big game were seen only as fodder for the stew pot, dollars for the marketeers, or competitors for grazing livestock.

In the last decade, disease issues have loomed large, particularly with regard to bison management in northern Alberta, winter ticks on moose, and the potential for chronic wasting disease (CWD) to establish in wild deer and elk. The Fish and Wildlife Division responded by hiring a full-time wildlife disease specialist [Margo Pybus] to deal specifically with the growing concerns and lack of disease information. Except for winter ticks, disease issues cross many jurisdictional and interest boundaries, which require on-going cooperative discussions with various stakeholders, partners, and federal and provincial departments. Solutions are elusive but can be achieved with a concerted effort by all parties.

99

MAJOR EVENTS IN BIG GAME MANAGEMENT
[ADAPTED FROM STELFOX (1993) HOOFED MAMMALS OF ALBERTA, P. 110]

1877	The NWT *Ordinance for the Protection of the Buffalo* is passed but later repealed.
1883	The NWT *Ordinance for the Protection of Game* is passed.
1887	Rocky Mountains Park, including the Banff hot springs, is established.
1889	The last free-ranging plains bison in Alberta is killed in Hand Hills.
1892	The first bag (harvest) limits are set for big game.
1895	Waterton Lakes park reserve is established.
1905	Alberta becomes a province.
1906	Elk Island Park east of Edmonton is established.
1907	Jasper Park reserve is established. The first *Game Act* of Alberta is passed. Dogs could no longer be used to hunt big game and could be shot on sight if caught doing so; hunting seasons for bighorn sheep, mountain goat, and elk were closed and limited for pronghorn. The sale of game heads now requires Government brands.

MAJOR EVENTS IN BIG GAME MANAGEMENT CONTINUED

1909	Wainwright Buffalo National Park is established.
1913	The hunting of pronghorn antelope is prohibited in Alberta.
1914	Nemiskam National Park is established for pronghorn preservation.
1922	The second *Game Act* of Alberta is passed. Wood Buffalo National Park is established.
1925-1928	6673 plains bison are shipped to Wood Buffalo National Park.
1930	The Province receives ownership of its wildlife with the *Natural Resources Transfer Act*.
1940	Ungulates are removed and Wainwright Buffalo National Park is turned over to Department of National Defence.
1944	Non-resident Big Game Licence fee is reduced to $50 with an additional $25 for a special licence to hunt in the forest reserves. A trophy tax is implemented ($25 big game, $15 deer) for trophy heads that are exported.
1946	Metal tags are required on harvested big game.
1947	Nemiskam National Park is closed.
1952	The province's first Game Biologist, George Mitchell, is hired. A hunter success questionnaire replaces the mandatory licence reports.
1953	The first hunter check station is operated.
1954-1955	Aerial surveys are conducted for elk, moose, deer, and antelope. The first female elk season is opened.
1956	Separate resident sheep and goat licences are introduced. A limited number of antelope permits are sold.
1958	The province is divided into 18 big game management zones.
1961	Party hunting is prohibited (each hunter has to fill his own tag). It is an offence to hunt under the influence of alcohol or drugs.
1964	Wildlife Management Units are developed to spread the hunting pressure and to allow for more refined management of specific populations.
1965	24 wood bison are transferred from Wood Buffalo to Elk Island National Park.
1980	The caribou hunting season is closed indefinitely.
1984	The *Wildlife Act* allows private ownership of wildlife for game farming activities.
1985	Wood Buffalo National Park is declared a World Heritage Site.
1986	A government white paper outlines the feasibility of farming big game in Alberta.
1988	The mountain goat hunting season is closed.
1990	Federal Environmental Assessment recommends removing and replacing diseased bison in Wood Buffalo National Park.
1991	The *Livestock Industry Diversification Act* moves administration of game farms to Alberta Agriculture. The Fish and Wildlife Division retains the authority to determine which species are farmed and to impose import requirements.
2001	A limited goat season is opened after 13 years of closure.

References • CHAPTER 3

1. Hewitt, C.G. 1921. The Conservation of the Wild Life of Canada. Charles Scribner's Sons, New York.

2. Longley, R.W. 1954. Temperature trends in Canada. Pp. 206-211 *in* Proceedings of the Toronto Meteorological Conference, Royal Meteorological Society, London, England.

3. Schulman, E. 1953. Climatic Change. Harvard University Press, Cambridge, MA.

4. Lothian, W.F. 1976-1981. A History of Canada's National Parks. Parks Canada, Ottawa. Volumes 1 - 6. This work appeared in instalments and provides a history of the National Parks from their beginnings. See also Marty, Sid. 1984. A Grand and Fabulous Notion: The First Century of Canada's Parks. Toronto. This work is an account of the origins and early problems of the National Parks. The main focus is Banff and, as it was the first Park, the problems of a young nation embarking on an entirely new concept are those of the first Park.

5. Foster, Janet. 1978. Working for Wildlife: The Beginning of Preservation in Canada. University of Toronto Press, Toronto.

6. Lothian, W.F., op. cit., vol. 1:20.

7. Canada. Department of the Interior Annual Reports, 1908-1930. These reports, particularly those of the Forestry Branch, provide a picture of conditions in the forest reserves in Alberta and elsewhere at that time. The foresters were expected to cope with the detection and suppression of fires, as well as to enforce game and fish regulations. Reports of the Dominion Parks Branch also appear, and provide valuable information on the growth of the National Parks.

8. Canada. Department of the Interior Annual Report, 1902-1903. Part VII, p. 6. Also quoted in Lothian.

9. Information from the Bo Holroyd Fonds (warden journals for 1920 to 1947), Whyte Museum of the Canadian Rockies, Archives and Library, Banff, Alberta.

10. Information from the Hubert Green Fonds, Whyte Museum of the Rocky Mountains, Archives and Library, Banff Alberta.

11. Green, H.U. 1949. The bighorn sheep of Banff National Park. National Parks and Historic Sites Service, Canada Department of Resources and Development, Ottawa.

12. Green, H.U. 1950. The productivity and sex survival of elk in Banff National Park, Alberta. Canadian Field-Naturalist 64:40-42.

13. Correspondence to the Controller, National Parks Bureau, Dept. of Mines and Resources, April 14, 1943. Located in the Hubert U. Green Fonds, Whyte Museum of the Rockies Archives, Banff, Alberta.

14. Millar, W.N. 1915. Game Preservation in the Rocky Mountains Forest Reserve. Forestry Branch Bulletin # 51, Department of the Interior, Ottawa.

15. Lothian, W.F., op. cit., vol. 4:48.

16. Warkentin, John. 1962. The Western Interior of Canada. McClelland Stewart, Toronto.

17. Millar, W.N. 1916. Big game of the Canadian Rockies: a practical method of preservation. Pp. 100-124 *in* Conservation of Fish, Birds, and Game, Proceedings of the Commission of Conservation in Canada, 1915. Methodist Book and Publishing House, Toronto.

18. Lloyd, H. 1927. Transfers of elk for re-stocking. The Canadian Field-Naturalist 41: 126-127.

19. MacEwan, Grant. 1995. Buffalo: Sacred or Sacrificed. Alberta Sport, Recreation, Parks and Wildlife Foundation, Edmonton.

20. Mitchell, J.A., and C.C. Gates. 2002. Status of wood bison (*Bison bison athabascae*) in Alberta. Alberta Wildlife Status Report No. 38, Fish and Wildlife Division and Alberta Conservation Association, Edmonton.

21. Lothian, W.F., op. cit., vol. 4:17.

22. Ogilvie, S.C. 1979. The Park Buffalo. National and Provincial Parks Association of Canada, The University of Calgary, Calgary, Alberta.

23. Hadwen, S. 1942. Tuberculosis in the buffalo. Journal of the American Veterinary Medical Association 100: 19-22.

24. Lothian, W.F., op. cit., vol. 1:62.

25. Cotton, E.J., with E. Mitchell. 1981. Buffalo Bud: Adventures of a Cowboy. Hancock House, North Vancouver.

26. North West Mounted Police. 1907. Annual Report.

27. Lothian, W.F., op. cit., vol. 1:62.

28. National Parks Branch. 1924. File Bull. 232-1. Vol. 1.

29. Ogilvie, S.C., op.cit.

30. van Zyll de Jong, C.G. 1986. A systematic study of recent bison, with particular consideration of the wood bison (*Bison bison athabascae* Rhoads 1898). Natural Sciences Publication No. 6, National Museum of Canada, Ottawa, Ontario.

31. Nishi, J. Pers. Comm. Government of the Northwest Territories.

32. Pybus, M.J. 2001. Liver flukes. Pp. 121-149 *in* W.M. Samuel, M.J. Pybus, and A.A. Kocan (eds.) Parasitic Diseases of Wild Mammals, Iowa State University Press, Ames, Iowa.

33. Pybus, M.J., D.K. Onderka, and N. Cool. 1991. Efficacy of triclabendazole against natural infections of *Fascioloides magna* in wapiti. Journal of Wildlife Diseases 27: 599-605.

34. Swales, W.E. 1935. The life cycle of *Fascioloides magna* (Bassi, 1875), the large liver fluke of ruminants in Canada. Canadian Journal of Research, Series D, 12: 177-215.

35. Hewitt, C.G. op. cit. Also Seton, E.T. 1953. Lives of Game Animals Volume III, Part II. Order Ungulata of hoofed animals deer, antelope, sheep, cattle, and peccary. Charles T. Brandford Co., Boston. Pp. 413-780.

36. Hewitt, C.G., op. cit.

37. Mitchell, G. 1980. The Pronghorn Antelope in Alberta. University of Regina, Regina, Saskatchewan. 165 pp.

38. Ibid.

39. Wishart, W. 1972. History and management of the pronghorn antelope in Alberta. Alberta Conservationist 1972: 20-22.

40. Stelfox, J. Brad. 1993. Hoofed Mammals of Alberta. Lone Pine Publishing, Edmonton, Alberta.

41. Hewitt, C.G. op. cit.

42. Pybus, M.J. 1999. Moose and ticks in Alberta: a die-off in 1998-99. Alberta Environment, Fisheries and Wildlife Management Division, Occasional Paper Series No. 20.

43. Ibid.

44. Samuel, B. 2004. White as a Ghost: Winter Ticks and Moose. Federation of Alberta Naturalists, Edmonton, Alberta.

45. Bjorge, R. 1996. Recent occupation of the Alberta aspen parkland ecoregion by moose. Alces 32:141-147.

46. Millar, W.N., op. cit.

47. Edmonds, E.J. 1986. Restoration plan for woodland caribou in Alberta. Unpublished report for Alberta Fish and Wildlife Division, Edmonton.

101

[48] Edmonds, E.J., and M. Bloomfield. 1984. A study of woodland caribou. Unpublished report prepared for Alberta Fish and Wildlife Division, Edmonton. See also Bloomfield. M. 1980. Closure of the caribou hunting season in Alberta: management of a threatened species. Unpublished report prepared for Alberta Fish and Wildlife Division, Edmonton.

[49] Douglas, D. 1914. Journal kept by David Douglas during his travels in North America 1823-27. W. Wesley and Son, London.

[50] Millar, W.N., op. cit.

[51] Wishart, W.D. 1986. The Wainwright deer herd (1966-1984): A comparative study of whitetails and mule deer. Edmonton. Unpublished report.

[52] Stelfox, J.B., op. cit., pp. 132-139.

[53] Alberta Elk Commission: www.albertaelk.com

[54] Stelfox, J.B., op. cit.

[55] Ondrack, J. 1985. Big Game Hunting in Alberta. Wildlife Publishing, Edmonton. An account of the status of big game and its hunting in Alberta from early settlement times to the present.

Chapter 4

THE ENFORCERS:
GAME LAWS AND THOSE WHO UPHELD THEM

Bob McClymont, Petra Rowell, Jim Struthers and Bill Wishart with contributions from
Jim Burns, Deryl Empson, John Girvan, Gordon Kerr, and Ernie Psikla

103

"Choose a job you love, and you will never have to work a day in your life."
CONFUCIUS

The First Game Guardians

Early in the 20th century, the newly created national parks and game preserves provided a safe haven for the game found within them. Nevertheless, something had to be done for fish and game populations outside of protected areas. As more and more settlers arrived in the province, it became apparent that hunting and fishing needed to be regulated to prevent overharvest. Otherwise, new Albertans would suffer the consequences of depleted local game supplies to sustain them.

While the first Territorial Game Ordinances were made in an attempt to stop the rapid decline of bison, they soon became useful for addressing other fish and game-related issues. In October 1883, the Northwest Territories Council passed its first *Ordinance for the Protection of Game*. This early legislation stated what big game and game birds could be hunted, and when they could be hunted. It also included provisions for hunting licences.

Poisons, narcotics, nightlights, nets, and similar devices were outlawed.[1] To uphold these new rules, deputized Council members in turn appointed Game Guardians to enforce the provisions of the Ordinance. Half a century later, these humble beginnings evolved into a full-time, salaried, and trained enforcement body. Game Guardians and, later, Fish and Wildlife Officers, would endeavour to ensure compliance with provincial game laws for the remainder of the century and into the next.

So the stage was set. Rules to regulate the harvest of fish and game species were legislated and a method to enforce those laws was set in motion. As the number of people and the complexity of rules grew, so did the number and duties of enforcers. Guardians not only monitored adherence to regulations, they also played an integral role in problem wildlife management, assisting biologists with collecting population data, and in educating the public to

GAME REGULATIONS
PROVINCE OF ALBERTA
PROHIBITIONS

SUNDAY SHOOTING IS PROHIBITED.
BUFFALO MUST NOT BE KILLED OR TAKEN AT ANY TIME.
MOUNTAIN SHEEP or GOATS must not be killed or taken between the 15th of December and the 1st of October of the following year.
ANTELOPE must not be killed or taken between the 15th of November and the 1st of October of the following year.
DEER including CARIBOU, MOOSE, WAPTI and ELK must not be killed or taken between the 15th of December and the 1st of November in the following year.
DUCKS, GEESE and SWANS shall not be killed between the 1st of January and 23rd of August.
CRANES shall not be killed between the 1st of January and the 1st of August.
RAILS and COOTS shall not be killed between the 5th of May and the 23rd of August.
SNIPE, PLOVER, etc., shall not be killed between the 5th of May and the 23rd of August.
PRAIRIE CHICKEN, PARTRIDGE, etc., shall not be killed between the 15th of December and the 15th of September following.
MINK, FISHER or MARTIN shall not be killed between the 1st of April and the 1st of November.
OTTER shall not be killed between the 1st of May and the 1st November.
MUSKRATS shall not be killed between the 15th of May and the 1st of November.
BEAVER shall not be killed at any time before the 31st of December, 1908.

The period of close season includes the first but not the last mentioned date in each case.
No person shall shoot or hunt on other person's property without permission.
No person shall shoot or hunt between one hour after sunset and one hour before sunrise.
No person shall destroy game by means of poison, narcotics, sunken punts, night-lights, traps, snares, swivel, spring, automatic or machine shot gun.
No person shall export game without a permit from the Minister of Agriculture.
No person shall expose for sale or buy any part of a mountain sheep or goat.
No person shall offer prairie chicken or partridge for sale unless killed by himself.
No person shall wilfully disturb, destroy or take the eggs of any game bird.
No dog shall be used by anyone to hunt deer.
LIMITS OF BAG. No person may shoot more that none of any species of deer.
No person may shoot more than 20 prairie chicken or other grouse in a day or more than 200 in a season.

PERMITS
Licenses entitling the holders thereof to shoot any kind of game (called General Game License) will be issued to non-residents upon application to Game Guardians and payment of the fee of $25.00 for each license. The fee for a license to shoot game birds only (Bird Game License) is $15.00. The holder of a General License may take heads, skins and hoofs of big game out of the country as trophies. All game licenses are good only if endorsed by the licensees and during the calendar year in which they are issued.

PENALTIES
FOR KILLING BUFFALO $50.00 TO $500.00 AND FOR OTHER VIOLATIONS $50.00 OR TWO MONTHS' IMPRISONMENT.
Department of Agriculture,
Edmonton, Alta., June 30th, 1906

GEO. HARCOURT
Deputy Minister

EARLY GAME REGULATIONS. COURTESY R. BJORGE

appreciate and respect Alberta's fish and wildlife resource. Enforcement, like biological considerations, grew into a major component of the overall fish and wildlife management process required by a growing province.

Alberta's Game Guardians
Alberta wasted no time in taking over wildlife enforcement duties shortly after becoming a province in 1905. In 1906, Benjamin Lawton, Alberta's newly appointed and first Chief Game Guardian inherited 218 volunteer Game Guardians appointed by the former territorial administration. Along with members of the newly formed Calgary Fish and Game Protective Association (established in 1908) and the North West Mounted Police, guardians monitored compliance to the game laws of the 1903 *North West Territories Game Ordinance*. Starting in 1909, in return for their efforts, guardians received an annual complimentary copy of *Rod and Gun*.

HUNTING AND FISHING LICENCES IN ALBERTA
In 1907, 450 game licences of two types (resident game and non-resident game) were sold to hunters in Alberta. In 1909, a game bird licence was added to the list. Three game bird licences were sold that year. An early trout licence was adopted prior to 1930 and a general sportfishing licence was introduced in 1956. Today, hunters and fishermen spend approximately $16 million each year ($11 and $5 million, respectively) buying approximately 456,000 hunting licences of 120 different types and 210,000 fishing licences of five different types.[2]

The number of hunters declined in the last 10-15 years across Alberta and North America. However, there is a recent rise in interest in hunting and the promotion of ethical hunting practice as a means of attracting new recreational hunters into the sport. The *Hunting for Tomorrow Foundation,* a not-for-profit organization, works to promote hunting in Alberta. Its vision is "…an Alberta where hunting continues to be a respected, traditional outdoor activity that remains a substantial and integral part of Alberta's heritage, culture, and environment". Its mission is "…to increase the level of public understanding, involvement, and support of hunting. We will increase opportunities for every Albertan to hunt within a management system that conserves the wildlife resource."

The number of sport fishermen purchasing licences in Alberta has also been on a steady decline. However, fishermen under 16 years of age or over 65 years old are not required to purchase a licence and the Government hosts at least two "free" fishing weekends each summer. Thus, the exact number of persons fishing in Alberta is not known. *Trout Unlimited Canada* has a local chapter in Alberta and uses hands-on volunteer activities to promote the wise use of fish resources in the province.

"The first officer for the protection of game appears to have been in Maine in 1852 (a moose warden) – now hardly a state and no province is without them."

BENJAMIN LAWTON, 1906 GAME BRANCH REPORT

From the volunteer Game Guardians, Lawton learned of enforcement difficulties and problem areas where game was scarce. However, in his first report (1906), he called for an end to the system of voluntary guardians—it simply wasn't working. As he pointed out, a volunteer game guardian might witness a neighbour violating the *Game Act* but if he attempted to report him, the guardian could expect to suffer dire consequences. As Lawton noted: "It is not in his interest to lay a charge against his neighbour alongside whom he may live for a number of years. Some are afraid to lay such information for fear they may be burned out."[3]

Clearly, being a volunteer guardian—however conservation-minded one might be—was a responsibility not to be taken lightly. Regardless of their lack of effectiveness, Lawton continued to see the volunteer force grow. By December 31, 1911, the list of volunteer game guardians reached 449, the largest number ever recorded.[4] Although he continued to recommend abolishing the voluntary Game Guardian system, Lawton didn't see it so in his lifetime.

Guardians weren't empowered to arrest persons for game law violations until 1910. Fortunately, the North West Mounted Police, as ex officio guardians, could lay and implement charges with impunity.[5] The number of ex-officio guardians later expanded. Section 41 of the *1932 Game Act* reads: "All members of the Royal Canadian Mounted Police and all forest rangers, and all postmasters shall be ex-officio game guardians and shall have the same powers and duties as are conferred or imposed upon a game guardian appointed by the Minister pursuant to this Act."

Lawton was successful in arguing that salaried Game Guardians were better off and could act without fear of reprisal, as they were usually not residents of an area. By 1916, along with the volunteers, Lawton had a small, but salaried seasonal staff of nine Game Guardians including J. Brewster, A. Campbell, J. McDonald, D. McEachern, H. Rivière, A.C. Ross, E. Simmons, P. Tompkins, and M.F. Webb. Additionally, two clerks, A.C. McFadyen and P.F. Bernard, and a stenographer, Annie Brown, rounded out operations.[6]

In those days, a Game Guardian often worked out of his home. Frequently he was a rancher, an outfitter, or both. He provided his own horses, tent, food, and horse feed. Money for operating expenses was strictly limited. He covered a large area and often spent a large amount of time away. In the summer, he travelled by horseback: in winter, on snowshoes. A guardian was successful if he covered his entire district once a year.

Lawton, for his part, did what he could to improve the working conditions of his field staff by urging the government to hire more guardians and to pay more of their expenses. In 1924, he made several requests for an additional salaried force to patrol outlying areas. However, money was scarce, particularly in the years following the First World War. The United Farmers Association, the Government of the day, walked a precarious fiscal path trying to satisfy its main backers, the farmers. In 1925, Lawton again mentioned in his annual report the difficulty of game law enforcement owing to a lack of salaried officers. This plea continued to come from the Game Branch for the better part of the next two decades.

105

HENRY STELFOX – VOLUNTEER GAME GUARDIAN AND OUTSTANDING CONSERVATIONIST

Henry Stelfox, one of Alberta's first game guardians and an ardent conservationist, must have been an adventurous soul! Born in 1883 in England, he spent time as a young man amidst the Zulus and Basutos of Africa.[7] Stelfox received his education at Manchester Grammar School before becoming an accounting clerk. He served in the South African Constabulary from 1903-1906 before emigrating to Alberta to homestead and raise a family in the Rocky Mountain House district. He arrived in Calgary during the exceptionally severe winter of 1906-1907 and began working for R. K. Bennett, owner of the Rushford Ranch, southwest of Red Deer Lake. In his autobiography, *Rambling Thoughts of a Wandering Fellow,* Stelfox described the harshness of that first winter when "snow drifted up over fences".[8] He also noted that many cattle and wildlife perished that year.

"I killed coyotes and lynx which came into the corrals, barnyards, and open buildings in search of food. Antelope and mule deer were decimated in large numbers. Moose, which yarded up in willow meadows, would have fared better than antelope and mule deer had it not been for the coyotes and wolves, which preyed upon them. Predators could travel on top of the frozen snow, whereas moose floundered if they left the beaten track. Ruffed grouse and sharp-tailed grouse were plentiful in the parklands and in the forest and survived the hard winter in plentiful numbers."[9]

Stelfox soon purchased his own homestead in the Battle Lake area. In the summers, he worked his land and in the winters he worked in logging camps to supplement his income. In 1908, he was elected Councillor for the Battle Lake Improvement District and was appointed Justice of the Peace, Notary Public, and a Game Guardian for which he received no salary.

Through the years, Henry Stelfox was a farmer, rancher, real estate agent, auctioneer, clerk, stock-raiser, and veterinarian. He befriended the local Indians and represented them on several councils and government associations. He was also a far-sighted individual when it came to wildlife. Throughout his lifetime, Stelfox worked tirelessly on wildlife conservation measures. He was actively involved in the founding of the Calgary Fish and Game Protective Association (and later, the Alberta Fish and Game Association). He also served as a member of the Game Advisory Council of the provincial Fish and Game Branch from 1945 to 1958.

For his efforts, Stelfox received the Julian Crandall Conservation Trophy in 1954, Canada's highest conservation award. In 1956, the Geographic Board of Alberta named Mt. Stelfox, overlooking the Kootenay Plains, in his honour. In 1958, the Royal Society of Canada appointed him a Geographer. He also received both the Fulton and Freeman trophies from the Alberta Fish and Game Association for his efforts on behalf of wildlife conservation. Close friend A. J. Hooke, provincial Member of the Legislative Assembly, described Henry, in later years, as "one of those rare characters born to love nature and to cherish every living thing be it animal or plant".[10]

Perhaps even more important his sphere of influence extended beyond his own generation. Henry was a great influence on sons Dave, a plant pathologist with Alberta Agriculture, and John, a wildlife biologist with Alberta Fish and Wildlife Division and the Canadian Wildlife Service. As well, grandsons Jim, Harry, and Brad are all actively contributing members to the wildlife management community. Henry Stelfox passed away in 1974 at the age of 91 but left Alberta a living legacy in his wildlife conservation efforts and in those who follow in his footsteps.

JOHN STRAWBERRY AND HENRY STELFOX IN THE ROCKY MOUNTAIN HOUSE AREA.
COURTESY PROVINCIAL ARCHIVES OF ALBERTA (PA 800/1)

106

TRAVEL EXPENSES?

[ADAPTED FROM JIM STRUTHERS, *LOOKIN' BACK*, THE ALBERTA GAME WARDEN, SPRING 1993]

Today, Fish and Wildlife Officers still occasionally use horseback and snowshoes but more often enjoy the use of sophisticated vehicles: four-wheel-drive patrol units, snowmobiles, all-terrain vehicles like quads, sonar-equipped boats, and fixed- and rotary-winged aircraft. The following excerpts from letters written to the Chief Game Guardian in 1916 give some idea of travel conditions for Alberta's pioneer game guardians.

On this trip to High River, I have been 17 days out of my district in order to do my work properly. I had to follow the game range at the base of the mountains where the trails were blocked with down timber and mud holes. You understand pretty near all creeks of any size have trails of some kind to their heads; the trouble is crossing from these trails to the next. Anyhow, I managed to cripple two horses out of three—one so bad I had to leave it behind. I had got these horses for this trip from a third party and had to get them shoed all around. Now don't you think that I should be entitled to pay for the use of these horses while out of my district? Kindly let me know what you think of this; no matter which way I figure it, I will come out loose anyhow.

Game Guardian Henry Rivière may have had more than a little trouble the next time he wanted to borrow a few horses! A second letter from Rivière details an investigation he conducted in December 1916 around the communities of Fawcett, Jarvie, Westlock, and Clyde. His report reveals that he hitch-hiked rides with dog and horse teams and took a train trip to complete the investigation.

A third letter from another game guardian describes a patrol made to investigate a complaint alleging residents of the Sullivan Lake District were taking goose eggs from wild nests and placing them under setting hens. Although the guardian inspected the premises of the suspect parties, he failed to find any evidence that any goose eggs had been taken unlawfully. His report seems to have been filed in support of a claim to be reimbursed for the livery (taxi) fare he had paid to accomplish the patrol. Apparently, he did not own a vehicle and could find no one willing to drive him through the countryside. Officers today occasionally claim expenses for cab fare but this is the only recorded request for reimbursement for cab fare for an extended rural patrol!

GAME GUARDIAN AND BIG GAME HUNTER, HENRI RIVIÈRE SITTING IN HIS CAMP NEAR PINCHER CREEK.
COURTESY GLENBOW ARCHIVES (NA-3051-3)

HENRY AND JAMES RIVIÈRE
[ADAPTED FROM AN INTERVIEW WITH ERIC HOLMGREN[11]]

James Rivière of Twin Buttes, near Pincher Creek, recalls what conditions were like for his father in the early years. Henry Rivière, born in Normandy, France, came to Canada in 1883. He was a game guardian in Alberta for 16 years between 1911 and 1928. Henry's assigned area was almost the entire foothills, which he patrolled, conscientiously.

Henry Rivière initially saw mountain sheep in considerable numbers in the area but later their numbers declined. He was also a National Parks Warden, involved in arresting a gang of illegal hunters shooting elk both inside and outside Jasper Park and selling the meat to coal miners. This was just one of many problems Henry encountered at the time. As well, Rivière was a big game outfitter, and in the course of his work, could appear seemingly from nowhere to apprehend a lawbreaker, or to warn an errant hunter. His knowledge of the country was said to be encyclopaedic. Henry died on June 30, 1956. He is buried on his ranch, Victoria

Peak Ranch, in the mountains. These words are inscribed on his headstone: "The trails that knew him shall know him no more."[12]

Like his father, James Rivière frequently took parties into the foothills and mountains to hunt elk. He noted the fluctuations in numbers from year to year. Both father and son were concerned with fire as the main threat to wildlife populations. A huge forest fire had ravaged the foothills areas near Pincher Creek in the 1880s and many elk perished. The area surrounding the Rivière ranch became a game preserve but it was some time before elk made a comeback. The Rivières were also deeply concerned about elk habitat loss due mainly to ranching. Elk just could not compete with cattle. James and Henry have been a continuous thread in the history of game watching in Alberta.

108

A FEW BAD APPLES
[ADAPTED FROM JIM STRUTHERS, *LOOKIN' BACK*, THE ALBERTA GAME WARDEN, SPRING 1992[13]]

Regrettably, there was the odd bad apple among the volunteer game guardians. As one local story goes, following the resignation of a particular volunteer game guardian after many years of service, the locals were anxious to learn of his replacement. Meat supplies were dwindling. The situation was becoming desperate for, without knowing who was the new guardian, the locals had to play by the rules which some viewed as a serious handicap if not an outright imposition. Few dared take a chance until they knew who was carrying the badge.

Long after the crops were in the bins and well past the time game was usually secured, butchered, and preserved, a neighbour on horseback stopped by to enlist the assistance of our storyteller's father. The neighbour had just spotted some deer in a coulee not too far away. The boy's dad was reluctant to be a party to the hunt since no one had divined the identity of the new game guardian. However, the

alternatives were few. Thus, he agreed and went to saddle up.

Soon the pair located the herd and downed a couple of deer. The afternoon was warm. The hunters shrugged out of their coats and rolled up their sleeves preparing to dress the carcasses. The boy's father stared wide-eyed at his partner. On the strap of his bib overalls hung a bright, new game guardian badge. The new game guardian realizing the object of his companion's interest chuckled: "It's a dirty job, but somebody's got to do it!"

Stories of this nature fostered and perpetuated a folk crime attitude respecting fisheries and wildlife violations. For many years, that perception was a serious barrier to the enforcement of the laws enacted to protect fish and game.

The First Fish and Game Officers

After the 1930 *Natural Resources Transfer Act*, Alberta also assumed responsibility for enforcing fisheries legislation from the federal government. A new Fisheries Service was created within the Department of Lands and Mines.[14] In May 1933, staff were assigned responsibility for regulating boats and other small craft.

By 1941, about 300 volunteer Game Guardians continued to work throughout the province. Now, when they made an arrest, volunteers were entitled to collect half the penalty paid by the guilty offender. However, the new Fish and Game Commissioner, like Lawson before him, also felt the volunteer system just wasn't working. Unlike Lawton, Eric Huestis was successful in arguing his case and in 1941, asked for, and received authority to dispense with the guardians over the next two years. More importantly, the money from their share of the penalty fees could now be re-directed towards other purposes.

After the creation of the Department of Lands and Forests in 1949, Commissioner Huestis continued to implement changes to the enforcement system. The term Game Guardian was changed to "Fish and Game Officer".[15] All such officers were permanent year-round employees of the provincial government. At first, the qualifications for the job of Fish and Game Officer were non-existent. Men who were war veterans, foresters, guides and outfitters, or former fish inspectors were preferred.

Under Huestis' leadership, Fish and Game Officers enforced game and angling regulations, recorded the numbers of kills during the hunting season, and patrolled their assigned area. Huestis continued to plead for more salaried officers to patrol outlying areas. In 1946-1947, the addition of five Game Inspectors posted to St. Paul, Vermilion, Camrose, Coronation, and Pincher Creek bolstered staff numbers. [The first game inspectors were hired by the province in 1923. As seen in the journals of Inspector Boag, the job of inspector was diverse, with considerable overlap with the duties of Game Guardians.]

However, there was still only a handful of Fish and Game Officers for the whole of Alberta in the early 1950s. Being an officer meant long periods in the field and little social life. As well, there was travel over incredible roads that were dusty in dry weather and one bog after another when wet. In winter, roads were often impassable and the Fish and Game Officer travelled (depending on which part of the province he patrolled in) either on snowshoes or by dog team. Charlie Dougherty, a Fish and Game Officer for many years, summed it up by saying that he "travelled on a half-ton truck and a prayer"![16] His recollections were not unique. Bob Forsyth, carrying out similar duties, recalled similar conditions.

The same conditions that frustrated Dougherty and Forsyth plagued other Fish and Game Officers as well. Gradually, however, their numbers increased and they continued to be supported by other institutions such as the police and forestry officers. In 1959-1960, for example, Forest Service and Eastern Conservation Board employees, in addition to Fish and Game Officers, reinforced the hunter checking station program.

GAME INSPECTOR BOAG [17]

Game Inspector T. A. Boag had a diverse job, requiring a great deal of travel. In the three and a half months between June 4 and September 17, 1937, Boag inspected beaver activity and a potential fur farm near Lamont; surveyed elk and range conditions in the Brazeau-Pembina Game Preserve; investigated complaints of ducks being hunted out of season at Lac St. Anne and Cooking and Hastings lakes; examined waterfowl crop damage near Magrath and Bruderheim; examined range damage by elk on ranches bordering Waterton Lakes National Park; visited G. Pickering who was then trying to garner support for the Inglewood Bird Sanctuary in Calgary; hunted for a problem bear in the Breton area; surveyed a potential deer preserve near Wainwright; manned a hunter check station near Sherwood Park; and investigated poaching in the Cooking Lake Forest Reserve!

OFFICER CHARLES (CHARLIE) DOUGHERTY
[ADAPTED FROM AN INTERVIEW WITH ERIC HOLMGREN[18]]

Charles Dougherty was one of the first officers hired by Commissioner Huestis as a newly named Fish and Game Officer. He started in 1952 and was assigned a large area stretching from Didsbury south almost to Crossfield, east along Highway 9 to Drumheller; north almost to Stettler, west to Sylvan Lake and south to the starting point. As well, Dougherty spent a winter at Wabamun Lake, enforcing commercial fishing regulations. In 1958, he was transferred to Brooks to oversee the commercial fishery at Lake Newell. He also counted ducks for Ducks Unlimited in the area south of Hanna. In addition, he oversaw the annual antelope hunt. Dougherty's duties also included stocking lakes with fingerlings. He left

Brooks in 1962 for Lethbridge, where his district was smaller, as more officers were being hired. His duties differed little, except that he also had to keep an eye on the pheasant population.

Dougherty also dealt with violators of the *Game Act*. If a prosecution were required, he did all the legal work, prepared the case, and presented in court. Until 1962, he performed these duties single-handed in his district, although, if necessary, he could get help from the RCMP. Only in 1962, did he finally get any staff: one full-time stenographer. Two years later, Gerry Tranter was hired as an assistant.

OFFICER BOB FORSYTH
[ADAPTED FROM AN INTERVIEW WITH ERIC HOLMGREN[19]]

Starting out as a Game Officer in Ontario, Bob Forsyth came to Alberta as a Fisheries Officer in 1950. His new territory extended from the Saskatchewan border to St. Paul, north to Lac La Biche, west to Smoky Lake and Vilna, and south to the North Saskatchewan River.

Forsyth recalled the early years when he oversaw the extensive commercial fishery in the St. Paul area which, even in the 1950s was still a pioneer area in Alberta. Roads were only beginning to penetrate this land to any degree. In the summer, he travelled by truck, often encountering roads that were impassable. In winter, he travelled by snowshoes and later, when it was available, snowmobile. Trapline registration was just being introduced in that area and it was his job to issue licences and persuade the trappers to accept the new system.

Forsyth also counted beaver houses in the area and imposed quotas on the number of animals that could be taken. He recalled that muskrat pelts were fetching a good price. Prime furs were the object, whether beaver or muskrat. In spite of the limitations of travel, impassable roads, and the isolation of the area, he managed to cover his area and perform his duties. Like other Fish and Game Officers, he issued hunting and angling licences and prosecuted violators of the *Game Act*. In 1952, Forsyth transferred to Calgary. A few years later, he became Regional Supervisor at Red Deer. He remained there until 1975, when he retired to Cardston.

OFFICER BILL WILLOWS CHECKING A HUNTER.
COURTESY B. STEVENSON

officer in Cardston, one in Claresholm, Bill Bell. There was Fred Aastrup in High River. Merv Heron was a Fisheries Officer. He was at Wabamun when I was there. Another one was Art Svenson. He was up to Cold Lake and Lac La Biche and then he moved into Edmonton about the same time as George Bray. In fact, I took the train to Edmonton to pick up a vehicle when I was supposed to go up north and Art Svenson is the one that met me and sort of gave me what little guidance and training I needed. All he said is: "Here's the typewriter and here's your briefcase. You know how to drive a vehicle? Hup to it."

In 1959, William C. "Rocky" Hales, was appointed the Head of Wildlife Law Enforcement where he was credited for much of the design and development of the enforcement program in the following years.[20] Hales entered Alberta's public service in the early 1930s. Much of his time as a Game Officer was spent in the Edson area. Those who worked with him knew him as a keen advocate for professionalism in wildlife enforcement. Hales believed that a game officer had a special place and role in the community he served. He was a person to whom the public looked for help, advice, and a professional response to all

111

The late Gerry Pelchat recalled many of the early officers:

I was the Game Officer for the Brooks area in charge of the pheasant hatchery. In fact, I was the only officer here until Forbes King came. He was my assistant. That would be in the mid-1950s. I was the youngest Fish and Game Officer at the time. I don't think there was any more than maybe twenty, twenty-five officers in total. There was Henry Bertelson in Medicine Hat and Dougherty came on after I did. There was a game officer in Medicine Hat, Brooks, and one in Lethbridge. In addition, there was an

OFFICER MILT WARREN WITH A NORTHERN PIKE
FROM FAWCETT LAKE, 1958.
CREDIT: J. STELFOX

FISH AND WILDLIFE OFFICER BERT FREEMAN
[INTERVIEWED BY PAT VALASTIN, SEPTEMBER 14, 2002 IN OLDS]

Bert Freeman was born December 20, 1928 in Winnipeg, Manitoba. "I was a Christmas bonus!" His parents moved west when he was five and he started his schooling in Calgary. When asked about his childhood activities, Bert said he liked to catch frogs and tadpoles. "I'd put them in little tubs of water. I also liked hunting partridges. Behind Scarborough Avenue was a wilderness area that broke out into a railroad, and I'd go down the track and trap weasels and rabbits. I'd bring them home, skin them, and sell them—75 cents for a weasel and two bits for a rabbit. They were trimming parkas with rabbit fur in those days. I would go out to the bush in the morning in the wintertime, and I'd cook some wieners over the fire, sit out there all day, and run my trap line..."

After he left school, Bert worked at a variety of jobs before turning to the fish and wildlife profession. "We went to Wilkie, Saskatchewan, drilling in the summer and back to Alberta in the winter. We had a layover; so I decided I'd go down and see if I could get a job as a Game Warden. I went to the Natural Resources Building in Edmonton and talked to Jack Jensen, Chief Timber Inspector at the time. I told him I wanted to become a Game Warden. He said: 'Well you can't just become a Game Warden. We'll put you on a tower.'" [The larger forestry Department provided many future officers their rite of passage into the Game Branch.]

"I went on Pasquaska tower, north of Calais, north of Sturgeon Lake. We [Bert and his wife Rose] were there about seven months. We lived in a log cabin up on top of the hill. The first fire that I reported, I thought I'd really done something. You had to report every smoke you saw in to Grande Prairie. I reported this fire, with the bearings, and the Ranger had to go out and inspect. It was burning garbage in the town of Valleyview. Don't think I wasn't embarrassed!

"I didn't want to come down! I would have stayed there all winter. However, it wasn't a winter situation. They offered me a job as an assistant ranger in Edson. I said I didn't want to be an assistant ranger in Edson; I wanted to be a game warden in the mountains! They said no that was the only opening. Well, I said I'd take it then. So I cruised timber all that winter.

"You had to do an estimate of how much timber was in a cutblock. You went around measuring trees. I'd never been on a pair of snowshoes before. I was on my ass more than I was on the snowshoes! I thought: what have I got myself into? But I got to the point where I could run with them, after a while. [This was the winter of 1952-53.] Then a Fish and Game Officer position came open at Camrose. Mr Huestis said to fire in an application, which I did. I got notice a week later that I had the job. So we moved to Camrose. That's where our two girls were born."

Bert stayed in Camrose for six years before being transferred to High River. He enjoyed taking part in the projects that the biologists were working on and remembers helping out a young Gordon Kerr. "Gordon Kerr was out of Lethbridge and he had to do pheasant crowing counts around High River. His wife was pregnant, and she was coming due. He came up to High River, the wind would start blowing, and he couldn't do the counts. He came up a couple of times, and then he came to me and said, would I mind doing them? So I did and sent the forms down to him. We were all there for the same thing. I enjoyed it. Spent six years in High River, and then spent 11 years in Olds."

When asked what kind of things he had to deal with, Bert replied: "Routine stuff. You know, checking hunters and anglers. Dennis Urban—he's still with the outfit—and I ran one of the first successful undercover operations in the province on a fish peddling deal at Sturgeon Lake. We got a couple of convictions up there in the early 1970s. After court was over, the Judge commended us on the great job we did. He said: 'It wasn't like a drug bust or anything, but it is a natural resource, and we've got to protect it. I've got to commend you on an exceptional job.' I thought that was pretty nice."

When asked what some of the stressful points of his career were, Bert replied: "One time at Camrose, some guys were shooting pheasants. One of them stuck a shotgun out the back window of the car. There were lots of things. I've often thought I'd like to write a book!"

According to wildlife biologist Bob Webb, Freeman was keen on the biological ideas being introduced and was very helpful to the biologists until at the age of 47, he left the Fish and Wildlife Division to pursue other opportunities.

A CLASS OF OFFICERS IN UNIFORM AT HINTON.
COURTESY B. STEVENSON

infraction situations. The public should expect the best and nothing less from an officer.

There was no room for shoddiness in appearance. Hales believed the public expected officers to present themselves in a manner that commanded respect. He knew the value of a strong, visual identity as a law enforcement agency. Initially, volunteer Game Guardians wore only a badge. Then in 1941, salaried game guardians and inspectors were provided with identification cards. Over the years, a number of shoulder flashes were designed but under Hales' direction, an easily recognizable uniform was eventually supplied to Officers.

Hales was one of the earliest proponents of community policing, although that catchy phrase was not in vogue for many years. He sponsored downtown offices for all district headquarters, each staffed with secretaries. Because of Hales' vision of an effective field organization, Alberta was set on a course that was leading-edge. From the creation of the Fish and Wildlife Division in 1959 to the present day, Alberta is recognized as having one of the finest fish and wildlife enforcement services in North America.

A COLLAGE OF OLD AND NEW CRESTS AND PINS.
COURTESY ALBERTA FISH AND WILDLIFE DIVISION

THE DEVELOPMENT OF OFFICER TRAINING

Rocky Hales was the prototypical modern officer. He wore the uniform proudly and expected others to do the same. Although he was a self-taught man with little formal education, he recognized academic credentials one day would be among the essential tools of the profession.

As Administrator of the Fish and Wildlife Division in the early 1960s, Hales coordinated a comprehensive training course for Alberta Fish and Wildlife Officers in aspects of wildlife, fisheries, and law enforcement. New recruits together with veteran officers attended courses held at the Hinton Forestry Training School. Officers were introduced to contemporary resource management principles, biological investigation and analysis, advanced law enforcement procedures and criminalistics. Some of the many activities undertaken at the school included mock trials, crime scene reconstruction and investigation, ballistics, tool marks, collection and preservation of evidence, taking statements, giving evidence, public speaking, criminal procedure, criminal code application, and prosecutorial responsibilities.

One of the mock trials featured Hales playing the prosecutor. The subject resulted from a lengthy investigation Hales conducted while stationed in Edson. For a considerable period, Hales had documented where a railroad conductor, not licensed to buy fur, made several purchases from trappers en route to Edson to sell their furs to legitimate fur dealers. In fact, one such dealer had put Hales onto the conductor. Apparently, the conductor was taking advantage of trappers who spent long periods in the bush and were more anxious to get their hands on some cash than they were to get the full value for their pelts.

At the mock trial, the officer (student) who played Hales' part presented considerable evidence relating to searches and seizure of furs in the conductor's possession. The student further testified that his check of government records revealed the conductor did not hold a valid licence authorizing the purchase of those furs. Other officers, playing the parts of trappers who had sold fur to the conductor, provided additional, damning testimony. Ultimately, and with considerable flourish, Hales in his role as prosecutor turned to the officer playing the magistrate and said: "Your Honour, the prosecution rests."

The officer playing the role of the defence attorney, considerably less dramatic, reviewed the evidence and

congratulated Hales the investigator and Hales the prosecutor for doing an admirable job of convincing everyone that the conductor had purchased fur on various occasions. He submitted, however, that the dynamic duo had not adequately proven the conductor did not hold the required licence. He made reference to the *Game Act* which outlines when it is necessary to prove whether or not a given individual holds a particular licence that a certificate, signed by a specified official, certifying with respect to that fact, shall be admitted in evidence as proof of the facts stated in the certificate. The defence attorney went on to suggest, given the ease with which Officer Hales could have secured the necessary certificate, the court should find in favour of the accused and dismiss the charges. The magistrate agreed and the case was dismissed.

Those who knew Rocky Hales were aware that admitting to such an oversight was a difficult thing for him to do. He did it in an effort to ensure that the students learned from his experience. Recognizing, however, that in-service training was, at best, an interim measure, Hales was instrumental in changing policy. Potential recruits soon had to be graduates of a recognized technical institution holding a diploma in fish and wildlife resource management. The first graduates from the Natural Resources Program at Kelsey Institute in Saskatchewan were hired in 1966. Over the years, academic requirements have increased. Most of today's candidates hold a Bachelor of Applied Science Conservation Enforcement from the Lethbridge Community College.

Additionally, recruits are now required to attend an in-service Academy, which occurs during an eight-week period prior to assuming field duties. Academies are conducted at the Forestry Training Centre in Hinton. The sessions include, but are not limited to: problem wildlife management and control; firearms training (rifle, shotgun and pistol); cross-cultural awareness; a water safety and awareness course relating to operation and maintenance of canoes, lake craft, and jet boats; similar instruction on various all-terrain vehicles, four-wheel-drive vehicles, and snow machines; specialized enforcement training in taking statements, obtaining and executing search warrants, preserving evidence, crime scene analysis, trophy sheep measurement, as well as forensics and related DNA applications. All officers hired prior to the inception of the academies were brought up to the same standards.

114

ROCKY HALES (FAR RIGHT) INSTRUCTING A CLASS FOR FISH AND WILDLIFE OFFICERS AT HINTON TRAINING SCHOOL.
COURTESY B. STEVENSON

Enforcement Issues through Time

Throughout the century, through ignorance of or simple disregard for the laws of the land, a small proportion of hunters and anglers failed to comply with the laws regarding seasons, bag limits, or licensing requirements. In the late 1960s, taking game without a licence and marketing game (outlawed in 1922) were common violations. Jacklighting—hunting at night with lights—was also becoming a serious issue. Various enforcement techniques were employed to deal with night hunting. In 1968-1969, 22 violators were apprehended for this violation. However, this illegal activity was again a problem the following year and would continue to be a serious problem for many years to come.

By 1970, the Enforcement Branch was well established and expanding to fill many specific needs in the on-going management of Alberta's fish and wildlife. This year, a new *Wildlife Act* came into force, which incorporated a number of changes designed around a "total wildlife concept." For example, M-E-D licences were introduced and for a cost of ten dollars they entitled the holder to take one animal of the moose, elk, or deer species. J. Donovan Ross, Minister at the time, imposed the MED Licence over the objection of the biological staff. Public lack of interest in its purchase caused it to be discontinued in about two years and following a change of Ministers.

Illegal trafficking in trophy big game animals was becoming a problem. Today, illegal hunting, trapping, and poaching continue to occur throughout the province. Poaching also occurs within the National Parks with poachers working

GAME WARDENS CAN SEE IN THE DARK!
[ADAPTED FROM JIM STRUTHERS, *LOOKIN' BACK*, THE ALBERTA GAME WARDEN, FALL 2004]

In the mid-1970s, the Fish and Wildlife Division acquired a night vision scope. The viewfinder was small, perhaps the size of the LCD monitor on today's digital cameras, and shaped like a common TV screen with rounded corners. The images it displayed were not pretty. They were bilious shades of green.

My first and only experience with this unique piece of equipment occurred during the 1977 migratory bird season. The Edmonton district office received numerous complaints alleging after-hours duck hunting on Big Lake. I teamed up with Steve Ewaschuk. We had the scope. Early in the evening, we went on patrol, primarily checking hunters' bags, licences, and shotguns to ensure they were properly plugged. At the same time, we were keeping an eye out for any hunters inclined to stay late. As the sun was setting, we happened on a party of six. They appeared to be dug in for the long haul. We left them undisturbed and retreated to a spot where we could, without our presence being detected, observe their activities.

All was quiet in our quarter as the legal time for hunting expired. Then, occasionally, we heard random shots from afar but our party of six remained silently hunkered in the reeds. One of their numbers, a guy with dark, curly hair and Buddy Holly glasses loosed a pack of Black Cat cigarettes from one of the many large pockets in his hunting jacket and lit up. I watched through the scope as the match flared. The cigarette was cork-tipped so I knew the package was blue. Everything looked weird in shades of green.

Ducks, returning from feeding in nearby fields in singles and pairs, slid by on cupped wings just out of range. They landed in the water well behind the guys lurking in the reeds. Many minutes passed. Sporadic shooting persisted at some distance. About the time the novelty of watching these guys on the small, green screen was wearing off, they began to stir. A large flock of ducks was approaching, silhouetted against the clear sky. Shotguns were shouldered. Wings whistled. Guns erupted.

It was over as quickly as it started. Some ducks fell. We helped the surprised six retrieve those that had not made it to the water. We wrote the guys up for hunting after one-half hour after sunset. As I handed Buddy Holly his ticket he said: "You'll never make it stick. Game Wardens can't see in the dark." We chose not to let him in on our little secret at that juncture but I couldn't resist saying: "You're the guy who smokes the Black Cat cork-tips, right?" That seemed to shake his confidence but only for the moment. He and the rest of the crew contested the charges. However, within the month all six were convicted. The wheels of justice rolled more rapidly in those days.

Those were the last tickets I ever wrote. The day after the trial, my supervisor phoned me and asked me where I had spent the last few days. When I told him I had been testifying in court and provided the details of the cases, he directed me to attend at his office forthwith, and to bring my ticket book. I complied. On my arrival, he gravely reminded me that I was now a Regional Officer and, therefore, not employed to chase violators and write tickets. He demanded my ticket book. I passed it to him. He was a big man. He tore that ticket book to shreds and handed it back to me. I spent another 20 years with the outfit and often missed the fieldwork…but I had proven game wardens could see in the dark, albeit with a little help.

for collectors for the head of an elk or a bighorn sheep. At Jasper National Park, wardens mark sheep horns so that if the heads are taken illegally, detection is more certain. Poaching is a worldwide problem and threatens several species.

Fish and Wildlife Officers were noticing other trends in enforcement. For example, the number of fishery prosecutions started to out-number those for wildlife. Angling without a licence was the primary infraction. Officers also noticed a relationship between the economic boom and the number of violations. Roads opened up in previously inaccessible areas and an influx of people into these areas inevitably increased the number of contraventions there. To deal with these and other issues, the Enforcement Branch grew into four sections: Enforcement, Problem Wildlife, Special Investigations, and Forensic Science Research. In 1981, 52 district offices dealt with 19,901 complaints, 4110 investigations, 3325 warnings, and 4417 prosecutions. As well, the Division fielded 8247 problem wildlife complaints. To meet these new demands, the Branch recruited several new officers, the first major increase in enforcement personnel in several years. Recruitment included Jacki Gerwing, the first female Fish and Wildlife Officer hired in Alberta.

As well as enforcing the *Wildlife Act*, Fish and Wildlife Officers also assisted with many biological programs in the province. The officers' interest and respect for wildlife was a common thread amongst them and the tie that bound them to many other wildlife-related duties. Officers often gathered biological data through observation of various species. For example, Fish and Game Officers conducted pheasant crowing counts as early as 1955 (see Bob Adam's book "*Fish Cop*" on the early days of pheasant counts around Brooks).[21]

Officers were often the first ones to respond to concerns from the public where problem or found wildlife was involved and the number of such complaints grew with an increase in the human population. In 1973 alone, officers participated in the removal or capture of 17,909 nuisance animals of various species and aided Department of Agriculture staff investigating claims of livestock loss attributed to predatory wildlife. Research into reducing or eliminating damage by using devices

OFFICERS DUANE KERIK, MATT EBERLE, AND ADRIANE TREPANIER ASSISTING BIOLOGIST JOHN STELFOX ON WINTER RANGE SURVEYS SOUTHEAST OF GRANDE PRAIRIE, 1965.
COURTESY J. STELFOX

JACKI GERWING, DISTRICT CONSERVATION OFFICER, HIGH LEVEL, ALBERTA
[INTERVIEWED BY JIM STRUTHERS]

"I was born and raised near Lake Lenore, Saskatchewan. We grew up on a farm and I guess we worked a lot as kids. I'm always talking to my kids about picking rocks because I'm an expert at that. We used to go fishing on Sunday. Dad would take all us kids out and we'd go to the north end of the lake. We had this old outboard motor and we'd rent a wooden boat. We caught perch by the five-gallon pail and hauled them all home.

"After high school, I went directly into the renewable resources course at Kelsey Institute in Saskatoon. When I graduated in 1975, I applied to get a job in Alberta because it seemed like the sort of thing that I would like. They interviewed me and sent me a letter saying that I wasn't strong enough to lift a moose into the back of the truck or pull 100 yards of net out from under the ice. I think they just had a pre-conceived idea when they were hiring back then, and I think a lot of that changed over the next few years. I just packed the letter away and went to work with Forestry in Saskatchewan.

"The job was quite interesting because there were only six of us working for the Department in the north half of the province. We did a little bit of everything. However, after six years there was no room for advancement. It just wasn't what I wanted to stick with. When Alberta advertised again in 1980, I applied again and that's when I was hired.

"My first posting [with Alberta Fish and Wildlife Division] was in Rocky Mountain House in April 1981. I felt like a fish out of water when I first got there. At Kelsey, and in six years with Forestry, I did very little enforcement. I did a lot of outdoors things and operated all types of equipment. So, I felt comfortable with that. But as far as dealing with somebody in an enforcement situation—I had never had that type of experience. As well, moving to Alberta, I didn't know a four-fifths curl (on a bighorn sheep) from a hole in the ground and ended up in Rocky Mountain House!

"I worked with Earl Dodsworth. He has a great sense of humour but he transferred out six months after I started. I was there through part of the hunting season and all winter by myself. I did a lot

of things the wrong way when I first started—as far as how to check a firearm safely and things like that. So I would constantly have people sticking guns out the window in my face. I guess once you do it for a while you learn to tell people to do what you want them to do.

"I was at Rocky for just over a year. I told them I wanted to go up north, so they sent me to Brooks! I drove down to Brooks that first time and thought I was going to die. It was such a desert to me. Nothing was green. There were no trees. I actually got to like the town of Brooks because I got involved with things in town. Tom Biglin was the District Officer. Some of it was interesting. I'd never seen antelope before. I'd never had anything to do with snakes. And just seeing the prairie, I mean, I appreciated that part of it. But there was something about no trees and the heat I didn't like. It was the longest three years of my life.

"I was in Brooks until 1985 and then I was transferred to Lac La Biche. I asked to go there and people thought I was nuts! Why do you want to go to Lac La Biche? Because there was water, lakes, and some bush, and that's what I wanted. I just loved it there but I was only there for 11 months. I got the promotion to District Officer in High Level and I've been here ever since.

"I'll tell you about my first interview for a District Officer position. That was when I was in Brooks. Everybody that had been on over a year was going for interviews to get their own district. I thought I knew what was going on, but I didn't have a lot of background on how legislation worked. I learned what to do in certain situations, but I never really learned why. So in my first interview that I went to, I knew when I was supposed to write a violation ticket instead of an appearance notice, but when they asked me why, I didn't know! I had to do a lot of work. It wasn't until I was in Lac La Biche when I passed the interview and got put on the list. The high point in my career was getting a District Officer position.

"For some reason, people seemed to accept me [as a female officer] within the Division, as far as I could see. There was probably some grumbling and people talking, but I never saw or heard any.

As far as problems dealing with people, I think people don't normally see me as a threat. So I've actually had an easier time, especially up in this area. People don't get their backs up as much when I'm out there by myself as they may if a couple of guys come out. I've never had a real serious situation that I couldn't handle. There was only one time I had to get help dealing with somebody, and other than that, I've always managed to deal with them myself.

"My career hasn't really been much different than anybody else's. I'm just sort of your average officer, and I haven't done anything that special. I'm just one of these people who do their job. Would I do it differently if I could do it all over again? You know, you learn from things, you learn from everything you do, the good and the bad, but it would have been nice to have been a little more prepared when I started.

[Today, Jacki Gerwing continues to work out of the High Level Fish and Wildlife office. "I have no interest in getting out of what I'm doing until I get to the point where I can't physically do it anymore. I'm still enjoying what I'm doing, and, will continue doing this as long as I can."]

that restricted the activities of wildlife was on-going. In 1975, the Problem Wildlife Service Operations was created to deal with a myriad of problem wildlife issues including the growing population of beaver, whose dams caused damage to agricultural land or road grades, or larger predatory furbearers, like wolf-livestock issues or black bear-beekeeper problems.[22]

Problem Wildlife Officers also dealt with ungulate complaints. Elk damage to forage crops and stored feed was a perennial problem, particularly along the foothills. In response to mounting pressure from agricultural producers, Regional Problem Wildlife Specialists supplied fencing materials (wire and posts), with labour provided by the ranchers, to decrease the loss of hay. The program was formally established in the winter of 1977-1978 when prolonged heavy snowfall resulted in increased ungulate complaints in southern Alberta. In 1982, 61,600 feet of wire fencing for problem elk and 30,000 feet of snow fencing for deer were used to mitigate the problem. Elk were also radio-collared to determine the effectiveness of electronic stack protectors to stop repeated visits to feedstacks. Today, the program continues to supply big game fencing for stack yards, plastic mesh fencing for temporary stack protection, and a variety of electronic noisemakers and scaring devices. Often, intercept feeding is used to draw elk and deer away from domestic feedstocks.

In the past, Alberta Agriculture administered and financed compensation programs for ungulate damage to standing and swathed crops; however, stacked or stored feed was not covered. Following a severe winter in 1996-1997 in which the Fish and Wildlife Division spent over $1,000,000 in efforts to protect stored feed, representatives from the Alberta Cattle Commission, Alberta Agriculture, Fish and Wildlife, Alberta Financial Services Corporation (AFSC), and Alberta Fish and Game developed a compensation program for stacked and stored feed. The program was funded through AFSC and implemented in 2000. Producers who take preventative measures are compensated for sustained ungulate damage to stacked and stored feed.

119

OFFICER DENNIS WEISSER
[INTERVIEWED BY PAT VALASTIN, AUGUST 30, 2002]

Dennis Weisser was born in 1934 in Camrose, Alberta. "I grew up on a farm just west of Camrose. East Bittern Lake is where I went to school for the first eight years and then to Camrose for high school. Thanks to the principal of the high school, I started with Fish and Wildlife. He called me in and told me I was missing too much school. Asked me where I was at and what I was doing. I said, well, probably hunting and fishing. He suggested to me that I think about doing something with Fish and Game. I had no idea there was such an organization! He gave me the address of E. S. Huestis, the Director of Forestry and Commissioner of Fish and Game. So, I wrote a letter looking for summer employment. I got a job banding geese, in 1951. And then I worked on a duck-banding crew the following summer, in connection with the U.S. Fish and Wildlife Service.

"Then I worked part-time with the Fish and Game Branch for a couple of years. Worked with the first game biologist the province had, George Mitchell, as his assistant for about one year: hunter checking stations, grouse surveys, a bit of big-game work." [Dennis, Bob Webb and Bill Weber ran the first biological check station in Alberta in 1954. This was for the first cow elk season in the Waterton Lakes Park area.]

"We trapped beavers, off and on, for a couple of years: live-trap and winter trapping in complaint areas. Then I applied for a job with the Enforcement Branch, got it, and was stationed at Slave Lake. Actually, the job was with the Fisheries Branch. There was a separate Commercial Fisheries Branch in those days. We had the whole lake to deal with.

"There were mink ranchers those days at Slave Lake: over one hundred. It was a pretty important lake. There were about 25 other lakes that we worked. It was interesting. You were dealing with people who were making their livelihood off of the resource. The other part of the branch dealt with sportsmen: anglers and hunters. I felt I'd sooner do that so I applied for a job in Edson and I got it. Then I was with the Fish and Game Branch. I was at Edson for approximately one year. I was a Fish and Game Officer level one—the first Assistant Officer position offered in the province."

"I went to Peace River in 1955 as a Fish and Game Officer. That was the first district that I was in charge of. I remained in Peace River until 1962 and

transferred to Claresholm. I stayed in Claresholm for five years and then left in 1967 back to Slave Lake. That was a straight transfer. Prior to 1966, they sent out a letter—anyone who was interested in doing a caribou survey in the Eastern Arctic—apply. You were going to be on loan to the Federal Government. They phoned and said: 'can you go in two days?', and two days later, I was in Churchill. I spent six weeks on a caribou survey. However, when I returned, they said: 'What do you think of Slave Lake?' I said, 'You know exactly what I think of Slave Lake.' That's about as low as you could go. They had nothing but trouble in Slave Lake. After Charlie Scott left, no one could really control the lake. So that's where I ended up."

When asked about the problems at Slave Lake, Dennis explained: "There was a great deal of problems between the commercial fishermen and the mink ranchers. The commercial fishermen blamed the mink ranchers for killing the lake by using too small of nets. And, of course, the mink ranchers had to have feed for their mink. As a result, there were a lot of hard feelings between the two factions. They quit allowing

WEIGHING BIG GAME CARCASSES AT A HUNTER CHECK STATION, ENTRANCE, 1962.
CREDIT: J. STELFOX

120

HUNTER CHECK
STATION AND
SIGN, 1958.
COURTESY
B. STEVENSON

121

them to use small mesh gear for mink feed. The mink ranchers were finished.

"Two and a half years later, I moved to Rocky Mountain House. I was there for a year and a half and then transferred to Hinton. We were in Hinton roughly three years. Then in 1974, a Problem Wildlife job came open in Calgary, which sounded interesting, so I applied and got it. We had lots of interesting incidents with bears [see more on the Bear Team in Chapter 5]. We did do quite a lot of ungulate work, too; elk depredation of hay stacks. This kept us pretty busy in the wintertime. We did quite a bit of experimenting with electric fences, and slab fencing, you name it. And we finally ended up using page wire. But it was hard to get money out of the government at that time. They wouldn't spend money on fencing. So, it was pretty tough to deal with the rancher when you didn't have anything to help him with. Eventually they started easing up with the money and we got a lot of fencing done. Just outside of Waterton Park, it's a classic example. All the ranchers down there now have permanent haystack fences to keep the elk out.

"I moved down to Lethbridge and did Problem Wildlife work there as well. That was just a change in location, really, working the same area pretty much. The Problem Wildlife Division was disbanded in 1983. There was a change in leadership. I transferred to Fort Chipewyan, back to Enforcement, as a Fish and Wildlife Officer. I always wanted to go up there. It's

isolated and a different world altogether. I wasn't disappointed. Enjoyed it. Different means of travel. Only had five miles of road, rest was by boat, or skidoo. different kind of work with the trap lines and some commercial fishing."

In 1986, Dennis transferred to Coronation where he remained until his retirement in 1993. "I kind of got back into Problem Wildlife work. There's one Problem Wildlife Specialist for each region. As a result, I did quite a bit of travelling around on the Bear Team. Two of us, who did most of the grizzly work, were both going to retire at the same time: Jan Allen and I. They wanted us to train some younger officers to do the grizzly work when we retired. Every time we had a grizzly incident somewhere, we'd take a couple of officers with us who'd never done it before. I put in a lot of travelling, the last three or four years—right from Grande Prairie to Pincher Creek."

"Jan was doing it as well, but in his absence, I ended going all the way down to Pincher Creek. It was kind of funny, the last bear I worked on, just outside Waterton Park. Two young officers that we had trained showed up there to work on the complaint. Mr. Wellman was the rancher there. He said: 'Where's Jan?' Well, he was on holidays. So he said: 'Where's Weisser?' Well, he's at home in Coronation. 'Well,' he said, 'you guys aren't working on it till you get either one of those guys.' We were very fortunate. We never had anybody get hurt on the crew although I ended up getting charged by a grizzly on a couple occasions."

When asked what the high and low points of his career were, Dennis replied, "I think the Problem Wildlife was the most enjoyable. I had some interesting experiences in Enforcement, as well. Some of the sheep investigations were interesting. There were some low points on the job I think due to management and some of their transfer policies. That was something I strongly disagreed with. They felt that if you liked the area and were getting along well with people, then you weren't doing your job. That was about the fastest way you could get a transfer. I could never really swallow that because, one man, in the district sizes we had, if you weren't getting any cooperation from the public, you may as well pack your tent and leave, because you weren't going to do anything at all. You really had to have the public on your side or you didn't accomplish anything. Enforcement work—all your best cases arise from tips from the public."

Dennis related a humorous event. In Slave Lake, there was a young officer who was quite gruff. He went to Wabasca Lake. The commercial fishermen have to number their nets, but they would get lax about it. This officer started jacking-up the fishermen on the law. When he came next morning to check the nets, all the numbers were very tiny, and on top of 35 foot high poles. No one could read them. The officer really had to work that day.

Dennis related another story. Around the Banff townsite, a grizzly bear had killed one person and hurt two others. The officers went to find the bear. They combed the area but Dennis always felt that this bear really knew what guns were (recognized them) because hard as they looked, the officers just couldn't find this bear. At this same time, some kid from Calgary had stolen a car and driven it to Banff. There was a roadblock just before Banff to warn people about this bear. The kid thought they were looking for him, so he got scared, left the car, and ran into the bush. The bear got him immediately. The kid managed to escape and he ran into two Officers (one was Dennis) who were out looking for the bear. They took him to the hospital. Dennis visited him in the hospital and he told Dennis that next time he'd take his chances with the cops: that the bear didn't have a sense of humour at all!

[Dennis Weisser spent 39.52 years with the Fish and Wildlife Service. They gave him his 40-year pin. This is still a record for Fish and Wildlife Officers.]

Communication, Transportation, and Firearms

Reliable communications are essential for safe, efficient, and effective enforcement. The Fish and Wildlife Division, using the services of Alberta Government Telephones, began to install two-way radios in patrol units in 1974. Prior to that, some officers were able to use radios provided by the Alberta Forest Service and a few utilized their personal citizens' band radios to coordinate special projects in local areas. Officers had to be innovative!

During the late 1970s, base stations were set up in district offices. Some officers maintained radio equipment in their homes, which facilitated operations outside office hours. In the early 1980s, Bob Adams, then Director of Enforcement, together with Lyle Marshall from Alberta Transportation, pushed for a provincial radio system. Their persistence was rewarded in January 1985 when the Multi-Departmental Mobile Radio System (MDMRS) was established. Les Douglas was the first manager with two operators: Tom Stobbs and Eric Newstead. Initially, this radio room worked an eight-hour shift, five days a week. By July 1985, the MDMRS control centre, served by a manager and six operators, functioned 24 hours a day, seven days a week. It was not until 1987 that the necessary switches and repeaters were installed to provide province-wide coverage.

Radio coverage provided security for the officers, who often worked alone and many miles from their district headquarters. It also facilitated communication during multi-officer patrols. Once the necessary security clearances were arranged, radios also provided ready access to motor vehicle information and records maintained by the Canadian Police Information Centre (CPIC), which improved enforcement efficiency markedly. Through time, the system has been enhanced with the addition of portable radios and telephone capabilities.

From the beginning, vehicles were scarce. In the early 1960s, the Division owned a few vehicles for use by officers: Dodge Dart station wagons equipped with a single rotating red light. Most of the officers drove their own private vehicles. Some chuckle as they recall officers well over six-feet tall unfolding themselves from Volkswagen bugs. Others may remember an officer who patrolled his district in a 1967 Mustang. Another drove a Mercedes Benz diesel and often had difficulty finding the appropriate fuel.

In 1969, the division began to procure Ford trucks for field officers. By 1973, the majority of the officers were driving government vehicles. In May 1975, marked units were phased in as the original trucks were replaced. The first of those marked units went to the Claresholm District. Officers there were initially reluctant to operate the unit fearing they would lose the element of surprise. However, the high profile outfit had just the opposite effect the first time it was used to patrol Chain Lakes. Reportedly, a group of anglers, subsequently charged with violations, failed to take any evasive action as the unit approached. They did not recognize the newly issued equipment but were confident it wasn't operated by Fish and Wildlife Officers.

Many will recall those mint green pick-ups with the white doors (affectionately known to staff as the "green and whites"). Some research had been done which suggested pastel colours were more acceptable for enforcement vehicles than the black and whites used by most police forces. Later, patrol boats were painted the same colours. These initiatives contributed significantly to the Division's identity and profile, particularly in rural communities. During the late 1990s, in the interests of economy, most enforcement agencies began utilizing white patrol units. These are in use today with distinctive decals on the doors and light bars on the cabs.

GREEN AND WHITE BOAT USED BY
FISH AND WILDLIFE OFFICERS.
COURTESY ALBERTA FISH AND WILDLIFE DIVISION

123

FIRST OFFICIAL FISH AND WILDLIFE
DIVISION VEHICLE: THE "GREEN AND WHITE".
CREDIT: E. PSIKLA

1960s INNOVATION!

J.D. Fallows spent some time at Grande Cache in the late 1960s. He patrolled that district alone and employed a number of creative practices in an effort to maximize his impact in fostering compliance. One such dodge employed a pen-like pointer, which extended to a length of about twenty-four inches. Fallows would excuse himself from a group of hunters, and discretely drift back some distance. With the appropriate distance between himself and curious ears, he would extend the pointer pen as if it were a radio antenna and make like he was conferring with colleagues. At some point during these simulated conversations, he would withdraw his notebook and make a few notes. He would return to the group after tucking the radio into his pocket. Once back with the others he would report that he had been called away to check some activity up north. Sometimes he pulled a similar stunt to indicate he had direct communication with passing aircraft. When equipment and manpower are scarce, something has to be done to foster at least an illusion that things are under control!

Today, the cost of leasing a single patrol unit for a year (together with all its specialized equipment) is $725/month or $8700/year; that does not include the cost of fuel or day-to-day maintenance. Currently, the Division maintains about 135 equipped units although operational budgets at times restrict officers' activity.

Fish and Wildlife Officers are Peace Officers. As such, the carrying of firearms (sidearms, rifles, and shotguns) while engaged in general duties was routine up until 1973. In that year, Division administrators issued orders for Officers to cease carrying sidearms while performing general duties. The use of other firearms continued.

Subsequently, a number of incidents occurred which demonstrated that in the interest of their personal safety, as well as the safety of those they served, officers required ready access to firearms to conduct their various duties. In 1974, all Fish and Wildlife Officers received formal training in the use of all firearms. By 1980, they were required to meet an annual firearms competency standard. Additionally, officers receive practical training in the appropriate use of force in accordance with an established standard recognized by the judiciary and enforcement agencies across North America. Each year, officers undergo a review of the appropriate use of force and are required to meet an established competency standard.

In 1985, one .357 magnum revolver was added to each of the five Bear Team Response Kits, available for use by Fish and Wildlife Officers responding to maulings and other serious incidents involving dangerous bears. By 1991, revolvers were issued to all field officers but their use was restricted to activities associated with bear control. A year later, the policy was modified to include cougar control. Finally, on March 15, 1995, with the support of then Minister for the Department of Environmental Protection, Ty Lund, policy was amended to authorize the carrying of sidearms for all general duties. So ended a battle that officers had fought for more than 20 years.

Politicians and bureaucrats had resisted the loosening of the sidearm restrictions, fearing a public backlash. Even the Chief of Enforcement and Field Services at the time, Jim Struthers, anticipated some resistance. In a memo to his staff he cautioned:

There is no doubt that during the coming months until the novelty wears off, officers will be asked by citizens or media why they are carrying sidearms. I believe it is in our collective interests to provide a consistent response. To that end, I propose, wherever the question surfaces, the initial response should take the following form: Fish and Wildlife Officers have been carrying sidearms since 1985. Recently, internal policy has been modified to permit the carrying of sidearms for most general duties as a final step in a logical progression that has taken place over the past ten years.

NEW WHITE ENFORCEMENT TRUCKS.
CREDIT: J. STRUTHERS

Ironically, there was hardly a ripple. The *Calgary Herald*, in a colour cartoon on its editorial page dated April 2, 1995, noted: "Fish and Game Officers become more police-like with sidearms." The cartoon showed a wildlife officer pointing a revolver at a fish that was standing on a rock, accusing it of breaking lines and running off with bait amongst other sins. A columnist for the same newspaper produced a diatribe on the new policy which, although intended to convince the world that sidearms were unnecessary for Fish and Wildlife Officers, served better to justify the matter. Otherwise, it was business as usual. In 1998, the revolvers were replaced with .40 calibre Glock pistols.

Report-A-Poacher

In 1974, to aid the Enforcement Branch, the Fish and Wildlife Division formally introduced the Outdoor Observer program. This program was developed in response to the Alberta Fish and Game Association's desire to become more active in aiding the Division in its law enforcement program and to protect the law-abiding sportsmen's interests in hunting and fishing. As well, the Fish and Game Association hoped that such a program would alleviate a perceived lack of field officers to enforce fish and wildlife legislation. The program was similar to a number of Civilian Wildlife Patrol programs popular in several states in the US. It was designed to prevent infractions by increasing hunter knowledge, teaching by example, and after-the-fact reporting of infractions.

Hunters and anglers in particular (but others as well) were encouraged to record relevant information relating to suspected violations of fish and wildlife protection legislation and to pass that information to a Fish and Wildlife Officer in a timely fashion. This program was deemed a preferable alternative, in modern times, to appointing fish and game association members as game guardians.

Until 1983, the Outdoor Observer communication materials existed primarily in kits containing two slide projectors and a series of

slides synchronized with a sound track. Fish and Wildlife Officers were encouraged to seek opportunities to promote the program at community events. Later that year, the presentation was transferred to videotape. In 1984, Lanny McDonald, a prominent national hockey league star from Alberta, was recruited to do a thirty-second television commercial encouraging citizens to report illegal activities, although in that advertisement the program was not named.

In the fall of 1985, the success of Outdoor Observer increased with the addition of a 24-hour telephone number (1-800-642-3800). The responsibility for answering calls went to the MDMRS Control Centre in 1986. Early in 1990, the Outdoor Observer Program became Report-A-Poacher (RAP) and cash rewards brought an increase of information leading to convictions. In 1992, RAP joined with the Rural Crime Watch Program in an effort to increase its visibility. Several communications products including highway signs, baseball caps, coffee mugs, key tags, whistles, licence plates, bumper stickers, static decals, rulers, balloons, pins, litterbags, posters, pencils, telephone stickers, and various brochures were distributed to promote the program.

Combined, these initiatives increased participation in the RAP program and seasonal staff were assigned at the control centre to handle the added pressure during the hunting season. Individuals recruited for these jobs are often students participating in resource management programs with the intention of becoming Fish and Wildlife Officers once their education is completed. In 1991, the RAP line received 5621 calls (then the greatest number to date), which resulted in 1181 charges involving resource-related violations. Often, the recipients of program rewards donate the funds they receive, or a portion thereof, back to the program. The largest amount of rewards, $48,850, was paid out in 2001.

At the outset, RAP was funded by licence fee appropriations, sale of forfeited items, donations, sale of promotional items, and the occasional

125

grant. Since 1997, the Alberta Conservation Association (ACA) has delivered the program. The ACA is a non-profit organization that receives funding through hunting and fishing licence fees to work collaboratively to conserve and enhance Alberta's wildlife, fisheries, and habitat.

Although it is impossible to quantify the deterrent effect of Report-A-Poacher, the program does significantly enhance the efficiency of Fish and Wildlife Officers by providing all Albertans with the opportunity to assist in the detection and apprehension of resource law violators. Despite some cynicism at the outset, the program continues to be one of the most successful of its kind in North America.

Eyes in the Sky

The use of aircraft in wildlife and fisheries enforcement was rather infrequent following the Second World War. By the mid-1960s, the Division issued letters authorizing the use of private aircraft on mileage to Officers Brown, Doonanco, Harle, and McDonald ('Old Mac') who held private pilot licences and either owned or had access to planes. This arrangement allowed these officers to fly on government business and be paid at the same rate they would have been reimbursed had they been operating their private automobiles (14 cents for each of the first 2000 miles and 7 cents per mile thereafter). On rare occasions, other officers with friends or acquaintances having access to aircraft conducted air patrols and, similarly, claimed road mileage to reimburse the pilots.

A few Fish and Wildlife officers used fixed wing aircraft during the antelope hunting season. Planes were equipped with large, soft (marshmallow) tires that enabled landing on prairie grass. Such craft did not require much ground support save for the transportation of large seizures. In the Stettler district, fixed-wing aircraft were used to find goose hunters and direct patrol units to nab those on the wrong side of the regulations.

By the early 1970s, the Division was beginning to use government-owned aircraft on a regular but limited basis. Twin-engine, fixed-wing aircraft were scheduled for night flights to patrol for those hunting unlawfully during the hours of darkness. At night, an airplane was particularly effective in locating vehicle lights in a field. Eventually, techniques were developed to monitor the activities of night hunters from the air and to bring in ground support to apprehend them in an efficient manner, securing the necessary evidence to convict them in subsequent trials. The courts often confiscated equipment, including vehicles, seized as evidence in night hunting cases.

By 1974, the Alberta Forest Service was sharing a portion of its annual allotment of helicopter time with the Fish and Wildlife Division for enforcement work. This time was initially allocated to investigations. Later, hours were routinely scheduled for patrol work associated with hunting activity but sometimes related to angling. Most of this time was in government-owned helicopters although some of it was in privately owned aircraft leased by the government.

EX-OFFICIO ENFORCEMENT OFFICERS

Enforcement Officers not only had to have an understanding of wildlife, they were often called upon to help biologists in their work. In turn, provincial biologists were ex-officio enforcement officers. When asked about his experience in enforcement, biologist Buck Cunningham recalled an incident on Chickadee Creek. "That was the one time I exercised my authority as an Ex-Officio Fisheries Officer. There were a couple of fishermen on Chickadee Creek, which is a little creek kind of northeast of Whitecourt. I just talked to them and asked them if they had had any luck. Oh yeah, yeah. They had this whole big cooler full; I think they had over eighty little Athabasca Rainbow and Arctic Grayling. So I seized the fish and their tackle, wrote them up a receipt on the back of a piece of paper, and turned it all over to Ed Langford in the head office. The one time I exercised my authority. Well, I mean eighty-seven fish out of this creek you could jump across. They cleaned it out for sure for miles literally."

126

LIVE AND LEARN
[ADAPTED FROM JIM STRUTHERS, *LOOKIN' BACK*. THE ALBERTA GAME WARDEN. SUMMER 2004]

Jim Nichols, a Fish and Wildlife Officer stationed at Athabasca in 1971, recalls the first time night hunters were apprehended with the use of an aircraft. Nichols was an observer in a government owned Dornier, a twin-engine plane affectionately called the *Doorknob*, with its motors mounted on stubs affixed to the fuselage below its wings.

During that patrol, Nichols spotted a vehicle operating a spotlight in a field not far from Vegreville. He called in the ground support units and continued to observe the suspect vehicle from a considerable height. At one point, all the lights went out and visual contact was lost. Later, the lights were switched back on and the aircraft followed the vehicle as it was driven from the field. Some distance down the road, one of the ground units met the errant hunters who had a loaded firearm and a freshly dressed deer carcass in their vehicle. They were arrested and the truck together with its contents was placed under seizure.

When these matters came to court, not-guilty pleas were entered on charges of hunting after a half-hour after sunset, hunting with the use of a light, illegal possession of wildlife, and having a loaded firearm in a motor vehicle. At trial, one of the accused testified that the deer had been taken earlier in the day, just after sunset, but during legal hunting time. When that witness was asked what they had been doing in the field with a spotlight, he informed the court they were searching for a hubcap that had fallen off the truck earlier in the day. While this testimony seemed far-fetched, the prosecution was unable to refute it. The charges relating to night hunting were dismissed. The charge respecting the loaded firearm suffered a similar fate. Apparently, several officers handled the rifle; as a result, continuity of the exhibits could not be established. The charge of illegal possession was successful because the deer was not tagged.

When the seized vehicle (which was within a fenced government compound) was checked, it was determined that all four hubcaps were in place. As a result, the dismissal of the night hunting charges was appealed. During a new trial, the individual who had testified respecting the missing hubcap was questioned in this regard. He reported the hubcap had been located after the truck was seized and that they had crawled over the fence of the compound to replace it. That testimony could not be refuted and the original dismissals were supported.

Apparently, the truck under seizure was not the property of the accused. A conviction for night hunting might well have resulted in the forfeiture of the vehicle. Valuable lessons were learned from this incident. For example, had the ground support units returned to the field, a practice that later became routine in such situations, a warm gut pile would likely have been discovered along with other evidence to counter suggestions the occupants of the vehicle had been searching for a missing hubcap. As the use of aircraft for wildlife enforcement became more prevalent, the airborne observers and their ground support developed sophistication and expertise. Routine night flights were judged a significant deterrent.

127

GOVERNMENT OF ALBERTA COURIER FIXED WING AIRCRAFT.
COURTESY PROVINCIAL ARCHIVES OF ALBERTA (PA 2757/2)

Retired officer Murray Bates recalls from the days when he was stationed at Medicine Hat:

In November 1981, we deployed an Alberta Government Jet Ranger helicopter during the prairie deer season. I arranged for a Medicine Hat News *photographer/reporter to accompany us for one day of the season to promote and advertise our new enforcement tool. I hoped for a successful day. The weather was cool and crisp: typical for November. Visibility was unlimited in the clear fall air. Hunters were numerous and widespread along the South Saskatchewan River, our chosen patrol area for the day. The coulees and river breaks held numerous mule deer. The southern and eastern borders of CFB Suffield were covered in a mere two hours at the 120-mile per hour cruising speed of the Bell helicopter. We had a range of two and a half hours plus a thirty-minute reserve. It would have taken two or three days by ground to cover the 300 miles we flew. If the area had been patrolled by truck it would not have included the deep draws and river shoreline that were easily monitored by air. According to my figures, I flew 265 hours, checked 1675 resource users and uncovered 137 violations with helicopters while I was district officer in Medicine Hat.* [23]

Wayne Brown, another retired officer who did his share of air patrols, notes: "The view from a

BIOLOGIST BOB WEBB USING GOVERNMENT AIRCRAFT TO CONDUCT GAME SURVEYS IN 1961.
COURTESY B. STEVENSON

129

helicopter affords an excellent opportunity to inspect the open boxes of pick-up trucks. Occasionally patrolling officers discover pre-season deer [deer taken before the hunting season opens] in the course of other flight duties."[24] Aircraft pilots were skilled and invariably found ways to set their aircraft down close to the hunters being checked despite difficult terrain or tricky winds. In 1994, in an effort to balance budgets and eliminate provincial debt, the fleet (including several fixed-wing aircraft) was sold. Since that time, the use of aircraft for routine fish and wildlife enforcement work has been minimal.

During the time the Fish and Wildlife Division regularly flew routine enforcement patrols, some of the aircraft were

unmarked. Since the hunting and angling public had difficulty determining which aircraft carried Fish and Wildlife Officers on patrol, the presence of unidentifiable aircraft in a given area often served to deter violations. It is unfortunate that fish and wildlife enforcement access to helicopters (and other aircraft) declined for routine enforcement work just as other enforcement agencies (notably police forces in Calgary and

OFFICER USES HELICOPTER TO MONITOR THE ANTELOPE HUNT.
CREDIT: E. PSIKLA

Edmonton) were learning the value of having eyes in the sky and making arrangements to have helicopters assigned for patrol work.

Evolution of Wildlife Forensics

Enforcement officers and biologists often worked hand-in-hand to tackle specific problems and their work combined to create a number of successful programs. Started in the late 1960s, the forensic science program was designed to refine enforcement efforts and big game management with a desire to increase the lawful harvest of female animals. Prior to that time, hunting regulations were designed around the harvest of male animals, almost exclusively.

The strategy to focus management on the total population required a great deal of groundwork and community relations to gain public understanding and support for the change. The concept of "harvestable surplus", for

WILDLIFE BIOLOGIST BILL WISHART WORKING WITH OFFICERS BOB ADAMS AND ERNIE PSIKLA.
COURTESY ALBERTA FISH AND WILDLIFE DIVISION

example, had to be understood and supported by the community. What eventually evolved was a complex licensing and zoning system that went

AIRCRAFT ENFORCEMENT PATROLS: ADAMS' ANGELS
[JOHN GIRVAN]

As more helicopters and airplanes became available, their use in wildlife and fisheries enforcement became more frequent. In 1982, the department looked at using helicopters for extensive enforcement during the hunting season. Volunteer officers were formed into two enforcement teams. One team started in the north and worked the east side of the province to southern Alberta. The other team started in the south and worked up the western side into northern Alberta. Unofficially the teams were called "Adams' Angels" and took to the air in November 1982 for a month-long period. The project was designed to record the number of hunters contacted and checked in each wildlife management unit, all infractions found, and the amount of time each team spent on actual helicopter patrol. The teams worked with the local officers to coordinate the flights in their districts and assist if there were any wildlife seizures resulting from an infraction. This project showed that the helicopter was a useful and effective tool for wildlife enforcement but economics limited its use.

Adams' Angels included Stan Hawes, Egon Larson, Keith Lindemann, Frank Koteles (deceased), Ken Speckeen and John (Scotty) Girvan. Our pilots were Cliff Hendrix (deceased), Gary Flath (Retired) and Roger Tessier. I remember most the camaraderie and friendship that developed within our particular team. Cliff Hendrix became a long-time friend and I flew with him often in later years. He was an interesting man and lived in very interesting times. He regaled us with stories from the Korean and Viet Nam wars. His career as a chopper pilot was quite long as pilots go, but sadly he is no longer with us. He used to say in his broad Wyoming drawl: "There are old pilots and there are bold pilots, but there ain't no old bold pilots." Cliff was a careful pilot and you never felt in danger when he had the stick.

from 20 big game hunting zones to 150 wildlife management units. The new program included gender- and species-specific licences that had to be supervised and enforced by officers. Separate licences were issued for male and female white-tailed deer, male and female mule deer, male and female elk, male and female moose, non-trophy, and trophy mountain sheep, non-trophy and trophy antelope, grizzly bear, black bear, caribou, and cougar.

Prior to the advent of this approach, enforcement of big game season regulations and licensing was relatively simple. Technical and scientific expertise was limited. For example, the R.C.M.P crime laboratory had the capability to determine if meat samples came from the deer family or not. The advent of gender- and species-specific licencing made these services insufficient. In the event of a court trial, enforcement had to be able to identify positively the meat, blood, hair, and bone of every big game animal, and both sexes, that was subject to separate licensing. If the licence was for female mule deer, then establishing at trial that the meat was from the deer family was no longer sufficient. The need for forensics was evident.

Aside from the requirement for gender and species identification, methods were also needed to identify how long meat had been frozen; hybrid specimens; the contents of commercially sold sausage; and the geographic origin of particular specimens. The geographic origin investigation was in response to the illegal taking of trophy mountain sheep—a problem involving non-resident hunters and resident poachers. Quite often, the case began long after the animal was taken. The horns and cape would be found in various places—garages and taxidermy shops in Canada and in the United States, in deep freezes, etc. A method to establish if the bighorn had been taken in a National Park or elsewhere was required.

To start this work, Bill Wishart in the winter of 1973-1974 asked Sandra Drummond and Bob McClymont to develop forensic techniques to identify tissue samples to species. Drummond investigated an immunological test that would be

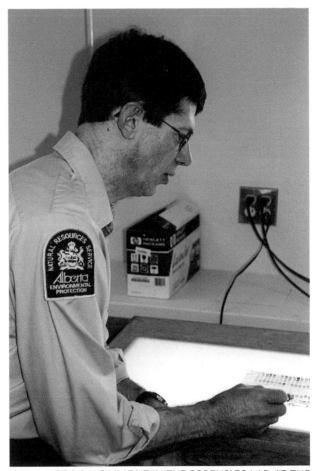

BOB McCLYMONT IN THE FORENSICS LAB AT THE O.S. LONGMAN BUILDING IN EDMONTON.
COURTESY ALBERTA FISH AND WILDLIFE DIVISION

131

more specific than the one being used by the R.C.M.P while McClymont looked into developing an alternate test for species-specific proteins.

At the time, animal taxonomists and geneticists were publishing scientific papers on the use of a technique called electrophoresis. The technique analyzed proteins to help determine differences between species. Various methods of electrophoresis were being employed. Through review of the scientific literature and discussion with other researchers, it appeared that acrylamide gel electrophoresis was the method of choice.

Tissue samples from various species were required for experimental work. At the time, Elk Island National Park was involved in a herd reduction program. Elk, moose, deer, and bison were being shot, processed, and distributed to aboriginal people throughout the province. From this, McClymont collected carcass cooling-rate information to use in making time of death estimates, as well as meat samples from the carcasses processed at the abattoir for use in the electrophoresis work.

At the same time, Dr. Jim Thompson from the Department of Animal Science at the University of Alberta was also collecting meat and fat samples from the Elk Island carcasses for a study he was planning on comparisons of fat composition. Dr. Thompson asked McClymont to continue the work. McClymont agreed and commenced his Master's program in the spring of 1975. His research dealt with comparing the composition of two kinds of fat in deer, moose, and elk and between the two sexes and different-aged animals within each species. The only definitive finding was that elk differed from the other species.

McClymont, along with Terry and Myra Fenton at the University of Alberta, also continued to work on developing an electrophoretic test for identifying different species using proteins. A specialized piece of equipment was designed and the chemistry shop at the University of Alberta was engaged to construct it. This and an improvised cooling system provided everything needed to get underway. The system progressed to where it was clearly possible to discriminate moose from other species.

The first application of these techniques to an enforcement investigation occurred in the fall of 1977. The Fish and Wildlife office in Calgary wanted some meat tested for species identification. Five samples were collected to determine fat composition and for running the electrophoresis. The fat composition indicated clearly that some of the meat was elk and the electrophoresis result showed that the remaining pieces were from moose. The results led to a court date to prosecute the suspects for poaching. A guilty plea was entered prior to the matter going to trial.

The new techniques were also discussed at the first wildlife forensic science symposium, hosted by Alberta Fish and Wildlife Division, in April 1977.

Scientists, wildlife managers, and wildlife enforcement people from all over North America attended. This symposium proved to be of tremendous benefit for networking and the exchange of information among those involved in wildlife enforcement, providing impetus for further development.

McClymont continued work on the electrophoretic test, which advanced to the point where it was possible to identify meat from most of the big game species in Alberta and various species of game birds, fish, and furbearers. Other areas where the lab provided expertise included the identification of bear gall bladders, species origin of hair and bone, age and sex of the animal that body parts came from, the number of animals represented by a collection of body parts, physical matching to see if separate body parts came from the same individual, cause of death, time of death, determination as to whether a wound was ante- or post-mortem, and determination as to whether a wound was caused by a bullet or an arrow.

For a while, Alberta was the only province with a government-run wildlife forensic laboratory. Because of this, other agencies including the provincial wildlife enforcement departments from Ontario, Manitoba, Saskatchewan, British Columbia, Yukon, and Northwest Territories; Parks Canada; Consumer and Corporate Affairs (federal and provincial); R.C.M.P.; municipal police; municipal health; and others sent evidence to the Alberta lab for analysis. As the forensic caseload continued to increase, help was needed. In 1990, Tom Packer was hired to assist McClymont. The province of Quebec subsequently started a wildlife forensic laboratory. Some other provinces make use of university labs for some types of analyses.

Techniques used in the lab continued to evolve and improve. The forensic application of DNA analysis burst onto the scene with a high profile case in the United Kingdom involving the identification of a specific person from analysis of body fluid. Subsequently, the R.C.M.P. developed a system of DNA analysis for application to their

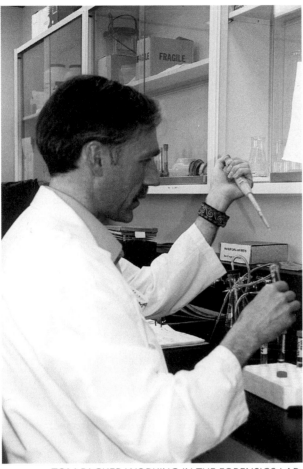

TOM PACKER WORKING IN THE FORENSICS LAB.
CREDIT: B. McCLYMONT

genetics. McClymont was invited to work in Dr. Strobeck's lab to learn such techniques. The initial focus was on applying one technique to examine species differences. Another technique being used could tell, with an extremely high degree of certainty, if two (or more) separate tissue samples came from the same individual. Dr. John Coffin, who oversaw the work in Dr. Strobeck's lab, worked on a number of cases for Alberta Fish and Wildlife using this technique. However, this lab was at the forefront in this type of work and started to get overburdened with cases from agencies throughout Canada and the United States. They advised Fish and Wildlife they would not be able to continue to provide regular service for Alberta wildlife forensic cases. So the Fish and Wildlife Division created a position for a DNA specialist in the forensic laboratory. In 2000, Rick Jobin was hired to fill this position.

Using a variation of the technique used in Dr. Strobeck's lab, Jobin is developing databases for various species for individual differences, gender determination, species differences, and differences between populations of the same species. Population differences are something that could also impact management decisions for game, non-game, and endangered species.

Forensics is a varied and fascinating field of study. The Fish and Wildlife Division has come a long way from the initial scientific laboratory techniques used to assist the enforcement field officers in poaching investigations. Instead of having to catch culprits with the smoking gun,

casework. The suitability of such analysis for wildlife forensics was obvious.

In 1991, Dr. Curtis Strobeck and his graduate students at the University of Alberta were applying DNA analysis to wildlife population

133

BONES AND FORENSICS
[JIM BURNS]

Bone identification with respect to forensic cases was part of Bob McClymont's territory, too. Pretty low-tech stuff. Occasionally, however, a bone retrieved in evidence stumped Bob and he would call on me, an Ice Age Paleontologist at the Royal Alberta Museum, Edmonton, to help out. One such case, about 15 years ago, involved a small, curved, white tooth that a chagrined customer found in food served to her at a local restaurant. The complainant blew the whistle, suggesting that the restaurant was guilty of not maintaining a clean facility and likely had a mouse problem. Bob received the tooth from Public Health and asked me to identify it, if I could. To our surprise, the offending specimen was an incisor of a southeast Asian shrew (genus *Suncus*). The facts of the case ultimately suggested that the tooth had come to Canada in a jar of imported hot pepper sauce! Thus, the restaurateur was exonerated in a twist on the story of the taming of the shrew(ish)!

they can now be caught months after the fact through the use of molecular evidence. Hopefully, the availability of modern forensics will serve as a deterrent to poachers as well as a means of aiding investigations and subsequent prosecutions.

Enforcement Issues Hit the News Stands

For an interesting look at the enforcement issues of today, one need only turn to the latest edition of *The Alberta Game Warden* magazine. This magazine was the brainchild of Guy L'Heureux, an Alberta Fish and Wildlife Officer with a hankering to tell a story. Many officers, past and present, recall with pride the day they first saw the magazine dedicated to them. The first edition, organized in 1987 and 17 pages, featured a number of stories that typify game warden problems everywhere including poaching,

bears, forensics, and enforcement techniques. With the success of the first edition, everyone looked forward to the next. With the help of Dave Hillary, a fellow officer in the Lethbridge district, Guy got busy with it, soliciting stories and photos from one end of the province to the other. Eventually, they gathered enough material (and money) to make the next run. With a little help from fellow officers and a lot of work, Guy and Dave pushed the little magazine along, publishing four more issues, sporadically released whenever they managed to secure the funds and the material to do so. The magazine sold for six dollars per year for four issues with about 600 magazines printed for each issue—all that could be afforded given the fact that advertising sales were minimal.

When Guy left Alberta for a job as a conservation officer in British Columbia, Daniel Boyco replaced him as editor. Boyco put together a dedicated team of officers to assist with regular columns, advertising sales, and circulation management. That first group comprised Glenn Chantal and Ken Speckeen (ad sales), Lyle and Charlotte Lester (circulation), Stan Webb (columnist), and Doug Nichols (illustrator). Boyco told the group that if they did not promote Alberta Fish and Wildlife Officers—their work and the issues important to them—no one would. They knew that Alberta Fish and Wildlife Officers could still drive down Main Street in any large urban centre in marked enforcement vehicles and people would look at them and wonder what they were. They decided that that was a shortcoming, and they would do their best to change it using a consumer magazine as their tool. After all, people were interested in what "game wardens" (Fish and Wildlife Officers) did; they wanted to hear their stories and read about the cases they worked on. They wanted to know about the contentious environmental issues of the day, from the perspective of frontline officers. Given that they were all Fish and Wildlife Officers, they felt they had a corner on the resource enforcement market—and it would sell.

The change from an internal publication to a consumer magazine was a giant step with a learning curve that seemed insurmountable. The group went

PICTURES OF EARLY COVERS OF *THE ALBERTA GAME WARDEN*.
CREDIT: J. STRUTHERS

hunting for writers who brought with them their own particular specialties: John Girvan (columnist and photographer), Miki Mann (columnist and photographer), Bob Machum (columnist), Jim Struthers (columnist), and Wayne Norstrom (columnist). A new feature section, "Head to Head", presented a series of in-depth articles that probed current and contentious conservation issues from stakeholders on all sides of the debate. The magazine crew knew they were treading on thin ice when it came to writing their own opinions on things related to government policy; however, they felt that it was important for them to inform as well as entertain. The strategy was to use the magazine as a forum for these articles and let an informed readership then choose which side they wanted to take. With full support from the membership of the Alberta Fish and Wildlife Officers Association, the group went to work on its first effort—a 40-page magazine that came out in the winter of 1989-1990. An Alberta Fish and Wildlife Officer from Calgary was featured on the cover.

The group secured a booth at the Edmonton Sportsman's Show and, with the help of officers, spouses and friends, sold hundreds of subscriptions, now upped to ten dollars a year. They mailed the magazine to every judge, justice, crown prosecutor, and MLA in the province, free of charge. Some of the recipients didn't appreciate the unsolicited material; however, many of them did.

As word got out about the magazine, subscription numbers began to mount, and the product garnered a loyal readership. With the addition of a number of new writers and a section dedicated to actual case files (*The Notebook*), readers began to write to the editor proclaiming their fascination with the material. There wasn't anything like it on the market, nor was it in direct competition with existing hunting and fishing magazines. It was unique. As the magazine evolved, it took on a different look and was eventually distributed to newsstands.

Fish and Wildlife Enforcement Today

Departmental changes made after the 1997 election resulted in yet another reorganization to a structure where Fish and Wildlife Officers and Park Rangers reported to the same management. In time, a decision was made to combine the two uniformed groups into a single entity. With the stroke of a pen, the *Fish and Wildlife Officers* of the past four decades became *Conservation Officers.* Conservation is a much more encompassing term aptly reflecting the more complex aspects and broad range of duties an officer will encounter. However, the new name did not reflect a long and proud history. Fortunately, following the 2001 election when the Fish and Wildlife Division and the Parks and Protected Areas Division were again reassigned to different departments, steps were taken to once again distinguish the two groups of officers. In 2003, officers in the Fish and Wildlife Division of Sustainable Resource Development became known, again, as Fish and Wildlife Officers; officers in the Parks and Protected Areas Division of Community Development retained the title of Conservation Officer.

Thus, after more than a century of evolution, today's Enforcement-Field Services Branch of the Department of Sustainable Resource Development comprises Field Logistics, Special Investigations and Forensic Services, Legislative and Advisory Services. There are four regions: northeast, northwest, southeast, southwest, ten areas and 60 District Offices. Within these regions reside ten managers and 117 Fish and Wildlife Officers trained to deal with a diversity of complex problems. Challenges facing today's officers are more varied and complex than those faced by the newly named Fish and Wildlife Officers of 1961! However, most of these challenges don't relate to the resource itself. Changes in individuals' rights under the Constitution, aboriginal rights, and laws respecting search and seizure are just a few complexities today's officers must deal with. As well, the increasing amount of access to and use of public lands, the increasing sophistication of violators involved in illegal commerce, and demands in areas of wildlife-human conflict add to the mix,

135

challenging today's officers to continually expand their knowledge, skills, and capabilities.

Today, non-compliance with fisheries and wildlife legislation is generally identified through proactive checking of hunters and fishermen in the field and following up on reports from the public. Site inspections (compliance assessments) are also carried out for commercial fishing operations, fish-processing facilities, commercial operators, and wildlife facilities (for example, zoos, elk farms, etc.). Reports through Report-A-Poacher and agency referrals can initiate investigations. The large number of users checked versus the small number of detected offences shows a high rate of compliance overall (in the range of 95 to 98 percent).

Some things never change, however, and, like Game Guardians earlier in the century, today's Fish and Wildlife Officers continue to lay charges in response to the illegal harvest and possession of fish and wildlife. In 2000-2001, Fish and Wildlife Officers gave 706 written warnings and laid 1957 charges under fisheries legislation; and gave 547 written warnings and laid 1584 charges under wildlife legislation.[25] Fishery charges resulted in 1351 convictions totalling $184,694 in penalties, nine licence suspensions, and three days in jail terms. Wildlife charges resulted in 951 convictions, $275,897 in penalties and 177 licence suspensions.

Today, officers work more closely than ever with resource managers, especially in identifying resource priorities that require the most attention. Officers and resource managers, in turn, work

OFFICERS CHECKING A MOOSE HUNTER.
CREDIT: J. GIRVAN

more closely with communities and, in particular, key stakeholders, to promote mutual understanding of public needs and resource issues. Part of maintaining high standards and traditions is seeking out and employing new techniques and tools. As noted, in the section on forensics where there has been an evolution of tools employed, there is a similar evolution in areas such as special investigations, research into the behaviour of users, and the effectiveness of various compliance assurance strategies (education, prevention and enforcement).

The pride, dedication, and *esprit de corps* among Fish and Wildlife Officers, evident in *The Alberta Game Warden* and other interviews and articles, are manifest over the past century and will continue to be so into the next. While the future of fish and wildlife management, and the enforcement component within it, is not easy to determine, it is apparent that enforcement in Alberta today is in peak form. It is also in good hands! With standards and traditions refined over more than a century, Alberta's force of highly skilled enforcement specialists will no doubt continue to uphold an excellence of service second to none, handed down from one generation to the next and in several

CHIPS OFF THE OLD BLOCKS

As the saying goes, sometimes the apple doesn't fall far from the tree. Today, like their fathers and sometimes grandfathers before them, the sons of several former or serving Fish and Wildlife Officers, are carrying on the proud tradition of serving in the Alberta Fish and Wildlife Division:

Dennis Weisser started out with the Division in the early 1950s (see his interview earlier in this chapter). Son Paul was hired as a junior officer at Strathmore in 1991. He served there until 1998 at which time he transferred to Evansburg, where he is today.

Lew Ramstead started as an Officer for the Division in 1962 at Claresholm. In 1966, he went to High Prairie as the officer-in-charge (today called District Officers), then on to Rocky Mountain House in 1971, to Medicine Hat in 1973, Ponoka in 1975 and Calgary in 1981. Later that year, he was promoted to the position of Regional Officer at Lethbridge. In 1983, Lew accepted a position as an Executive Officer for the Assistant Deputy Minister where he stayed until his retirement in 1993. Lew wasn't the first of the Ramsteads to work with wildlife in Alberta. His father, Gordon Ramstead, was a Summer Ranger with the Forest service at

A CLASS OF YOUNG FISH AND WILDLIFE OFFICERS AT THE HINTON FORESTRY TRAINING SCHOOL, EAGER TO FOLLOW IN THE FOOTSTEPS OF THOSE WHO WENT BEFORE THEM, ca. 1960s.
COURTESY B. STEVENSON.

Drayton Valley from 1934 to 1941. From 1941 until his death in 1949, he was a Forest Ranger at Edson. In those capacities, he did some wildlife enforcement. As well, two of Lew's daughters, Marj and Vivian, worked as stenographers for the Fish and Wildlife Division and the Forest Service. Son Shane assumed duties as a junior officer at Rocky Mountain House in 1983. He served there until 1986 when he transferred to Cold Lake. In 1989, Shane was promoted and transferred to Grande Cache as the officer-in-charge where he is today.

Gary Pollock commenced duties at Lac La Biche in 1962. In 1965, he was promoted to officer-in-charge at Fort McMurray. He transferred to Drumheller in 1969 and then to Bonnyville in 1978. He resigned from the division in 1981 but returned to the outfit in 1985 to work with Conservation Education. In 1990, he got back into uniform at Fort McMurray and in 1991 became the officer-in-charge at Swan Hills where he served until his retirement in 1996. Gary's son, Harvey, assumed duties as a fisheries technician at the Raven Rearing Station in 1980 and worked there until transferring to Cold Lake in 1985 and Calgary in 1989. Harvey returned to Cold Lake as a fisheries technician in 1991 and continues to serve there today.

Ron Hanson commenced his duties with the division in 1964. During three years in Edson, he was promoted and became the officer-in-charge of that district. He also served in Stettler from 1967-1972 and St. Paul from 1972-1974. Ron then specialized in problem wildlife control and worked out of Edson from 1974-1983, at which time he moved to Foremost and assumed district office duties. In 1985, Ron moved to Edmonton to assume various duties in headquarters. He retired as the Chief of Field Services in 1994. Ron's son, Jason Hanson, did some time in the Multi-Departmental Mobile Radio Room Control Centre fielding Report-A-Poacher calls prior to being hired as a junior officer at Barrhead in 1989. Jason was sworn in by his father on November 19, 1989. After three years at Barrhead, Jason went to Camrose, Red Earth, and Wetaskiwin, where he remains the officer-in-charge today. He is also president of the Alberta Game Warden Association.

Jack Morrison joined the Division in 1967 at High Prairie. In 1969, he became the officer-in-charge of the Slave Lake District. He subsequently served in High River, Calgary, and Cochrane, before retiring in 1996. In 1981, Rob Morrison joined his father on the force, serving in Olds until 1983 at which time he transferred to Peace River. From there, he went to Bonnyville in 1986 and Foremost in 1989. Currently, Rob is the District Officer of the Foremost District.

Lyle Lester started as an officer at Lac La Biche in 1988. In 1990, he transferred to Hinton. He was promoted to officer-in-charge at Oyen in 1992. He served there until his transfer to Cardston in 1998. Today, he remains in Cardston. Son Kyle commenced officer duties in Slave Lake District in 2000 and remains there today.

There is also at least one more father-son duo waiting in the wings. Glen Rowan commenced as a Fish and Wildlife Officer at Cold Lake in June 1968. The late C. W. (Chuck) Scott was his supervisor. Glen was posted to Vegreville as officer-in-charge from June 1970 to September 1971, whereupon he was transferred to Grand Prairie. In January 1975, he went to High Prairie and in May that year moved to Peace River as Regional Officer for the Peace River Region. In September 1981, he transferred to Red Deer and became the Regional Superintendent of Enforcement. Reorganization in 1998 resulted in his relocation to Fort McMurray as Area Manager and finally Rocky Mountain House from August 2000 until retirement in June 2001. Glen's son, Cameron, graduated from Lethbridge Community College and completed a practicum in January 2005. He worked summer jobs for Ducks Unlimited and Alberta Conservation Association before working as an Outdoor Skills Instructor at the Alfred Lake Hunter Training Camp in 2001. In 2005, he worked on the Chronic Wasting Disease Border Project and is temporarily located at Lloydminster.

MAJOR EVENTS IN FISH AND WILDLIFE ENFORCEMENT ACTIVITIES IN ALBERTA

1887   The Territorial Government appoints game guardians to enforce game laws.

1892   The first bag limits are established for big game.

1894   Permission is required to hunt on fenced or cultivated lands.

1903   Hunting is prohibited on Sundays.

1906   The first salaried Game Guardian in Alberta, E. Simmers, is hired to patrol Island Park Preserve.

1907   Alberta's first *Game Act* supersedes the 1903 *NWT Game Ordinance*. A resident hunting licence costs $2.50 and reporting hunter success is mandatory.

1909   A Bird Game Licence is required for hunting upland game birds.

1910   Game Guardians are granted authority to arrest game law violators.

1918   Legislation requires hunters to wear white. [This is changed in 1932 to scarlet; and again in 1968 to orange (blaze); then overturned in 1985 and there is currently no specified colour requirement except for the hunt on Camp Wainwright.]

1920   The *Game Act* is amended.

1922   The second *Game Act* of Alberta is passed.

1930   The *Natural Resources Transfer Act* gives the province ownership of its natural resources.

1932   The *Game Act* (1922) is re-written. Cabinet is empowered to make hunting regulations.

1941   The *Game Act* of 1932 is re-written. Loaded firearms in vehicles and shooting of swimming ungulates is prohibited.

1945   A new *Game Act* is passed.

1947   The federal *Migratory Bird Act* and Provincial *Game Act* are amended—shotguns must now be plugged to a maximum of three shells. Metal tags are required on harvested big game.

1950   New three-day angling, game bird, and big game licences are designed to include written notes, especially the number of animals taken. The licence is returned to Division personnel at the end of the season.

1957   The province is divided into ten hunting zones, each with its own seasons and bag limits.

1959   The Fish and Wildlife Division comes into being with Curt P. Smith as its first Director.

1961   Fish and Game Officers officially become Fish and Wildlife Officers. Party hunting is prohibited (each hunter has to fill his own tag) and it is an offence to hunt while under the influence of alcohol or drugs.

1970   Alberta's first *Wildlife Act* is proclaimed.

1980   A hunter test is required to regain suspended hunting privileges.

1984   A revised *Wildlife Act* and regulations are implemented.

1987   A first-time hunter test becomes mandatory. Regulations for the new *Wildlife Act* (1984) are released.

1992   A new *Fisheries (Alberta) Act* passed but not proclaimed.

1993   A Lifetime Wildlife Identification Number (WIN) card is issued to all hunters and anglers.

1994   A new definition for loaded firearm includes live rounds in the magazine.

1995   A 1-900-telephone service is created for draw applications.

1997   The *Fisheries (Alberta) Act* is proclaimed; General Fisheries (Alberta) Regulation is passed; and Fisheries (Ministerial) Regulation is passed.

1998   Recreational licence sales are privatized and automated. All hunting licences now expire on March 31 following their date of issue.

139

MAJOR EVENTS IN FISH AND WILDLIFE ENFORCEMENT ACTIVITIES IN ALBERTA CONTINUED

2002　Crossbows are removed from the list of weapons prohibited for hunting big game. Use of crossbows is restricted to physically challenged persons (under licence) during archery-only big game seasons.

2003　Penalties in the *Wildlife Act* are increased markedly. Case length is no longer a criterion to determine legal cartridges for hunting big game. Youths are allowed as hunting partners for all special big game licences held by adults.

2004　An interim harvesting agreement is signed with Métis groups to allow similar harvesting rights as First Nations throughout Alberta.

References • CHAPTER 4

[1] Northwest Territories. Council Journals. September 9, 1883 and October 4, 1883.

[2] Fish and Wildlife Division records, April 2005. Edmonton.

[3] Alberta Department of Agriculture. 1906. Annual Report. Edmonton. This includes the report of the Chief Game Guardian.

[4] Alberta Department of Agriculture. 1911. Annual Report. Edmonton.

[5] Provision for the North West Mounted Police (after 1920, the Royal Canadian Mounted Police) to act as ex-officio game guardians was made in all subsequent Game Acts.

[6] Struthers, J.B. 1994. Lookin' Back. Alberta Game Warden. Summer 1994:2.

[7] Government of Alberta. 1969. Alberta Lands-Forests-Parks-Wildlife. Summer 1969. Vol. 12(2): 6-7.

[8] Stelfox, John (ed.). 1972. Rambling Thoughts of a Wandering Fellow, 1903-1968. IDB Press, Edmonton, Alberta.

[9] Ibid. pg. 18

[10] Ibid. p. viii.

[11] Holmgren, Eric. 1986. Fish and Wildlife Management in Alberta: A History. Alberta Fish and Wildlife Division, Edmonton, Alberta.

[12] This is also recorded in Prairie Grass to Mountain Pass: a History of Pincher Creek and District. Pincher Creek Historical Society, Pincher Creek.

[13] Adapted from Jim Struthers, Lookin' Back, Alberta Game Warden, Spring 1992. Originally from a story told to Glen Rowan, Superintendent at Red Deer, by an old gentleman at the Legion.

[14] Department of Mines and Minerals. Annual Reports of the early 1930s. Edmonton.

[15] This changed to Fish and Wildlife Officer in 1961 after the Division changed from Fish and Game to Fish and Wildlife in 1959. However, Game Officer, Wildlife Officer, and sometimes even Fish Cop or Game Warden, are often used interchangeably, depending on who's telling the story!

[16] Holmgren, Eric. 1986. August 27 1985 interview with Charles Dougherty at Lethbridge *in* Fish and Wildlife Management in Alberta: A History. Alberta Fish and Wildlife Division, Edmonton, Alberta.

[17] Information was obtained from the carbon copies of several reports filed by T.A. Boag to then Game Commissioner W.H. Wallace, in the Department of Agriculture. These copies were loaned to the project by Dr. Dave Boag, former Professor of Ornithology, University of Alberta, and currently retired and living in British Columbia.

[18] Holmgren, Eric. 1986. Fish and Wildlife Management in Alberta: A History. Alberta Fish and Wildlife Division, Edmonton, Alberta

[19] Ibid.

[20] Struthers, Jim. 1996. *The "Rocky" Story—A Man of Vision*. Alberta Game Warden, Winter 1996.

[21] Adams, Robert. 1999. Fish Cop. Megamy Publishing, Spruce Grove, Alberta.

[22] Read more about problem furbearer and predator management in Chapter 5.

[23] Bates, Murray. 2002. Game Warden. Murray E. Bates Publishing Company, Sundre, Alberta.

[24] Brown, Wayne. 2004. Personal communication with J.B. Struthers.

[25] Alberta Environment. 2002. Compliance Assessment and Enforcement Activities: Annual Report April 1, 2000 – March 31, 2001. Edmonton, Alberta.

Chapter 5

FURBEARERS:
TRAPPING, FUR FARMS, AND PROBLEM WILDLIFE

Margo Pybus with contributions from
John Bourne, Randy Flath, Michelle Hiltz, Floyd Kunnas,
Fred Neuman, Blair Rippin and Francine Wieliczko

141

There were marten and mink to be trapped in the winter, an occasional fisher,
and muskrats were plentiful. Lynx and foxes but no beaver…Beavers had been
over-trapped as the demand for their pelts by the Hudson's Bay Company
hunters made no provision for their natural increase.[1]

PETER ERASMUS COMMENTING ON THE BEAVER HILLS, NEAR EDMONTON

Furbearers in the 20th Century

The numerous and valuable pelts of beaver, fox, wolf, and other furbearers are what first attracted European exploration into Alberta. Yet by the time this area was named a province in 1905, the once great fur trade, started two centuries earlier, was all but over. Beaver were scarce over large tracts of previously occupied range. While many fur-trading posts continued to operate for some time (Dunvegan closed in 1918 and parts of the post at Fort Chipewyan were in use until 1964), it was never again at the fever pitch seen previously.

Regardless, wild furs continued to provide economic activity in many parts of Canada well into the 20th century. The viability of furbearer populations was an important concern for early provincial wildlife managers whether they were monitoring the fur harvest (trapping) industry, supporting the new industry of domestic fur farming, or managing problem species that came into conflict with human activities.

The Registered Trapline System

Early territorial legislation provided initial game laws to regulate the harvest of furbearers and avoid harvest when pelts were not prime. The *1883 Territorial Ordinance for the Protection of Game* set a closed season on "hare" between the first day of February and the first day of September in any year; on mink and marten between the fifteenth day of April and the first day of November; on otter, beaver, and fisher between the first of May and the first of October; and on muskrat between

142

CASH FOR FURS: FUR TRADERS LOADED UP AND READY TO HEAD NORTH FOR THE SEASON.
COURTESY PROVINCIAL ARCHIVES OF ALBERTA (B5703)

the fifteenth of May and the first of November. The province's first *Game Act* (1907) held similar provisions with the exception that beaver were fully protected under a five-year moratorium on any harvest (which was extended repeatedly).

Aside from these restrictions, it appears that little thought was given to the trapping industry in Alberta during the first two decades of the century. The next attempt at any regulation occurred in

1920, when the *Game Act* was amended to require that all fur dealers, buyers, and exporters purchase licences before trafficking in the pelts of wild animals. Reports and returns were also required from trappers. The information from these

A TRAVELLING FUR BUYER ASSESSING RAW FURS AT FORT McKAY, 1919.
COURTESY UNIVERSITY OF ALBERTA ARCHIVES (77-84)

documents helped fur managers from the Game Branch of the Department of Agriculture set seasons, quotas, and furbearer policies. By this time, managers and trappers had realized that furbearers needed proper management to ensure their continued harvest. Trapping was prohibited when pelts were valueless on the market, thereby leaving animals to breed in future years. To support fur management, a fur tax was imposed on any pelt or fur exported from Alberta, and by 1928, a Fur Marketing Service facilitated the industry.

Issues at this time included the number of furbearing animals being harvested, the trapping practices in use, and the scarcity of furbearers in some areas. Trapping areas were not designated and since many resident and non-resident trappers came and went, trapping became indiscriminate. In some areas, furbearers were depleted and in some cases, unqualified trappers set, but failed to pick up, their snares, thus wasting valuable fur. The system was too competitive with no emphasis on conservation of the resource. As early as 1929, the idea of establishing registered traplines began to take hold.

As a conservation measure, a large portion of the furbearer areas of Alberta was organized into a system of assigned registered traplines and trapping areas in 1938-1939. A similar system of registration in the federal forest reserves was proving beneficial for conservation as well as for fire protection. At first, the major furbearer area in the far north (north of the 25th baseline) was organized into a registered trapping system on a trial basis. This was soon extended in 1941 to include all crown lands north of the Brazeau and the North Saskatchewan rivers (north of the 14th baseline). Under the guidance and direction of Fish and Game Commissioner, Eric Huestis, and Superintendent of Game, Don Forsland, province-wide registration of traplines and areas began in 1942 and was completed by the end of 1944. The number of registered traplines peaked in 1946-1947 at 3023.

The registered trapline system allowed a licensee exclusive trapping right to his assigned territory. The trapper, in consultation with Fish and Game officials, selected the line. It was his responsibility to trap it and also to maintain it. Registered traplines were held for life and usually changed hands only on the death of the holder or through inheritance. If a holder for any reason gave up his line, it was reallocated by a draw. Registered owners, realizing that maintenance of a good trapline meant a healthy return in furs, made a conscientious effort to conserve furs and forested lands: the latter by reporting fires. Fewer uncontrolled fires meant more furbearers. Lightning fires continued to be a threat, but were often detected more quickly.[2] As well, trappers made every effort to take only prime furs. The

143

POPLAR POINT PATROL
[ADAPTED FROM J.B. STRUTHERS, *LOOKIN' BACK*, THE ALBERTA GAME WARDEN, SUMMER 1995[3]]

Prior to the registration of traplines, there were many disputes over whose trapline was whose. In an Alberta Provincial Police Crime Report of October 20-24, 1924, Corporal J.G. McDonald reported: "I left McMurray on patrol to Poplar Point to investigate the complaint received from the above named Harry G. Covey. I arrived at this man's shack at Poplar Point on the morning of the 16th. I interviewed Harry Covey regarding his complaint and then proceeded to the shack occupied by the man complained about, Amos C. Lindsay, which is situated about one mile further on."

"Upon hearing the grievances of both these men, I came to the conclusion that it was a case of dog eat dog over a piece of trapping ground which one man had as much right to trap on as the other. I then brought these men together and gave them fifteen minutes to decide the halving up of the trapping ground in dispute...I left them on friendly terms with themselves."

itinerant trappers, previously the scourge of traplines and forests alike, suddenly found themselves without any source of furs. Eventually, they disappeared.

The registration system served furbearers and fur managers well and continues today. Currently, registered trapline licences are issued on a five-year basis, with annual renewal. While trappers often retain their licences for many years, licences can be relinquished to someone of the trapper's choice. Partners often take over a trapping area.

Fluctuating Furbearer Populations

Like many wildlife species, furbearer populations fluctuate from time to time. In 1942-1943, registered traplines were doing well with a steady increase in registrations. Hares and squirrels made up 49% and 42%, respectively, of the nearly 12 million pelts sold that year. Market demand was

driven in part by the influx of women into the work force during the Second World War. These women had cash to spare and could finally buy that fur coat they always wanted! The following year, furbearers continued to do well, although the quantity of fur trapped decreased, in part due to reduced effort. The manpower required just wasn't available as many men had gone to war.

It was then well known (but poorly understood) that snowshoe hare numbers peaked about every ten years. During such a peak in the early 1940s, Fish and Game Commissioner Eric Huestis noted: "You could go out into a field with a .22…and keep on shooting…and never run out of rabbits."[4] Because of the war, rabbit fur was unavailable from Europe or Australia, but was in high demand in New York for men's felt hats. Alberta trappers filled the gap with six million hare hides in one year! William Rowan and a bus load of students from the University of Alberta estimated 32,000 hares per sq. mi. in an area north of Edmonton.[5] This estimate was questioned by others but was confirmed two weeks later by another researcher from Rowan's department. During the same period, hares wreaked havoc on forestry seedlings planted in the Cooking Lake Forest Reserve.

In the mid-1940s, and in the years following the war, the Fish and Game Branch worked in cooperation with the federal wildlife authority (a forerunner of the Canadian Wildlife Service) on the problems of snowshoe hare fluctuations.

A LADY MODELLING A FUR COAT.
COURTESY PROVINCIAL ARCHIVES OF ALBERTA (PA1566/1)

A SNOWSHOE HARE.
CREDIT: L. KEITH; COURTESY: B. WISHART

When hares were scarce, lynx and other predators turned to other furbearers, with serious results for trappers. The object was to determine the cause of these cycles. In those days, disease was considered an important factor.[6]

Though not synchronous, fluctuations also occur in beaver populations. Prized for their luxurious pelt for more than 400 years, beaver are unquestionably the most commercially important furbearer. Beaver graced Canada's first postage stamp, in recognition of the pivotal role the species played in developing the nation. Yet beaver have not always fared well in Alberta. Trapping, in concert with natural changes on the landscape, resulted in enough concern that beaver came under legislative protection as early as 1883 when the *Ordinance for the Protection of Game* placed the first closed season on beaver (the season was closed between May 1 and October 1). By 1907, the Alberta *Game Act* placed a five-year moratorium on any beaver harvest ("No person shall hunt, trap, take, shoot at, wound or kill…any beaver at any time before the thirty-first day of December, 1912.").

145

DAMAGE FROM SNOWSHOE HARES TO THREE-YEAR OLD PINE IN THE FORT McMURRAY DISTRICT IN 1961.
COURTESY ALBERTA FISH AND WILDLIFE DIVISION

WILDLIFE POPULATION CYCLES
Peter Fidler, who travelled throughout Alberta, was the first to document the evidence of synchronous eight-to-ten-year cycles in snowshoe hare and lynx. These cycles fascinated conservationists, managers, and researchers alike for generations, including prominent Albertans Henry Stelfox, Professor William Rowan, Lloyd Keith, and a number of wildlife biologists.[7]

In 1913, short open seasons were used where northern beaver populations had recovered sufficiently or where they were causing flood damage. In 1918, regulations were amended to allow trapping of those beavers that were a nuisance to farmers in southern Alberta. A permit was granted if proven damage existed. Skins were obtained and sold by tender by the Province with returns of 75% to the owner and 25% to the government.

After the drought years of the 1930s, beaver were again scarce in some areas and were again protected by a closed season. About the same time, individuals like the infamous Grey Owl promoted the idea of beaver reintroduction programs. While this idea never gained much support in Alberta, there was a shift in thinking in the war against beaver. In some locations, nuisance beaver were now live-trapped and relocated, rather than killed.

BLOWING A BEAVER DAM NEAR EDSON, 1957.
COURTESY ALBERTA SUSTAINABLE RESOURCE DEVELOPMENT
(ALBERTA FOREST PROTECTION CATALOGUE)

During the 1950s, beaver numbers were considerably higher, but as pelt prices declined, trapping was not economical. Interest in trapping beaver and muskrat on farmlands waned but something still had to be done where flooding was a problem. J.B. Stewart, a Second World War veteran and explosives expert, became the first provincial problem beaver control officer responsible for removing beaver dams. This work was greatly enhanced in 1960 with the addition of two full-time staff and a limited number of expert trappers hired to help District Fish and Game Officers remove unwanted beaver.

In time, improvements in beaver management were made. In the mid-1960s, Fred Conibear, a trapper from Fort Smith, NWT designed a trap (now bearing his name) that was more humane than previous traps. The Conibear trap reduced the number of crippling losses and could be used more selectively to catch older beaver. In addition, repellents for nuisance beaver were tested and later, perforated culverts were developed to prevent some of the flooding problems. These options reduced the need to completely remove beavers from some areas.

By 1977, a comprehensive joint Beaver Flood Control Program was developed by the Fish and Wildlife Division, Alberta Agriculture Service Board, municipalities, counties, and improvement districts. The Division managed the complaints, authorized the removal of beaver and their dams, and hired and trained dam blasters. The trapper/blaster worked for the municipalities and responded to beaver problems along road allowances and on private lands. Most municipalities with significant numbers of beaver

GREY OWL

After the dry years of the 1930s, there was movement afoot to reintroduce beaver into areas where they could play a role in watershed retention. Leading this effort was the infamous Grey Owl—an Englishman (Archibald Belaney) who successfully passed himself off as native. Operating out of Prince Albert National Park in Saskatchewan, Grey Owl corresponded extensively with other beaver enthusiasts, including A. Norquay (Dominion Lands Agent in Edmonton) and J. Dewey Soper (federal Migratory Bird Officer) who also appeared to have been sympathetic towards the beaver's plight. Soper wrote:

"Protection of the beaver in Alberta has not had the consideration and support that the importance of the matter demands. There are several very cogent reasons why this should be done, possibly the greatest through the necessities of these small animals for an ample supply of water, and their ability to create their own swimming pools..."[8]

CONIBEAR TRAP

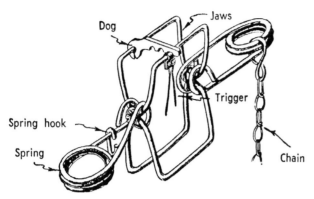

DIAGRAM OF A CONIBEAR TRAP.
COURTESY ALBERTA FISH AND WILDLIFE DIVISION

complaints participated in the program. The Agriculture Service Board Grants provided 60% of the funding; the municipalities provided 40%.

As costs escalated and provincial support eroded, participation declined until the program ceased to exist in the late 1990s.

Today, while the stylish beaver hats of the past have all but faded from fashion, the status of beavers in Alberta is secure. Good to high populations occur throughout most of the province.[9] As well, the beaver is recognized and appreciated as an important component in water management and wetland habitat retention.

A Fur Coordinator for Alberta

The early 1970s were heady years for the Fish and Wildlife Division. The economy was good and interest in fur management and support of the fur industry was high. Responding to this interest, the Division created a Fur Coordinator position in

147

DAVE UNGER, TRAPPER AND FUR MANAGER EXTRAORDINAIRE
[FLOYD KUNNAS]

Dave Unger had an interest in trapping all his life. As a Fish and Wildlife Officer stationed in Lac La Biche in the 1960s, he spent a great many days on the trapline with many of the trappers in his area. Later, as Fur Coordinator, it was an ideal relationship between Unger and the Fish and Wildlife Division. The job fit into his personal interests perfectly: he had a budget of sorts, and there was no job description. He used flexibility to get the job done. Trappers were touched by the efforts of the first Fur Coordinator and it brought this unique client group into closer contact with far-off Edmonton. If you can't get the trapper to come to you, then you go to the trapper.

In the early 1970s, the Canadian Association of Humane Trapping started a trap exchange program across the country. Unger was the first officer to carry out the program in Alberta. A trapper could bring in a steel-jawed leg-hold trap (judged to be inhumane) and exchange it for a comparable approved Conibear trap. The program was so successful that Unger was seconded to establish a similar program in the Northwest Territories. He also travelled extensively over the western arctic setting up trapper education classes in remote communities. With his ears tuned to what trappers had to say, Dave could teach and learn at the same time. His approach simply made sense—to him and to trappers. He also worked with the Ontario Trappers Association and the U.S. National Trappers Association to keep abreast of changes. In the early 1980s, Dave left government and took a position with the Edmonton Fur Auction.

Gordon Kerr recalls: "Humane trapping was a serious issue as it impacted the fur industry which was of greater dollar value than was the commercial fishery. Dave Unger was instrumental in bringing humane trapping into practice through organizing trappers and holding trapper education workshops. He also played a pivotal role in shifting trapping seasons to better produce prime fur (versus fur of low quality) and to ensure quality handling of the pelts."

The stories and antics of Unger are widespread and endless. However, the impressions he left on northern trappers in Alberta, Saskatchewan, Manitoba, Yukon, and Northwest Territories linger to this day. The legacy of his efforts is, in part, the reason why trapping still thrives in these areas. For his efforts, Unger was made a lifelong member of the trappers' associations in Alberta, Saskatchewan and Manitoba.

1973 to provide instruction on humane trapping and proper fur handling. Fish and Wildlife Officer Dave Unger, Lac La Biche District, had the skills and connections, and became the province's first Fur Coordinator. His role was not well defined, which fit in well with the way Dave operated: after all, trappers don't punch time clocks!

About the same time, various trapper organizations in the province were discussing the possibility of combining under one roof. In the words of Rance Curtis: "If we don't hang together, we are going to hang separately."[10] It would take someone with a persuasive personality and common bond with trappers to draw independent-minded trappers together. Building on his previous contacts with trappers

in the Lac La Biche area, and the considerable efforts of strong leadership in existing local trapper groups, Unger was able to knit together the disparate interests and personalities into one large group, the Alberta Trappers' Central Association. The name later changed to the Alberta Trappers' Association (ATA) and in 1998, the ATA celebrated "25 years of cooperation among people responsible for the continuation of the only true practice of sustainable development in North America".[11] The new organization provided the trappers of Alberta with one strong voice to talk to Government regarding their concerns and also allowed fur managers to consult with this one group on matters dealing with trapping. Emphasis was on liaison with local groups, instruction on humane trapping methods, and proper fur handling.

AMALGAMATION OF THE FUR TRAPPERS' ASSOCIATIONS
[ADAPTED FROM SUMMARIES BY DEWEY MILLER[12] AND AUGUST PETERS[13]]

Prior to 1945, trappers perceived a lack of government interest in trappers and furbearer management. Diminished budgets and a lack of staff resulted in what appeared to be arbitrary trapping seasons that bore little relationship to differing ecosystems throughout the province, constant quarrels over trapline boundaries, and failure to provide sustainable furbearer harvest.

Eric Huestis, Commissioner of Fish and Game, enlisted the help of the trappers to bring some organization to fur management. The Edson Registered Trappers' Association was born in 1945, with Dewey Miller as the first President and Norman Willmore (then a Member of the Legislative Assembly, for the area) as voluntary Secretary-Treasurer. Eighty-nine members signed up. In 1946, the Peace River Trappers' Association formed and included several locals in northwest Alberta. In 1947, eleven local associations, including Edson, Peace River, Athabasca, and Lac La Biche, formed the Alberta Registered Trappers' Central Association, led by August Peters. The Central Association had a good cross-section of trappers and worked closely with the Game Branch in Edmonton to make recommendations regarding regulations and administration of the fur harvest.

As disputes and concerns were addressed through the 1950s, interest in the trappers' association waned. By the 1960s, only four locals remained in the fold. However, renewed interest in humane trapping, a growing anti-trapping lobby across North America, and issues regarding proposed gun control in the mid-1960s, generated new concerns and a desire yet again to have a strong voice for trappers in Alberta. The Alberta Trappers' Association, led by Ken Pratt, was created in southern Alberta, with membership largely from resident trappers. The Kanata Trappers' Association, led by Ken Belcourt, was formed as a united voice for First Nations trappers.

In October 1973, the Central, Kanata, and Alberta trappers' associations agreed to amalgamate into one strong central force under the name of the Alberta Trappers' Central Association, later to become the Alberta Trappers' Association. The group held their first annual convention in Whitecourt in June 1974. Finally, provincial trappers were represented by a single rapidly growing organization devoted to improving the image of the trapper and the conservation of Alberta's furbearing animals by selective and humane trapping techniques.

With one voice established for trappers throughout the province, Unger and a new fur biologist, Arlen Todd, began to meet with trapper groups to improve wild fur management. Alberta led the way in trapper education in the mid-1970s. With full support from the Alberta Vocational Centre (AVC) at Lac La Biche, a three-week trapper instructors' course was held in 1976. This was a precedent-setting event as the first ever such course in North America. Ralph Bice (a long-time trapper instructor from Ontario), Gerald Plamondon (a local trapper with many years' experience) and Dave Unger were instructors. Twenty trappers from different parts of Alberta attended the course which covered all aspects of trapping including humane trapping techniques, pelt preparation, equipment repair and maintenance, fur marketing, and legal issues.

In conjunction with the trapper instructors' course, AVC and Fred Neuman of the Fish and

TRAPPER EDUCATION COURSE, FORT McMURRAY, 1998.
COURTESY ALBERTA TRAPPERS' ASSOCIATION

Wildlife Division developed a Standardized Basic Trapping Course in 1981. In 1983, AVC hired Emiel Robertson to provide a comprehensive Trapper Education Manual in cooperation with the Division. The manual consolidated trapping information for the basic and instructors' courses, and provided a standardized approach to course content. It became the model for manuals to guide trapper education courses across Canada and parts of the U.S. To reach a broader audience, it was translated into Cree. This course has been the focus of trapper education for the last 20 years, with over 5000 participants in Alberta. In conjunction with specialized workshops, it continues to provide ongoing trapper education.

The basic course was enhanced in 1990 when it became mandatory for all first-time trapper licence holders to either receive instruction or write an exam prior to setting their first trap. At this time, Emiel Robertson, Don Currie, and Fred Neuman developed the *Wild Fur Study Guide* to facilitate the exam. The guide was developed from funds ($25,000) originating from the Humane Trapping Trust Fund.

Markets and Management

By the early 1950s, declining fur prices, generally improved economic conditions, and opportunities in forestry and petroleum provided the stimulus for many trappers to leave their traplines to try other occupations. Interest in trapping beaver and

ALBERTA TRAPPING GUIDE

ᐊ�̇ᐳᔾᐨᒋ ᑊᖅᐡᐊᐟᐊᐤᐟᐦᖅ

ᒍᒥᖿᐟᔥᐊᐧ ᐡᐢᐤᐦᔥᐤᐟᖸᐢ

Alberta
RECREATION, PARKS
AND WILDLIFE
FISH AND WILDLIFE DIVISION

ALBERTA TRAPPING GUIDE.
COURTESY ALBERTA FISH AND WILDLIFE DIVISION

149

INSTRUCTORS JOHN ROSS AND DON CURRIE LEADING A TRAPPING COURSE.
COURTESY B. STEVENSON

150

Frankfurt, and other European cities to try to stimulate more interest in Canadian products. As well, trapping seasons were adjusted to assure pelt quality and prevent off-prime pelts from depressing the market.

Overall, the combined total number of Alberta pelts of all species sold into the fur industry increased 20-fold from 1920-1921 to 1941-1942 and then declined by the same magnitude by 1977-1978.[14] Markets continued to fluctuate, reaching an all-time provincial high of $15 million in 1979-1980. The general trend was towards increased value for fewer pelts. This reflected a shift from large-quantity, low-value species such as red squirrels and hares, to less numerous but more valuable species such as coyote, lynx, and beaver.

muskrats on farmlands also waned and programs to stimulate trapping interest in farm youths were largely unsuccessful. Still, trapping remained a viable industry and, in 1960-1961, Alberta exhibited wild furs at World Trade Fairs in Paris, London,

GERRY WILDE, TRAPPER AND EDUCATOR

In the mid-1980s, there was growing demand among western Canadian fur managers to develop and promote a uniform program which stressed humane trapping, fur handling, and fur-management concepts. Because of Alberta's active trapper education program, the Fur Institute of Canada (FIC) selected Gerry Wilde, a wildlife instructor at the Hinton Forestry Training School, to consult with native and non-native trapping groups and develop a standardized trapping course with curriculum suitable for use across Canada. With Wilde's driving energy, and support from the forestry school, three national courses for trappers from across Canada were conducted in Hinton in 1986-1987. Additional courses came later.

The Northlands School Division held three trapping programs for students with academic learning disabilities. The Fur Institute saw this as an opportunity to introduce trapping education into formal school programs and contracted Wilde to develop the course content. Although he completed a draft of a curriculum, his waning health hampered further work on the project and the initiative died.

Gerry Wilde was a tireless advocate of trapping and responsible stewardship of the land. He spent many long hours in wild country and was an astute observer of all things natural. Whenever he had access to books or knowledge, Gerry constantly sought answers to explain what he had seen in the bush. He willingly passed this knowledge and enthusiasm on to countless students who attended the forestry training school and anyone else who took the time to listen and learn.

Management efforts focussed on improving the sustainability of desired species. When market prices were low, trappers voluntarily took fewer animals to conserve the resource for another day; besides, there was limited return for a lot of hard work. When prices were high, quotas were kept low to protect the resource from overharvest. By 1980, long-haired fashions were in style and even coyotes became valuable and consequently required monitoring. In 1983, lynx also required special management as pelt prices were high and trapping pressure was intense in some areas.

GAME OFFICER ED LANGFORD AT A FUR DISPLAY AT FORESTRY WEEK EXPO, EDMONTON, 1959.
COURTESY ALBERTA SUSTAINABLE RESOURCE DEVELOPMENT (ALBERTA FOREST PROTECTION CATALOGUE)

151

In the late 1970s and 1980s, attempts were made to get an overview of trapping efforts in the province. Province-wide trapper questionnaires, now conducted for about ten years, were summarized. A major report, *Fur: Major Review of Alberta Fur Production from 1920-21 to 1977-78*, summarized historical perspectives, trapper numbers, fur harvests, average pelt prices, and harvest regulations. A zoning system for the harvest of fur was introduced in the 1979 Trapping Regulations. Zones were based on the distribution and relative abundance of the fur-bearing species so that the fur resource was more effectively managed. Otter and wolverine quotas were established because of population declines.

A concerted effort to find and validate humane trapping devices began in 1981. The Wildlife Branch provided the initial financial support for the Federal-Provincial Committee for Humane Trapping to create a major installation and trap-testing program at the Alberta Environmental Centre in Vegreville. This was formalized in 1985 with a renewed commitment between the province and the national Fur Institute. Morley Barrett was instrumental in making the facility and its programs operational. Similarly, Gilbert Proulx was the principal researcher who established the approach and the credibility of the centre's research. In 1989, the program was realigned under the administrative direction of the Alberta Research Council in Edmonton (although the operational component remained in Vegreville), with Proulx as the primary administrator and researcher. This changed yet again when administration moved back to Vegreville in 1993, with Larry Roy heading up the humane trap programs.

Occasionally, completely external factors drive the markets. Early in 1987, the fur harvest was relatively high and generated $7.4 million. Beaver, coyote, marten, muskrat, and squirrel production rose substantially with fur prices rising for all except squirrel. High returns were available for marten (sable), fisher, and lynx pelts. But markets quickly fell to $2.3 million following the stockmarket crash in October 1987. This was the greatest single-year decline since 1940 and muskrat, beaver, fox, coyote, mink, and marten harvests each declined in the range of 50%-70%. Money was scarce and fur markets bottomed out. World fur prices (especially long-hair furs) fell 20%-40%, the number of trappers decreased 30%, and unusually heavy snow conditions early in the season restricted access to traplines. There was also a limited quota on valuable species such as lynx and fisher.

In 1989-1990, quotas on the number of lynx and fisher that could be trapped were increased, but registration was required. Throughout the 1990s, registration programs for lynx, fisher, and wolverine provided a sound basis for setting quotas. Markets continued to fluctuate but remained at the $2-3 million range throughout

the decade. Today, furbearer markets continue to have their ups and downs.

The Trapper Compensation Review Board

In the latter part of 1980, Bud Miller, the Minister responsible for Fish and Wildlife, created a Trapper Compensation Review Board to oversee payments to trappers where fur harvests were negatively affected by industrial activity. Board members were to arbitrate disputes between registered trappers and the conventional oil and gas industry in Alberta. The Board was initially made up of one representative from the ATA (August Peters), one from the oil industry (Lorne Grimson), and one member representing the public at large (Dave Unger). Unger, the general manager of Edmonton Fur Auctions in Edmonton at the time, chaired the Board and was in charge of developing the program. The board later

152

THE TESTING AND ADVANCEMENT OF HUMANE TRAPPING METHODS
[MICHELLE HILTZ]

Trapping techniques evolved throughout the century and Alberta was, and is, a national leader in developing humane trapping methods. In 1981, the Federal-Provincial Committee for Humane Trapping received $25,700 from the Wildlife Management Branch to develop humane traps and trapping methods. In the following year, 126 traps of ten different designs were tested in Alberta. In 1985, the Province of Alberta and the Fur Institute of Canada signed a five-year agreement to research and develop humane trapping systems.

The Humane Trapping Program is located at the Alberta Research Council (formerly Alberta Environmental Centre) in Vegreville, Alberta. The facility, which cost over $1 million to build, was designed as an outdoor laboratory. Its purpose was to develop and test new and modified humane trapping systems for Canadian fur-bearing animals. Animal behaviour and trap performance were monitored remotely using infrared cameras within the simulated natural setting of the compound.

The primary objective of the Trap Effectiveness Project evolved from development of humane traps to development and application of technologies to rate trapping systems against the *Agreement on International Humane Trapping Standards* established in 1997. Trapping systems used in Canada must conform to these standards in order to maintain the European Union wild fur markets and keep Canada's fur trade viable. The national fur trade contributes $800 million to the Canadian economy annually and approximately 80% of Canadian fur ends up in Europe.

In the last ten years, the project has developed several innovative methods for rating trapping systems. The program now uses its extensive research database, which contains information from over 600 compound tests involving 12 different species, and computer simulation models to replace testing on live animals. The models use mechanical properties to rate trap designs against the international standards at significantly less cost than using live-animal testing. In addition, trap optimization routines assist manufacturers by suggesting trap modifications that better meet international standards.

FISHER: THE ELUSIVE FURBEARER

Fisher is traditionally an important furbearing species in Alberta. As with other species, the extent and value of the fisher harvest differed widely from one decade to the next and trappers were concerned that quotas did not always match the availability of animals. Seasons were closed from 1938 to 1955 but reached a maximum annual harvest of 5500 in 1985-1986.

Current fisher management is based on population data reconstructed from carcasses submitted by trappers. Each year, trappers provide the Fish and Wildlife Division with 300 to 500 carcasses, at $5 apiece. Using x-rays, one canine tooth from each fisher is examined to determine the condition of the pulp cavity (a reflection of age). Adapting a program initiated by Marg Strickland in Ontario, the reproductive success of the previous year is determined from the annual juvenile/adult female ratio in the carcasses. The goal is to maintain a ratio greater than 2:1, indicating stable or increasing populations. If the ratio drops below 2:1, quotas are reduced to protect reproductive females. Thus quotas can be adjusted in near real time and some of the dramatic fluctuation in fur harvest seen in early years is avoided. The program is well received by trappers, and the current annual harvest is in the range of 1600 fisher pelts at commercial values of nearly $73,000.

As well as the northern forests, fisher originally inhabited the aspen parklands of central Alberta; however, they were extirpated in these habitats by the turn of the 20th century. Major changes to the landscape due to logging, fire, and land clearing in association with human settlement contributed to the loss of these populations. To try to return fisher to the parklands, 20 wild-caught fishers were released into sites within Elk Island National Park, Cooking Lake Blackfoot Recreational Area, and Ministik Lake Bird Sanctuary east of Edmonton.[15] Groups of animals were released in March and June 1990 and August 1991. There were many unknowns at the time, including the effects of time of year, group size, and fidelity to aspen parkland habitats. Many individuals released in March left the area and moved long distances, perhaps in conjunction with breeding behaviours and lack of suitable cover. However, those released in June and August stayed in the vicinity of the release. The groups were monitored for a few years and there was some evidence of successful reproduction. However, sightings soon tailed off and eventually all individuals died without establishing a viable population.

153

RIVER OTTER: THE PLAYFUL FURBEARER

Similar to beaver, river otter have a luxurious thick pelt designed to insulate animals that spend much of their time in cold water. However, otters are more secretive and far less numerous than beaver. They primarily eat fish and thus are restricted to habitat that includes fish-bearing waters. Suitable habitat for otter has become relatively scarce in Alberta and the species has largely disappeared through much of its former range.

In the early 1980s, Don Reid, a graduate student at the University of Calgary, provided basic information regarding the ecology of river otter in northeastern Alberta.[16] In the mid-1980s, the Fish and Wildlife Division used this information to identify Lac des Arcs, near Canmore, as a suitable site to try to re-establish an otter population. Eight otter were released at the lake. There was some evidence of reproduction for the first few years, but the

introduction was not successful in the long run. Similarly, a small number of surplus otters from the humane trapping programs at Vegreville were released into the Clearwater River in the central foothills region in the late 1990s. The fate of these otter is unknown.

Otter generally occur in northern Alberta and are slowly expanding their geographic distribution southwards along the foothills. They are increasingly seen south of Edson and west of Rocky Mountain House. Otter are managed on a quota basis by registered fur management area; however, they are difficult to catch and trappers take them opportunistically in beaver sets. There is a general concern among trappers that otter prey on beaver, but food habit studies indicate this is not a common occurrence.

expanded to allow broader input from trappers and industry. Industry was assessed a levy based on the number of hectares allotted to each company for exploration and development.

The Fish and Wildlife Division created three positions responsible for field delivery of the program and a secretary-manager to oversee its administration. The positions were called Trapline Resource Officers (TRO). On April 15, 1981, the positions were staffed by Bill Johnson (Peace River), Pat Rhude (Rocky Mountain House), and Floyd Kunnas (St. Paul). Each person was provided with a tent, metal detector, backpack, and a new Citation 4500 snow machine as well as a job description flexible enough to allow for unrestricted work anywhere within the Region. TROs assigned fur management areas and assisted with trapper education or whatever local fur management was taking place. They gradually took over much of the trapping administration and management. Fred Neuman was the first Secretary-Manager of the Review Board.

Each compensation claim was submitted to the TRO, who in turn completed a report that was reviewed by the Board. At the outset, there were no guidelines, and claims from trappers were sometimes frivolous and exaggerated. In general, unresolved expectations of trappers contributed to an ongoing dissatisfaction, which still lingers today. Although compensation guidelines were developed, they are linked directly to historical fur harvests on record; but trappers felt they had inherent land rights to trap. Nevertheless, the program was the first of its kind in Canada and has solved many actual and potential conflicts.

The TRO positions officially ended in 1995. In 1997, the compensation program was moved to the Alberta Trappers' Association where it still resides today. Currently, claims are submitted via the District Fish and Wildlife Officer and forwarded to the Alberta Trappers' Association to address through the compensation board.

Fur Farms

As early as 1913, live foxes were captured in Alberta and sold to stock fur farms in eastern Canada and the U.S. By 1914, regulations were enacted governing the operation of 148 fur farms (mostly fox but some mink) operating in Alberta. In 1921, the possibility of establishing "muskrat farms" as a means of supplementing income of farmers south of the North Saskatchewan River was introduced but never really caught on.

The fur farm industry really took off in the 1930s. Interest in fur farms continued to grow and emphasis switched from foxes to mink. The Government established a summer fur farm inspector position in 1932. In 1938, an Experimental Fur Farm was established at Oliver to aid the development of the fur industry in Alberta and to provide breeding stock for farms in other areas. Fur Farm Field Days, with pelting demonstrations and lectures, were held throughout the province and became very popular. By 1939, Alberta fur ranches were supporting quality furbearing animals and fur farm pelts assumed great importance in the world fur market because of their excellent quality. Alberta ranked third among the provinces in domestic fur production and value.

While the Fish and Game Branch assisted in establishing local fur farmer associations, the Alberta Fur Breeders Association organized activities such as field days, and live animal and pelt shows. Fur farm organizations also provided input into legislation dealing with fur farms. By 1943-1944, fox and mink farms were well established, but muskrat and beaver farms were in their formative stages. Ongoing problems included finding adequate fencing to keep wild populations out and captive animals in. Occasional outbreaks of disease, largely canine distemper, were a problem. On April 1, 1946, the management of fur farms was transferred to the Department of Agriculture as a specialized industry emphasizing stock, breeding, and animal husbandry. Beaver and muskrat farms

154

FUR FARM INSPECTOR BOB GILLIES VISITING MONTGOMERY MINK RANCH, WETASKIWIN, 1965.
COURTESY PROVINCIAL ARCHIVES OF ALBERTA (PA1570/2)

remained with the Fish and Game Branch since interest was minimal, and most individuals of these species were still part of a wild population.

At the height of the fur farm industry in the middle decades of the 1900s, the large number of fur farms in north-central Alberta had a significant effect on the commercial fishing industry. All coarse fish (tullibee and burbot) from Lac La Biche and Lesser Slave Lake were regarded as the primary source of food for fur farm mink and foxes, supplemented by other coarse fish from other lakes. The quantities needed to supply the farms were enormous. By 1944-1945, fur farmers were allowed to take coarse fish during the closed season in order to feed their animals, and to use nets of a smaller mesh size than those of commercial fisherman. Needless to say, this level of fish harvest was not sustainable over the long run and a collapse in fish production in the mid-1960s was a severe blow to hundreds of local fur farmers.

"During and after the war years, George Meyers and Henry Blake would sit all day in a boat in the summer [on Island Lake] and catch pike for their mink, which they were farming. However, this came to an end in 1947 when the price of mink dropped."[17]

A number of fox farms operated in the Morinville area in 1952 mainly because cheap feed was available from the Edmonton Meat Packing plants. However, the fox's long fur was soon to go out of fashion and the fox pens disappeared thereafter. Mink ranches farther north around Lesser Slave Lake and Calling Lake prospered for a few more years. Today, there are fewer than a half dozen fur farms in Alberta. One of the larger mink farms in Canada, holding some 50,000 animals, is located near Wetaskiwin. Interest in and success of fur-farming tend to wax and wane with the whims of economics and social attitudes at home and abroad.

MEMORIES OF A FUR FARM IN NORTHERN ALBERTA, 1905 TO 1975
[BLAIR RIPPIN]

My great-grandfather, Fred Leeman, was a carpenter who moved his family from the Maritimes just after Alberta became a province. After working in Edmonton and building barges at Waterways, he eventually settled at Widewater, on the south shore of Lesser Slave Lake. With the promotion of commercial fishing by the Alberta government after the First World War, he began building toboggans, sleighs, and boats to meet the demand by commercial fishermen operating on Lesser Slave and many smaller lakes across north-central Alberta, including Peerless, Trout, Utikuma, Wabasca, Calling, and Cold lakes and Lac La Biche.

Great-granddad's boats (Leeman boats) were fashioned after east-coast fishing boats with round-bottomed displacement hulls capable of transporting up to 10,000 pounds of fish. Early models were open hulled, powered by Easthope single-cylinder engines, capable of about five miles per hour. His later models were closed deck with wheelhouses, powered by six-cylinder and V8 car motors, and capable of 10-15 miles per hour with about the same payload. His sleighs and toboggans were pulled by dog teams and horses and were designed to carry cargo or "cabooses" (on-ice living quarters for fishermen). My father came on the scene in the early 1930s and eventually acquired both a Leeman boat and dog-team sleigh outfit. Although serving fishermen well for several years, the old-style equipment was replaced in the 1950s with faster commercial boats of aluminum and fiberglass, Bombardiers, 4x2 and 4x4 trucks, and snowmobiles. Powered ice augers replaced the needle bars, and jiggers were equipped with electronic homing devices.

Commercial fishing during the late 1920s through to the 1940s was largely for food markets in the northeastern United States and was a welcome hedge against the cash-poor society created by the Great Depression. Lake trout, whitefish, pickerel (walleye), and jacks (northern pike) were in great demand seasonally for the Jewish holidays in Chicago and New York. Entrepreneurs A. P. Burwash and W. R. Menzie set up fish-packing plants along the south shore of Lesser Slave Lake and outfitted fishermen to provide year-round supply for the plants. In summer, fish were shipped by rail, unfrozen and on ice. In winter, horses, dogs, trucks, and aircraft transported fish to the plants and the

railhead. Indeed, in 1932 Grant McConachie, one of the founding fathers of aviation in Canada, received the first contract to fly frozen fish from Cold Lake to the railhead and thus established a business venture that eventually gave rise to Canadian Pacific Airlines. The war slowed the progress of the fishing industry somewhat, but it remained a primary source of income for many families through the 1940s and 1950s, and annual whitefish catches reached one million pounds.

The advent of fur farming in the 1930s had a major effect on the commercial fishing industry. Starting in the late 1930s and early 1940s, residents on the shores of Lesser Slave Lake (including my father) augmented their fishing income by raising mink and a few foxes. Subsequently, some of the commercial fishermen began using nets with smaller mesh sizes and baited hook lines to catch tullibee (cisco) and ling (burbot), respectively. These two species were considered excellent mink and fox food. Other fish species were used but generally they commanded higher prices as human food. In contrast, there was no market for the long-nosed and red-horse suckers caught in commercial nets. They were considered too high in iodine for mink diets and generally were discarded.[18]

Mink farming expanded greatly in the late 1940s and 1950s, and the quest for tullibee and ling changed the focus of commercial fisheries. Fishing for mink food ruled the day. Small wooden piers, fishing boats anchored offshore, commuter rowboats pulled up on shore, and hand-made wooden rotary net dryers became common sights along the lakeshore from Slave Lake west to Faust and Joussard. The early cotton nets required treating with tar or "bluestone" (copper sulphate) to increase rot resistance. They also had to be dried and cleaned to rid them of algae and pondweed. With the advent in the late 1950s of nylon nets that did not need treating and drying, net dryers quickly disappeared.

Fish and Wildlife Officers were run off their feet trying to maintain compliance with legal net mesh size, quotas, and seasons. My first memories in that regard are mainly of Charlie Scott and later Ralph Harle, who were each respected and despised, depending on what part of the industry local residents were involved in. Charlie had very meagre resources but great determination, and was the only Fisheries Officer in the area for several years. He walked in frigid winter weather for many miles along the ice to check on commercial fishermen. Although he endorsed his enforcement function, he was also somewhat sympathetic with the often-difficult plight of local fur farmers and fishermen. As a result, he became a respected member of the community.

I also recall the problem of dealing with fish in summer before large-scale refrigeration was available. Fish are very perishable and become inedible by humans or mink if left without ice for only a few hours in summer. Each winter during the 1940s and into the 1960s, fishermen and fur farmers used horses, dogs, and later trucks and tractors to harvest large chunks of lake ice, which were piled in insulated icehouses or merely stacked in the back yard. Piles were about ten feet high covering an area of about 400 square feet. The whole pile was heaped high with sawdust or shavings from the local sawmills. Ice secured in this way lasted until the next winter and provided the critical cooling of fresh fish caught in the summer. In the mid-1950s, a cooperative community cold storage operation was built at Canyon Creek. It served the needs of fishermen and mink farmers for several years until they could afford to build their own cold storage facilities.

By the early 1960s there were 300-400 licensed fur farmers along the south shore of Lesser Slave Lake, with an annual production of over 200,000 mink pelts. Although most farmers kept a few hundred animals, our ranch reached a peak of 4000, requiring about 2000 pounds of fish per day for about five months of the year. Several ranches also operated at Lac La Biche, Cold Lake, Primrose Lake, and Wolf Lake, and mink and foxes were raised during that time near Edmonton and Red Deer.

Annual tullibee catches of several million pounds at Lesser Slave Lake reached a peak at this time; however, fish production was unreliable by the mid-1960s. To make up for low catches, fur farmers imported frozen fish from the west coast

via rail. With the lack of reliable local feed and the added expense of freighting coast fish, many ranchers went out of business or moved their ranches to British Columbia where mink food was cheaper and readily available. My father's operation was among those that moved to Aldergrove, B.C. Lesser Slave Lake was closed to tullibee fishing in 1970 and the fur-farming industry in northern Alberta declined rapidly thereafter.

At present, there are no mink being raised along Lesser Slave Lake, and the tullibee and ling resource goes largely untapped by commercial interests. However, the fur-farming industry did not die. Some of the ranches that moved to B.C. in the late 1960s and early 1970s continue to operate and expand. At present our ranch (now operated by my brother and his son) has nearly 20,000 mink, but ranches with 30,000 to 100,000 mink also operate in the vicinity.

157

ABANDONED MINK HOUSES. CREDIT: B. RIPPIN

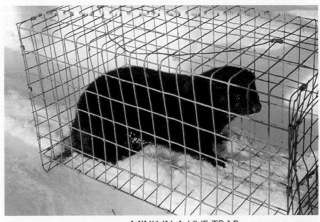

MINK IN A LIVE TRAP. CREDIT: B. RIPPIN

Managing Problem Wildlife

It was readily apparent to early settlers that some wildlife species could have a significant impact on agriculture. Random control actions towards such "vermin" or "pests" often included shooting, trapping, snaring, and poisoning, with little effective interference from government. Legal authority for control of species such as coyotes, wolves, cougars, crows, and magpies lay with the Department of Agriculture. This changed when the Fish and Game Branch was transferred to the Department of Lands and Forests in 1941, although responsibility for control of coyotes in the settled areas was transferred back to the Department of Agriculture in 1951. Control of agricultural pests such as pocket gophers, ground squirrels, rats, and mice remained the responsibility of Agriculture.

While trapping is usually associated with desirable commercial furbearers, it was also used as a management tool for dealing with problem wildlife, those pests or predators that were unwelcome near human settlement. In the first part of the century, many duties of the Chief Game Guardian revolved around the payment of bounties to encourage the trapping or shooting of certain undesirable species. Predators included any wild mammal or bird of prey that killed domestic livestock (cattle, sheep, pigs, or poultry). As well, the removal of predators from an area was thought to increase the number of game animals. Of course, a predator to some may be a beneficial mammal or bird to others, and the list of those species considered to be pests has changed through time.

Heading the early list of undesirables was the timber or gray wolf, with the coyote a close second, and the cougar third. Birds of prey including almost all hawks and owls were shot even though not all of them killed domestic poultry. In the eyes of farmers, the goshawk was the chief culprit. However, on many farms chickens were not adequately protected: many simply ran wild and were easy prey for hawks. Bears gained an early reputation as cattle killers,

without the realization that bears, especially grizzlies, will also eat carrion. A steer or cow might die of natural causes on the range; a grizzly would soon find the carcass and eat it. If seen by a farmer, the bear was immediately shot even if it had not killed what it was eating. It took many years to modify such attitudes.

The first provincial *Game Act* in 1907 established the province's first bounty regulations. A bounty on both wolves and coyotes was paid directly by the Department of Agriculture. Wolf Bounty Inspectors (stock inspectors appointed under the *Stock Inspection Ordinance*) were employed in the summer south of 55°N; North West Mounted Police served as inspectors north of 55°N. In 1909, the *Wolf Bounty Act* established that Wolf Bounty Inspectors could now be employed north of 55°N. The bounty on coyotes was discontinued in 1910. In 1916, bounty legislation changed such that all bounties were discontinued between January and May. However, this lasted only a short time and bounties were quickly re-established on wolves. Another management option, strychnine, was used to poison coyotes. After 1916, bounties came and went like the changing seasons of the year.

In the late 1930s, bounties were also used to try to get rid of crows, magpies, and gophers (ground squirrels). In eastern Canada, Jack Miner led the campaign of war against such species and the crow was his favourite species to hate. In western regions, magpies and crows earned the dislike of farmers and sportsmen because they were thought to damage crops and eat young barnyard fowl and wild birds. Ground squirrels were particularly detested for their direct damage to crops and the indirect risk of injury to livestock that might trip on their burrows. Bounty programs to remove such pests were run by the Fish and Game Clubs using government funds to pay the bounties. In 1938 alone, bounties were paid out for more than 88,000 crows and magpies, 600,000 ground squirrels, and 145,000 crow and magpie eggs to a total cost of $4,188.[19] In 1939, the annual totals were 83,000, more than 780,000, and 118,000, respectively, at a cost of $4,647.[20]

ALBERTA'S RAT CONTROL PROGRAM
[JOHN BOURNE]

In 1950-1951, weasels were protected in the eastern part of the province in the hopes that they would stop the spread of Norway rats entering from Saskatchewan. At the same time, Alberta Agriculture began an ongoing war on rats—the Border Rat Control Program. As we still have no established rat population in Alberta, these actions seem to have been effective!

Norway rats first arrived in North America in sailing ships on the east coast about 1775. They spread westward with European settlers, arriving in Saskatchewan some 100 years later. By the mid-1900s they were eating their way into eastern Alberta. The province is protected from rat invasion in the south by open, relatively unsettled, short-grass prairie, in the north by boreal mixed-wood forest, and in the west by the Rocky Mountains; none of which is favourable habitat for Norway rats. The only route of invasion is overland from the east along a sparsely populated rural area, itself a limiting factor to rat migration. Relatively inhospitable climate on the western prairies also works against these large rodents. For about half the year, the province is snow covered with daytime temperatures well below freezing. The harsh climate limits rat activity to occupied man-made structures and discourages rat colonization in isolated areas.

In 1950, Norway rats were discovered along the eastern border of Alberta during a Department of Health field survey of sylvatic plague in Richardson's ground squirrels. By chance, a rat colony was uncovered on a family farm near Alsask. The findings brought immediate action by the provincial government. Rats were a potential health risk and could contaminate or destroy crops, stored grain, feed, and foodstuffs. As such, war could be waged under the provisions of the *Agricultural Pests Act*. A rat control zone was quickly established along the eastern

border from Montana to the relatively uninhabited boreal forests of the north, a distance of 380 miles (610 km). The zone covered three Ranges west from the Saskatchewan border, a distance of 18 miles (29 km).

Most Albertans knew little or nothing about rats or how to control them, so public education was the first order of the day. Residents were encouraged to destroy rat colonies, eliminate shelter sites and potential food sources, and rat-proof farm buildings and rural structures. Initially a variety of toxic chemicals and traps was used, but methods were later refined to better target rats only. However, the quick knockdown of rat populations and termination of rat migration gave the province time to organize a responsible and defensible rat control program.

Thus, appropriate legislation was in place before rats invaded the province and provided a basis for zero tolerance. Alberta Agriculture, in cooperation with municipalities along the border, developed a universal strategy of detection and control of rats on agricultural lands. All farmsteads, nuisance grounds, and other potential rat habitat were identified and inspected regularly and consistently throughout the year. This organized and systematic strategy of rat surveillance and removal, in conjunction with public information, was the mainstay of rat control. The program is still in place as we enter the 21st century and the province continues to keep the unwanted pests at bay.

Many changes to prairie agronomy over the last 50 years, such as specialization, diversification, and intensive livestock production, also had a positive effect on rat control. The "mixed farm" of the 1950s became either a grain or livestock operation in the 1970s. In the process, many buildings whether functional or obsolete were altered or removed, resulting in reduced rat habitat. Similarly, the development of new and more effective rat baits also improved rat control in Alberta. Inexpensive and versatile bait formulations, such as those designed with extended field life, high moisture resistance, and requiring only a single feed to cause death, are commonly used. These baits have added features of environmental safety, reliability, and diversity.

NWT

BRITISH COLUMBIA   ALBERTA   SASKATCHEWAN

30 km

600 km

PREDATOR BOUNTIES: A CHECKERED HISTORY

Through time, bounties seemed to come and go as social or political pressures waxed and waned in the province. A gradual shift from a frontier to a new-age attitude also is apparent in later years.

1907	*Game Act* establishes bounties for wolves and coyotes.
1909	*Wolf Bounty Act* pays $10 for adults, $1 for pups, and $1 for coyotes.
1910	Coyote bounty is discontinued.
1916	Bounties are discontinued from January to May; wolf bounty is reinstated.
1917	Coyote bounty is for females only; wolf female bounty is twice as much as males.
1920	*Wolf Bounty Act* is repealed; bounties on all species are discontinued.
1920s-1930s	Wolf bounties come and go.
1938-1939	A bounty is put on cougar.
1941-1942	Competition bounties are put on crows, magpies, and gophers (ground squirrels).
1942-1943	Bounty on wolf pups is increased in western Alberta (west only so as to avoid illegal bootlegged pelts from NWT and Saskatchewan where bounties are discontinued).
1943-1944	Bounty placed on coyotes.
1944-1945	Bounty placed on snared wolves.
1946-1947	Agricultural pest bounties expanded to include goshawks and owls; competition bounties are discontinued but bounties still paid through Fish and Game Association.
1947-1948	Nuisance beaver and muskrat could be shot, trapped, or sent to fur farms.
1948-1949	Coyote bounty is discontinued.
1949-1950	Agricultural pests are again restricted to crows and magpies (does not include hawks and owls).
1956-1957	Bounty on wolves is discontinued (although wolf control was not).
1964	Bounty system eliminated due to lack of effect on pest management.
1965-1966	Predator control is continued in the north, largely by targeted poisoning of specific wolf packs; coyotes in central and southern areas taken by hunters.
1966-1967	Wolf control limited to cases of specific livestock damage, public safety, or scientific research.

Every farmer and school child was encouraged to help rid the province of these agricultural pests. In order to attract as much attention and to kill as many individuals as possible, the program was redesigned in 1942 as a trophy competition.[21] The contest was divided into four sections. Competition 1: rod and gun clubs and similar organizations; Competition 2: individuals; Competitions 3 and 4: schools and individual pupils. The program began early in spring and terminated at the end of November. Prizes were awarded on a point system: four points for a pair of feet for each crow or magpie; one point for each gopher tail; two points for each crow or magpie egg. Whoever accumulated the greatest number of points received first prize. The group or individual had to file an affidavit stating that he, she, or they killed the magpies, crows or gophers whose feet, eggs or tails were presented. Prizes differed—in Competition 1 the maximum was $200; whereas in Competition 4 it was $75.

Throughout this time, the Game Branch continued to grant funds to the Fish and Game Association as it had done since the Association's establishment. In the late 1940s, the monies were based on membership numbers. The funds were used for educational programs for sportsmen and to continue the bounties on agricultural pests, which by then were expanded to include goshawks and owls. To encourage trapping when pelts were valueless, coyote, wolf, and cougar bounties continued, but wolf and cougar bounties applied only during the summer.

As the 1950s dawned, it was evident that bounties were not achieving the intended goal. They were ineffective in predator control and often were not affecting the animals that were menacing livestock. Also, there was no discrimination between the furbearers of the north and the farmer's menace of the south. Besides, a continent-wide study showed that bounties were largely unsuccessful due to the innate biological factors that often produce an increased number of young when predators, particularly mammalian predators, occur at reduced population density. Thus, individuals that were removed by the bounty system were replaced during the following

reproductive season. In addition, reduced density of highly mobile predators can lead to immigration from adjacent populations and this reduces the effect of removing the individuals for which the bounties were paid.

In 1964, bounties were finally abandoned as being ineffective in controlling numbers and because they were an administrative headache. Magpie and crow numbers did not appear to decrease to any great extent, proving that these two species were (and still are!) capable of surviving in the face of persecution and indeed they seem to profit from their association with humans. As for the ground squirrels, neither did they decrease to any significant degree. The bounty system was also unsuccessful at eliminating predator species or increasing game species.

Bounties have not entirely gone out of vogue. Local competitions occasionally crop up even in the 21st century. These are generally promoted and justified as reducing the numbers of ground squirrels or coyotes. However, they are conducted by private interests and are more about tourism and recreational activities than wildlife management. While legal, wildlife managers do not condone such competitions as a means of population control. However, municipal governments occasionally institute bounties as an attempt at local pest management of coyotes and beaver.

Problem wildlife management shifted towards methods of individual pest/predator control rather than outright attempts to eliminate an entire species. In the late 1960s and 1970s, predator control was limited to only those cases where livestock damage occurred, public safety was threatened, or specimens were collected for scientific purposes. Fish and Wildlife staff responded to many problem wildlife complaints by attending the site and, where necessary, setting traps or snares to catch offending animals ranging from smaller furbearers such as foxes, beaver, and badger to large carnivores such as wolves, bears, and cougars. By the late 1970s, the number of problem wildlife complaints reached the point where the Division could no longer provide

161

control services for small animals. Municipal control programs and private enterprise subsequently filled much of the void.

The Fish and Wildlife Division concentrated specifically on waterfowl, bears, wolves, and elk in conflict with human interests. In 1973, a Joint Problem Wildlife Committee was created with Dave Neave (Director of Wildlife) and Ernie Psikla (Director of Field Services-Enforcement) representing Alberta Recreation, Parks and Wildlife. Mike Dorrance (Head, Zoology Section) and G. Whenham (Head, Veterinary Field-Services Branch) represented Alberta Agriculture. Together, committee members developed the *General Principles of Problem Wildlife Management* and a *General Agreement on Code of Operations for Joint Programs*. These documents identified the roles and responsibilities of the two Departments in the delivery of problem wildlife programs.

In 1974, Vic Sigurdson became the first Provincial Problem Wildlife Coordinator, heading up the newly established Problem Wildlife Section within the Field Service-Enforcement Branch of the Fish and Wildlife Division. Fish and Wildlife Officers Jan Allen, Ron Hanson, Dennis Weisser, and Carl Roscovich took up Regional Problem Wildlife Specialist positions. They were responsible for program development, field delivery of problem wildlife programs, equipment testing, and staff training in problem wildlife control techniques. In 1984, Ron Hanson replaced Vic Sigurdson as the Provincial Problem Wildlife Coordinator.

From 1974 to 1993, Alberta Agriculture financed and administered a Livestock Predator Compensation Program. The program varied over the years but generally provided compensation for 80%-85% of the value of a confirmed kill and 50% for a probable kill. The program applied to wild predator kills of any livestock or fowl raised primarily as food-producing animals. Fish and Wildlife Officers investigated and submitted claims for all livestock killed in the green zone [remote areas]

and livestock killed by wildlife other than coyotes in the white zone [settled areas], while Alberta Agriculture and municipal inspectors investigated all coyote kills in the white zone.

In 1996, the Fish and Wildlife Division developed and implemented a Wildlife Predator Compensation Program that was far more limited in scope and budget than the Alberta Agriculture program it replaced. The new program provided compensation only for cattle, sheep, pigs, goats, and bison killed or injured by grizzly bear, black bear, wolves, and cougar. Eagles were later added to the list of predators. Initially the program used the previous 85% and 50% compensations; however, this was amended to 100% of the value of a confirmed kill. Currently, the Division administers the program in conjunction with the Alberta Conservation Association. Fish and Wildlife Officers conduct the investigations. The Division also provides public information on prevention and control methods and lends traps to the public to take care of problem animals themselves. Fish and Wildlife staff continue to provide the primary response to bear, wolf, and cougar complaints.

Wolves—Ups and Downs in Alberta

When European explorers entered present-day Alberta, wolves were widespread and abundant. Anthony Henday observed many wolves in association with bison herds in 1754 and recorded in his diary that he could not say whether wolves or buffaloes were more plentiful. More than 100 years later, the famous Palliser expedition (1857-1860) noted numerous wolves in the Battle River and other areas, and reported native claims of occasional outbreaks of rabies in wolves. A few years after that, the Reverend John McDougall described abundant wolves preying on horses at bison hunters' camps.

However, the tide for wolves soon began to change for the worse. The first phase of their demise was the slaughter of bison. The 1860s and 1870s saw the once great herds extirpated across most of the western plains. Other ungulates

163

BLACK WOLF.
CREDIT: G. KUZYK

suffered, too—from overhunting by settlers, as well as market hunters supplying the expanding towns, railways and mines. Severe winter weather and uncontrolled fires also took their toll on wild species. Without their usual prey, the wolves were hard-pressed to survive.[22]

For a good discussion of wolf numbers in Alberta, see the 1969 review article written by John Stelfox.[23] Stelfox cited several references from early explorers and hunters who found that despite the use of strychnine and the activities of "wolfers" like Kootenai Brown (wolfers harvested about 1000 wolves each winter), wolves appeared to be numerous in much of Alberta between 1800 and 1875. Then, as one might expect with the decline of the bison and other large ungulates and the continued use of poisoning and trapping

programs, wolf numbers declined between 1875 and 1915.

The pressure on wolves continued into the 1900s through control actions in agricultural areas and bounties throughout the new province. The government at times promoted increased wolf harvest by distributing snares and using many special education programs to teach effective wolf trapping methods. The last wolves were removed from Waterton Lakes National Park in southern Alberta in 1922 because of depredations of livestock in neighbouring regions.

In the north, Dewey Soper, one of Canada's great early mammalogists, reported abundant numbers of wolves in Wood Buffalo National Park in 1925. A southerly expansion of these northern wolves, and an influx from far western Alberta and eastern British Columbia during the 1930s, laid the foundation for the gradual build-up of wolves in northeastern Alberta during the 1930s and 1940s.[24] These wolves apparently spread south during the war years when hunting and trapping pressures were lower and ungulates more available, despite periodic removals associated with the wolf bounty. The low market value of wolf pelts discouraged trappers and by the late 1940s, the species achieved a remarkable comeback throughout much of forested Canada. But it was to be short-lived.

Farmers and ranchers soon reported severe depredations of livestock, and hunters began to complain of poor survival of game herds. By the mid-to-late 1940s, wildlife managers were concerned about the loss of game to wolves. With the approval of the Game Commission, a group of sportsmen conducted a pilot wolf control program in the Clearwater Forest in 1951. Snares were legalized for the trapping of wolves and coyotes, and cyanide "coyote-getters" were distributed to forestry personnel. Control even resumed in the national parks.

Wolves probably reached their peak population in 1952 with approximately 5000 wolves in the province. In 1952, hard times returned with a vengeance for wolves in all of Alberta when rabies spread from arctic foxes into coyotes and wolves. The province took management actions that included control of large carnivores. Thousands of wolves were killed, mostly by poisoning in 1952-1956. Stelfox estimated a provincial population of 500-1000 wolves at the dawn of the 1960s. For the second time since the beginning of settlement, wolves in Alberta were at a low point. However, the ever-resilient wolf again rebounded, reaching approximately 3550 animals in the province by 1969.

In 1972, the Fish and Wildlife Division again initiated a wolf control program as a response to escalating incidents of livestock depredation. If wolf predation were confirmed, individual control was carried out primarily through the use of toxicants (poisons). Although control methods were limited to shooting and trapping along the southern foothills

in the late 1990s, toxic baits are the only effective means of control and are used on a limited basis throughout the rest of the province. Today, the status of wolves in Alberta is considered secure, with a population of between 3000 and 5000 animals.[25]

The Sheep River Cougar Story

Another large furbearing predator, the cougar historically ranged throughout the United States and southern Canada from coast to coast. However, strong frontier anti-predator attitudes came with European settlement in the 1800s and anti-cougar sentiment was widespread. William Hornaday, Director of the New York Zoological Society, repeatedly railed against puma (cougar) as a deplorable curse of immediate urgency. Bounty payments were instituted in Alberta in 1938 and ranged from $15 to $40 for each cougar pelt: an annual average of 40 cougars was turned in for bounties between 1937 and 1964.

In 1969, hunters were required to have a moose, elk, or deer licence to kill a cougar. The season ran from September to March and hunting with dogs was permitted in February and March. When cougars were designated a big game species in 1971, a separate cougar licence was introduced (though hunters with an elk licence were able to hunt cougar until 1972), requiring that all cougars killed be registered, only one cougar per person per year was permitted, and dogs could be used from early December to the end of January. To reduce hunting pressure in southern Alberta, the use of dogs was limited to January in certain areas in 1978, and then in all areas in 1981.

In 1982, kittens accompanied by females or with spotted fur were protected. Fall cougar hunting season (i.e., without dogs) ranged between 66 and 100 days, but in 1985 it was abolished. In 1990, after extensive research in Alberta, the cougar season was increased to three months (December to February) in conjunction with a quota system of regional kill goals. Once the local quota was met, the season closed in that region. In 1996, the effectiveness of the harvest quota system was evaluated. The total province-wide cougar harvest

RABIES IN ALBERTA: A HISTORY

The provincial rabies control programs have served the province well in limiting rabies in wildlife (primarily furbearers) and reducing the subsequent risk to humans and livestock. Rabies is a viral disease that can potentially kill any mammal or bird. In Alberta, the virus initially swept southwards out of the arctic in arctic foxes and spilled over into red foxes, wolves, and coyotes in the early 1950s. This invasion was met with a massive control response coordinated by the Department of Agriculture under the direction of E.E. Ballantyne and J.G. O'Donoghue. Trapping, poisoning, shooting, and gassing were used to remove virtually any carnivore that could pose potential risk to humans and livestock in farming and urban areas. Systematic eradication of predators resulted in killing at least 35,000 coyotes, 50,000 foxes, 4200 wolves, 7500 lynx, 1850 bears, 500 skunks, and 64 cougars in forested regions and an additional 60,000 to 80,000 coyotes in agricultural regions of Alberta in a period of 18 months![26] In concert with the massive removal of potential hosts, the virus itself killed many wild canids. The combined result was a period of 12 years in the late 1950s and throughout the 1960s during which no case of rabies was detected in wildlife in Alberta.

Rabies again invaded the Canadian prairie regions in 1959, but this time as a movement northward out of North Dakota in striped skunks. The virus moved into southwest Manitoba and reached eastern Saskatchewan by 1962-1963 and western Saskatchewan by 1969. Not wanting to repeat the mass eradications of the 1950s, J.G. O'Donoghue and G.R. Kerr hired Ernie Ewaschuk to initiate a limited control program. Targeted control efforts in Alberta continue to this day. Removal of skunks to reduce the population density appears to keep rabies at bay and stops its spread at the Alberta/Saskatchewan border. Similar vigilance is kept along the Alberta/Montana border.

Since the 1970s, rabies in Alberta has occurred primarily in skunks and bats. Recently, there have been a few cases found in skunks. Although rabies-positive bats continue to be collected each year, the annual average is less than five. Rabies in livestock is virtually non-existent. Alberta has recorded one fatal human rabies case since the disease was first detected in the early 1950s.

H.R. THOMPSON, A TRAPPER EMPLOYED DURING THE 1950s RABIES SCARE, RAM RIVER AREA.
COURTESY ALBERTA FISH AND WILDLIFE DIVISION

165

Through the years, a series of wildlife biologists started their careers in rabies management programs. These included, but are not limited to, Ron Bjorge, John Gunson, Per Anderson, Dave Schowalter, Dave Hobson, Rick Rosatte, and Margo Pybus. The program was a great proving ground—it seems if you could work with skunks, you could take on just about anything!

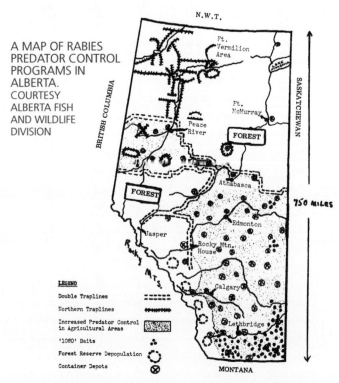

A MAP OF RABIES PREDATOR CONTROL PROGRAMS IN ALBERTA. COURTESY ALBERTA FISH AND WILDLIFE DIVISION

MAP II. -- Rabies Control in Wildlife in Alberta

had increased but the number of females harvested remained stable, hunter success rates increased, and the total harvest north and south of the Bow River increased. The program was considered successful and thus, continues to date.

Cougars are elusive solitary creatures and their habits in the province were largely unknown. Since the foothills of Alberta are the northern limit of cougar distribution and ecological conditions can significantly affect population characteristics, data collected from other parts of North America could not simply be applied to Alberta. Extensive recreational development in Kananaskis Country in the 1980s added to management concerns and the need for better information. Thanks to one of the longest running and most intensive studies in North America, cougars in Alberta are now better understood and managed more effectively. The Sheep River Cougar Project is the only large predator project that allowed researchers to detect long-term changes in population size and composition.[27] Orval Pall, Martin Jalkotzy, and Ian Ross were key players in the research team conducting the 14-year study on cougar population characteristics, food habits, and habitat use in Alberta. These three researchers were instrumental in persuading the Alberta Government to create a management plan to regulate cougar hunting.

Orval Pall, a wildlife technician with the Fish and Wildlife Division, initiated cougar work in 1981 when he was put in charge of the field portion of the project. His contribution wasn't limited to field work however as he also presented many

RESEARCHERS ORVAL PALL, IAN ROSS, AND MARTIN JALKOTZY WITH A SEDATED COUGAR AND ORVAL'S DOG, TARKA, 1986.
CREDIT: ARC ASSOCIATED RESOURCE CONSULTANTS LTD.

slide shows and lectures, believing that strong public support and good science were essential to long-term cougar survival. In 1986, at the age of 34, Orval and his pilot were killed when their single-engine plane was caught in a thunderstorm and went down in Kananaskis Country while radio tracking bighorn sheep. Eleven additional lives were lost while searching for the downed plane in the rugged mountain area.

Martin Jalkotzy and Ian Ross, partners in ARC Associated Resource Consultants Ltd., joined Orval Pall in his research efforts in the winter of 1984-1985. After Pall's death, the two consultants took over the study so the cougar management plan could be completed. Jalkotzy has been described as knowing "more about cougars than almost anyone, anywhere". Ross was internationally respected for his expertise on cougars, lions, bears, and other large predators. In 2003, at the age of 44, he too was killed in a plane crash while tracking lions north of Nairobi, Kenya. As many colleagues commented: "He died doing what he loved best."

One other individual who was integral to the success of the study was not a professional

IAN ROSS AND MARTIN JALKOTZY WEIGH A COUGAR, 1986.
CREDIT: ORVAL PALL/COURTESY OF MARTIN JALKOTZY

about their reproductive strategies, range, and food habits. Habitat characteristics were recorded for each radio location. When conditions allowed, the research team tracked cougars on the ground in order to identify the prey they killed, determine the reproductive status of the females, collect cougar scats, and seek cougars that were not yet collared.

167

biologist, but rather a volunteer who helped to ensure the researchers had data to collect. Ralph Schmidt, a captain with the Calgary Fire Department, was involved in the research project for many years and became an essential part of the field crew after Orval Pall died. He volunteered his time and his cougar hounds to find, pursue, and tree cougars. He fixed everything that broke and used his considerable interpersonal skills to raise funds for the project. His volunteer efforts were recognized in 1992 when he was named a recipient of the *Order of the Bighorn* for his outstanding contributions to fish and wildlife conservation in Alberta.

From 1981 to 1994, cougars within 780 sq. km of the foothills in southwestern Alberta were studied intensively. Human intrusions into the area included paved highways, gravel roads, campgrounds, equestrian/hiking/all-terrain vehicle trails, hunting/trapping/livestock grazing, and several natural gas wells. Eighty-seven different cougars were captured, marked, and measured; over 3400 radio locations were recorded between 1981 and 1989; 368 cougar kills were examined; and the movements of 61 different cougars were tracked in order to learn vital facts

Based on this information, we now know that, in Alberta, cougar home range size depends on age, sex, and female reproductive status, and that the most important criteria for establishing female home ranges are food requirements and availability. Survival of young cougars (greater than 97%) is considerably higher than reported elsewhere. The data also indicated that the provincial cougar population was not overhunted, but harvests in individual areas were excessive in some years. A cougar management plan for Alberta was developed, which in turn resulted in responsive control of hunting, the largest single source of cougar mortality.

In an investigation of cougar/prey relationships, mule deer account for 55% of the prey and 38% of the biomass consumed. In winter, adult male cougars prey heavily on moose calves, but avoid adult moose. Females kill moose less frequently and usually select mule deer and elk. Cougars rarely kill bighorn sheep in the Sheep River study area, although predation loss in small herds can be high when individual cougars specialize in preying on bighorns. One cougar killed 9% of the sheep and 26% of the lambs in the Sheep River study area during one winter. Males and females lead very separate and different lives, both in their hunting patterns and in their use of territory. Even among females, predation and consumption rates differ depending on whether a female is alone, with kittens, or with food-demanding juveniles.

A final phase of the study was designed to better understand the effects of human disturbance on the activity and movements of cougars in the Sheep River drainage. Because recreational use, residential development, livestock grazing, and oil and gas exploration increased significantly in the 1980s, there were concerns regarding the possible disturbance and displacement of cougars from this area. However, despite varying levels of human activity, cougars appeared to adapt during the summer, although areas of high human use were avoided. The Sheep River area is closed during the winter and thus the cougars are provided security from human disturbance. It is apparent that maintaining a healthy cougar population means preserving large tracts of undisturbed land along the eastern slopes of the Rocky Mountains, as well as a healthy number of cervids [members of the deer family] as a food source for cougars.

Despite early efforts to rid the land of these "vermin", the cougar has survived. Today, cougars occupy most of their historical range in Alberta, except the major river valleys east of the foothills. Indeed, there is recent evidence to suggest that cougar populations are expanding geographically and, perhaps, numerically. Prior to 1980 there were relatively few cougar complaints. However, by 1993, annual cougar complaints rose to more than 100 incidents. By 2002, they exceeded 700. Complaints now come in from all parts of the province including major cities. Targeted control is carried out when and where required, usually through the use of contracted cougar houndsmen and their hounds, or by Division staff using leg snares.

Bear Management in Alberta

Grizzly bears once roamed widely throughout the province. Prior to European settlement, they were abundant across Alberta's prairies, including the Cypress Hills, and throughout major valleys like those of the Peace, Bow, and North and South Saskatchewan rivers. However, with increasing

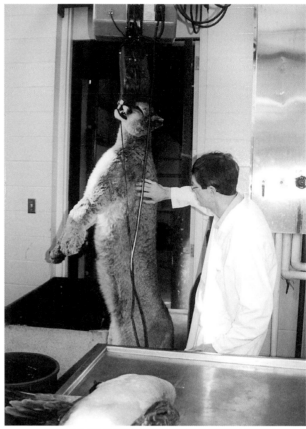

BOB McCLYMONT COLLECTS INFORMATION ON A COUGAR TURNED INTO THE O.S. LONGMAN WILDLIFE LABORATORY.
COURTESY ALBERTA FISH AND WILDLIFE DIVISION

numbers of explorers and fur traders, as well as improved firearms, grizzly bear numbers began to decline.

The vast majority of reductions in historic range occurred during the pioneer era of unrestricted market hunting and rapid conversion of natural lands to agricultural fields. In the past, a grizzly bear was prized by hunters and outfitters eager to find and battle this "King of the Wilderness". At the same time, they were also shot indiscriminately by ranchers threatened by their presence near livestock. Farming, ranching, and settlements in the 1870s overtook the grasslands and led to the final extirpation of the prairie-dwelling grizzly bears. Ranchers from the eastern reaches of the Bow and Highwood rivers had a similar effect by the 1890s. Additional "rancher control" in the 1940s, abetted by rabies control programs in the 1950s, greatly reduced grizzly bears in the Front Ranges of Kananaskis Country.

For many years, the isolation of the mountains and northern forests provided grizzlies some sanctuary where humans rarely entered. However, by the late 1950s and early 1960s, the need for increased protection of grizzly bear populations was recognized. Today, habitat loss and human disturbance are a significant part of the daily life of grizzly bears. In conjunction with limited reproductive potential and generally low survival rates, grizzly bears are at risk. The overriding cause of the species' decline is increased access and the loss of habitat as a direct result of human encroachment into formerly isolated wilderness areas. Such disturbance is currently a common problem for all furbearers in the foothills, and is increasing in the boreal forests of the north.

Grizzlies continue to persist in areas where human disturbance is minimal—relatively uninhabited portions of British Columbia, the boreal forest of Alberta, Yukon, and Northwest Territories, and a band of mountains and foothills between the plains and the Continental Divide of the Canadian Rockies. In 1990, the Fish and Wildlife Division published a provincial *Grizzly Bear Management Plan*, which included the first population estimates of grizzly bears in the province. This plan also divided the province into 21 Bear Management Areas with population estimates for each unit. A major research project aimed at understanding how grizzly bears use the landscape and how they interact with human disturbances began in the Hinton/Jasper area in the late 1990s. This program will also provide improved population estimates and new methods for assessing the environmental health of the grizzly bear population in Alberta.[28]

Like their cousins, black bears also once roamed the prairies, forests, hills and valleys throughout the province. However, early populations were likely kept in check by the larger, dominant grizzly bears. European settlement soon changed the balance in favour of the smaller black bear, but then the European guns also turned on the black bears. Black bears were not even mentioned in Alberta's first *Game Act*. They were gone from Cypress Hills by 1911, and by 1920,

were pushed back to the foothills and the forested areas north of the North Saskatchewan River.

Today, black bears maintain good populations and are not a significant concern. Though reduced in settled areas, the species is well adapted to living in proximity, but not too close, to humans and as such poses only local or individual concerns. Management programs have focussed on appropriate hunting seasons, problem bear management, and public safety. Fish and Wildlife Division enforcement staff continue to spend considerable time and effort responding to problem black bear complaints throughout the settled northern and western regions of the province.

With the shift from frontier eradication attitudes towards conservation came the need for extensive study in order to understand the species to be managed. As evidenced below both black and grizzly bears are well studied in Alberta:

1971	Study to examine black bear biology. Home ranges, movements, age distribution, food habits, and parasite loads assessed.
1972	Evaluation of beekeeper/black bear conflicts and control efforts.
1972	Study of the population dynamics of black bears at Cold Lake.
1977	Studies of black bear-human conflicts.
1981	Black and grizzly bears: ecological studies in Kananaskis Country to determine population dynamics, habitat preferences, and spatial relationships of the two species. Studies designed to minimize future human-bear conflicts, particularly in many recreational areas throughout Alberta.
1983	Bear Management Task Force initiated to develop recommendations concerning bear response teams, bear equipment kits, extension programs, biological records of problem bears, relocation policy guidelines for handling nuisance bears, release sites, hunting management, and research.
1990s	Major grizzly bear research program initiated in the Hinton/Jasper area.
2000	Major black bear study initiated in Cold Lake area to determine effects of hunting on black bear populations.

169

In the past, when it was necessary to move them, most problem bears were captured in culvert traps. However, these traps were limited in their effectiveness, particularly with grizzlies. Increased expertise in the use of spring-loaded Aldrich leg snares significantly enhanced the ability of staff to capture bears in a wide variety of locations and situations. Introduction of immobilizing agents enabled staff to relocate bears caught in snares. Initially grizzlies were relocated hundreds of kilometres away, but are now radio-collared and relocated within 100 km of where they were captured. Both snares and traps are now used widely.

A SEDATED BLACK BEAR BEING RELEASED FROM A CULVERT TRAP, 1972.
COURTESY B. STEVENSON

From 1974 to 1977, Alberta Agriculture provided a $100 subsidy for each of 605 electric fences constructed to keep bears out of bee yards. Wildlife biologist John Gunson, Fish and Wildlife Division, was instrumental in developing an effective program. From 1979 to 1993, the Agriculture department financed and administered a program of compensation for bear damage to bee yards enclosed by a functioning 4-wire electric fence. Fish and Wildlife Officers inspected damaged yards and completed the compensation application. The program held a high profile for a number of years and highlighted the change from just shooting bears to trying to find other solutions.

A fatality inquiry of a bear mauling in southern Alberta in the early 1980s recommended that the government develop a more effective response to mauling incidents. In May 1985, the Fish and Wildlife Division established a Bear Task Force, Bear Response Teams and standby kits. A new policy required that Bear Response Teams respond to all dangerous bear situations which included maulings, all grizzly bear control attempts, and any other situation that local officers deemed to be dangerous. The kits contained the equipment necessary to respond to a dangerous bear incident and were strategically located in Edson, Rocky Mountain House, Pincher Creek, Lac La Biche, and Grande Prairie. Team leaders were officers who received additional training in bear capture techniques, bear attack investigations, and firearms. A team consisted of a Bear Response

DENNIS WEISSER – PROBLEM WILDLIFE OFFICER

The officers received the complaint, and if they thought they'd need assistance from Problem Wildlife, we would take it on. The complaint may be anything from elk in a haystack, to beaver control, or bear control. In Calgary, surprisingly, we had a lot of wolf trouble with severe stock depredation around Cochrane. School buses would stop on the road to let kids watch wolves on the hillsides. Wolves killed cattle right in the rancher's yard. It was quite the thing.

An important step in managing problem wildlife was taken when the government began to pay for domestic livestock killed by wildlife (the Livestock Predator Compensation Program). We paid 80% of the market value of the animal killed by a bear, wolf, coyote, or other predator. Of course, we had to inspect the dead animal to be sure that a predator had killed it and was not just feeding on it. Most of the problems happened in fall, when bears were laying on fat for their winter sleep. They would kill a cow and gorge themselves until it was gone.

The compensation program helped grizzly bears a lot. Ranchers in the southwest corner of the province generally did their own bear control. The program was the first assistance offered them. Along with paying for the dead animal, we also trapped the bear and moved it to a non-stock area. As a result, we moved a lot of grizzlies for a while. It worked pretty well and certainly saved the lives of a lot of bears.

Leg snares came along and we started using them for black bears. Cable snares allowed us to release bears that were not associated with an animal kill. We also used culvert traps. Generally grizzlies would not enter the culverts, but we had good success with leg snares for catching them. There are not a lot of places where grizzlies were a

problem in Alberta. It was bad around Pincher Creek where there are no foothills. It's mountains, and then it's ranch land, so there's very little buffer between. This is very different from Rocky Mountain House where you've got mountains and then miles of foothills before you get into the farmland. As a result, we had stock kills all along the mountain slopes from Grande Prairie to the border, but far more in the south.

I stayed active as a Bear Response Team Leader and trained quite a lot of new officers in handling bears. Sure, I took part in quite a few dangerous situations and we had a few human fatalities. I remember Wilf Etherington [a retired pharmacist who got a degree in biology and went to work for CWS as a technician]. A photographer really wanted a picture of a drugged bear waking up and they lingered too long with the bear. Mr. Etherington was killed by the grizzly. I also worked with the wardens in Banff. They had never used leg snares, so I gave them advice on several instances.

Bears are a lot smarter than we give them credit for. All bears. But you always show a little more respect for the grizzlies. They are quicker to retaliate. A black bear in a snare will 90% of the time try to run away from you. A grizzly is just the opposite: 90% will try to get at you!

A SMALL BLACK BEAR LOOKING FOR AN EASY MEAL NEAR A CONSTRUCTION CAMP IN NORTHERN ALBERTA, 1987.
CREDIT: P. ROWELL

171

Team Leader (BRTL) and other BRTLs and/or officers. Jan Allen, Dennis Weisser, Ron Hanson, Stan Hawes, Andy Davison, Jack Braden, and Randy Flath were identified as the first team leaders when the program was implemented in July 1985.

In addition to the BRTL program, recommendations of the Bear Task Force resulted in the re-establishment of Regional Problem Wildlife Specialists (PWS), usually district officers willing to accept the additional responsibilities. Today both PWS and BRTL must qualify for the added responsibilities of the positions through structured training programs.

The bear control program evolved into a bear/human conflict prevention and control program with an emphasis on prevention. Due to the high volume of bear complaints in the city of Fort McMurray, a bear intercept program was established in 1987. This involved baited snares set around the outskirts to intercept bears before they ventured into the city and to relocate them to uninhabited areas. In response to ongoing conflicts between bears and ranchers, Fish and Wildlife biologist Richard Quinlan spearheaded the South West Alberta Grizzly Bear Management Strategy in 1998. As part of the strategy, carcasses of road-killed wildlife were relocated to strategic high-country locations to hold grizzly bears near their dens until cattle finished calving in the ranch lands below. In 2001, the Division acquired two Karelian bear dogs for use throughout the Southwest Region with the goal of conditioning bears to avoid specific locations and/or experiences.

The Future of Furbearers in Alberta

As we begin a new century, gone are the days when the livelihood gained from trapping sustained entire families, and even if it did, such rural ways are quickly diminishing in favour of urban lifestyles. This change cuts across the full spectrum of occupations, and trapping is no different. Even the close link of aboriginal people to the use of furbearers is weakening as fewer

participate in trapping. The overall cost of harvesting furs versus financial returns further reduces the potential for a commercial enterprise.

The historical impact of the fur industry on Canada is becoming a story for school textbooks or else, largely forgotten. The fur industry as a whole has undergone significant change, most notably the recent but complete severance from the once mighty Hudson's Bay Company. The Company no longer promotes or sells fur in their stores. This largely urban-oriented decision was seen as a major blow to the earliest and longest-running Canadian industry.

Regardless, the use of fur will continue in the coming years. Much of the fur will come from fur farms, where the perceived cruelty aspect of trapping is not an issue. However, with emerging markets in China and the Far East, wild fur species in Alberta will continue to fill a unique and specialty fur demand not available from farms. Trapping of our wild species will readily satisfy consumers in areas where cruelty issues do not elicit the sensitivity they currently do in Europe (where ironically the industry started so long ago). However, trappers will need to continue to be pro-active and willing to change to meet public sentiment. With the *Agreement on International Humane Trapping Standards* now in place, a framework exists that should lead to reducing perceived cruelty in trapping.

Trapping is also likely to continue only as a part-time occupation practised by individuals whose love for the wilderness and strong hunting desires outweigh the costs. As of 2002-2003, there were approximately 2500 trappers in Alberta, of which 1603 were trapping in 1669 Registered Fur Management Areas (RFMA). An RFMA is a parcel of public land allocated to the holder of a Registered Fur Management Licence. About 800 holders of Resident Fur Trapping Licences trap on private and public lands not included in RFMA. Both types of licences allow spouses and children to trap. The remaining 105 trappers in the province hold aboriginal licences to trap on Mètis settlements and First Nation reserves. Each trapper is responsible for managing the furbearers on his or

her trapping area and much of the information used to manage furbearers is obtained from these stewards of the land.

MAJOR EVENTS IN FURBEARER MANAGEMENT IN ALBERTA

1883	The *Territorial Ordinance for the Protection of Game* sets closed seasons on "hare" between the first day of February and the first day of September in any year; on mink and marten between the fifteenth day of April and the first day of November; on otter, beaver, and fisher between the first of May and the first of October; and on muskrat between the fifteenth of May and the first of November.
1907	The first provincial Game Act places a five-year moratorium on the harvest of beaver and bounties on wolf and coyote.
1914	Approximately 148 fur farms (mostly fox but also mink) are operating in Alberta.
1918	Regulations are amended to allow trapping of those beavers that are a nuisance to farmers in southern Alberta.
1920	All fur dealers, buyers, and exporters are required to purchase licences; a tax is levied on all exported pelts; the export of non-prime pelts is prohibited; and trapping permits for muskrat are authorized.
1942	The fur farm licence schedule is redrafted—higher fees are set for established farmers.
1942-1944	Province-wide registration of traplines and trapping areas is completed.
1946	Authority over fur farms is transferred to Alberta Agriculture.
1950-1951	Weasels are protected in the eastern part of the province in hopes that they stop the spread of Norway rats.
1952-1956	A major rabies outbreak occurs with thousands of furbearers, particularly carnivores like wolves, killed in a rabies control program.
1953	Spring bear licences are re-instated.
1950s and 1960s	Alberta wild furs are exhibited at World Trade Fairs in Paris, London, Frankfurt, and other European cities to promote Canadian fur products.
1973	A Provincial Fur Coordinator position is established; several trapping organizations join to form the Alberta Trappers' Association; and trapper education and humane trapping methods are promoted.
1974	A Provincial Problem Wildlife Coordinator and Problem Wildlife Section of the Field Service-Enforcement Branch are created. A Livestock Compensation Program is established.
1977	A Beaver Flood Control Program is established jointly by the Fish and Wildlife Division, Alberta Agriculture, and municipal governments.
1979-1980	Fur harvest reaches an all-time provincial high of $15 million. A zoning system for fur harvest is introduced in regulations.
1980	A Trapper Compensation Review Board is established.
1981	A humane trap research program is initiated in Vegreville. The Sheep River cougar study begins.
1985	A Bear Task Force and Bear Response Teams are established.
1990	A quota system is established to regulate cougar hunting.
1998	The South West Alberta Grizzly Bear Management Strategy is established.
2001	The Fish and Wildlife Division obtains two Karelian dogs for bear aversion programs.
2002	There are approximately 2500 trappers in Alberta.

173

References • CHAPTER 5

1. Erasmus, Peter. 1999. Buffalo Days and Nights. Fifth House Ltd., Calgary (Original manuscript resides at the Glenbow Institute in Calgary.)

2. Huestis, E. 1943. Annual Report of the Fish and Game Commissioner. Department of Lands and Mines, Edmonton.

3. Struthers, J.B. 1995. Lookin' Back. Alberta Game Warden, Edmonton. Summer.

4. Huestis, Eric. 1986. Talk given at the Forest Technology School in Hinton, 1972. Edited by Peter Murphy, University of Alberta, Department of Forestry, Edmonton.

5. Ibid.

6. Huestis, E. 1943-1944 to 1945-1946. Annual reports of the Fish and Game Commissioner. Department of Lands and Mines, Edmonton.

7. See Chapter 7 for more details of this intriguing aspect of wildlife biology.

8. Soper, J.D. ca. 1935. Letter donated by John Stelfox, Canadian Wildlife Service, to the Musèe Hèritage archives, St. Albert, Alberta.

9. Alberta Fish and Wildlife Division. 2000. The general status of Alberta wild species, 2000. Edmonton. Online version available at: www3.gov.ab.ca/srd/fw/wild/index.html

10. Curtis, R. 1973. As related in the Alberta Trappers' Association 25th Anniversary publication, 1998.

11. Ganske, T. 1998. President's Address, Alberta Trappers' Association, 25th Anniversary publication, 1998.

12. Miller, D.W. Date unknown. A history of the organized trappers' movement in Alberta. Typed report in the files of the Alberta Trappers' Association, Westlock, Alberta.

13. Peters, A. 1974. Alberta Trappers' Central Association. Canadian Trapper 3: 4-5.

14. Todd, A. W., and L. C. Giesbrecht. 1979. A review of Alberta fur production and management, 1920-1921 to 1977-1978. Fish and Wildlife Division, Alberta Energy and Natural Resources, Edmonton.

15. Badry, M.J., G. Proulx, and P.M. Woodard. 1997. Home range and habitat use by fishers translocated to the aspen parkland of Alberta. Pp. 233-251; in G. Proulx, H.N. Bryant, and P.M. Woodard (eds.). Martes: taxonomy, ecology, techniques, and management. Provincial Museum of Alberta, Edmonton.

16. Reid, D. G. 1984. Ecological interactions of river otters and beavers in a boreal ecosystem. M.Sc. Thesis, Department of Biology, University of Calgary, Calgary, Alberta.

17. Valastin, P., and M. Sullivan. 1996. A historical survey of the sport fisheries in northeastern Alberta. Natural Resources Service, Alberta Environmental Protection, Edmonton.

18. R.B. Miller later discovered an enzyme in the skin was creating the problem. This enzyme could be broken down easily by boiling the fish before consumption.

19. P. 50 in the Report of Fish and Game Commissioner. 1938. Department of Agriculture, Edmonton.

20. P. 47 in the Report of Fish and Game Commissioner. 1939. Department of Agriculture, Edmonton.

21. Alberta Department of Agriculture. 1942. Regulations Relating to Awarding of Prizes for Destruction of Agriculture Pests: Gophers, Crows and Magpies. Edmonton.

22. Adapted from Alberta Government website: www3.gov.ab.ca/srd/fw/wolves/index.html

23. Stelfox, J.G. 1969. Wolves in Alberta: A History 1800-1969. Alberta Lands, Forests, Parks and Wildlife 12:18-27.

24. Ibid.

25. Alberta Fish and Wildlife Division, op. cit.

26. Ballantyne, E.E. and J.G. O'Donoghue. 1954. Rabies control in Alberta. Journal of the American Veterinary Medicine Association 125: 316-326.

27. The following information is based on various publications by Ian Ross, Martin Jalkotzy, and associates.

28. Partially adapted from the Fish and Wildlife Division website (www3.gov.ab.ca/srd/fw)

174

Conservation

Conservation is a state of harmony between men and land. By land is meant all of the things on, over, or in the earth. Harmony with land is like harmony with a friend; you cannot cherish his right hand and chop off his left. That is to say, you cannot love game and hate predators; you cannot conserve the waters and waste the ranges; you cannot build the forest and mine the farm. The land is one organism. Its parts, like our own parts, compete with each other and co-operate with each other, the competitions are as much a part of the inner workings as the co-operations. You can regulate them – cautiously – but not abolish them.

THE *second* ERA

OF FISH AND WILDLIFE MANAGEMENT IN ALBERTA:
Conservation Aldo Leopold Style

By the middle of the 20th century, the peak of the era of preservation was beginning to fade but not before leaving Albertans with a legacy of protected wildlife and wild spaces in a National Parks system that today makes up approximately eight percent of Alberta's landbase.

These nationally protected areas preserve portions of three of the province's six ecoregions (Jasper, Banff and Waterton in the mountains, Elk Island in the parkland, and Wood Buffalo in the boreal forest). While the province has added another four percent to this landbase through its various parks and protected areas programs over the century, including sizeable additions like the Willmore Wilderness Area, the political will for large-scale protection in Alberta has not been present since the formation of Wood Buffalo National Park in 1922. As well, the level of "protection" has varied through time within both nationally and provincially designated areas where resource extraction and other activities may continue to occur on and underneath such lands.

Thus, the second era of fish and wildlife management saw the need to *preserve* overtaken by the desire to *conserve* a manageable and renewable resource. New surveys and studies were needed to better define population parameters, particularly in the management of fisheries (Chapter Six *Fisheries: Research and Management*). The Province contracted R.B. Miller to initiate a study of several Alberta lakes for fish production. Soon, it would hire its own biologists to continue this work on both fish and game populations. The Game Branch, soon to be the Fish and Wildlife Division, matured like the rest of the young province. Trained wildlife biologists familiar with Leopold's game management techniques gathered the information required. In response to new knowledge, fish and game management became more refined, hunting and fishing laws became more sophisticated, and harvest regimens, for the most part, more

sustainable. Even the general public were more aware that collectively fish and game was not an endless bounty to be overexploited. Rather, this renewable resource needed to be managed properly. "Conservation is the wise use of resources in perpetuity" became the accepted slogan of the day.

In addition to government, a number of non-government organizations were also interested in conserving Alberta's fish and wildlife. These organizations, sometimes in partnership with the province, undertook a number of projects to enhance certain game species and/or their habitat. The Alberta Fish and Game Association promoted upland game bird management very early on (Chapter Seven *Upland Game Birds: Study and Enhancement*). Active since 1906, the Association introduced several non-native species including pheasants, Hungarian (gray) partridge, bobwhite quail, and chukar partridge. While releasing non-native species may be viewed in a negative light today, habitat and census programs for these species also benefitted many native upland game birds. Similarly, Ducks Unlimited Canada, growing out of an American hunting industry, came to Alberta to undertake projects that would enhance waterfowl populations and their habitat (Chapter Eight *Waterfowl and Wetlands: Cooperation in Conservation*).

While these early programs benefitted many species, the focus at the time remained, for the most part, on game species. Benefits to non-game species were largely incidental. However, the recognition of the critical wildlife-habitat connection was coming and the incorporation of programs to address habitat loss would soon benefit many species.

Chapter 6

FISHERIES:
RESEARCH AND MANAGEMENT

Margo Pybus and Petra Rowell with contributions from Cheryl Croucher, Ken Crutchfield,
Vic Gillman, Gordon Haugen, Carl Hunt, Gordon Kerr, Dennis McDonald, George Sterling,
Michael Sullivan, George Walker, Francine Wieliczko, Kevin Wingert, Bill Wishart and Ken Zelt

177

In a cool curving world he lies, and ripples with dark ecstasies.
The kind luxurious lapse and steal, shapes all his universe to feel
And know and be; the clinging stream, closes his memory, glooms his dream,
Who lips the roots o'the shore, and glides, superb on unreturning tides.

EXCERPT FROM "THE FISH" BY RUPERT BROOKE[1]

■ ■ ■

DEDICATION

When we first started thinking about a fisheries chapter for this book, it wasn't long before the name Martin Paetz came up in conversation. A few phone calls later, and Martin was at one of our early meetings. At first, he appeared a bit sceptical at the few notes I had quickly sketched together about the topic. But he soon came around after I assured him the fisheries chapter could grow in any direction he saw fit to take it. Soon the stories, and the laughter, began to fill the room....

A winter of poor health and Martin's subsequent passing robbed the project of his further guidance. But Martin continued to be on our minds as we, with the help of some of his colleagues, pieced together the story of fisheries research and management in Alberta. While the following provides only a brief overview of events when we could indeed have filled entire volumes, we hope that it provides a starting point and that Martin would have approved.

We dedicate this chapter to Martin Paetz—Alberta's first provincial fisheries biologist hired in 1952 and rising to Director of Fisheries before his retirement in 1983—a respected colleague, mentor, and cherished friend.

■ ■ ■

PROVINCIAL FISHERIES BIOLOGIST MARTIN PAETZ AND ASSISTANT HATCHERY SUPERINTENDENT STU SHAW PLANTING FISH,
EDMONTON BEACH, 1962.
COURTESY ALBERTA FISH AND WILDLIFE DIVISION

Jurisdiction in the Early Years

Aboriginal peoples, fur traders, explorers, and eventually settlers, all benefitted from Alberta's seemingly abundant fish stocks. As with other wild resources, there was, initially at least, little thought given to its conservation. Before long, however, Albertans would start to see the need, first, to learn more about this resource, and second, to manage it accordingly.

Fisheries management began, as Canada began, with the *British North America (BNA) Act* of 1867, which provided for federal control over all fisheries. The new nation established its first federal *Fisheries Act* in 1868. Fisheries

management, in the area that was to become Alberta, first came under serious consideration in 1890 when two North West Mounted Police officers submitted a report on the condition of several trout streams in the Calgary and Pincher Creek districts. They noted the fish in these streams were "suffering greatly from the want of proper protection and authorized officials to enforce the laws for such protection".[2] The use of unlawful and unsporting traps and nets for sport fishing had become common. As well, a number of dead fish were found with sawdust in their gills. Dumping such material into the nearest water body was a common practice of local sawmills at the time.

A NICE CATCH OF CUTTHROAT TROUT OUT OF THE BOW RIVER, 1924.
COURTESY ALBERTA SUSTAINABLE RESOURCE DEVELOPMENT
(FOREST PROTECTION IMAGE LIBRARY)

provided recognition of both provincial and federal rights pertaining to Alberta fish stocks suitable for domestic, sport, and commercial uses. Even today, Alberta fisheries are administered jointly under the federal *Fisheries Act* and the provincial *Fisheries (Alberta) Act* and Regulations.

As they are today, early fisheries managers were faced with the problem of a growing number of fishermen and not enough fish. Compared to other parts of Canada, Alberta has a relatively small number of fish-bearing waterbodies. Approximately 800 lakes in the province have naturally occurring game fish populations. And while there are approximately 63 species of fishes in Alberta, only 18 of them are preferred for food or angling, including pike, walleye, perch, whitefish, arctic grayling, and several trout species. In the early part of the century, fish culture and the planting of exotic, preferred trout species in mountain lakes and rivers, was seen as the solution to this perceived piscatorial deficit.

Both Officers called for stricter fishing regulations and the establishment of fish hatcheries so that affected streams could be restocked. There was only one problem: the authority for fisheries was controlled from afar by the federal government in Ottawa—managed through its Department of the Interior. Even when Alberta became a province in 1905, it did not have the authority to manage the fish found within its borders, and gained only a shared responsibility for fisheries under the 1930 *Natural Resources Transfer Act*.

After 1930, the federal government continued to maintain a role in some aspects of fisheries management, including the right to determine the acceptability of fishing equipment, techniques, and seasons. It also maintained a presence in managing commercial fisheries. For its share of the transfer agreement, the province gained ownership of its fisheries and determination of who could access the resource. The provincial authority for fisheries was placed in the Department of Lands and Mines, with R.T. Todd as Director. Several provincial Fisheries Officers would now carry out enforcement activities. The provincial *Act Respecting the Rights of Fishery*

The Early Trout Hatcheries

Fish culture, the artificial propagation and rearing of fish, became popular in Alberta early in the 20th century, as it did in many jurisdictions across North America. Park managers, looking to enhance the recreational angling experience in the national parks, wanted to stock game fish into mountain lakes devoid of native trout. The first federal trout hatchery, established in Banff in 1913, produced rainbow, cutthroat, brook, and to a lesser extent lake, splake, and brown trout.[3] At the same time, an egg-collecting station for the

EXCERPT FROM THE 1930 *NATURAL RESOURCES TRANSFER ACT*
"Except as herein otherwise provided, all rights of fishery shall, after the coming into force of this agreement, belong to and be administered by the Province, and the Province shall have the right to dispose of all such rights of fishery by sale, licence or otherwise, subject to the exercise by the Parliament of Canada of its legislative jurisdiction over sea-coast and inland fisheries."

main hatchery was established at Spray Lakes within the early boundaries of Banff National Park. Native bull trout were viewed as a predator on preferred trout stocks and early managers were interested in eliminating it in favour of cutthroat and rainbow trout. Exotic, non-native fish like brook and brown trout were introduced because of their reputation with anglers as challenging game fish.

THE DOMINION GOVERNMENT FISH HATCHERY AT BANFF, 1924.
COURTESY ALBERTA SUSTAINABLE RESOURCE DEVELOPMENT
(ALBERTA FOREST PROTECTION CATALOGUE)

Additional fish hatcheries followed at Waterton and Jasper and by 1936, the federal hatcheries were well established. Outside the national parks, James Cross, President of the Calgary Brewing and Malting Company, was about to conceive the idea for the first provincial game fish hatchery. When Alfred Ernest Cross built the Calgary brewery in 1892, he found an aquifer flowing parallel to the Bow River.

Although the water was of exceptional purity, it was used only to cool the beer prior to aging. James Cross thought this water should be put to some productive use before being discharged. A fish hatchery seemed perfect. The water warmed by the cooling cycle would be ideal for hatching and rearing fish fry and fingerlings.

A GAME FISH "RE-INVENTED" IN ALBERTA
[MICHAEL SULLIVAN]

One of the more interesting outcomes from the early years of fish hatcheries was the development of splake. This hatchery cross between brook trout (also called speckled trout) and lake trout was described as early as the late 1800s, but little became of developing the hybrid as a viable hatchery fish or game fish until much later. During the 1940s, J. E. Stenton (father of Ernie Stenton, provincial Director of Fisheries in the 1980s) was a park warden working at the Banff Fish Hatchery. He experimented with crossing lake and brook trout and eventually developed successful techniques for large-scale production of this hybrid. His success came in crossing male brook trout from Third Vermilion Lake and female lake trout from Lake Minnewanka.

Techniques for creating and raising splake were duly published in the *Canadian Fish Culturalist* in 1950 and 1952, and were quickly adopted by hatcheries in Quebec, Ontario, and Wyoming. Based on its rapid growth and good game fish qualities, this unusual and new game fish was soon in demand by anglers. Federally managed lakes throughout Banff, Jasper, and even Wood Buffalo national parks were stocked. In Jasper, splake were of particular interest to anglers, and from 1953 to 1971, 15 different lakes were stocked a total of 51 times with over a quarter of a million splake. Going one step further, Lac Beauvert in Jasper National Park was stocked with a hybrid backcross of splake and brook trout in 1957.

Biologists managing Alberta's provincial waters appeared less enthusiastic about spreading this unusual fish. George Sterling (fisheries biologist, Edson) recalls: "Two lakes were stocked with splake in 1968: Emerson Lake (north of Edson) received 4800 fingerlings, and an unnamed lake (a.k.a. Splake Lake; north of Hinton) received about 2000 fingerlings. There was a complete winterkill in the unnamed lake the following winter. Emerson Lake produced a few splake for anglers until about 1973 and then brook trout were introduced to the lake in 1974."

Cross went to Banff to learn how the federal hatchery was operated, returned to Calgary, and laid his plans accordingly. A new building was erected with appropriate troughs and suitable piping. Cross then approached the government and struck a deal. The province gladly agreed to supply fish eggs and manpower to operate the facility; the Brewery would look after construction and maintenance. By 1940, the Calgary hatchery produced enough individuals of several species to begin distributing them to lakes and streams throughout the province. In his annual reports of the time, Fish and Game Commissioner W.H. Wallace noted that the brewery hatchery was one of the most up-to-date in North America and, even in its early years, some two million fish were reared annually. Operating for 32 years, it underwent many improvements and expansions. However, on September 5, 1972, the Brewery closed its fish-rearing facilities after the new, modern Sam Livingston Fish Hatchery was ready to open in William Pearce Estate Park, just across the railroad tracks from the brewery.

Expansion and Improvements of the Provincial Hatcheries

In 1941, provincial hatchery managers started distributing older fingerlings instead of young fry, releasing them in the spring rather than summer, to achieve better survival rates. The program was well received and the resultant demand for more fingerlings required the development of more rearing ponds. These were established in Calgary within the grounds of the Brewery and at the Inglewood Bird

Sanctuary. By 1942, with a capacity for four million fish, the Calgary Brewing and Malting hatchery was the largest game fish hatchery in the Dominion of Canada.

Satellite sites were also enhanced to aid fish production and transportation around the province. Rearing ponds had been established in 1926 at the junction of Beaver Creek and the Raven River near Caroline, using water from clear springs particularly conducive to rearing fish. In 1937, the springs and a quarter section of land surrounding them were dedicated as the Raven River Rearing Station. In 1942, four large ponds were added to the site. Trout fry were initially brought from the Banff hatchery, but after 1941, they were brought from Calgary. In 1959, alterations improved the water flow in the ponds and in 1962 the station was again enlarged. In 1975, this facility was changed to a brood station,

EARLY SIGN AT THE RAVEN RIVER FISH REARING STATION.
CREDIT: K. LUNGLE

181

FISH STOCKING - A FAMILY AFFAIR
[GORDON KERR]

I was fascinated by the stories my father told of how he (James Kerr) and my grandfather (John Kerr), picked up rainbow trout fry from the federal park hatcheries at Banff and Waterton Lakes. They then released them into streams and beaver ponds from the Castle River to the Oldman River headwaters. Starting about 1917, they did this with five-gallon milk cans in the back seat of the family car, stopping frequently at streams to replace the water, ensuring it remained cold and oxygenated.

This was at their own time and expense over countless miles of gravel and dirt (gumbo) roads. James and his sons continued trout stocking, working with the provincial government staff and the local Fish and Game clubs well into the 1950s. The result was the presence of rainbows throughout the Crowsnest River system, which provided for some spectacular fishing!

THE SAM LIVINGSTON FISH HATCHERY
[FRANCINE WIELICZKO]

The Sam Livingston Fish Hatchery, at a start-up cost of $5.7 million, was named after one of the first farmers in the Calgary area. Sam Livingston was born in Ireland and came to North America in 1847. Along with introducing mechanized equipment, he made many contributions to the community and is considered a founding father to the region now called Calgary.

Another historical figure in Calgary, William Pearce, the Superintendent of Mines for the Federal Government, established his office in Calgary in 1884. Pearce purchased a block of land on the south bank of the Bow River and built a 14-room mansion called the Bow Bend Shack. Upon his death, this land was bequeathed to the City of Calgary. In light of his abiding interest in irrigation and parks, the City decided that a fish hatchery was a perfect fit with Pearce's original intentions for this land.

When it opened in 1973, the Sam Livingston Fish Hatchery was designed to produce up to five million fish each year for stocking approximately 200 locations throughout the province. Alex Sinclair,

previously superintendent of the Calgary Brewing and Malting Hatchery, oversaw the development of the new operation. The design was well ahead of its time and had several cutting edge features. It was the first totally enclosed hatchery in North America, which meant temperature control of the water was more economical, fish could be reared throughout the winter, and birds and other predators could be kept away from the fish. Whereas most fish hatcheries could only rear one species at a time, the Sam Livingston could rear eight different species simultaneously. The facility incorporated a recycling and reconditioning system that required new water for only ten percent of the total water flow. It was also designed to include public viewing galleries, theatres for school children, and interpretive signage.

In July 1989, disaster struck: fish at the Sam Livingston Fish Hatchery contracted infectious pancreatic necrosis virus (IPNV). The virus produces high mortality in young trout and surviving fish can become lifelong carriers. Although this was not the first time IPNV had gotten into Alberta's hatcheries,

FISH HATCHERY AT CALGARY BREWING AND MALTING. COURTESY PROVINCIAL ARCHIVES OF ALBERTA (P4738)

(brook trout eggs brought IPNV into the hatchery in the late 1960s with the result that 300,000 brook trout were destroyed), it was by far the most serious outbreak.

In 1989, IPNV had entered the hatchery system through infected wild lake trout eggs collected from a lake in northern Alberta and sent to the Cold Lake hatchery. While the virus was unknowingly incubating, brood stock recruits were transferred to the Raven station. By the time the virus was detected, it had been spread to three of the four provincial fish culture facilities (only the Allison Creek station was spared). To make matters worse, the Sam Livingston was bursting at the seams with fish (between 3.5 and 4.8 million fish ready to go). Fish were dying at an incredible rate, but the survivors also posed a risk as potential carriers of the virus.

A provincial task force decided to eradicate IPNV in the hatcheries. At the Sam Livingston that meant taking new precautions to prevent further outbreaks and destroying all the fish in the facility. From 1989 to 1991, tons of dead fish were buried in dead-animal disposal sites in Calgary. This was hard on staff, as expressed by Dave DePape, the current hatchery Superintendent. "We knew we were doing the right thing but still…we were supposed to raise fish, not kill

WORKERS MONITOR THE EGG INCUBATION TRAYS AND TROUGHS IN THE CALGARY BREWING AND MALTING FISH HATCHERY, ca. 1950.
COURTESY SAM LIVINGSTON FISH HATCHERY

them. It was a very traumatic experience. You could talk to any of the technical staff involved … and get some pretty emotional responses."

The virus was eradicated after ponds, storage, and administrative areas of the Sam Livingston were disinfected (at a cost of $2 million) and the incubation, trough, and pond areas were repaired. Production was restored in late 1991 and full production of rainbow, brown, and brook trout resumed in 1992. On April 24, 1992, the official reopening of the Sam Livingston Fish Hatchery was celebrated. Eradication at the Raven station was also successful with full return to egg production after 1992. Today, the Sam Livingston Fish Hatchery remains the flagship of Alberta's fish culture program.[4]

183

FISH REARING PONDS OUTSIDE OF THE CALGARY BREWERY FISH HATCHERY, ca.1943.
COURTESY PROVINCIAL ARCHIVES OF ALBERTA (P4740)

RAVEN RIVER REARING STATION IN 1963 BEFORE
CONVERSION TO A TROUT BROOD STATION.
COURTESY ALBERTA FISH AND WILDLIFE DIVISION

184

Associations were the first sports groups to maintain rearing ponds, but other local groups soon joined them. In 1946, five ponds on the Hunter Brothers Ranch west of Fort Macleod were chosen for trout brood stock ponds after being treated with rotenone to remove pike and suckers. By 1953, it became more cost-efficient to purchase fertilized eggs from large commercial trout hatcheries in the U.S., and the ranch ponds and other sites were closed.

supplying fertilized eggs to the new Sam Livingston Hatchery in Calgary. A new dimension was added to the Raven Station in 2000 when ponds were used to incubate and grow eggs of the provincially endangered leopard frog.[5]

A second satellite brood station was established in the Crowsnest Pass. Gordon Kerr recalls: "Then as the head of the fish and wildlife program in the 1970s, I recommended a brood station be developed on Allison Creek in the Crowsnest Pass at a site I had been familiar with since childhood. Engineering studies proved the site to be very suitable, with favourable water conditions and security from disease. Thus the Allison Brood Trout Station was developed."

Fish culture also grabbed the attention of several fish and game associations. In 1941, the Cardston and Claresholm Fish and Game

Technical training of hatchery personnel was non-existent in the start-up years of the provincial hatcheries. Winfried Schenk, who spent nearly 40 years at the hatcheries and was the Superintendent of the Sam Livingston from 1976 to 1998, reflected that you could "work seven years for the Calgary Electric Department and come into this [hatchery] with no knowledge. All the knowledge you had, you

CALGARY FISH HATCHERY STAFF INCLUDING ALEX SINCLAIR, WINFRIED SCHENK, RUSSELL SINCLAIR, AND STU SHAW, 1963.
COURTESY ALBERTA FISH AND WILDLIFE DIVISION

acquired in the business". Technical training in fisheries management was first offered in Alberta in 1970 at the Lethbridge Community College and in 1973 at the Northern Alberta Institute of Technology. Gradually, academic standards changed and in 1983, the hatchery hired its first employee who held a university degree.

Transporting fish from the hatcheries to the drop-off points was always a challenge and methods changed over time. Originally, fish were moved without oxygen. Transport tanks were iced down and employees went as fast as they could to get to their destination. This required small satellite stations (including facilities at Pincher Creek, Edson, and Caroline) where fish were dropped off for further re-distribution. Beginning about 1960, oxygen was supplied in the transport trucks but there was still no way to carry oxygen into remote areas. The trip to high mountain lakes was arduous, to say the least. Using packhorses or backpack

containers full of fish, employees stopped at creek crossings. The fish no doubt appreciated being replenished with fresh mountain water and those carrying them appreciated the rest. Since the early 1970s, helicopters have made life much easier for stocking remote lakes.

Over the years, fisheries management shifted to an increased focus on declining species and the overall health of native fish populations, in particular walleye and bull trout. The fish culture program shifted as well. More native species were raised, including cutthroat trout, arctic grayling, walleye, and bull trout. Bigger fish were also produced. Terry McFadden, Head of the Fish Culture Section from 1976 to 1996, played an important role in shaping the development and expansion of the fish culture program. He was a strong advocate of fish culture and invested a great deal of energy in ensuring that the resources needed to expand the Sam Livingston hatchery were secured.[6] Ken Zelt

185

TANK TRUCK PLANTING HATCHERY FISH AT EDMONTON BEACH, 1962. COURTESY PROVINCIAL ARCHIVES OF ALBERTA (PA219/4)

TERRY MCFADDEN, FISHERIES CULTURE SPECIALIST
[INTERVIEWED BY PAT VALASTIN]

Terry McFadden was born in 1938 in Flin Flon, near the Saskatchewan/Manitoba border. "My father was in copper and zinc mining and refining. Flin Flon was tremendous country—lots of beautiful lakes, and lots of fishing and outdoors activities. It was a good healthy upbringing."

Terry obtained a Bachelor's and a Master's degree from the University of Manitoba. "In the Flin Flon area, there were concerns about heavy metals and their impact on fish. The Department of Health and the Fish and Wildlife group were interested in pursuing it, so I studied toxicity in brook trout. Then I went off to do a Ph.D. at the University of Toronto. I was working with the former Associate Director of Connaught Lab (an affiliate of the university) trying to develop vaccines for some fish diseases. He and I were constantly back and forth to Connaught Labs, just a few miles south of my office at Maple, Ontario. We both inadvertently picked up one of the germ-warfare bugs that Connaught was working on for the U.S. military. But we didn't realize it at the time. I had some extremely competent medical attention at Toronto, but without knowing exactly what we were dealing with and where it had come from…we just knew that he and I had it and my wife, Darlene, picked it up. We checked the kids—they didn't. We even went so far as to check the dog. It took us about three years under stressful circumstances to get over that and in the process I kind of lost interest in the Ph.D."

"In 1970, I moved to a satellite campus of Sir Sanford Fleming College in Lindsay, Ontario. I was there for five years and eventually set up a two-year fish and wildlife technician program and a three-year fish and wildlife technologist program. We also built a fish hatchery training facility there."

"I came to Alberta as Section Head for Fish Culture with the Fish and Wildlife Division in 1976. I spent the first year in Calgary so I could get familiar with the Sam Livingston Fish Hatchery which was unique. Sam Livingston was a big recirculation hatchery. The Fisheries Director, Martin Paetz, knew that any new hatcheries would have to be recirculation hatcheries because of the climate. Gordon Kerr was the Assistant Deputy Minister of Fish and Wildlife. I had quite a lot of confidence in both those fellows. And Ernie Stenton, too, who was responsible for the field biologists.

"The federal government wanted to implement some rules and controls on fish movements. I'd had some experience there, so I was involved along with people from other provinces and the federal government. We stopped the free movement of cultured fish in and out of Alberta from other provinces, and in and out of Canada from the United States and elsewhere. There were some importations of salmon before I'd arrived and it scared the daylights out of me, because I knew what those salmon carried. I became the administrator for fish health in Alberta, which drew all the other health areas together. Veterinarians and microbiologists actually dealt in the lab with fish. It was a fascinating period and I think we did manage to keep out a lot of fish diseases. There were times when we'd detect something that was getting away from us and bring it under control. We worked very closely with the veterinary lab at the O.S. Longman Building.

"One other good thing involved a federal survey on the benefits of keeping angling nearby rather than having people go outside the province. I looked at the data and pointed out that based on what you got from the fisheries, not only keeping the fish shops in business, the sporting equipment sales, the hotels, restaurants, all these other things, was in fact about an 18 to 1 return on every dollar invested. You were getting back about twenty times what you put into it. That didn't take long to get to the Premier's office. It made sense to the politicians.

"There were times when it was hard to go to work optimistically, I guess, because there were changes. Certainly when they started to cut back, it was hard to see competent employees let go. We had an excellent group that could run things and I had just about enough anyway. The last few years there was a lot of rear-guard action. Reduced funding made it difficult to do much more. That was true in many other areas of Fish and Wildlife as well. I really empathized with the Director of Fisheries and the Assistant Deputy Minister at the time for what they had to put up with. I wasn't prepared to do that."

As for the future of the wildlife profession, Terry reflected: "I think it's maturing, although it's getting a lot more complex, like everything else. We're getting more specialized. I think we'll have to do more planning. It's very difficult at the provincial level to do the planning we need to do to identify where the problem areas are. However, with a reduced staff, it's super-critical to select the key issues and which way to go. At the same time, we have to try to predict how other things are going to diminish." Summing up his career, Terry stated: "Overall, I had a chance to utilize a lot of skills. I was very happy and certainly very happy with the people I worked with."

186

FRANK SOMERVILLE, LAWRENCE SCHEFFELMIAR, AND JOEY COCCIOLONI
TRANSPORTING FISH INTO LOWER BARNABY LAKE, 1959.
CREDIT: C. GORDON

an important tool to support the provincial fisheries management program.

R. B. Miller and Early Fisheries Research

While the hatchery and stocking programs continued to grow, more information on the state of Alberta's fisheries, and any potential opportunities to expand this resource, was desired. Early in the 1940s, the Fish and Game Division hired Richard B. Miller, a professor at the University of Alberta, to study several streams and lakes, gathering the first fisheries data ever collected at most of these locations. Several members of the Fisheries Branch and some enforcement officers, such as Mervyn Heron of Lac La Biche, assisted Miller. Much of Miller's work was duly recorded in the Division's annual reports.

187

and Morley Barrett, with the Fish and Wildlife Division, also significantly influenced the fish culture industry. They were instrumental in breaking down some of the management barriers and allowing the fish culture program to become

Over several summers, Miller made a number of observations and recommendations to fisheries managers. For example, in 1946, he undertook a survey of Cold Lake and suggested it would support a good sport fishery, if commercial net

DR. R.B. MILLER NOTES FROM THE 1943 FISH AND GAME DIVISION ANNUAL REPORT:

Ghost River Reservoir:	Physical, chemical, planktonic, and bottom fauna observations made; meagre plankton and poor bottom fauna show very low productivity.
Gadsby Pond:	Only supports summer life, unsuitable for fish.
Baptiste Lake:	Summer stagnation (low oxygen in deep water, high temperature in surface water) likely responsible for tullibee deaths.
Jamieson (Johnson) Lake:	Near Brooks, suitable for stocking with pickerel [walleye].
Whitewood Lake:	Suitable for stocking with perch and pickerel.
Lake Eden:	Lack of fauna due to low oxygen in deeper water.
Lake Newell:	Poor food conditions for fish.
Raymond Sugar Refinery Pond:	Freezes during winter; will not support fish.
McLeod River drainage:	Poor supply of natural trout food due to winter ice scouring.
Obed Lake:	Trout, northern pearl dace, and suckers present.

fishing were abolished. Similarly, he thought the Elbow River was useless for rainbow trout stocking since the physical habitat was not suitable due to poor food, cover, and water fluctuations.[7] Surveying the McLeod and Jumping Pound drainages, Miller found the Upper McLeod River was too large to warrant remedial measures and recommended that it be left alone. However, Jumping Pound Creek often flooded and had limited pools and cover. Miller suggested that cutthroat stocking be continued in this water body, as they appeared to survive there.

While these early lake and stream inventories focussed on lake ecology, productivity, and stocking potential, attention soon turned to other aspects affecting waterbodies in Alberta including excessive weed growth, winter kill, pollution, bank erosion, and proposed hydro-electric developments. A survey of the Spray River in 1948 indicated that a proposed hydroelectric development would greatly alter the ecological picture, although the main reservoir would be good for lake trout.

In the late 1940s, Dr. Miller refined his research, looking specifically at the life histories and taxonomies of several trout species. To do this, he needed a location where he could conduct several experiments on trout. In 1950, Miller established the Gorge Creek Biological Station near Turner Valley.[8] The object was to learn as much as possible about Alberta fisheries; why some species stocked in certain watercourses failed to survive, and why released hatchlings did not result in a corresponding increase in the population. Early results indicated 31% mortality in stocked hatchlings. In fenced experimental pens in Gorge Creek, hatchery fish died but wild fish did not. Apparently, there was considerable competition for secure space between hatchery fish and wild fish.

Martin Paetz and the Fisheries Branch

With the major oil finds of the 1940s, Alberta's economy boomed in the 1950s and Fish and Game Commissioner Huestis was able to hire a number of professional fisheries and wildlife biologists. The first of these was Martin J. Paetz, a fisheries biologist and former student of R.B. Miller. In 1952, Paetz was based in Edmonton but, in the course of his work, travelled to various parts of the province. Throughout the 1950s, Miller and Paetz both continued their work, amassing a large body of data on the lakes and streams of every major drainage system in the province. More specific biological research was also conducted through fish stocking, hatching, and rearing experiments.

As popular streams became increasingly crowded with anglers, stocking trout into reservoirs and pothole lakes became more important. In some cases, native fish (perch and/or pike) in these ponds were eradicated before the waters were stocked with trout. In 1954, Grassy Lake Reservoir was stocked with the largest single trout planting at that time (25,000 trout). To increase angling success in pothole lakes, experiments were undertaken in 1955 and a new trout stocking policy was formulated. Additional studies focussed on the survival of pond-raised trout in quiet brown-water streams and the inhibition of algal growth in earthen ponds. Carl Hunt, retired Fisheries Biologist in Edson, recalls: "Pothole stocking was an innovative use of waters that would not support native species or provide natural reproduction. Today, we take it for granted but, at the time, the public wanted to stock creeks and thought Miller and Paetz were nuts when they insisted on stocking sloughs!"

D.S. RAWSON

A contemporary of Dr. Miller, D.S. Rawson also carried out a number of early studies and experiments on fish in the lakes of the mountain parks and elsewhere in Alberta. One such experiment involved reducing the population of longnose suckers at Pyramid Lake in an effort to improve local angling efforts. Rawson published several papers describing such experiments and the alpine lakes he studied.[9] The naming of Rawson Lake, a high mountain lake in Kananaskis Country, recognizes his early contributions to Alberta's fishery resource.

FISHERIES RESEARCH AT GORGE CREEK

In his book, *A Cool Curving World*, Dr. Richard Birnie Miller describes the beginnings of a world-class ecological research institution: "Early in May of 1950, Mac and I, in Gertrude II, laden with lumber, tools, and tents, set out for the location we had chosen late the previous fall. This was Gorge Creek."[10] ["Mac" was W.H. Macdonald, a Fisheries Officer, and "Gertrude II" was an International 4x4 truck.]

Born in Weyburn, Saskatchewan, Miller graduated from the University of Toronto and became permanent staff at the University of Alberta. For ten summers, Miller assisted the Department of Lands and Forests with fisheries inventories and studies of various waterbodies. In time, he came to believe that the many management problems of the day could be solved only by careful, long-term investigation. During the winter of 1949-1950, Miller and Eric Huestis, the Game Commissioner, discussed these research problems and the method by which they might be tackled. Huestis agreed that a biological station should be established. Together with H.B. Watkins, the Superintendent of Fisheries, the problem of trout stocking was selected as a subject of study. Miller's task was to determine why hatchery-reared trout did not survive in streams where wild trout were living. If the results proved valuable, plans would be made to establish a full-fledged biological station.

The Provincial Government provided funds for the building and operation of the field station. Meanwhile, Robert Newton secured permission from the University of Alberta Board of Governors for Miller to use university material to equip it. University grants provided $900 to compensate students employed there for the summer. Huestis obtained permission from the Eastern Rockies Forest Conservation Board for a station on Gorge Creek, considered an ideal location to study hatchery-raised trout.

On May 8, 1950, W.H. Macdonald and R.B. Miller selected a site for the camp in the current Sheep River Wildlife Sanctuary west of Turner Valley. Mahlon Mangan, and Martin J. Paetz, both undergraduate students in zoology and interested in fisheries, were employed to help build the station. In a week, the four researchers constructed a rustic campsite consisting of two tent platforms with four-foot wooden walls and tarps. The larger building (14'x16') was furnished with a stove, tables, and benches for use as a combined cookhouse and laboratory. The smaller building (10'x12') was a dormitory equipped with a heater and bunks. The site, named the Alberta Biological Station, could be accessed only via a rough dirt road.

After the first year of research, Miller recommended that they conduct further experiments on hatchery-raised fish; that they replace the tents with winterized buildings so that gear could be stored over winter and experiments

GORGE CREEK RESEARCH STATION, 1950. COURTESY B. STEVENSON

189

could be run year-round, and that they secure funds to expand research to birds, big game, and other mammals. Subsequently, Miller's innovative trout research brought significant understanding to the survival of hatchery-raised fish in streams, and led to significant changes to fisheries management in subsequent years. After his death in 1959, the site was renamed the R.B. Miller Station (in 1965) in his honour. Initially, the University of Alberta managed the station. When the

FISH FENCING FOR EXPERIMENTS ON GORGE CREEK, 1958.
COURTESY B. STEVENSON

University of Calgary gained full autonomy in 1966, both universities shared management until 1991, when operation was given solely to the University of Calgary, Kananaskis Field Stations. To many who worked and learned here, the Station is simply known as Gorge Creek.

Directors of the R.B. Miller Station:

R.B. Miller	1950-58
Dave Boag	1958-60
Victor Lewin	1960-63
Dave Boag	1963-90
Ross Lein	1990-91
Edward Johnson	1991-present

DR. RICHARD B. MILLER AT A FISH CAMP, ca. 1943.
COURTESY M. SULLIVAN

DR. MARTIN PAETZ, FISHERIES BIOLOGIST
[ADAPTED FROM AN INTERVIEW WITH CHERYL CROUCHER, INNOVATION ALBERTA]

When R.B. Miller established the first biological research station in Alberta, among his students was a bright young biologist named Martin Paetz. Paetz worked at the Gorge Creek Station and completed his Master's thesis under Miller's supervision. Dr. Miller also paved the way for Paetz to become the first staff fisheries biologist hired by the Province of Alberta. His career was to span the gamut from a basic inventory of fishes and fish habitat in Alberta's rivers, lakes, and streams, to developing and setting regulations to protect Alberta's fish populations. Along the way, he and Dr. Joe Nelson of the University of Alberta co-authored *Fishes of Alberta*.

The 1950s were a great time to be a fisheries biologist in Alberta. Much of the land was still untouched wilderness, industry was just beginning, and the lakes and streams were brimming with trout, pike, and perch. A visit with Dr. Paetz reveals much about Alberta's world of fishes.

Paetz was asked what first interested him in fish. He replied: "I'm not entirely sure. I guess it goes back to my days in public school and high school when I had a teacher for many years who was a naturalist. We used to go out on field trips and observe birds and mammals. Then a neighbour sort of took me under his wing because he was a fisherman and he taught me about angling. We made quite a few trips together. Then later, in my university days, I met Dr. Miller and fisheries became the guiding force in what I chose to do."

"Dr. Miller approached the government some years before I came along, for the need for some biologists. I think he was instrumental in actually selling them the idea that they needed not only consultants, but also some staff who worked in the biological field. The first position came up and he suggested I apply for it. I did and I think his references stood me in very good stead.

"There was a massive amount of work to be done. There were so many streams that the government didn't really know very much about their characteristics or fish populations. So, we went around the province and looked at a large number of streams. Dr. Miller actually started that and we continued. And the same applies to lakes. There were so many lakes that were simply on the inventory but nothing really was known about them. So my work for the next ten years was to survey a lot of these waterbodies and determine their suitability or otherwise for fish."

When asked about which big events in his career had real meaning for him, Paetz recalled: "Well, after I was more or less through with the fieldwork (we never were through with it!), I was asked to take a higher position in the administrative end of things and that took me away from the fieldwork to quite a large degree. But the use of scientific material and so on in drafting fishing regulations was perhaps where I received the most satisfaction."

"I also harken back to my days in the field with Dr. Miller. We did a lot of fish collecting as we went about our work and so we developed quite an inventory of what fishes were in the province and to some extent, their abundance. This laid the groundwork for the book *Fishes of Alberta*. Dr. Miller and I talked about this as a matter of fact but it never came to fruition until some time later. I started putting this material together and got Dr. Nelson, who was rising in the Zoology Department at the time, to collaborate with me and we eventually produced a book and a subsequent revision."

When asked to compare the state of the fisheries in Alberta today with that of the time when he was in the field stations and tromping around the streams and rivers and lakes, Paetz hedged: "That's a bit of a difficult question, but I guess I was there at a time when the angling population was growing. The fish populations were relatively stable and, in short, it was a good time to be around. Since then, the angling population has grown by leaps and bounds. The habitat for fish has deteriorated to a fairly marked degree through various things…to some extent climatic change, industrialization and its subsequent effect on habitat, construction of hydro dams, building of pulp mills, and so on—all had an impact on the fishery. And so I think it's fair to say that the fishery declined mainly for those reasons. Also, angling took a lot more of the fish population each year."

Paetz was asked what message he would pass on based on his life and experience. "Well, I would advise fisheries managers to make their regulations on the basis of science. That, of course, coupled with the needs of the angler and the conservation needs of those fishes that aren't angled for. But yes, I think we must know what the habitat will produce, the life history of the fishes, their requirements, and then develop the regulations from there. I think scientific investigations must play a real part in today's fish or regulation development."

Dr. Martin Paetz became the Chief Fishery Biologist in 1961 and was Director of Fisheries when he retired in 1983. When he passed away in July 2002 at the age of 81, the fishes of Alberta lost a remarkable ally and advocate.

To provide even more fishing opportunities, two types of fish farms were introduced to Alberta in the 1960s. Commercial game fish farms raised fish to stock private farms or to enable limited sport fishing for a fee. Similarly, a private game fish farm was defined as a small privately owned pond, which provided a source of personal recreation and food supply where there was no sale of fish or angling rights. A feasibility study in 1970 looked at the production capability of 20 ponds in western Alberta from Pincher Creek to Grande Prairie. The province stocked these ponds with fingerling rainbow trout in July 1970 and again in 1971. The ponds were harvested in late fall of both years by commercial operations and the harvest was sold to the Freshwater Fish Marketing Corporation. Researchers concluded that raising fish was a "high risk" business affected by a number of uncontrollable variables such as weather and pond characteristics. Also, variable survival rates made the profitability of fish farming questionable.

Despite these findings, private game fish farms showed a sharp increase in numbers, from 24 in 1973 to 121 in 1974. In 1975, the Fish and Wildlife Division responded with a new biologist, Bruce Barton, to administer game fish farming activities. An information brochure for fish farmers was produced and a survey of fish farmers was completed. More formal education in aquaculture was carried out through seminars provided by District Agriculturists or through a course at Olds Agricultural College. Today, approximately 100

commercial fish farms provide stock for approximately 3600 private fish ponds.

Commercial Fisheries Management and Research

Like Alberta's recreational anglers, Alberta's commercial fishermen were also active early in the 20th century. The commercial fishing industry focussed largely on the fisheries in Lake Athabasca and Lesser Slave Lake. Like recreational fishing, it too was augmented by hatchery fish. In 1928, a federal hatchery had been built at Canyon Creek, on the south shore of Lesser Slave Lake, to incubate large numbers of fertilized whitefish eggs to within several weeks of hatching. With the transfer of resources in 1930, the province took over responsibility for running this facility. Fry from the hatchery were released into Lesser Slave, Cold, Lac La Biche, Wabamun, and other lakes.

After the drought and Depression of the 1930s, a healthy commercial fishing industry was seen as an

EARLY COMMERCIAL FISHING. COURTESY B. STEVENSON

STOCKING TYRRELL LAKE
[GORDON HAUGEN]

In the early days, Tyrrell Lake was a large, productive lake located southeast of Lethbridge. Stocking the lake with trout was deemed a good idea . However, it would take the bulk of the fingerling rainbow trout produced at the lone fish hatchery in Calgary to achieve the recommended stocking rate, leaving little else for lakes in the rest of the province. To overcome this obstacle, sportsmen in Magrath and Milk River formed the Tyrrell Lake Fishermen's Association. The Association worked with government staff to secure over 1.5 million fingerling rainbow trout from a private fish hatchery in Montana. Although there was good survival of the initial stocking, angler success was only fair. Abundant fresh water shrimp as a food source and dense aquatic vegetation made harvesting by the conventional hook and line methods slow.

THE CANYON CREEK FISH HATCHERY, LESSER SLAVE LAKE, 1931.
COURTESY PROVINCIAL ARCHIVES OF ALBERTA (A7046)

economic opportunity for the struggling province. To stimulate interest in it, public information programs delivered through demonstrations, public lectures, and radio shows were given on the preparation, cooking, and nutrition of native fish species. Sales figures increased and high market prices encouraged even more residents to take out commercial fishing licences. Whitefish made up the bulk of Alberta's commercial catch. This species was exported to markets in Chicago and New York, where they were highly prized and in great demand. Other species were sold in local markets. Commercial fishing opportunities eventually expanded to 120 lakes in the province, but hard times were coming.

Just as the whitefish export industry started to take off, the United States became increasingly alarmed at the possibility of introducing tapeworm-infected fish into its market. In order to prevent an import embargo, all commercial lakes in Canada were surveyed for wormy whitefish. No Alberta lakes were closed; however, products from borderline lakes were examined closely for parasites before shipping. In 1938-1939, the

tapeworm concern made export markets unstable and all coarse fish (whitefish and tullibee) were marketed within the province where they were used largely as feed on mink farms.[11] By this time, Fish and Game Commissioner Eric Huestis had contracted Dr. Miller to work for the Fisheries Branch during the summer months. In 1941, Miller conducted his first fish survey of Lesser Slave Lake and thus began his investigation of the tapeworm *Triaenophorus crassus*.

COMMERCIAL FISHERMEN AT WORK.
COURTESY PROVINCIAL ARCHIVES OF ALBERTA (PA 214/2)

WORMS IN WHITEFISH: MUCH ADO ABOUT NOTHING

[MICHAEL G. SULLIVAN]

Despite its image as a drought-ridden prairie province, Alberta's commercial fishing industry was vigorous and economically important in the early to mid-decades of the 20th century. Fisheries in northern lakes provided much-needed employment, largely to supply lake whitefish for export to the lucrative big-city markets in the United States. However, in 1932, inspectors for the U.S. Pure Foods Administration began to refuse imports of whitefish that contained parasite cysts, even though the cysts were harmless to humans. According to Miller: "…this led to all manner of unfortunate trade practices". It also resulted in large federal infusions of cash and a wide-open book for scientific investigations that might help reopen the borders or control this parasite.[12]

At the centre of this international economic dispute was *Triaenophorus crassus*, a naturally occurring tapeworm in many northern lakes across Canada. R.B. Miller unravelled the complex life cycle of this tapeworm by rigorous scientific lab work, field experiments, and widespread data collections. He determined that adult worms live in the intestine of northern pike, eggs hatch in water, and larvae live in the flesh of ciscoes, with spill-over into whitefish.[13]

Characteristically concerned not only with basic science but also with useful applications of science, Dr. Miller used his new knowledge to design and test methods of controlling the tapeworm. Using large Alberta lakes as part of his field experiments, Miller investigated three main areas of breaking the life cycle of *T. crassus*: reducing the abundance of pike, reducing the abundance of cisco, and killing free-swimming larvae.

In his experiment to control pike numbers, Miller used a chemical fish poison (rotenone) to kill adult pike concentrated in spring in the spawning areas at Square Lake, near Lac La Biche. From 1947 to 1949, Miller managed to kill approximately 85% of the adult pike in Square Lake. However, once the poisoning campaign stopped, the pike population quickly recovered and Miller concluded this was not a cost-effective control measure!

To control cisco numbers, Miller convinced the Fish and Game Division to remove the quota controls on the expanding commercial fishery at Lesser Slave Lake. From 1941 to 1948, up to four million pounds of cisco were netted annually from this lake. Miller described a "great reduction" in cisco numbers.[14] He also described what now would be recognized as classic symptoms of overfishing (e.g., smaller size and younger population

age structure of the remaining fish). The number of cysts in whitefish also declined considerably. Things were looking good. Unfortunately, reduced numbers of small cisco (primarily used as feed for ranched mink) likely contributed to the extirpation (local extinction) of the local population of lake trout, as well as collapse of the walleye fishery in Lesser Slave Lake (which didn't recover until the late 1980s). This was not so good, and the approach was abandoned.

Perhaps the most ingenious, and in today's terms controversial, efforts were directed at control of the tapeworm larvae. Miller, in conjunction with Dr. M.J. Huston (Director of Pharmacy at the University of Alberta), conducted lab experiments using hundreds of *T. crassus* larvae. He found that increased acidity killed the free-swimming larva soon after the egg hatched. Consequently, field-tests were conducted at Baptiste Lake during the spring of 1945. Twenty tons of concentrated sulphuric acid, delivered by railway car to the lake, were released in spring into the shallow pike spawning areas along the shore, a time and place where the tapeworm eggs were most abundant and likely to hatch. But the heavily buffered water failed to acidify. Surface water pH returned to normal within a half-hour, lake bottom pH was normal within 12 hours, and the tapeworm larvae were unaffected. Undeterred, Miller continued his research into possible chemical treatments and, with his graduate student M.L. Libin, found that Dow K604 was very effective at killing larvae in the lab.[15] During the spring of 1952, Miller poured 2000 pounds of Dow K604 into the waters of the long-suffering Square Lake. The lake water "turned bright yellow, which was very useful in marking the area of the lake that had been treated".[16] Miller learned that the water was toxic after 24 hours, but returned to normal within two days and the larvae remained unaffected. He was thwarted again.

These aspects of Miller's work may seem heavy-handed and environmentally harsh to present-day ecologists trained in the ethics of "light ecological footprints" and rigorous standards of animal care. However, current and future Alberta biologists could do well to spend a few days poring over Miller's extensive publications. His amazing breadth and precision of work in fisheries science and management, parasitology, and statistics set very high standards for future scientists. His untimely death on February 23, 1959 (at the young age of 43) was an incalculable setback for fisheries research and management in Alberta.

In 1945, tapeworm larvae in the muscles of Canadian freshwater fish were still having a detrimental effect on fish markets. Surveys showed that 80% of whitefish could be marketed readily, without processing by candling or filleting. But, the remaining 20% were an ongoing concern. In 1946, federal whitefish Inspection Regulations were instituted. This move increased the confidence of the U.S. Food and Drug Administration in the quality of Canadian whitefish and eased some of their concerns. In Alberta, however, overfishing, and competition from the Great Slave Lake Commercial Fishery in the Northwest Territories, was putting the province in a critical position.

In contrast to unstable export markets, the growing demand for fur farm feed at first stabilized the whitefish markets for Lesser Slave Lake and Lac La Biche fisheries. However, fur farm demand soon exceeded the commercial supply and fur farmers were allowed to fish for coarse fish during the winter. Commercial fishermen complained that fur farmers were reducing the poundage allowed to others throughout the rest of the year. To add to the commercial fishermen's woe, a fishing royalty was instituted in Alberta in 1946.

Low market prices continued to negatively affect the commercial fishing industry in Alberta. To try to bolster the industry, the Federal Government and the prairie provinces met to discuss the situation. New regulations were added to the federal *Fish Dealers' Act* to improve packing, handling, and processing of commercial fish, primarily to reduce the number of infected whitefish sent to market.

Along with the new regulations, there was also a recognized need to study fish populations, habitats, and diseases to learn why commercial fish stocks were declining. It was soon discovered that there were too many fishermen looking for too few fish. A proposal to reinstate fish quotas, restrict licences, and enforce mesh sizes was met with instant protest. A softer approach was called

for. So, instead, no new commercial licences were issued and attrition took its course, licences were renewed annually, and mesh sizes were limited. Also, two seasons—winter, from December 1 to March 31 depending on ice conditions, and summer, from May 1 to September 1 were established. These changes were generally met with approval from all concerned. Later, recommendations would support the move to more controlled production, with fewer fishermen but increased individual net returns. Modern processing and freezing plants also helped to provide a more constant supply of fish to local and export markets.

In 1958, an agreement between the Minister of Lands and Forests and Alberta Fish Products Limited granted exclusive commercial fishing rights on Winifred, Touchwood, and Marie Lakes for specified quantities and species of fish. This agreement did not interfere with the rights of anglers, aboriginals, or local fur farmers. In the Fish and Game Division annual report, it was noted:

Construction of adequate processing and storage plants, together with minimum production limits of whitefish, pickerel, pike, and perch on each of the said lakes should tend to regulate marketable supplies with respect to value and quantity and thus provide a more constant flow to consumer outlets. Utilization of large fish resources, now unexploited, except for local and animal food purposes, will become possible by establishment of approved processing plants.

A decade later, the Freshwater Fish Marketing Corporation was given federal-provincial sponsorship and licensed as the sole buyer of commercially caught fish in Alberta, Saskatchewan, Manitoba, Northwest Territories, and western Ontario. The Fish and Wildlife Director in Alberta was a director of the Corporation, and Fish and Wildlife Officers in Alberta were corporation inspectors. The Corporation established agents at strategic points across Alberta and set lake prices for fish.

195

Fishermen sold their catch to the Corporation or directly to the consumer, and benefitted from the increased prices and market stability.

In the mid-1960s, the largest remaining commercial fishing operation in Alberta was McInnes Fish Products Limited. McInnes had an entire fish processing plant built on barges, which were dry docked in Fort McMurray over winter. Each spring, the Northern Transportation Company tugboats towed the barges down the Athabasca River to the delta near the entry to Richardson Lake and Lake Athabasca. Here, the fish plant operated through late spring and early summer

processing the fish taken from the Alberta side of Lake Athabasca. In mid-summer and fall the plant was relocated near Uranium City to process fish from the Saskatchewan portion of the lake. Canadian Fish Products Limited also operated a fish plant in this area.

Commercial fishing remained a viable industry in Alberta throughout the remainder of the century. By 1985, the main commercial fish was whitefish; however, northern pike, tullibee, lake trout, perch, and walleye were also marketed. A total of 92 lakes were fished commercially and 15 fish packing and processing facilities were licensed. Game fish species for recreational

FRESHWATER FISH MARKETING CORPORATION BUILDING OUTSIDE AND INSIDE.
COURTESY PROVINCIAL ARCHIVES OF ALBERTA (J976/1 AND J976/2)

anglers were protected in commercially fished lakes by low production quotas, regulated mesh size of gill nets, as well as depth limits and closure of areas frequented by game fish during commercial fishing operations.

More Hatcheries

In the mid-1980s, fisheries management focus was turning to artificial walleye rearing to meet the popular sentiment of "just stock more fish" to meet growing demand. To produce walleye and other fish stocks, work on the Cold Lake Fish Hatchery was started in 1983 and completed in 1986. The new hatchery was slated to produce upwards of 20 million fishes, mainly walleye. In its first year, walleye fingerlings were successfully raised in ten outdoor rearing ponds, and lake trout were incubated and reared. However, the following year, the station was contaminated with a viral disease and was temporarily closed until it could be completely disinfected. By March 1988, the hatchery was again rearing lake trout and was ready to receive walleye eggs. But the trout operation was closed again that winter owing to another virus outbreak. Following a four-year shut-down, the Cold Lake Fish Hatchery returned to normal operations in February 1993 and achieved full production in 1994, this time with an ozone disinfection system in place.

The walleye enhancement program continued to expand, requiring more and more manpower and budget. Many fisheries staff spent a considerable amount of time examining walleye populations and potential egg collection sites like Brett

McINNES FISH PRODUCTS LIMITED FISH PROCESSING PLANT BUILT ON BARGES AND PART OF THE FISHING FLEET IN THE ATHABASCA DELTA NEAR RICHARDSON LAKE, 1964.
CREDIT: D. MCDONALD

197

Creek, before transporting eggs back to the hatchery. Eggs were then incubated and hatched before transporting fry back to release sites. Staff also spent time working to improve pond-rearing and stocking methods.

At the same time that the Cold Lake hatchery was being built in the mid-1980s, a new fish-rearing facility on the south shore of Wabamun Lake was designed to use the warm water from the Sundance Power Station. In 1985, a private operator was contracted to operate the Sundance Trout Rearing Station which reared 175,000 yearling rainbow trout that year. Combined, Alberta's fish hatcheries reared 9.3 million fish in 1985, releasing primarily rainbow trout, walleye, eastern brook trout, brown trout, yellow perch, cutthroat trout, lake trout, arctic grayling, and golden trout into 308 waterbodies throughout the province.

DID YOU KNOW?
Alberta has 177 lakes and reservoirs that contain walleye. However, this species, commonly known as pickerel, is the most sought after sportfish in the province. Recreational fishing is considered the major factor in the drastic decline of provincial walleye stocks.

BRETT CREEK WALLEYE SPAWN CAMPS, 1985-1999
[GEORGE WALKER]

The Brett Creek walleye-spawning project came about as part of the provincial walleye enhancement initiative. Spawn sources were needed to support the supplemental stocking of beleaguered walleye populations at many of Alberta's lakes and reservoirs. While fisheries workers in the Northwest Region started collecting eggs at Bistcho and Lesser Slave lakes, the Northeast Region got busy looking for a large, stable walleye egg source close to the hatchery at Cold Lake. Primrose Lake was the obvious choice, but it had some unique challenges: Alberta shared the lake with Saskatchewan, and likely spawning runs were located deep in the federal Cold Lake Air Weapons Range. It took delicate, convoluted negotiations to secure the needed permissions and it helped immeasurably to know military-speak!

Permission to enter the area was granted in time for the 1985 spring spawning season and fisheries staff mobilized to monitor walleye movements in Shaver River, Ferrier Creek, Calder River, and Brett Creek. All were well into the Saskatchewan end of Primrose Lake and since the main lake stayed ice-covered, access was by helicopter only. To top it off, the timing overlapped with *Operation Maple Flag*, a major fighter jet exercise with international participation that created a logistical nightmare for us and our civilian helicopter!

And then there were the bears! Very bold and unafraid of us puny humans, bears in the area were habituated to loud sounds of air traffic, bombs, and rockets, but rarely saw two legged creatures—and certainly were not afraid of them. Being in a protected area, they were a high-density population and were regularly in our face, breaking into traps and just being a general threat.

Journal entries for Shaver River 1985 documented the bear problem:

Apr 26, 1700 hr: 55 northern pike (NRPK), 12 white sucker (WHSC). Big brown bear at trap watching us.
Apr 27, 1900 hr: 33 NRPK, 0 WHSC. Trap partially collapsed, bear damage.
Apr 28, 1000 hr: 40 NRPK, 1 WHSC. Rebuilt trap, severe bear damage.
Apr 30, 1500 hr: 404 WHSC, 5 NRPK. Bear tore trap apart.
May 1, 1630 hr: 19 NRPK, 55 WHSC. Bear damage severe. Bear arrived and threatened to jump in the boat with us. Severe and fatal damage to the bear!

In the spring of 1986, we geared up for more intensive surveys of Ferrier Creek, Calder River, and Brett Creek. Boats and equipment were pre-positioned over the ice in March and operations began on May 1 when the creeks opened up. Living conditions were extremely primitive! As the muskeg thawed, the plywood tent platforms holding the tourist-type tents shifted and sank. The crews lived in their waders, and the cold spring of 1986 went on and on. The only dry ground was aboard the boats. There was also a suite of "bonus" experiences. A bear made an extra door in the tent and ate the seat off the jet boat, and the mobile substrate on the Calder River kept burying the pound trap!

Eventually, we did find walleye. An expert spawning crew was called in from the Fisheries Culture Section to research spawning techniques that would work for the site. After battling low temperatures and little to no shelter in which to work, fertilized eggs began to flow to the new Cold Lake Fish Hatchery. In all, 16.2 million eggs were shipped that year. Although only 32% hatched, it was a start!

Lessons learned, in 1987 we concentrated on Brett Creek. Three floating platforms were built and brought in to overcome the muskeg conditions. The 20'x20' platforms accommodated "spacious" wall tents in which to work and live. The system worked great and allowed us to move closer to the natural spawning site. With advice and construction from fish culture staff, the spawning tent was fitted with upwellers, pumps, lights, and generators. The floating sleeping platform attached to the floating living/cooking platform was comfortable provided you didn't sleep walk or get concerned by the wet foot prints of a bear who investigated the snoring occupants! Great strides were made with pound traps and the fish holding facilities installed adjacent to the spawning tent. Refinements in spawning techniques and egg handling gave 50% hatching success from the 12.8 million eggs shipped to the hatchery that year.

However, bear problems continued in 1987:

May 4, 0415 hr: Awakened by bear intrusion at spawning tent, rushed down in our shorts to scare him off with shell crackers—must now take turns at night shift riding shotgun.

One team member, wearing chest waders and floater coat, was assigned to this night shift. He lay down on the wet platform and after gazing at the stars—fell asleep. Two hours later, and after a heavy frost, he woke to find himself frozen solid to the deck. Good thing the bruin did not visit that night!

The Brett Creek site was also a wonderful place for us naturalist types. Sightings and interactions with local mammals and returning spring birds were common. Birds of another kind often were too common. Our site was located between two major targets used by the military war birds for the biggest multi-national air combat exercise in North America. Our work area on Brett Creek looked like a mock-up of a jungle village—we worried about that. But the aerial display was spectacular as the latest fighter jets from around the world tried to out top gun each other in dog fights right above our heads. The tranquillity of mixing walleye eggs and sperm in the spawning process often was shattered as silent jets approaching Mach 1 speeds screamed over at 100 feet altitude. You slammed your hands over your ears and felt the compression waves in your chest—all while trying not to spill the precious eggs!

Improvements in the process and the facilities continued as annual spawning camps produced a targeted 35 million walleye eggs. We were proud of ourselves and the Cold Lake Hatchery as we regularly achieved hatching rates of 75%— probably better than anywhere in North America. Permanent staff of the Northeast Region and Cold Lake Hatchery provided the manpower backbone of the spawning camps; however, we could not have operated without a number of temporary staff and dedicated volunteers. We also played host to many working visitors like regional directors, managers, Saskatchewan environment staff, and even a CBC film crew.

The final years of the camp in 1998 and 1999 were a bit disappointing. The drought throughout the northeast and a local forest fire left the muskeg drier than usual and water levels lower in Brett Creek. The spawn camps and the walleye enhancement program were discontinued due to changing priorities in provincial fisheries management.

New Species Experimentation

Attempts to expand Alberta's limited fisheries by introducing new species was a common practice from very early on in the century. As soon as they could be procured, or produced at the early hatcheries, new trout species were being introduced by the province to its waterbodies, including splake, brook, brown, and rainbow trout. These early introductions were done in order to increase species diversity and to expand the province's fishing opportunities. It also satisfied the demands of new Albertans familiar with such species from Europe and other parts of North America.

This thirst for new species continued throughout the middle decades of the century. In 1959, golden trout, a high-altitude native of the Sierra Mountains of the southwestern U.S., was stocked into the Crowsnest and Kananaskis areas. Twenty-five hundred eggs were obtained from Wyoming by hatcheries Superintendent Alex Sinclair. The eggs were hatched and the fry were introduced into Southfork Lakes (Barnaby Ridge Lakes) just north of Waterton Lakes National Park. Fish and Wildlife Officers Lawrence Scheffelmiar, Frank Somerville, and Chuck Gordon used Wajax backpacks, normally used by firefighters, to carry the fish up the arduous trail. An avid local fisherman, Joe Coccioloni also made the trek. The next year, fry were released into Three Isle Lake and Galatea Lake in case the Barnaby plantings proved unsuccessful, but this time, the fish were flown in by helicopter! Fisheries biologists Buck Cunningham and Brian Hammond and officers Chuck Gordon and Dave Unger monitored these lakes. In 1969-70, eggs collected at the Barnaby sites were used to stock a few high alpine lakes near Pincher Creek, including Rainy Ridge Lake in the Castle drainage. Today, a limited fishery exists on self-sustaining populations of golden trout at several alpine lakes, including Barnaby and Rainy Ridge lakes.

Kokanee, landlocked sockeye salmon from British Columbia, were introduced into the Glenmore Reservoir in Calgary in 1961 but the planting was unsuccessful. In 1963, the Raven Rearing Station

199

produced kokanee salmon; however, after three years of stocking various central Alberta lakes, there was no apparent success with this species. Between 1964 and 1968, kokanee were introduced into Phillips Lake (Pincher Creek) and Narrow Lake (Athabasca) but these, too, were unsuccessful.

Coho salmon were introduced into Cold Lake in May 1970 in the hopes of adding a new fisheries element to the northeast part of the province. This Pacific salmon had been introduced into Lake Michigan with success. Many were hopeful that similar results could be gained in Alberta. Cold Lake is deep (maximum depth 370 feet or 113 metres), relatively cold, and unproductive. Early in the 1900s, the lake was recognized for its lake trout fishery but by the 1970s, it produced few pike, walleye, or lake trout. However, it had good numbers of ciscoes (tullibee), which theoretically should have provided prey for the salmon. In 1968, the State of Alaska gave Alberta 100,000 eyed coho eggs.[17] These eggs were hatched in Calgary and reared at the Raven

Rearing Station. Later that year, ninety-three thousand coho smolts were held for three weeks in holding ponds on the Medley River and then allowed to migrate down to Cold Lake. Commercial fishing for ciscoes was cancelled on Cold Lake in the fall of 1970 and 1971 because too many coho were caught in the nets. Introductions continued with additional coho releases into the Medley River in 1971. But the population did not take off (although some fish did take off to downstream lakes in Saskatchewan). This population was never self-reproducing and the experiment was discontinued.

Finally, in 1976, Island Lake (north of Smoky Lake) was assessed for a small-mouth bass introduction that was carried out in 1977. These small but feisty fish are relatively easy to catch and provide abundant fishing recreation in eastern North America. Established populations of crayfish and spot-tail shiners should have provided adequate food. A remnant population still exists but is not managed and will not be restocked if it disappears.

SUNDANCE STATION
[KEVIN WINGERT]

The province was booming in the 1980s and the environmental pressures on government also were strong. What better way to soften the image of coal-generating power plants than to use the warm-water effluent to grow fish? A site was chosen at the Sundance Power Plant and John Bilas, a long-time technician from the Sam Livingston Fish Hatchery, was sent by Winfried Schenk to build a new station. I was a wildlife technician in Edson at the time. When that position was abolished in 1984, I transferred to the Sam Livingston staff roster and went to help John with the new station. Together, we built a siphon system rearing station using ten circular tanks with plastic pond liners. We put headers in each tank and spray dispersal bars dispensing water from the power plant's cooling pond. It took the better part of a year to get all the hand construction completed. By January 1985, water was flowing and all the tanks were ready to receive trout.

As with all complicated systems, precautions were taken to assure continued smooth operation and to prevent the interruption of the water flow. Yet the unexpected still happened. In one such case, a curious muskrat was sucked into the intake pipe and lodged at the elbow bend leading to the first tank. Not surprisingly, this reduced the water flow and some fish were lost. Extreme fog over the warm water was a recurring problem and made it difficult to navigate motor equipment during cold winter mornings. One particularly foggy morning, we hit and punctured one of the tanks. We quickly transferred trout to the other tanks while it was repaired and luckily no fish were lost. On yet another occasion, one tank overflowed when the outlet screen became plugged with algae. Of course such problems only happen when no one is around. The next morning, trout were swimming in shallow water all over the parking lot! Having worked the bugs out of the system, so to speak, the station was eventually turned over to a private operator. However, with shifting priorities, the station was subsequently abandoned.

BUCK CUNNINGHAM, FISHERIES BIOLOGIST
[INTERVIEWED BY BILL WISHART]

Buck Cunningham was born in 1932 and grew up near Riverton, a small town on the banks of the Wind River in central Wyoming. "I spent the summers with a couple of uncles that were bachelor farmers. They let me do whatever I wanted. I was about ten years old and I had a little single shot .22 rifle to hunt cottontail rabbits and shoot prairie dogs…kind of an ideal Huck Finn life."

"I graduated from high school in 1950 just as the Korean War started. I volunteered and spent four years in different Air Force postings throughout the U.S. and a year or so in the Philippine Islands on Clark Air Force Base before it was annihilated when Mount Pinatubo blew up. I spent some time as a cryptographer dealing with secret codes and ciphers in a highly classified job literally locked in a room with a vault door. That was interesting. It got me out into the world and I was able to go to university after that."

Cunningham returned from Korea and completed a BSc and MSc at the University of Wyoming before he was hired as a Fisheries Biologist in Alberta in 1959. "I did basic biophysical inventories of streams mostly in north and west Alberta. Oil development was getting under way and a lot of streams were becoming accessible. We did surveys around Rocky Mountain House, Edson, and Hinton as the Forestry trunk road was put in. Most of it was pretty superficial: look at what's there, describe the characteristics of the stream, collect some fish, do an age and growth study. Some of the streams, particularly in central Alberta, like the North Raven, Dogpound Creek, Crooked Creek, and Schroeder were deteriorating, primarily owing to agricultural practices. I also recall places where drilling sumps were cut loose in the Swan Hills. In the Swan River, for example, you could see this oil mark on the vegetation about two feet above the present water level: during high water there had been a pretty good gush of oil go down the creek. In one of the front canyons near Pincher Creek where they drilled a gas well, the contractor hired to clean up the well site simply let the sump go into the Drywood River and killed all the fish, several miles downstream."

"I also looked at quite a few lakes in southern Alberta. When we surveyed Three Isle Lake, Brian Hammond and I backpacked up there, constructed a little raft using our air mattresses, and paddled out on the lake. Very primitive I must say. Real seat-of-your-pants biology. When I was moved to Calgary, I was

FISHERIES BIOLOGIST BUCK CUNNINGHAM AND OFFICER JOHN DOONANCO.
CREDIT: J. STELFOX

responsible for the South Saskatchewan drainage. My district stretched from the Blindman River north of Red Deer to the US border, and from BC to Saskatchewan, so I spent an enormous amount of time on the road. I guess I got weary of the travel. It was frustrating because it was difficult to get any help and the equipment was basically a stream thermometer and an oxygen kit. The contortions I had to go through to get a boat! I decided to leave the Fish and Wildlife Division.

"We did have some fun though. A member of the Calgary Fish and Game Association caught some big trout at the upper end of Glenmore Reservoir, where the Elbow River ran in. He was convinced the reservoir could be a fantastic trout fishery. So we went to see what was there. I can't remember how many hundred yards of net we strung out in the lake, maybe 400 or so. The next day we hauled in…boat loads of suckers! Enormous numbers of longnose and white suckers. It was a great sucker-picking party!"

"Looking back [at early fish surveying techniques], I wonder how we didn't electrocute ourselves. We had a 230v DC generator which took two people to carry. A big roll of insulated wire was hooked to the negative pole which was a wand with a paddle. A shorter wire was hooked to the positive which was dropped in the water. Then you worked this thing up and down the stream, dragging the cord behind. Brian Hammond made a really neat carrier with one bicycle wheel underneath a frame with handles coming out of each end. We'd set this big generator on it and go hooting up and down the stream! The design was taken out of a journal someplace—it was the very early days of electrofishing. There was a biologist killed in South Dakota using this kind of equipment and that kind of got everybody thinking we needed to use a little bit more caution.

"One of the scariest moments I had was when Brian Hammond and I hiked up to Three Isle Lake with my dog Bots. We went up a fairly narrow, little canyon…looked across and there was a female grizzly and her cub. They were several hundred yards away and we just sat and watched them. They were going down the valley and we were going up. Anyway, they came to a little gully that was full of snow and the cub lay on its belly and tobogganed right down this thing, scrambled back up to the top, and went down again. Did this three or four times! After watching for a while, we continued on and made our camp. The next morning we put together our little fabricated raft using our air mattresses, did our survey, and then packed up and left. In the back of my mind was that sow grizzly down in the valley. We were going through this really dark, thick timber and all of a sudden my dog stopped and growled. The hackles went up on his back and the hair on the back of my neck

went up too! I was convinced that sow grizzly was right there. Anyway, we stopped and looked carefully and it turned out to be a moose! I was never so happy to see a moose in my life!"

In 1965, Cunningham left the Division and spent four years with the National Parks. In 1969, he joined the Lethbridge Community College where he was instrumental in developing an Environmental Science program. This program received the *Minister's Special Award in the Order of the Bighorn* in 1993.

"It's probably through that program that I've had the greatest impact on fish and wildlife. I've had the privilege of training or teaching a good portion of the officer staff and many of the technicians that work in Alberta. I used to tell my students that the fishery profession will probably always be around because fish are recognized as a food resource, rather than a recreational resource, and so they'll always receive some emphasis. But in Alberta at the present time, I don't think things look very good. You know, I think it's pretty sad what's happening here in a sense that fish and wildlife are still regarded as kind of a fringe benefit: nice to have but not worth sacrificing anything for."

BUCK CUNNINGHAM, R.J. ADAMS, AND W.E. WILLOWS SAMPLING FISH BY ELECTROFISHING, 1962.
COURTESY B. STEVENSON

202

In addition to these government-sponsored introductions, Fish and Game Association clubs and private individuals dallied with species such as large-mouthed bass, small-mouthed bass, Atlantic salmon, and arctic char. For the most part, these activities had limited success and these introduced species have not persisted in Alberta.

Growth of the Fisheries Branch

Throughout the latter half of the century, the tasks and staff of the Fisheries Branch of Alberta Fish and Wildlife Division had grown in response to the issues and needs of the day. Martin Paetz, hired in 1952, was joined by Ron Thomas in 1954. In 1959, a Sports Fisheries section was added with Buck Cunningham and Rod Paterson in charge of streams and lakes, respectively. Gordon Haugen and Dennis McDonald were hired to assist Paterson in 1963.

In 1967, Paterson was promoted to Senior Management Biologist and supervisor of regional fisheries staff. By 1970, this included regional biologists stationed in Lethbridge (Gordon Haugen), Calgary (Dennis McDonald and Gerald Thompson), Red Deer (Mel Kraft and Carl Hunt), Edson (Chuck Lane), St. Paul (Bryant Bidgood, Dave Buchwald), and Peace River (Frank Bishop). In 1973, a regional biologist in Edmonton, Ken Zelt, was added and given the responsibility for fisheries management in the heavy demand area adjacent to the city. Regional fisheries biologists were responsible for fish inventory, aquatic habitat protection and development, fish stocking programs, fish regulation recommendations, and public information.

On the Commercial Fisheries side, lab technician Don Barwise was hired in 1960 to assist Ron Thomas. Barwise worked in the lab ageing fish scales as a tool in population studies. In 1961, Morley Riske became the second commercial fishery biologist. In 1967, Fisheries Officer Charlie Scott was appointed to the new position of Commercial Fishery Coordinator in Edmonton.

All in all, the tasks of these new staff were diverse during these exciting times. Despite the early work of Miller, Paetz and others, little was yet known about Alberta's fishery resource, particularly in the north. In 1966, the Fisheries Branch received funding from the Northern Alberta Development Council (NADC) to survey all the major water bodies in Alberta north of the 55th parallel. The first year focussed on lakes in the Canadian Shield area in the northeast corner of the province. In following years, lake and rivers in the Peerless Lake area, Caribou Mountains, Buffalo Hills and Bistcho Lake region were surveyed.

Starting in 1968, staff also undertook a Sport Fish Capability Study as part of the Canada Land Inventory initiative of the Agricultural Rural Development Agreement (ARDA). Lakes and streams in Alberta were classified according to their ability to produce fish. Ken Zelt led the team, with additional work later done by Jim O'Neal and many others. Following three years of extensive fieldwork, a series of map overlays with coded ratings for fish production potential on various waterbodies was produced.

A third major undertaking was the comprehensive Tri-Creeks study. Started in 1965, this project would evolve into a 20-year cooperative research effort involving the forestry industry and several provincial and federal government agencies. It was initially approved as a project of the International Hydrological Decade.

As the province's demand for a vibrant fishery grew, so too did the number of major development projects that could potentially impact this resource. To better understand such concerns, a research component was added to the growing Fisheries Branch. Bryant Bidgood was hired in 1967 to be the first Fishery Research Biologist, joined shortly thereafter by Dave Berry. This team began an investigation on the Oldman River, conducting a review of water flows, fish management, and pollution control. They also examined a proposal for irrigation reservoir management that included monitoring pesticide

203

REFLECTIONS OF A FISHERIES BIOLOGIST
[DENNIS MCDONALD]

I started work as a summer student on several fisheries projects for Buck Cunningham and Ron Thomas, two of the original fisheries biologists with the Fish and Wildlife Division. Gordon Haugen and I were both hired full time late in the summer of 1963.

In 1964, I was assigned responsibility for fisheries management in the area from the North Saskatchewan River to the Northwest Territories and from Edmonton east to Saskatchewan. I conducted surveys on many lakes in this region including Lake Athabasca and the Canadian Shield lakes in the far northeast. This was the heyday of commercial fishing in the region. There were no fishing lodges offering sport-fishing opportunities until Dick York of Cold Lake built the first one on Grist Lake north of the Cold Lake military base. Summer road access north of Lac La Biche or Cold Lake was non-existent although winter snow and ice roads were built into a few lakes. Access to Fort McMurray was by plane or the railway from Lac La Biche and access to Fort Chipewyan was by boat down the Athabasca River from Fort McMurray or up the Slave River from Fort Smith, Northwest Territories.

1964, the Great Canadian Oil Sands project was proposed as the first commercial oil sands plant in Alberta. At that time, the Boreal forest between Fort McMurray and Lake Athabasca bore little evidence of human activity.

From 1964 to 1967, much of my work was basic fisheries surveys of key lakes in the northeast. However, I also undertook a few interesting studies, including an extensive study of movement and catch rate of walleye and yellow perch in Moose Lake near Bonnyville. Another experiment entailed clearing snow off a portion of Jackfish Lake north of Vermilion to see if this would prevent winterkill of the trout population.

At the time, we also tried to improve our elected officials' understanding of basic fish and wildlife biology and management principles. We did this by developing and teaching a short course one evening each week for several weeks during the winter session of the legislature and inviting all interested MLAs to attend. As I recall, more than half of them did and they expressed considerable appreciation for this enlightenment. It was very important, in our

It was exciting being one of the earliest fisheries biologists to explore many of the waters in northeastern Alberta. Later, Bryant Bidgood joined me as Regional Fishery Biologist for the northeast. Tar sands development was not yet underway except for a small experimental plant near Fort McMurray. In

DENNIS McDONALD COLLECTING INFORMATION DURING A FISH SURVEY ON A LAKE IN NORTHEAST ALBERTA, 1964. PHOTO COURTESY D. MCDONALD

view, that politicians understand the developing scientific basis of modern fish and wildlife management.

In 1967, I became the Regional Fishery Biologist for the Calgary Region (the Bow-Highwood watershed). During my time there, Gerry Thompson and Percy Wiebe joined my staff. With new staff across the Division, we moved beyond setting regulations and doing inventory. We began in-depth studies of the impact of a whole spectrum of human activities on wild populations, and the ecological requirements of key fish and wildlife species. One of these studies involved a major pollution investigation of refinery discharges into the Sheep River in the Turner Valley. Eventually, charges were laid against the company—the first major prosecution for water pollution in the history of the oil and gas industry in Alberta. The company was found guilty, leading to a dramatic awareness through the entire industry of the need to change practices.

Government agencies responsible for public health, water management, pollution control, and oil and gas industry regulation began to work more cooperatively with the Fish and Wildlife Division. A similar investigation of pollution of the Bow River from the Calgary sewage treatment plant led to improved sewage treatment to protect the fishery in the river below Calgary. In another study, a proposed dam downstream from the Bow-Highwood River junction would flood the river valley all the way upstream into the City of Calgary. A study of the potential impact of this project on some of the key fish and wildlife resources of the area became the focus of my Master's degree thesis from the University of Calgary. This may have been the first in-depth environmental impact assessment of a proposed major dam project in Alberta. The dam was never built.

Emphasis in the 1970s within the Fish and Wildlife Division was directed increasingly toward maintaining, protecting, enhancing, or rehabilitating critical fish and wildlife habitat. In the fall of 1972, I became Head of Fisheries Habitat Protection and Daryll Hebert was the first Head of Wildlife Habitat Protection. From the outset, we both realized the need to work co-operatively to achieve our objectives. Together, we assessed the potential impact of a wide range of development proposals and land-use activities on fish and wildlife habitat, and outlined habitat protection requirements.

In the fall of 1973, I left the government and went into private consulting. I was Program Manager of the Save Habitat and Restore Pheasants Program (SHARP). This initiative was an attempt to reduce loss of critical pheasant habitat due to intensive agricultural development in southern Alberta. I managed Phase I in 1974 and Morley Barrett managed Phase II. A 45-part series on pheasant management written by SHARP staff appeared as a weekly column in 18 newspapers throughout southern Alberta. Despite these efforts, pheasant habitat continued to decline due primarily to agricultural practices and changing irrigation practices.

In September 1974, I returned to the Fish and Wildlife Division as Director of the newly formed Extension Services Branch responsible for public relations, information and education, as well as hunter and trapper training programs. Among other things, we prepared a mandatory hunter testing proposal, developed an award-winning Hunter Training Manual, and organized the first international symposium on the application of forensic science to fish and wildlife law enforcement. The unit also worked with the Department of Education to incorporate wildlife conservation content into the K-12 curriculum in Alberta schools.

In 1978, my responsibilities expanded to include planning and co-ordination within the Department of Recreation, Parks, and Wildlife. Shortly thereafter, I also co-ordinated Divisional input into development of the East Slopes Land-use Planning process and the Kananaskis Country land-use strategy. These initiatives marked the beginning of an extremely important era in fish and wildlife management in Alberta. For the first time, habitat requirements received equal consideration and importance with water management, livestock grazing, forest harvesting, recreational development, and non-renewable resource development.

In 1979, I left Alberta and joined the B.C. government as Regional Director, Kootenay Region for the Ministry of Environment, Lands, and Parks.

205

TRI-CREEKS: A LASTING LEGACY

[GEORGE STERLING, WITH INPUT FROM GORDON HAUGEN, KEN ZELT AND CARL HUNT]

Gordon Haugen was one of several graduate fisheries biologists to join the Fish and Wildlife Division during the early 1960s. He used his exposure to watershed studies in the U.S. to initiate fisheries research relevant to the Alberta scene. North Western Pulp and Power, holder of the first Forest Management Area (FMA) in the province, had been clear-cutting trees for a decade on a big chunk of western Alberta landscape around Hinton. Based on the U.S. experience, we suspected adverse changes to area streams and the trout that lived in them were imminent. North Western Pulp and Power, and the Department of Lands and Forests (Forestry Division and Fish and Wildlife Division) agreed that research was needed.

In 1965, Haugen, as Edson Regional Fisheries Biologist, initiated the Tri-Creeks project, a 20-year before-and-after logging study. Chuck Lane, Carl Hunt, and George Sterling further developed the project. Hunt recalls: "It was possibly one of the longest-running and poorest-funded fish research projects in Alberta!" The purpose of the investigation was to measure and record the effects of land use, pulpwood extraction and its associated activities, on the physical, chemical and biotic characteristics of small western Alberta trout streams.

The partners settled on a research design incorporating three watersheds: a control, an experimental treatment (clear-cut with no streamside buffers), and a conventional treatment (clear-cut with streamside buffers). Wampus, Deerlick, and Eunice creeks south of Hinton appeared to meet the requirements of similar biological and physical characteristics, and were close to each other. The three creeks constitute the Tri-Creek Basin and are tributaries to the McLeod River, which in turn is a tributary of the Athabasca River.

The Tri-Creek study evolved into a cooperative effort by several provincial and federal agencies. In 1966, projects included establishing extensive instrumentation to record stream flows, water temperatures, and weather events. Surficial, bedrock, soil and ground water surveys were carried out as a joint venture with the Alberta Research Council and the University of Alberta. Don Currie conducted the field program.

In 1970, the emphasis was on assessing natural stream conditions prior to pulp harvest. The Fisheries Branch was responsible for determining fish populations (primarily rainbow trout) and their characteristics, measuring stream bottom material and channel patterns at permanent sampling stations, measuring and classifying stream fauna, and monitoring water temperatures.

As research objectives broadened, Tri-Creeks spawned a number of graduate fisheries managers who tackled various elements of the program. One of the first, Ken Zelt, implemented an invertebrate research project. The main objectives of the project were to determine what species were present, to describe the life histories of common species, to document community structure, and to assess the standing crop. The field component of the project was completed in June 1968.[18] Ken went on to work for the Fisheries Research Section and retired from the Branch in 2000 as Head of Fisheries Allocation and Use.

Karl Dietz, in 1968 and 1969, described the fish community and life histories of the major fish species.[19] He, too, went to work for the Fisheries Research Section. Additional work was carried out by Chuck Lane and Carl Hunt. In 1971, George Sterling was part of the seasonal crew at Tri-Creeks and in 1974 became Project Fisheries Biologist tasked with delivering the fisheries component and coordinating several expanded research elements with the Alberta Forest Service, Alberta Environment, and Alberta Research Council. Sterling undertook graduate studies in 1980 and compared the spawning success and recruitment of rainbow trout before and after logging.

Several other Fish and Wildlife staff spent part of their early careers at Tri-Creeks. Dennis Surrendi characterized selected study sections in 1965 and went on to become Assistant Deputy Minister of the Division. Gary Erickson was there in 1966 and 1967, but went on to a career in wildlife management. Following seasonal employment at Tri-Creeks in the early 1970s, Ken Crutchfield, Daryl Watters, and Larry Rhude went on to careers as fisheries biologists with the Branch. Ken aspired to be the "boss of us all", and succeeded in becoming the Director of Fisheries in 2003. Daryl and Larry aspired to other things and became, the provincial "sturgeon" and "EIA" kings, respectively.

At one time or another, many of the current provincial fisheries staff did time at Tri-Creeks by assisting with population estimates—folks like Rudy Hawryluk, Don Hildebrandt, Glen Clements, and Mike Sullivan. Others, names now mostly forgotten, cycled through seasonally but contributed to the "colour" at Tri-Creeks. Those more permanently attached to the project (namely me) endured a vast array of personalities; including one guy with aspirations of eco-terrorism (now a Federal Parks employee), one who didn't know a rotary gas engine wouldn't run on white gas (now a car salesman), one who suggested I should "take my job and shove it" after being chastised for responding much too slowly during electrofishing (now owns a photo shop), and one who fell asleep regularly while leaning on his dip net handle (now an instructor). However, the project continued and science happened.

Field programs at Tri-Creeks concluded in late summer 1985 to allow time for data analysis and reporting; by March 1987 several important fisheries papers were published. With no commitment for funding beyond 1987, considerable amounts of data were simply archived; however, the completed work increased the understanding of native Athabascan rainbow trout and provided important insights into the adverse effects that logging had on their natural habitat. The results had direct relevance to land-use guidelines and fisheries regulations in the province.

Nearly 20 years later, there is anecdotal evidence that significant changes in fish habitat and fish populations are happening— so Tri-Creeks remains on the radar screen. Periodic fish sampling allows maintenance of the long-term data set and specific projects occur through partnership with the Foothills Model Forest and more recently, the Alberta Conservation Association. Those who can still remember Tri-Creeks and value the many benefits of long-term ecological studies, lament the fact that bureaucracies are often much too shortsighted.

levels in whitefish. Other development-related issues of the day included court action against a major oil company for polluting the Sheep River near Calgary and studying Wabamun Lake to determine the effect of warm water effluent from the proposed Sundance Thermal Generating plant.

Bidgood and Berry also explored the use of new research techniques using floy tags and surgically implanted radio tags to track migratory fish movements. This opened the door for new opportunities to study and understand fish movement patterns. One such project involved intercepting, tagging, and releasing spring spawning migrations of walleye into Buffalo Bay on Lesser Slave Lake. Additional information was gleaned from marked walleye captured by anglers and in commercial nets throughout the year. Eventually, goldeye, walleye, northern pike, and suckers in the Red Deer River were tracked, as were walleye and northern pike in the Athabasca River delta. A study of spawning walleye at Richardson Lake in the Athabasca River delta directed by Bidgood and Karl Dietz showed that these fish originated in Lake Athabasca. The possible reduction in water level by the proposed Bennett Dam on the Peace River in B.C. could potentially affect this fish population. The Peace-Athabasca Delta Study was a major federal/provincial program that involved Fish and Wildlife, the Canadian Wildlife Service, and various consultants over several years in the 1970s.

To address the increased demands on the Fisheries Research section and to study land management practices alongside several waterbodies, an Aquatic Pollution Research Section was established in 1968-69. The new section, directed by Paul Paetkau, continued to monitor fish in the Oldman River for accumulated pesticide residues. They also initiated a new study to look at the effects of cattle grazing on fisheries in the Red Deer River. In addition, the group examined coal mining in the Crowsnest Pass and Coal Branch areas, oil spills, seismic operations, and land clearing adjacent to rivers. As a result of their activities, several companies and individuals were prosecuted

207

for their actions, and increasing time was devoted to the inspection of coal, gas, and other industrial operations.

The Aquatic Pollution Research Section also established a biological monitoring program including most of the major rivers in the province. A bioassay laboratory, established in conjunction with the Department of Agriculture, was used to assess pollution damage in cases where harm to the aquatic environment was suspected. Fish were analyzed for pesticide contamination from drainages throughout the province. In addition, fish samples from a number of locations were sent to the federal Fisheries Research Board Laboratory in Winnipeg for mercury analysis. One result was a health advisory issued to the public in the late 1960s not to eat walleye, pike, sauger, and goldeye from the North Saskatchewan River downstream of Edmonton.

In 1970, fish samples from several locations along a 120-mile stretch of the Peace River were used to determine species presence and distribution. Pesticide contamination was looked at—the pesticide DDT was present but concentrations were very low. Biological surveys of other major rivers were used to determine their ecological health and any changes owing to industrial or domestic waste discharges. Toxicity determinations (bioassays) were conducted on a number of effluents. Vic Gillman worked with the Pollution Section and later transferred to the St. Paul District as a wildlife technician. He joined the federal Department of Fisheries and Oceans in 1972 and is currently Director, Ontario Great Lakes Area.

With increasing industrial development, and a growing public concern for the environment through the late 1960s, the Fisheries Branch was also enlarged to address the effects of development on fish habitat. In 1972, the Fisheries Habitat Protection Section, headed by Dennis McDonald, became involved in reviewing various applications and development plans submitted to public land and water regulators.

DEAD FISH RESULTING FROM AN OIL SPILL.
COURTESY ALBERTA FISH AND WILDLIFE DIVISION

Without legislative instruments to directly regulate activities that affected fish and wildlife and their habitat, Division staff could only provide advice and recommendations about possible concerns and mitigations the regulator could consider when deciding to permit the development.

Larger scale development demanded innovative approaches to protecting the environment. An example of this was the initiation of the multi-agency, multi-faceted Alberta Oil Sands Environmental Research Program (AOSERP). The major field investigations associated with this comprehensive study embraced work in ecology, geology, hydrology and air quality monitoring. All told, several million dollars were spent in northeastern Alberta looking at the impact of oilsands development on local fisheries and other environmental factors.[20]

Throughout the early 1970s, the Fisheries Habitat Protection Section refined its approach to dealing with a burgeoning demand for its advice. In a few short years, staff created a series of maps that detailed fish distribution and timing windows for

REFLECTIONS ON THE POLLUTION CONTROL SECTION—EARLY DAYS!
[VIC GILLMAN]

We all owe our careers to a certain degree to happenstance. In the summer of 1967, I was a water resources technician doing land survey in the Coronation and Consort areas of Alberta. During a lunch break one day, I sat with a Fish and Wildlife Officer and, having always had an active interest in hunting and fishing from a boyhood spent on a small farm in the Vermilion area, I was enthralled with his stories. With his encouragement, I applied to the Northern Alberta Institute of Technology (NAIT) in their newly formed Biological Sciences Technology program.

In September 1969, I landed a job with the newly formed Pollution Control Section of the Fish and Wildlife Division. Paul Paetkau (the biologist in charge) and I, along with an old Travelall truck, and an 18-foot aluminum SmokerCraft boat, set out to establish the first biological monitoring program in Alberta. Given the limited resources, and the multitude of rivers in Alberta, it was no easy task. We started by identifying the major industrial contaminant sources and setting up index stations above and below their outlets. Baseline invertebrate studies on certain rivers added to our case for changing and improving industrial practices. On a map of Alberta, I tracked all the stations and highways and rivers that I travelled during those first years—there was not a lot left unmarked!

It was pretty straightforward stuff, but it had its moments—from dogs set on you by unfriendly landowners, to scary moments working alone in less than ideal conditions! While sampling one day, I had the misfortune to slip—instantly filling my waders with rushing water. Within moments I was swept into some deep pools, I found myself calmly bouncing along the bottom of the Bow River thinking this was an inglorious way to meet one's maker. Fortunately the pool-riffle ratio was constant and I calmly floated into the next series of shallows, where I came up spluttering and gasping for breath. I emerged unscathed, but a lot more cautious!

In 1970, there was a major spill at the Great Canadian Oil Sands (GCOS) project near Fort McMurray. The Pollution Response team kicked into action! Rod Patterson called on Friday afternoon and I was at Fort McKay the next morning with the SmokerCraft, a balky outboard motor, numerous ten gallon kegs of fuel, and our emergency sampling routine! Media interest blossomed and I recall with great pride hearing Martin Paetz refer to the professionally-trained response team that was onsite and working effectively! The enormity of the spill and the task of sampling soon struck home. Reinforcements were called in to bolster the initial samples—samples that proved effective in influencing the GCOS recovery plan.

Pre-assessment surveys and pulp mill effluent work on the Smoky, Wapiti, and Peace rivers prompted an upgrade in equipment. A 26-foot aluminum inboard jet boat was purchased from Northwest Jet in Grande Prairie—No. 3 off their line! Considering how tough it was to get a new vehicle, let alone a new boat, there must have been some creative memo-writing, I'm sure! With improved transportation, a combined fish and benthic monitoring program was soon underway, matched by a lab investment in static and flow-through bioassays. This was pretty new stuff and when it proved impossible to purchase the flow-through dilution equipment, we got out the Plexiglas, plastic tubing, and silicon seal, and built one from scratch! It was one of the first working models in the country, much to the dismay of the many rainbow trout who fell victim to our effluent testing.

It was also a great time to be working at the O. S. Longman building in Edmonton with fellow graduates from NAIT, Jim Allen and Des Smith among them. There was real pleasure in how everyone worked together and, often as not, you found yourself doing your job as well as helping out on wildlife projects. I enjoyed working with Eike Schefler, Mark Quadvlieg, Bill Wishart, Jack Nolan, Gary Erickson, and others. As a result, I transferred to St. Paul District and worked with Gerry Kemp on trapping and tagging whitetails in the Rochester study area, studying black bears at Cold Lake, and studying moose and wolf as well. Boiling bear and beaver skulls is a memory that will stay forever!

In 1972, I joined the federal Department of Fisheries and Oceans, largely lured by the prospect of arctic adventure. However, in much of what followed, it was the basic grounding I got in Alberta that equipped me to handle new situations with confidence. And all because of a lunch conversation with a Fish and Wildlife Officer!

209

permissible activity. By 1978, the program was gaining recognition and respect within Alberta for its proactive efforts to work with industry in spearheading innovative approaches to mitigate the effects of development. In addition, the unit produced a series of public habitat protection guidelines covering a range of activities including road construction, pipeline crossings, culvert design, seismic work on waterbodies, and gravel extraction.

The Fisheries Habitat Protection Section received a tremendous boost in 1973-1974 when anglers paid an extra dollar on their fishing licences. The proceeds were directed towards the Fish and Wildlife Trust Fund for re-investment in habitat protection and development. Starting in 1973, the *Buck for Wildlife* program made a wide range of projects possible, including improving reservoirs,

building fish barriers, creating new reservoirs and dugouts, as well as regulating and improving stream flows. The work attracted other supporters from outside government providing the foundation for what is today the work of the Alberta Conservation Association and its partners.

During the late 1970s and early 1980s, the Division was inundated with public complaints regarding access to public fisheries. In many instances the access was either non-existent or poorly developed. There was also a growing concern about sanitation around heavily used sites, like stocked lakes. A new Fisheries Access Section, headed by Ernie Stenton with staff Glen Clements and Cam Wallman, had the task of compiling an inventory of needs, and developing plans to address the problems methodically. Together with other government agencies, municipalities, and

STURGEON CAUGHT IN THE INTAKE OF THE EDMONTON WATER TREATMENT FACILITY.
COURTESY PROVINCIAL ARCHIVES OF ALBERTA (BL770/2)

other regional staff, they worked to improve public access to fisheries.

Standards for access and site improvement included hardened road access, parking, sanitary facilities, signage, as well as garbage management. In some cases, adjoining lands had to be acquired to provide access points. Throughout the three-year program, approximately 30 fishery sites were improved including McKinnon Flats, North Raven River, Dolberg Lake, Tyrrell Lake, Bathing Lake, Blood Indian Reservoir, Cow Lake, Millers Lake, Lamberts Pond, Windy Lake, Star Lake, Boyle Pond, and many other favourite fishing spots. Provincial forestry, parks, environment, transportation, and recreation agencies as well as the Special Areas Board and numerous counties throughout Alberta operated the access programs. Seniors groups and private individuals often contracted the maintenance of these facilities. In 1984, the Fisheries Access Section was dismantled with program funding turned over to the Habitat Section. Many of the improvements implemented by a small group of dedicated staff are still in evidence today and are maintained from levy funds administered by the Alberta Conservation Association or local municipalities and industry.

Habitat management remained a focus throughout the remainder of the century. What began in 1973 with a special start-up grant of $280,000 and a $1 levy on every fishing licence (a $2 levy in 1977, $5 in 1981) grew to an investment of $1.1 million by 1994-95. Funds this same year supported 93 new or continuing projects. It also provided for 16 habitat grants for private organizations, sportsmen's clubs, and individuals involved in a wide range of habitat enhancement projects like lake enhancement (aeration and shoreline protection), stream enhancement (bank stabilization and beaver management), and streambank fencing.

Fisheries Today

Throughout the 20th century, Alberta's fisheries managers faced several challenges. The growth of fur farming, with farmers turning to readily available fish stocks as a source of mink food, proved incompatible with a commercial fishing industry. Fur farmers contributed to over-fishing of some lakes but fishery managers addressed the issue with catch and mesh size restrictions. The eventual downturn in the fur markets and subsequent reduction in fur farms also put an end to the problem.

The fur farmers were largely gone but competition for Alberta's fish stocks didn't seem to lessen any. Despite repeated plantings, a lack of sportfish, particularly in the streams of western Alberta, was at odds with a rapid increase in sport fishing pressure. Similarly, there appeared to be too many commercial fishermen for the available commercial fish stocks. These problems wouldn't be resolved quite so easily. In response, fisheries managers would see the allocation of lakes between commercial fishing and recreational angling and tourism dominate fisheries management over the remainder of the century.

In 1975, the mission of the Fisheries Branch of the Fish and Wildlife Division was "to research, manage and perpetuate the fish resources and aquatic ecosystems of the Province for the benefit and enjoyment of the people". Specifically, objectives were "to maintain and enhance fish population levels so that the recreational, commercial, scientific, and educational domestic use and intrinsic value needs of the people will be met; to ensure the capability of surface waters in Alberta to meet the needs identified in the previous objective; and to inform and educate people on the conservation and management of aquatic resources". While this mission has

211

STAUFFER CREEK
Stauffer Creek, flowing into the North Raven River, was the earliest successful project to restore a high quality trout stream affected by poor land clearing, drainage, and grazing livestock. Much of the initial work was organized and carried out by Mel Kraft with the support and assistance of the Alberta Fish and Game Association.

remained relatively unchanged, in 1982, the province endorsed the *Fish and Wildlife Policy for Alberta*, a groundbreaking document that was the first of its kind in Canada. *A Fish Conservation Strategy for Alberta 2000-2005* expanded and strengthened the policy and gave greater clarity to the direction of future fisheries management. A decade in the making, the strategy was well worth the effort and continues to guide fish management decisions today with an overriding goal to sustain the abundance, distribution, and diversity of fish populations at the carrying capacity of their habitats. In other words, it outlines how a province short on fishes and long on fishermen will continue to manage this resource.

Throughout the last part of the 20th century, recreational fisheries continued to focus on trout populations in southwestern Alberta; grayling in the north; and pike, perch, and walleye in the east and north. Despite declining licence sales, a widespread interest and concern for fisheries management was evident in the strong public support to add a $5 levy to sport fishing licences. Ken Zelt managed the levy dollars under guidance of a Fisheries Advisory Committee with representatives from Trout Unlimited Canada (Lloyd Shea), Alberta Fish and Game Association (Darryl Smith), Western Walleye Council (Bob Brewster), and the public (Ron Beck). The work began with a 1990-1991 revenue base of $1.2 million, used to supplement many fisheries management programs, most notably the heavy focus on walleye. At the same time, the greatest commercial fish production came from the central and northern areas of the province. Throughout the 1990s, the commercial fishing annual harvest varied around two million kilograms with total landed values to fishermen in the range of $2-3 million a year from 85 to 100 lakes.

Fish culture practices were continued, with approximately 122 million walleye, 12 million trout (rainbow, brown, brook, and cutthroat), and a small number of perch (30,000) stocked into Alberta lakes between 1990 and 1993 alone. In 2004, this number would drop to nearly three million fishes, largely rainbow trout, reflecting a change in management focus away from the heavy stocking of walleye to managing more stabilized natural populations. As well, a new licensing policy aimed at making the commercial fishing industry more profitable and market-driven was implemented in 1993, making it more viable for those that remained, and less in

COMPUTERS AND MODELLING – FISHERIES GOES HIGH-TECH

The widespread use of computers was a major change in fisheries management during the late 1980s. Fisheries science always was a mathematically intensive field of study and the advent of powerful desktop computers allowed Alberta fisheries managers to analyze more data, faster, and with greater effectiveness than ever before. The Walleye and Northern Pike Task Forces owed much of their success to the computerized analysis and presentation of huge data sets. Computer modelling formed an integral part of the regulation design process and the angling public became more and more literate about complex issues such as cumulative effects and long-term sustainability.

These changes coincided with an influx of young, computer-savvy fisheries biologists and closer working relationships with students and professors at Alberta universities. Award-winning research out of the University of Calgary with John Post and Andy Paul focussed on population dynamics of the recovering bull trout in Lower Kananaskis Lake, as well as studies examining stream ecology. At the University of Alberta, a variety of fisheries projects involved professors Bill Mackay, Ellie Prepas, Dave Schindler, Mark Boyce, and Lee Foote. Several Fish and Wildlife fisheries staff, including George Sterling, Travis Ripley, Jordan Walker, Michael Sullivan, Trevor Rhodes, and Stephen Spencer, undertook graduate degrees during this time.

The computer-aided advances in fisheries scientific rigour were tempered with birthing pains. Internet access and e-mail sped communication, but led to unrealistic expectations about swift responses to the growing volume of demands. However, centralized computer databases became absolutely essential to manage the increasing mass of fisheries data and the many difficulties were solved when field biologists and systems analysts learned to work together.

conflict with recreational angling. The new policy carried the support of the Alberta Fish and Game Association and the Commercial Fishermen's Association.

Research also continued as a necessary component of fisheries management throughout the 1990s. Basic fisheries research laid the foundation on which management plans, seasons, and catch goals were developed and implemented. Ultimately, the information gained from studies was used to assess species status. For example, species abundance and distribution of shorthead sculpin were assessed in the Milk and Oldman river drainages and the information used to develop a provincial management plan. Other management plans based on research findings included arctic grayling in the Little Smoky River (1990), bull trout (1995), golden trout (1996), St. Mary's sculpin and the shortjaw cisco (begun in 1996), and northern pike (1999). The Bull Trout Task Force played a lead role in having the species declared Alberta's official fish emblem.

Today, Alberta has the highest ratio of anglers per lake and the third highest angling pressure in Canada. An estimated 300,000 recreational anglers and 800 commercial fishing operations visit Alberta's favourite fishing holes each year. Recreational fishing contributed more than $350 million to Alberta's economy in 2000 and commercial fishing provides $5 million annually to the provincial economy. That we still have subsistence, recreational, and commercial fishing in Alberta is testimony to the success of the many individuals and efforts carried out over a century of fisheries management. There were challenges in the past and there will be challenges yet to come. Angling

pressure, degraded or lost habitat, potential diseases, and at-risk species will continue to dominate management issues in the new century.

While there are many, many more stories to tell involving more than a century of fisheries management in Alberta, we close this chapter with just one more tale, *The Crooked Lake Campaign*. We tell it in the hopes that it will provide a somewhat humorous example of the challenges, adventures, and frustration facing those who chose this particular profession. And that it demonstrates the dedication with which they responded.

FISHERIES BIOLOGIST MICHAEL SULLIVAN FISHING ON THE BOW RIVER NEAR CALGARY.
CREDIT: M. PYBUS

213

WHIRLING DISEASE THREAT

In 1997, measures were taken to protect Alberta's wild trout from the threat of the fatal whirling disease found in Montana. The tiny parasite that causes this disease can survive in live fish, dead fish, water, and riverbed mud and can devastate lake, river, and watershed populations of wild trout. The province's borders were closed to the importation of live fish as of October 1997. Alberta began the most concerted surveillance in Canada and also delivered a public education campaign to warn travellers of the risks of bringing the parasite into the province. As of early 2005, the disease has not been identified in Alberta, although surveillance programs are not as extensive as some U.S. jurisdictions where it has been documented. Provincial trout populations remain at risk.

THE CROOKED LAKE CAMPAIGN, 1977-1979
[CARL HUNT]

Crooked Lake, northwest of Fox Creek, is famous for an abundance of large perch. It attracts fishermen from obscure corners of the province but only during the winter months. In the summer, the fishery is adequately protected from angling pressure by 15 miles of muddy roads unsuitable for the family trailer and six miles of muskeg unsuitable for hip waders.

With increasing conflict between anglers and net fishermen, a summer lake survey was imperative in 1976. Crooked Lake is in the Edson Region and it was the responsibility of the fisheries biologist [Carl Hunt] to complete this task, which undoubtedly required extensive experience and great perseverance. The job was promptly assigned to regional technician, Rudy Hawryluk.

1977 – Preparation
The Crooked lake Campaign commenced in 1977. The first strategy was to avoid the trip until fall—so the road would dry up and the muskeg would drain. But the valiant volunteers (not exactly volunteers) were not idle. They requested a soft-wheeled trailer to drag the old freighter canoe behind the Passe Par Tout (a cantankerous ATV with good traction, rubber tracks, and grinding brakes). Fish and Wildlife's equipment specialist in Edmonton, Ron Boyer, recommended and even offered to weld a travois contraption made of pipes that would slide over lily pads. Well, that's what he claimed!

September 19th. The field action began. The roads had dried for a week and the forecast was all sunshine but on Sept 19—it poured. "Never fear, they'll persevere." Besides, Rudy had borrowed Enforcement's Bombi, which was a better track vehicle than the Passe Par Tout. Things didn't quite proceed on schedule. First the 4x4 mired down because it was towing the heavier trailer, so the intrepid crew drove the Bombi off the trailer and got about a mile down the road before it threw a track. Now the truck had to be winched to the trackless machine so the latter could be winched out of the mud and back onto the trailer so the track could be replaced. Along about this time (midnight), Rudy realized the front hubs on the 4x4 were not doing their thing. At 2 a.m., the troops made camp in the mud. Erwin (Mentz) realized he'd forgotten his sleeping bag and spent a miserable night wrapped in tarps and a smelly seine net. From here on everything went to heck. They spent the rest of the week winching the truck back to Fox Creek to get the hubs repaired so they could go back to get the Bombi on the trailer and return to Edson.

October 25th. On the second attempt, the road was conquered but the travois contraption carrying the canoe sank in every bog hole and buried the track vehicle. Finally, everything was unloaded and without as much as a fishing rod our guys finally stood on the shore of Crooked Lake.

The following week the lake froze over. So what…this is next year country!

1978 – Practice
June 8th. Things got off to an early start. Why wait for the fall rains? On June 8th, a lightly equipped high-speed commando unit went on a scouting mission to explore a rumoured access route into the northeast corner of the lake. No one knew if they succeeded. Infiltrators might be a problem so everything was kept top secret. Rumour had it that Frank Bishop and his "Peace River Rebels" might attempt a boundary expansion and take over Crooked Lake if Edson fisheries didn't complete their assignment.

June 26th. Things proceeded rapidly. This was "C Day" and all available men and equipment were assembled for the final assault. This included Rudy and our only summer student. Equipment included the Ford 4x4 towing the Passe Par Tout and our old ³⁄₄-ton Dodge hauling the Bombi. The crew made Fox Creek with few problems and advanced on Tony Creek only to find that a flash flood had washed out the bridge during the weekend. They surveyed Meekwap Lake just for practice. "C Day" and the Tony Creek Bridge was a bust.

August 20th. The fifth trip to Crooked Lake. Erwin recovered sufficiently from his first trip to once again assist Rudy, and the Tony Creek Bridge was repaired. With little effort, the crew made fast time to road's end. Success was close; they could feel it in their bones. Warm days, cool nights, and no rain. The Bombi stubbornly refused to leave the trailer—it had a broken clutch. The crew returned to Fox Creek and netted Smoke Lake, which was the only waterbody within 50 miles that remotely needed a survey—except for Crooked. Crooked Lake was beginning to get to Rudy. He spent the fall in a rehab program (i.e., he went moose hunting).

1979 – Performance
April 3rd. Why wait for spring thaw? Using an old double-track snowmobile, new exploration led to the discovery of a complicated but fail-safe route on high(er) ground.

June 11th. Now equipped with modern equipment (a 12-ft. aluminum car-top borrowed from the Habitat Section) and new technology (a set of 1946 aerial photographs borrowed from Forestry), the crew was prepared for the 7th attack. Two trucks towed two track machines to the end of the road and after two days and many relays the equipment was cached on the shores of Crooked Lake. Despite two days of heavy rain, the routine lake survey was a breeze. Both men and most of the equipment returned to regional headquarters without further casualties. The seventh campaign was a success and Crooked Lake was secure (and finally surveyed!).

214

MAJOR EVENTS IN FISHERIES MANAGEMENT

1867   The *British North America Act* gives Canada ownership of its fisheries resource.

1868   The first federal *Fisheries Act* is administered by the Department of the Interior.

1892   Alfred Ernest Cross builds the Calgary Brewing and Malting Company, future site of the first provincial fish hatchery in the late 1930s.

1913   The first federal trout hatchery is established in Banff.

1926   Rearing ponds, established at the junction of Beaver Creek and the Raven River near Caroline, become the Raven River Rearing Station.

1930   The *Natural Resources Transfer Act* is passed.

1931   Alberta establishes a Fisheries Service within the Department of Lands and Mines, with R.T. Todd as Director. A provincial *Fisheries Act* and regulations are passed.

1940   The Calgary fish hatchery produces enough individuals of several species to begin distributing them to lakes and streams throughout the province.

1942   A new 3-day angling permit is introduced to attract tourists and people with limited leisure time.

1944   A *Fish Dealers Act* and *Alberta Fish Inspection Act* are passed.

1946   A commercial fishing royalty is charged. The *Fish Dealers Act* is operative—all persons dealing in or with fish must be licensed and regulations are designed for the protection of the industry and the export trade.

1950   A new comprehensive *Fisheries Act* is passed repealing the former Alberta *Fisheries Act (1931)*, the *Fish Dealers Act (1944)* and the *Alberta Fish Inspection Act (1944)*.

1952   Martin Paetz, Alberta's first fisheries biologist, is hired by the provincial government.

1962   The Alberta *Fisheries Act (1950)* is repealed and replaced by the *Fishery Act*.

1969   The *Fish Marketing Act* is passed repealing the *Fishery Act (1962)*.

1970   Technical training in fisheries management is offered for the first time in Alberta at Lethbridge Community College (NAIT would follow by 1973.)

1972   The Calgary Brewing and Malting Company closes its fish-rearing facilities after the modern Sam Livingston Hatchery is ready to open in William Pearce Estate Park.

1982   A *Fish and Wildlife Policy for Alberta* is released.

1989   Fish at the Sam Livingston Fish Hatchery contracted infectious pancreatic necrosis virus (IPNV).

2000   *A Fish Conservation Strategy For Alberta, 2000-2005* is released.

215

References • CHAPTER 6

[1] Brooke, Rupert. 1916. *Collected Poems*. John Lane, New York.

[2] Historical Society of Alberta. 1983. Fishing in Southern Alberta. Alberta History. Vol. 31(2):36-38. Both these officers were in the NWMP. McIlree's report on Maple Creek was dated July 29, 1890. White-Fraser's report was dated October 12, 1890.

[3] Paetz, M. and J. Nelson. 1970. The Fishes of Alberta. Government of Alberta (The Queen's Printer), Edmonton. This book provides an overview of the history of the early hatcheries.

[4] Other references for this article include the Sam Livingston Fish Hatchery Self-Guided Tour Brochure; display signage at the facility; the William Pearce 1848-1930 booklet—printed by Alberta Environment—no date available; and Sam Livingston Fish Hatchery—Operating Procedures and Precautions—Background Information.

[5] See Chapter 10 for more information on species at risk in Alberta.

[6] Taped interviews and conversations between January 23 and June 26, 2003 with David DePape, current Superintendent of Sam Livingston Fish Hatchery, and Winfried Schenk, past Superintendent.

[7] Miller, R. B. 1950. Preliminary Biological Surveys of Alberta Watersheds, 1947-1949. Edmonton, Alberta.

8   Alberta Department of Lands and Forests. 1994. Annual Reports. Also, interview with M. Paetz by Eric Holmgren, Edmonton, November 19, 1985.

9   Rawson, D.S. and C. A. Elsey. 1950. Reduction in the longnose sucker population in Pyramid Lake, Alberta, in an attempt to improve angling. Trans. Am. Fish. Soc. 78:13-31. See also Rawson, D.S. 1942. A comparison of some large alpine lakes in Western Canada. Ecology 23: 143-161.

10 Miller, R.B. 1962. A Cool, Curving World. Longmans Canada, Toronto.

11 See Chapter 5 for more details

12 Miller, R.B. 1952. A review of the *Triaenophorus* problem in Canadian lakes. Bulletin No. 95, Fisheries Research Board of Canada.

13 Alberta Fish and Wildlife Division. 2004. *Triaenophorus crassus* factsheet.

14 Miller, R.B. 1948. Reduction of *Triaenophorus* infestation in whitefish by depletion of the cisco population. Canadian Journal of Research, D, 26, 67-72.

15 Libin, M.L. 1951. Laboratory experiments on the control of the tapeworm, *Triaenophorus crassus*. M.Sc. thesis, University of Alberta, Edmonton.

16 Miller, R.B. 1952. op. cit.

17 Paterson, R. J. 1970. Coho for Alberta. Alberta Lands-Forests-Parks-Wildlife vol. 13:33-34.

18 Zelt, K.A. 1970. The Mayfly (Ephemeroptera) and Stonefly (Plecoptera) Fauna of a Foothills Stream in Alberta, with Special Reference to Sampling Techniques. M.Sc. Thesis, University of Alberta, Edmonton.

19 Dietz, K. 1971. The fish populations of three streams in the foothills of Alberta. M.Sc. Thesis, University of Alberta, Edmonton.

20 The many volumes of reports generated during this massive undertaking are available from the Fish and Wildlife Division.

Chapter 7

UPLAND GAME BIRDS: STUDY AND ENHANCEMENT

Blair Rippin and Bill Wishart with contributions from
Sue Clarke, Ken Lungle, Margo Pybus and John Stelfox

217

"You must not know too much, or be too precise or scientific about birds and trees and flowers and water-craft; a certain free margin, and even vagueness—perhaps ignorance, credulity—helps your enjoyment of these things."[1]
WALT WHITMAN

Early Years

Before Alberta took shape during the first part of the 20th century, there was little in the way of active "game management". The bison were long gone and other wildlife species were recovering from several harsh winters associated with the "little ice age" of the late 1800s. In particular, minimal effort was directed towards the eight native upland game bird species in Alberta. These included blue grouse, spruce grouse, ruffed grouse, willow ptarmigan, white-tailed ptarmigan, pinnated grouse (greater prairie-chicken), sharp-tailed grouse, and greater sage-grouse.[2]

However, British hunting attitudes were soon to have a profound effect on the province. Alberta had the greatest variety of native grouse in the world in 1905.[3] Yet these species did not present the hunting challenge that early European sportsmen were looking for. Such hunters were more familiar with birds moulded by centuries of interactions with people: birds that were more wily and swift of wing like the Chinese ring-necked pheasant and the Hungarian (gray) partridge. This common sentiment fuelled efforts to introduce more sporting species to the province. Many people also believed that the introduction of new species would ease the pressure on existing game species. Over time, new species would also prove to be more adaptable to habitat changes than native birds. While upland game bird habitat was relatively intact at the start of the century, this too, would soon change with the rapid settlement of the parklands and prairies.

ALBERTA'S NATIVE GROUSE

1 WILLOW PTARMIGAN.
CREDIT: E. JONES COURTESY ROYAL
ALBERTA MUSEUM

2 RUFFED GROUSE. CREDIT: G. COURT

3 SPRUCE GROUSE. CREDIT: B. McGILLIVRAY
COURTESY ROYAL ALBERTA MUSEUM

4 SHARP-TAILED GROUSE. CREDIT: G. COURT

5 BLUE GROUSE. CREDIT: J. KEISER COURTESY ROYAL ALBERTA
MUSEUM

6 GREATER PRAIRIE CHICKEN (ALSO KNOWN AS PINNATED
GROUSE, NOW EXTIRPATED). CREDIT: F. LAHRMAN

7 WHITE-TAILED PTARMIGAN. CREDIT: R. CARSON COURTESY
ROYAL ALBERTA MUSEUM

8 SAGE-GROUSE. CREDIT: G. COURT

218

Hungarian Partridge: they came, they stayed

In the winter of 1907, Austin de B. Winter and his friends, Fred J. Green and George Wood, privately imported 15 pairs of bobwhite quail. These were brought from the U.S. to Alberta in heated cars. The birds were released near Dan Patton's ranch at Midnapore. Unfortunately, a severe blizzard struck the following day and all the birds died. Other releases of quail were made in 1929 in High River and the 1930s near Leduc, but none was successful in establishing this species in Alberta.[4]

Undeterred by the quail setback, Winter spearheaded formation of the Calgary Fish and Game Protective Association in 1908. After receiving permission from Chief Game Guardian Benjamin Lawton, Association members immediately pooled their financial resources to purchase and "import wild game birds best suited to the climatic conditions of Alberta".[5] The Hungarian partridge, more affectionately known as "the hun", was the bird of choice. Fifty-five pairs were imported directly from Hungary at a total cost of $416.72. The first 15 pairs were liberated at the Patton ranch in April 1908. In November, six sets of five pairs each were released at locations where there were birds from the original release of 15 pairs. In December, the remaining ten pairs were freed at John Hamilton's place at the head of Pine Creek, southwest of Calgary. Additional birds were imported that fall and in the spring of 1909, and again in 1911 and 1914. While the sportsmen covered the majority of the cost ($2,400), the Alberta

Government contributed $500 towards the effort. Eventually 175 pairs were released in the Calgary area and another 50 pairs were released around Edmonton.

The hun experiment was highly successful. The original stock of birds established themselves and reproduced such that there were sufficient numbers to open a hunting season in the autumn of 1913. As well, Winter and his associates received numerous hun sightings from as far away as Saskatchewan and Montana. Even J.B. Harkin, Commissioner of National Parks, inquired about introducing huns to Elk Island Park. However, a national park was not a suitable setting for a species rapidly expanding its range in association with expanding agricultural crops. Some years after their introduction Winter wrote, "Huns in the Eastern Irrigation District are literally as thick as flies."[6]

The Hungarian partridge introduction was not without controversy. Some folks alleged that the huns "drove the prairie chicken out". Research later showed that the prairie chicken disappeared because of a loss of their habitat as the prairies

GORDON KERR AND BUCK CUNNINGHAM CAPTURING HUNS NEAR EDMONTON FOR RELEASE IN THE GRANDE PRAIRIE AREA, 1962.
CREDIT: B. WISHART

219

were broken up and cultivated. Regardless, the huns thrived in Alberta and throughout the midwestern U.S., becoming an international success story.

Hares, Upland Game Birds, and Conservation Stamps

During the 1940s, Austin Winter carried on a continuous correspondence with William Rowan, Professor of Zoology at the University of Alberta. Rowan was noted for his work on bird migration, but was interested in almost any aspect of wildlife. Although he often was regarded as an eccentric, many of his ideas were later proven correct.

Rowan and Winter were each astute observers of nature. One recurring theme in their letters was a mysterious series of cyclical crashes seen in upland

AUSTIN DE B. WINTER AND THE CALGARY FISH AND GAME PROTECTIVE ASSOCIATION
[SUE CLARKE]

Austin de B. Winter, a lawyer and conservationist, was born in 1882 in Exeter, England. He studied law in London before arriving in Calgary in 1903. He was admitted to the bar in 1909, was deputy clerk of the Supreme Court until 1910, and practised law until 1952. He died in November 1969.

Winter was an avid sportsman and passionate conservationist. He was a founding member and guiding spirit behind the Calgary Fish and Game Protective Association and had a lifelong association with its provincial counterpart, the Alberta Fish and Game Association. As a member of the Upland Game Birds Committee, he played a significant role in the introduction of several species of upland game birds to Alberta including Hungarian partridge, Chinese ring-necked pheasant, Mongolian pheasant, and bobwhite quail. In 1942, Winter and several other Association members supported the idea of game bird stamps. Hunters and anglers were encouraged to buy stamps with their licences, with the proceeds from sales used to address wildlife problems.

As with any organization, there was always a pressing need for funds. Money was raised by membership dues and gradually the Calgary Association and its counterpart in Edmonton came to work closely with one another. In dealings with the government, Winter was the spokesman. In a letter to the Honourable C.W. Fisher, Speaker of the Legislature and Member for Cochrane, Winter inquired whether something could be done about a grant. He pointed out that the Association was doing work that should receive more than lip service from the government. Following repeated back and forth correspondence with Duncan Marshall, Minister of Agriculture, Winter was able to formally thank the Minister in 1917 for a grant of $100.[7]

During the late 1920s and throughout the 1930s, the Alberta Fish and Game Association was performing a variety of wildlife work including collecting and incubating game bird eggs, releasing young birds, acting as volunteer game guardians on occasion, and assisting with annual fish stocking operations. (See "To Conserve a Heritage", a history of the Alberta Fish and Game Association for more details.[8]) However, things changed in 1940. The Provincial Fish and Game Branch was made a permanent part of the Department of Lands and Mines, and government assumed a more active role in many aspects of wildlife management. Eric Huestis, appointed as the first Fish and Game Commissioner, soon made it clear what government would do and what the Association could do. When the Association informed the government of its intent to trap pheasants and collect eggs in 1945, it in turn, was informed that J.A. Morden, a government employee, would organize this work. The Association could assist if it wished.

Despite the new role of government, the Association continued with its game bird programs. From 1937 to 1941, southern sportsmen repeatedly introduced chukar partridge and government instituted new regulations for their protection. Although releases were made in 1937, 1939, 1941, 1953, and 1954, only remnant populations persisted near the release sites.[9] In 1961, it was reported that annual surveys since 1959 failed to demonstrate that chukars still resided in the province. Attempts to establish chukar partridge in Alberta were deemed to have failed. Similarly, repeated attempts to introduce bobwhite quail into Alberta also proved unsuccessful.

game bird populations in Alberta.[10] In Rowan's assessment, populations were high and people complained about the super-abundance of birds in some years and some seasons. Then, just as suddenly and inexplicably, the birds disappeared. It was a biological mystery, "the conundrum of the century", that Rowan the scientist and Winter the sportsman-conservationist struggled to solve. Unfortunately, Rowan did not live to see the solution. Slowly the pieces of the puzzle came into focus many years later, as summarized and synthesized by Lloyd Keith, a former student of Rowan's.[11]

When Winter and associates began introducing Hungarian partridge to Alberta in 1908, the huns were largely unseen for the first three years. Indeed, it was not known whether they would even survive, let alone thrive in the Alberta climate. Amazingly, they established themselves within the unbelievably short period of five years.[12] According to Rowan, these early Hungarian partridge populations increased steadily. No fluctuations were observed until 1925 when diseased partridges were sent in to him from hunters from several parts of the Province, most notably, the Wainwright district.

By 1934, huns were again so abundant that the Game Department provided the most generous bag (harvest) limits in Alberta partridge history. Rowan, ever the scientist, kept meticulous bag records, including details of age, sex, weight, and crop contents of each individual bird. He also made use of his partner's bag for additional data. As the hunting season advanced that year, Rowan

221

WHAT'S GOING ON? October 6, 1943
[REPRODUCED COURTESY OF THE GLENBOW ARCHIVES] From a letter found in the Austin de B Winter fonds.

Dear Winter:
I hate to send you depressing news, but I am afraid the ruddy worst has befallen our feathered natives. The reports I am now getting from all over the shop suggest that chicken and ruffed grouse hunters, at least, needn't worry about the shells that aren't there [ammunition was directed to the war effort], for there is nothing to shoot with them. Most of the north seems to have been decimated, as well as the general Red Deer area and the country west of Edmonton. Huns look very sad to me also. I haven't been out much, but there are too many pairs of birds without any young at all and I have only seen one decent-sized covey this fall. What is even worse, one does not hear Huns except at infrequent intervals. Maybe as the fall progresses things won't look so black, but there is certainly no reason for optimism. I expect, as usual, it will take a year for the thing to be noticeable in the south, but it looks very bad here. I think I told you of the chaps who camped on a spot near Lac St. Anne in October, 1941, (4 of them, one presumably a cook) and bottled 300 sealers of ruffed grouse without shifting camp (in a week) which is a bit of a contrast when one considers that seven ruffed grouse go into one quart sealer (i.e. if one cuts the meat off the bones).

I have not yet discovered how the pheasants are weathering this crash, (I fear the worst) but there seems to be a lot of them right now. However, they are more difficult to judge. There are lots of late broods and one cannot yet spot the young cocks in many of them, so I shan't be wasting gas on them 'till November when the second half of the season comes off up here. It will be interesting to see if we at last have a permanent upland game bird that can weather the ten-year depression. People are complaining now about their super-abundance. If they really stick out the cycle successfully, I can foresee a veritable uproar from the country yokels before many more years have elapsed...

Hoping to see you again one of these days,

Yours ever,
William Rowan

noted that 70% of the harvested birds were adult. In other years, the exact opposite was true: 70 to 80% were juveniles. Rowan immediately sent a questionnaire around the province to investigate this alarming pattern. Some farmers reported that in many situations, resident coveys (flocks) of young, some of them with 20 birds, dwindled to nothing until only the parents remained. This was during August in perfectly normal weather. Meticulous post-mortem examinations by Rowan revealed no evidence of disease or parasite that could account for this decimation of juveniles.

By 1936, Rowan noted that the huns reached their lowest ebb and that depletion was general over the prairies. Low populations also occurred in snowshoe hares and grouse. "The great point of interest is, of course, whether all of this is mere co-incidence or something much more fundamental that might lead us to expect a repetition in about 1944."[13] He thought the latter seemed more likely.

Sportsmen, conservationists, and government officials expressed grave concern over these alarming trends for which there seemed no explanation. They feared the worst: decimation of the upland game bird population. The mystery of these cycles required at least an explanation, and at best, a solution. Biological research was still very much in its infancy and Rowan found himself at the leading edge. Funding for research was practically non-existent yet this cyclical mystery required resources for its successful resolution. Where could they get the money so desperately needed for research?

In 1942, in a letter of response to Winter's deep concerns regarding the nature and impact of these cycles, Rowan provided his best scientific opinion

LLOYD KEITH: PUTTING THE PIECES TOGETHER

The intriguing phenomenon of cyclic abundance of snowshoe hares, grouse, and their predators was the subject of considerable research from 1960 to 1975. Lloyd Keith began working on the ten-year game cycle as a student of William Rowan at the University of Alberta. Building on the information gathered by Rowan, C. Gordon Hewitt, P.A. Taverner, and others, Keith and his students, including Mike Dorrance, Gerry Kemp, Ron Weatherill, Lamar Windberg, and Arlen Todd, examined numerous aspects of the riddle near Rochester, Alberta. Eventually, they made the link between snowshoe hares and upland game birds. In years of good habitat, fair weather, and numerous hares, the hares are the preferred prey species of lynx, goshawks, great-horned owls, and other predators. As hare numbers peak, habitat and food become limiting and the population takes a nosedive. As hare numbers decline, predators turn to other prey like upland game birds, and game bird populations in turn take a downward spiral. Keith and several students conducted many studies and published many papers detailing this phenomenon.

BILL WISHART AND LLOYD KEITH EXAMINING A STARVED HARE NEAR ROCHESTER.
COURTESY B. WISHART

Based on the evidence, reducing predators to stabilize grouse fluctuations seemed like a good idea to hunters. However, such action was deemed impractical, biologically unsound, and distasteful to the general public. Therefore, the idea of predator control to enhance grouse survival was abandoned.

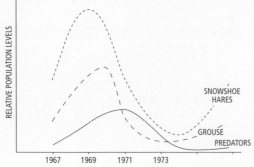

A CONCEPTUAL MODEL OF THE 10-YEAR GAME CYCLE.
FROM KEITH (1971)

while offering a possible solution to the research funding dilemma:

Whatever may be the underlying basis of these cycles for which there exists no satisfactory explanation at present, it seems that they are visible indications of a fundamental factor of the northern environment whose influence on human activities may be more direct than we at present suspect. The subject has had much serious attention during the past two decades both on this continent and in Europe, but the solution is not yet in sight. In order to prosecute the research on an adequate scale here at home, the very headquarters of these cycles during the impending "crash", it is now hoped to issue a "conservation stamp" during the summer. This will be sold (on a purely voluntary basis) to sportsmen and others sufficiently interested in the project and the proceeds devoted entirely to the investigation. A suggested design for the first of these stamps is herewith submitted.[14]

A SAMPLE OF ROWAN'S GAME STAMPS.
COURTESY UNIVERSITY OF ALBERTA ARCHIVES

Rowan was a superb artist in addition to his superior talents as an ornithologist. He designed a set of five conservation stamps portraying the Hungarian partridge, the Canada goose, the ruffed grouse, the mallard duck, and the ring-necked pheasant. The stamps were issued as a private venture of the Science Association of the University of Alberta, with approval and co-operation of the Alberta provincial game department. Sets of stamps were issued to licence vendors, along with a memorandum dated August 1942, which stated the purpose of the stamps:

The problems involved are complex, but it is obvious that if this regularly recurring depression could be prevented, hunting would be both better and more consistent. It has recurred since the prairies were first settled and is due again in the

near future. Considerable research has already been done on various aspects of this problem, but it is hoped that the funds derived from the sales of the stamps will see its conclusion. There are many other analogous problems in the general field of conservation that can only be solved by trained men, who are available at the Universities, but the funds are not. These stamps issued to provide the means to make such work possible during the war, when the conservation of animal life, and particularly the question of diseases, takes on an important aspect.[15]

Participating vendors were offered 10% commission on all sales along with instructions for

223

224

A PAIR OF RING-NECKED PHEASANTS.
COURTESY ROYAL ALBERTA MUSEUM

promoting and advertising the conservation stamps. *The Albertan* newspaper in Calgary ran an article on September 10, 1942 explaining the purpose of the stamps and the need to undertake appropriate scientific research on these game cycles. It noted that the prairies were at the peak of the regular ten-year game cycle and the hares and upland game birds were very abundant. Interestingly, the article stressed that if the next cyclical decline occurred as predicted disease would sweep across the Dominion and more or less wipe these species out.

The Reign of the Ring-necked Pheasant

Several groups, including various Fish and Game and Rod and Gun Club members, started introducing the popular and remarkable ring-necked pheasant into Alberta in 1909. Indeed, many of the same folks responsible for bringing Hungarian partridge to the province were also involved with pheasant releases. Repeated releases continued over the next 25 years. Introductions were supplemented with eggs purchased from the U.S. or gathered from "dump" nests (where hens lay and then abandon eggs) of wild pheasants. These eggs were then provided to co-operators for incubation and hatching, and at one-month of age, the young chicks were released to the wild.

Pheasant populations built slowly and it wasn't until the 1930s that ring-necks became well established, particularly in the Eastern Irrigation District (EID). The species thrived on irrigated lands because of a network of ditches, canals, and wetlands interspersed through a variety of

WHAT'S IN A NAME?

When early explorers first encountered the ruffed grouse on the Atlantic coast, they called it a "pheasant." Thus began a confusing litany of names and misnomers for upland game birds in North America. Audubon continued with "pheasant" in 1830.[16] Nuttall did the same in 1891.[17] To add confusion, Nuttall used the correct scientific name, but provided two common names: ruffed grouse and pheasant. Nuttall also used pinnated grouse and sharp-tailed grouse correctly, but unfortunately applied the common name of "prairie chicken" to both species. No wonder there was confusion with ruffed grouse and sharp-tailed grouse prior to Nuttall's book, and ever since!

The 1883 Ordinance for the Northwest Territories included a hunting season (but no bag limit) for all our native grouse referred to as "pheasants, partridge, prairie chicken and grouse". (Of course, there were no real pheasants in Alberta until they were introduced in 1909.) Bag limits of 20 per day for "grouse" were introduced in 1895. In 1906, a list of game regulation prohibitions stated, "No person may shoot more than 20 prairie chickens or other grouse in a day or more than 200 in a season."

In 1908, a handbook published for tourists to Alberta stated there was a hunting season for "prairie chicken and partridge" which probably was the vernacular for sharp-tailed grouse and ruffed grouse since the Hungarian partridge was only introduced in 1908 and there was no hunting season for it until five years later. Ptarmigan were included in the list with "pheasants, partridge, prairie chicken and grouse" in 1907. In 1927 "pheasant" was finally changed to ruffed grouse, probably as a result of Taverner's *Birds of Western Canada* published in 1926.[18] The amended provincial regulation in 1927 stated "as to paragraph (d), by striking out 'pheasant' and adding…that 'no person shall kill ruffed grouse, commonly called partridge…at any time'". Thus, while clarifying one point (pheasant), this statement created more confusion (partridge).

After the introduction of Hungarian partridge in 1908, this species was so named and duly protected in the regulations of 1909. In the 1927 regulations, the "hun" was given its correct common name "European gray partridge, commonly called Hungarian partridge" as it appeared in Taverner's book. The name Hungarian partridge persisted in the regulations until it was changed to gray partridge in

the upland bird regulations in 1989 after 80 years as a "hun".

In 1910, a year after its introduction, the ring-necked pheasant was referred to as "Hungarian pheasant"! In 1913, when the season opened on Hungarian partridge, the "Hungarian pheasant" was listed separately as protected and remained so for several years. With probable thanks to Dr. Rowan, an ornithologist and avid "hun" hunter, the name "Hungarian pheasant" was finally struck from the regulations, and the introduced ring-necked pheasant was placed correctly in the pheasant family in the *Game Act* of 1932.

The name "prairie chicken" was used interchangeably for sharptails in hunting regulations and popular usage. But this, too, was confusing: the amended regulations of 1927 stated "no person shall…kill sharp-tailed or pinnated grouse, commonly called prairie chicken at any time". This was the first time the pinnated grouse was named in Alberta regulations and it was protected *per se*. However, the summary of 1930 game regulations added to the confusion by stating there was no open season on pinnated grouse, but there was an open season on prairie chicken (north of the Red Deer River) and sharp-tailed grouse throughout the province. This was despite the disappearance of pinnated grouse/greater prairie chicken from Alberta in the early 1930s![19] Apparently, "prairie chicken" was well-established vernacular for sharp-tailed grouse and it seems few folks knew the difference! In 1934, the regulations stated that ring-necked pheasants and grouse were protected except sharp-tailed grouse commonly called prairie chicken. As late as 1958, the game bird regulations stated: "The holder of a Game Bird Licence may hunt and kill sharp-tailed grouse, commonly but erroneously referred to as prairie chicken."

The remaining "grouse" in the original list of 1883 must have applied to blue grouse and sage-grouse. Not until 1930 were all of Alberta's upland birds listed specifically, with the exception of ptarmigan, in a summary of Alberta game regulations as follows: "No open season on ruffed grouse (native partridge), pinnated grouse, sage, spruce, and blue grouse, also ring-necked pheasants." Seasons were declared for Hungarian partridge, sharp-tailed grouse, and/or prairie chicken.

croplands. Pheasants and ditches were synonymous, whether they were irrigation ditches, drainage ditches, roadside ditches, or railroad ditches. Ditches were usually moist and provided vegetative cover as well as interconnected travel lanes where the birds could "ditch" the hunter!

The first pheasant hunting season occurred in 1939 and consisted of a two-day hunt with a limit of six roosters per hunter. Season length and bag limits rose steadily in the following years until 1947 when the upland bird season was closed except for pheasants, and the bag limits dropped to three per day and 18 per season. During peak years in the 1940s and 1950s, densities of pheasants in the EID (two birds per acre) exceeded those of Pelee Island, in Lake Erie, Ontario, famous for its pheasants and pheasant hunting opportunities. Bag limits in Alberta soared to five birds per day and 30 per season. The town of Brooks was central to the pheasant bonanza and attracted hunters from all parts of North America. The average annual harvest of cock pheasants in Alberta during the mid-1950s was 145,000 birds! (By the 1990s, the average

annual harvest of cock pheasants dropped to fewer than 20,000 birds.)

The interest in pheasants and other upland game birds prompted a number of studies to determine better management practices. In 1947, released pheasants carried leg bands that allowed the Province to study their survival and movement. In 1949, Roy Anderson and Bud Gau from the University of Alberta conducted a pheasant survey.[20] They found that cover was the principal factor underlying the great variation in pheasant density among seven irrigation districts in southern Alberta. Also, the amount of pheasant habitat available in the irrigation districts was directly proportional to the length of the irrigation period per year and the amount of water directed through the system. And finally, the amount of cover available was inversely proportional to the degree of ditch maintenance. Therefore, the Eastern Irrigation District offered the finest cover for pheasants because the irrigation period lasted from April to October, the amount of water used was 3.2 acre-feet, and ditch maintenance was low. Taber and Vauxhall

DENNIS McDONALD, DON HARFORD AND BILL WISHART WITH A NICE BAG OF PHEASANTS NEAR BROOKS, 1968.
CREDIT: B. CUNNINGHAM COURTESY D. McDONALD

A PHEASANT HATCHERY IN BROOKS

In some ways, introducing pheasants to Alberta was the easy part. Establishing a viable provincial population proved more complicated. The wild hens were erratic nesters and often abandoned their nests. They tended to lay their eggs where they were vulnerable to farming operations. As a result, additional methods were needed to enhance the growth of pheasant populations. For a while, pheasants were live-trapped in areas where they were numerous and transferred to less populated areas. Fish and Game members often did this work. But this was labour-intensive and limited by the finding and collecting of wild birds.

It was readily apparent that eggs were much easier to find. And to collect! A somewhat uncoordinated pheasant raise-and-release program worked reasonably well for a number of years, but a central

AN AERIAL VIEW OF THE BROOKS PHEASANT HATCHERY, ca. 1965.
COURTESY THE PROVINCIAL ARCHIVES OF ALBERTA (PA 827/4)

pheasant-rearing station would be even more efficient. Late in 1945, a facility was built at Brooks, with Game Inspector George Bray as superintendent of the new pheasant hatchery. The hatchery soon achieved a 70% hatching rate and young birds were released at seven weeks of age. In some years, there was difficulty getting enough eggs—some people in the Eastern Irrigation District were opposed to the collection. In other years, surplus eggs were sent to B.C., Saskatchewan, and Manitoba. By 1957, the Brooks "game bird farm" was operating at capacity. The next year, in addition to regular releases of adult pheasants from the Brooks pheasant farm, day-old chicks were distributed to private individuals for raising and releasing. The hatchery was well established and became an integral part of game bird management in Alberta. It served the needs of pheasants and hunters alike for many years.

GAME COMMISSIONER ERIC HUESTIS AND OTHERS RELEASING PHEASANTS FROM THE BROOKS PHEASANT HATCHERY, ca. 1950.
COURTESY ALBERTA FISH AND WILDLIFE DIVISION

Irrigation Districts were rated good and the four other districts were rated poor based on the above criteria and occurrence of pheasants.

The standard for estimating pheasant numbers in the 1950s and 1960s was the pheasant crowing count (counting male mating calls). Each spring, starting one-half hour before sunrise, counters followed a 20-30 mile route (transect) through a stretch of suitable pheasant habitat. They stopped and listened for two minutes (the average crowing interval for cock pheasants) then proceeded to the next stop one or two miles down the road. During the peak years, you could hear 20-30 crowing cocks in a two-minute period in good habitat. [However, in the 1970s, the pheasant crowing counts declined in concert with declining habitat, to the extent that most of the crowing transects were discontinued throughout the province.]

Spring surveys also provided cock-to-hen ratios, and when combined with summer brood surveys, provided a cumulative picture used to forecast the annual fall harvest. Other upland bird indices, such as drumming counts from ruffed grouse and dancing ground (lek) counts of sharp-tailed grouse, were used for predicting fall populations.

Although these upland bird population surveys were interesting and useful at the time, they served primarily to record the steady decline of upland birds throughout the agricultural areas of the province.

For better management of upland game bird populations, the Province was divided into three hunting zones. In 1961, hunter check stations for upland game birds were established to determine hunter success. Check stations also allowed biologists an opportunity to determine the age of harvested birds and thus, confirm or disprove the harvest forecast. Feather replacement patterns in wings collected from harvested birds were used to determine the dates of hatch, which could then be related to weather conditions during the laying, nesting, and brooding period.

An experimental hen pheasant season in 1967, demonstrated that hunting hens had no effect on subsequent pheasant production, a pattern seen also in other upland game birds. Hunting simply removes a portion of the birds that normally would have died during the winter (winter mortality is in the range of 60%-80%, with or without hunting). As a result, a limited hen season (one hen in a daily bag of three pheasants and three hens in a possession limit of nine) was introduced throughout the province in 1971. However, the "sacred hen" season proved so unpopular with hunters that it was closed in 1973. As Dave Moyles, Fish and Wildlife Division, Peace River, observed, "Many Albertans were convinced that the conservative season on hen pheasants, rather than the subtle but steady loss of

AN IRRIGATION CANAL WITH GOOD COVER FOR PHEASANTS.
COURTESY ALBERTA FISH AND WILDLIFE DIVISION

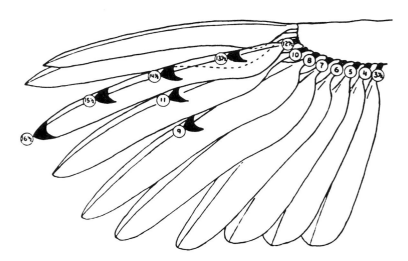

A DIAGRAM OF WING MOULT IN HUNGARIAN PARTRIDGE. THE STAGE OF MOULT IS EQUAL TO THE BIRD'S AGE IN WEEKS.
CREDIT: K. WESTERSKOV COURTESY B. WISHART

and concluded that it was neither sustainable in the long run nor cost-effective in the short term. Instead, the province adopted the Midwest approach and resorted to put-and-take pheasant hunting. This move was similar to a management decision to establish a "put-and-take" fishery in stocked dugouts, ponds and other "potholes".

The popularity of hunting pheasants led to an interest from several entrepreneurs and the *Game Act* of 1955 included provisions to allow private individuals to rear pheasants for sale as food or for subsequent breeding purposes. By 1970, the new *Wildlife Act* contained provisions for the operation of Pheasant Shooting Grounds, the forerunner of current Game Bird Shooting Grounds.

Pheasant Shooting Ground Licensees were exempt from a provincial prohibition against charging hunters an access fee. Operators could sell opportunities to hunt their pheasants any time of the year. The popularity of shooting grounds increased as the number of wild pheasants decreased. Over time, hunting on shooting grounds allowed harvest of other introduced

229

cover in southern and central Alberta, coupled with the severe winters of the early 1970s, led to the overall decline in the numbers of pheasants."

Pheasant production for stocking various parts of the province was the norm until the mid-1960s when it became apparent that modern agriculture and suitable habitat for pheasants were not compatible. Stocking pheasants to increase populations where good habitat was already occupied or where good habitat no longer existed was a futile exercise. Some midwestern states experienced a similar dilemma. The agricultural landscape could not be restored to the earlier pheasant hunting glory days, so these states resorted to put-and-take releases. Alberta examined the cost of land purchase and land easements to recreate productive pheasant habitat

HERDING PHEASANTS AT THE BROOKS WILDLIFE CENTRE FOR LOADING AND EVENTUAL RELEASE. COURTESY ALBERTA FISH AND WILDLIFE DIVISION

upland game birds such as bobwhite quail and chukar partridge. Currently, pheasants and wild turkeys also may be hunted on nearly 100 Game Bird Shooting Grounds in Alberta. Owners also may market these four game birds as meat products.

In the 1970s, hunting success on pheasant roosters the day following their release was tested. Return rates ranged from 65-75% and were considered very cost effective. As a consequence, the Brooks hatchery expanded to become the Brooks Wildlife Centre in 1978. The Centre was able to produce up to 100,000 pheasants a year for release to the wild. Most of the cocks, and melanistic pheasants of both sexes, were used for put-and-take releases on Buck for Wildlife properties.[21] Charging a separate fee for pheasant-hunting licences covered some of the costs; however, in the mid-1990s, Fish and Wildlife no longer could provide sufficient funding and no longer felt the need to operate the facility. Under the banner of privatization, the Centre was sold eventually to The Canadian Pheasant Company with the provision that some of the birds produced would continue to be released for public hunting.

In 1982, pheasant hunters in the U.S. united to form Pheasants Forever. One of their co-founding members stated, "I think the low water mark on habitat loss has finally been reached." Several chapters were formed and over the course of 20 years, the organization was able to dedicate $106 million to 250,000 habitat projects to improve 2.7 million acres of land vital to wildlife. Their funds are directed toward food plots, nesting cover, woody cover, wetlands, land acquisitions, controlled burns, equipment, public awareness, and education. In recent years, a number of chapters of Pheasants Forever have formed in southern Alberta and are making efforts to reserve and create habitat for the "wily ring-neck".

The Plow, the Cow, and the Shotgun – A Changing World

The march of agriculture across the prairies and parklands, particularly between 1920 and 1940, was the most significant upland game bird management event of the century. A similar pattern was seen during the 1950s and 1960s in the Peace River parklands. In the early stages of agricultural development, farming practices actually enhanced the food and cover benefits for upland game birds. Fields were small with strips of brushy cover (including lots of wild rose) along the fencerows, irrigation ditches, and roadsides. During the harvest, a horse drawn binder cut and bound the grain before dumping it onto the

ON THE WAY TO A THRESHING MACHINE LOADING BUNDLES OF GRAIN FROM A STOOKED FIELD.
CREDIT: C. GORDON

A PERSONAL STORY OF PHEASANT INTRODUCTIONS
[AS TOLD BY THE LATE GERRY PELCHAT TO BILL WISHART]

Gerry Pelchat was born in Phoenix, Saskatchewan in 1923. His Dad ran a mixed farm with cattle, pigs, chickens, and grain until 1939 when the family moved to the Rolling Hills area of Alberta. The devastating prairie droughts of the 1930s were largely over and it was the beginning of a new era in farm practices, one based largely on irrigation. It also was the dawn of expanding pheasant populations as a result of previous releases. Gerry's life and pheasant management became synonymous in Alberta:

"When we came on the place, it was all raw land except for a hundred acres that had been broken. The farmstead was located in the new Eastern Irrigation District and our water was provided from Lake Newell for flood irrigation. We were allotted two acre-feet. In those days, if you had first water right, they had to guarantee you one acre-foot. With second water right, you got water only when water was available.

"The first few years, there were no pheasants. They came after the area became established with farmers and habitat. When we first came there were no willow ditches and very little cover on what we referred to as wetlands. But after we had been there for two, three years, the willows and cattails started growing and we had quite a few pheasants by the time I left home.

"After discharge from the Navy, I had a number of jobs, some with poultry, before working for George Bray, who raised pheasants for the Government. George was a returned air force officer discharged in 1945, just as Brooks opened up as a game district for a game officer. He got the job and was also put in charge of the new pheasant-raising program. They started off with 12 rooster houses and increased each year until in 1950 when I came, it was up to 49 houses. The pens were scattered amongst the orchards in a horticultural station just east of town. Annual maximum production was less than 3,000. I helped George in the hatchery and then he kept me on during the hunting and commercial fishing seasons.

"In the spring of 1951, they sent me up north to relieve a Fisheries Officer at Calling Lake. On my way home (March 15-17), a blizzard hit just as I got to Bassano. There were areas on that highway where the snow was piled up eight feet on each side of the road. I got up the next morning about 8 o'clock and couldn't find my truck—it was completely covered!

We lost about 95% of our pheasants. We had just gone through a three-day Chinook. The fields were fairly bare and the Chinook continued into the night so the pheasants didn't look for good areas to roost. When the storm hit, they were caught in the open. The wind blew so hard that the pheasants faced into the storm because of their feathers. But the storm started as wet snow and it plugged their nostrils. We found all kinds of birds with their mouth wide open, full of ice. Some took off and then the wind took them and we found them all over the place. Most of the pheasants we picked up showed severe bruises, broken backs, and broken wings. They'd been hammered against the ground or someplace when the wind picked them up. We took a few hundred to the University in Edmonton. This was in the days of Professor Rowan.

"When I started to work for George Bray, all the pheasant eggs were collected from school kids. We used to cover every school in Newell County once a day, five days a week. We gave the kids a nickel an egg: one girl one year, with her family, collected over 800 eggs! That's how many pheasants used to be around here in those days. I used to collect anywhere from 12–14,000 eggs a year from the kids. Hatchability was around 50% because a lot of them were frozen. They'd either been laid too early or were infertile."

George Bray soon moved on to become Senior Game Officer in Edmonton. There was no one else who had any experience with raising pheasants, so Gerry got the job in Brooks. Besides, he really wanted the job:

"In 1952, we picked up about 41 acres west of Brooks. We built pens in the summer and moved after the pheasant season was over. In 1953, we started operations at the new site with a capacity for 6,000 birds. In 1954, we increased that again and reached 60-some houses. We kept all our parent stock at that time, but I still collected about 1,000 eggs from the wild to keep up the wild genes, mixing captive and wild breeding hens and roosters. We kept about 600 laying hens for egg production.

"George Mitchell came down to Brooks about 1952 to do a study on game bird density and reproduction. We dragged a light cable with a bunch of dangling chains across alfalfa fields and recorded everything that flushed, whether it was

231

pheasants, ducks, or Hungarian partridge. The government was deciding whether to have a three-bird season, should it open at ten o'clock, this kind of stuff. Fish and Game did most of the field work. George analyzed the crowing counts and number of birds on transects.

"The changes in habitat started in the 1950s. The biggest change came with herbicides. The next thing was centralized school systems. With the shift from little country schools all over the place, they had to upgrade all the country roads. So where we had a trail between two fences with all kinds of cover, we now had an elevated all-weather road. Ditches were drained and willows were cut down or sprayed so they wouldn't hold the snow.

"Then farmers became a little more affluent. They could clean up wet areas that grew a lot of weeds and cattails and fill or drain them to make the area 'productive'. And finally, they came up with sprinkler systems for irrigation. They took the ditches out and levelled the fields. The biggest loss of cover was during the 1950s to the late 1960s. I say we lost probably 70% to 80% of our cover in that period of time. In the early 1950s, there were travel lanes all over the place and winter concentration of 3000-4000 pheasants was not unusual. They picked up food left after harvest. One little change at a time and pretty soon you'd find only a few birds. They were just gradually whittled down.

"We paid about $80,000 for five quarters near Millicent in the late 1960s in an attempt to recover some habitat. [This was one of the first provincial Buck for Wildlife projects]. The idea was to develop pheasant habitat on a fairly large parcel of land. Harold Carr, the biologist in Calgary, was in charge for the first year. In 1972, it was turned over to me to design the shelterbelts and the type of trees to grow. I convinced Gordon Kerr, Director of Wildlife, to give me a few extra bucks so we could level some land and direct the water to specific areas to grow trees. We tried to establish border habitat areas and leave the inside clear for grain farming.

"The first year we planted over 3000 trees. And if I remember correctly about June 6 or so, we had a heavy frost and lost most of our fruit trees. So, we replanted the following year. We eventually had some good shelterbelts but the surrounding area was mostly bare. It was an island and didn't work out as well as it should have. I guess we decided we couldn't buy enough land to develop enough of these areas. They'd have to be close enough to be joined, with travel lanes in between. And there's no way you can grow enough pheasants without cooperation of the farmer: it just doesn't work.

"So about 1975, we came around to the idea that we should raise pheasants in mass production for put-and-take operations. We bought 200 acres of land east of Brooks, built new houses and pens, and moved onto the place in 1978. We produced in

FISH AND WILDLIFE DIVISION DEVELOPING UPLAND GAME BIRD HABITAT NEAR MILLICENT.
COURTESY ALBERTA FISH AND WILDLIFE DIVISION

province. And chicken heads. We also had a parrot or two. Quite a menagerie. We had a pretty good Administration and Interpretive Centre as well as an interpretive person. One year we had in excess of 4000 tourists come through. We had buses from Europe—German, Swiss, French, and English. A lot of Americans and a lot of people from down East. Those were the heydays through the 1970s and early 1980s.

"I retired in 1983. I had my 35 years in. I saw the money drying up and that's the biggest reason I left. We had a lab technician and they closed that down. They cut most of the research in 1992. The only thing left was raising pheasants. Tom Archer took over from me: he was well qualified and did an excellent job but he only stayed a couple of years. Les Trip took over for him and Dale Jacobson stayed on. Then the government sold it.

"The high point of my career was when the government agreed to expand the Brooks Wildlife Centre. That was quite a challenge. Those were probably the best six or seven years that I enjoyed the most. I had an excellent supervisor who gave me a free hand. There weren't too many people in the Fish and Wildlife Division who did what I was doing. And very few who were in a position to give me any guidance or advice or criticism. I pretty well got a free hand in a place far removed from government."

[After retirement, Gerry remained in Brooks. He passed away in 2003.]

233

GERRY PELCHAT RELEASING A MELANISTIC PHEASANT.
COURTESY ALBERTA FISH AND WILDLIFE DIVISION

excess of 100,000 birds a year in the new facility. The hatchery initiated new programs with the Fish and Game Associations and with agricultural 4-H Clubs. Chicks were raised at the hatchery for the first six weeks and then shipped to volunteers for eventual release. We were also releasing birds from the wildlife centre.

"The Brooks facility grew to include the production area, a new administration building, a waterfowl area, and outdoor game pens. We also produced 60,000-70,000 quail per year as feed for a birds-of-prey centre (later removed from the site). We built a bunch of cat pens to accommodate illegal animals seized by Fish and Wildlife. We had a lion, two Bengal tigers, and four cougars. To feed the cats, we always had a truck going steady picking up road kills from Fish and Wildlife Offices all over the

BOB McFETRIDGE, BLAIR RIPPIN AND DAVE NEAVE RELEASING PHEASANTS.
COURTESY ALBERTA FISH AND WILDLIFE DIVISION

FIELDS OF STOOKS PROVIDED "TABLE TOPS" OF GRAIN FOR UPLAND BIRDS.
CREDIT: K. LUNGLE

stubble. The bound bundles were gathered by hand and placed into small groups of pyramid arrangements called stooks. Stooks were left in the field until the grain dried before being delivered to the threshing machine. Cereal grains were harvested by parked threshing machines fed bundles of grain delivered from the fields by horse drawn wagons. A steam-powered or motor-driven threshing machine sorted the grain into a wagon and the straw into a large straw pile.

Although tractors and trucks gradually replaced horses and wagons, the era of stooks and straw stacks were bonanza years for upland birds in the form of a readily available source of high quality food near escape cover. Unharvested stooks were often left out over winter for a variety of reasons and provided fully provisioned "table tops" of grain. Straw stacks with some unthreshed grain heads were particularly beneficial when they occurred in a waste area on the farm, such as a willow swale. As such, they provided all the essentials of food, cover, and a roosting site: a "winter condominium", so to speak. In addition, wooden granaries, frequently leaky or with spilled grain around them, often were placed in farm shelterbelts or beside woodlots near the fields. In

winter, the wind scoured away the snow around these buildings and exposed the waste grain for huns and pheasants to find.

However, as the ratio of cropland to native vegetation changed, pinnated grouse disappeared and sharp-tailed grouse declined, while the introduced game birds (i.e., pheasants and huns) seemed to reap the benefits of change. Early recognition that upland bird habitat was declining is reflected in the Fish and Game Branch's annual reports. In 1938, Commissioner W.H. Wallace stated, "Not only have ill-advised projects [referring to some drainage projects] caused distress [to agricultural interests], but areas suited admirably to the sustenance of wild life of great economic value, and to the retardation of floods, have been spoiled for these uses." In his 1944 report, Commissioner Eric Huestis stated, "As man came into the picture and proceeded to farm and ranch, the scene changed. Where upland birds and ducks once had plenty of cover in the way of grass and shrubs and trees, these disappeared as more land was broken."

A crushing blow to prairie and parkland upland game birds was the arrival of the combine. Early combines were mobile threshing machines that picked up and threshed rows of grain swaths left to dry by swathing machines. These rows of swaths, if left unharvested, provided winter food for game birds, but not as effectively as stooks, particularly if the snow was deep. Straight combines that cut and threshed at the same time soon appeared and all that was left behind were trails of straw. But not for long. Following behind, balers packed and wrapped the

LEAKY GRAIN BINS NEAR SHELTERBELTS PROVIDED FOOD FOR UPLAND GAME BIRDS.
CREDIT: B. WISHART

straw into impenetrable "bricks" and these were tightly stacked in big bale stacks. The birds could no longer find either food or cover. In a similar fashion, the big round straw bales that came later were too tightly bound or were wrapped in plastic. Either way, they no longer provided easy access to food for upland game birds. Thus, with new methods and more efficient machinery for harvesting cereal and forage crops, farm fields increased in size and, effectively created a large barren landscape for wildlife.

Gordon Kerr recalls these landscape changes: "The country changed a lot since my teenage years when we hunted pheasants, Hungarian partridge, and the occasional sharp-tailed grouse near Fort Macleod, Claresholm, and Nanton. In the 1950s, birds were everywhere. You could get your limit by driving slowly along the country roads and spotting them in the stubble. In 1963, there were still lots of pheasants and "huns", but the sharp-tailed grouse were gone, and a number

of marshes where we used to hunt ducks were gone as well. When I travelled that area again in 1971, the change was striking. There were very few places that even looked like they would support pheasants, and the low numbers of birds we saw was proof of the habitat lost due to changes in agriculture practices."

TODAY'S EFFICIENT AGRICULTURAL PRACTICES LEAVE LITTLE HABITAT FOR UPLAND GAME BIRDS AND OTHER WILDLIFE. CREDIT: M. PYBUS

A New Era of Upland Game Bird Management

During this period of agricultural change, managing upland game birds in Alberta was mostly a matter of setting bag limits based on perceived abundance. The abundance was strongly influenced by the "ten-year game cycle". Native grouse, as well as central and northern populations of Hungarian partridge, are profoundly cyclical in numbers. As a consequence, so was the number of birds available for hunters to harvest.

In the 1950s, the province hired its first trained wildlife biologists whose work included research on upland game bird populations. By then it was evident that habitat was the key to survival. An Upland Game Bird Shelterbelt Program was initiated in 1957. This program was expanded in 1959 with shelterbelt plantings near Ponoka, Edmonton, and Redwater. In 1960, this program continued with three new projects north of Edmonton. Provincial biologists selected the sites, the Department of Agriculture provided trees and shrubs, Fish and Game Association members planted them, and cooperating farmers were responsible for any further care of the plantings. The shelterbelt program showed that suitable habitat for upland game birds could be produced in four years. In 1968, the first major land acquisition was made for fish and wildlife habitat development near Brooks, when 771 acres of farmland were purchased under the Land Assembly Program through the Alberta Department of Agriculture. The lands were to be farmed as well as developed for pheasant habitat. During the 1970s and 1980s, several programs were undertaken to retain or enhance remaining habitat.

With the dawn of the 1960s came a variety of studies to enhance and refine the management of Alberta's upland game birds. A preliminary study of the life history of the sage-grouse began in 1959. Ongoing studies listed in the annual reports of the Fish and Wildlife Division in the early 1960s included behaviour and courtship of blue (Richardson's) grouse and ruffed grouse at Gorge Creek, distribution of a race of spruce grouse (Franklin's grouse) in western Alberta, population surveys of ptarmigan, and breeding behaviour of sharp-tailed grouse in the Peace parklands and eastern parklands. These studies were done under the direction of ornithologists from the University of Alberta.

Introduction of Merriam's Turkey

In the early 1960s, Wildlife Biologist Bob Webb negotiated a trade of 12 Alberta bighorn sheep, captured by Bill Wishart at Sheep River, for 24 Merriam's turkeys from South Dakota. Twenty-one turkeys survived the trip and were released in the Cypress Hills in 1962. The introduction was initially successful and the population grew to an estimated 70 birds in 1963 and 200 birds in 1965. However, severe winter conditions, limited habitat, and competition for food with cattle, deer,

THE MERCURY STORY[22]

On September 19, 1969, a startled public heard that the fall hunting season on pheasants and Hungarian partridge was closed in Alberta until further notice because of mercury contamination. The Canadian Wildlife Service found mercury in the tissues of birds of prey and suggested it may have been coming from seed-eating mammals and birds. The Fish and Wildlife Division proceeded with a year-long collection of approximately 400 upland birds and found that huns and pheasants in the spring contained mercury at four and a half times the acceptable level for human consumption. They got it from eating seed grain treated with mercury to prevent fungal infection. The mercury was concentrated as it passed up the food chain into the birds of prey, where it reached levels that affected the hatchability of their eggs. Fortunately, mercury quickly clears from the tissues of upland birds and levels dropped to less than 10% of acceptable human consumption levels in the fall. Organochlorines such as dieldrin, aldrin, and heptachlor were also found in the upland bird tissues. The provincial Department of Agriculture immediately proceeded to phase out the use of alkylmercury seed treatments and organochlorines, and moved towards less toxic and persistent pesticides. The season on pheasants and huns was opened again in the fall of 1970.

UPLAND GAME BIRD POPULATIONS IN NORTHERN ALBERTA
[JOHN G. STELFOX]

As a provincial Wildlife Biologist during 1952 and again from 1955 to 1966, I was involved in research and management of upland game birds north of Highway 16 from Lloydminster to Hinton. Objectives included monitoring the abundance, distribution, and habitat preference of native grouse and introduced ring-necked pheasant and Hungarian partridge; introducing pheasants and huns into suitable new farmland habitats; and enhancing farmland habitat by establishing Farmstead Wildlife Shelterbelts.

To achieve these objectives, a cooperative program was established among the provincial Wildlife, Forest Service, and Agriculture agencies plus the Alberta Fish and Game Association and farmers. Under the wise leadership of Eric Huestis, Director of Forestry and Wildlife, I was able to work closely with district Forest Officers and Fish and Game Officers and share equipment and facilities. Together we gathered wildlife information to build up a knowledge base that previously was limited.

Game bird observations were best during the first two and the last two hours of daylight so working 8 a.m. to 5 p.m. was not logical. Long working days were also typical for Forest and Fish and Wildlife Officers so we were all in the same boat. Government unions and overtime pay did not exist and as we all enjoyed the great outdoors and the fairly independent working arrangements, long working days were not drudgery. During our many travels, if accommodation was not available in a forestry cabin, we often slept by a campfire near a stream or burrowed into a straw stack (motels were scarce and budgets small). I vividly remember the night in a straw stack on top of a pig shelter with biologist George Mitchell and his Labrador pup, Brant, in late October 1952. All night the pigs below us shuffled and squealed. This scared the pup, which kept George awake. In early morning light, while drinking coffee and munching sandwiches by a small campfire, we kept busy extracting straw from our clothing and various body parts.

A number of sources of information revealed that sharptails, ruffed grouse, and Hungarian partridge were numerous. Small-scale farming interspersed with native habitat provided a greater diversity of food, escape cover, and shelter than did the original native vegetation. Grain harvesting with binders and threshing machines resulted in numerous straw stacks, granaries, piles of weed screenings, as well as bundle stacks and stooks in the field over winter, providing a vital source of food for many birds and small mammals. An abundance of native trees provided roosting habitat and food (buds and seed), while manure spread on stubble fields during the winter provided an additional food source. Numerous ponds, lakes, and muskeg bogs were not yet drained and provided important food, water, shelter, and cover. Small homestead farms had many outbuildings and much shrub and tree cover. Herbicides and pesticides were used sparingly on fields but not on fencerows, or railway and road rights-of-way; so considerable herbaceous and shrubby native cover existed to hide and shelter game birds. Pheasant and Hungarian partridge numbers also increased in urban and suburban areas where many undeveloped lots and acreages existed and where grain elevators, feed mills, and railway yards provided a good source of spilled grain.

The abundance of sharp-tailed grouse, ruffed grouse, and Hungarian partridge was revealed from

237

JOHN STELFOX RELEASING HUNGARIAN (GRAY) PARTRIDGE NORTH OF GRANDE PRAIRIE, 1956.
CREDIT: BARNEY HAMM COURTESY JOHN STELFOX

GOOD GAME BIRD HABITAT IN THE SHELTERBELTS SURROUNDING THIS SMALL FARMING OPERATION.
COURTESY ALBERTA FISH AND WILDLIFE DIVISION

population surveys using roadside counts and flush-out study areas (areas about 200 acres in size where surveyors counted birds by flushing them out of their cover) plus annual wildlife reports from Forest and Fish and Wildlife Officers. From 13 upland game bird study areas between Cold Lake and Edson during October 1952, sharptails were seen in all 13 districts. They were the most abundant game birds in 54% of the districts compared with Hungarian partridge in 46%, ruffed grouse in 8%, and pheasant in 0% of the districts. Six study areas within prime sharptail habitat in October 1956 and 1957 yielded an average flock size (for groups of 5+) of 11.2 birds. Many large flocks of 35-40, 40-50, 65, and 90-125 birds were recorded. When five study areas, each 200 acres of semi-farmland, were censused in October 1959 with a flush-out count, a total of 290 sharptails, 43 Hungarian partridge, and 11 ruffed grouse were counted: a total of 344 upland game birds.

Another example of upland game bird abundance in the 1950s occurred when I was live trapping Hungarian partridge between Edmonton and Nisku for transplanting to the Grande Prairie area.

Between February 24 and March 18, 1957 I was able to trap 57 birds using one small funnel trap. Each quarter section (160 acres) had two to four coveys of huns. Annual fall harvests of Hungarian partridge in Alberta during the 1950s ranged between 80,000 and 150,000 depending mainly on how favourable the weather was during and after the nesting season.

Now in 2002, I realize how much the habitat for upland game birds changed north of Highway 16 over the past 50 years. Much of the native habitat was displaced by extensive cultivated land and by more efficient cultivation, harvesting, and storage systems. I suspect that native grouse populations, in particular sharptails and huns, are now considerably smaller than they were during the 1950s. A comparison of habitat conditions in the 1950s versus those today would be most interesting and easy to determine using remote sensing techniques such as aerial photography interpretation. Relative differences in upland game bird abundance could also be compared by repeating the census systems used in the 1950s and documented in the biologist reports of 1952-1966.

GERRY PELCHAT DISPLAYING A CAPTURED MERRIAM'S TURKEY.
CREDIT: D. MOYLES

and elk resulted in a dramatic decline so that only a few turkeys remain in Cypress Hills today.

Subsequent releases also did not fare so well. In 1967, 12 turkeys live-trapped in Cypress Hills were released in the Porcupine Hills. During the early 1970s, Fish and Game clubs released turkeys from various sources in a number of areas including the Battle River, Milk River, Oldman River, and Belly River. However, none of these releases was successful. The last major release of Merriam's turkeys in Alberta was in 1973, when 88 birds were reintroduced to the Porcupine Hills. Thirteen were wild-trapped turkeys from Nebraska picked up by Morley Barrett and Gerry Pelchat in exchange for 30 Hungarian partridge (which was a much better deal pound for pound than trading away 12 bighorn sheep!). The remainder of the release was the Merriam's parent stock raised at the Brooks pheasant hatchery.

Based on observations of marked birds, most if not all of the existing turkeys in the Porcupine Hills are progeny of the wild Nebraska birds.

The Porcupine Hills turkeys increased steadily and became a problem when they started eating livestock feed on local farmsteads. In 1990, the first hunting season was opened on wild turkeys in the southern half of the Porcupine Hills. The limit was one "bearded" (male) turkey per hunter during a short season in the last two weeks of May. There were 1156 applicants for 50 permits and 19 "bearded" turkeys were harvested. Since then, the season has been extended to the whole month of May, and the area expanded south and west of Pincher Creek to encompass the offspring of an earlier release of turkeys into the Lees Lake area. The number of permits remains 50, with annual applications ranging from 500 to over 2000 in recent years. Obviously, the desire of Alberta

A FAMILY GROUP OF MERRIAM'S TURKEYS IN ALBERTA.
COURTESY ROYAL ALBERTA MUSEUM

hunters to stalk a gobbler is great considering that the odds of being drawn for a permit are less than three in 100.

Tracking Our Native Grouse through the Century

PINNATED GROUSE: THEY CAME, THEY WENT

The rise and fall of the pinnated grouse (greater prairie-chicken) in Alberta and indeed across the prairie provinces was coincidental with the interval between the disappearance of the bison and their replacement with domestic livestock. Early populations of pinnated grouse were confined primarily to the tall grass prairies in the midwestern U.S. and the species was scarce or entirely absent on much of the western Great Plains. Without grazing animals during the wetter than normal 1880s, the northern prairies produced a cover of grass the likes of which had

never been seen before and which may never be seen again. The geographic spread and eventual arrival of the pinnates into Alberta appeared to follow the railroads into a relatively undisturbed prairie/parkland that was interspersed with a patchwork of grain fields during the late 1800s and early 1900s. Nearly all pinnate specimens and nest records in Alberta are from the prairie and parkland areas north of the Red Deer River.

Pinnates became increasingly more abundant as cultivation began in earnest.[23] As the homesteaders settled and raised small cereal crops on small farms, pinnated grouse thrived. They peaked during the teens and early 1920s. However, when cultivation and heavy grazing expanded, when farms were abandoned and there were no grain crops, or when small farms were incorporated into larger holdings with intensive agricultural practices over large areas, pinnates decreased dramatically. Eventually, they succumbed under the pressure of the cow and the plow, and finally disappeared during the drought of the 1930s. The rise and fall of the pinnates was consistent from Manitoba to Alberta.[24]

The last specimen of pinnated grouse from Alberta was shot in 1929 near Youngstown. It was preserved as a mount by the parents of provincial Fisheries Biologist Martin Paetz and donated to the Provincial Museum of Alberta by the Paetz family in 2004. Surveys in 1958-1959 confirmed that pinnated grouse no longer occurred in Alberta.

In 1983, the feasibility of reintroducing greater prairie-chicken into Alberta was assessed.[25] Due to the progress of agricultural practices, the biological prognosis for a successful introduction was poor. Similar situations occurred across the prairie provinces and the pinnated grouse was officially listed as extirpated in Canada in 1990.

THE RISE AND FALL OF SHARP-TAILED GROUSE

Sharp-tailed grouse were the prominent, native upland bird species on the prairies and parkland of Alberta in 1905. Their elaborate courtship display and striking plumage were unique and so profound that they played an important role in traditional aboriginal ceremonies. The species also provided early European settlers with an accessible and important food source.

Sharp-tailed grouse received much less attention from wildlife managers during the first half of the century than did a whole host of other hunted species, including the introduced upland bird species. From 1905 to 1944, the average annual number of licensed upland bird hunters (for all species) was about 8400, and bag limits were generous. Although there was no province-wide census prior to the 1960s, William Rowan gleaned useful information on sharptail numbers, distribution, and trends from trapper questionnaires circulated in the 1930s and 1940s as part of his study of the ten-year game cycle phenomenon. As Fish and Wildlife biological staff came onto the scene in the 1950s, local sharptail

population trends were tracked effectively using field census methods which included "dancing ground" or lek counts, harvest assessments, hunter reports, and field observations.

By the late 1950s, one in four adult male Albertans hunted upland birds and 90,000 licences were sold annually. Upland bird hunting was "big business", with an annual value of nearly $200,000.[26] The upland bird harvest in 1957 was estimated at 450,000 birds! The main factor behind this phenomenal interest was the economic recovery of Alberta after the war, coupled with the amazing success of the introduced pheasants and Hungarian partridge as described earlier. About two-thirds of the upland birds harvested in the middle decades of the century consisted of these two species. Less than 20% were sharp-tailed grouse, despite the tremendous periodic peaks in sharptail populations.

The growing popularity of upland bird hunting in the 1950s and 1960s prompted a more systematic approach to sharptail censusing. Contributors to some of the early District reports tried to estimate the number of grouse per square mile. In retrospect, considering the methods of the day and the biology of the birds, the accuracy of those reports is highly suspect. However, the records were sufficient to track upland game bird abundance and population cycles, and to adjust the seasons and bag limits accordingly. The management objective at this time was to offer the maximum hunter harvest possible while retaining sufficient breeding stock for the following year's production.

The pervasive "ten-year" cycle of abundance was strong in sharp-tailed grouse at this time. In about four years of each decade, sharptail numbers were high, with peaks in 1932, 1942, 1951, and 1962. Although the cyclic phenomenon was part of the picture, sharptail numbers were also bolstered by ideal habitat conditions created by early agricultural development in central Alberta from the late 1930s to the 1950s, and in the Peace River block during the 1950s and 1960s. In the 1960s, Roger Evans documented sharptail densities in

241

242

A "COCK FIGHT" OR BORDER CONFLICT OF SHART-TAILED GROUSE ON A DANCING GROUND (LEK).
CREDIT: G. COURT

various habitats and began "dancing ground" counts as a monitoring technique. He reported a count of more than one lek per sq. mi. over several townships in the Wanham area. At the same time, local hunters reported flocks of several hundred

"sharpies" moving about the area during the fall and winter.

However, with intensified agriculture, game bird cycles became less pronounced and reliable. After the 1970s, sharp-tailed grouse distribution and overall abundance declined dramatically over most of the agriculturally developed area. In addition, a general decline in the popularity of hunting was seen in Alberta towards the end of the 20th century. A telephone questionnaire system initiated in 1985 provided consistent information on upland bird hunters and their harvest. A cyclic game bird high in 1988 saw 12,182 hunters harvest 54,025 birds. In contrast, the next high, occurring in 1998, saw only 4566 hunters harvest 18,050 birds.[27] This downward trend is likely to continue as hunting becomes increasingly unpopular and sharptails less abundant because of land-use changes.

The conversion to intensive agriculture and its affect on sharp-tailed grouse populations was evident by the early 1980s. Where habitat was highly altered by years of agricultural development, sharptail density in the east-central parkland declined from one lek per section (1 sq. mi.) to one lek per township (36 sq. mi.) over a large area east of Edmonton between the Battle and North Saskatchewan rivers. However, several large provincial cattle-grazing reserves covering one or two townships, in addition to Camp Wainwright, remained as foci of viable populations of sharptails in the region. Other

productive populations persisted in a few parts of the prairie region and along the forest/agriculture transition zone of the foothills extending from the U.S. boundary well into the Peace River country. Sharp-tailed grouse were a difficult management challenge. On one hand, they occurred throughout the province in a wide variety of habitats. On the other hand, they attained huntable numbers only in areas that contained a specific mix of tree/shrub cover interspersed with open grassland. The Peace River Parkland during the 1950s and 1960s presented an excellent example of the optimum sharp-tailed grouse habitat mosaic. For a relatively brief period (about 20 years), gradual forest clearing created the suitable patchwork pattern of tree cover and open fields over hundreds of townships and resulted in a tremendous explosion of sharp-tailed grouse. However, as in the central parkland, this "bonanza" was followed by a steady decline in sharptail numbers and distribution as the agricultural development skewed the pattern toward fewer trees and more open areas. In the late 1960s and early 1970s, Blair Rippin and Dave Moyles investigated various aspects of sharptail behaviour, recruitment, nesting, and production within Camp Wainwright, a 650 km^2 military training area of sandy parkland habitat that continues to support a viable sharp-tailed

243

MALE SHARP-TAILED GROUSE DANCING AND COOING WHILE STATIONED AT THEIR BOUNDARIES ON A LEK.
CREDIT: G. COURT

grouse population. Lek location and numbers of attending males in spring have been monitored there for more than 35 years to date, and is still going strong—probably the longest-running field dataset of any species anywhere in Alberta. Each fall, hunter effort as well as the number, sex, and age of birds harvested is recorded. Surprisingly, sharptails within Camp Wainwright appear to reach a cyclic abundance every three to four years, unlike the provincial average of ten years.

Lek counts of territorial breeding males in mid-to-late April require the observer to be at the dancing ground before sunrise. But, the unappealing task of rising at 4 a.m., well before breakfast, is easily offset by the opportunity to hear the sights and sounds of spring returning to the parkland. Early morning is by far the noisiest time of any spring day! Many regional biologists conducted annual counts on dancing grounds in their areas over the past 30 years, although we now know that the number of males attending leks is not always a reliable indicator of population trends. Recent research by Doug Manzer continues to show that the species has considerable difficulty dealing with today's agricultural practices in the northern prairies: agricultural disturbance of the landscape was linked directly to lower reproduction and survival of sharptails in 2003.[28]

In the mid-1990s, Bob Goddard headed up a project in the southern foothills that targeted sharp-tailed grouse. It began with an extensive lek inventory and habitat mapping initiative in and around the Porcupine Hills. Cooperation and involvement of local landowners was a key element that resulted in the preparation of range management plans tailored to the unique operating regime of individual land holdings. Habitat improvements for sharptails included strategic fencing, modified cattle-watering sites, and improved tame pasture in lieu of overgrazing native range. Since 1995, the program expanded to include the Milk River Ridge area and evolved under the direction and involvement of many Fish and Wildlife staff. Presently the Alberta Conservation Association conducts this program.

The land-use changes resulting from this program were significant and provided a higher degree of landscape health, although agreements often were not binding and the commitment of some landowners was short-term. Regardless, these efforts can be held up as an excellent template for developing effective initiatives to address habitat loss through landowner-based stewardship programs.

Over the past 25 years, the value that sharptails offer to the public was also recognized, and organized opportunities to watch the unique display of males on their dancing grounds during April are still provided in a few locations around the province. Sharp-tailed grouse are used also as indicators of large expanses of lightly grazed shrubland, their optimal habitat. Pressures from agriculture, and more recently, urban, suburban, and infrastructural development, result in a steady decline of habitats with the characteristics required by sharptails. It is predicted that the species will continue to be a part of Alberta's rich endemic fauna, but with a much-reduced distribution and population than it enjoyed prior to 1960. Reasonable numbers will persist within suitable sites in the forested areas, within well-managed larger grazing reserves, and at a few locations in the prairies and foothills where grazing management maintains native vegetation characteristics.

It would be wise to delineate areas that continue to support viable sharp-tailed grouse populations, and to make arrangements with land stewards to preserve the vegetative pattern and growth forms that favour the species. Periodic census counts, combined with locating and preserving the suitable lek and brooding sites, also would be beneficial.

When Alberta became a province in 1905, ruffed grouse dominated the forested habitats of the boreal mixed-woods, much of the parkland, and some of the bottomlands of prairie rivers. They shared the northern and western forested habitats with spruce grouse, which have strong ties to conifers, particularly lodgepole and jack pine. A small enclave of spruce grouse within the Willmore Wilderness Park area and along the forested eastern slopes south of the Ram River lack the cinnamon tip on their black tail feathers and are known as Franklin's grouse. Also unique to Franklin's grouse, breeding males make a loud clapping sound by touching their wings together over their backs during courtship display. Blue grouse, with a spectacular strutting and hooting courtship display, are confined to the forested portion of the alpine/subalpine zones. The present population of ruffed grouse in the Cypress Hills arose from a release there in the 1920s.

Aboriginal people and early European settlers used forest grouse extensively as an easily accessible, savoury, and important food source. However, the cycle between grouse super-abundance and extreme scarcity was a phenomenon familiar to both user groups. Written records begin with ruffed grouse population peaks in 1932 and 1942, and a substantial hunter harvest for 4-5 years around those dates. After the Second World War, the popularity of upland bird hunting greatly expanded and peaked around 1959. Despite the greater number of hunters, the harvest of ruffed grouse continued to vary with their cyclic population numbers. They were hunted extensively on a local basis during times of abundance, but given almost no attention during times of low numbers.

Over the period 1949 to 1959 (which included a cyclic high in 1951), average annual ruffed grouse harvest accounted for only 16% of the total upland bird harvest: the introduced ring-necked pheasants and Hungarian partridge dominated the bag count. Spruce and blue grouse made up a small portion of the forest grouse hunter's bag. Seasons were set and bag limits adjusted according to the ruffed grouse cyclic phase as determined by Fish and Wildlife staff, with input from local hunters. In general, little attention was paid to forest grouse management until the late 1950s when university research stations were established at the R.B. Miller station at Sheep River and Rochester (near Athabasca). Professors Fred Zwickel, David Boag, and Lloyd Keith along with their students, added to our knowledge of forest grouse behaviour and population dynamics.

Ruffed grouse drumming counts were conducted each spring by regional biologists and technicians across the province. The characteristic hollow sound of ruffies beating their wings with increasing rapidity and blending into a final blur was easy to recognize and easy to distinguish from everything else in the forest. The resulting information, combined with harvest assessments, provided a reasonable tracking mechanism to determine the phase of the game cycle during the 1960s and 1970s. Hunting seasons remained open, but bag limits were reduced during periods of low grouse numbers, and then raised upon their recovery. Similar hunting regimens were applied to spruce grouse even though population census was limited due to their small portion of the bird harvest, difficult access to occupied habitat, and lack of easy census methods.

Establishing the length and timing of upland game bird hunting seasons and bag limits resulted in considerable debate among biologists over the years. Many felt hunting was not a primary limiting factor and the law of diminishing returns reduced the harvest during periods of low bird numbers. Others maintained that hunting was significant and hunting limits should reflect current bird populations. The debate was particularly relevant to ruffed grouse, which has dramatic periodic fluctuations in density. However, the natural cycle is not synchronous over the province. The decline in peak grouse numbers generally begins in northeastern Alberta then continues as a slowly progressing wave, reaching the extreme southwest one to three years later. In 1987, the debate eventually resulted in stabilized bag limits regardless of cyclic phase. Overall, this satisfies the concerns of hunters and is compatible with grouse population dynamics over much of their range.

Since 1970, the combined evidence collected through harvest information, hunter reports, and field investigations indicates an overall decline in ruffed grouse abundance and less pronounced cyclic changes in agricultural areas of the parkland and fringe boreal areas. In addition to direct habitat loss, grouse populations may be unable to

A WHITE-TAILED PTARMIGAN. CREDIT: ALBERTA FISH AND WILDLIFE DIVISION

expand because of increased predation in their remaining highly fragmented habitat. In spite of this, ruffies still occupy the boreal and foothills zones in numbers similar to those in 1905, and with a strong ten-year cycle. Substantial expansion in fibre production (lumber and pulp) and petroleum extraction has undoubtedly favoured ruffed grouse by reducing the conifer component and the age of the deciduous component of the forests.

Blue grouse were studied intensively in only a few small areas, and relatively little attention was directed at determining numbers and distribution on a provincial basis. Blue grouse hunting has never been popular as much of their range is difficult to access. Most harvest is incidental to big game hunting in the eastern slopes. There is little doubt that logging, fires, and fire suppression alter the forest component in alpine and subalpine zones, and thus influence blue grouse numbers. However, predation, weather, and forest succession likely are the primary limiting factors, whereas hunting has almost no effect on blue grouse population dynamics. This species will undoubtedly continue to occupy Alberta's alpine/

subalpine habitat as long as reasonable forest conservation practices continue.

PTARMIGAN: IGNORED BUT NOT FORGOTTEN

Of all our native upland birds, the two ptarmigan species in Alberta received the least management attention. White-tailed ptarmigan inhabit alpine habitats and willow ptarmigan occupy alpine and far northern boreal habitats. They are the only grouse that undergo major change in plumage colour for camouflage in summer and winter. For management purposes, the two species were identified separately from 1961 to 1973, but were then lumped together thereafter and differentiated only by geographic location and timing of hunting seasons. Neither species is highly sought by hunters, partly because of the inaccessible terrain they occupy, and partly because of their low numbers and sporadic distribution.

A small resident population of willow ptarmigan occurs in the alpine region largely within the Willmore Wilderness area. The species also makes irregular winter forays from the barrenlands of the Northwest Territories into the boreal mixed-wood region of northern Alberta, often reaching Fort

McMurray and High Level on an annual basis. The southern movement generally occurs after the end of regular grouse hunting seasons, which prompted an extension of the hunting season into December to allow some recreational use of the species. Individual birds are recorded as far south as Edmonton, Camrose, and Sylvan Lake.[29]

White-tailed ptarmigan occur sporadically down the spine of the mountains from Kakwa River to Waterton in national parks and on provincial lands. They are truly an alpine species and receive hunting attention only by a few bighorn sheep or mountain goat hunters on provincial lands. As a result, there is limited management attention.

The habitats occupied by these two well-adapted grouse species are considered harsh, but relatively stable and likely to continue to support viable populations. For the same reasons, it is likely that their ecology in Alberta also will remain largely unknown. However, they are an interesting and valuable component of Alberta's extensive biodiversity.

GREATER SAGE-GROUSE: COCK OF THE PLAINS

In the days of Audubon and the early explorers, the largest grouse species in North America was known as the "Cock of the Plains". Sage-grouse appears in *A Catalogue of Canadian Birds* (1887).[30] However, it is surprisingly absent in the revised edition of Nuttall's *Birds of Canada* (1907).[31] In the ordinances of the Northwest Territories and the early hunting regulations of Alberta, sage-grouse were simply part of the "grouse" listed along with "partridge and prairie chicken". Thus they were subject to very generous bag limits of 10 to 20 per day or 100 to 200 per season. However, since the birds use sagebrush as their main food source, they were never considered particularly tasty and probably were not a significant food item, at least in human diets.

Sage-grouse was not listed separately from other grouse until the summary of game bird regulations in 1930, when the season was closed except for sharp-tailed grouse and Hungarian partridge. Thereafter, sage-grouse were lumped with other protected "grouse" or specifically excluded from upland game bird regulations until a season was opened in 1967. The possession limit of two in 1967 changed to a season limit of two in 1976. The spring population estimate in 1968 was approximately 2000 birds, with over 600 males counted on 21 strutting grounds (leks). Good numbers of sage-grouse prevailed into the 1980s, with estimated annual harvests ranging from 100 to 400 per year.

In the 1990s, there was a significant decline in sage-grouse, with numbers down to just over 100 males on eight leks. The sage-grouse season

MALE SAGE GROUSE STRUTTING ON A LEK WITH A DIMINUTIVE HEN IN THE MIDDLE.
CREDIT: B. WISHART

continued, although harvest was minimal. The season was closed in Alberta in 1996. Despite a closed hunting season in Saskatchewan, there was a similar decline in sage-grouse during the same time period. Current population estimates in Alberta are in the range of 300-400 birds in a confined area south and east of Manyberries.

To investigate this decline, an interprovincial Sage-grouse Recovery Team was formed in 1997. Intensive studies revealed that growth of the oil and gas industry, increased cultivation, grazing within the critical sage-grouse range, and prolonged drought adversely affect grouse production. In 2002, in cooperation with local ranchers, grazing practices were manipulated in order to demonstrate that agriculture and sage-grouse can be compatible. In addition, sage-grouse leks and adjacent nesting habitat on public lands were protected from human intrusion and restrictions were imposed on bird dog-training activities in critical areas. Since most leks are on crown land, conservation and management takes place through regulations and negotiation with those with dispositions on or leases to use crown land. Successful conservation of sage-grouse habitat on private land will only be achieved through the active involvement and cooperation of landowners. This is not a new concept. In 1926, Taverner noted with respect to the sage hen: "In general, the large ranch holders have shown an admirable spirit of protection towards it and have done much to perpetuate the species." Without major changes, sage-grouse is a species on the road to extirpation in Alberta.

Upland Game Birds, Bird Dogs, and Field Trials

The companionship and assistance of trained bird dogs are integral components of hunting upland game birds. A well-trained dog contributes substantially to the enjoyment and efficiency of each bird hunting experience and the relationship between dog and owner seems to give considerable pleasure to both. A trained dog can locate game birds, reduce loss of wounded birds, and increase the harvest, thereby enhancing the aesthetics and public perception of game bird hunting. The dog constantly reminds the hunter of past field activities and may be important in retaining active game bird hunters—an important consideration as hunter numbers decline across North America.

There is a long tradition of using dogs to find and retrieve game birds, and basic aspects of bird dog training are considered in regulations. Professional trainers and individuals who train their own dogs require space and access to birds. Organizations associated with bird dogs often require the use of live upland game birds in competitive field trials to test the training, abilities, and discipline of bird dogs. The trials provide a direct link between the recreational and commercial aspect of dog training and hunting opportunities. In Alberta, dog trainers focus on native sharp-tailed grouse and introduced Hungarian partridge. While private individuals train dogs throughout the province, commercial training and field trial activities traditionally concentrate in grassland and southern parkland areas.

SAGE-GROUSE AND WEST NILE VIRUS: A NEW CONCERN
In the summer of 2003, West Nile virus arrived in Alberta. During ongoing cooperative research by the University of Alberta and the Fish and Wildlife Division, several sage-grouse near Manyberries were found dead in late July and August, a time when mortality is uncommon in adult grouse. But in 2003, it was also a time when the viral population peaked in one species of local prairie mosquitoes (*Culex tarsalis*). Diagnostic tests revealed that the birds died as a direct result of West Nile infection. Similar deaths occurred in Wyoming and Montana. Again, a sage-grouse planning team was struck, this time with an international perspective, and this time focussed on understanding and limiting the risk to sage-grouse. As of this writing, we hold our breath and cannot predict the outcome of this new mortality factor facing endangered sage-grouse in Alberta.

Trainers may obtain an annual commercial permit to train bird dogs anywhere in the province except within sage-grouse range. They may not train bird dogs on wild birds during the nesting and early brood season (before August 1), but they may release and use (but not shoot) pheasants and other selected non-native species outside the open season as well as release and shoot non-controlled species (bobwhite quail, chukars, and pigeons) at any time. Personal dogs can be trained anywhere in the province except public lands in sage-grouse range from April 1 to July 31. Field trials may be held on any lands except sage-grouse range, but a permit is required on unoccupied public land or Provincial Grazing Reserves. Organizers of non-shooting field trials may release pheasants, and gray partridge. Shoot-to-kill field trials may use non-controlled birds, and can be held anytime on a licensed game bird shooting ground or be held during the open seasons with licensed hunters shooting legal bag limits of wild or released game birds. These regulations appear to work well and support the camaraderie associated with dog training and dog field trials.

Upland Game Birds in Alberta Today

Over its first 100 years of existence, upland game bird management in Alberta included an eclectic array of events and activities that cover the gamut from facilitated and controlled exploitation; introduced exotics; raise-and-release or put-and-take hunting; preservation of dwindling habitat; and finally, attempts to avoid local extinctions.

These actions reflected major land-use (habitat) changes; major human population expansion; and more recently, significant shifts in public attitude toward hunting and the natural environment. Habitat changed significantly in the prairies and parklands, but continues to support sustainable populations of sharp-tailed and ruffed grouse. Altered habitats in boreal, subalpine, and alpine forests continue to support sustainable populations of ruffed, spruce, and blue grouse, as well as ptarmigan. Introduction of exotic species resulted in viable populations of pheasants in some prairie areas, Hungarian (gray) partridge over much of the

249

A HAPPY BRITTANY EARNING HIS KEEP RETRIEVING A RUFFED GROUSE.
CREDIT: B. WISHART

prairie and parkland, and wild turkeys in small enclaves in Cypress Hills Park and in the Porcupine Hills. Over the century, we lost only one of eight native grouse species (pinnated grouse), but perhaps are about to lose another (sage-grouse). The natural phenomenon of the ten-year cyclic abundance continues to play out in the forested habitats, but to a much lesser degree in the agricultural zone.

Considering the dramatic change in the natural environment that occurred over much of the

province in the past century, our ability to retain most of the species we were entrusted with in 1905 stands in good stead. Upland game bird hunting remains a viable option for those who desire such activity, and these species continue to enrich Alberta's natural heritage by adding diversity and recreational viewing opportunities. With continued attention to their management, upland game birds should make up a significant portion of the province's wildlife heritage well into the future.

MAJOR EVENTS IN UPLAND GAME BIRD MANAGEMENT IN ALBERTA

1883　The first hunting season on native grouse is declared from September 15 to March 15 with four ambiguous names for eight species of grouse.

1895　The first bag limits are introduced as 20 grouse per day from September 15 to December 15.

1907　The first introduction of bobwhite quail is made. Ptarmigan are added to the game bird list.

1908　Hungarian (gray) partridge are introduced in Alberta. They are protected until 1913.

1909　A Bird Game Licence is added to those previously established in regulations.
The first of several ring-necked pheasant introductions is made. Pheasants are protected until 1939.

1913　The first Hungarian partridge season is opened.

1929　The last pinnated grouse in Alberta is collected. Ruffed grouse are introduced into the Cypress Hills area.

1933　Hungarian partridge bag limits are 50 per day and 200 per season. There is an open season on all grouse species except ruffed grouse. Grouse bag limits are 5 per day and 25 per season.

1936　There is a closed season on all upland game birds except Hungarian partridge.

1937　The first of several unsuccessful introductions of chukar partridge. All grouse are protected except ruffed grouse.

1939　The first season on ring-necked cock pheasants is held by permit for two days with a limit of six birds per person.

1942　Hunter bag limits increase to 5 pheasants per day and 30 per season. Huns increase to 20 per day and 250 per season.

1945　A pheasant hatchery is constructed at Brooks.

1946　The grouse season is closed.

1947　The upland game bird season is closed except for pheasants with a bag limit of 3 per day and 18 per season.

1948　An upland game bird season is resumed on all species except ptarmigan and sage-grouse.

1953　Ptarmigan are added to upland game bird season regulations.

MAJOR EVENTS IN UPLAND GAME BIRD MANAGEMENT IN ALBERTA CONTINUED

1961	White-tailed ptarmigan and willow ptarmigan are listed in the regulations separately for the first time.
1962	Merriam's turkey is introduced into the Cypress Hills.
1967	A sage-grouse season is opened with a season limit of two birds per hunter.
1969	Mercury contamination leads to a closed season on pheasants and Hungarian partridge.
1973	Wild turkeys are successfully introduced into the Porcupine Hills. They are protected from hunting until 1990.
1978	The Brooks Wildlife Centre, formerly the Brooks Pheasant Hatchery, is officially opened.
1986	An upland game bird phone questionnaire is introduced. (George Mitchell used mail questionnaires in the 1950s.) Pheasant bag limits are reduced to 2 per day and 6 per season.
1987	Bag limits are set and remain unchanged for upland game birds into the next century.
1989	The name change from Hungarian partridge to gray partridge is reflected in Alberta's hunting regulations.
1990	A turkey season is opened in the Porcupine hills. Fifty permits are offered to 1156 applicants.
1996	The hunting season on sage-grouse is closed.
2000	Sage-grouse are declared endangered.
2003	Several sage-grouse die from infection with the West Nile virus.

251

References • CHAPTER 7

1 Whitman, Walt. 1892. Birds - And a Caution *in* Specimen Days, Prose Works. David McKay, Philadelphia.

2 A new species of sage-grouse was identified in 2004 and the birds in Alberta are now designated as greater sage-grouse. Official bird list. American Ornithological Union May 18, 2004.

3 delHoyo, J.A. Elliott, and J. Sargatal (eds.). 1994. Handbook of the birds of the world. Vol. 2. Lynx Edicons.

4 Salt, W.R., and J.R. Salt. 1976. The Birds of Alberta. Hurtig Publishers, Edmonton.

5 Memo to the Calgary Fish and Game Protective Association, Calgary, Feb. 21, 1909. Austin de B. Winter Fonds, Glenbow Archives, Calgary. Winter's papers contain valuable information on the pioneer Calgary Fish and Game Protective Association, the introduction of the Hungarian partridge into Alberta, and the creation of game stamps, which appeared during the Second World War.

6 Lewis, M. 1979. To Conserve a Heritage. Alberta Fish and Game Association, Calgary.

7 Letter from Winter to the Hon. Duncan Marshall, March 8, 1917. Austin de B. Winter Fonds, Glenbow Archives, Calgary.

8 Lewis, M., op. cit.

9 Salt and Salt., op. cit.

10 Correspondence between Rowan and Winter. Austin de B. Winter Fonds, Glenbow Archives, Calgary.

11 Keith, L., and L.A. Windberg. 1978. A demographic analysis of the snowshoe hare cycle. Wildlife Monographs #58.

12 Winter, A. de B. 1942. Hungarian partridges and the grouse cycle in Alberta (an address given before the Alberta Fish and Game League, Calgary, February 7, 1942). Glenbow Archives, Calgary.

13 Ibid.

14 Ibid.

15 Memo to licence vendors from Dr. H.E. Rawlinson, Secretary, Science Association, University of Alberta, Aug, 31, 1942. Austin de B. Winter Fonds. Glenbow Archives, Calgary.

16 Audubon, J.J. 1830. The birds of America. Published by the Author. Plates reprinted in 1953 by the Macmillan Company, New York.

17 Nuttall, T. and M. Chamberlain. 1891. A Popular Handbook of the Ornithology of the United States and Canada. Little, Brown and Company, Boston.

18 Taverner, P.A. 1926. Birds of western Canada. Canada Department of Mines, Museum Bulletin No. 41. Ottawa.

19 Houston, C.S. 2002. Spread and disappearance of the greater prairie-chicken, *Tympanuchus cupido*, on the Canadian prairies and adjacent areas. The Canadian Field-Naturalist 116(1):1-21.

20 Anderson, R.C. and B. Gau. 1950. Preliminary report of the pheasant situation in the irrigation districts of southern Alberta. Unpublished report prepared for the Alberta Fish and Game Branch, Edmonton.

21 See Chapter 11 (Habitat) for more information about the Buck for Wildlife program.

[22] Wishart, W. 1970. A mercury problem in Alberta's game birds. Alberta Lands, Forests, Parks, Wildlife 13:4-9.

[23] Johnston, A. and S. Smoliak. 1976. Settlements of the grasslands and the greater prairie chicken. Blue Jay 34: 153-156.

[24] Houston. 2002, op. cit.

[25] IEC Beak Consultants Ltd. 1984. The feasibility of reintroducing a viable population of greater prairie chickens (*Tympanuchus cupido pinnatus*) to Alberta. Unpublished report prepared for the Alberta Fish and Wildlife Division, Edmonton.

[26] Mitchell, G. 1959. Upland bird resources. Alberta Land, Forest, Wildlife Resources Conference, Edmonton, Alberta. Proceedings printed by the Department of Lands and Forests.

[27] Alberta Fish and Wildlife Division records, Edmonton.

[28] Manzer, D.L. 2004. Sharp-tailed grouse breeding success, survival, and site selection in relation to habitat measured at multiple scales. Ph.D. Thesis, Department of Biological Sciences, University of Alberta, Edmonton. 158pp.

[29] Salt and Salt. 1976., op. cit.

[30] Chamberlain, M. 1887. A catalogue of Canadian birds. J. and A. McMillan, Saint John, N.B.

[31] Chamberlain, M. 1907. New revised and annotated edition of: A popular handbook of the birds of Canada and the United States, by Thomas Nuttall. The Musson Book Company Limited, Toronto.

Chapter 8

WATERFOWL AND WETLANDS:
COOPERATION FOR CONSERVATION

Bruce Turner with contributions from Brett Calverley, Sue Clarke, Ernie Ewaschuk,
Gordon Kerr, Ken Lungle, Margo Pybus, Nyree Sharp, Pat Valastin, Bill Wishart, and Ken Wright

253

"The duck was all jewels combined, showing different lustres as it turned on the unrippled element in various lights, now brilliant glossy green, now dusky violet, now a rich bronze, now the reflections that sleep in the ruby's grain." [1]
HENRY DAVID THOREAU

A Bounty of Waterfowl

A bounty of waterfowl across the geographic region we now call Alberta was well recognized and appreciated by the aboriginals who used this area. Everywhere and abundant, waterfowl provided a readily accessible source of food and added beauty to an already appealing landscape. This wealth of waterfowl was also impressive to the first Europeans who penetrated the prairie and parkland regions of the province.

Today, we know that the density and diversity of waterfowl, and the quantity and quality of their habitat, is directly linked to climate and geological forces. In the distant past, expansion and withdrawal of the Tropical and Boreal Oceans, and ultimately, the retreat of the Inland Sea, created a nutrient-rich organic base on which flora and fauna thrived. Later, retreating glaciers

transformed the terrain into a multitude of depressions, some concentrated in a "knob and kettle" topography. These basins eventually developed into lakes and potholes, becoming the productive waterfowl habitats that are a prominent feature of the current landscape.

Aided by a mid latitude continental climate, waterfowl populations prospered, developing life history strategies that saw them increase production during wet periods when wetlands were abundant, and decrease in times of drought. Fortunately, the effects of drought are temporary and waterfowl numbers increase under weather conditions favourable to wetlands. Waterfowl populations and their habitats across Alberta are world class, and though paralleled in some areas of the Canadian prairies, they are not surpassed.

CANADA GOOSE GOSLINGS JUST HATCHED.
CREDIT: D. MCDONALD

The Treaty to Protect Migratory Birds

At the turn of the 20th century, waterfowl populations in Alberta enjoyed an environment that was thinly populated by humans and subject to few man-made pressures. However, such was not the case in more southern areas of the continent, where waterfowl concentrated over winter. In these areas, waterfowl were vulnerable to hunting, and many populations were decimated by unregulated, excessive, and sometimes wanton harvests driven by the commercial interests of market-hunters intent on supplying society's culinary demands.

In the early 1900s, conservationists on both sides of the International Boundary noted that migratory birds were not protected equally across the continent. Regulations for migratory bird hunting were administered exclusively by the provinces and states, with each having its own game laws, and these differing from one jurisdiction to the next. In 1913, the U.S. government passed its own federal *Migratory Bird Law*, which provided for a standardized open season in that country. Most states amended their game legislation to conform to the federal Act, but some openly opposed such a law, and others simply did nothing. No such unified approach existed in Canada. Given the disparate local views and the lack of coordination among jurisdictions, this haphazard system was inadequate and underscored the need for international cooperation.

Conservation groups, largely comprised of sport hunters, began to mobilize public opinion and lobby governments for action. In 1914, W.S.

A MARKET HUNTER WITH A DAY'S BAG, ca. 1920s.
COURTESY ALBERTA FISH AND WILDLIFE DIVISION

Britain (as Canada had no control of such matters until after the First World War when it established its own Department of Foreign Affairs) was a major achievement in conservation. The treaty recognized the migratory nature of waterfowl and affirmed the need for joint management of a shared resource.

The corresponding *Migratory Birds Convention Act* enabled the provisions of the treaty in Canada. The Act included a closed season on migratory wildfowl from March 1 to

255

Heskell, counsel for the American Game Protection and Propagation Associations, addressed the Commission of Conservation in Ottawa and explained the benefits of an international migratory bird law. The combined lobby efforts were successful and that same year draft treaties were drawn up. Along with officials from the departments of Agriculture and the Interior, C. Gordon Hewitt, Dominion Entomologist and Consulting Zoologist, carried out the negotiations for Canada. Drafts of the proposed treaties were sent to the provincial governments for examination with only a few minor objections noted.

Finally, on June 29, 1916, a treaty was recommended and, on August 29, was signed. The *Treaty to Protect Migratory Birds* between the United States and Great

September 1 except for certain Indian and Inuit bands, an open season of 3 months with specified bag (harvest) limits, and a closed season on all insect-eating birds. The provinces quickly initialled the Treaty and the Act, and amended their game legislation accordingly. Having proven its inherent value for many decades, the Treaty was modernized in 1995 to include, among other things, recognition of harvesting by First Nations peoples of Canada and Indigenous peoples in Alaska. The 1995 revision (the Parksville Protocol) was the only amendment ever made to the original document.

Bird Sanctuaries

The importance of protecting waterfowl habitat was recognized in Canada long before Alberta

---

MIGRATORY BIRDS TREATY: EXCLUSIONS AND IMPLICATIONS

Keeping with the sentiments of the day, some migratory bird species were excluded from the *Treaty to Protect Migratory Birds,* as they were not seen as useful to human interests. In fact, they were seen as harmful or in competition. This included hawks, eagles, falcons, crows, and a number of other "undesirable" species.

The treaty also left an interesting twist for future managers. The legislative authority for migratory bird harvest rested with the Government of Canada, while ownership of the birds, and management of the land and habitat upon which they depend, rested with the provinces. Despite these restrictions and almost 90 years later, the Treaty is still the fundamental legal tool that guides international cooperation not only for waterfowl but all migratory birds in North America.

became a province. In 1887, an Order in Council established the Dominion bird reserve at Last Mountain Lake in Saskatchewan. This was followed by an order from the Minister of the Interior in early 1911 establishing a reserve on "all vacant lands in the vicinity of Ministik Lake, Alberta and other lakes in that locality".[2] This was followed in 1915 with a ministerial order that approved federal reservations on "all the vacant quarter-sections immediately adjoining the following lakes in Saskatchewan and Alberta, with a view to the future establishment of permanent bird reserves".[3] The Order withdrew 14 lakes in Alberta from settlement. R.M. Anderson, zoologist with the Geological Survey of Canada, was given the task of assessing which sites were suitable for full sanctuary designation.

Sanctuaries for waterfowl continued to be a priority under the 1916 *Treaty to Protect Migratory Birds* when both national governments assumed greater responsibility for migratory bird hunting regulations, population assessments, and habitat protection. The Dominion Government, often in conjunction with the provinces, established a series of reserves. Both Federal Migratory Bird Officers and provincial Game Guardians were hired to administer them. The majority of these reserves occurred on the prairies. In 1917, sites in Alberta included Birch Lake (Innisfree), Big Hay Lake (Leduc), Miquelon Lake (Camrose), Oliver Lake (Camrose), Ministik (Edmonton), Pakowki (Foremost), Many Island (Medicine Hat), and Buffalo Lake (Stettler). In 1925, another 25 sites were added to the provincial list including a parcel near Lethbridge known as Henderson Lake Park

(now within the Lethbridge city limits). In 1929, the area that would become Inglewood Bird Sanctuary along the Bow River in Calgary was added to the growing list. And finally, in 1943, new sites included St. George's Island in the Bow River (Calgary), Hall's Coulee (Crossfield), and Cygnet Lake (Red Deer).

Waterfowl Population Surveys

The first waterfowl surveys were triggered in the 1920s as a responsibility under the *Treaty to Protect Migratory Birds* and the demands of organized conservation groups. Surveys were carried out by the U.S. Biological Survey and involved regional appraisals by knowledgeable fieldmen initially only in the United States. Although the significance of prairie Canada as a duck production area was well appreciated, the region was not surveyed until 1935. At that time, a comprehensive survey of the major waterfowl production areas of the mid-continent, including North and South Dakota, Minnesota, Manitoba, Saskatchewan, Alberta, and a portion of the Mackenzie District of the Northwest Territories, was carried out by members of the More Game Birds in America Foundation, the precursor of Ducks Unlimited Incorporated and Ducks Unlimited Canada.

This monumental effort of conducting ground counts in settled agricultural areas and aerial coverage of forested regions required the participation of thousands of people. Arthur Bartley was the survey coordinator for Alberta and later became executive director of Ducks Unlimited Inc. Of the 42.7 million ducks counted

FRANK FARLEY AND MIQUELON LAKE BIRD SANCTUARY
In the 1920s, local Alberta naturalist Frank Farley was placed in charge of the bird sanctuary at Miquelon Lake. He was paid ten dollars a month for his efforts. Following the transfer of natural resources in 1930 and the limited provincial monies to deal with the new responsibilities, Farley became an early casualty of budget cuts. After a decade of superb care, he was released from his duties. The lake and the sanctuary suffered, as evidenced by an increase in illegal killing of waterfowl and big game, stealing of timber, and uncontrolled burning. As well, the spread of cattle and horses into the area damaged vegetation that provided cover for the nesting birds the sanctuary was originally designed to protect.

INGLEWOOD BIRD SANCTUARY
[SUE CLARKE]

The Inglewood Bird Sanctuary, a unique urban oasis nestled in the heart of downtown Calgary's east end, consists of 160 ha (395 acres) bordered on three sides by the Bow River. The history of the Sanctuary—a haven for migratory birds and other wildlife—dates back to early pioneer days. In 1883, Colonel James Walker, an officer of the Northwest Mounted Police, carved a homestead out of this piece of land.[4] Eventually, he built the large brick mansion called Inglewood which stands intact on the property today.[5] The rich natural history of the area with its riverine forest, abundant shrub understorey, and a spring-fed creek that never froze, was highly attractive to the ducks that frequently over-wintered there.

Upon Walker's death, the estate was left to his son, Selby—the true hero in the development of the Inglewood Bird Sanctuary. Wildlife conservation was not a popular subject at the time, and creating a sanctuary likely caused a stir among local farmers. Concern over waterfowl feeding on surrounding crops was the major source of dissension. In addition, the increasing number of waterfowl hunters and land squatters on the property was becoming a problem.

Several local groups and businesses expressed interest in acquiring the Walker land. Austin de B. Winter, Secretary of the Calgary Fish and Game Protective Association, wrote: "It is of extreme importance that this land and the buildings on it be procured for the benefit of this Association."[6] Later that year, Selby succeeded in having 59 ha (146 acres) designated as a Migratory Bird Sanctuary. On his insistence, "the killing, hunting, capturing, injuring, taking of migratory game, migratory insectivorous, or migratory non-game birds, or the molestation of their nests is prohibited at all times at the said Sanctuary".[7] Soon after, the area was re-named the Inglewood Bird Sanctuary.

In 1932, the Sanctuary was increased to 162 ha (400 acres) with the addition of lands on both sides of the Bow River, including the Canadian Pacific Railroad property and what is now the Inglewood Golf Course. These lands were legally protected as a federal sanctuary and a provincial game park.[8] The Sanctuary's first employee, George Pickering, a former Banff park warden, tended the grounds for 26 years and earned the reputation as Calgary's "Jack Miner". [Miner loved waterfowl and dedicated his property in Kingsville, Ontario, as a private bird sanctuary. In his honour, *National Wildlife Week* was legislated under a federal Act by the House of Commons in 1947 and is held annually the week of April 10.]

By 1933, Inglewood Bird Sanctuary was the largest urban bird sanctuary in Canada and the only acknowledged waterfowl winter sanctuary in the country.[9] Today, 270 bird species have been recorded, most of which use the area during spring and fall migration. The Calgary Bird Banding Society carries out an active bird banding and monitoring program. In fall, the riparian forest is particularly busy with large numbers of warblers, vireos, chickadees, kinglets, nuthatches, and woodpeckers. In winter, birds using the open water include Canada geese, mallards, common goldeneye, common merganser, lesser scaup, bufflehead, and the occasional bald eagle.[10]

MALLARDS IN FRONT OF THE INGLEWOOD BIRD SANCTUARY, 1988.
CREDIT: T. SADLER COURTESY DUCKS UNLIMITED CANADA

257

258

G. HORTON JENSEN, U.S. FISH AND WILDLIFE SERVICE, AL SMITH, CENTRAL FLYWAY BIOLOGIST FROM UTAH, DENNIS
WEISSER, ALBERTA GAME BRANCH, ALLAN BROOKS, CANADIAN WILDLIFE SERVICE AND AN UNIDENTIFIED MAN
UNLOADING GEAR PRIOR TO TRAPPING AND BANDING OPERATIONS, LAKE NEWELL, 1951.
CREDIT: REX GARY SCHMIDT COURTESY ALBERTA FISH AND WILDLIFE DIVISION

across North America in 1935, 38% of the total
and 40% of the Canadian portion occurred in
Alberta, thus establishing the province's
importance as a waterfowl production area.[11]

In 1947, a waterfowl survey of prairie Canada was
carried out by the U.S. Fish and Wildlife Service
(USFWS), the Dominion Wildlife Service (soon
to become the Canadian Wildlife Service), and the
Game Branches of the provinces of Manitoba,
Saskatchewan, Alberta, and British Columbia. In
1949, a joint migratory waterfowl survey was again
conducted, this time by Alberta and the USFWS.

In 1955, the USFWS started using aerial censuses
to assess breeding waterfowl populations

throughout the prairie and parkland regions of
Canada and the United States. However, biases in
aerial visibility presented a major limitation. The
USFWS had been conducting studies on
waterfowl populations at Lousana, Alberta and a
number of other sites across prairie Canada since
1952.[12] From this research, a system of air-ground
transects were implemented to correct for biases.[13]
This was a major improvement in the accuracy of
breeding population estimates and continues to be
the cornerstone of survey methodology.

After 1961, USFWS personnel carried out both
aerial and ground components of the annual
breeding population survey in Alberta. In addition
to the breeding adult population surveys in the

A MALLARD HEN AND HER BROOD.
COURTESY DUCKS UNLIMITED CANADA

259

prairie, parkland, boreal, taiga, and tundra regions, they also introduced aerial surveys to assess waterfowl brood (a family or group of young) production numbers. Brood surveys were limited to the prairie and parkland regions and lacked the precision of breeding population counts. Nonetheless, over time, they yielded excellent trend data on the annual number of broods, mean brood size, and the number of broods per 100 breeding pairs.

From Alberta, participation in annual waterfowl surveys was provided by CWS staff out of Edmonton including Mike Sorensen (1968-1970), Harold Weaver (1971-1973), Bruce Turner (1975-1994) and Dave Duncan (1995-2002). After 1970, Alberta Fish and Wildlife Division staff, including Harold Weaver (left CWS), Ken Lungle, Ken Froggatt, Jim Allen, Reg Russell, Leo Dube, and Ed Hoffman, participated with some regularity in waterfowl surveys. Similarly, DUC staff, including Mike Barr and Brian Ilnicki, added to the roster of survey participants.

Waterfowl Banding Programs

In 1959, to learn more about waterfowl populations, the USFWS added a waterfowl-banding component to their work in Alberta. Bird banding is a technique in which small, individually numbered or coloured aluminum bands or plastic rings are placed on live-trapped birds and later recovered when the bird is harvested or found dead. Data on the bird, including where it was banded and where it was subsequently recovered, are kept in central databases by the Bird Banding Office, Environment Canada and the U.S. Fish and Wildlife Service. This practice has been used to learn more about the longevity, migratory patterns, breeding and wintering sites, and other life history characteristics of many bird species worldwide. The Alberta program expanded throughout the 1960s to include seven crews of naturalists, biologists, students, and enforcement officers: three crews were operated by the Fish and Wildlife Division, one by USFWS in the northern parklands, and one by DUC in the Brooks area.

DUCKS UNLIMITED CANADA: THE BEGINNINGS
[BRETT CALVERLEY]

Ducks Unlimited Incorporated (DUI) was founded in 1937 in the United States out of concern for waterfowl and their nesting habitats at a time when many wetlands were severely reduced by agricultural practices and high evaporation rates brought by drought. The organization's main purpose was to raise money in the United States for rehabilitating, preserving, and developing waterfowl habitat in Canada.

In 1938, Ducks Unlimited Canada (DUC), a sister company of DUI, opened its first office in Alberta. Its first task was to investigate Many Island Lake in southeastern Alberta, a bird sanctuary since 1917. With settlement and water demands on inflowing creeks, together with the drought of the 1930s, the lake was drying up. By 1936, its water level fell to such an extent that closure of the sanctuary was considered. DUC built a dam at the outlet, which raised the level and enabled the lake to continue its useful role in providing waterfowl habitat.[14]

Similarly, DUC investigated Ministik Bird Sanctuary. This area, including Ministik Lake and some adjacent small ponds southeast of Edmonton, became a federal bird sanctuary in 1911. H.E. Williams, a local farmer, was paid an annual honorarium of $125 for his warden services. In 1930, the Sanctuary became the responsibility of the Alberta government, but little was done in the lean years of drought and depression that followed. The Sanctuary faced local pressure from grazing leases and poaching, and fires were becoming a concern. In 1938, DUC recommended that the provincial government fence the area, eliminate grazing, and appoint a game guardian to administer it.

Fish and Game Commissioner Huestis suggested that DUC could provide a valuable service by managing such reserves. Under authority of a letter from the Minister of Lands and Mines, DUC was put in charge of the Ministik Sanctuary. Although the area was soon fenced, poaching remained a struggle to solve. Francis Williams, one of the sons of the original game guardian, took up the task of warden (at first, without remuneration but later on a small salary). He applied himself diligently to the tasks at hand until his death, when his brother, Keith Williams, took over and later became a long-time employee of DUC.[15] As a result of this activity, Ministik Bird Sanctuary remains a relatively unmodified area for waterfowl.

MINISTIK LAKE.
COURTESY DUCKS UNLIMITED CANADA

Williams expanded his responsibilities and became Area Manager for central and northern Alberta. He was responsible for hundreds of wetland projects throughout this vast region, eventually supervising all DUC habitat activities north of the Alberta prairie biome. Williams' counterpart in the grasslands of southern Alberta was the flamboyant George Freeman from Strathmore. Freeman supervised all southern Alberta field staff and together they built hundreds of wetland projects in both the irrigated and dryland portions of the south. He particularly loved goose-banding operations and, later in his career, the annual Greenwing events for DUC youth members. Freeman is perhaps the longest standing DUC employee. He started his award-winning career in 1948 and remains on contract to DUC at the time of writing. Keith Williams, George Freeman, and Fred Sharp were all veterans of the Second World War. Dedication to their country was applied equally to their work with Ducks Unlimited Canada.

AN EXAMPLE OF MARSH ENHANCEMENT AT A DUCKS UNLIMITED SITE.
COURTESY DUCKS UNLIMITED CANADA

A CANADIAN WILDLIFE SERVICE

In 1920, all RCMP officers in participating provinces (including Alberta) became *ex officio* game officers under the *Migratory Birds Convention Act*. A network of Honorary Federal Game Officers was also established with the goal of communicating conservation values and the importance of compliance with federal hunting and fishing laws. James (Jim) Munro became the Chief Migratory Bird Officer with authority to oversee conservation and enforcement activities in British Columbia, the three prairie provinces, and the Northwest Territories. Munro was both peace officer and justice of the peace, with the power to arrest, hear, and adjudicate summary conviction cases under the Act. With such a large area under his jurisdiction, he focussed on B.C. and Alberta, where he not only coordinated conservation and enforcement activities, but also conducted on-going research that led to numerous publications and public lectures. In 1934, this large territory was divided up and Dewey Soper became Chief Migratory Bird Officer for the Prairies.

Building on the early work of the migratory bird officers, the Dominion Wildlife Service was established by the federal government in 1947 and renamed the Canadian Wildlife Service in 1950. Wildlife management was its key function, with a research role partially filled by the National Museum. Biologists hired after 1947 required formal training and some had postgraduate degrees. In response to a need for greater enforcement, Ron Mackay became the Regional Supervisor of Surveys and Enforcement for the Western Region in 1966, and Jack Shaver was appointed as co-ordinator for the Western Region in 1967. Chuck Gordon joined him in 1975. In the early 1980s, the roles and responsibilities of governments with respect to wildlife management were re-evaluated. Closer teamwork between the federal and provincial agencies was emphasized and some federal responsibilities were delegated to the provinces. In 1985, federal enforcement officers took on a more active policing role and became responsible for enforcing the *Convention on International Trade in Endangered Species of Wild Fauna and Flora* (CITES), and in 1992, the *Wild Animal and Plant Protection and Regulation of International and Interprovincial Trade Act* (WAPRIITA).

CWS Edmonton

From a diminutive one-person office manned by Dewey Soper in the 1940s and Ron Mackay in the 1950s, the Edmonton office of CWS grew to over 30 employees in the heady days of the 1960s and 1970s. This growth coincided with increased public awareness of environmental issues and a stronger federal commitment to resource management and conservation issues. Programs included research and management of mammals on federal lands (national parks and northern territories), endangered species, and waterfowl, as well as habitat protection, environmental assessment, and investigation of contaminants.

Several well-respected biologists, supported by field technicians and administrative support, spent some or all of their careers in the Edmonton office of CWS. Among these, biologists Lu Carbyn, Richard Fyfe, John Kelsall, Ernie Kuyt, Ron Mackay, Frank Miller, George Scotter, Ed Telfer, and Ian Stirling gained international recognition in their respective fields; Art Pearson became Commissioner for the Yukon Territory; Jim Patterson provided the vision, direction, and leadership to bring the North American Waterfowl Management Plan to fruition; and Dennis Surrendi served as Assistant Deputy Minister in both Manitoba and Alberta. These individuals reflected the quality and dedication towards fish and wildlife management issues in Alberta demonstrated by many Edmonton CWS staff over the past five decades.

261

BIOLOGISTS GATHERING DATA AT BASSANO DURING BANDING OPERATIONS OF THE 1951 WATERFOWL SURVEY.
THE GEESE ARE TRAPPED, BANDED, AND INFORMATION RECORDED AS TO AGE, SEX AND SPECIES.
CREDIT: REX GARY SCHMIDT COURTESY ALBERTA FISH AND WILDLIFE DIVISION

262

By the late 1960s, CWS assumed responsibility for the duck-banding program, initially in the Vermilion area, but later extended it to include Edmonton-Bashaw, Grande Prairie, Fairview-Peace River, and Calgary-Brooks regions. Banding programs became more structured, quotas were established for target species (usually mallard and pintail), and banding stations operated for a minimum of five years. Across the prairies, Alberta banders usually led the way in terms of numbers of ducks banded, often in the range of 12,000-15,000 birds annually. Much of this success is due to the experience and expertise of CWS biologist Paul Pryor who, since the 1970s, has overseen the work of a number of summer students operating banding stations.

Banding programs were also used to understand goose populations better. Historically, Canada geese nested throughout the mid-latitudes, including southern and central Alberta. However, by the turn of the last century, excessive exploitation had taken its toll on this species. Settlement and the draining of wetlands also limited productivity. During the 1960s and 1970s, Canada geese remained limited all across western North America. To better protect the remainder, the Fish and Wildlife Division conducted fall goose surveys throughout central and southern Alberta to determine their timing of migration. Hunting season dates were then adjusted to provide protection to snow, Ross', locally breeding large Canada, and white-fronted geese.

In addition to geese surveys, in 1960, a central flyway crew (composed of members of state agencies in New Mexico, Colorado and

BAND BEING ATTACHED TO LEG OF YOUNG CANADA GOOSE
DURING THE 1951 WATERFOWL SURVEY.
CREDIT: REX GARY SCHMIDT COURTESY ALBERTA FISH AND WILDLIFE DIVISION

Canada geese from Alberta used both the Central and Pacific flyways. This led to a cooperative goose-banding program among the Fish and Wildlife Division, CWS, and managers from the states of Idaho, Utah, Colorado, and Wyoming from 1975 to 1979 to define the breeding range of Rocky Mountain (Pacific) and Hi-Line (Central) populations.

Annual goose drives occurred in early July when adult geese were moulting and young were not yet flight-worthy. While most goose drives yielded 100–300 geese, one particular effort at Hays Reservoir in 1975 netted 749 geese in one trap. Goose banding data yielded valuable information about mortality, flyways used, and wintering areas: information put towards direct management application. The banding operation also provided

263

Nebraska) spent 30 days in Hanna, Alberta, gathering data on the migration timing of lesser Canada geese. Evidence indicated that large

PAUL PRYOR, CWS BIRD BANDER EXTRAORDINAIRE
[BRUCE TURNER]

Paul Pryor joined the Canadian Wildlife Service in Saskatoon in 1964 and transferred to Edmonton in 1967. Initially involved with the habitat program, in 1972 he began a long career with waterfowl population management programs including breeding population, production, and habitat surveys, and banding projects. Pryor's responsibilities included training banding crews, something at which he excelled and for which he was eminently qualified. Meticulous to the last detail, he never set a duck trap without a thorough consideration of all factors, including substrate, shoreline vegetation, water depth, the extent of emergent and submergent vegetation, the positioning of the trap in relation to the shoreline, the width and height of the trap entrance, and last but not least, the manner in which the trap is baited.

Owing to the thoroughness of the training, it was a rare occasion when a banding crew complained about low catch rates. However, in 1988 I received a plea for help from the Brooks crew who had a problem: ducks were abundant at the trap sites but the crew was unable to catch them. Paul went to Brooks, promptly repositioned the traps, strategically baited each site, and then went to High River to check out another crew. Three days later at 11 o'clock at night I received a call from a distraught student in the Brooks crew: they needed help because they were catching between 1000 and 1200 ducks per day and running out of daylight before all the birds could be processed! Needless to say, they never asked for Paul's assistance again.

Many students passed under the watchful eye of Paul Pryor, enjoying and benefitting from his thoughtful and patient guidance. Without exception, every summer student who arrived as a stranger in May, and enjoyed his tutelage over the summer, departed as a friend in September. As he enters his 41st year with the Canadian Wildlife Service, this dedicated and durable employee continues his work with an enviable youthful enthusiasm.

an excellent opportunity for field crews and wetland managers to gather and discuss current waterfowl strategies. Crews from CWS (Bruce Turner, Paul Pryor, and many students) and Alberta Fish and Wildlife (Harold Weaver, Ken Lungle, Jim Allen, Ed Hofman, Dave Moyles, and Bob Goddard) continued banding geese in southern Alberta and the Grande Prairie areas until 1987.

GEESE CAUGHT IN A TRAP ARE BEING ROUNDED UP FOR BANDING.
CREDIT: ERNIE PSIKLA

264

Banding programs also provided goslings and adults for a Canada goose translocation program. In the 1960s, resource agencies developed programs to restore goose populations by transplanting birds from remaining breeding stocks. Most breeding Canada geese in Alberta were confined to larger lakes and reservoirs in the prairie region. Under the guidance of Bill

Wishart, the Fish and Wildlife Division translocated geese from these areas to unoccupied suitable habitat elsewhere in the province.

Expanding Goose Numbers

The Canada goose translocation project was an overwhelming success. Birds quickly established themselves and populations expanded, their

BRUCE TURNER ON WATERFOWL BAND RECOVERIES...
[FROM AN INTERVIEW WITH PETRA ROWELL]

After his many years of banding waterfowl in Alberta, I asked Bruce Turner where some of his most interesting band recoveries came from. He relayed the following: "I still have band recoveries coming to my office after not having banded for ten years now, but perhaps the most interesting one was a bird which I had banded in the Cooking Lake moraine. I forget which year it had been banded. But I used to take my children out hunting. We were out at Beaverhill Lake and I tended to get a little bit fussy about what I shot. I would shoot only males and generally it was male mallards. So we had been in the canoe for quite some time and the kids were getting bored, getting into their lunch, and my young fellow was saying: 'Dad, shoot that one, shoot that one.' So finally, to appease them, a pintail came by and it was partially coloured up with breeding plumage. So I shot him. I picked up the bird only to find out it had been a bird that I had banded about seven years before at Cooking Lake. So that was an interesting one!

"Other interesting returns were from Mexico and South America. Generally the South American recoveries were blue-winged teal. They seem to travel farther than any of the other ducks. A lot of the mallards banded here, depending on where they were caught in the province, would often be recovered in Washington, Idaho; some went down to Colorado—that seemed to be where most of the gadwall went. Pintail, of course, most of them would have been taken in California. In the eastern part of the province, most of the mallards were taken in the central flyway—the Mississippi flyway—Louisiana, Texas, Arkansas were big harvest areas for mallards banded in eastern Alberta."

CANADA GOOSE TRANSLOCATIONS
[BILL WISHART]

In my early days, there weren't that many Canada geese around. We had good goose habitat in Alberta, but the geese were being harvested—by robbing nests for eggs or by catching birds when they were flightless. Dennis Surrendi experimented by translocating geese from southern Alberta to the Hanna area. He collared these geese [put a coloured plastic neck band on them], and we tracked where they went. We learned that a goose would return to wherever it learns to fly. So we started translocating goslings.

Beginning in 1965, Canada geese were trapped and translocated to a number of areas. The largest releases occurred at Oliver Lake (New Sarepta). Other releases occurred at Bushyhead Lake (Wainwright), Vermilion Reservoir, Big Lake (St. Albert), Driedmeat Lake (Camrose), Chain Lakes (Claresholm), and Waterton Reservoir. Although not very successful initially, translocations continued through the late 1960s and eventually geese were seen nesting on many release areas. Approximately 1000 individuals (mainly goslings) were moved.

We moved young geese without the adults, but soon learned that they were very vulnerable to hunting. So we moved adults with the goslings. I'd take either an adult male or an adult female but not a pair. We did not want to leave orphan goslings on the source lake.

Once the young learned to fly, the adults took the goslings back to where they had been trapped and then led them safely to the winter sites. Come spring, the adults flew back to where we trapped them, and the young ones flew back to where they learned to fly. This was exactly what we wanted them to do.

A CANADA GOOSE WEARING A NECK COLLAR FOR EASY IDENTIFICATION AT A DISTANCE.
COURTESY DUCKS UNLIMITED CANADA

265

growth enhanced by nesting structures (primarily hay bales) provided by DUC and the Alberta Fish and Game Association. The Canada goose breeding population expanded in Alberta from approximately 33,000 in the mid-1900s to over 130,000 in the last two decades. Drought conditions in southern Alberta in the 1980s contributed to the northward expansion and growth of the population as geese began to use wetlands in the parkland and boreal-fringe areas. Reduced hunting pressure also had an effect as the number of waterfowl hunters in the province declined after the late 1970s.

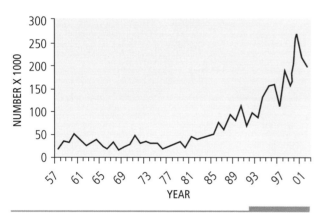

CANADA GOOSE NUMBERS IN SOUTHERN ALBERTA, 1957-2001

In addition to local populations of Canada geese, Albertans are also privileged to experience massive spring migrations of other goose populations that pass through the province on their way north to nest in Arctic regions. Small Canada geese breed across the Northwest Territories and Nunavut. White-fronted geese breed across much of the inland areas of the Northwest Territories. Snow geese and Ross' geese breed in colonies along the coast of the Northwest Territories and on islands in the Arctic Ocean. As well, white-fronted geese that breed in Alaska regularly migrate through northwestern Alberta each fall.

During the 1960s, waterfowl managers were concerned about low population numbers for some northern migratory flocks. To address this concern, the province had three major waterfowl-

hunting zones and added a goose-management zone on fall staging areas (areas where birds feed and rest before migrating) in east-central Alberta. Special seasons in the goose management zone were timed to protect species of concern by limiting their harvest, particularly that of "white" geese (lesser snow and Ross' geese). However, white-fronted geese were also considered vulnerable to overharvest.

While no single factor controls goose populations, it appears the special seasons contributed significantly to the overall increase in these northern populations. Since the 1970s, the mid-continent population of white-fronted geese has grown considerably. East-central Alberta wetlands and the reaches of the South Saskatchewan River that form Diefenbaker Lake in Saskatchewan regularly provide an important staging area for migrating white-fronts. During late September, the entire mid-continent white-fronted goose population can be found in these areas. Cooperative fall surveys conducted by USFWS and CWS indicated the white-front population exceeded one million birds for several years. As a result, jurisdictions that harvest white-fronted geese liberalized the bag limits. However, white-fronted geese, like other Arctic-nesters, are subject to boom and bust production and there is some indication that population numbers are again declining in the early part of the 21st century.

In contrast to their low numbers during the 1960s, snow goose and Ross' goose numbers have skyrocketed in recent years. The mid-continent snow goose populations along the west coast of Hudson Bay and adjoining Arctic coast demonstrated the most pronounced exponential growth, but similar increases occurred among western Arctic populations. There are several factors contributing to this population growth. Hunter numbers declined considerably throughout North America and, correspondingly, the harvest rates for snow geese are low. Habitat on the snow goose wintering grounds has changed significantly. Large

MORE CANADA GOOSE RESEARCH
[ERNIE EWASCHUK]

The lack of Canada geese on their historical breeding areas in the parkland, together with subsequent survey, banding, and translocation programs, stimulated further research on this species. Dennis Surrendi, Alberta Fish and Wildlife Division, had an interest in sub-speciation/races of Canada geese and we began to look at whether the large Canadas breeding in Alberta were actually *Branta canadensis maxima* or not. During banding sessions and surveys of northern rivers we measured a lot of Canada geese and eventually concluded that there was a gradation in size from south to north with the largest birds occurring in southern Alberta. We also weighed a lot of geese at fall hunter check stations during the 1960s and 1970s, but rarely had geese over 10–12 pounds. Later, after the population explosion, it was common to find geese in the 12–15 pound range.

The 1967 discovery of a large concentration of Canada geese nesting on an island in Dowling Lake, near Hanna, provided another research opportunity. Charles Lacy, a DUC biologist for Alberta, told us about these geese he saw from the air. We checked it out and found approximately 180 nests on the 16-acre island. Many nests failed to hatch and the immediate thought was predation; however, the density of nests also raised the question of possible territorial behaviour affecting nesting success.

From an observation tower, we watched goose pairs during the breeding season of 1969. Water levels were normal and predation was not a factor. But the ability of the gander to defend his territory and ensure his mate was undisturbed during incubation

appeared to influence hatching success. This, in turn, was influenced by the density of vegetation: nests in dense vegetation required smaller territories and received less harassment from neighbouring pairs.

Following this study, Bill Glasgow, Fish and Wildlife Division, studied "creching" (crib or nursery) behaviour of Canada geese at Dowling Lake. Territorial behaviour of Canada geese was important to Ducks Unlimited since they were constructing nesting islands for waterfowl in all their wetland restoration projects. Jean-François Giroux further examined factors affecting territorial behaviour on islands in the Brooks area and was able to entice two pairs to nest on a small island by establishing a barrier (four-foot-high plywood wall) that visually separated the two pairs of geese.

DIFFERENT RACES OF CANADA GEESE RANGE IN SIZE CONSIDERABLY.
COURTESY E. EWASCHUK

SNOW GEESE ON THEIR ARCTIC BREEDING GROUND.
CREDIT: G. BEYERSBERGEN

268

proportions of mid-continent populations traditionally used winter ranges restricted to coastal areas along the Gulf of Mexico. However, over the past 20 years, inland cotton fields were converted to more lucrative rice crops. Flooded rice fields are much more attractive to snow geese than dry cotton fields and the geese rapidly adjusted their prime feeding areas. The abundance of waste grain in rice fields also meant that snow geese left their wintering areas in excellent body condition and arrived on Arctic breeding areas in good condition. Thus, current annual production and survival of first-year birds greatly exceeds previous levels.

Exponential growth of the snow goose populations, or any wild species, cannot be sustained over the long term. Snow (as well as Ross') geese grub in the soil to unearth tender roots of grasses, sedges and forbs. This practice, compounded by massive numbers of geese, is denuding the habitat on their traditional nesting grounds. As huge areas of Arctic landscape are destroyed, nesting geese move inland to fresh, vegetated areas. The cycle continues year after

year as an increasing number of healthy geese wing their way north from wintering grounds to nest in the disappearing Arctic habitat.

To avoid a catastrophic population crash, North American jurisdictions have taken drastic measures to increase the harvest of mid-continent snow geese. Liberal fall hunting seasons are in place in most jurisdictions, some with unlimited daily bag limits. Under new special provisions in the *Migratory Birds Convention Act*, "conservation hunts" for snow geese are held in several provinces and states during spring migration. To encourage hunters to harvest as many birds as possible, conservation hunts allow some unusual rules including unplugged shotguns and no bag limits.

In Alberta, fall seasons for white geese are maximized and bag limits are extremely liberal, but there is no spring conservation hunt. A small, precarious population of snow geese nesting on Wrangell Island, off the northeast coast of Russia, migrates northward through Alberta in the spring. Because this population may not be able to withstand additional harvest,

SNOW GOOSE STORM!
CREDIT: G. BEYERSBERGEN

269

a spring hunt for white geese cannot be held in Alberta.

Waterfowl Harvest Management

Obviously, the waterfowl we enjoy represent shared, international resources that do not recognize provincial or national borders. Thus, waterfowl populations and their harvest cannot be managed in isolation from surrounding jurisdictions. Waterfowl production in Canada provides huntable surpluses within the United States, and we depend on U.S. jurisdictions to control their harvest so that ample breeding populations return to Canada the following spring.

The *Treaty to Protect Migratory Birds* provides the primary framework for management of waterfowl populations and waterfowl harvests between Canada and the U.S. The Treaty appoints the two federal governments as ultimately responsible for

preservation of North American waterfowl resources. That responsibility is assumed by the U.S. Department of Interior (U.S. Fish and Wildlife Service) and Environment Canada (Canadian Wildlife Service).

For decades, these agencies worked collaboratively with no formal process for direct involvement by individual provinces or states in setting hunting seasons and bag limits. This management regime began to change somewhat in the 1940s with the splitting of North America into four flyways (Pacific, Central, Mississippi, and Atlantic) along a north-south axis that roughly represented waterfowl migration patterns. The flyway system provided an opportunity for USFWS to meet with and discuss management objectives and options with individual states in each flyway.

In Canada, managers in each province could align themselves with the flyways that represented the

A HUNTER AND HIS DECOYS AT DUSK.
COURTESY DUCKS UNLIMITED CANADA

Under the terms of the *Migratory Birds Convention Act*, the federal government has the ultimate authority for protection of migratory birds in Canada. Seasons and bag limits within each province are determined as a result of annual consultation between each province and CWS. Even though Alberta sets its season and bag limits by virtue of the Alberta *Wildlife Act* and Regulations, the province cannot unilaterally determine season dates or bag limits without consensus with the federal government. Annual regulations are published each year in the federal Migratory Birds Regulations and the Alberta Wildlife Regulations.

greatest commonality in terms of species and populations managed in their home province. For instance, various ducks and geese produced in Alberta migrate to and are harvested in each of the four flyways; however, the greatest proportion spends its winters in the Pacific Flyway, with the Central Flyway a close second. Hence, from an Albertan perspective, it is prudent to become involved in management discussions with colleagues in the Pacific and Central Flyways. Annual flyway meetings constitute a forum for collaboration and international agreement on management initiatives and objectives for each species of waterfowl and some individual populations. Within the U.S., the flyway meetings are also where state waterfowl seasons and bag limits are discussed, bearing in mind the overall international management objectives.

Survey work throughout the 1950s to the 1970s showed that waterfowl populations in the productive prairie and parkland regions fluctuated in response to wetland availability. After this period, populations continued to

A GOOD DAY'S BAG OF GREENHEADS.
COURTESY DUCKS UNLIMITED CANADA

reflect changes in wetland numbers, but the overall population was significantly less. Population declines were not unique to Alberta but were widespread throughout the mid-continental region. Not surprisingly, people began to wonder why.

The relative importance of hunter harvest and changing habitat as the cause of waterfowl population decline became the source of heated debate. Extensive analysis of mallard survival rates concluded that above certain threshold levels, hunting mortality is "additive".[16] That is, hunting mortality occurs in addition to natural mortality. Below the threshold, the effects of hunting are "compensatory"—hunting replaces other forms of natural mortality. This finding raised doubts about previous harvest management strategies. While it was generally believed that it was not necessary to adjust hunting regulations if harvest was below estimated threshold levels, these threshold levels were not easily identified.

The discussions around these issues successfully exposed a number of problems and deficiencies that hampered the development of sound waterfowl management programs. First, the role of hunting in regulating population numbers was uncertain and controversial. Second, the role of land-use changes on waterfowl was not fully understood. And third, varying harvest regulations in response to population changes obscured any relationship between hunting and population size. In order to enhance waterfowl management, these issues had to be addressed.

The Stabilized Duck Hunting Regulations Program of the USFWS and CWS, in conjunction with state and provincial resource agencies, was developed as a solution. Implemented from 1979-

1984, the program set constant or stabilized hunting regulations on duck harvests and then looked at other factors like production and land-use changes that could be influencing populations. The principal findings of the program were that harvest rates were high and in some instances hunting mortality was additive (in addition to natural mortality). Hunter success remained high when populations were low, thus conservative regulations were needed when populations were in decline. In addition, land-use changes were compromising the relationship between wetland numbers and waterfowl reproductive performance which was below levels required to maintain stable populations. The findings of the Stabilized Hunting Regulations Program emphasized that together with harvest management, habitat conservation would have to be a principal focus of waterfowl management across North America.

271

Waterfowl Habitat in Alberta

The prairie and parkland regions exemplify the best waterfowl-breeding habitat in North America. Knob-and-kettle pothole complexes with abundant upland nesting cover of grasses and forbs are capable of supporting high densities of breeding waterfowl. No less important are the plentiful large marshes and lakes that provide

A POTHOLE COMPLEX. COURTESY DUCKS UNLIMITED CANADA

critical habitat during staging and moulting periods. Waterfowl density and productivity traditionally are higher here than anywhere else.

Periods of drought, like the severe drought that prevailed across Alberta over the first three years of the new millennium, can ravage waterfowl breeding, production, moulting, and staging habitats. However, drought impacts are relatively temporary and the ecological function of these wetlands is usually restored as water levels are recharged. In contrast, the effects of intensified agricultural activities,

A SCENIC MARSH IN THE BOREAL FRINGE.
COURTESY DUCKS UNLIMITED CANADA

272

urban expansion, road construction, and other industrial activities have a far greater impact.

Wetland loss is influenced by a number of factors including politics, economics, attitudes, and

PRIME WATERFOWL HABITAT IN ALBERTA

In Alberta, high quality Class 1 and 2 waterfowl habitats hold 85 ducks per sq. km compared to 80 ducks per sq. km in Manitoba and 69 ducks per sq. km in Saskatchewan. Similarly, Class 3 habitats, with slight limitations to waterfowl breeding, hold 62 ducks per sq. km in Alberta compared to 36 ducks per sq. km in Manitoba and 47 ducks per sq. km in Saskatchewan.[17]

In addition, 8 of 13 nationally significant and 11 of 32 regionally significant prairie habitats for breeding ducks are found in Alberta.[18] These include the Rumsey Upland, Battle River Upland, Birch Lake Plain, Killam Plain, Beaverhill Lake Plain, Buffalo Lake Plain, and Bashaw Upland. Excellent waterfowl breeding habitat is not confined to central Alberta. High quality waterfowl breeding habitat occurs across the breadth of the province, from the Cypress Hills Benchlands and Milk River Ridge in the south, to the Peace-Athabasca delta and Zama Plain in the north.

In addition to breeding habitat, large wetlands and marshes are required by staging ducks and geese during spring and fall migration and during the post-breeding moult. Beaverhill, Buffalo, and Utikuma lakes and the Peace-Athabasca delta are nationally significant moulting sites. Other important moulting sites include Pakowki, Ribstone, Bittern, Bearhills, Cooking, Miquelon, Kimiwan, Lac Magloire, Lac Cardinal, Irricana, Whitford, Hay-Zama lakes, and many other named and unnamed wetlands. Nationally significant staging wetlands, where waterfowl rest and feed prior to migration, include Many Island, Erskine, Kenilworth, Wavy, Beaverhill, Buffalo, Bearhills, Manawan, Sullivan, Vermilion Lakes, Smoky, Flat, Kimiwan, Lac Magloire, Bear, Utikuma, Peace Athabasca Delta, Hay-Zama, and La Glace lakes [although some of these lakes actually dried up in recent years].

climate.[19] Wetlands rarely provide tangible benefits to landowners, but instead represent an impediment to increased production and a source of higher operational costs. In addition, government policies such as the Canada Wheat Board Quota system and Municipal Tax structures directly conflict with wetland retention and hence, with supportive waterfowl management. Early settlers soon realized that drainage was an effective and efficient means of increasing arable lands and many large shallow wetlands were turned into cropland or pasture. Although the *Northwest Irrigation Act* of 1884 and the Alberta *Water Resources Act* of 1931 existed as legal instruments to regulate water use, they served more to facilitate wetland drainage than control or limit it. In fact, until 1993 when the province of Alberta issued the *Wetland Management in the Settled Area of Alberta—Interim Policy* and launched the Beyond Prairie Potholes program, wetlands, particularly prairie sloughs, were considered wastelands.

This dismissive and negative attitude toward wetlands was no doubt rooted in misguided

impressions of a cornucopia of wetlands and perhaps an ignorance of the long-term effects of drainage. The attitude is captured succinctly in an article in the Alberta Agriculture *Agri-News*, January 19, 1987, stating: "…drainage is not as big an industry in Alberta as in other provinces, but with an estimated 11 million acres of wetland in the agricultural areas of Alberta, there is no shortage of need."

In addition, widespread drought conditions and changes in equipment allowed landowners to cultivate up to and into previous wetlands. One of the first researchers to note the devastating impacts of agriculture on wetlands observed: "In the case of the Lousana Study Area, biologists were on hand to record how farmers, with the help of drought, farmed the ducks out of existence. This is a tragic commentary on the future of one of our great natural resources but its inevitability is as certain as the permanence of the plough, the ditcher, the brusher, and the match."[20] Between 1940 and 1970, there was a 13% decline in wetland area and a 4.5% decrease in wetland numbers for the Black Soil Zone of the Prairie

273

A TRACTOR CULTIVATING ALONGSIDE A WATER BODY.
COURTESY DUCKS UNLIMITED CANADA

CROPS TILLED AND PLANTED RIGHT THROUGH WETLANDS.
COURTESY DUCKS UNLIMITED CANADA

274

and Wildlife Division signed *Wetlands for Tomorrow*, a five-year plan to secure and enhance the 20 most important waterfowl staging and moulting lakes in Alberta. The plan applies to Beaverhill, Bens/Watt, Big, Big Hay/Bittern, Buffalo/Spotted, Chip, Cygnet, Hay-Zama, Kleskun, Manawan, Many Island, Marion, Stirling, Tyrrell/Rush, Utikuma, and Whitford/Rush lakes as well as Buffalo Bay/Heart River, Little Red Deer, and Vauxhall marshes, and the Peace-Athabasca delta. The Division was to secure the land base for all listed lakes and DUC would conduct the enhancement activities and long-term management. Although *Wetlands for Tomorrow* has met with some success and was extended well beyond its initial time frame, significant purchase, enhancement, and management challenges remain in 2005. In the meantime, damage to wetlands continues, as drainage rates are largely unchanged since the 1970s.[24]

Provinces.[21] Degradation and destruction of wetlands accelerated thereafter, facilitated by larger and more powerful farm machinery. By 1986, it was generally accepted that 40% of the original wetlands in prairie Canada were gone.[22]

Recognizing that the reproductive performance of ducks was compromised by changes in habitat, that agricultural impacts on wetlands were not documented, and that concrete data were required to change policy or legislation, the Canadian Wildlife Service implemented a program in 1980 to collect information on the incidence and extent of transitory and permanent agricultural impacts on wetlands in prairie Canada. It found that 66% of the basins and 93% of the wetland margins in Alberta were affected to some degree; grazing and cultivation accounted for most of the transitory changes. The annual drainage rate in Alberta was 0.53% compared to 0.19% in Saskatchewan and 0.25% in Manitoba.[23] Not only were wetlands drained but, in addition, upland nesting cover around remaining wetlands was lost at an alarming rate.

To address some of these concerns, in 1981 Ducks Unlimited Canada and the Alberta Fish

The North American Waterfowl Management Plan

Responding to the severe decline in waterfowl numbers across the continent during the 1980s, the North American Waterfowl Management Plan (NAWMP) was created in 1986. An international partnership, the Plan recognized the key relationship between waterfowl and wetlands and introduced programs to mitigate habitat loss. Today, the plan is an example of successful cooperation among government and non-government partners for addressing common concerns.

"It is often said (and corroborated by history) that crisis is the catalyst for change. Excessive exploitation prompted the development of the Treaty for the Protection of Migratory Birds in the early part of the 20th Century, drought spawned the creation of Ducks Unlimited in the 1930s, and drought in the 1980s prompted the development of the North American Waterfowl Management Plan."

GORDON KERR

The plan, a blueprint for waterfowl habitat enhancement, called for $1.5 billion-worth of habitat improvement and restoration including 3.6 million acres of Canadian prairie before the year 2000. Goals also included a breeding population of 62 million ducks and a fall flight total of 100 million, as well as individual goals for 37 duck species. (Fall flight numbers were greater than 100 million in the 1970s but fell to 66 million by the end of the drought-ridden 1980s. The all-time low was less than 27 million.)

In 1990, provincial activities were coordinated by the Alberta NAWMP Centre, with Morley Barrett as the first Executive Director and a Board of Directors chaired by Alberta Fish and Wildlife Division. Ducks Unlimited Canada, Alberta Agriculture, Environment Canada (Canadian Wildlife Service), and Wildlife Habitat Canada also held seats on the board. Key funding came from U.S. sources including the *North American Wetland Conservation Act* and Ducks Unlimited Incorporated.

Upland nesting success was identified as the major factor in Alberta affecting breeding success and recruitment of ducks into the fall flight. Thus, the plan focussed on working with landowners to secure upland nesting habitat in association with high wetland and waterfowl densities. Habitat work started in 1989 with the Buffalo Lake Moraine–First Step Project. Full implementation

275

A NORTHERN WATERFOWL GEM
[KEN WRIGHT]

The Hay-Zama Lakes complex is recognized internationally as a critical staging and nesting area for waterfowl and shorebirds that funnel in and out on three of the four continental migration pathways. This spectacular wetland complex spans more than five townships in the northwest corner of the province. Its unique hydrology—a river flowing through the middle of two large lakes—includes a matrix of flooded lakes and ponds separated by elevated banks of the Hay River. The ecological values of the complex are recognized by the Dene Tha' First Nation who live nearby, as well as by conservation and management agencies. The area was designated a RAMSAR site (Wetland of International Importance) in 1982, designated a provincial Wetland For Tomorrow in 1985, nominated as a World Heritage Site in 1990, and provincially legislated as a Wildlife Provincial Park in 1999.

The complex has a unique management history. For generations, members of the Dene Tha' respected the wetland for its abundance of hunting, fishing, and trapping opportunities. An Order in Council in 1939 gave Ducks Unlimited Canada (DUC) the authority to actively manage the wetland complex.[25] This was amended in 1958 to include the provincial Water Resources Branch. Significant oil and gas reserves lie beneath the complex and have been tapped since the 1960s. In 1968, the Dene Tha' passed a Council resolution to cooperate in the management of the wetland. Thus began a cooperative working relationship that remains a model of successful management of crown lands among differing interests. The success is based firmly on a foundation of transparent consultation and consensus decision-making.

began in 1991 when programs were established in priority landscapes in the Prairie, Aspen Parkland, and Peace Parkland biomes.

Initial funds were contingent upon evaluating the effects of various land management treatments on ducks and other wetland-dependent species. Multi-species teams were developed to evaluate these treatments with Ernie Ewaschuk as team leader, Reg Arbuckle in Grande Prairie, Andy Murphy in Red Deer, Tom Sadler in Strathmore, and Bob Goddard in Lethbridge. Other Centre personnel included Ken Gurr (Communications Specialist), Lori Neufeld (Administrative Assistant), Brett Calverley (Habitat Delivery Specialist seconded from DUC half-time), and Dave Prescott (Research Scientist).

In 1996, the Alberta NAWMP program underwent some changes. Alberta Fish and Wildlife Division closed the Alberta NAWMP Centre and invited DUC to take over coordination of the plan in Alberta. Wildlife Habitat Canada left the Board, but Alberta Environment, The Nature Conservancy of Canada, and Agriculture and Agri-Food Canada were added. In 1996, Brett Calverley was appointed the Alberta NAWMP Coordinator. During 2001, the Board formally adopted the name "Alberta NAWMP Partnership".

Since 1986, the Alberta NAWMP partners have spent $213 million and have secured 486,000 ha (1.2 million acres) of upland and wetland habitat. However, these statistics do not tell the whole story of the effect the plan has had on the province. Highly successful crop damage prevention and compensation programs; waterfowl population and habitat monitoring programs; wetland, waterfowl and biodiversity evaluations; input into government policy; and communications programs were initiated. In addition, the Partnership's organizational structure is touted as the model to follow in other provincial NAWMP jurisdictions.

Crop Damage

With the dual distinction of being the "bread basket" as well as the "duck factory" of the continent, crop damage is a significant problem for Alberta's agricultural and waterfowl managers. Most waterfowl have an appetite for cereal grains, and several species (mallard, northern pintail, Canada goose, white-fronted goose, snow goose and Ross' goose) readily adjust foraging strategies to access this rich food source. The conflict is most prevalent throughout central and northern Alberta as the fall staging and migration of northern breeders coincides with the peak period of cereal grain harvesting in these regions.

A GRAIN SWATH BEFORE AND AFTER WATERFOWL HAVE FED ON IT.
CREDIT: K. LUNGLE

SWATHS OF GEESE FEEDING ON SWATHS OF GRAIN.
COURTESY DUCKS UNLIMITED CANADA

No doubt waterfowl ate cereal crops since their initial cultivation on the Canadian prairies. However, the traditional, labour-intensive practices of stack and stook threshing afforded limited opportunity for waterfowl damage. Circumstances changed quickly around the 1950s when combine harvesting came into general use and crops became vulnerable after they were swathed and left on the ground in windrows. Because this practice affords uniform dryness, reduces seed loss, and reduces frost damage to unripened kernels, it is widespread and entrenched in cereal crop management. Inclement weather often lengthens the period during which crops are left exposed in fields and any delay in harvest increases the likelihood of depredation by waterfowl. When foraging waterfowl damage swathed crops, losses accrue from consumption of seed, but also from trampling and shelling of grains before combines can harvest the field.

As early as 1942, Migratory Bird Regulations were amended to provide for hunting permits to farmers who were losing grain to ducks. A farmer could ask for assistance from hunters, providing he gave each a letter showing his authorization for shooting on his land. Despite a bag limit of 20 ducks per day and 150 for the season in 1945, the problem of ducks eating grain again arose in the Eastern Irrigation District the following year.

The first efforts to estimate the value of crop losses to waterfowl were undertaken in 1955 in Saskatchewan by the federal and provincial departments of agriculture. Prairie-wide surveys from 1959 to 1961 determined that annual losses ranged from $4.3-$12.6 million with 24-45 thousand farmers affected. This prompted the creation of a crop damage insurance program made available to Alberta farmers in 1961. The premiums were set at 5% of the insured value.

The Alberta Fish and Game Association promoted the expansion of the program and supported hunter licence fees to help fund compensation. The insurance program was replaced in 1964 by a program of paying direct compensation for losses with monies from the Wildlife Damage Fund.

In 1969, waterfowl damage to unharvested crops was the worst on record. The Wildlife Damage Fund paid out over $900,000 as compensation, representing only a small fraction (less than 25%) of the millions of dollars in losses that actually occurred. In response to the escalating conflict between waterfowl and agricultural producers, an innovative Crop Damage Control (CDC) program was carried out from 1970–1972 in an effort to prevent losses of crops to waterfowl. Under the direction of Tom Burgess and Ken Lungle, the Fish and Wildlife Division conducted an experimental CDC program in the Grande Prairie area, consisting of waterfowl feeding stations, dry and flooded lure crops, and a field scaring program. A similar lure crop program was also carried out in the Beaverhill Lake area.

The experimental program identified that a damage prevention program could be both effective and economical in controlling waterfowl damage of unharvested crops. Plans were formed immediately to expand the CDC program to all areas of Alberta wherever the degree of economic loss warranted prevention programs. Between 1973 and 1975, the program expanded into the Peace River, St. Paul, and Red Deer areas.

Recognizing crop damage as a major hindrance to waterfowl conservation, Alberta, Saskatchewan, Manitoba, and Canada entered a comprehensive cost-shared crop damage agreement in 1973. In Alberta, responsibility for the compensation program was transferred to the Hail and Crop Insurance Corporation (now the Agriculture Financial Services) under Alberta Agriculture in 1993. The Fish and Wildlife Trust Fund (former Wildlife Damage Fund) continued to fund Alberta's share of the prevention program. Federal government administration of the CDC program was handled by Raymond "Jerry" Prach

(1973-1979), Bert Poston (1979-1993) and Paul Gregoire (1993 to present). Alberta's programs were managed by Tom Burgess/Ken Lungle (1970-1973), Harold Weaver/Ken Lungle (1973-1987), and Ken Lungle (1988-1997). In 1997, the Fish and Wildlife Trust Fund and the responsibility for delivery of the CDC program were transferred to the Alberta Conservation Association.

The CDC program represents the first coordinated and organized government effort to address waterfowl damage to cereal crops. Given the broad geographic extent of the problem, several coordinators were needed for program delivery: Ken Lungle was Provincial Crop Damage Coordinator, Jim Rosin was hired for the northwest, Grant Gunderson (and later Daryl Cole) in the northeast, and Daryl Cole (and later Jim Allen) for the central region. Over the years, the CDC program was the entry level where a surprising number of Fish and Wildlife employees cut their teeth with the Division.

A LURE CROP SIGN.
CREDIT: K. LUNGLE

During the life of the CDC program, lure crops were purchased, field staff patrolled control areas in search of marauding waterfowl, scare cannons were set in fields at the farmer's request, and feeding stations were established within each control area if suitable locations existed. To some degree, all initiatives were successful; however,

A SCARE CANNON IS USED TO SCARE WATERFOWL AWAY FROM A CROP.
CREDIT: K. LUNGLE

the success of lure crops was compromised when birds opted to select another field or consumed all the feed in the lure crop before crops in the surrounding area were harvested. Scare cannons, while effective deterrents, sometimes were a source of problems when exploding propane ignited tinder-dry swaths. Feeding stations were by far the most effective and efficient preventative measure, often holding in excess of 30,000 ducks for six to eight weeks. Grain (barley) was delivered to the station daily and the amount of grain offered was adjusted to reflect the number of birds being fed, or to an assessed maximum of what the wetland could safely hold without creating significant potential for diseases.

When water levels and waterfowl populations were high in the 1970s, active feeding stations included Lac Cardinal, La Glace, Bear, Buffalo (west of La Glace), Beaverlodge, Magloire, Duck, Flat, Beaverhill, Whitford, Mantoken, Brosseau, McCullough, Bittern, Edberg, Buffalo, Erskine, and Kenilworth lakes. Over time, drought conditions and disappearing lakes resulted in the demise of several feeding stations, and programs in many areas now operate with only an active waterfowl-scaring program without any feeding stations or lure crops.

It is difficult to say whether the crop damage program minimized resentment of farmers towards waterfowl that damage cereal crops and encouraged a generally more favourable attitude to waterfowl and wetlands. In many areas, the CDC program elevated the value of waterfowl from a negative to at least a neutral value. If nothing else, the program prevented crop losses worth hundreds of millions of dollars. The program also demonstrated that the amount of

A TRUCK UNLOADING GRAIN AT A WATERFOWL BAIT STATION.
CREDIT: K. LUNGLE

AVIAN BOTULISM IN ALBERTA: HISTORY AND MANAGEMENT
[MARGO PYBUS]

Avian botulism is a naturally occurring food poisoning in many aquatic ecosystems throughout the world and in some years is a primary cause of mortality in waterfowl and shorebirds throughout the prairie regions of North America. No one knows how to prevent outbreaks and once a major outbreak gets going there is not much short of draining a lake that will change the natural course of the mortality event.

In Alberta, *botulinum* spores occur commonly in soils in aquatic environments. They are eaten regularly by dabbling ducks with no effect. However, under the conditions found in a duck after it dies, the spores can produce a potent toxin (poison), which interferes with nerve transmission to the muscles. When this toxin is eaten by a healthy bird (via fly maggots that have fed on a toxic carcass), the bird becomes paralyzed and eventually dies from drowning, suffocation, or predation. Generally, mammals are unaffected by the toxin and thus coyotes and foxes that eat sick or dead ducks usually are not at risk. Similarly, hunting dogs are not at significant risk—besides, good hunting dogs don't eat ducks!

A forest fire offers a direct analogy to a botulism outbreak. Not every lightning strike in a forest starts a raging inferno. Similarly, not every dead bird that falls into a wetland starts a die-off. Factors affecting the outcome of death in a marsh are extremely complex. In general, fluctuating water levels, high air and water temperatures, heavy contamination with botulism spores, and large numbers of waterfowl and shorebirds set the scene. Avian carcasses provide the spark, and later the fuel, for the wildfire to take off. However, if any of the factors is missing or is below the threshold level, the dead birds are simply resorbed into the marsh ecosystem.

The earliest record of large-scale waterfowl mortality in Alberta involves large numbers of dead birds at Lake Newell in the summer of 1924 and 1925.[26] The clinical signs, distribution of carcasses, and species composition were consistent with botulism poisoning. Blue-green algae, which also produce lethal toxins, were

present in large amounts. Unfortunately it seems we have not progressed much in the intervening years: a die-off at Pakowki Lake in 1994 appeared almost identical to the one at Lake Newell.[27]

The number of botulism outbreaks and the concerns of waterfowl managers come and go with the general water conditions on the prairies. For example, the mid-1980s were relatively dry years and some of the lakes with traditional problems were too dry to support waterfowl production or botulism outbreaks. With the return of moisture in the early and mid-1990s, botulism mortality soared in the prairie and parkland regions. In recent years, mortality occurred repeatedly on Beaverhill, Buffalo, Frank, Hay-Zama, Pakowki, Utikuma, and Whitford lakes. Usually, outbreaks are limited to a few hundred birds and occur primarily in dabbling ducks; however, large-scale waterfowl and shorebird losses were detected at Pakowki Lake in 1994 to 1997 (100s of thousands of dead birds) and at Beaverhill, Kimiwan, Stobart, and Utikuma in 1998 (thousands). An apparent increase in mortality in northern areas (Hay-Zama, Utikuma) since the early 1990s may reflect increased surveillance and control effort.

Management of botulism mortality traditionally focussed on breaking the cycle of toxin-passing from carcasses to live birds. Early detection and carcass cleanup were the order of the day. In 1991, Alberta developed a provincial Waterfowl Disease Contingency Plan, which formalized the traditional working arrangement among Alberta Fish and Wildlife, Ducks Unlimited Canada, and the Canadian Wildlife Service. [The Alberta Conservation Association later joined the partnership.] The cooperative effort worked well for identifying and responding to waterfowl mortality events. Ken Lungle, Brett Calverley, and Bruce Turner were instrumental in developing the plan for their respective agencies. A myriad of dead-duck-pickers from each agency carried out the plan.

In the late 1990s, the Alberta effort was expanded to a regional cooperative effort among various provincial wildlife agencies, federal agencies, and non-government organizations throughout the prairie region of Canada. The Botulism Working

Group of the Prairie Habitat Joint Venture of the North American Waterfowl Management Plan assessed the efficiency and efficacy of carcass collections, investigated factors associated with initiation/ perpetuation of outbreaks, and assessed the impact of losses on bird populations. In a nutshell, it was apparent that control measures were ineffective in large outbreaks. There was some evidence that Central Flyway mallard populations were adversely affected by the extensive botulism mortality during the mid-to-late 1990s when prairie regions were in the wet portion of the long-term moisture regime. The annual botulism mortality in these years was estimated to be more than a million ducks and shorebirds at each of three large prairie lakes: Pakowki in Alberta, Old Wives in Saskatchewan, and Whitewater in Manitoba. As the new century dawned, the prairies slipped back into a dry cycle and botulism losses declined significantly. However, when the moisture regime turns favourable again, botulism poisoning also will return to plague waterfowl in Alberta.

A WORK CREW HEADS OUT TO PICK UP BIRD CARCASSES IN THE HOPES OF REDUCING FURTHER BOTULISM BREAKOUTS.
CREDIT: M. PYBUS

281

crop damage in any given year is directly related to the type of harvest weather experienced rather than the size of local or provincial waterfowl populations. The CDC program levelled the playing field, providing a reasonable base on which other habitat programs could be delivered. In testament to the effectiveness of the program, agricultural producers continue to insist on establishment of feeding stations as an integral component of any major wetland habitat enhancement initiative.

Trumpeter Swans

At the turn of the 20th century, it was feared that the trumpeter swan, the largest of all waterfowl in North America, would soon become extinct. Dewey Soper, Chief Migratory Bird Officer in Edmonton from 1948-1951, reported on the status of the species and offered some eloquent retrospective comments about its plight:

"Owing to its great size and snow white plumage, it is a creature of rare and arresting beauty. One could never forget the nobility of beauty and form, and immaculate purity of dress displayed, as groups of these birds majestically wing their way against the azure of the sky in their native habitat. Not so long ago its fate seemed to be trembling in the balance...a royal entity whose total extermination seemed only a question of time. Was it inevitably to join the long line of vanished and vanishing species of the world? Too many rare and beautiful creatures had already taken that dark and fateful course."[28]

The trumpeter swan was exploited for its feathers during the height of the "fancy hat" trade of the late 1800s.[29] By the early 1900s, only a few small populations remained in isolated and remote areas of the west. During the 1920s and 1930s, efforts to preserve this species focussed on campaigns to solicit public information about the distribution of wintering

A FAMILY OF TRUMPETER SWANS.
COURTESY ALBERTA FISH AND WILDLIFE DIVISION

birds (the location of breeding birds was unknown). In addition, guardians were hired to protect those flocks that were endangered by possible human intervention.

It is unclear when officials first learned about trumpeter swans breeding in the Grande Prairie area, but in 1944, Dewey Soper reported 64 adults and 14 cygnets in the population. Following Soper's assessment, the Dominion Wildlife Service hired Bernard Hamm as Migratory Bird Officer to protect the Grande Prairie birds. Hamm collected biological information about the swans and sought the cooperation of local residents in conserving the species. His efforts, and those of others who followed, were clearly successful. As the bison is

282

J. (JOSEPH) DEWEY SOPER (1893-1982), CHIEF MIGRATORY BIRD OFFICER
[NYREE SHARP AND MARGO PYBUS]

Joseph Dewey Soper was born in 1893 on a farm near Guelph, Ontario. It was always his dream to visit the Arctic—the land of the Inuit and polar bears—and he read voraciously about arctic exploration. Soper realized his career aspirations required formal training, so he worked as a builder to earn enough money to study Zoology at the University of Alberta.

In 1920, Soper met his first true arctic biologist-explorer, R. M. Anderson, head of the Natural History Division of the Victoria Memorial Museum in Ottawa. In 1923, Soper was appointed naturalist for the federal Arctic Expedition of the National Museum of Canada. Several expeditions led to many "firsts", countless miles travelled, and hundreds of natural history collections. He was the first explorer to successfully cross Baffin Island and return, and three geographical features on the island are named for him: Soper River, Soper Highlands, and Dewey Soper Bird Sanctuary. But it was the mystery of the blue goose (a dominant colour phase of the snow goose) breeding grounds that captivated him and took him the longest to discover.[30] He started looking for the breeding grounds in 1924, but it was 1929 when he finally found a small colony with eight blue goose nests with juveniles. This nesting territory was set aside in 1957 as the 5500 sq. km federal Dewey Soper Bird Sanctuary.

Soper made his last expedition to the arctic in 1930-31 and then moved on to other challenges. In 1932, he began two years of fieldwork in Wood Buffalo National Park reporting on the status and life history of bison. In 1934, he accepted a position as the federal Chief

Migratory Bird Officer, a position he held for 18 years. He was initially stationed in the Prairie Region in Winnipeg (1934-48) and then the Yukon and western Northwest Territories in Edmonton (1948-51). Among other things, he set migratory game bird hunting seasons and bag limits, conducted biological surveys, identified concerns for waterfowl, expressed the need for sanctuaries, and wrote detailed natural histories of the national parks. However, he missed the freedom of field work and took early retirement in 1952 to pursue his passions as a naturalist.

BIOLOGIST DEWEY SOPER IN THE FIELD.
COURTESY UNIVERSITY OF ALBERTA ARCHIVES

283

In 1959, Soper met with Bill Fuller at the University of Alberta.[31] He expressed his desire to have his natural history specimens (over 300 specimens were collected each summer in the early years) remain in Alberta instead of going to Ottawa. In the following year, the University granted Soper an honorary Doctor of Laws and a research associateship in recognition of his zoological contributions to Canada. The Department of Zoology gave him a small honorarium and, in return, Soper spent the next 20 years depositing his natural history specimens in the university's Zoology Museum. He maintained his independence even as he passed his 70th birthday. He was repeatedly offered undergraduate assistants, but always declined.

Soper made astounding contributions to Canadian natural history: incredible miles travelled, publications and reports written, maps produced and corrected. He provided uncounted pen and ink sketches, paintings, photos, and meticulous field notes. He contributed notebooks, diaries, catalogues, memorabilia, and almost 2500 mammal and bird study skins to the University of Alberta.

Much of this material, including an album of hand-tinted colour photos, are safely preserved in the university Archives. His publications include over 130 scientific and natural history articles as well as *The Mammals of Alberta* (1964).[32] The latter remained the authoritative reference for several decades. He named subspecies of birds and mammals, provided baseline knowledge about the bison in Wood Buffalo National Park, and explored not only the arctic but also the prairies, the Rocky Mountain parks, and portions of Northwest Territories and Yukon. In 1971, the Federation of Alberta Naturalists made Dewey Soper their first honorary member, and in 1980 the Canadian Nature Federation granted him the Douglas H. Pimlott Conservation Award.

Despite these many achievements and an international reputation as explorer, naturalist, and writer, Dewey Soper was a quiet, unpretentious, and unassuming man. When living in the arctic he learned all he could about the Inuit way and lived there as a northerner rather than a visiting scientist. His life-long passion to explore and understand arctic environments sustained him even during his retirement. His legacy is truly amazing. J. Dewey Soper died in Edmonton on November 2, 1982.[33]

284

SOPER'S CAMP AT NEMISKAM NATIONAL PARK, CREATED FOR THE PROTECTION OF ANTELOPE IN 1914.
COURTESY UNIVERSITY OF ALBERTA ARCHIVES

revered in Wainwright, the trumpeter swan is entrenched as a symbol of civic pride in Grande Prairie and local landowners remain protective of swans on or near their property.

In the face of the wider species decline, the persistence of the population near Grande Prairie was associated with three factors: some swans nested in isolated areas while others were likely protected by local residents; the birds migrated through sparsely or non-populated areas in spring and fall; and a portion of their wintering habitat was fortunately protected within the confines of Yellowstone National Park.

In 1950, Ron Mackay was hired by the Dominion Wildlife Service to "find out how many trumpeter swans there are in Canada and where they are located".[34] These responsibilities soon brought him to the Peace River District, the only known nesting area for the species in Canada at that time. The trumpeter swan became a career passion for Mackay and he regularly censused the population from the mid-1950s to the mid-1970s. After Mackay, trumpeter swan management activities sequentially passed to Harold Weaver, Bruce Turner, Leonard Shandruk, and Gerry Beyersbergen, all of the Canadian Wildlife Service.

From 1950 to 1972, Mackay assessed the status of the population at 100 to 150 birds. Periods of growth followed invariably by declines indicated that density dependent factors and habitat limitations were affecting the population. This was not surprising since the principal wintering area was a short stretch of open water downstream of a dam along Henry's Fork of the Snake River in Idaho. The utility company operating the dam agreed to adjust the winter water releases to increase the amount of open water in winter, thereby increasing the amount of habitat available to the birds. The experiment was successful and the population entered a growth phase and pioneered new habitats. The Grande Prairie flock

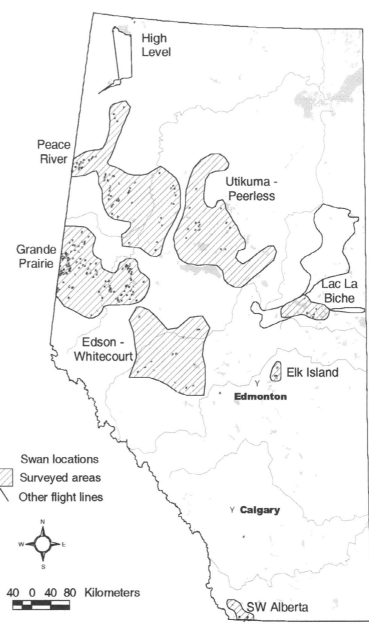

MAP OF CURRENT (2000) LOCATION OF TRUMPETER SWANS IN ALBERTA.
COURTESY G. BEYERSBERGEN

currently numbers over 600 and has expanded to other breeding areas including Peace River, High Level, Utikuma Lake, Peerless Lake, Edson-Whitecourt, Lac La Biche, and southwest Alberta.[35] Today, the total population in Alberta numbers about 1000, including a flock at Elk Island National Park that was successfully established by translocating swans from Grande Prairie.

285

TRUMPETER SWAN SURVEYS AND RECOVERY EFFORTS
[NYREE SHARP]

The Canadian population of trumpeter swans is a subpopulation of the Rocky Mountain population that breeds in scattered flocks in northeastern B.C., southeastern Yukon, southwestern Northwest Territories, and Alberta. From 1957 to 1995, the Canadian Wildlife Service (CWS) mounted annual fall aerial surveys for trumpeter swans (with some variation in effort). International trumpeter swan surveys were conducted in 1968 and every five years since 1975. The Alberta population makes up about 30% of the Canadian population and is spread throughout the province in lakes and marshes in the Aspen Parkland and Boreal ecoregions. The majority breed near Grande Prairie.

Despite short-term fluctuations, the Alberta population increased gradually since 1944 and benefitted from research and management attention, protective legislation, hunting restrictions, public education, land-use guidelines, and reintroductions. For example, research by the Alberta Fish and Wildlife Division revealed that human disturbance and habitat loss threatened the long-term survival of trumpeter swans in the Grande Prairie area. It was important to establish new foci of breeding swans in the province. Building on the experiences with Canada geese successfully returning to the areas where they fledge, a similar approach was taken with swans.

In a co-operative project with Parks Canada, CWS, and Friends of Elk Island National Park, the Fish and Wildlife Division released cygnets hatched from eggs from Grande Prairie into Elk Island National Park in 1987 (the species was extirpated there in the late 1880s). The birds had been overwintered in captivity at Camrose and released early in the season so they could spend most of the summer in the park and get thoroughly used to it. In the early 1990s, cygnets and adults, and later cygnets only, were captured annually at Grande Prairie and released directly into Elk Island. CWS continued the efforts until 1999. The first sign of success occurred when one male cygnet, translocated in 1987, returned to the park the next year and each year after until 2004.

Trumpeter swans are slow to reach reproductive age and setbacks in the Elk Island population have occurred, primarily from coyote predation of cygnets. However, swans released in the park have finally returned to breed and family groups of magnificent trumpeters can again be seen in Elk

Island and the adjoining Cooking Lake-Blackfoot provincial recreation and grazing area. It appears the population crossed a threshold in 2004 and is likely to be maintained without further releases so long as no new limiting factors come into play.

One of the goals of the transfers to Elk Island National Park was to establish a breeding population that would winter on the Pacific coast rather than in the limited tri-state region. A plan was hatched to use adults from Powell River, B.C., to guide Alberta youngsters to the west coast. Unfortunately it did not work and the concept of using west coast guide birds was abandoned. For a year or two, some cygnets from the park joined migrating tundra swans on their way to the west coast. However, this did not last either, as the Alberta birds succumbed to peer pressure and eventually followed the majority of coastal swans to Alaska. The over-mountain path to Elk Island Park was abandoned.

Recovery efforts have been largely successful in many parts of trumpeter swan range and most populations have increased in the last 50 years. The North American census in 2000 recorded 23,467 swans—an increase of 20,000 since 1968. The trumpeter swan, listed by the Committee on the Status of Endangered Wildlife in Canada (COSEWIC) as a species of *Special Concern* in 1978, was downgraded to a listing of *Not at Risk* in 1996. However, in Alberta the species is still considered *Threatened*, and on-going management is required to ensure persistence of the provincial population.

Provincial biologists in the Grande Prairie region continue to make land-use recommendations in decisions affecting public lands. However, these recommendations are not legislated and do not apply to private land (although their use is encouraged there as well). Recommendations include applying protective notations (PNTs) on many of the lakes in the Grande Prairie area and any new breeding lakes found on public land. In the U.S., the Trumpeter Swan Society, state and federal management agencies, and other conservation groups continue with attempts to expand the wintering destinations of the Rocky Mountain population, along with existing protection, survey, and management efforts.[36]

The Changing Role of Ducks Unlimited Canada

During their early days in Alberta, Ducks Unlimited Canada focussed on large wetland projects, particularly in southern Alberta where irrigation spillwater was available. The DUC philosophy was to impound water to create or restore large wetlands in turn increasing their capability to produce ducks. Large projects were funded provincially or cost-shared with the local government or the landowners; DUC provided the local share to a project if the stabilized water level met their criteria for waterfowl production.

Eventually, large wetland complexes were constructed in the irrigation districts including Tilley A and B reservoirs, Kinninvie, and Kitsim. Later, nesting islands, constructed before projects were flooded or on the ice in existing projects, were added to wetland projects based on relatively new evidence of high duck nesting concentrations and success on naturally inhabited islands. Charles Lacy was the first Provincial Biologist hired in the mid-1960s in Alberta (followed by Ernie Ewaschuk in the 1970s) complementing DUC's engineering and naturalist staff. Fred Sharp, George Freeman, and Bill Campbell were some of the other early and intrepid DUC employees. Another colourful character was Martin Jolitz, the "unquestioned boss" of the goose drives.

Smaller wetland projects were begun in the Hanna area under the guidance of Bruce McGlone. These projects captured spring runoff or summer rains behind small dams and created a stockwater source important for local ranchers, as well as a wetland for duck production. In the mid-1970s, Bruce came up with the idea of running siphons over these dams to keep the creek below alive during the summer. Again, this proved beneficial for both waterfowl and cattle.

By the early 1980s, declining nesting success appeared to be the primary factor reducing waterfowl recruitment throughout the prairie pothole region of North America. DUC scientists designed studies to corroborate this information, while habitat managers, led by Gary Stewart,

DUC Provincial Biologist, tested new land management treatments to improve the quality of upland nesting cover for ducks. DUC undertook a major shift in approach: no longer were engineering solutions the order of the day. Agrologists were hired and primary agronomic solutions adopted throughout much of the province. In southern Alberta, geographic features, cooperative landowners, and availability of water in Alberta's 13 Irrigation Districts dictated that traditional wetland impoundment projects continue. But even there, upland habitat improvements went hand in hand with wetland construction activities.

The new approach was incorporated into the goals of the North American Waterfowl Management Plan (NAWMP) to restore waterfowl populations to average sizes seen during the 1970s. New funds, administered by the U.S. Fish and Wildlife Service through the *North American Wetlands Conservation Act*, were instrumental in moving DUC into its era of habitat conservation. Local fund-raising was equally important and has been an on-going activity for DUC in Alberta since 1960. Alberta's hunting community, with a vested interest in waterfowl habitat, began to join DUC as volunteers for the cause. The local DUC-Dinner and Auction became the event to attend in many Alberta communities, and still is today.

Throughout the 1990s, DUC continued its focus on improving upland nesting cover. The Institute for Wetlands and Waterfowl Research (IWWR) conducted a comprehensive assessment of waterfowl habitat treatments. However, even as the Assessment Study ended, it was apparent that waterfowl did not respond to land-management treatments as originally predicted by the planning models. Further IWWR investigations revealed that the cumulative loss of wetlands over the past decade has been a major contributing factor to the inability of waterfowl populations to recover. The initial NAWMP plans assumed that protective government policies would provide stable base habitat conditions; however, continued wetland loss since 1989 is readily apparent. Therefore, beginning in 2004, DUC dedicates more

287

MORLEY BARRETT: A CAREER AND A HALF!
[FROM AN INTERVIEW WITH PAT VALASTIN, OCTOBER, 2004]

"I was born in Orangeville, Ontario in 1944, the baby of the family. My dad just loved hunting, fishing, and the outdoors. Going out with him and my brothers whetted my appetite for wildlife. Hockey also was a big part of our family. I had a hockey scholarship for the States, but I didn't take it. I decided to take the Fish and Wildlife Program at the University of Guelph instead.

"The first day I went to university I decided to go into wildlife biology. I did my Bachelor's and Master's at Guelph. Alex Cringan and Tony DeVos started the program there and along with Lars Karstad, head of Wildlife Diseases at the Ontario Veterinary College (on the University of Guelph campus), provided me support. My Master's work involved looking at the metabolism of pheasants under wintering conditions and ecological use of different habitat types. I looked at different cover types and some of the survival rates of released birds. It wasn't always that high. Like many biologists, the field work was one of my favourite parts.

"In 1969, there was an opening in Alberta, a one-year term position filling in as a Regional Biologist in Lethbridge while Gaylen Armstrong took a sabbatical in Africa. When he came back, I was given the opportunity to stay in Lethbridge, while Gaylen went to Edmonton. We had six regions in the province: the Southern Region went from Saskatchewan to B.C., roughly from a line north of Medicine Hat and Vulcan down to the Montana border. It was pretty much a one-man show in wildlife. There was the Fisheries Biologist (Gord Haugen), the Wildlife Biologist (me), and five or so enforcement officers scattered around the region. Frank Sommerville was the Regional Supervisor, Charlie Dougherty was the District Officer, and we had officers in Medicine Hat, Foremost, Claresholm, Pincher Creek and Cardston. We were allocated a budget, sort of, for field operations. We had an old Travel-All trailer and an old double-track skidoo and usually enough money to hire a summer student. Fish and Game clubs helped us a lot.

"I maintained my position in Lethbridge while I went back to university. I started working on a Ph.D. on pronghorns in 1975 with Bill Samuel at the University of Alberta. Samuel and Bob Hudson, also on my committee, were both very supportive. Pronghorns here are at the northern limits to their range and move huge distances trying to find snow-free areas. In 1982, many died following repeated heavy snowfall. I saw herds where virtually all the kids (young) and most of the males died. Most of the females resorbed or aborted their fetuses. The pronghorn travelled along vulnerable places like roads and railway tracks. Here they often ended up in a tunnel through really deep snow and a train or vehicle just mowed them down like bowling pins. I recall picking up truckloads of dead pronghorns. I worked closely with Dr. Gord Chalmers at the Department of Agriculture Regional Diagnostic Lab in Lethbridge.

"Meanwhile, in 1979, I formally left the Division and Lethbridge and went to head up the new Wildlife Biology Group at the Alberta Environmental Centre in Vegreville. I worked with people like Alex Hawley, Mike Dorrance, Larry Roy, and Jim Sommers. My favourite program was one on grizzly bears north of Hinton. We looked at the ecology, distribution, productivity, and habitat use of bears over a four-year period. John Nagy was a big part of that study. One of the most controversial and difficult programs, both biologically and politically, was work on humane trapping.[37] The Centre was selected by the Fur Institute of Canada, Environment Canada, and a consortium of agencies and provinces to do research involving behavioural work on how animals approach traps, mechanical work on the efficiency of traps, pathology work on the effects of traps on captured animals, and field work to test traps that met certain criteria of success. Initially, Gilbert Proulx was the lead research scientist on the project. Larry Roy and Jack Nolan were involved, too. The work led to all kinds of off-shoots such as trap replacement programs, new regulations regarding species-specific trap types used across Canada, as well as legislated provincial and international standards.

"In 1989, a partnership among federal and provincial agencies was setting up something called the Alberta office of the North American Waterfowl Management Plan (NAWMP). It was a new, extensive program with a lot of optimism and potential, and I became the Executive Director. Fish and Wildlife, Canadian Wildlife Service, and Ducks Unlimited Canada (DUC) were the big players. Agriculture, Environment, the Nature Conservancy of Canada, and others were also involved. My job was to bring them all together for the common good and develop provincial and specific delivery plans to benefit waterfowl. I took great comfort in helping people from the different agencies develop a close working team. The Buffalo Lake Moraine (near Stettler), one of the best Parkland waterfowl areas, was chosen as a 'first step' area, a flagship program in North America.

"After three years, change came again when I threw my hat in the ring for the provincial Director of Fisheries position. At NAWMP, I missed some of the operations in the Fish and Wildlife business. I remember the first day of the new job, being introduced to all the Fisheries staff, and wondering, "What am I doing here?" I had a burning interest in Fisheries, but damn little technical knowledge. But staff were very tolerant and supportive. In particular, Duane Radford, Regional Director for Southern Region, was a great help to me. I learned to appreciate the Regional Fisheries Biologists and I just sort of helped them chase their dreams in terms of management. We overhauled the whole East Slope trout fishery—Dave Christianson [Fish and Wildlife Division, Rocky Mountain House], Barry Mitchell [Trout Unlimited] and Carl Hunt [Fish and Wildlife, Edson] were highly involved. The same thing was done with regulations for walleye and pike throughout

the province. Mike Sullivan was so instrumental in his folksy way at public meetings and with the ministers of the day. He led everyone through his models and helped them understand what we were trying to achieve and why. The strong, tremendously knowledgeable staff and their effort and willingness to make changes resulted in reforms that helped recover a fishery failing due to over-exploitation.

"After three or four years, Jim Nichols [Assistant Deputy Minister of Fish and Wildlife] was promoted to Deputy Minister and I was chosen as the new ADM. The job of the ADM is largely care and feeding of ministers, but can be a very positive thing when you get on the same wavelength. There are a lot of demands, a lot of things to balance, a lot of political management issues. After a while and you've given it your best, it's time to move on.

"In 2002, Ducks Unlimited Canada called to see if I would consider being their Director of Regional Operations for the Prairie-Western Boreal (PWB) Region, which includes Manitoba, Saskatchewan, Alberta, the Northwest Territories, the Yukon and a little bit of northern British Columbia. I thought I was ready to retire,

289

FISHERIES BIOLOGIST MICHAEL SULLIVAN (SECOND FROM LEFT) SHARES HIS ENTHUSIASM FOR HIS WORK WITH A COUPLE OF YOUNG COLLEAGUES.
COURTESY ALBERTA FISH AND WILDLIFE DIVISION

but this was too good to miss. The prairies are the number one region in Canada for breeding waterfowl. The number two region is the Western Boreal Forest. In good years, up to 70% of the continental waterfowl population are produced in this region. I took the job.

"At DUC, we have outstanding staff, a commonness of purpose, and good supporting research and information. We're very unified and closely connected, streamlined and effective. All the work we've done on the ground with landowners, developing wetlands and other direct actions, established a good, credible reputation as a 'can-do' group. You can't win the battle quarter-section by quarter-section. You have to get out there and be effective on some big-picture stuff, like working with agricultural agencies to make programs water- and watershed-friendly. Such programs are sustainable and they're good for people, waterfowl, soil, and water.

"When I came from Guelph, it didn't take me long to be glad I'd made that decision. I had worked as a summer student in 1965 in Saskatchewan and I loved the west. So I took that one-year term position in Alberta. I worked with Gordon Kerr [Director of Wildlife], Dave Neave [Head of Wildlife Management], Bill Wishart [my mentor, but he takes every opportunity to disavow this], and Brent Markham [a classmate from Guelph who worked with Alberta Fish and Wildlife his whole career]. These were good people and I sure made the right decision. One I've never regretted."

RESTORING WETLANDS AND BUILDING PARTNERSHIPS IS WHAT DUCKS UNLIMITED CANADA DOES BEST AND PEOPLE LIKE MORLEY BARRETT MADE IT HAPPEN!
CREDIT: P. ROWELL

GEESE FLYING EAST AGAINST A PRAIRIE SUNSET.
COURTESY DUCKS UNLIMITED CANADA

resources to encouraging new government policies to protect native and naturalized wetland as well as upland habitats. In target areas, efforts are directed at protecting existing wetlands and quality upland nesting cover while restoring drained wetlands and converting marginal cropland back into land-uses that rely on perennial cover.

As of December 2004, DUC has secured or manages 566,500 hectares (1.4 million acres) of wetland and upland habitat in Alberta and protects an additional 342,000 hectares (845,000 acres), with an investment of $159.3 million alone between 1986 and 2003. In addition to its role in direct habitat conservation, DUC actively promotes voluntary adoption of sustainable land-use practices such as

planting winter wheat into standing stubble, improving grazing management plans, and retaining wetlands.

The success of the North American Waterfowl Management Plan set the stage for collaboration within the wildlife habitat conservation community. The Agriculture Policy Framework, jointly delivered by Agriculture and Agri-Food Canada and Alberta Agriculture, Food and Rural Development is another example of collaboration in which federal and provincial governments work closely with conservation organizations to promote environmentally, economically, and socially sustainable agriculture. The draft Wetland Policy of Alberta Environment is another promising initiative. This progressive policy will protect wetlands in the province and, through partnerships with conservation organizations, will strive to restore many wetlands already drained. A detailed inventory of existing and drained wetlands is already underway. Similarly, the Alberta *Water Act* is key to improving water quality and quantity in Alberta watersheds.

And finally, partnerships among governments, conservation organizations like DUC, and locally organized watershed groups can magnify the corresponding resources and use them more effectively to conserve and restore natural capital on a watershed basis throughout the province. Through the combined efforts of partnerships like these, there is optimism that challenges can be met and that once again waterfowl populations equal to those flying over the province during the 1970s will become a reality.

The Future of Waterfowl in Alberta

The crystal ball predicting the future of waterfowl in Alberta is about as clear as the fog that settles around the goose pits at dawn. There was a time during the 1970s when it seemed reasonable to predict harvestable surpluses of waterfowl for many generations. But, the history of waterfowl abundance over the past 100 years shows that nothing is certain. Quite surprisingly, waterfowl populations can and do change rapidly.

Overall, systematic and standardized methods used since 1955 provide a reliable picture of the distribution and abundance of waterfowl, variability in surface-water conditions, contribution of Alberta to continental waterfowl populations, and population response to variable wetland and upland habitat conditions. From 1955 to 1980, breeding duck populations in the productive prairie and parkland regions of Alberta averaged 5.3 million, varying from a low of 2.9 million in 1962 (a severe drought year) to an all time high of 7.6 million in 1974 (an extremely wet year). Alberta contributed over 25% of the continental mallard and the pintail populations. As well, over 20% of all ducks normally surveyed throughout the mid-continent occurred in Alberta.

Less than a decade later, the cumulative loss and degradation of breeding habitats finally overwhelmed the adaptive ability of waterfowl and populations declined. After 1980, the population size was markedly lower, averaging three million. Similarly, brood surveys indicated a long-term decline in the number of broods, mean brood size, and number of broods per 100 breeding pairs.

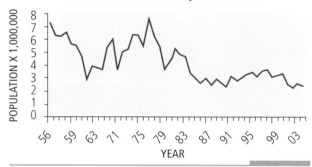

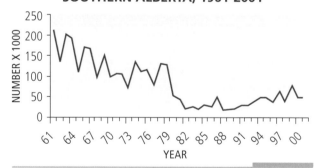

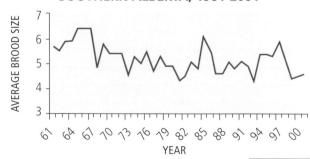

292

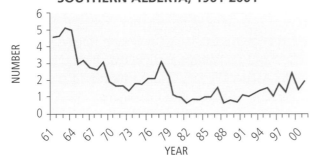

BROODS/100 BREEDING DUCKS IN SOUTHERN ALBERTA, 1961-2001

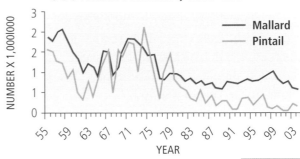

MALLARD AND PINTAIL NUMBERS IN SOUTHERN ALBERTA, 1955-2004

With the decline in population numbers, and the abundant evidence that reproductive performance of waterfowl breeding was impaired, jurisdictions were casting their lot with the North American Waterfowl Management Plan. They hoped that concerted habitat initiatives would fix the landscape so that the record low duck populations could once again grow to the abundance experienced earlier.

NAWMP successfully restored and secured considerable waterfowl breeding, migration, and wintering habitat. Duck population growth during wet years in the late 1990s demonstrated that NAWMP is working with the right formula; that when there is water, ducks, especially mallards, will capitalize on the availability of enhanced habitat and populations will rebound. However, unlike mallards, pintails that nest in the grasslands of southern Alberta do not show significant ability to respond with increased production. Similarly, lesser scaup populations that nest in the parkland and boreal forest areas have not responded to recent wetter conditions. The waterfowl management community recently embarked on critical research into lesser scaup biology and landscape influences to determine environmental or other factors that may be impeding lesser scaup recovery. The NAWMP recipe needs to be retooled to address the specific management requirements of these and other species.

On the opposite end of the spectrum, rising goose numbers present a different suite of management challenges. Hunters across North America appear unable to control rapidly growing snow goose populations and it remains to be seen if managers can reduce these populations before the inevitable population crash occurs. Similarly, an excess of locally breeding Canada geese is a significant management issue in almost every major urban centre in North America. Canada geese welcome the security and safety of environments created by humans in urban centres. Production is good, hazards are few, and living is easy! As conflicts between cantankerous geese and frustrated humans increase, the relative value of large populations and the habitat required to support them may decrease in the public psyche.

Crystal ball gazing does not have to be far-reaching to perceive potential concern for the mid-continental white-fronted goose population. This population from the Arctic interior is subject to exploitation and is a desired species taken in preference to other geese. Current harvest regimes evolved around an abundance of white-fronts: they are currently harvested at the maximum sustainable rate. However, this population is subject to "boom and bust" production depending on climatic conditions during nesting seasons. Population surveys already show declines in population numbers, both in terms of annual-trend and long-term averages. It is not unrealistic to speculate that a couple of bust production years could result in population

293

numbers below pre-determined thresholds that will trigger substantial harvest reduction.

If and when this occurs, the call for harvest reduction is likely to result in acrimonious international debate about where major harvest reduction should occur. Traditionally, harvest of white-fronted geese was 50% Canada (primarily Alberta and Saskatchewan) and 50% U.S. (Texas and Louisiana). However, due to harvest liberalizations over the past 15 years, the proportion of harvest changed to about 80:20 in favour of the U.S., with major harvest increases in Texas, Louisiana and Alabama. International concerns about population declines and calls for harvest reduction may meet resistance in Alberta and Saskatchewan until the harvest proportion again approaches 50:50.

There is early indication that the Arctic-nesting population of small Canada geese may be declining. Current efforts to maximize harvest of Canada geese to control growth of locally nesting large Canada geese may be adversely affecting the status of small Canada geese as these two groups of birds mix during harvest seasons. Waterfowl managers of the future, including those in Alberta, may be faced with the dilemma of having to reduce harvest of small Canada geese while still attempting to maximize harvest of large Canada geese to avoid human-wildlife conflicts.

The foregoing examples clearly indicate the future for waterfowl in Alberta is anything but clear! To compound the uncertainty, we may need to factor in the potential impact of climate change. In the near term, global warming may result in increased occurrences of extreme weather events. Extreme weather events can have significant impact on breeding populations, particularly those that nest in the Arctic. We may also see increased occurrences of drought phenomena, which have substantial impact on species like pintails. Gradual changes in ecozones may occur over the long term, with corresponding shifts in boundaries between prairies, parklands and boreal forests. As a result, we may see substantial shifts in areas of prime waterfowl production areas—with unknown implications.

Perhaps the only certainty about waterfowl in the future is that these species will respond to whatever habitat that we, as custodians of the landscape, provide for them. If we want the current diversity of viable and healthy waterfowl populations, we need to look holistically at the habitat base required to support these populations, a critical issue of regional, national, and international concern. Alberta is but an island, albeit a critical island, in the continental sea of waterfowl production, migration and wintering habitats. What happens on this island affects the rest of the continent, as actions on the rest of the continent affect our small world. In the end, the future of waterfowl and waterfowl habitat in Alberta may reflect the effort we expend on protecting this resource—a reflection of how and what we value and when.

MAJOR EVENTS IN WATERFOWL AND WETLAND MANAGEMENT IN ALBERTA

1911	The Minister of the Interior establishes a reserve on "all vacant lands in the vicinity of Ministik Lake".
1915	A federal Ministerial Order withdraws 14 lakes in Alberta from settlement. R.M. Anderson, zoologist with the Geological Survey of Canada, is given the task of assessing which sites are suitable for designation as bird sanctuaries.
1916	The *Migratory Bird Treaty* is signed by Great Britain (on behalf of Canada) and the United States.
1922	Market hunting is declared illegal.
1929	Inglewood Bird Sanctuary is established in Calgary.
1930s	Drought hits the prairies negatively impacting waterfowl habitat.

294

MAJOR EVENTS IN WATERFOWL AND WETLAND MANAGEMENT IN ALBERTA CONTINUED

1935   The first waterfowl surveys are conducted by a precursor of Ducks Unlimited.

1938   Ducks Unlimited Canada comes to Alberta.

1942   Migratory Birds Regulations are changed. Shooting permits are issued to those farmers losing grain to ducks.

1944   The first population census of trumpeter swans is conducted by Dewey Soper in the Grande Prairie area.

1947   General regulations are added to the *Migratory Birds Convention Act*—all legal shotguns must be plugged to a maximum of three shells in all provinces. The *Game Act* is amended so that plugged shotguns can be used for shooting of both upland and migratory birds. A new bird sanctuary is opened at Kirkpatrick Lake. The Dominion Wildlife Service is formed and soon becomes the Canadian Wildlife Service.

1955   The U.S. Fish and Wildlife Service introduces breeding population surveys using aerial censusing of waterfowl in Canada.

1961   Air-ground transects are implemented to correct for visibility bias in aerial waterfowl surveys.

1965   Canada geese are trapped and translocated to areas where they formerly occurred.

1974   A prairie-wide crop-damage compensation program is implemented to encourage waterfowl preservation and habitat conservation.

1979-1984   The Canadian Wildlife Service and the U.S. Fish and Wildlife Service implement the Stabilized Hunting Regulations Program in response to a decline in waterfowl numbers.

1986   Approximately 40% of original wetlands have been lost in Canada.

1995   The Migratory Bird Treaty is modified under the Parksville Protocol, to include, among other things, recognition of harvesting by First Nations peoples of Canada and Indigenous peoples in Alaska.

1999   A federal ban is placed on the use of lead shot for waterfowl hunting—the province does not follow suit with its own regulation.

References • CHAPTER 8

[1] Hill, J. 1999. An Exhilaration of Wings: the literature of birdwatching. Penguin Books, New York.

[2] Hewitt, C.G. 1921. The conservation of the wild life of Canada. Charles Scribner's Sons, New York.

[3] Ibid.

[4] Sherrington, P. 1975. Calgary's Natural Areas: A Popular Guide. Calgary Field Naturalists' Society, Calgary.

[5] Elphinstone, D. 1990. Inglewood Bird Sanctuary. Rocky Mountain Books, Calgary.

[6] Austin de B. Winter Fond, A W784, File 41, Glenbow Archives, Calgary.

[7] Elphinstone, D., op. cit. p. 22.

[8] Sherrington, P., op. cit. p. 107.

[9] Campus Calgary (website). October 2003. History of Inglewood Bird Sanctuary. http://www.campuscalgary.ca/birdschool_teacherresources.cfm#sanctuaryhistory

[10] Government of Canada (website). September 2003. Canada's Digital Collections. http://collections.ic.gc.ca/sanctuaries/alberta/ingelwood.htm

[11] Leitch, W. G. 1984. Response of the private sector. *In* Flyways: Pioneering Waterfowl Management in North America. U.S. Government Printing Office, Washington, D.C. pp. 15-17.

[12] Smith, A.G. 1971. Ecological factors affecting waterfowl production in the Alberta parklands. U. S. Fish and Wildlife Service, Resource Publication 98.

[13] Diem, K.L., and K.H. Lu. 1960. Factors influencing waterfowl censuses in the parklands, Alberta, Canada. J. Wildl. Mgmt. 24: 113-133.

[14] Leitch, W.G. 1978. Ducks and Men—Forty Years of Cooperation. Ducks Unlimited, Canada. Winnipeg. This work provides useful information on the beginnings of this organization.

[15] Ibid. ,pp. 54-61.

[16] Anderson, D. R. and K.P. Burnham, 1976. Population Ecology of the Mallard VI. The effects of exploitation on survival. U.S. Fish and Wildlife Service, Resource Publication 128.

[17] Patterson, J.H. 1978. Canadian Waterfowl Management Plan. Canadian Wildlife Service, Environment Canada, Internal Report, 88 pp.

18 Poston, B., D.M. Ealey, P.S. Taylor, and G.B. McKeating. 1990. Priority migratory bird habitats of Canada's prairie provinces. Canadian Wildlife Service Report, Edmonton, Alberta.

19 Leitch, R.W. 1983. Economics of prairie wetland drainage. Transactions of the American Society of Agricultural Engineering 26: 1465-1470.

20 Smith, A.G., and E. Bosniak. 1963. Factors affecting waterfowl populations and the production of young in the parklands of Canada: breeding ground study, Lousana Study Area. U.S. Fish and Wildlife Service, Unpublished Report.

21 Goodman, A.S., and S.P. Pryor. 1972. Preliminary study of the methods and rates of alteration of waterfowl habitat in the black soil zone of western Canada. Canadian Wildlife Service Report, No. 2578. Edmonton.

22 Canada/United States Steering Committee. 1986. North American Waterfowl Management Plan. May 1986. Canadian Wildlife Service, Ottawa and U. S. Fish and Wildlife Service, Washington, D.C.

23 Turner, B.C., G.W. Hochbaum, F. D. Caswell, and D.J. Nieman. 1987. Agricultural impacts on wetland habitats on the Canadian prairies. 1981-85. Trans. 52nd North American Wildlife and Natural Resources Conference. Pp. 1206-1215.

24 Watmough, M.D., D.W. Ingstrup, D.C. Duncan and H.J. Schinke. 2002. Prairie habitat joint venture habitat monitoring program phase 1: recent habitat trends in NAWMP targeted landscapes. Technical Report Series No. 391. Canadian Wildlife Service, Edmonton, Alberta.

25 Hay-Zama Wildlife Park Management Committee. 2002. Hay-Zama Wildlife Park Management Plan. Unpublished report prepared for the Department of Community Development, Parks and Protected Areas, Edmonton.

26 Munro, J.A. 1927. The waterfowl sickness at Lake Newell, Alberta, 1925-1926. Canadian Field-Naturalist 41:77-84.

27 Pybus, M.J. 1994. Botulism and blue-green algae poisoning at Pakowki Lake, 1994. Alberta Fish and Wildlife Division, Internal Report.

28 Soper, D. 1944. The Trumpeter Swan and its perpetuation. Canadian Wildlife Service, Unpublished Report No. 442. Edmonton, Alberta.

29 Munro, J. A. 1944. Conservation of the Trumpeter Swan in Canada. Canadian Wildlife Service, Unpublished Report No. 455.

30 Martin, C. 1995. Search for the blue goose: J. Dewey Soper; the Arctic adventures of a Canadian Naturalist. Bayeux Arts Incorporated and the Arctic Institute of North America, Calgary.

31 Burnett, J.A. 1999. A Passion for Wildlife: The History of the Canadian Wildlife Service. UBC Press, Vancouver.

32 Soper, J.D. 1964. The mammals of Alberta. Hamly Press, Edmonton, Alberta.

33 Several references were used, including Ealey, D.M. 1982. J. Dewey Soper–naturalist-explorer, 1893-1982. Alberta Naturalist 12: 189; Stevens, W.E., and G.W. Scotter. 1983. Joseph Dewey Soper, 1893-1982. Canadian Field-Naturalist 97:350-353; Scotter, G.W. 1982. Publications of J. Dewey Soper. Canadian Field-Naturalist 97:353-355; and http://www.thecanadianencyclopedia.com

34 Quote by Harrison Lewis in Burnett, J.A. 1999, op. cit.

35 Hawkings, J.S., A. Breau, S. Boyd, M. Norton, G. Beyersbergen, and P. Latour. 2002. Trumpeter swan numbers and distribution in western Canada. Waterbirds 25 (Special Publication 1).

36 Burnett, 1999, op. cit. Also James, M.L., and A. James. 2001. 2000 survey of the trumpeter swan (Cygnus buccinator) in Alberta. Alberta Fish and Wildlife Division, Species at Risk Report No. 5. Edmonton. http://www3.gov.ab.ca/srd/fw/riskspecies/pdf/SAR_5.pdf

37 More information on the humane trapping program is provided in Chapter 5.

296

Shared Stewardship

We are a unique kind of animal, conscious, able to reflect on what we do, gifted in wondrous ways. But at the same time, we are tied tightly to the surrounding ecological system from which our talents, physical and psychological, are drawn. Ignorance of our source and, too often, disdain for it, lie at the root of humanity's major predicament. Politics and economics continue to centre on the individual and the collectivity, on free enterprise and social welfare, neglecting ecological necessities of a higher order.

Humanity is clearly issue of the earth, physically from Nature's water, soil, air, sunlight, and plants; and psychologically from Nature's animal kingdom by some generative miracle. The fiction of Nature-as-Other can only be maintained with eyes firmly closed, denying ecological realities.

J. Stan Rowe [1990][1]

■ ■ ■

THE *third* ERA

OF FISH AND WILDLIFE MANAGEMENT IN ALBERTA:

Linking Fish and Wildlife to the Landscape through Shared Stewardship

Today, as we enter into a third era of fish and wildlife management, information and education about Alberta's natural resources, or as some call it, natural capital, has resulted in an increasingly better-informed public (Chapter Nine *Informing Albertans: Education, Information and Natural History Research*).

Hunter education programs, popular in the past and still today, have helped build an appreciation for wildlife and the outdoors in many Albertans. Similarly, in response to an ever-increasing urban audience, watchable wildlife programs have widened the scope to include non-consumptive uses such as photography, birdwatching, and backyard "naturescaping".

Like conservation education, endangered species management has grown in response to an increasingly aware and concerned public (Chapter Ten *Managing Species at Risk: Maintaining Alberta's Biodiversity*). The Fish and Wildlife Division took its first step towards a broader mandate in the early 1980s with the creation of a Non-game Branch. At first, this Branch was limited to recovery work for several endangered species, particularly those caught up in the national processes of the Committee on the Status of Endangered Wildlife in Canada (COSEWIC) and its associated recovery programs. Eventually, however, the Non-game Branch expanded its role, developing the present-day species assessment process that strives to rank the status of all vertebrate and invertebrate animals and vascular and non-vascular plants in Alberta. While there has been progress, there is still much to be done before management systems completely embrace a more comprehensive approach to measuring, monitoring, and maintaining all of Alberta's biodiversity.

Education and endangered species management have led to a growing appreciation for all things wild and all wild places. Yet, at the same time, the habitat available to this diversity is shrinking (Chapter Eleven *Habitat: Integrating Fish and Wildlife into Multiple Land-Use Planning*). The need for adequate fish and wildlife habitat protection was recognized in the 1970s and fish and wildlife biologists and researchers have spent the last three decades identifying in detail wildlife's relationship to their surroundings. However, efforts to fully integrate fish and wildlife habitat needs into other land-use planning processes have been limited in their success. Retaining wild species and wild spaces may be the biggest challenge facing conservationists in the 21st century. To meet this challenge, many fish and wildlife managers are turning to the philosophy of *shared stewardship*—making the case that taking care of entire ecosystems and the ecological processes they are a part of, including the production of drinkable water, breathable air and productive soil, is in the best interests of both wildlife and humans.

---

[1] Rowe, J. Stan. 1990. *Home Place*. NuWest Publishers Limited, Edmonton.

Chapter 9

INFORMING ALBERTANS: EDUCATION, INFORMATION AND NATURAL HISTORY RESEARCH

Don Meredith and Petra Rowell with contributions from Tom Bateman, Ron Bjorge, Sue Clarke, Cam Finlay, Joy Finlay, Bill Glasgow, Gordon Kerr, Margo Pybus, Martin Robillard, Bill Samuel, Heather Wheeliker and Pat Wishart

"History is a race between education and catastrophe."

RALPH WALDO EMERSON

Early Days

Throughout the past century, public information and education played an increasingly larger role in the management of fish and wildlife. During the first few decades, early visionaries like Ben Lawton, Austin de B. Winter, C. Gordon Hewitt and others, all too aware that natural resources were indeed exhaustible, spread their conservation message by whatever means they could. Eventually, public attitudes changed and there came about more tolerance for protected areas, game laws, and other measures imposed for the good of everyone to ensure the fish and wildlife resource was maintained in perpetuity.

Perhaps one of the earliest attempts at conservation education in Alberta was initiated in 1914 when the government, encouraged by the fledgling fish and game associations, organized a demonstration train. Full of mounted fish and wildlife specimens, the train travelled throughout the province in an attempt to interest Albertans in this resource. Copies of the *Game Act* (1907) were distributed because many folks were then unaware of this legislation. Overall, the train was met with great approval.

The newly created national parks were also a good source of fish and wildlife information. Park literature promoted the protection of natural landscapes and the fish and wildlife found within them. Federal, provincial, and local museums also provided wildlife information to a growing public audience.

A public fisheries information program in the early 1930s was designed to increase the interest in the commercial fishing industry during difficult

BEN LAWTON (FRONT ROW, SECOND FROM LEFT) AND OTHER DEPARTMENT OF AGRICULTURE STAFF
IN FRONT OF THE WILDLIFE DEMONSTRATION TRAIN. ca. 1914.
COURTESY GLENBOW MUSEUM (NC-4-59)

economic times. Exhibitions, demonstrations, public lectures, and radio shows provided information about the preparation, cooking, and nutrition of native fish species. The program was deemed highly successful as sales of fish increased. Later, fisheries interpretation would be enhanced by signage, publications, displays, and public tours offered at the various fish hatcheries in the province. Similar programs and exhibitions promoted trapping as an alternate income opportunity and a useful service to the public.

By the mid-1950s and early 1960s, wildlife biologists were following up on the philosophies and guiding principles set out by Aldo Leopold, who pleaded with simple eloquence and compassion for an understanding of our

connection to the land and for the rational management of our game species. New wildlife management strategies were proposed, including restricted hunting seasons and bag limits. Public support was needed for these new ideas. Early provincial biologists—Mitchell, Webb, Stelfox, Wishart and others—recall the many hours spent in public meetings explaining the antlerless (female) season for ungulates and other aspects of game management. These early public information sessions were often delivered to members of the Alberta Fish and Game Association (AFGA), representing many of the province's hunters and fishermen. Over the years, the Government also granted funds to the AFGA to carry out their own educational programs for Alberta's sportsmen.

THE VIEW INSIDE THE WILDLIFE DEMONSTRATION TRAIN.
COURTESY: B. STEVENSON

301

ENVIRONMENTAL EDUCATION AND INTERPRETATION IN ALBERTA'S PARKS
[SUE CLARKE]

Environmental education and interpretation of natural history in a park setting has been used throughout the last century to convey the importance of our natural resources. Public wildlife education was introduced in the federal parks early on. At first, Park Rangers carried out this duty unofficially during the normal course of their day. Then, in the early 1940s, rangers like Hubert Green lobbied the federal government for officially sanctioned wildlife education programs in Banff National Park. Green also authored several pamphlets and booklets geared towards educating the public about wild animals, their habits, and habitats. Museums, park interpretive centres, and a wide range of information programs and products continue this tradition in national parks today.

Through time, the field of natural history interpretation has grown. Today, interpretation is defined as "...a communication process that forges emotional and intellectual connections between the interests of the audience and the inherent meanings in the resource".[1] Songs, stories, puppets, hands-on displays, slide and video presentations, and theatrical productions convey the messages and bring natural science to people at a personal level. According to Ron Chamney (former Kananaskis District Interpretation and Environmental Coordinator), "If people don't identify with their environment, they will not protect it." Chamney, one of the first government interpreters in Alberta, believes that interpretation can enlighten the public while enhancing and protecting our natural resource. Likewise, Brad Tucker (Program Development Coordinator for the Royal Tyrrell Museum Cooperating Society) believes that a function of interpretation is to provide an understanding of ecology and our impact on it.

In Alberta's provincial parks, seasonal interpreters were at work unofficially as early as 1974. Chamney was originally hired to deliver interpretive programming at Dinosaur Provincial Park under the job classification of Equipment Operator! As awareness, understanding, and scientific knowledge of the significance of wildlife preservation and conservation grew, public education messages were increasingly specialized and formalized. Within the provincial Parks Division, these services evolved into the Environmental Education and Interpretation Section in 1975 with Jim Butler and Ed Andrusiak in charge. Initially, interpretation occurred on a limited basis in only a few provincial parks; however, it later became a province-wide program centred at site-specific locales.

For more than 25 years, and despite numerous departmental changes and many years of fiscal restraint, interpretive programming has remained a priority in provincial parks. Interpretive programs are delivered throughout Alberta in the summer at major provincial parks like Writing-on-Stone, Dinosaur, Peter Lougheed and Bow Valley, and other locales with significant cultural, historical, or heritage interest.

A FISH AND WILDLIFE EDUCATIONAL DISPLAY AT THE 1956 SPORTSMEN'S SHOW IN EDMONTON.
COURTESY B. STEVENSON

Hunter Training

After the Second World War, a large supply of surplus firearms available at a low price made recreational hunting an attractive activity throughout North America. Many hunters, however, were not familiar with basic firearm safety or animal identification, raising concern among farmers and the non-hunting public. Governments throughout Canada and the U.S. responded by creating hunter safety courses, the first of which was developed in New York State in 1949. Some of these programs became a prerequisite for obtaining a hunting licence.

Early in 1963, Minister Norman Willmore, Deputy Minister Eric Huestis, and Director of the Fish and Wildlife Division Curt Smith moved to forge a program on hunting safety for Albertans. Squadron Leader Paul J. Presidente, the Commanding Officer of the Royal Canadian Air Force Survival School at Namao,

was hired to head up the program. Six months of research and writing led to a training manual and course program, which consisted of animal and habitat recognition, gun safety, first aid, survival, and tips to increase hunting success.

When presented to the AFGA in February 1964, response was mixed. Many ideas in the manual were new and some hunters thought the program was too involved. Later that year, a second, more acceptable manual was completed. It featured a wide range of topics, including sections on game fish, raptors, archery, fly-tying, waterfowl identification, and mammal hoof and paw prints. In addition, a hunter instructor course, additional training aids, and wallet-sized identification cards for qualified instructors were introduced. By this time, 283 instructors and 736 students had qualified through the program. Although only one year old, the Alberta program received an Award of Merit for outstanding

PAUL PRESIDENTE (LEFT) AND OTHER DIGNITARIES INCLUDING MINISTER HENRY RUSTE (RIGHT)
AT AN EARLY HUNTER EDUCATION COURSE, ca. 1967.
COURTESY B. STEVENSON

303

achievement from the U.S. National Rifle Association in 1965.

After two and a half years, 4000 students and 763 instructors had passed the hunter training courses conducted in 164 different centres in Alberta. The course took five evenings to complete and required students and instructors to pass the written examination with 70% and 85%, respectively. Course subjects were expanded to include game management, hunting rules and regulations, the *Game Act*, general prohibitions, safe gun-handling, sportsmen's responsibilities, hunting courtesy, prevention of forest fires, care of firearms, a code of ethics, hunting hints and techniques, first aid and survival, archery techniques, as well as species, habits, and habitat identification of big game, upland game birds, waterfowl, predators, and fish of Alberta. The course used 26 films and 200 colour slides during 22 hours of instruction. The legal age to hunt in

Alberta, set at 16 years of age since 1950 and lowered to 14 in the company of parent or legal guardian after 1955, now also required students to take the hunter training course and pass the exam of 100 questions.[2] Successful students received certificates and crests.

Hunter training staff took part in many television, radio, and public engagements to promote the program. Even politicians were targeted. Dennis McDonald recalls: "A course was prepared by several Fish and Wildlife staff specifically for MLAs called *The Basic Principles of Fish and Wildlife Management*. This course was given over several weeks in the evening for all interested MLAs and was well received by the 50% plus who took advantage of it." Biologists also made several noon-hour presentations at the Legislature Building. Locally, several Fish and Wildlife Officers like Lew Ramstead in Ponoka and Wayne Brown in St. Paul, delivered the program to communities around the province making hunter training in Alberta, on a per capita basis, the most extensive program of its kind in Canada.[3]

Conservation Education

As the hunter training program grew, so too did the need for broader conservation information and education programs. To meet this need, in 1974, the Extension Services Branch of the Fish and Wildlife Division was formed in Edmonton. Its goals were to deliver the hunter training program, and to increase public knowledge and understanding of fish and wildlife management. By 1976, Extension Services had nine permanent staff positions including a Branch Manager (Dennis McDonald), Resource Education Biologist (Norm Gaelick), six Hunter Training Officers (Lionel Dunn, Tom Bateman, Dave

Paplawski, Jo-Anne Hewko, George Diduck and Leo Ferrar) and a Chief Hunter Training Officer, C. Red Hasay. Hasay's many ideas are credited with guiding the program for many years. Additional assistance came from Wally West, the Division's Public Communications Officer, and Sylvia Bieneck, an artist who along with Lionel Dunn provided much of the artwork for course and communication materials.

Conservation education has long been a component of the Alberta school system. Many Alberta schools used the Conservation and Hunter Education course as part of their curriculum, and teachers often asked Fish and Wildlife staff to assist on field trips. Wilderness survival, fish and wildlife identification, firearms safety, archery, outdoor cooking, and map and compass reading

HUNTER EDUCATION PROGRAM LOGO.
PROVINCIAL ARCHIVES OF ALBERTA (PA 5626)

A HUNTER EDUCATION TRAINING CERTIFICATE WAS ISSUED TO THOSE WHO SUCCESSFULLY COMPLETED THE COURSE.
COURTESY B. STEVENSON

HUNTER EDUCATION
MANUAL COVER AND BROCHURE
COURTESY ALBERTA
FISH AND WILDLIFE DIVISION

became so popular that in 1970 the Division established an outdoor camp at Narrow Lake, near Athabasca. Schools and other groups booked three-day time slots to attend the camp, receive basic outdoor and recreational instruction, and practise some of the activities and course topics. Students were provided with the opportunity to cook their own food over an open fire and sleep in a plastic shelter they built for themselves.

In November of 1972, a second camp was established at Alford Lake, just west of Caroline. The original camp at Narrow Lake was closed and the site turned over to the Alberta Fish and Game Association. Camp programs continued to be very popular with schools, scouts, Junior Forest Wardens, military personnel, church groups, aboriginal groups, and others. But travel was a problem for some; so in 1983, a portable camp was developed and operated during the spring and summer months, first at Sharples Creek in the Porcupine Hills, then later at McGillivray Creek north of Blairmore. About the same time, the Extension Services Branch led the formation of an Interdepartmental Committee on Environmental Education with the Alberta Ministry of Education in an effort to increase the fish and wildlife conservation component taught to students inside the classroom.

Between 1964 and 1975, nearly 46,000 successful students completed the hunter training course and countless other people received fish and wildlife conservation education messages in written materials, oral presentations, and one-on-one discussions with staff and volunteers. Working together with Division officers and biologists, extension staff set up public displays and delivered illustrated lectures to schools, service clubs, Scouts and Guides, fairs, sportsmen's shows, and other public meetings, in addition to the traditional

presentations to rod and gun and fish and game clubs. Besides photographic slides and brochures, staff used a host of props to enhance their presentations, including a variety of skulls and mounted specimens, and a fur kit—a suitcase filled with a selection of skins from various furbearers in the province. Though programs have waxed and waned over time, similar educational activities continue today, with informal delivery by staff in local offices or volunteers from non-government organizations and associations.

Over the years, a number of other courses were developed to assist traditional fisheries and wildlife user groups. A turkey seminar at Claresholm corresponded with the first hunting season for wild turkeys. Similarly, white-tailed deer hunting seminars were held in Calgary, Stettler and Edmonton. A first-time hunter program paired up new hunters with a mentor and a compulsory hunter test was implemented for suspended hunters. Archery and firearms courses were provided for members of the public, instructors and government staff. A major effort to communicate with trappers involved a Trapper Improvement Training Course held in conjunction with Alberta Advanced Education, as well as the production of several articles on fur trends and humane trapping methods written in Cree. During 1975, Fur Coordinator Dave Unger alone attended 40 meetings associated with fur industry activities.[4]

In 1983, the Alberta Conservation and Hunter Education course was selected by a panel of experts as the most outstanding of its kind in North America. A rising interest in the fishing resource led to the separate development of the Alberta Fishing Education program in 1988. And in 1989, a huge undertaking at the Edmonton Convention Centre celebrated 25 years of hunter

305

THE FIRST FEMALE HUNTER TRAINING OFFICERS IN CANADA
In 1975, a reclassification of positions in the Hunter Training conservation program led to the two Hunter Training Clerk positions becoming Hunter Training Officers (Fish and Wildlife Officer I-II). This change made Mrs. J. Hewko and Miss L. Badgeley, the first female Hunter Training Officers in Canada.

training and conservation education in Alberta. Despite these apparent successes, the programs and staff of the Extension Services Branch were downsized throughout the economic downturn of the 1980s and 1990s. Today, hunting in Alberta continues to be a very safe recreational activity, a lasting tribute to Alberta hunters and to the ongoing success of the Alberta Conservation and Hunter Education programs, as well as the thousands of volunteer instructors who delivered it.

Privatizing Hunter Education

With the 1990s budget-tightening and headlong drive to reduce government deficits, Bob Gruszecki, President of the Alberta Hunter Education Instructors' Association (AHEIA),

proposed to provincial authorities that the Association take responsibility for administering all the fish and wildlife conservation education programs. This proposal was eventually accepted, and on April 1, 1996 these programs, including the camp programs, were turned over to the AHEIA.

The next years were very exciting as enough money was raised to purchase a 14,000-square-foot building that became the Calgary Conservation Education Centre for Excellence. An Edmonton Conservation Centre for Excellence was also soon opened. A couple of years later, the Calgary Trap and Skeet Club asked AHEIA to take over their property near Calgary and the Calgary Firearms Centre was added to the

CONSERVATION EDUCATION SERIAL PUBLICATIONS

In 1958, Norman Willmore, Minister of the Department of Lands and Forests, proudly announced a new bi-monthly publication entitled *Land-Forest-Wildlife*, a periodical with the goal of informing the public about the "state of Alberta's renewable resources; its land, its forest cover, and the mammals, birds, and fishes it contains". Further goals were to "provide enlightenment and understanding of the duties of the Department and its administration of these resources…and to…enhance the liaison that exists between people and their government". Willmore also stated: "the continued interest [of the public] in the subjects of our stewardship can be our greatest asset". In 1967, the provincial Parks Section was raised to the level of a full Division and recognized as such by addition to the name of the publication, which became *Lands-Forests-Parks-Wildlife*.

For thirteen years, *Land-Forest-Parks-Wildlife* was small in size, but huge in its content and impact. The publication provided a treasure chest of information about any and all aspects of natural resource management, including personal stories and incidents, biology basics, legislative regulations and their inevitable changes, enforcement activities, survival skills, and outdoor training opportunities. W.H. MacDonald, publicity officer for the Department of Lands and Forests and editor for the first nine years, set the standards which subsequent editors W.A. West and C.E. Haglund upheld and expanded. [MacDonald also published specific booklets for public education on topics such as *Fishing in Alberta*.]

Subsequent government periodical publications regarding natural resources in Alberta have not had nearly the lifespan or success of *Land-Forest-Parks-Wildlife*. *Land for Living* was short-lived (one or two years) in the early 1970s and *Alberta Conservationist*, which made a great start in 1972, was unable to generate the support to continue beyond 1973.

Non-government periodicals met with greater success. Ducks Unlimited Canada's *Conservator* was in its 25th volume at the time of this writing. Although it contains articles of local and provincial interest interwoven with basic biology and conservation messages, it is published on a national scale for the thousands of DUC members and partners. As well, *The Alberta Game Warden*, initiated in 1987, continues to provide an informative and entertaining look at some of the issues Fish and Wildlife Officers encounter during the course of their work. In 2003, the Alberta Conservation Association launched *Conservation*, a semi-annual magazine aimed at informing "hunters and anglers, conservation groups, government, industry, academia, landowners, and citizens of Alberta". One can only wish the editors success in this newest venture of providing outdoor and conservation information to residents of the province.

growing number of facilities available to promote conservation principles.

In 2002, all camp operations were brought together at the Alford Lake Conservation Education Centre for Excellence. The camp was completely re-built by AHEIA, with enough winterized cabins to accommodate 70 people. The facility includes world-class shooting ranges, archery ranges, map and compass courses, as well as excellent fishing opportunities and hiking trails. The camp is very popular and often is booked more than a year in advance. In June 2002, the federal Justice Department asked AHEIA to administer the Canadian Firearms Safety (CFS) Courses in Alberta. These programs relate directly to hunting activities and safety; so an agreement was negotiated and the CFS courses were added to AHEIA's programs.

The provincial government further devolved its fish and wildlife education component when it contracted the preparation and publication of the hunting, fishing and trapping regulations to a private company in 1996. A tremendous commitment of time, the annual production of these guides had been the primary responsibility of the information unit within the Fish and Wildlife Division. After 1996, production costs, previously borne by the Fish and Wildlife Division, were offset by the contractor through the sale of advertising space in these commercial publications. Government retained an oversight role to ensure legal and factual accuracy.

The Fish and Wildlife Division was then able to turn its attention to other educational initiatives. In 1996, it became one of the first Alberta government agencies to launch a Web site. *Hunting in Alberta* provides accessible information about recreational hunting in the province and explains what can be hunted and how. *Fishing in Alberta* soon followed. The Division's fishing pages contain, among other things, a quick and easy identification quiz to learn the difference between a bull, rainbow, and a brook trout (and any other sport fish species found in Alberta). Information on the bull trout, Alberta's provincial

fish and an endangered species, raises public interest in fishes as well as awareness of our diminishing fish resources. The web sites are well received by Albertans and people around the world. They provide an inexpensive but effective means of distributing information. More recently, the *Species at Risk* and *Wildlife Disease* web sites have become well used by government staff and the public.

Fisheries interpretation also has a rich history in Alberta starting with R.B. Miller and carried on by Martin Paetz. In addition to the many scientific papers each wrote, they both went out of their way to explain and interpret the details of fishes and fish habitats in Alberta to anyone who would listen. Paetz was particularly proud of *Fishes of Alberta*, which he co-authored with Joe Nelson from the University of Alberta. Following in their footsteps, Mike Sullivan's recent book *Fish of Alberta* goes one step further in bringing readable fish information and natural history details to public notice.

The Sam Livingston Fish Hatchery, nestled on the Bow River near downtown Calgary, also has a long history of public education. The hatchery currently produces up to three million trout annually for release into accessible waterbodies across the province.[5] Visitors can see millions of fish in stages from eggs to fingerlings. A new visitor centre will incorporate hatchery operations with innovative hands-on interactive displays to engage the visitor in a multi-faceted learning experience.

Adjacent to the hatchery, the award-winning Pearce Estate Park Interpretive Wetland is an Alberta Centennial Legacy Project scheduled to open in spring 2006. This interpretive wetland is one of the largest projects of its kind in Canada, the result of a successful partnership among industry, non-profit conservation organizations, governments, and a small army of volunteers and supporters. It will contain a series of ponds, streams, and backwaters lined with natural vegetation and populated with a multitude of aquatic species. It is destined to become the

307

A VOLUNTEER LEADS A GROUP OF CHILDREN THROUGH AN EDUCATIONAL PROGRAM AT THE SAM LIVINGSTON FISH HATCHERY.
COURTESY SAM LIVINGSTON FISH HATCHERY

the public and help them identify a wide variety of wild species in the province. The full-color, poster-sized brochures were easy to display on a classroom wall and were particularly popular with teachers and students alike. Youth groups, naturalists, and outdoor education instructors also found them useful.

At first, posters featured game animals—Cloven-hoofed Animals, Upland Game Birds, Puddle Ducks, Diving Ducks, Fishes of Alberta—but later, other brochures included Large Hawks and Eagles, Rabbits and Large Rodents, Weasels, Leaves and Trees, and Invertebrates. Lionel Dunn, Sylvia Bieneck, and Andrew Raszewski produced the original artwork. Written text about species habits and habitats appeared on one side, and more detailed descriptions of life histories and management on the other. Despite a minor public outcry at their loss, the series is now out-of-print. However, its content is available on the Division's Watchable Wildlife web site (www3.gov.ab.ca/srd/fw/watch).

Between 1982 and 1984, the Fish and Wildlife Division helped the Canadian Wildlife Federation develop a Canadian version of *Project*

primary information and education tool for wetland interpretation in Alberta. Trails and signs will provide self-guided learning opportunities as well as an outdoor classroom for organized school programs. Combined, the Sam Livingston Fish Hatchery, the Visitor Centre and the Pearce Estate Park Interpretive Wetland make up the Bow Habitat Station.

Public Information—Reaching Out to a Broader Audience

During the late 1970s, it was apparent that hunters, trappers, and fishermen were not the only ones interested in wildlife and the places they live. Responding to a broader audience, the Fish and Wildlife Division created a series of brochures, later titled *Alberta's Watchable Wildlife*, to inform

HINTERLAND WHO'S WHO

Similar to the *Watchable Wildlife* material, the *Hinterland Who's Who* series was developed and delivered by the Canadian Wildlife Service across Canada. This series was extremely popular and included radio and television clips. The series was resurrected, updated, and given a more upbeat tone early in the 21st century and the haunting yet recognizable introductory tones of the background music can again be heard on TV and radio since 2004. As popular as ever, it is evident that the public thirst for such information continues to grow.

BIRD WATCHING AT THE WEIR AT BEAVERHILL LAKE NATURAL AREA.
CREDIT: H. STELFOX

309

to use these "Monday-morning-ready" activities that required minimal preparation. The guidebooks, lesson plans, and activity manuals were designed to reduce teacher workloads, rather than add to them. In 1990, The International Convention of Project Wild Coordinators was hosted in Lethbridge at the Lethbridge Community College. Martin Robillard recalls: "This was likely the best single event Alberta Fish and Wildlife Division ever put together where delegates from North America were invited." Although initially very popular, Project WILD was not continued in Alberta, despite its continuing success in other jurisdictions across Canada and the U.S.

WILD (Wildlife in Living Design), a U.S. program intended to introduce wildlife topics to classrooms. Activities were designed to help teachers use wildlife as a motivator and example in presenting their regular curriculum: "…rather than counting apples and oranges, let's count rabbits and ruddy ducks." The Division held workshops to show teachers how

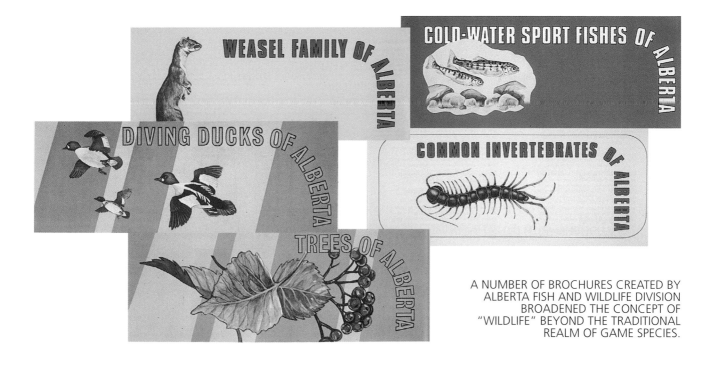

A NUMBER OF BROCHURES CREATED BY ALBERTA FISH AND WILDLIFE DIVISION BROADENED THE CONCEPT OF "WILDLIFE" BEYOND THE TRADITIONAL REALM OF GAME SPECIES.

By the late 1980s, increasing attention was being given to urban wildlife and urban audiences. Information on programs aimed at enhancing the exposure of urban residents to wildlife in Alberta and elsewhere was examined by staff of a new Watchable Wildlife Section in the Wildlife Branch. Under the combined efforts of Harry

BIRD WATCHING AT THE COLD LAKE PROVINCIAL PARK VIEWING PLATFORM.
CREDIT: H. STELFOX

Stelfox, Doug Culbert and Don Meredith, programs set out to encourage the public to enjoy Alberta's wildlife in non-consumptive ways, such as birdwatching, wildlife photography, and attracting backyard wildlife. The program resulted in production of the *Alberta Wildlife Viewing Guide* which details 60 of the best wildlife-viewing sites throughout Alberta, as well as *Alberta's Watchable Wildlife: A Directory of References*.

A comprehensive 80-page manual titled *Developing Your Wildlife-Viewing Site* was prepared as a step-by-step guide for communities and other organizations to develop their own wildlife-viewing sites. The Watchable Wildlife Program complemented this manual with a series of low-cost interpretive signs for over 100 different wildlife species and natural history topics. Electronic copies of these signs are still available on the Fish and Wildlife Division's Watchable

Wildlife web site. The *Watchable Wildlife Calendar* was one of the most popular products to come out of this group. The calendar was sprinkled liberally with seasonal natural history notes, viewing tips, and engaging photos of plants, animals and landscapes found in Alberta. Using images voluntarily provided by amateur photographers, the calendar was an instant success and was offered to wildlife and natural history clubs for fund-raising purposes.

In 1990, the Watchable Wildlife Program conducted a survey of Alberta residents regarding their wildlife viewing interests and activities: 64% of Albertans (approx. 1.15 million) participated in wildlife viewing activities either in their backyards or local park, or on trips farther away from home. Surveys since this time indicate similar high participation and interest values.

DID YOU KNOW?

In 1990, Albertans spent an estimated $350 million on various types of wildlife-viewing equipment and guides and an additional $583 million on expenses related to wildlife-viewing trips.[6]

Education and Information in the Conservation Community

Throughout the century, many conservation organizations played a strong role in providing the public with conservation information and education. Ducks Unlimited Canada (DUC) has a long and successful history of combining natural history observations, public interest in wildlife, and sound scientific evidence into products and materials that are easily accessible to a wide range of audiences. The award-winning *Greenwing* program, aimed at children up to 17 years old, brings youngsters face-to-face with wetlands, their inhabitants, and their problems. It was also a favourite program of many DUC staff. Dennis McDonald recalls: "George Freeman of Strathmore spent his career in Alberta with Ducks Unlimited and, throughout that period (1950s-1980s) and into his retirement, he has probably put more children through the *Greenwing* Program than anyone else in the prairie provinces!"

Species identification, habitat needs, and the interconnectedness of wetland ecosystems are the primary focus of all DUC programs. A recent winner of the prestigious Emerald Award, DUC made perhaps its greatest mark on the landscape by increasing wetland awareness and understanding for thousands of people. Many Albertans became more familiar with marshes, lakes, ponds, sloughs, and rivers because they visited a DUC facility, project site, demonstration, lecture, presentation, or information booth. Many also read *Conservator* (or in French, *Conservationniste)* or *Puddler* magazines, or the many other publications and web-based conservation education products available from DUC.

Similarly, the conservation group Trout Unlimited Canada (TUC) distributes materials regarding the health of coldwater fishes and their habitats. The *Yellow Fish Road* is perhaps their best-known program and focusses youth-oriented environmental action aimed at increasing awareness about fishes and watershed issues. TUC also works to identify current and potential threats to cold waters in the interests of improved understanding of such hazards. With its national office in Calgary, TUC expends considerable energy in Alberta. For example, the popular "fish rescues", aimed at salvaging fish put in jeopardy when irrigation canals are dewatered each fall in southern Alberta, serve to educate and inform.

311

ENVIRONMENTAL EDUCATION—GOING BEYOND WILDLIFE

Starting in the 1970s, not only was the public becoming more informed about all wild species, they were also more aware of a broader suite of environmental issues beyond just fish and wildlife. In response to this increasing public awareness and desire for information, in 1976 the provincial government added an Education Branch within the Department of Environment. The Education Branch would provide products to educate a wider audience on a wider range of environmental topics involving air, land, water, waste, and pollution. When housed in the same Department (Environmental Protection) as the Fish and Wildlife Division in 1992, the Education Branch broadened its mandate to increase public awareness of fish and wildlife and their habitat. In 1994, the *Alberta's Threatened Wildlife* series was launched with teacher's guides accompanying a series of colourful brochures on the northern leopard frog, bull trout, and trumpeter swan. In addition, videos were produced on bull trout and walleye and a number of other species were added to the growing list. This series was well received then and is still in use today.

Over the years, a large number of brochures concerning different programs or species were printed or posted to the Environment web pages. Currently, the Education Branch again resides in a department separate from the Fish and Wildlife Division. Although the Education Branch still distributes fish and wildlife educational material, it no longer has a mandate to present or update fish and wildlife educational material. Instead, it is focussing its attention on producing materials relating to the growing issues of air, water, land protection, and waste reduction.

Alberta has always had a strong natural history community to collect and disseminate information about the province's wildlife and wild spaces. Outstanding individuals, like Elsie Cassels McAlister, Kerry Wood, W. Ray Salt, and A.L. Wilk and more recently, Joy and Cam Finlay, spent entire lifetimes learning about the province's flora and fauna and sharing that knowledge with others. Unusual bird sightings, in particular, have been noted throughout the century. For example, about 1950, Mrs. P. Cox, Secretary of the Edmonton Bird Club, was the first person to report sighting a white-breasted nuthatch in Alberta. This species was common to the northwestern states and southeastern B.C., but was not yet common in Alberta.[7] Salt and Wilk would eventually undertake the collection of many such sightings, producing the comprehensive *Birds of Alberta* in 1958, a reference and field guide still very much in use today.[8]

While many of the early naturalists focussed their efforts on vertebrates and plants, efforts were also made to document the province's invertebrate fauna. Edmund Murton Walker, entomologist of the Royal Ontario Museum, travelled to Alberta in 1913. During his visit, Walker and an associate described "ice-bugs" (Grylloblatta) on Sulphur Mountain, the first time a new Order of insects had been found in Canada. Grylloblatta species have since been found in the northwestern U.S., Russia, and Japan.[9]

Today, field guides depicting the many butterflies, dragonflies, damselflies, beetles, pill bugs, sow bugs and other insects and spiders are readily available and many of these species are now recorded as part of May Day Species counts. John Acorn, a.k.a. the *Nature Nut*, is the latest in a long lineage of esteemed entomologists and wacky bug guys from Alberta. Acorn's unique and disarming style can make anyone forget their fears and misgivings as he weaves his stories in song and rhyme in syndicated television programs aired around the world. Robin Leech, a.k.a. "spiderman", retired from the Northern

ELIZA (ELSIE) CASSELS McALISTER AND THE ALBERTA NATURAL HISTORY SOCIETY

Eliza (Elsie) Cassels McAlister, one of the first women to hold an official position in a Canadian natural history society, was a member of the Alberta Natural History Society (ANHS) from its founding in 1906 until 1926. She was vice-president between 1917 and 1924.[10]

Like a true naturalist, Elsie carried out extensive fieldwork involving the flora and fauna of the Red Deer and Sylvan Lake regions of Alberta. She corresponded with friends William Rowan and Percy Taverner, and with several respected amateur naturalists and ornithologists including Frank Farley, Tom Randall, and Charles Snell. However, she was strongly opposed to shooting wildlife for the purpose of collection or identification, which must have placed her at odds with these gentlemen. In conjunction with the ANHS, Elsie helped establish purple martin colonies at Sylvan Lake; campaigned in 1906 (unsuccessfully) for the creation of a provincial park to encompass the Red Deer River Canyon; and formulated plans for the Gaetz Lake Sanctuary in Red Deer (then known as the Red Deer Bird Sanctuary). The latter became a Dominion Wildlife Refuge in 1924. For a short time, Elsie was a Game Officer for the Canada Bird Protection Service of the Dominion Parks Branch.

Elsie kept a field journal between 1920 and 1935 and used her observations to contribute several ornithological notes to the *Canadian Field-Naturalist* on subjects such as the Hudsonian [boreal] chickadee, gyrfalcon, rufous hummingbird, and red-breasted nuthatch. She also wrote articles and lectured about birds for naturalist societies and the general public and kept the records of the migratory bird count for ANHS. "She was a sensitive and energetic woman who lived an almost penniless existence her entire adult life. Those who knew her well called her a woman of charm and spirit."[11]

Alberta Institute of Technology, and Terry Thormin, invertebrate zoologist at the Royal Alberta Museum, have also contributed tremendous amounts of time and enthusiasm introducing the world of invertebrates to school children and other interest groups.

Whether they studied birds, bugs or plants, the work of these early naturalists and collectors, from Alberta and elsewhere, set the stage for a provincial natural history club. The Alberta Natural History Society was founded in Red Deer on March 14, 1906 and was the successor of an earlier Territorial Natural History Society. A number of clubs soon followed, starting with the Edmonton Natural History Club (ENHC) that grew out of a University of Alberta botany club in 1937; the Edmonton Bird Club in 1949 which in 2004 joined the ENHC to form the Edmonton Nature Club; the Calgary Bird Club in 1955 which evolved into the Calgary Field Naturalists Society in 1969; the Bow Valley Naturalists in 1967; the Lethbridge Natural History Society in 1967; and the Cold Lake Bird Club over the period between 1967 and 1970. These first seven natural history clubs then came together under one umbrella, forming the Federation of Alberta Naturalists (FAN) in 1970. One of the major goals of the Federation is to foster and assist in the formation of additional natural history clubs and

313

KERRY WOOD 1907-1998: OUTSTANDING NATURALIST AND COMMUNICATOR
[RON BJORGE]

Outstanding naturalist, historian, gifted and prolific writer, great storyteller, conservationist, and humanitarian are some of the words that come to mind in considering the life and contributions of Kerry Wood.

I attended the opening of the Kerry Wood Nature Centre one warm summer afternoon in 1986. As I arrived, the Master of Ceremonies was introducing none other than Mr. Kerry Wood, a slight man, with mischievous eyes, a warm smile, and a very quick wit. He held the audience in the palm of his hand as he talked of the early days in the Red Deer area and a variety of community-based conservation initiatives. He gave much praise to everyone in the audience, never drawing attention to his numerous personal accomplishments.

This was just a small personal glimpse into the character and life of an outstanding communicator who brought the wonder and reality of nature to thousands. Wood decided to become a writer when he was seven years old. He received strong encouragement from his scholarly father, other family members, and one special high school teacher. As he began to write, he also became an outstanding naturalist. By 1919, the 12-year old Wood could identify 300 species of birds. Before the age of 20, he collected detailed data on the population cycles of field voles, snowshoe hares, and ruffed grouse, and submitted much of it to the Canadian Wildlife Service. For this work, he was offered an honorary doctorate from a university in California. He declined this award. He was offered an honorary position from the Cree Chief, Sam Goodeye of Hobbema. He also declined this honour, but did accept over 40 herbal plant secrets passed on to him by Cree medicine men.

Kerry Wood's writing accomplishments are indeed impressive. He wrote more than 20 books, 6200 short stories, 8000 articles, and 9000 newspaper columns. He wore out at least 19 typewriters! Starting in 1939, he began regular radio shows with CBC and other stations, and continued for about 35 years. Most of his stories held an incredible appeal for children, but were eagerly read or listened to by all ages. They tended to weave humour with natural or historical fact combined with exciting insights into life. In 1969, an informal survey among librarians estimated that 500,000 Canadians read Kerry Wood books through libraries each year. Through his writings, he is credited with influencing the creation of more than 20 wildlife sanctuaries.

Over the years, Kerry Wood received numerous awards including the *Order of Canada*, the *Order of the Bighorn*, the *Distinguished Service Award* from Interpretation Canada, two Governor General's medals, an Honorary Doctorate from the University of Alberta, and an *Alberta Achievement Award*.

societies in Alberta. Today, there are 24 such clubs working throughout the province to promote the conservation of Alberta's natural history.

With publication of *The Atlas of Breeding Birds of Alberta* in 1992, FAN also began providing the public with a number of books that highlight an amazing array of natural history topics. Myrna Pearman and Ted Pike's *NatureScape Alberta* is a perfect example of interpreting natural systems and encouraging the public to provide for other species in landscaping projects ranging from improving the backyard to restoring cultivated fields and reclaimed roadways. In 2004, FAN launched a new Natural History Series with Bill Samuel's *White as a Ghost*, a book about mighty moose and mini-marauders in the form of winter ticks. Wildlife information education is alive and well in Alberta!

Collections and Databases: Adding to our Natural History Knowledge

With its role to inform the public about our fish and wildlife resources, the Provincial Museum of Alberta (now the Royal Alberta Museum) has always had a strong tie to Alberta's natural history community. As a central repository for the work of many naturalists and researchers, its extensive bird and mammal collections contain a wealth of information. These collections are used to verify the occurrence and distribution of particular species in Alberta. Every specimen is catalogued with collector, location, and date of collection. The assembled lists provide a good understanding of the geographic and morphometric range of species in the province and how these may have changed over time. The museum itself has made significant contributions to natural history information, undertaking its own collecting expeditions and research, particularly in more remote areas of the province.

The museum is perhaps best known for its realistic wildlife dioramas, which contain intricately painted backdrops that meld seamlessly into actual rocks, dirt, and preserved plant and animal specimens in the foreground. The dioramas, first constructed in the early 1970s, maintained their popularity over the last three decades and recently benefitted from an upgrade to a new interactive gallery called *Wild Alberta*. The representative scenes let visitors learn which species are plentiful and which are not; what special adaptations native species have for existence in a northern climate zone; what threatens natural ecosystems in the province; and a wide range of other biological and geographical aspects of wild plants and animals in Alberta. The museum engenders a healthy curiosity about the flora and fauna of the province, and in so doing increases public awareness, which in turn makes a significant contribution to conservation.[12]

The University of Alberta is another source of natural history collections. During his tenure there, Professor Rowan collected many vertebrate specimens from throughout Alberta. In addition, through his own efforts and his vigorous trading

ALBERTA SPORT, RECREATION, PARKS AND WILDLIFE FOUNDATION

The Alberta Sport, Recreation, Parks and Wildlife Foundation has been a major partner in and supporter of natural history research and initiatives. The late "Boomer" Adair, Minister of Recreation, Parks and Wildlife, had the idea for this organization and made it happen. For many years, the foundation was a boon to wildlife and fisheries projects such as *The Atlas of Breeding Birds of Alberta*. Tom Drinkwater was the first Chair of the Board of Directors, and the Assistant Deputy Ministers of the Recreation, Parks, and Wildlife Department were Board Members. Through time it became truly a public board and Chuck Moser became Executive Director. Wildlife biologist Gordon Kerr served for many years as a science advisor to the grants programs, both as a provincial and then a federal employee and later on his own as a retiree. While the foundation later expanded to include a larger sports component, it continues today to receive grant applications and provide monies to natural resource initiatives.

RECOLLECTIONS BY JOY AND CAM FINLAY OF THE EARLY DAYS IN ENVIRONMENTAL EDUCATION IN ALBERTA
[COMPILED BY CAM FINLAY]

Cam began his career in natural history interpretation in 1965 when he joined Elk Island National Park, east of Edmonton, as one of the first permanent park naturalists in Canada. With very little direction (few superintendents knew what a naturalist was supposed to do) he began leading nature walks, evening slide talks, and car caravans in search of big game for his audiences of young and old, singles, couples, and families. Wildlife viewing and environmental concerns were coming into vogue and park programs were well attended. People would drive out from Edmonton, weekend after weekend. In addition, Cam contacted several Edmonton schools since he thought city kids needed nature education. Soon he was overbooked and giving four walks a day.

That same summer, Edmonton Parks and Recreation, wanting to expose urban people to natural history, hired Joy to give nature walks in Whitemud Park. Joy soon expanded these walks to school groups and before long was leading four to six sessions a day. Joy's winter walks became extremely popular since she incorporated both outdoor recreation (snowshoeing) with natural history (magpie and snowshoe hare tracks, snow studies, and food chain games). Growing up on the western prairies and reinforced by courses in boreal ecology, Joy knew that Alberta mammals and some birds were adapted to live in winter. She drafted up a small booklet for leaders, teachers and parents, which discussed winter, snow conditions, and how local animal life had adapted to survive. She called it *Winter Here and Now*. This booklet was so well received, it went through several revisions and printings until finally Scholastic Books ordered 7500 copies, making it available to schools across the country and into the northern U.S.

By this time, Joy had also been involved in a number of other conservation education initiatives. Edmonton Parks and Recreation had asked her to start a Junior Naturalist program. This group started one of the first Bluebird Trails in Alberta. Lieutenant-Governor Grant MacEwan came out to dedicate the trail and later helped with banding the first three clutches of nestlings. Alberta Culture, Youth, and Recreation asked Joy to visit and evaluate a number of outdoor camps run by school districts to find out if grant monies were well spent. These trips put her in touch with teachers across Alberta. Soon, they

united to form the Environmental and Outdoor Education Council of the Alberta Teachers Association, with Joy as their first president.

In the late 1960s, the Blue Lake Outdoor Centre near Hinton was built with Joy a part of the planning team for both site and program development. Later she taught many courses at the centre on winter ecology, berry finding, and jelly making. Soon, Joy was in demand across Alberta, providing workshops for teacher and leader groups showing them how to extend classroom activities beyond four walls. When *Project Wild* came to Alberta, Joy helped to adapt it to the province and encouraged teachers to use the program. Joy and Cam also wrote a weekly nature column for the *Edmonton Journal* for ten years and the *Calgary Herald* for three years in the late 1970s and 1980s. ACCESS Radio and TV soon joined the natural history trend. Joy, as a well-known naturalist, was often called in to write scripts and be part of program preparation.

Cam, after a year at Elk Island, joined the City of Edmonton to develop Fort Edmonton Historic Park. This was a full time job for the first few years with little time for natural history, other than to sometimes join Joy in her programs. In the early 1970s, at an executive meeting of Edmonton Parks and Recreation, John Janzen, the superintendent, turned to Cam and asked: "Would you like to build a Nature Centre?" He took the matter to City Council but had a hard time selling it. Most politicians were of the old school and had not yet awakened to the need for environmental education. It was a close vote, winning by one, but they were off.

A sod-turning event took place in the fall of 1973. Horst Schmidt, Minister of Culture, Youth and Recreation, broke the first ground saying he had no idea what a nature centre was but thought it would be a good thing! By the fall of 1974, the building was done. There was only enough money to hire one secretary and pay the utilities and related costs. (The first full-time secretary at the Centre was Pat Clayton, today a well-known contributor to Alberta's natural history community.) There were no funds for programming! So, being part of the Edmonton natural history community, Cam appealed for volunteers to give the school programmes. Pat Wishart stepped forward as the first volunteer and school programs began that fall. The Centre never looked back. Soon it began offering public courses in wildlife with volunteers including instructors from Fish and Wildlife. Attendance quickly rose in all facets of the operation until 50,000 participants a year were attending sessions. Later, annual attendance topped 100,000.

When the budget was established, monies were set aside to build exhibits. By the spring of 1975, displays were ready and the official opening took place in 1976. As programs developed, Fish and Wildlife Division materials including the many brochures and other written items were the main resource. Division staff continued to give talks. They were also exceedingly helpful when exhibits were being prepared. When Alberta naturalists began building bluebird trails in the later 1960s, there was a great demand for more nest boxes. Edgar T. Jones obtained a grant to build these boxes and Cam suggested the Nature Centre would be the ideal place for construction and distribution. Over the next three years, more than 5000 bluebird boxes were made at the Centre and distributed across the southern and central half of the province. Almost all of the older and longer Trails in the province can trace their start from this supply.

The high point of the Finlays' work was *Wildlife 87* with the motto *Gaining Momentum.* This was the 100th birthday of wildlife conservation in North America. The celebration began at Last Mountain Lake in Saskatchewan where the first major wildlife sanctuary on the continent had been established in 1887. With contacts across Canada (Joy in providing workshop presentations and programmes across the country in environmental education and also on the Board of the Canadian Nature Federation, and Cam as past president of the Canadian Museums Association), they had many ties. With no funds initially (later on, the federal government and some provinces provided some monies) Joy got on the home phone to make contacts and on the plane to travel across the nation to make this event a grassroots movement. Soon she had volunteer organizations

established in every province and territory in Canada.

In Alberta, Cam called representatives of the various government and non-government conservation organizations together to establish a provincial group. Shortly thereafter, Don Sparrow, Minister responsible for the Fish and Wildlife Division visited the Nature Centre and Cam cornered him to explain about *Wildlife 87*. Soon the province would set aside five times as many natural areas in one stroke as had been established in Alberta before that year. Similar actions took place right across Canada. Today, Cam and Joy Finlay are retired but no less busy and living on the coast of British Columbia.

NEST BOXES PROVIDED MANY RESEARCH OPPORTUNITIES AT BEAVERHILL LAKE, DESIGNATED A NATURAL AREA AS PART OF *WILDLIFE 87* ACTIVITIES IN ALBERTA.
CREDIT: P. ROWELL

316

habits, he acquired specimens from many regions of the world for comparative purposes in teaching vertebrate anatomy and biology. Unfortunately, much of his collection was sold to the University of California–Berkeley and only a small portion remains in Alberta. On the other hand, J. Dewey Soper, federal game officer in the early and mid-1900s, lodged a wealth of scientific specimens, observational notes, and annotated photographs in the University of Alberta archives and zoology museum.

The University of Alberta Museum of Zoology also benefitted from the work of David Boag, Vic Lewin, Nick Panter, and Wayne Roberts, who contributed specimens from 1959 to the present day. Further surveys to fill the gaps in knowledge of vertebrate distributions within Alberta were undertaken by Bill Fuller, Jan Murie, and their many graduate students. More recently, acquisitions result from collections made by consulting companies, government agencies,

university staff, and graduate students during their respective programs or studies.

Today, the Mammalogy Collection consists of 7300 specimens representing 16 Orders, and 76 Families, largely from northwest Canada. Fish specimens are housed in the museum's Ichthyological Collection. It consists of over 7400 lots and more than 200,000 specimens representing 40 Orders and over 200 Families, including a complete systematic collection of fishes from Alberta with extensive examples of sticklebacks. The material consists largely of research material collected by J. Ralph Nursall, Joe Nelson, Martin Paetz, Vic Lewin, Wayne Roberts, and several graduate and undergraduate students.

The University museum also houses the largest number of reptiles and amphibians collected within Alberta. The collection contains more than 3000 amphibians (including specimen lots of eggs

317

MYRNA PEARMAN AND THE ELLIS BIRD FARM—CONSERVATION EDUCATION SUCCESS!

The Ellis Bird Farm is a conservation and education success story, recognized internationally for its education programs and several popular books including *Winter Bird Feeding – an Alberta Guide, Nestboxes for Prairie Birds, Water Gardening – a Prairie Guide,* and *Backyard Wildlife Habitat Manual.* This last publication gave rise to the very informative *NatureScape Alberta – creating and caring for wildlife habitat at home*, co-published by the Red Deer River Naturalists and the Federation of Alberta Naturalists, and co-authored by Ted Pike and Myrna Pearman. Pearman is a long time biologist for the Ellis Bird Farm.

The Ellis Bird Farm itself arose out of individual drive and commitment combined with responsible farming practices and a particular love of bluebirds. The Ellis family arrived in Alberta in 1886. In 1906, John and Agnes Ellis bought a tract of land southeast of Lacombe and subsequent Ellis generations grew to love the land and animals that reside there. Charlie Ellis had an abiding interest in mountain bluebirds and a concern over their declining abundance in the mid-1950s. He put up a bluebird box on his lawn and established what became a trail of more than 300 bluebird, chickadee, purple martin, and flicker nest boxes. His initial winter-feeding efforts expanded into a large feeding operation using up to two tons of sunflower seeds some years.

The bluebirds responded to the boxes and it became common in summer to see them hawking insects over the fields, or standing guard from fence posts and power lines. However, Charlie and his sister Winnie were not satisfied with their success and went on to improve the habitat for many wild terrestrial, aquatic, and aerial species throughout the farm. In 1980, Union Carbide purchased the farm, but not until Charlie got a commitment that much of the land become the primary asset of a non-profit company (Ellis Bird Farm Ltd.) and thus would provide habitat for bluebirds long after he was gone. Today, the farm continues to successfully marry the interests of industry and naturalists, and fosters a partnership from which wildlife, humans, and landscapes benefit.

and larvae) and 900 reptile specimens, as well as valuable historical records providing baseline data for studies involving declines in amphibian populations. These records were instrumental in identifying the disappearance of the northern leopard frog from much of its range in Alberta and currently serve a similar function in a study of the declining Canadian toad.

The Freshwater Invertebrate Collection, housed in the Biological Sciences building, has a historic collection of leech specimens collected by J. E. Moore in the 1940s. In the 1960s, researchers working on rivers, streams, and lakes primarily in Alberta, but also in parts of northwest Canada, recognized the need to preserve biological specimens. By then, freshwater invertebrates were being used as bio-indicators to assess ecological changes and the University's collection continues to provide pioneer baseline studies for waterbodies that have undergone major changes, such as Kananaskis and Wabamun lakes. Hugh Clifford, the Curator of the Freshwater Invertebrates Collection, used the specimens as a basis for his book *Aquatic Invertebrates of Alberta*.[13] At present, the Freshwater Invertebrate Collection consists of more than 5000 lots of one to uncounted thousands of specimens per lot.

In 1996, the need to track the growing body of data concerning Alberta's natural history was recognized with the creation of the Alberta Natural Heritage Information Centre (ANHIC). This Centre is a co-operative initiative between the Alberta government, Canadian Heritage, and the Nature Conservancy. The database is housed and maintained by the provincial Parks and Protected Areas, Department of Community Development. The Centre maintains biodiversity data to help the province set priorities for the preservation of its natural diversity. Other databases maintained by the Fish and Wildlife Division (the Biological Species Observation Database), the Federation of Alberta Naturalists (Bird List), and Bird Studies Canada/Audubon Society (Christmas Bird Count and Project FeederWatch) provide repositories for many wildlife sightings recorded in Alberta.

As well as storing records, natural history databases provide an opportunity to identify where the gaps in knowledge are. These gaps can be successfully filled when government agencies and researchers team up with Alberta's vibrant volunteer naturalist community. The Alberta Bird Atlas Project started with the goal to identify the distribution and relative abundance of breeding birds across Alberta. This was a huge task and would not have succeeded without the cooperation of the Federation of Alberta Naturalists, Alberta Fish and Wildlife Division, the Canadian Wildlife Service, the Provincial Museum of Alberta, Alberta Sport, Recreation, Parks and Wildlife Foundation and more than 1000 dedicated and intrepid volunteers. Similarly, volunteer events like the Christmas Bird Count and May Day Species Counts, with participation from hundreds of volunteers, significantly add to the knowledge base. Such projects are not only successful in collecting data, they also foster an appreciation for the bounty of wildlife and wild spaces in Alberta.

Educating Ourselves—Wildlife Biologists Unite

Recognizing that management in a vacuum rarely leads to good management, wildlife professionals in Alberta became members in existing national and U.S. groups in the hopes that group dynamics would inevitably lead to greater strength, fertile discussion, consistent approach, and broader impact. As the ranks of the wildlife profession grew in the 1960s and 1970s, many biologists became active members in the Canadian Society of Wildlife and Fisheries Biologists (CSWFB) and The Wildlife Society (TWS). The CSWFB was established in the late 1950s as a Canada-wide organization of fish and wildlife biologists. It had annual meetings but struggled to deal with issues all across the country without the benefit of provincial or local chapters. Alberta members, always a relatively large group, met monthly during the winter in Edmonton, often at the university. They tackled issues and provided statements of concern usually to the Alberta government. The national group decided to broaden its scope to embrace all biologists focussed on environmental issues and the name changed to the Canadian Society of Environmental Biologists (CSEB). Initially, Alberta had over 400 members. Although the broadening of scope seemed like a good idea, the society lost focus nationally and provincially, particularly from a wildlife perspective. Many wildlife biologists felt that the CSEB in Alberta was not meeting their professional needs as a practical forum to exchange ideas and address issues.

The Wildlife Society was established in 1937 and is a United States-based international society with strong regional sections and local chapters. The Northwest Section (NWS), which includes Alberta, has an annual meeting that Alberta has hosted regularly over the past three decades. In the 1960s and 1970s, many wildlifers in Alberta were drawn to TWS by access to its high quality publications (*Journal of Wildlife Management, Wildlife Monographs, Wildlife Bulletin*) and annual meetings. Many of the issues were closer to home than those addressed by the CSEB and provided Alberta wildlife biologists with a forum more in line with activities undertaken within a wildlife profession.

Basic biology also played a role in establishing an organization of wildlife professionals. Ecosystems in Alberta have much more in common with those in Montana, Wyoming, British Columbia, and Washington than with those in eastern Canada: natural affinities were western rather than national. As evidenced at the annual meetings, the program and expertise of NWS members involved the same species, issues, and concerns as those in Alberta. It seemed a natural fit to develop a strong Alberta Chapter that followed the ideals of TWS and NWS, but had a home-grown focus to exchange ideas, engage students, and address issues as expertise and energy permitted.

Hence, the charter of the Alberta Chapter of the Wildlife Society (ACTWS) was proclaimed at the

Northwest Section meeting in Banff in April 1989. The Founding Committee (Morley Barrett, Mike Dorrance, Bill Glasgow, Larry Roy, and Bill Samuel) conducted the business of the Chapter through 1989, establishing bylaws and recruiting a slate of nominees for the 1990 Executive. Other achievements in that first year included development of a logo, organization of the first Annual Meeting of ACTWS, and the first issue of *The Alberta Wildlifer*. There were 61 registered members in the first year.

Today, the Chapter gathers wildlife professionals from across the province annually to share information, ideas, problems, and solutions. ACTWS has established itself as an important vehicle to connect with wildlife professionals and share information. It continues to host annual meetings and Northwest Section meetings, and in 2004 it hosted the first Canadian meeting of the parent TWS. The Chapter regularly communicates wildlife management concerns to politicians and has representation on a range of provincial and local wildlife management advisory committees. Membership includes professionals employed by governments, universities, industries, and businesses throughout Alberta, as well as in British Columbia, Yukon, and Northwest Territories.

ACTWS is also a strong advocate of student involvement and recognition. Student Chapters of TWS exist at the Lethbridge Community College and the University of Alberta. When the NWS requested assistance in raising funds for a NWS student scholarship, the Alberta Chapter pitched in. Blair Rippin, a premier duck-carver, offered a hand-carved widgeon as a raffle item for the first fund-raiser in 1992-1993. Successful annual fund-raising efforts led to offering the first ACTWS student scholarship to Phil McLoughlin (U of A) in 1995. As of 2003, the Chapter offers three scholarships available to students in technical, undergraduate, and postgraduate levels. In addition, awards are presented for the best student oral and poster presentations at annual meetings. Looking back, formation of a strong local organization for wildlife professionals was the right thing to do. The successes of ACTWS speak for themselves. A comparable focus, the American Fisheries Society, offers similar opportunities for fisheries biologists.

The Challenges of Conservation Education Today

One of the greatest challenges facing fish and wildlife conservation education today is the change to a largely urban audience. Having left our rural, agricultural roots, more than 80% of Albertans live in cities where they may become disconnected from the land and an inherent understanding of natural ecosystems. People who are protected from natural realities often have little knowledge of wildlife, its benefits to humans, or what it needs in order to exist.

Concern about wildlife in Alberta's cities is often driven by incidents such as coyote sightings, too many geese on a golf course, or too many deer killed by vehicles on city roads. In Edmonton, an outdoor education centre was temporarily shut down following an eruption of harmless aphids that filled the air. The depth of misunderstanding and disconnection from wildlife and things wild in some cases is enormous.

Future biologists and naturalists must make a concerted effort not only to inform, but also to instil understanding of the interconnectedness of life, the implications of altered ecosystems, and the ramifications that wild species have on the very safety and quality of the soil, air, and

water that urban populations use. Wildlife does not live simply for us to watch and be entertained. They have an integral role in the very existence and sustainability of the province. Whether they are the decomposers that scrub water and soil clean again; whether they are the "canaries in the coalmine" that warn of dire environmental changes; whether they are the living evidence that systems are healthy or stressed or collapsed; whether they are simply part of the psychological relief provided by a walk in a natural area, a paddle down a quiet river, or a ski into wilderness back country; they are of value to all of us, no matter where we live. This value in wild species and wild spaces must be communicated in every manner to help all Albertans understand that we do not live on this planet alone, that we cannot live at the expense of all the other species, and that there is good reason to keep the full complement of fish and wildlife around.

The challenge is large. Our system responds with financial resources to the things Albertans care about. Somehow wildlife, fish, and the places they live in must become more important to Albertans. Citizens must be made aware of the contribution wildlife and fish make to the quality of our lives. Alberta is a better place to live because we have such a variety of natural wild resources. May it always be so!

Final Words...

In closing, Pat Wishart, Edmonton naturalist and co-author with Dianne Hayley of *Knee High Nature* offers the following advice:

320

WILLIAM ROWAN AWARD FOR DISTINGUISHED SERVICE
Outstanding contributions of wildlife biologists in Alberta are recognized by the Alberta Chapter of The Wildlife Society in the form of the William Rowan Award for Distinguished Service.[14] Rowan Award recipients include Bill Fuller (Canadian Wildlife Service [CWS] and University of Alberta [U of A], retired), John Stelfox (Alberta Fish and Wildlife Division [F&W], CWS, retired), Bill Wishart (F&W, retired), Ed Telfer (CWS, retired), Morley Barrett (F&W, North American Waterfowl Management Plan, currently Ducks Unlimited Canada), Dave Boag (U of A, retired), Ernie Kuyt (CWS, retired), Bill Samuel (U of A), Ian Stirling (CWS), Valerius Geist (University of Calgary, retired), Don Thomas (CWS, retired), Ludwig Carbyn (CWS, retired), Gordon Kerr (F&W, CWS, retired), and Detlef Onderka (Alberta Agriculture, retired).

THE POSSIBILITIES FOR EXPLORATION IN THE NATURAL WORLD ARE ENDLESS!
CREDIT: D. FAIRLESS

Our very lives depend on understanding our environment. But we must all be more aware of our natural world before we can learn about its intricacies. As more and more of us now live in an urban setting with development outpacing our natural spaces, we, as adults, must take time to discover the joys of nature with children. Children already have a built-in fascination with their natural world and learn through all their senses. They delight in small and large creatures and happily share their lives with all plants and animals from dandelions to dragonflies and magpies to moose.

Experiences in nature should be fun and interesting. Start with the familiar such as a small garden in the backyard or in the school grounds. Take time to enjoy the fresh air by walking in the local parks. Simple activities such as feeding the birds, listening for frogs, picnicking, climbing a tree, and watching a bee are easy ways to enjoy nature. National and provincial parks can provide wonderful experiences in a natural environment. Even smart-growth cities are realizing that they must save some of their fast-dwindling natural spaces for health, scientific and aesthetic reasons.

322

We will all be the better for it! Recent research shows that direct exposure to nature is essential for physical and emotional health.[15] More than 100 studies confirm that one of the benefits of spending time in nature is stress reduction. Other studies show that nature can be therapeutic for a number of disorders including depression and obesity. When adults and children hike in the woods, they feel relaxed and at peace. And the sight of an animal in that environment adds to the joy.

CLIMBING A TREE IS A GREAT WAY TO GET A NEW PERSPECTIVE!
CREDIT: D. FAIRLESS

Because of their knowledge and dedicated work in the field, fish and wildlife enthusiasts, whether they be biologists, naturalists, or researchers, need to expand their role in conservation education. They can best assess the changes in nature and can alert and educate the rest of us to problems affecting wildlife and their habitat. But they desperately need the help of parents, educators, city planners, farmers, developers, industry, in fact, all Albertans. They need to leverage their work, building stronger partnerships with schools, universities, curriculum designers and other educators, as well as hunters, trappers, Fish and Game clubs, nature centres, stewards, naturalists,

museums, and environmental and conservation organizations. They also need to use a variety of electronic and print media including courses, publications and television programs. Teachers are also a part of the solution and should be required to take more than one course on environmental issues. They should be encouraged to undertake schoolyard naturalization projects so that children can have daily opportunities to study ecosystems close at hand.

And finally, we all need to learn that healthy ecosystems are an important part of our world and a heavy human footprint can harm these ecosystems. If our children become more aware of our natural world, they can build on that awareness, leading to respect, appreciation and understanding of our natural environment. Then they will be able to make the best decisions about the natural heritage of Alberta, today and in the future.

JOHN STELFOX INSTRUCTING A CLASS OF
JUNIOR FOREST WARDENS.
COURTESY ALBERTA SUSTAINABLE RESOURCE DEVELOPMENT
(FOREST PROTECTION IMAGE LIBRARY)

323

MAJOR EVENTS IN CONSERVATION EDUCATION

1906	The Alberta Natural History Society is formed.
1914	A Wildlife Demonstration Train travels throughout the province.
1958	Minister Norman Willmore initiates *Lands-Forests-Wildlife*—a publication for fish and wildlife management issues in Alberta.
1963	Minister Norman Willmore, Deputy Minister Eric Huestis, and Director of the Fish and Wildlife Division Curt Smith, move to forge a program on hunting safety.
1970	The first outdoor conservation camp is established at Narrow Lake. Several natural history clubs form a provincial umbrella organization called the Federation of Alberta Naturalists.
1974	The Extension Services Branch is formed to house hunter training and conservation education.
1975	An Environmental Education and Interpretation Section is added to the Parks and Protected Areas Division. Mrs. J. Hewko and Miss L. Badgeley become the first female Hunter Training Officers in Canada.
1976	The John Janzen Nature Centre is opened in Edmonton.
1976	An Education Branch is added to Alberta Environment.
1983	The Alberta Conservation and Hunter Education course is selected by a panel of experts as the most outstanding of its kind in North America.
1987	The 100th birthday of wildlife conservation in North America is celebrated with *Wildlife 87*.
1989	The Alberta Chapter of The Wildlife Society is established. Alberta celebrates 25 years of conservation education.
1990	The International Convention of Project Wild Coordinators is held at Lethbridge. The Watchable Wildlife Program conducts a survey: 64% of Albertans (approx. 1.15 million) view wildlife in their backyards, neighbourhoods or elsewhere.
1996	Conservation education and camp programs are handed over to Alberta Hunter Education Instructors' Association (AHEIA). AHEIA opens Alford Lake Conservation Education Centre for Excellence. *Hunting in Alberta* and *Fishing in Alberta*, two websites produced by the Fish and Wildlife Division, use a new forum, the internet, to inform Albertan's about these activities.
2004	Environment Canada's *Hinterland Who's Who* series is updated and rebroadcast on national television. The Federation of Alberta Naturalists launches a new natural history publication series.
2006	The Bow Habitat Station Interpretive Centre will open as a premier fisheries and wetland educational facility.

References • CHAPTER 9

[1] As defined by the National Association for Interpretation (http://www.interpnet.com/)

[2] In 1970, regulations were broadened to allow hunting at the age of 14 if accompanied by a parent, legal guardian or authorized person over the age of 18.

[3] Alberta Fish and Wildlife Division. 1967. Annual Report. Edmonton.

[4] For more on furbearer management, see Chapter 5.

[5] More detail provided in Chapter 6.

[6] Stelfox, Harry. 1993. Alberta's Watchable Wildlife. *Alberta Game Warden*, Summer, 1993:32.

[7] Höhn, E.O. 1981. History of the Edmonton Bird Club. *Alberta Naturalist*. Special issue No. 1:48-51.

[8] Salt, W.R., and A.L. Wilk. 1958. The Birds of Alberta. Hurtig Publishers, Edmonton.

[9] Leech, Robin. Personal communication, February 2003, Edmonton.

[10] Sterling, K.B., R.P. Harmond, G.A. Cevasco, and L.F. Hammond [eds.] 1997. Biographical Dictionary of American and Canadian Naturalists and Environmentalists. Greenwood Press, Connecticut. p. 145

[11] Ibid.

[12] Smith, Hugh. Curator of Mammalogy, Provincial Museum of Alberta, Interview with Eric Holmgren. February 12, 1986.

[13] Hugh Clifford. 1991. Aquatic Invertebrates of Alberta. University of Alberta Press, Edmonton.

[14] Rowan's own achievements are highlighted in Chapters 2 and 7.

[15] Louv, Richard. 2005. Last Child in the Woods. Algonquin Books of Chapel Hill, North Carolina.

Chapter 10

MANAGING SPECIES AT RISK: MAINTAINING ALBERTA'S BIODIVERSITY

Petra Rowell with contributions from Lu Carbyn, Sue Cotterill, Gordon Court, Gordon Kerr, Gerry Kuzyk, Guy L'Heureux, Nyree Sharp, Pat Valastin and Francine Wieliczko

325

"In the end, our society will be defined not only by what we create, but by what we refuse to destroy."

JOHN SAWHILL, THE NATURE CONSERVANCY

A New Conundrum

In today's world of increasing information and communication, Albertans are becoming more and more aware of the broad array of flora and fauna that grace our province. Whereas traditional fish and wildlife managers focussed primarily on game species (big game, upland game birds, furbearers, and fish) today's managers increasingly appreciate and understand all of our biological diversity (biodiversity) including the mammals, birds, fishes, amphibians, reptiles, invertebrates and plants found within our borders. Biodiversity is also now recognized as a cornerstone of our natural capital, contributing to the functioning of ecological systems that provide us with the breathable air, drinkable water, and fertile soil we all depend upon.

But as biodiversity gains importance ideologically, in reality, fish and wildlife managers are spending a larger proportion of effort on just a small fraction of that diversity—the growing number of individual species at risk of decline, extirpation, or extinction. These species—some precipitously close to the brink like sage-grouse and some caribou herds—eat up a tremendous amount of time from very limited staff resources. In addition, the habitat required to maintain healthy populations of these and other species is shrinking. Wildlife habitat needs do not compete well with other land uses like agriculture, mineral extraction and even recreation. In the 1950s, Professor Rowan declared the peaks and valleys of the ten-year game cycle the "conundrum of the century". Perhaps the ability to preserve entire suites of species (biodiversity) on a shrinking habitat base while sinking the majority of our resources into intensively managed, at-risk single species, is the new conundrum of the 21st century.

Early Efforts at Managing Species at Risk

Throughout the first half of the 20th century, fish and wildlife managers focussed their efforts primarily on species that were harvested either for consumptive or commercial purposes. When and where a particular game species declined, the harvest season was limited or closed. Sometimes, an area was made into a game preserve, until such time as the species' natural increase returned the population to its former abundance. As discussed in chapter three, pronghorn antelope and the creation of the Nemiskam Reserve in southern Alberta in 1914 is an example of where this approach was successful and the park was no longer needed after 1947.

Where a species became locally extinct (extirpated), individuals were translocated or "reintroduced" from healthier populations. This worked particularly well for species like elk, deer and mountain goats. In the 1930s, beaver were being translocated in Ontario, Saskatchewan, and parts of the United States. In Alberta, Mr. A. Norquay of the Dominion Lands Office in Edmonton carried on a correspondence with the renowned author and naturalist, Grey Owl. The

two men discussed at length the beaver's biology and habitat requirements, as well as the best methods for capturing and reintroducing them to areas where they could no longer be found.

Joseph Dewey Soper, an employee of the Dominion Wildlife Service in the 1930s, also entered into these beaver discussions. Soper produced a memo outlining the benefits that propagation and protection of beaver would bring to Alberta. These included maintaining the water supply and eliminating drought, minimizing flooding, protecting against forest fires, creating fish habitat, and providing habitat for big game and waterfowl. In later years, the province would use beaver translocations as a method of controlling unwanted beaver activity—moving problem beaver to areas where they were scarce.

The Whooping Crane: Alberta's First Endangered Species

Like the beaver, the whooping crane had once been a game species but declined to the point where it was no longer harvested. The last known nest of migratory whooping cranes in the United States was noted in Iowa in 1894. The eggs and birds at this nest were collected for a museum.

GREY OWL: FRIEND TO THE BEAVER
Grey Owl, a strong proponent of beaver reintroductions, was an Englishmen who adopted an aboriginal lifestyle. For much of his life, he resided in Prince Albert, Saskatchewan where he became an eloquent author and naturalist.

Man will always lack something of being a really good woodsman, in the finer sense, until he is so steeped in the atmosphere of the wild, and has become so possessed with long association to it, of a feeling of close kinship and responsibility for it that he may even unconsciously avoid tramping on too many flowers on his passage through the forest. Here and then only can he become truly receptive to the delicate nuances of a culture that may elude those who are not so tuned in on their surroundings.[1]

GREY OWL. (ARCHIE BELANEY), 1888-1938

DAN VIGAR, BILL WISHART'S GREAT-GRANDFATHER, WITH A YOUNG OF THE YEAR WHOOPING CRANE SHOT NEAR ROSEBUD, ca. 1900.
COURTESY B. WISHART

time, verified the sighting and returned the next spring to determine that the birds were indeed nesting within the park but to the north of the Alberta-Northwest Territories border.

The discovery of the whooping crane nesting grounds led to the development of a recovery strategy for these birds. Soon, their nesting grounds would be surveyed every summer by the CWS. The U.S. Fish and Wildlife Service (USFWS) would survey their wintering grounds in Aransas, Texas. By 1966, a captive-breeding program was managed jointly by the CWS and USFWS. Nick Novakowski, initially tasked with the Canadian portion of this work, left CWS on education leave and Ernie Kuyt found himself in charge of the program for the next 25 years. Between 1967 and 1991, 128 eggs were collected from wild nests and sent to the Patuxent Wildlife Research Center in Maryland where they were incubated, hatched and reared. By 1992, only 72 birds had been successfully produced.

Although it was believed that whooping cranes still nested in Alberta, and some migratory sightings had been made, initial research efforts were severely impeded because the actual location of the nesting ground was not known. After 1926, whooping cranes appeared to be extirpated in Alberta. Then in 1954, a sighting was made in Wood Buffalo National Park. Dr. Bill Fuller, a Canadian Wildlife Service (CWS) employee at the

Eggs were also sent to Grays Lake National Wildlife Research Center in Idaho to be raised by sandhill cranes. Although rearing was successful, the fostered whooping cranes didn't seem to recognize their own species and failed to pair and produce young of their own.

Meanwhile, Kuyt had been manipulating the egg collecting to increase the productivity of the

ALBERTA'S BIODIVERSITY
Within Alberta's six natural regions (mountains, foothills, prairies, parkland, boreal forest, and Canadian Shield) there are 91 species of mammals, 309 breeding birds, 63 fish, 10 amphibians, and eight reptiles. Although they have not all been identified yet, there are an estimated 20,000 insect species in Alberta. The province is also home to more than 1650 flowering plants, 650 species of moss, about the same number of lichens, and 450 fungi species.

DISCOVERING THE NESTING GROUNDS OF THE WHOOPING CRANE
[DR. WILLIAM (BILL) A. FULLER]

The date is June 30, 1954. The last nest of a Whooping Crane had been seen about 1926 in Saskatchewan. Members of the U.S. Fish and Wildlife Service (USFWS), and others, had searched from central Saskatchewan to the delta of the Mackenzie River without success. Each year, Bob Smith and a partner came through Fort Smith on a waterfowl survey. I was usually invited to join them on one of their flights. They always kept their eyes open for whoopers when they were not actually counting ducks.

I spent most of the day in my office. Late in the afternoon Dr. Ward Stevens, Superintendent of Wildlife in the Northwest Territories came into my office with a message. There was a fire on the northern boundary of Wood Buffalo National Park. George Wilson, who was in charge of everything about forests, including forest fires, had gone out by helicopter earlier in the day to find out how the battle was going. He radioed in to Fort Smith on his way back that he and the

pilot, Don Landells, had seen some large white birds, which they thought might be whooping cranes. They were also bringing in a pump that had failed on the job. They were to be met on landing by someone with a working pump, and Landells would turn around and take the new pump back to the fire. Furthermore, if I was at the landing place at 5:00 p.m., I could go back with the pump and perhaps see the birds.

I *was* at the landing place and ready to go at 5:00 p.m. Landells took us back over the same route he had followed on his first trip. We did see the white birds, and they were certainly whooping cranes. Furthermore, there were young birds as well as the adults, so there was reason to believe that the nesting grounds were not far away. I've forgotten the numbers that we saw, but something tells me it was nine whoopers on this trip. I believe they had seen fewer than that on the first trip. Communication with the "outside" world in those days was through the Army. Telegrams went out in Morse code. We sent a

AN ADULT AND A JUVENILE WHOOPING CRANE.
CREDIT: LORNE SCOTT COURTESY ALBERTA FISH AND WILDLIFE DIVISION

328

short account of the finding to Ottawa that evening. July 1 was, of course, a holiday, but one person was on duty at Canadian Wildlife Service (CWS) headquarters. He was Dr. David Munroe. His reply to me was "What price bird watching now?"

Later on, word came from Ottawa that I should keep a watch on the birds up to the time they left for Texas. I made several more flights in a regular aeroplane over the suspected nesting area. On one occasion, I saw 13 cranes: almost half the birds in the Texas flock at the time.

The Whooping Crane Society and the USFWS were very excited about the discovery, and talk began about a ground survey in the following year. The CWS did not want to commit to that until there was proof of nesting, so I was to have a look the next spring. In the 1950s, single engine aeroplanes were required to fly to Edmonton in spring and fall in order to change from skis to pontoons in spring or pontoons to skis in fall. The government plane was out getting pontoons on so I had some difficulty finding transportation at the critical time. However, I was able to get a ride with a pilot from Yellowknife on his way out to Edmonton. I got another ride in the plane that belonged to the Mounted Police. On that flight, I saw what could only be a crane sitting on a nest. So, the ground survey was on. Robert P. Allen of the National Audubon Society was to lead it. When Allen arrived in Fort Smith, we made one flight over the area so I could show him, and mark on a map the location of the known nests. I then left to attend a Scientific Conference in Alaska. (The attempted ground study was a story of its own, but it does not belong here.)

In 1956, I moved from Fort Smith to Whitehorse in the Yukon. Nick Novakowski, and later Ernie Kuyt, both of CWS, took over the whooping crane work. I have received a lot of credit for the discovery, but I try to tell people that had it not been for the fire and George Wilson's observation I would not have gone out to identify the birds. I had flown over the area many times, and I had seen tracks in the mud at the bottom of the lakes, and I had wondered what kind of MAMMAL could leave such tracks. Big birds never entered my mind. On the other hand, no actual nests were seen in 1954, so I was the first person (along with the pilot) to confirm that it was a nesting area.

[Born in Moosomin, Saskatchewan in 1924, Dr. William (Bill) Fuller spent 12 years with the Canadian Wildlife Service in Fort Smith and Whitehorse, before joining the University of Alberta in 1959. As a Professor of Zoology, Fuller carried out long-term studies on the fluctuating populations of small mammals, developing an interest in winter ecology of northern forests and the effect of winter on mammals. In pursuit of his interest, Fuller developed a year-round biological station at Heart Lake, near Hay River, NWT. He is also the first recipient of the William Rowan Distinguished Service Award (awarded by the Alberta Chapter of The Wildlife Society) with a long list of outstanding contributions to wildlife at the local, provincial, national and international levels. Fuller was a contributor to the landmark book *Alberta—A Natural History*. Though he retired in 1984, Dr. Fuller continues his research and teaching at the University of Athabasca and as Professor Emeritus at the University of Alberta.]

329

natural population. Novakowski's research had revealed that of the two eggs laid, whooping crane pairs would only successfully rear one chick, leading to the conclusion that removing one of the eggs for captive rearing could double the productivity of the population. What was learned after analysis, however, was that one or both of the eggs were often infertile. The pairs were often wasting a whole season trying to hatch an infertile egg. Concerned by the wasted effort, Kuyt developed a method of testing the viability of the eggs in the field, and could thereby ensure at least one fertile egg was left in each nest. Due in large part to these efforts, the wild flock began making a slow but steady recovery, and Kuyt was awarded the *Order of Canada* for his efforts.

The international recovery of the whooping crane was also due in large part to public awareness campaigns, the fact that both the

wintering and breeding grounds are in protected areas, and the development of joint agreements between Canada and the United States to manage both wild and captive populations. Academic institutions, corporate sponsors, governments and non-governmental agencies worked together to provide research and funding. Canada adopted a national whooping crane recovery plan in 1988, and a 1996 census confirmed that the range of the breeding population had extended south of the Northwest Territories-Alberta border. This flock is now believed to be large enough to be at low risk of extinction. Numbers are still low enough, however, that the species is still considered endangered.

Today, the whooping crane is a symbol of successful species preservation in North America. The migratory flock which nests in Wood Buffalo National Park has gone from a

THE CALGARY ZOO—EDUCATION AND ENDANGERED SPECIES RECOVERY

Though not often linked to the traditional role of fish and wildlife management, zoos have played an important educational role since they started and, more recently, have taken on a role in endangered species breeding and reintroduction efforts. The Calgary Zoological Society celebrated its 75th year in 2004. Humble beginnings in 1929 saw a number of animals housed on St. George's Island on the Bow River in the heart of Calgary. Heavy run-off that year nearly flooded the island and several animals had to be removed for safety. By 1932, plans were developed to create a Prehistoric Park, and construction began on the first dinosaur model. The Monkey House, the zoo's first heated building with public indoor viewing, quickly followed in 1933.

By the early 1940s, the animal collection consisted of about 500 individuals, and between 150 and 200 species. By 1948, attendance approached an estimated 400,000 visitors per year. The 1950s and 1960s saw many additions including the Feline House, a cable-suspended foot bridge to the zoo over the north arm of the Bow River, a children's zoo component, a conservatory, two giraffes, and a large mammal building.

With public education and the welfare of the animals a priority, the 1970s saw the zoo enter a new planning phase that included promoting the animals' social needs and natural behaviours, enhancing captive reproduction efforts, and expanding teaching opportunities about wildlife. While many new animals were added, the zoo became equally well known for its natural surroundings and barless enclosures. Education was further enhanced when the Karsten Discovery Centre, with a 150-seat theatre and a number of classrooms, opened in 1992. The zoo linked education more directly to Alberta's wildlife with the opening of the *Canadian Wilds* project with its aspen woodlands, mountains, and northern forest exhibits.

And finally, the zoo opened its Centre for Conservation Research. Here it engages in captive-breeding programs and reintroductions in an attempt to re-establish endangered or extirpated (locally extinct) species. Currently, the Calgary Zoo is involved in breeding and reintroduction programs for three Alberta species—leopard frogs, swift fox and whooping cranes.

AN ADULT PEREGRINE FALCON UP CLOSE
COURTESY ALBERTA FISH AND WILDLIFE DIVISION

331

low of 15 to 194 individuals. Across North America, 312 wild birds were counted in the winter of 2003-04. Another 119 birds were then in captivity, the majority of these located at five different breeding facilities, including the Calgary Zoo. Threats to the whooping crane remain, however. While they receive protection in the Park, their migration south is subject to habitat loss and degradation through wetland conversion and exploitation, agricultural conversion of grasslands, dams and water diversions, land development, urban expansion, coastal marsh and shoreline erosion, pollution, and oil exploration and development. Therefore, continued management is critical to ensure their survival.[2]

Peregrine Falcons—Flagship of Endangered Species Recovery Efforts

In 1973, Gary Erickson, a young provincial biologist, joined the work of several federal counterparts in what was to become another intensively managed migratory bird species in Alberta (and across North America), the peregrine falcon. Although not technically a game species for consumption, the peregrine falcon has been the favourite species of falconers for centuries. This interest from a small but committed user group helped to draw attention to its plight. Unlike whooping crane recovery efforts, which were largely carried out by federal agencies,

Alberta's peregrine recovery efforts would become a long-term partnership between both federal and provincial governments, with additional support from conservation organizations, corporate sponsors and key individuals.

The continental *anatum* peregrine falcon was once a fairly common breeding resident across most of North America, but as early as the late 1950s, was no longer occupying many traditional nesting sites. Thinned eggshells, that cracked during incubation, and other symptoms of widespread reproductive failure were evident. At the 1963 Federal-Provincial Wildlife Conference, Canadian Wildlife Service biologist Richard Fyfe presented a paper stating that DDT and other organochlorine pesticides had been found in high concentrations in unhatched peregrine falcon eggs in Britain.

Further research soon confirmed the presence of these pesticide residues in North American peregrines. In 1969, the use of DDT was banned in Canada (and in the United States three years later). Raptor researchers recommended that the peregrine be designated as endangered throughout its range. They also proposed a continent-wide survey in 1970, to be repeated every five years thereafter. Survey results revealed that the continental *anatum* sub-species was particularly threatened compared to west coast (*pealei*) and northern (*tundrius*) populations. Only one *anatum* pair was confirmed to be nesting south of 60°N and east of the Rocky Mountains, and two pairs were found in Labrador.

A number of intensive strategies were employed to save the *anatum* peregrine from extirpation. The core of this management was a captive-breeding program, initiated in 1970 by the CWS. Richard

Fyfe, with the help of a keen young technician, Harry Armbruster, located the last nesting *anatum* peregrine pair in Alberta. Eggs from this pair were taken and hatched in captivity to start the program at Fyfe's farm in Fort Saskatchewan. Young captured from other parts of Canada, and falcons donated by falconers, served to establish additional breeding stock.

By 1972, the breeding program had expanded into a facility established at Canadian Forces Base Wainwright, and CWS added Phil Trefry to the team to help pioneer captive breeding techniques. More eggs of wild pairs were taken for hatching in captivity. Taking the first set (clutch) of eggs from a nest induced wild pairs to lay second clutches—a technique known as "double-clutching". The first clutch was then taken to the captive-breeding facility in Wainwright to be hatched, and the young were returned to the nest and exchanged for the second set of eggs, which would be hatched and kept in captivity. The aim was to maximize the productivity of the remnant wild population, while supplementing the captive breeding program and maintaining high levels of genetic diversity in both.

There were many who believed that falcons could not be bred on a large scale in captivity. But by 1976, enough young birds were being produced that experimental reintroductions could be initiated. "Hacking", a technique using artificial nestboxes to acclimatize young to their wild surroundings, was used to release young birds back into their former range in central Alberta. Young peregrines were also fostered back to wild remnant pairs in northeastern Alberta by wildlife technicians Rick Beaver, Pat Paul, and Lizzane Johnstone-Beaver.

PAT PAUL—A LIFE TOO SHORT

Pat Paul went to work for Alberta Fish and Wildlife Division after working with Richard Fyfe and Harry Armbruster on peregrines in the north. Here his tasks were diverse. He worked on bighorn sheep in the Mount Allen-Wind Creek area, trapped bears and deer with Brian Pelchat, counted Highwood elk with Harold Carr, and conducted peregrine releases in Kananaskis with fellow technician and wife-to-be, Julie Bauer. Tragically, about three months after the aircraft crash that claimed fellow worker Orval Pall, Pat Paul died in a commercial Air Mexico jet crash on his way to a holiday climbing volcanoes in Mexico. He was just 31 years old.

With the help of Fish and Wildlife research personnel Bill Wishart and Gary Erickson, the CWS crew also experimented with the first release of peregrines in an urban situation in Canada, using the top of the O.S. Longman Laboratory Building in Edmonton starting in 1976. One of the four birds released that summer, a male, was recovered later that year in Belize, Central America—a very early demonstration of the effectiveness of the reintroduction techniques used. Erickson recorded several adult birds at the building by 1979. More success came in 1980 when Alberta Fish and Wildlife summer student, Gordon Court, discovered the nesting site of a pair of peregrines in downtown Edmonton on the Alberta Government Telephone Toll building. This pair became the first captive-produced peregrine pair to breed in Canada. It also provided the foundation for an on-going urban education and fostering program that expanded as the number of urban pairs increased

333

HACK BOX INSTALLED ON THE O.S. LONGMAN BUILDING IN EDMONTON FOR PEREGRINE RELEASES.
COURTESY ALBERTA FISH AND WILDLIFE DIVISION

FORT CHIPEWYAN PEREGRINES

In his account of the birds of the Mackenzie Basin, Robert MacFarlane describes the skin of a peregrine, or "duck hawk", shot at Fort Chipewyan in the spring of 1885 and two eggs collected on June 18th of the same year from the edge of a cliff "at some distance north of the establishment".[3] MacFarlane also noted that "the duck hawk makes a great row when its eggs are taken" and well it should! Perhaps if MacFarlane had known of the vital role this small northern population would later play in re-establishing the nearly extirpated *anatum* peregrine falcon across Canada, he would have re-considered his vigorous collecting habits. MacFarlane sent such a great number of peregrine eggs to the U.S. National Collection in Washington they believed the species was "fairly common" throughout the north at the turn of the century.

Whereas in 1970, the peregrine was thought to be extirpated in Alberta, a subsequent re-discovery of a small population of birds in the Fort Chipewyan area brought renewed hope. Lizzane Johnstone-Beaver, known as a driven and resilient field technician, worked in Fort Chipewyan as a contractor for CWS from 1975-1978 and for Alberta Fish and Wildlife from 1978-1979. She was responsible for the nest manipulations (exchanging eggs and chicks) of the northern pairs. As these were now the only nesting peregrines remaining in the province, the project was ripe with potential for disaster.

In fact, the project proved extremely successful. In 1977, Johnstone-Beaver, and summer student Gordon Court, discovered one of the birds they had fostered back into a nest in 1975 breeding at a nest site near Fort Chipewyan—a female banded *P21*. This bird was the first known captive-raised peregrine falcon in the world to return and breed in the wild: a tremendous feather in the cap of the Canadian peregrine recovery effort. From five known breeding pairs in the Fort Chipewyan area in 1975, there are now more than 25 breeding pairs, and the young that were taken into captivity provided most of the stock for the breeding program that raised peregrines for reintroductions across Canada.

in both Edmonton and Calgary. Fostering of young to wild pairs also continued to occur in northeastern Alberta, and with the combined efforts of the Alberta Fish and Wildlife Division, CWS, and Wood Buffalo National Park staff, the northern population also began to show positive signs of growth.

With the growing vitality of northern and urban populations, the early 1990s brought a renewed vigour to peregrine re-introduction in Alberta. Steve Brechtel and Bruce Treichel, Alberta Fish and Wildlife Division, with the assistance of long-time peregrine expert, Gary Erickson, evaluated the state of pollutants in peregrines and their prey to see if continued releases would re-establish peregrines in historical sites in central and southern Alberta. Buoyed up by declining pesticides, and considerable corporate sponsorship from PetroCanada, a large-scale release program was initiated in the early 1990s with hack boxes installed at rural sites on the Red Deer and Bow rivers. Geoff Holroyd, Ursula Banasch, Helen Trefry, and Phil Trefry continued to run the CWS Wainwright facility, largely on a cost-recovery basis, and provided all of the young for the stepped-up Alberta releases. Alberta Fish and Wildlife biologists Petra Rowell and David Stepnisky acted as project coordinators over the five-year period, which was to see the southern Alberta population grow from two to more than 20 pairs in less than a decade. Several young biologists took part in this extensive release program and many of them now hold positions in conservation agencies across Canada.

Intensive management efforts for the peregrine falcon were also supported by on-going surveys and recovery work. The *Anatum Peregrine Falcon*

BRUCE TREICHEL PLACES A YOUNG PEREGRINE CHICK FROM WAINWRIGHT IN THE HACK BOX AT THE O.S. LONGMAN BUILDING IN EDMONTON.
COURTESY ALBERTA FISH AND WILDLIFE DIVISION

Recovery Plan was released in 1988 by the National Peregrine Falcon Recovery Team and included goals for population size and productivity levels. Annual monitoring has been conducted by federal and provincial wildlife agencies since 1970 and continent-wide surveys have been carried out every five years since 1970. Although survey methods sometimes varied, the long-term trend is

BRUCE TREICHEL AND DAVE MOORE BAND
A YOUNG URBAN PEREGRINE.
COURTESY ALBERTA FISH AND WILDLIFE DIVISION

management by federal and provincial bodies have led to a near-full recovery of the *anatum* peregrine falcon. The falcon was down-listed to *Threatened* in 2000 by the Committee on the Status of Endangered Wildlife in Canada (COSEWIC), which had listed the peregrine as *Endangered* in 1978, when status designations first began. The peregrine was also downlisted from *Endangered* to *Threatened* in Alberta in 1999. By 2000, the population in Alberta had increased from only one productive pair to 40 productive pairs. In that same year, the natural productivity from wild nests in southern Alberta exceeded the greatest number of captive-bred young released in any year.

335

The peregrine population still faces challenges as productivity has to remain at an annual average of about 1.5 young per territorial pair to make up for mortality. Monitoring is vital to ensure the peregrine's full recovery. Surveys are still needed in Alberta, as populations show wide annual fluctuations in productivity. Alberta Fish and Wildlife, Wood Buffalo National Park and CWS intend to continue annual monitoring of three study areas in northern Alberta. With continued co-operation both within Canada and across the continent, there is reason to believe that the peregrine falcon's recovery will continue.

clear. Consistently low numbers of peregrines were recorded until the early 1990s, after which the number of known breeding pairs more than tripled over the next five years. It was at this time, in 1992, that analysis of declining pesticide residues in peregrine eggshells carried out by Gordon Court showed conclusively that eggshell breakage would no longer be a limiting factor.

The Canadian Wildlife Service Peregrine Falcon Breeding Facility was closed in 1995 after having raised more than 1500 peregrines over 25 years. At that time, there were enough released peregrines to assure sufficient reproduction in the wild (a decision hastened by budget cuts). Bans on the use of DDT in Canada and the United States and close to three decades of intensive

The Return of Swift Fox to Alberta

Unlike the whooping crane and the peregrine falcon that retained remnant populations in the province, the swift fox had completely disappeared from Alberta by the late 1930s. The last individual in Canada was captured in 1928. The last verified sighting in Alberta dates to 1938. This diminutive little fox, about the size of a house cat, was once abundant but couldn't compete with the human settlers sharing its prairie habitat. Causes of the swift fox's disappearance included the loss of its native

GARY ERICKSON—PROFILE OF ALBERTA'S FIRST NON-GAME BIOLOGIST
[GARY ERICKSON AND FRANCINE WIELICZKO]

"I was born and raised in Edmonton, on the southern city limits (62nd Avenue), where I spent much of my time in the forests and fields south of my home. I was forever bringing home live frogs, hawks and owls. The Boy Scout movement also played an important role in my early years. I was fortunate to be in a troop where camping and hiking were a regular part of the program. My love for hunting also started as a young boy. I spent a lot of time with a schoolmate shooting my BB gun. My father, Vic, was an avid fisherman and hunter who introduced me to the ways of the great outdoors. Vic was always looking for that pristine fishing hole far off the beaten trail. Fall and winter hunting trips for moose and elk were some of my favourite times.

"I later chummed around with fellow biologist Bill Glasgow. The two of us would take off on bird hunting forays after school (or sometimes during school!). One of our favourite haunts was the Blackfoot Grazing Reserve just east of Edmonton. This area was great for ruffed grouse. I attended the University of Alberta from 1965 to 1968 where I obtained a Bachelor of Science Degree, with a major in Zoology. Dr. David Boag and Dr. Jan Murie were advisors and mentors.

"In 1966, while still in university, I landed a summer job as a fisheries technician with Alberta Fish and Wildlife Division, working for Gordon Haugen in the northwest of the province. The work involved stream and lake surveys in the Edson area. I also worked with Ken Zelt on the Tri-Creeks watershed study. After graduating, I was employed year-round as the crew chief for the Agricultural Rehabilitation Development Act (ARDA) Sports Fisheries survey led by Ken Zelt. In 1969, I went to work with Bill Wishart on the Wildlife Research Team."

As the province's first non-game biologist, Gary was tasked with developing and coordinating the provincial non-game and endangered species program. He became the Province of Alberta representative on a long list of federal and provincial endangered species programs, including the Committee on the Status of Endangered Wildlife in Canada (COSEWIC), Convention on International Trade in Endangered Species of Wild Fauna and Flora (CITES), the National Swift Fox Recovery Team, the National Burrowing Owl Recovery Team, the National Whooping Crane Recovery Team, the National Loggerhead Shrike Recovery Team, the Piping Plover Recovery Team, and the Peregrine Falcon Recovery Team. In addition, Gary

was responsible for developing a provincial policy for the management of threatened wildlife in Alberta.

Gary started working with peregrines after Richard Fyfe asked him to participate on the Western Raptor Technical Committee in the early 1970s. This committee had representation from the Yukon, Northwest Territories, British Columbia, Saskatchewan, Manitoba, Alberta and CWS. It had the mandate to develop a national recovery plan for the peregrine falcon—the first recovery plan ever formulated for an endangered species in Canada. Gary was involved in many aspects of the peregrine recovery project and maintained his involvement after moving to work in the southern region in 1988.

"I took a position in Lethbridge as the Regional Wildlife Biologist. Here, I was responsible for the implementation and administration of wildlife programs in the southern region, specifically in the Lethbridge, Medicine Hat, Hanna and Drumheller

GARY ERICKSON IN THE FIELD NEAR BOW CITY COLLECTING PEREGRINE PREY SPECIES FOR PESTICIDE ANALYSIS, 1991.
CREDIT. S. BRECHTEL COURTESY G. ERICKSON

Resource Management Areas. I stayed in this position until 2002 when I retired after 35 years of service.

"Throughout my career, I enjoyed all fieldwork but my most memorable time was spent on the Ram Mountain Bighorn Sheep Study with my close friend, Kirby Smith. In this study, sheep were captured, marked and released, and the survival of orphaned lambs was studied. Other significant projects, aside from peregrine work, included the Camp Wainwright deer and sharp-tailed grouse studies, Canada goose transplanting program, and ring-necked pheasant research where radioactive tracers were used to compare survival rates of wild and captive-raised birds."

During his career, Gary also became more and more involved with working with industry, agriculture, transportation and others to ensure that issues and concerns for wildlife were not ignored. He worked with colleagues to develop consistent and fair land-use guidelines. However, he notes that the most disappointing aspect of his career was when the Habitat Branch was disbanded and integrated into the Wildlife Branch. The Habitat Branch had evolved into a very specialized group of tenacious individuals who had fine-tuned the art of managing people and industry to ensure that the fish and wildlife habitat needs were protected. As Gary recalls: "The Habitat Branch was a force to be reckoned with if the landscape was to be altered in any way." During and after the disbanding of the Habitat Branch, Gary and his team found themselves in a difficult position because they had no legislated mandate to be working on the land base to preserve habitat for fish and wildlife.

When reflecting on his career, Gary pointed out that the biological profession is fraught with danger and he did not escape from finding himself in a few precarious situations. When he was a fisheries technician, he spent a long cold night on a capsized boat tangled in fish nets on Wabamun Lake. He also remembers climbing and rappelling down cliffs using "improvised" equipment, or worse, often not using any safety equipment at all. But perhaps the most dangerous situations that Gary recollects were flying low-level aerial surveys, as he clearly remembers six colleagues who lost their lives while conducting similar surveys (four in Alberta and two in the Yukon).

But there were humorous situations as well. Gary recalls: "I had the opportunity to assist Roy Nowlin with a moose capture/tagging project in the Ministik Lake area. Things went really well—we darted a couple of cow moose, processed them and applied the tags necessary for future identification. However, we encountered our first real test when we 'under-dosed' a small bull moose. Giving a second dose of drugs could result in death to the animal. Rather, it was better to just go out and tackle the under-dosed animal once it started running in circles. Roy was back in the bush about 100 yards shaking his head and mouthing out the words 'No way'. When the moose came by on its next circuit, I sprang up onto its shoulders. Roy mustered up a pile of adrenaline and leapt right up onto me! Eventually our combined weight brought the animal down to the ground. Who says all that we do is science?"

Since retiring from government in 2002, Gary has started his own company, Buteo Environmental Consulting Incorporated and conducts pre-development inventories for the oil and gas industry. When asked about mentors that shaped his career, he feels that Bill Wishart played a significant role in this regard. Gary considers Bill's knowledge and understanding of wildlife ecology to be outstanding. In addition, he admires Bill's ability to stimulate thought-provoking discussions. On a more global level, Gary feels that Aldo Leopold, best known as the author of *A Sand County Almanac* (published in 1949), is the individual who most shaped the development of the field of wildlife management. It was Leopold's view that it is "a human duty to preserve as much wild land as possible, as a kind of bank for the biological future of all species". Gary Erickson has taken this statement to heart.

GARY ERICKSON CLIMBS A TREE TO AN OSPREY NEST ON SWAN LAKE TO BAND THE YOUNG, 1977.
COURTESY G. ERICKSON

337

A RADIO-COLLARED SWIFT FOX READY FOR RELEASE.
COURTESY B. STEVENSON

grassland habitat, competition with other species (especially coyotes), its vulnerability to trapping and poisoning programs, and the drought of the 1930s.[4]

The process of returning the species to its former range was a lengthy one. The first attempt at captive breeding was undertaken at Al Oeming's Polar Park near Edmonton during the 1960s. The foxes (also referred to as kit foxes) that were used as breeding stock originated from Utah. Some of the Polar Park foxes were given to the Cochrane Wildlife Reserve in 1976. The Reserve had previously imported two pairs of swift foxes from Colorado in 1972.

These humble beginnings grew into a major recovery program involving four government agencies (both provincial and federal) and six non-government organizations. The Canadian Wildlife Service and Alberta Fish and Wildlife Division officially became involved around 1976, when the Committee on the Status of Endangered Wildlife in Canada (COSEWIC) classified the swift fox as

Extirpated. Steven Herrero and a number of his graduate students from the University of Calgary also became involved in 1976 and initiated research into the feasibility of reintroduction.

Initial work was guided by letters of agreement between the provincial and federal governments drafted and renewed in 1984, 1989 and 1994. The National Swift Fox Recovery Team was established in 1989. Membership included representatives from Alberta, Saskatchewan, the Canadian Wildlife Service, the Calgary Zoo, and Parks Canada. Lu Carbyn, Canadian Wildlife Service, was the first Recovery Team Chairman. Steve Brechtel (Alberta Fish and Wildlife Division) was the first provincial chairman. The committee was subsequently co-chaired by Pat Fargey (Parks Canada) and Axel Moehrenschlager (Calgary Zoo).

The first release of a swift fox into Alberta occurred in 1983. In total, there were 942 captive-

A SWIFT FOX HARD RELEASE.
CREDIT: LU CARBYN

the official downlisting of the species from *Extirpated* to *Endangered*. It was estimated that there were 279 individuals in the two small wild populations.

An extensive survey was performed in the winter of 2000-2001 in Canada and northern Montana. The census was a follow-up to the 1996-1997 census; several groups participated, including the Calgary Zoo, Alberta Conservation Association, Alberta Sustainable Resource Development, Parks Canada, and the Montana government. The census confirmed that the Canadian population had strengthened and even expanded into Montana. The fact that 99% of captured foxes were unmarked (i.e., born in the wild) was strong

raised and wild-captured foxes (from Wyoming, Colorado, and South Dakota) released from 1983-1996 in Alberta and from 1984-1997 in Saskatchewan. In 1989, foxes were also released into the Milk River Ridge area in Alberta (61 individuals), but this area was abandoned for reintroduction efforts because of high predator numbers and intensive predator control programs.

A Canadian census during 1996-1997 revealed that the core distribution of foxes centred in an area along the Alberta-Saskatchewan border. A smaller population became established in the Grasslands National Park-Montana border area. By 1998 the work of the team and its many co-operators, resulted in

A SWIFT FOX SOFT RELEASE ENCLOSURE.
COURTESY B. STEVENSON

A SWIFT FOX AT HOME ON THE PRAIRIE.
COURTESY B. STEVENSON

340

evidence of successful reproduction within the population. In the 2000-2001 survey, there were three times as many captures as there were during the 1996-1997 census and the sex ratio was better balanced. The Alberta-Saskatchewan border population was estimated at 560 (from 192 in the previous census), the Saskatchewan population at 96 (from 87), and the Montana population at 221.

These census results are very encouraging, and draft guidelines for industrial development and activity in the grassland natural regions of Alberta have been developed which include year-round setback distances from swift fox dens. Populations remain relatively small and vulnerable to decline, however, and their ability to persist is still uncertain. The swift fox is dependent on relatively flat, short or mixed-grass prairie habitat with low ground cover to enhance mobility and visibility, and on the presence of burrowing animals such as Richardson's ground squirrels for food and badgers for dens. It is also potentially vulnerable

to those same impacts that were responsible for its initial decline including loss of native grassland habitat, competition with coyotes, trapping and poisoning programs, and drought. Continued cooperation between the participating government agencies and protective guidelines for industry should help to ensure the lasting recovery of this species. In the short-to-medium term perspective, however, it is clear that the swift fox story is a success story.

Branching Out to Non-Game Species Recovery Work

While the sighting of nesting whooping cranes in the 1950s triggered some of the first endangered species work in the province, the focus of wildlife management remained largely on game species for the next two decades. Wildlife managers would not actively manage non-game species until the 1970s (although the province did make note in its 1955-1956 annual report of the importance of wildlife for

DID YOU KNOW?
Alberta identified its first insect at risk, the Yucca Moth, in 2003. This species is found only in parts of southern Alberta and has been recommended for listing under the Wildlife Act as *endangered*.

"recreational and aesthetic outlets" as well as for harvest).

Work carried out by biologist Steve Brechtel in 1976 was one such example of early non-game species projects. In this year, surveys were organized to locate the nesting sites of American white pelicans, great blue herons, black-crowned night herons, and double-crested cormorants. A few years later, surveys would include western grebes. These colonial species required specific habitat. They were also considered to be low in number and susceptible to human disturbance. Hence, Brechtel was also to investigate various methods for their protection.

In 1977, the *Designation and Protection of Endangered Wildlife Regulations* listed the double-crested cormorant and the American white pelican as endangered species and provided for their protection in Alberta, the first such species to be so designated by the province. Within two decades, management actions would be deemed to be so successful that these two species were removed from the endangered list in Alberta. In particular, the cormorant would do so well as to spark the age-old enmity between this fish-eating bird and its rivals—the fishermen. In 2002, the MLA of Lac La Biche introduced legislation allowing for the culling of any species, including the cormorant, deemed a threat to fish stocks in Alberta.

With the door to non-game species work open, wildlife managers suddenly had many more responsibilities to add to their list. Some reorganization was needed to recognize these new tasks. In 1982, Alberta Fish and Wildlife Division's Wildlife Management Section was broken down into four subsections: Big Game, Bird Game, Commercial Wildlife, and for the first time, a Non-game Management unit. This new unit, largely responsible for amalgamating endangered species programs, wasted little time. In 1985, it released *A Policy for the Management of Threatened Wildlife in Alberta*, followed by changes in 1987 to an updated *Wildlife Act* and associated *General Wildlife Regulation*. Provisions under the

Act now enabled the listing of species at risk as either endangered or threatened. At the time, twelve species were listed. A number of these occurred on the prairies including swift fox, ferruginous hawk, burrowing owl, piping plover, and mountain plover. However, species at risk were not limited to the south with woodland caribou, wood bison, peregrine falcon, whooping crane, and trumpeter swan also listed. The Act and its associated regulations contained provisions to protect endangered and threatened animals year-round. They also provided for the first legislated habitat protection. Nests and dens of endangered species and migratory birds defined under the federal *Migratory Birds Convention Act* were to be protected throughout the year, while hibernacula used by snakes and bats were protected during hibernation periods.

By this time, work on species at risk of extinction or extirpation in Alberta had not only grown in the number of species under examination, it had also grown in the partnerships and methods being used. A page out of the 1986 Fish and Wildlife Division Annual Report (on the following page) provides a glimpse of the species, the partnerships, and the techniques being employed to manage species at risk. Concurrent with this growth in the Fish and Wildlife Division was a similar expansion in the Canadian Wildlife Service under the leadership of Director Gerry McKeating, previously a non-game biologist familiar with species at risk, urban and habitat issues.

Overall, however, the Non-game Management section of the Fish and Wildlife Division remained small and chiefly under the influence of its single permanent non-game biologist, Steve Brechtel (Erickson moved to Southern Region in 1988). With a small amount of provincial funding and the successful leveraging of dollars and manpower from federal and conservation agencies, Brechtel successfully juggled the responsibility of managing a handful of threatened and endangered species, while setting the foundation for what would become a much larger process of species-at-risk assessment and recovery in Alberta.

1986 ALBERTA FISH AND WILDLIFE DIVISION'S ANNUAL REPORT:

Swift Fox

Fish and Wildlife Division continues to work with the Canadian Wildlife Service and the University of Calgary to reintroduce the swift fox to southern Alberta. 59 foxes have been released since 1983 (8 released in 1986). 17 foxes were radio-collared and released in the fall of 1983. As of January 1986, 2 of these foxes are alive. Three pairs released in 1983 produced 12 offspring in the spring of 1984. 10/14 known cases of mortality are suspected coyote or bobcat kills.

Peregrine Falcon

Province wide survey of all historical peregrine falcon nest locations conducted in May 1986. 59 historical eyries were surveyed; none were active. Eight young captive-raised peregrines from the Canadian Wildlife Service facility at Wainwright were fostered to three of the pairs. Total production (including fostered birds) was three young.

Burrowing Owls

Initiated an inventory of nesting locations in 1986. 3-year survey funded by World Wildlife Fund (Canada), Alberta Recreation, Parks and Wildlife Foundation, Coaldale Insurance Company, Robinson's Camera (Lethbridge), and Alberta Fish and Wildlife Division. Coordinated by Colin Weir, a public volunteer from Coaldale. The project relies on public response to a media campaign requesting that individuals report sightings of burrowing owls to Mr. Weir or District Fish and Wildlife offices. Approximately 200 different nest locations were reported in 1986. Mr. Weir and Mr. Dan Wood of Castor banded 345 owls at 101 nests.

Prairie Buteos

South of Hanna, Dr. J. Schmutz of University of Saskatchewan continued population studies. 309 nesting and adult ferruginous hawks were colour-marked, as were 256 Swainson's hawks. A province-wide survey will be conducted in 1987 to determine current population levels and population trends since the last provincial survey in 1982.

Raptors

Six individuals or institutions have entered into agreements with the Fish and Wildlife Division to provide volunteer rehabilitative care for sick, injured or orphaned raptors. These individuals received approx. 200 birds of 16 species in 1985, of which 88 were released. Forty-four were undergoing treatment or care at the end of the year while the remainder died or were euthanized.

Wild West

An endangered species and habitat program initiated by World Wildlife Fund (Canada) in the Canadian prairies. Designed to initiate and co-operatively sponsor projects, which contribute to the well being of endangered species. Projects directed by steering committee comprised of representatives from provincial and federal wildlife agencies, non-profit organizations, and private landowners. In Alberta, projects for burrowing owls, ferruginous hawks, and swift foxes are currently active.

342

GERRY McKEATING: NON-GAME AND SPECIES-AT-RISK WITH THE CANADIAN WILDLIFE SERVICE
[INTERVIEWED BY PAT VALASTIN, OCTOBER 14, 2004, EDMONTON]

"I was born in Montreal in 1936 but grew up in Toronto. As a teen, I spent a lot of time in Algonquin Park camping and fishing with friends. Then I met several bird-banders at Long Point on Lake Erie. This got me involved in the Federation of Ontario Naturalists. I worked with them for five or six years with birds of prey, songbirds, and bird-banding.

"I went back to school and finished a B.Sc. and eventually a M.Sc. from York University dealing with wildlife policy in urban environments. We wanted to know how to get urban people involved in wildlife issues and what wildlife departments could do in urban areas from a management perspective. At the same time, I was working on urban issues with the Wildlife Branch of Ontario Ministry of Natural Resources. I worked with them for five or six years. This gave me some good insights as to what concerned provincial wildlife folks. When I joined the Canadian Wildlife Service (CWS), I brought that experience with me.

"I joined CWS in 1979 and was posted to London, Ontario for five years. As one of the first non-game biologists, I helped to develop provincial endangered species and interpretation programs. I worked with Val Maicins, out of the District office at Kenora, on white pelicans. I also was responsible for the first peregrine falcon introduction program in Algonquin Park. Then I became a Habitat Biologist and we dealt with a lot of the large wetlands around Lake St. Clair.

"I left for Ottawa and did eight or nine months of French training before running into the budget cuts of 1984. I stayed in Ottawa for a couple of years after that, and then, when the Head of Habitat position was available in the Prairie and Northern region, I applied. I came here [Edmonton] in 1986.

"Running the Habitat Program, I spent a lot of time with the National Wildlife Areas in Saskatchewan, Manitoba, and a few that were in Alberta and the Arctic. In those days, there also was a lot of pioneering work going on with the North American Waterfowl Management Plan, both nationally and internationally. Bob Andrews, Wildlife Director for Alberta Fish and Wildlife

Division, and Gordon Kerr, Director for CWS, both played very active roles. Under this program, there ended up being a lot of money for wetland and wetland bird science and some of our Habitat Management programs as well. There has been a lot of land secured, one way or another.

"When Kerr left CWS, I filled his position as Director. I worked to get the Prairie Habitat Joint Venture program up and running, working out the details as to what should be the provincial and federal roles, where non-government organizations, like Ducks Unlimited Canada and a number of others, fit, and how programs were to be delivered in each of the prairie provinces. There were endless meetings. We eventually came out with implementation plans and delivery structures in each province. In Alberta, the 'first-step' project was at Buffalo Lake. I felt that that whole experience, while it was tough slogging right up to the day I left, was a very positive and cooperative venture. My successor, Bill Gummer, is now Chair of the Prairie Habitat Joint Venture.

"In 1984, the federal government and priorities changed, and the CWS budget came under attack. There were about 80 positions deemed surplus nationally and laid-off. This region suffered immensely. Then in late 1980s, there was another period of belt-tightening. We had to lay off another 18 people. So our ability to do some of our work was lessened considerably. We couldn't really manage those kinds of cuts without it affecting some of the money we were getting for the North American Plan. Cuts aren't always one hundred percent bad, because they force you to focus. Some of the stuff that we got out of perhaps was tenuous, for a federal focus anyway. Those views may not have been shared, but that was part of the way I approached it.

"I always wanted to be in the position with my colleagues that we could phone each other up and say: 'What the hell are you doing?' in a constructive way and work that through. I got along with Brent Markham [Fish and Wildlife Division] very well. But often a lot of the stuff came from Ottawa. Our country is very different. Alberta is different from Saskatchewan, as it is from British Columbia. And I don't think they

[Ottawa] do a very good job of reflecting those regional differences. I felt fairly strongly that the wounds of the National Energy Program as it affected Alberta were still very apparent. They still are today.

"But overall in Alberta, with the peregrine falcon program, work on other birds of prey, and other species, the end result was positive. Peregrine falcons are doing very well now. We can look at Alberta Fish and Wildlife Division and Canadian Wildlife Service—our role and theirs—and it's worked out very well. I can think of a lot of people in Alberta Fish and Wildlife, people like Gordon Court, that are very dedicated, as there

are in the Wildlife Service. The challenge is how we can make sure that these folks continue to work together for the common goal.

"I left CWS [retired] at the end of June, 2004 because I didn't want to leave facing November on the doorstep. At last, I would have a summer off. And the time has really flown by. I've been quite involved with Bird Studies Canada, a national bird science group based at Long Point. I was Chairman of the Board of Directors for a couple of years. We do breeding bird surveys in Alberta, and I'm also Chair of the Management Committee for the Alberta Bird Atlas. So I'm doing those kinds of things for fun and interest, plus playing a lot of tennis."

[When Gerry McKeating retired from CWS, several members of Alberta Fish and Wildlife came to his retirement party where Brent Markham presented him with a plaque thanking him for 17 years of dedicated service in wildlife conservation work in Alberta.]

Wild Species 2000—The Expansion of Species Status Assessment

Throughout the 1980s, public opinion was changing and the number of non-consumptive users of wildlife—like bird watchers, photographers and hikers—was growing. With this growth came the emerging awareness of the need to protect all wild plant and animal species, eventually emerging as today's awareness of our biodiversity.

The development of the *Guidelines for Wildlife Policy in Canada* led by Anthony Keith of the CWS and formally approved at the Wildlife Ministers' Conference of 1982, with input from representatives from the provinces and territories, formally expanded the definition of wildlife to include all non-domestic species of plants and animals. This policy was a significant turning point in the evolution of wildlife management in Canada. Further activities by national agencies such as the Committee on the Status of Endangered Wildlife in Canada (COSEWIC), which examined and listed at-risk species, and the Recovery of Nationally Endangered Wildlife Committee (RENEW), which implemented recovery plans for endangered and threatened species listed by COSEWIC, also helped to foster this new awareness.

A RESEARCHER USES TELEMETRY TO TRACK THE MOVEMENT OF NORTHERN LEOPARD FROGS.
CREDIT: L. TAKATS COURTESY ALBERTA FISH AND WILDLIFE DIVISION

345

By 1990, work in Alberta's non-game unit was also expanding from its traditional base of birds and mammals. The western hognose snake and the northern leopard frog were some of the first reptiles and amphibians to come under scrutiny by the province. Later, the western blue flag and cottonwood habitat would become the first plant species and first ecosystem to be recognized as requiring research and management action.

A comprehensive assessment of the biological status of all wild species in Alberta was first undertaken in 1986. In 1991, a more defined evaluation process ranked species into categories, reflecting the degree of threat they faced. Further, it highlighted those species for which a more

detailed status assessment was needed and those species for which insufficient data existed. In 1996, the Fish and Wildlife Division released the second five-year assessment of *The Status of Alberta Wildlife*. This assessment and ranking system has now grown into today's ongoing *General Status Assessment Process*.

In 1997, just short of a decade since the endangered and threatened designations had been added to the *Wildlife Act*, the Government of Alberta amended the Act and added a new *Wildlife Regulation* that broadened the definition of wildlife. The legislation now made provisions to include the designation of at-risk plants, fungi, algae, invertebrates and fish. The ability to list non-game and non-traditional (plants and invertebrates) wildlife represented a huge step forward in the evolution of species-at-risk protection in the province and in recognizing the importance of preserving biodiversity.

Changes to the provincial act were in line with a national approach outlined in the *Accord for the Protection of Species at Risk*, developed in co-operation with the other provinces, territories, and the federal government in 1996. The Accord initiated the refinement of the general status assessment process across Canada.

In Alberta, the most recent general status assessment report, *The General Status of Alberta Wild Species 2000*, was released in 2001 and reported that, of 832 species assessed, 1.44 percent (12) were classified "at risk". However, the percentage varied depending on which group of species was examined, with 15 percent of the province's birds, 100 percent of reptiles, 21 percent of mammals, 70 percent of amphibians, 12 percent of butterflies, 19 percent of fish, 63 percent of ferns and 58 percent of orchids assessed at some degree of risk in the province. Alberta's general status ranks were compiled with those of all other provinces and territories to produce national general status ranks, published in March 2001 in the *Wild Species 2000 Report*.

The 1997 regulatory reform of the provincial *Wildlife Act* also provided for greater public participation in species-at-risk determination with the creation of the Endangered Species Conservation Committee (ESCC) and its Scientific Subcommittee (SSC). The ESCC, a stakeholder group composed of land users and managers, industry, scientists, conservation organizations, and government, was established by then Minister Gary Mar to provide advice on the identification and protection of species at risk in the province. The SSC was created to conduct detailed status assessments for high priority species. For species considered at risk, these assessments form the basis for potential legal

A RESEARCHER CAPTURES A PRAIRIE RATTLE SNAKE—A SPECIES AT-RISK.
CREDIT: D. ESLINGER COURTESY ALBERTA FISH AND WILDLIFE DIVISION

listing under the *Wildlife Act* as *Endangered* or *Threatened*.

To date, Alberta's SSC and the ESCC have reviewed approximately 50 species including a diversity of small and large mammals, raptors and songbirds, game and non-game fish, most of Alberta's reptiles and amphibians, several unique plants and a few invertebrates! The SSC uses assessment criteria developed by The International Union for the Conservation of Nature (IUCN). The same criteria are used by COSEWIC to assess the national status of species, providing a good parallel between provincial and national processes.

The Species at Risk Act

The provincial species-at-risk program continued to evolve and received its biggest boost in 2000 with an enhanced budget that enabled the hiring of 11 biologists. With the assistance of many regional Fish and Wildlife Division staff and numerous other partner agencies, advancements were made in the identification and recovery of at-risk species. In 2002, the first provincial recovery teams had produced recovery plans for western blue flag and piping plover. These plans were formally approved by the provincial government and the recovery implementation phase begun. Numerous other stakeholder-based recovery teams were initiated and although many of them deal with complex land-use issues, they have continued to make progress in recovery-plan development and implementation. As of 2004, 14 recovery teams were working on developing and implementing plans for Alberta's threatened and endangered species.

For the most part, recovery teams are single-species focussed. A single-species approach is necessary in some situations where species are in extreme peril; however, in many cases it may be beneficial to pursue a multi-species approach, or even better, a landscape approach that is aimed at preventing species from becoming at-risk in the first place. By 2002-2003, the Species-at-Risk Program started to move in this direction with the initiation of three multi-species landscape-level projects (MULTISAR: The Milk River Basin Project; SHARP: Southern Headwaters at Risk Project; and Habitat Stewardship Program for Species-At-Risk In Special Areas 2, 3 and 4). These initiatives focus on conservation of species-at-risk at the landscape-level through voluntary stewardship actions with land users. In addition, a multi-species approach has been adopted for recovery planning for the soapweed and yucca moth, and for several at-risk fish species that occur in the Milk River.

After more than a decade of discussion, the federal *Species at Risk Act* (*SARA*) was passed by Parliament in December 2002 (under then

Environment Minister David Anderson). SARA focusses on preventing species from becoming extirpated or extinct, and recovering species that have been listed as endangered and threatened, as well as extirpated species if recovery is feasible. The Act includes actions to protect species at risk and their "residences". SARA defines residence as a dwelling-place, such as a den, nest or other similar area or place, that is occupied or habitually occupied by one or more individuals during all or part of their life cycles, including breeding, rearing, staging, wintering, feeding or hibernating. It also incorporates measures to protect critical habitat through the recovery planning process.

Perhaps one of the greatest perceived weaknesses of the Act is that, while protection is in most cases mandatory on federal lands and for species under federal jurisdiction (aquatic species defined as fish under the federal *Fisheries Act* and migratory birds listed under the *Migratory Birds Convention Act*), it relies on discretionary use of protective measures for individuals, residences and critical habitat on provincial crown and private lands. (SARA defines critical habitat as the habitat that is necessary for the survival or recovery of a listed wildlife species and that is identified as the species' critical habitat in the recovery strategy or in an action plan for the species.) While it remains to be seen how effective SARA will be, it has raised awareness of species-at-risk protection within all levels of government, industry, land managers, landowners and the general public.

Future Challenges of Biodiversity Management

Over the first half of the century in Alberta, the role of managers was largely to understand population size and trends such that the allocation of game species for subsistence, commercial and recreational purposes was sustained. The early biologists' unequivocal success at setting bag limits, seasons, and other regulations, was equally matched by enforcement and forensics staff and techniques that ensured that allocation rules were followed. Even today,

347

the "recreational and economic importance" of the resource is a cornerstone of the provincial government's business plan and maintaining suitable amounts of harvestable species like walleye and moose continue to take up a large proportion of provincial time and resources.

"Fish and Wildlife Management manages Alberta's fish and wildlife resources to preserve their intrinsic value to the environment as well as their recreational and economic importance to Albertans."

SUSTAINABLE RESOURCE DEVELOPMENT BUSINESS PLAN 2003-06

348

Through time, however, the role of fish and wildlife managers has expanded. By the late 1960s, the impact of traditional human activities, like hunting and fishing, were becoming much smaller in relation to other resource extraction issues. The large-scale development of industries for grain, cattle, trees, and oil and gas took a toll on fish and wildlife habitat. Responding to these changes, fish and wildlife managers had to expand their repertoire. They now had to understand land-use planning and management processes. And they had to define precisely what habitat it was they were trying to include, and why, in these processes. To do this, biologists examined the habitat needs of fish and wildlife in closer detail. Perhaps this, in turn, triggered a greater understanding and appreciation not only of biodiversity but of the strong interconnectedness between all species and the ecosystem of which they are an integral component.

Today, the goal of most fish and wildlife agencies is to manage for "biodiversity" or, at the very least, keystone or indicator species of biodiversity and general ecosystem health

where we can define it. However, the reality is that it is getting harder and harder to manage traditional species that we know a great deal about, in the limited habitat that remains, and with limited resources for such work.

The story of caribou perhaps best exemplifies this new conundrum. Successfully managed for more than a century under traditional game laws and bag limits, broad-scale landscape changes tipped the scales in the 1970s and caribou decline was noted. Caribou harvest was discontinued in 1980. The species was listed as *Threatened* in 1987. In the last two and a half decades, the population has continued to decline, and despite intensive research, predictions are dire, particularly for small western foothills herds. Among the root causes of the caribou's decline are its shrinking old growth forest habitat, its increasing number of encounters with humans or the footprint they leave behind, and the change in predator-prey cycles triggered by this footprint. Even if dollars for research and recovery efforts were unlimited, finding a solution to the paradox of maintaining healthy caribou populations, and many other species for that matter, with less and less old growth forest available to them—is no small feat.

How, then, do we solve this conundrum and manage for all of Alberta's biodiversity, on a land base that is likely to have less and less habitat available to it in the future? On an international front, similar concerns led to the negotiation of the United Nations Convention on Biological Diversity (the Rio Convention) in 1992. Canada was the first industrialized country to ratify the Convention, developing its own *Canadian Biodiversity Strategy* to guide efforts in this country. In 1995, the Government of Alberta committed to supporting the strategy. Today, more than a decade after the Rio Convention, the province is working towards fulfilling its obligations. At a policy level, an Alberta Biodiversity Strategy is in development but objectives are unclear and

RESEARCHERS COLLECTING INFORMATION ON A TRANQUILLIZED WOODLAND CARIBOU.
CREDIT: BOB WYNES

349

progress seems slow. At the research level, there are efforts to determine biodiversity measures and monitoring techniques but resources are limited. And at the ground level, there are efforts to restore more than two-dozen species identified as at-risk but efforts are hampered by a lack of resources and an inability to address the protection of existing habitat or the replacement of habitat already lost.

One of the most important needs recognized in the Canadian Biodiversity Strategy is the need to increase our understanding of ecosystems and increase our resource management capability. We would add to that the need for commitment—from governments, from industry, land managers, and the public—and the need for action, for to change our ways is the true measure of our understanding.

GUY L'HEUREUX: EVERYTHING IS CONNECTED

I'm reminded of a comment given by a rancher in the Oyen area who stood in the middle of a conference discussing the extermination of the feared coyote: "If the day ever comes, when you go out onto your veranda in the evening to enjoy a cup of coffee, and you don't hear a coyote on your ranch, then you'd best sell your cows, because they will not be able to live there either." Somehow, we need to find a way to re-establish in the minds of those powers that be that everything in nature is connected, and necessary for our survival. What could be more important than that?

WOLF RESEARCH ON CARIBOU RANGES IN WEST-CENTRAL ALBERTA
[GERRY KUZYK]

Woodland caribou is a "threatened" species under the Alberta *Wildlife Act* and special management considerations are necessary to maintain its numbers and habitat. In September 1999, the West-Central Alberta Caribou Standing Committee initiated a wolf study to run concurrently with new and long-term caribou research projects. A number of wolf studies have been conducted in the foothills and mountains of western Alberta, but none of these was directed at wolf movements on caribou ranges. This study was to provide information on wolf distribution and movements in relation to land-use developments on caribou ranges in west-central Alberta.[5]

Densities of 11 wolves/1000 km^2 were found on caribou ranges in west-central Alberta, which is well above the 6.5 wolves/1000 km^2 that some suggest is required to cause a caribou decline. One management option would be to conduct a wolf control program to increase caribou numbers, but simply reducing wolves to benefit ungulate populations is controversial. Further, wolves are able to repopulate quickly and could attain their pre-reduction levels within five years, leading once again to a potential caribou decline. Also, such a reduction has the potential to greatly increase moose numbers, which is contrary to what some suggest would benefit caribou.

The wolves in this study were preying predominantly on moose, with kill rates averaging one moose every three to five days. There are opposing views as to how moose abundance can affect caribou. One view states that increasing moose numbers will translate into a corresponding increase in wolf numbers, and thus result in more wolves preying on caribou. The alternate view suggests that more moose in the system will benefit caribou, as moose provide more biomass (meat) for wolves. A Yukon study found that the wolf pack size and number of wolf packs remained similar, despite a two to three-fold increase in the number of ungulates in the area.[6] Results from the west-central Alberta study conformed to the view of moose being beneficial to caribou. Wolves travelled about four times less far when near moose kill sites than when they were away from them. Therefore, an abundance of moose in the system *may* benefit caribou

because wolf packs preying primarily on smaller prey, such as deer, may travel farther and increase their chances of encountering caribou.

Although wolf predation may be one cause of caribou declines in west-central Alberta, a greater threat to caribou survival may be the amount of remaining old-growth forest. As the amount of forest continues to decrease, caribou will be forced to live in residual patches, and may be at increased risk to wolf predation. The amount of natural forest in this study area ranged from 60%-86% between wolf pack territories. The threshold amount of forest that caribou need to avoid population-limiting predation by wolves is currently unknown.

Wolves in this study preferred forest cutblocks to either forest or anthropogenic (pipelines, wellsites) features. How cutblocks are developed on caribou ranges may have important consequences for wolf predation risk to caribou. Decisions must be made about the spatial relationship of cutblocks and other preferred wolf habitats to the habitats preferred by caribou. Ideally, creating aggregated cutblocks away from caribou habitats that receive special management consideration may attract other ungulates and thus wolves to the cutblock and away from caribou areas. This would also allow more access to resident hunters and trappers, which could increase the opportunities to legally harvest wolves.

Obviously, future research on wolves is needed to answer some important questions related to caribou conservation. Recent estimates suggest there are about 4000-6000 woodland caribou in Alberta, with an adult sex ratio of 53% females, an 85% birth rate, and a survivorship of 22% for original calves surviving to March. To estimate the impact of predation on caribou calves conservatively using the above data (4000 caribou), we could calculate 2120 female caribou (55%), producing 1802 calves, of which 901 calves (50%) are killed by predators in the first month, leaving only 396 (22%) of the original calves remaining by March. Thus, predation alone could account for about 1700 caribou calf deaths per year. This direct impact on caribou deserves much greater research attention.

A PACK OF WOLVES TRAVELLING DOWN A CUTLINE.
CREDIT: GERRY KUZYK

During this study, several wolves dispersed as individuals or in small groups (less than three) from their natal territories. These lone wolves, or small groups, may be an important factor when assessing predation risk to caribou. These wolves could represent 10%-30% of the wolf population, and would be travelling great distances to establish new territories. If, at a large scale, wolf packs are generally avoiding caribou habitats because of a lack of moose, then dispersing wolves may "select" these habitats to avoid being killed by pack wolves defending their territories, which is a primary cause of natural wolf mortality. Conducting research on single or small groups of wolves would be logistically difficult because of low sample size, difficulty in tracking, and high natural mortality of wolves, but resulting information could lead to important insights into caribou predation risk from wolves.

Limited study has been conducted in Alberta to examine causes of caribou calf mortality; thus, it is unknown if wolves are the main cause of death for young caribou. Results from caribou calf mortality studies in Alaska have found that death to caribou calves less than 30 days old is normally 40%-50% due to wolves and 40%-50% to bears. While wolves may be the primary cause of caribou declines in Alberta, further predator research must address the effects of other important predators of caribou calves, such as bears, coyotes and lynx. The importance of bear predation on caribou should not be overlooked.

In summation, future, long-term research will provide meaningful information on wolves for caribou managers. Resource managers must consider wolves and their relation to caribou, in the context of the entire system. Single-species research can provide useful information, but it has the potential to be misleading. In west-central Alberta, wolves are intent on hunting moose in certain areas and deer and elk in others; caribou occur as available prey, but in such low numbers that they could not possibly support the present wolf densities. Future research on wolves and caribou in Alberta should be conducted in the context of the system in which they live: a dynamic multi-predator/multi-prey system.

MAJOR EVENTS IN AT-RISK SPECIES MANAGEMENT IN ALBERTA

1926 Whooping Cranes are believed to be extirpated in Alberta.

1938 The last verified sighting of a swift fox in Alberta is made.

1954 Whooping Cranes are sighted in Wood Buffalo National Park.

1966 A captive-breeding program is initiated for Whooping Cranes.

1969 The use of DDT is banned in Canada. Raptor researchers recommend that the peregrine be designated as "endangered".

1972 The Canadian Wildlife Service Peregrine Falcon Breeding Facility opens at Wainwright (closed in 1995).

1977 Female peregrine P21 is the first known captive-raised peregrine falcon in the world to return to and breed in the wild. *Designation and Protection of Endangered Wildlife Regulations* lists the double-crested cormorant and the American white pelican as endangered species.

1980 The hunting season for woodland caribou is discontinued.

1985 A *Policy for Management of Threatened Wildlife* is released.

1987 *General Wildlife Regulations* now enables the listing of species-at-risk as either endangered or threatened. Woodland caribou are listed as threatened in Alberta.

1988 The Recovery of Nationally Endangered Wildlife (RENEW) is created to undertake recovery planning for COSEWIC-listed species.

1992 The United Nations Convention on Biological Diversity (the Rio Convention) is held.

1995 Alberta commits to the Canadian Biodiversity Strategy.

1997 The Endangered Species Conservation Committee and Scientific Sub-committee is formed.

2000 Endangered species programs are implemented and expanded to include fish, plants, and endangered invertebrates.

2002 The Federal Species at Risk Act (SARA) is enabled. Recovery plans for western blue flag and piping plover are completed.

352

References ▪ CHAPTER 10

[1] Found in the John Stelfox fond at the Musée Heritage Archives in St. Albert. Fond contains two handwritten letters by Grey Owl to Mr. Norquay, agent for Dominion Land Administration in Edmonton, a newspaper clipping, excerpt from Grey Owl's book on beavers, and typed correspondence of John Dewey Soper, an employee of the Canadian Wildlife Service in the 1930s. Donated by John Stelfox, a retired employee of the Canadian Wildlife Service in Edmonton.

[2] Burnett, J.A. 1999. A passion for wildlife: a history of the Canadian Wildlife Service, 1947-1997. UBC Press, Vancouver. (Also published in Canadian Field-Naturalist 113:1-214). Also see White, J.L. 2001. Status of the whooping crane (*Grus americana*) in Alberta. Alberta Sustainable Resource Development, Fish and Wildlife Division, and Alberta Conservation Association, Wildlife Status Report No. 34. Edmonton. (http://www3.gov.ab.ca/srd/fw/status/reports/whooper/index.html)

[3] Mair, Charles and MacFarlane, R. 1908. Through the Mackenzie Basin. William Briggs, Toronto.

[4] Burnett, J.A. 1999, op. cit. See also Cotterill, S. 1997. Status of the swift fox (*Vulpes velox*) in Alberta. Alberta Environmental Protection, Wildlife Status Report No. 7. Edmonton. (http://www3.gov.ab.ca/srd/fw/status/reports/swfox/index.html) and Moehrenschlager, A. and C. Moehrenschlager. 2001. Census of swift fox (*Vulpes velox*) in Canada and northern Montana: 2000-2001. Alberta Sustainable Resource Development, Fish and Wildlife Division, Alberta Species at Risk Report No. 24. Edmonton, AB. (http://www3.gov.ab.ca/srd/fw/riskspecies/pdf/SAR_24.pdf).

[5] Kuzyk, G.W. 2002. Wolf distribution and movements on caribou ranges in west-central Alberta. Masters of Science thesis. University of Alberta, Edmonton, Alberta. 125 pages.

[6] Hayes, R.D., R.S. Farnell, R.M.P. Ward, J. Carey, M.M. Dehn, G.W. Kuzyk, A.M. Baer, C.L. Gardner and M. O'Donoghue. 2003. Experimental reduction of wolves in the Yukon: ungulate responses and management implications. Wildlife Monographs No. 152.

Chapter 11

HABITAT:
INTEGRATING FISH AND WILDLIFE
INTO MULTIPLE LAND-USE PLANNING

Petra Rowell and Gordon Kerr with contributions from Gary Byrtus, Dave Ealey, Archie Landals, George Mitchell, Margo Pybus, Nyree Sharp, John Stelfox, Nadine Stiller and Bill Wishart

353

*The law locks up both man and woman, who steals the goose from the common
But lets the greater felon loose, who steals the common from the goose.*
ANONYMOUS ENGLISH POEM[1]

A Fixed Land Base

In 1967, the authors of *Alberta - A Natural History* appeared to be divining the future when they wrote: "In today's Alberta, overpopulation, serious encroachment on the habitats of plant and animal life, and the pollution of air, soil, and water may seem remote possibilities. A half-century hence, they may be problems crowding in upon us."[2]

Today, one needs only to look at the decline in caribou and grizzly numbers in the north and west, or similar declines in burrowing owls, piping plovers and sage grouse in the south, to concur that yes, a half-century later, encroachment on wildlife and their habitat has become a serious problem. Today, virtually all of Alberta's natural ecoregions have been

modified to some degree. Most visible are the stark changes on the southern and central landscapes, where native prairies were put to the

IN THE PAST, BRUSH AND SPILLED GRAIN ALONG A ROADSIDE PROVIDED FOOD AND COVER FOR UPLAND GAME BIRDS AND OTHER WILDLIFE.
CREDIT: B. WISHART

AGRICULTURAL FIELD THAT IS TILLED THROUGH
THE DITCH AND RIGHT UP TO THE ROADSIDE.
COURTESY B. WISHART

As Brad Stelfox, founder of Forem Technologies and the ALCES project, emphatically makes the point, Alberta is composed of a fixed land base that is not getting any bigger. However, competition for that land base from a multitude of users is increasing rapidly. Although somewhat dated, the *1997 State of the Environment Report–Terrestrial Ecosystems* makes an effort to quantify some of the man-made pressures placed on Alberta's 661,185 sq. km landbase. In 1996, 12% of the province was under protected area status. Only 2.5% of Alberta was

plough and wooded parklands were felled to make way for grain fields stretching across the horizon. Renowned Edmonton birder and Order of Canada recipient Edgar Jones decries the loss of even that small amount of roadside vegetation that once lined every lane—the shrubby brush of yesteryear that once harboured rodents, songbirds, and the odd upland game bird or small furbearer. Similarly, a quick inspection of any current access map or, better yet, aerial reconnaissance, will reveal an ever-expanding web of linear corridors, resource extraction projects, industrial installations, and clearcut forest blocks sweeping across the province making once remote areas now accessible to an increasing number of recreating humans.

classified as open water, making it one of the most water-poor regions of Canada. At the same time, 32% of the province was under some form of agricultural use, 4% was crown lands under grazing lease dispositions, and 27% was crown land under Forest Management Agreements. A further 2% was impacted by urban areas, surface mining (coal, oil sand, sand and gravel) sites, well sites, roads, pipelines, rail lines and other linear disturbances. Since 1997, additional protected areas have been declared; however, the growth of industrial development and disturbance has also intensified.

While human activities do not always preclude all wildlife, they can have a significant impact on local

THE ALCES PROJECT

In Alberta, numerous landscapes are undergoing rapid transformation in response to many overlapping land uses including forestry, agriculture, mining, oil and gas, transportation, intensive recreational use, and the growth of cities, towns, and acreages. Collectively, these land uses can compromise ecological goods and services (like clean air and water, fertile soils, and healthy wildlife) and can lead to unsustainable natural resource management (for example, shortages of merchantable wood, or increases in the number of species at risk). Designed by Brad Stelfox, Forem Technologies, *A Landscape Cumulative Effects Simulator* (ALCES) is an effective simulation tool for assessing cumulative effects and exploring the consequences of different land-use strategies. Government, industry, and conservation agencies use ALCES to explore ecological and economic risks associated with different development trajectories. Mitigation strategies can then be developed to minimize adverse effects. As the pressures on fish and wildlife and habitat management become more complex, so must the tools that are used to manage them.

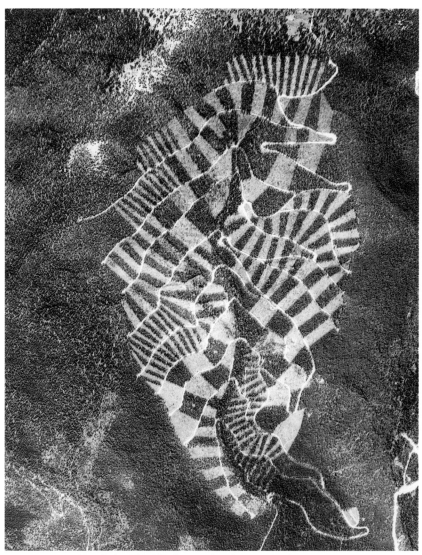

MOSAIC OF FOREST CLEAR CUTS IN WEST CENTRAL ALBERTA, 1958.
COURTESY B. STEVENSON

populations. In some areas, fish and wildlife habitat (the food, shelter, and space plants and animals need to survive) has decreased substantially, or outright disappeared. In many instances, fish and wildlife managers are caught in the middle between conflicting interests: conservation versus agriculture, forestry, oil and gas and other mineral extraction, urban expansion, recreation and other interests. Even where society has made fish and wildlife habitat a priority, a clear course of action is often clouded by a lack of information and understanding of fish and wildlife habitat needs, the ecological processes they are a part of, and the suite of issues they face under the reality of existing on today's fragmented landscape. Many of the underlying issues are complex and evolved over time. Similarly, attempts at habitat management were equally complex over the past century.

DEFINING HABITAT

Habitat is not only the place where organisms live, it is the food, shelter, and space both plants and animals need to survive. This includes the sum total of complex interactions between the air, soil, and water, tempered by climate, latitude, the sun, the moon, and ocean currents.

Habitat undergoes change constantly. In some cases, change occurs a little at a time over a very long period. In other cases, it follows dramatic spontaneous modifications on a local or landscape level. In Alberta, forest fires and extreme weather events like flooding or drought are agents of change. Human activity is also a significant cause of habitat change. Whether it is forestry in the north, agriculture in the south, or linear disturbance and recreational pursuits throughout the province, there has been no shortage of their effects on landscapes and habitats in Alberta during the last 100 years.

A FOREST FIRE NEAR RAM RIVER.
CREDIT: J. JORGENSON COURTESY B. WISHART

356

SEVERAL HUNTERS AROUND A "PLAINS GRIZZLY" KILLED NEAR INNISFAIL.
COURTESY GLENBOW ARCHIVES (NA-103-5)

Habitat Loss through the Century

In 1901, Alberta's human population of 73,022 was only a small fraction (2.4%) of the approximately three million we are today. Predominantly a rural society, pioneers were concerned with wresting a living from the land. Early homesteaders ploughed up the prairie grasslands; those in the parkland belt cleared the trees to prepare the land for farming. Much of the local habitat was destroyed and those species that were not shot, trapped, or poisoned, existed only in more remote areas. Some, such as the coyote and the crow, adapted well to farmsteads. Others, such as the plains grizzly and pinnated grouse, vanished. In spite of regulated hunting seasons, mammals, birds and fishes continued to fall prey to the hunter, whose plea was all too often that he needed the game for food. The volunteer Game Guardians, engaged in the first decades of the century to enforce game laws, were few and far between.

By 1931, agriculture dominated the province with a largely rural population of 700,000. After drought and depression, irrigation projects and community grazing pastures were seen as the saviour of prairie farms. Created under the newly established Prairie Farm Rehabilitation Administration (PFRA), such projects extended the ability of land to sustain crops and livestock, with mixed results for wild populations. Ranchers also demanded more land in the foothills for grazing domestic herds and thus infringed on grazing range once used by elk, deer, and bighorn sheep. Additionally, where predators like bears, cougars, wolves and coyotes, hawks and other birds of prey were perceived as a threat to domestic herds, they were routinely destroyed.

Gordon Kerr recalls: "In many cases, they were different types of impacts. Drainage was fairly widespread. In the southern mixed grass prairie,

THE HISTORY OF THE PRAIRIE FARM REHABILITATION ADMINISTRATION

It is said that a dependable water supply can increase productivity of the land by 500 times and no time was wasted trying to prove this statistic in Alberta. Several small irrigation projects, started as early as 1879, led to the federal *Northwest Irrigation Act* of 1894. However, no projects of any major proportions occurred until after provincehood had been attained in 1905. Formed in 1906, the Southern Alberta Land Company began construction in 1909 on the main diversion on the Bow River near Carseland. After financial difficulties and the outbreak of the First World War, the first delivery of water took place in 1920. By 1921, 9400 acres (3804 ha) were being irrigated in what was to become the Bow River Irrigation District: one of 13 such districts that today dominate a large portion of southern Alberta. The area under water had increased to 30,000 acres (12,141 ha) by 1930 but it wasn't enough to soften the blow of the dirty thirties.

Responding to the desperate needs of the farmers during a period of drought and depression, the *Prairie Farm Rehabilitation Act* received Royal Assent on April 17, 1935. This Act established the Prairie Farm Rehabilitation Administration (PFRA) with a mandate to "secure the rehabilitation of the drought and soil drifting areas in the provinces of Manitoba, Saskatchewan and Alberta" with an operational boundary following Palliser's Triangle in the southern Prairies. The following year, the Act was amended to add land utilization and land settlement. The first PFRA office opened at Medicine Hat, but later moved to Swift Current and then to Regina. The agency's first activities included efforts to control soil drifting by ridging, strip cropping and planting shelterbelts. Local Agricultural Improvement Associations were organized to demonstrate new farming practices.

357

WILDLIFE BIOLOGIST JOHN STELFOX AND W.H. MACDONALD WORKING WITH REDWATER FISH AND GAME CLUB AND ALBERTA AGRICULTURE PLANTING FARMSTEAD SHELTERBELTS TO IMPROVE WILDLIFE HABITAT, 1958.
COURTESY J. STELFOX

To meet the growing needs of producers, the Community Pasture Program was born in 1937. Sixteen community pastures across the prairies were fenced and seeded by December and opened for grazing the following year. By 1999, 87 community pastures encompassed an area of 2.3 million acres or 930,810 ha. Pasture quality was also improved over time. In 1938, one cow needed 58.7 acres (23.8 ha) of land to graze; by 1948, it required only 20.5 acres (8.3 ha).

BUILDING A FISH LADDER AT THE NEW WESTERN IRRIGATION DISTRICT WEIR ON THE BOW RIVER IN CALGARY, 1975.
CREDIT: D. MCDONALD

The PFRA also lost little time getting its first water projects underway. In 1935, farmers were paid $50 to construct dugouts. This amount would rise to $250 by 1959. In 1936, the PFRA's first irrigation work was started. Farmers were then resettled on or near these projects. For example, in 1939, 38 families were resettled to the new Rolling Hills irrigation area. Work slowed during the Second World War between 1940 and 1945, but eventually expanded again. In 1959, 162 families from Saskatchewan and Manitoba were resettled in the Hays District of the Bow River. Other projects included renovation and expansion of the Bow River Irrigation Project in 1950; diversion of the Waterton and Belly rivers into the St. Mary Irrigation Project in 1951; and Travers Dam on the Little Bow River in 1954. The prairies experienced an unusually dry period between 1957 and 1962.

This kept community pastures stocked to capacity and also dramatically increased the demand for water development projects.

In 1959, PFRA saw the official opening by no less than Prime Minister Diefenbaker of its largest project to date—the South Saskatchewan River Project (Gardiner Dam). Although located downstream of Alberta's border, the dam affected the upstream ecosystem particularly for fish populations that once moved freely between the two jurisdictions. Between 1960 and 1973, the PFRA did upgrades on Carseland Weir, Brooks Aqueduct, Western Irrigation District Headworks and Bassano Dam. By 1990, these works were turned over to the Province, as had the St. Mary and Bow River irrigation projects in 1974. Today, the PFRA continues to be a strong player in rural Alberta and is involved in many shelterbelt and watershed conservation programs.

we would see the impacts of grazing, as well as the impacts of intensive cultivation. The rates of degradation seemed to accelerate during the years of drought, particularly with the cultivation of wetland basins. This occurred at the same time that many farmers were getting into larger equipment that increased their capacity to inflict change on the landscape. Both grazing and cultivation impacts could be seen throughout the parkland. As one moved into the north, one saw a lot more clearing of agricultural land, particularly up in the Peace River country around La Crete and Fort Vermilion. And of course those changes affected some responses on the part of the wild populations. The traditional staging area for geese was the Hay-Zama Lakes wetland complex. But then many of the birds moved east to the agricultural lands around High Level and Fort Vermilion. They also staged for a longer period of time in those areas where they had easy access to a rich source of protein."

By the late 1950s, forestry operations had spread from the western foothills north into the boreal

LAND CLEARING IN NORTHERN ALBERTA.
CREDIT: B. RIPPIN

359

forest. The first of the great oil strikes had occurred in 1947, and oil and gas royalties were flowing into government coffers. Seismic crews were bulldozing their way through the bush. Highways and district roads were improved. Four-wheel-drive vehicles and, later, all-terrain vehicles made access into remote areas even easier. Hunters were now able to reach previously inaccessible locations. John Stelfox remembers: "In rural Alberta, the Depression really didn't end until the 1950s with the advent of rural electrifications, oil and gas exploration, and more jobs at better salaries."

There is no more beautiful place than where the prairie meets the mountains in southwest Alberta. The people strong and self-reliant. Where it mattered more what a person could do than where they came from. We didn't have much money; we struggled, but like so many Canadian farm families, we lived on the land we loved and we did what ever was required to make a living from it.

CHIEF JUSTICE BEVERLY McLACHLIN, SUPREME COURT OF CANADA

A BULLDOZER WORKING ON THE
NORDEGG-BRAZEAU ROAD IN 1962 STUCK IN THE MUD.
CREDIT: BOB STEVENSON

came an increasing need for sound management. However, few decision makers at the time gave much thought to the impact these incursions into the wilderness might have. "Progress" would continue throughout the second half of the century. It would be the early 1970s before habitat management would gain as much attention as traditional game harvest management and another decade after that before a habitat branch would be established within the government.

Although our frontier ethic still runs deep, the days of endless wilderness waiting to be subdued are long gone. However, today's recognition that Alberta is sitting on a fixed land base is not an entirely new concept. In the spring of 1969, Deputy Minister of the Department of Lands and Forests Dr. V.A. Wood wisely stated: "In the physical sense, the amount of land available on the earth is fixed. Man cannot increase the physical amount although he can increase or decrease the usable amount by the way he manages and takes care of the land available."[3] Wood, and presumably his department, was already aware of the need for what was then called "multiple land-use planning". Alberta at the time, and still today, retained more than half of its geography as crown land: land that the government would hold and manage for the public good, its bountiful natural resources and multiple uses identified then as outdoor recreation, timber, forage, water, fish and wildlife, minerals and petroleum products.

More people poured into Alberta, and more people ventured into the great outdoors. With scenic areas close at hand, local chambers of commerce pushed for hard-surfaced all-weather roads to service such areas. Camping, hiking, canoeing and hunting increased in popularity. As well, cottages appeared around small lakes with the associated impacts on shorelines, waterfowl, colonial nesters, fish populations, and other wildlife.

The First Efforts at Multiple Land-use Planning

In short, fish and wildlife and their habitat came under pressure simply because a larger population was now carrying out a larger range of activities across many parts of the province. With the increase in activity on the landscape

Like game managers, land managers engaged in three basic steps. They inventoried the land to determine what resource potential was available. They developed policies, legislation, regulations and plans on how they would harvest these resources. And finally, they implemented their plans. Perhaps one of the biggest inventory projects ever undertaken in the province (or across Canada, for that matter) was done under the auspices of the *Federal-Provincial Agricultural Rehabilitation and Development Act Agreement* of the early 1960s. This work was prompted by passage of the 1962 *Agricultural Rehabilitation and Development Act* (ARDA) that encouraged the reversion of submarginal farms to "natural" habitat but also identified undeveloped lands which could be converted to agricultural use. Much of rural Canada was to be assessed as to its land-use capability. The inventory was divided into five sectors (Agriculture, Forestry, Recreation, Wildlife and Present Land Use) and would determine land suitability for farming,

forestry, recreation and the production of hoofed mammals, waterfowl, and game fish.

In Alberta, provincial biologists participated by assessing fisheries capability in our lakes. They also assessed hoofed mammals and their habitat under the "Canada Land Inventory-Ungulate Wildlife Capability Classification Project" led by Ron Weatherill. Similarly, the Canadian Wildlife Service under the leadership of Harold Weaver led a team that carried out waterfowl surveys. At this time, aircraft, first used in fire spotting and suppression, were being used to

361

A MAN HAD A COW...
[DEAN VOLENAC, WISCONSIN CONSERVATION DEPARTMENT OFFICER[4]]

A man had a cow, a horse and a few acres of land. He had a gun and a dog. When he wanted a pheasant or a rabbit he went out and shot it. He had a small stream flowing through his land where he could catch a trout if he wanted one. He thought he lived quite comfortably.

One rainy day he went to town. There he took himself a wife. He lived a little more comfortably now because he didn't have to carry the water, get his meals, or wash his clothes.

Then one day his wife said she was through carrying the water from the spring and she wanted a pump in the house. She also was tired of cooking over an open fire. She said other women had stoves they could put wood into and cook on top of and inside of. The man finally got more cows so he could sell a little more milk, and when he did he bought his wife the things she wanted and had the pump installed.

Soon he found he could not produce enough food to feed the cattle through the winter without another horse and some more machinery. With more machinery and horses he cleared more land for planting crops. Now he produced more, so he added more cows.

He was getting along quite comfortably now. A few years passed and electricity came through the country. The wife wanted lights in the house. By now they had four children. They needed a bigger house. He would have to build one. The wife was tired of the wood stove. Other women had stoves you could turn on with buttons. They had hot and cold water that came out of a faucet. Yes, these things would all be nice.

More cows were bought. Then a milking machine. The horses were worn out and had to be replaced with a tractor. As time passed the flat lowlands where the pheasants used to be were ploughed. The once bushy wooded hillsides were now bare and scarred with deep ditches. Ridges could be seen around the hillsides, caused by too many cattle walking. Overgrazing had left the steep slopes bare, with nothing to break the fall of the raindrops. The once beautiful clear stream was now an ugly deep ditch that ran brown with muddy water after each rain.

One day the man was seen at his table writing a letter. It was to the State Conservation Department. It read as follows: "I buy hunting and fishing licences every year and I think you guys should do more than you are doing to get good hunting and fishing. I can remember when..."

map waterfowl habitat—notably
wetlands. Inventory data were then
used to develop plans for marginal
and sub-marginal agricultural
lands. Land that was not suitable
for farming would be managed for
water retention, wildlife habitat, or
other purposes.

After inventories were completed,
the next step in multiple land-use
management was planning. To
develop a land-use plan, managers
had to determine the needs and
demands of the public and try to
develop a plan to use the land
according to its capability to satisfy
those needs. Where the land was
suitable to be used for more than
one purpose, as identified in the
survey, a multiple-use plan was
called for. This, too, was not a new idea and had
been carried out in the Eastern Rockies Forest
Conservation Area since 1947. This area was
managed primarily for watershed protection but
also for timber production, grazing livestock, the
production of game, and recreation such as
camping and fishing.

LUMBERING OPERATIONS IN THE CROWSNEST FOREST, 1901.
COURTESY ALBERTA SUSTAINABLE RESOURCE DEVELOPMENT
(FOREST PROTECTION IMAGE LIBRARY)

The Eastern Rockies Forest Conservation Board

In his 1931-32 report for the Alberta Fish and
Game Branch, Game Commissioner W.H.
Wallace expressed concern regarding water
pollution from portable sawmills, coal mines, oil
wells, refineries and urban centres. The practice
of dumping sawdust into the nearest river had
been noted as early as 1890. Several others
echoed Wallace's concern for watershed
protection. However, money was scarce. A
shortage of funds prevented any further action
until 1947. In this year, the federal government
passed the *Eastern Rocky Mountain Forest
Conservation Act* creating the Eastern Rockies
Forest Conservation Area. To administer the area,
the Eastern Rockies Forest Conservation Board
was legislated in 1948.

The Area and the Board likely arose out of
recommendations of the 1943 federal report by
R.C. Wallace which, among other things, called
for the "resumption by the Dominion
Government of administrative control and
management of the eastern slopes of the Rocky
Mountains and the creation of national forests
thereon, in order to provide effective protection
for the headwaters of the great rivers of the
plains". By this time, however, the Dominion
had turned control of the resources over to the
province with the 1930s *Resource Transfer Act*,
and the "resumption" of complete federal
control was unlikely to occur. As a compromise,
the new Board became a federal-provincial body
with a budget supplied by both governments.
The Board's prime objective was watershed
protection, keeping in mind the growing
irrigation needs in the southern part of the
province, the water consumption needs of
downstream communities such as Calgary, and
power generation needs of utilities such as
Calgary Power.

The Board was made up of three members at
large, two appointed by the federal government

and one by the Province.[5] One of the principal provincial members was E.S. Huestis, Director of Forestry, who was also the Fish and Game Commissioner, representing the Department of Lands and Forests. Another Chief Officer of the Board was W.R. (Wally) Hanson, Chief Forester of the Board from 1949-1955.[6]

The Board hired its own staff of foresters, engineers, technicians and others and much of their work was taken up with engineering problems such as the construction of roads for forest and watershed protection access. Their task was to make inventories of the timber on the east slopes from Waterton Lakes National Park to the Athabasca River. But work also included all aspects of the multiple use of the region including grazing, lumbering, mineral, and petroleum exploration and development, as well as recreation, fish and game.

One of the major issues within the Eastern Rockies Forest Conservation Area was that of grazing permits. Ranchers were requesting more grazing permits and allotments of crown land for summer range for their cattle herds while others requested that consideration be given to wildlife. In January 1948, the Calgary Fish and Game Association argued for the conservation of streams and forests on the Bow River watershed. The Board, in reply, instructed the secretary to acknowledge receipt of this brief and to inform the Administration that the Board, along with technical experts, would study the points raised in greater detail.[7]

It was generally believed that cattle and wild ungulates, particularly elk, could not compete evenly for grazing range. In the winter of 1949-1950, the Board conducted a game winter range survey in the Castlemount and Livingstone rivers districts. The winter was one of severe cold and heavy snow and it was thought that the range would be overgrazed. Winter range types were classified and those animals that used them were listed. Some ridges, thought to be used by cattle as summer range, were in fact not being used by cattle at all, but were providing good winter range for elk. By spring, much of the range was trampled when the snow melted, making it difficult for cattle to use it. The report concluded that there was a need to balance the number of elk in the southernmost parts with the carrying capacity of the winter range.[8]

At a public meeting held in 1954, ranchers again complained of overgrazing by elk.[9] The biologists from the Department of Lands and Forests were again asked to study the situation. The area south of Highway 3, the Crowsnest Pass, primarily in the Castle and Carbondale river watersheds, had seen a dramatic increase in elk as a result of earlier elk transplants from Yellowstone National Park. Protected and expanding populations— particularly in times of high populations or poor range conditions from dry summers or cold, snowy winters—were now moving out on to ranches in direct competition with private pastures and feed stacks meant for domestic herds. Later that year, it was recommended that the elk reserves be cancelled and an elk hunting season be implemented. The Board also worked to re-zone areas in order that elk and other wildlife would have as little contact with livestock as possible.[10]

In the 1970s, there came the inevitable clash between the Fish and Wildlife Branch and the ranchers. The latter argued that although habitat preservation may have been a worthy object, grazing leases brought in more money. This controversy generated much argument as witnessed by the creation of the Blackfoot Grazing Reserve in the old Cooking Lake Forest Reserve south of Elk Island Park. The Eastern Rockies Forest Conservation Board continued its work until 1973, at which time it was disbanded. The Province would now look after the eastern slopes with its own staff from the Department of Lands and Forests and its successors.

363

THE RANCHER—ELK ISSUE
[GEORGE MITCHELL]

The years 1952-1960 were years of in-depth study and management of wild ungulates and their rangeland condition in the Forest Reserves in Alberta. Early in that period, I studied bighorn sheep and conditions of range parcels used by elk, moose, mule deer and whitetail deer in Forest Reserves south of the Bow River.

The Crowsnest Forest prior to 1954 had a very small annual elk harvest. The Carbondale Game Preserve in the Castle district in this Forest had not been legally hunted previously. The result was that elk numbers had increased dramatically over the years while range conditions declined. In 1953 and 1954, the Castle and Carbondale areas did not have the necessary winter range to support a high density of elk, nor did the private and leased land to the east. The result was an annual exodus of elk to the east from the Forest Reserve and Waterton Lakes National Park. Ranchers just east of these reserves had suffered losses of stacked hay each winter.

In 1953, I was directed to visit Max Bradshaw, a very concerned rancher bordering on the east boundary of Waterton, to assess his concern over the annual damages by elk to his property. I discussed with him a number of management procedures to reduce elk numbers and alleviate the damage elk can do. These procedures and others were implemented in 1954 and included assessing the numbers and distributions of elk, moose and deer in the Crowsnest Forest District during 56 days of aerial and ground censuses. Range conditions in the Forestry Districts showed heavy use of vegetation by game animals and or livestock, and prior to a late April storm, many elk appeared in poor physical condition. Elk carcasses necropsied were infested with ticks and lungworms and had signs of malnutrition.

Poor winter conditions can directly influence herd composition. It is the younger animals that are most affected when food is scarce and snowfall is heavy. The herd composition of healthy elk herds approximates 80% adult and yearling animals and 20% calves. In the Castle District, where the elk herd had been allowed to increase for years with no harvesting and range conditions were poor, the herd composition in 1954 was 87% adult and

yearlings and 13% calves. In the West Porcupine District of the Crowsnest Forest where range conditions were less severe, the elk herd composition was 75% adults and 25% calves. Hence, our recommendation in 1954 for the Crowsnest Forest Big Game Season was to abolish the Castle-Carbondale reserve status and allow the harvesting of elk and other big game; declare an either-sex elk season in the Crowsnest Forest for an extended period; set up a network of hunter checking stations to provide data on hunter effort and success, and collect elk lower mandibles and uteri; set up a study of winter range conditions in the Crowsnest Forest to assess the vigour and distribution of grass and browse species and establish exclosure plots on key sites to study the use of range vegetation by livestock and wild ungulates; and to repeat the ground and aerial surveys in 1955.

The on-site management and control objectives of the Crowsnest Forest hunting season in 1954 were a resounding example of total personnel cooperation and effort. The hunter check stations at Mill Creek and Castle River received excellent assistance from members of the Fish and Game Branch, the RCMP, and members of the Eastern Rockies Forest Conservation Board who also made roving patrols checking hunting parties. An estimated 700-750 either-sex elk were harvested in the Castle-Carbondale District.

This approach to ungulate management in the Forest Reserves was expanded in 1955. That year, botanist Dr. Cormack and I conducted an evaluation of winter range vegetation at three locations in the Crowsnest Forest that documented the misuse of these ranges by elk and livestock. Even though elk numbers had been reduced by some 70% in 1954, we recommended the reduction of cattle on key wintering areas to improve range conditions. The 1954 and 1955 aerial and ground censuses in Forest Reserves, the tabulation of hunter harvest data, the assistance of Fish and Game Officers, Forestry Officers, and biologists at hunter check stations and on roving patrols became a "modus operandi" of accepted procedures in subsequent hunting seasons.

GORDON KERR AND THE 1954 ELK SEASON

My first big game hunting experience I would call a "successful disaster". It was 1954, I was 14 years old, and the Castle River Game Preserve (created primarily for elk protection) was opened for the first time. Cows were legal to shoot but calves were not. I believe this was the first female big game season planned and organized by the first team of provincial biologists. There was no control on hunter numbers, the weather was fine and all roads were open.

When daylight came that first day the gunfire sounded like a war. You could tell where the elk were by the sounds of gunfire moving up and down the valleys. By the time the barrage died away about 1:00 PM, we had taken two female elk, but we had also seen three which others had wounded. We observed several calves running aimlessly, apparently without their mothers. It seemed every car or truck had an elk or two on it. This season went on for a month but fortunately there was not a repeat like opening day.

Our ranch where we had lived since 1950 was 50 miles to the north. Prior to the Castle season, we had not seen an elk in that valley, not even a track, but that winter about 50 head took up residence. We were convinced they had been displaced from the Castle River area. The first hunt experience was a success in that I got my elk, but as a hunting experience it was disappointing. This type of uncontrolled antler-less season, known locally as "Mothers' Day Seasons", was a serious factor which motivated landowners to close their lands to hunting. Much was learned and systems changed leading to the very orderly seasons governed by wildlife management units and the special licence draw systems of the 1960s and 1970s and onward.

Balancing Development with Wildlife Habitat Needs

Although multiple land-use planning seemed like a good concept, it would quickly come under pressure in other areas as well as the eastern slopes. As Dr. Wood explained in 1969:

We are continually faced with the problem of weighing the relative values in returns to the people and in satisfying their needs when the land is used for different purposes. In making the decision of what land-use to follow for a particular area of land we must also consider principles of conservation to ensure the land can be used for whatever purpose that is decided, for an indefinite period, without a loss in its productive capacity. This certainly increases the problem of the land administrator as each land disposition is likely to be challenged not only by the people who compete for use of the land for the same purpose but by other persons who wish to use the land for other purposes. This usually means that no decision is acceptable to all of the intended land users.

Making the right land-use decision required a great deal of thought. Studies were required to obtain a more thorough understanding of all the factors influencing the landscape under examination. Initiating a study on the effects of logging on wildlife was noted by John Stelfox as the most significant contribution of his career with the Fish and Wildlife Division. The study, initiated in 1956 with the Northwestern Pulp and Power Company in the Hinton area (which would later become Weldwood of Canada Limited), was ongoing for a remarkable 40 years. It was successful at defining forest types and conditions and their suitability as wildlife habitat.

Indeed, picking and choosing the best, or several best, uses for public lands gave rise to the complex system of land allocations we have today. Initially, managers divided up crown lands into three broad categories based mainly on soil classification: green, yellow and white. Yellow and white areas comprised the "settlement zone" and came to be administered under the *Public Lands Act* and the Public Lands Division, which currently resides in the Department of Sustainable Resource Development. White areas suitable for agriculture were sold in a manner to create "economic farm units". Yellow

JOHN STELFOX
[INTERVIEWED BY PAT VALASTIN, OCTOBER 4TH 2002, ST. ALBERT]

John Stelfox was born at Rocky Mountain House in March 1929. His parents farmed and ran a livery stable and feed mill. Like many youngsters at the time, John enjoyed a lot of "fishing and hunting, and horseback riding". John took his early schooling in Rocky Mountain House: "…then two brothers and one sister were in the war, so I had to take their places running the farm because Dad was running the livery stable. There wasn't much time for studying for exams and getting homework done". John started his formal education at Olds Agricultural College. "I was interested because it was a good practical education. I enjoyed it and as we see today, Olds College is one of the best technical colleges in Alberta."

John continued his education at the University of Alberta. "I took Agriculture. They would find you work in the summer, which meant you would be able to make a little money and see some other places. I met a lot of very interesting people, like Dr. William Rowan, Dr. Fred Bentley, and Drs. Moss and Cormack in Botany. I think my favourite professor, who had quite an influence on me, was Dr. Reuben Sandin who taught organic chemistry."

After spending time in the Yukon on a federal experimental farm, John came to work for the Province of Alberta in 1955. "Mr. Eric Huestis, Director of Fish and Wildlife, offered me a summer job working with biologists George Mitchell and Bob Webb. Then I was offered a permanent position as a wildlife biologist. The first year I started was interesting because, up until that time, timber management involved primarily selection-type logging on a small scale, where you are harvesting the most mature, best timber, and leaving everything else. Then in 1955, the first clear-cut logging operation opened up at Hinton, and Northwest Pulp and Power established the first pulp mill. Huestis and I used to talk about how this new forest management was going to impact wildlife and their habitats. We decided we should do a study."

"We initiated a study in 1956 looking at the effects of clear-cut logging and scarification on forest structure and biota in three different forest types of west-central Alberta. The study eventually showed that there are other ways of harvesting forests that are much better ecologically. These methods are also

economically sound, and employment wise, superior." John continued to work on the study until 1996 when a summary report was released, entitled *Long term (1956-1996) Effects of Clearcut Logging and Scarification on Forest Structure and Biota in Spruce, Mixedwood and Pine Communities of West-Central Alberta* by J.G. Stelfox, J.B. Stelfox, W.C. Bessie and C.R. Clark. Today, this same study area is a part of the ongoing Foothills Model Forest.

John remained with the Division until 1966, "…at which time I was offered a permanent job with the Canadian Wildlife Service in Edmonton. I worked for 20 years as a research scientist. Work included some of the first studies on prairie dogs in the Val Marie area that is now the Grasslands National Park. And then there was other work in the Fort Walsh area in southwestern Saskatchewan. Research studies were done on bighorn sheep, caribou, elk, bison, and their habitats plus livestock/wildlife competition within Suffield Military Reserve. During that period, I was seconded to the Canadian International Development Agency for three and a half years to establish an ecological monitoring program in Kenya."

John returned to Edmonton in 1982 and retired from CWS in 1986. "I did some contract work on a rangeland-oriented recovery program in southeast Ethiopia. The purpose was to get 115,000 refugees re-established in their homeland after they were forced out by drought and war. Then I did some work in Peru field-training graduate students from the University of Lima. We moved to BC in 1989. I continued to do contract work in Alberta and BC until the year 2000."

When reflecting on his career, John recalls: "We were quite fortunate in the 1950s and 1960s because there weren't so many government agencies or industries competing on the same parcel of public land as there are today. Basically, we had the Forest Service who was the boss on forested land, and then Agriculture and the Lands Branch who were bosses on arable, agricultural land. Roads were very few and pretty poor. The energy industry was just getting active in the northern half of Alberta. During those early years, the main job was to obtain initial information on the abundance, seasonal distribution, production and harvest of primarily big game, then upland game species, as well as predators, large carnivores, and to a limited extent waterfowl.

"We spent a good 75% of our time in the field. So you really knew what was going on. It was a stern policy by our director Eric Huestis that you work as a team with the Forest Service and Fish and Wildlife Officers. Throughout the year, they kept information on what there was in their districts for caribou, moose, deer and elk, bighorns and goats. When I started working all of northern Alberta until 1958, I set up a system for them to provide monthly wildlife reports from their districts for the winter period. That gave us a lot of information, especially for areas that weren't opened up to roads yet. That really helped in getting that preliminary, initial information for the northern half of the province.

"It wasn't until the late 1950s and the 1960s when they really started putting a lot of roads through for energy development. One that made a big difference was the Forestry Trunk Road (started the last year or two of the 1940s), especially in the 1950s to 1958 when it was pushed north eventually right up to Grande Prairie. By 1956, it had reached north of Hinton, and up to Muskeg. Then seismic operations started working from the Forestry Trunk Road, putting other roads in, which increased access for hunters and fishermen. Word started to get out that there was good fishing back there. In the spring, after the grain crops were put in, a lot of farmers and others would go back there. Some would take big washtubs and 50 to 75 pounds of salt, and they would pull those big bull trout out of those pools, salt them down and take home hundreds of pounds of them. Now, the bull trout is on the endangered list."

When asked who most influenced his career, John replied: "I've got to mention that Dad certainly did, because he was one of the few major naturalists and conservationists in the period between 1920 and 1950. He was always advising the provincial and federal governments and the public to get involved in better conservation programs. He was way ahead of his time. Eric Huestis was a wonderful person to work for. He was a forward-thinking person who believed strongly in a cooperative, unified approach to managing all natural renewable resources, rather than having a number of separate, competing agencies. He would say that the only way that could be done was if you had all the natural resource

agencies under one department of Natural Resources, and they were compelled to work together and to come up with cooperative, unified plans. The more time goes by, the more you realize that's the right approach. Today, it seems we really have more of a competitive approach among natural resource agencies."

When the discussion turned his thoughts to the future of wildlife management, John said: "I really have mixed thoughts on it, because it has changed so much. The computer plays such an important role today. There are so many uses of public crown land by various government and private organizations, as well as public organizations. They are all vying for an important role on the same chunk of public Crown land. Now there's a need for so much office work handling referrals, and trying to come up with reasonable compromises. I believe there is now much more political intrusion into the management decisions that it's more difficult for biologists to develop and implement wise wildlife management programs than it was in the 1950s and 1960s. I think that today we've had to go more into people management than into wildlife management.

"So I don't see the future today being as bright as we saw it in the 1950s and 1960s. But I still think that what a professor at Utah State University (Dr. Wagner) emphasized in the late 1950s and 1960s is correct: that in order to have a sound Wildlife Management Program, and one that can be maintained, the wildlife resource has to have a strong financial basis. Wildlife resource agencies have very little power in decision-making on public lands, because there's no large economic benefit. What he also said, that I think tends to be true throughout the world, is we have to lose that wildlife resource, or almost entirely lose it, before the public and the government realize that it was important, and we're able to make any headway managing it."

[Today, though officially retired, John remains as busy as ever.]

367

THE OLIVER TREE NURSERY, ca. EARLY 1950s.
COURTESY B. STEVENSON

areas classified as unsuitable for agriculture (usually because of poor soils or potential erosion) were reserved from sale and where suitable, leased for grazing domestic herds.

All lands in the green area were classified on the basis of timber potential and came to be administered under the *Forests Act* and the Forest Services Division, also currently residing in the Department of Sustainable Resource Development. The quota system was implemented and, as of 1969, reforestation of areas that were cut over became mandatory. Within a few years, oil and gas, and hence the department responsible for energy development, would also become major players in managing dispositions across the province.

During the last few years, the forest or green areas of the province have been used for purposes other than forestry, namely for oil and mineral development and for recreational purposes. This has required increased emphasis on planning and management of our forested areas and has necessitated a fairly intensive control of the use of the lands in these areas.

DR. V.A WOOD, 1969

"In wildness is the preservation of the world."
HENRY DAVID THOREAU

Habitat Preservation in Parks and Protected Areas

While recreational activity was at one time limited by the inconvenience of travel and the lack of free time, by the mid-1950s, Albertans were interested in travelling farther afield. The advent of the five-day work week and an increasing availability of the automobile and improved roads, entrenched the Sunday drive, weekend camping, and other recreational events as favourite pastimes for many Albertans. At the same time, concern for man-made forest fires arising from impromptu campsites led to the need to have contained sites in areas that could be monitored and accessed quickly by firefighting personnel and equipment if need be. Destinations with the appropriate facilities were required.

Thus while Forestry and Public Lands were divvying up the white, yellow and green zones, another branch of the government was working to protect those areas that were best suited for the "pleasure, recreation and general benefit of the inhabitants of the province".[11] Provincial parks and protected areas, eventually to become approximately 4% of Alberta's land base, were also created for the production of native plant and animal life and for geological, ethnological, historical and other scientific interests. This interest in protected areas was noted as early as 1927 with the result being the *Provincial Parks and Protected Areas Act* of 1931. The first provincial park, Aspen Beach on Gull Lake near Lacombe, was established in 1932. It included approximately 69 acres (27.9 ha). A Parks Board consisting of members of the Department of Public Works administered this and 19 subsequent parks.

In 1951, administration of provincial parks was transferred to the Department of Lands and Forests and a new provincial *Parks Act* was passed. By this time, there were 20 provincial parks although all were relatively small. Up until 1955, the parks were operated through the use of local advisory committees, consisting of public members who assisted in their development and management. Between 1951 and 1958, another 16 areas were reserved to relieve congested conditions in the original parks. In 1958 alone, 750,000 patrons used the provincial parks.

In 1959, Mr. E.P. Shaver was appointed Provincial Parks Commissioner and in 1964 he was elevated to the position of Director of the newly formed Parks Division. Changes to the *Parks Act* included provision for the establishment of Natural Areas and Wilderness Areas, which now joined the categories of Parks and Historical Sites. (There were then 24 historical sites also under the control of the Parks Division.)

By 1967, there were 42 sites listed as provincial parks in Alberta comprising 196.06 sq. mi. (507.8 sq. km) or 0.12% of Alberta's area. The largest of these was Cypress Hills (49,620 acres; 20,081 ha) and Dinosaur provincial parks (22,072 acres; 8932.5 ha). The smallest was Ma-Me-o Beach (4 acres; 1.62 ha) on Pigeon Lake, 100 km southwest of Edmonton. In the same year, three-and-a-third million people visited Alberta's provincial parks.

Other designations were also used to protect significant areas from development starting

369

with *Willmore Wilderness Park Area*, established under its own legislation in 1959. *Siffleur, White Goat* and *Ghost River Wilderness Areas* followed in the 1960s. In addition, *Ecological Reserves*, like the Wainwright Dunes Ecological Reserve, can be designated for unique or particularly sensitive landscapes or key habitat of an endangered species. *Wildland Provincial Parks* are a sub-category of *Provincial Parks* established under regulations in 1996. Both wildlands and provincial parks can be managed for a wide range of activities, as can *Natural Areas* and *Recreation Areas*. And finally, *Heritage Rangelands*, a new class of protection, was developed to protect native rangelands that were managed by ranchers to ensure lasting ecological integrity and biological diversity using livestock as the primary grazers.

Partly because of this mixed bag of designations and partly because of the widely publicized *Endangered Spaces Campaign* led by World Wildlife Fund Canada in 1989, the province undertook the *Special Places 2000* program to establish a coherent network of protected areas by the year 2000. Ralph Klein, then Environment Minister, announced the initiative when Prince Philip, the Duke of Edinburgh and president of World Wildlife Fund International was visiting Alberta in 1995. A total of 81 new and 13 expanded sites, adding up to two million hectares,

were named as special areas under this program. Unfortunately, with a large proportion of Alberta already layered with both surface and subsurface dispositions (Forest Management Agreements, timber quotas, mining permits and licences, and oil and gas leases) special areas were not necessarily protected from development. The entire Special Places 2000 process was hampered in its efforts to find and retain sites with intact ecosystems free from industrial interests who would develop the same land. The tenuous situation surrounding some of these "protected" areas was highlighted even more when, in 2004 the Department of Energy became mired in controversy when it posted for sale mineral leases in the Rumsey South Natural Area, designated as such under the Special Places 2000 process.

At the same time as Special Places 2000 was established, the province started to investigate the possibility of consolidating legislation under a single statute for Alberta's protected areas. Alberta's parks and protected areas fall under eight different classifications with varying degrees of protection. While legislation addressing this issue was developed, it disappeared in a shift of priorities before it could be passed and implemented. Some of the changes in the draft legislation have been instituted through regulations.

ALBERTA'S LAST GREAT WILDERNESS—WILLMORE WILDERNESS PARK AREA

In 1959, noting the rapidly expanding economy and number of developments in the Hinton area (that would eventually grow to include a new Kraft pulp mill, completion of the four-lane divided Yellowhead Highway between Jasper and Edmonton, and coal development at Grande Cache), the provincial government under Premier Ernest Manning declared a large tract of land (4600 sq. km or 1840 sq. mi.) on the east slopes of the mountains as a "wilderness park". This was done in an attempt to protect the area's wilderness from the rash of developments.

Renamed in 1965 after its champion, MLA and Minister of Natural Resources Norman Willmore, the park was to have no roads built inside its boundaries and all motorized vehicles were to be banned. Minister Willmore reasoned that, "The broad basic problem is whether or not the government should condone and encourage the industrialization of Alberta at the expense of the rivers, the air and the countryside of our Province through a lack of policy and foresight, or should we endeavour to promote in an orderly manner which will bring the greatest possible benefits to all the people in Alberta without necessitating the improper exploitation of our greatest natural resources—which are the air we breathe and the water and the soil."[12]

Today, Willmore Wilderness Park is referred to as one of Alberta's last great wilderness areas and is still only accessible on foot or horseback. Amendments to existing legislation in 1995 ensured industrial activity was categorically prohibited from this park.

Today in Alberta, approximately 12% of the province's land base is listed under some form of federal or provincial parks and protected areas. While the national parks contribute the lion's share of this area, there are now 13 provincially protected areas larger than 500 sq. km and more than 100 provincial protected areas that are larger than 10 sq. km. On the national front, the creation of wildlife areas is still occurring as witnessed by the recent designation of the Suffield National Wildlife Area, an area important for its relatively intact native prairie ecosystem and its prairie species like antelope, burrowing owl, and kangaroo rat.

Both national and provincial parks, although established for a variety of reasons, play an important role in the conservation of Alberta's fish and wildlife. The mountain national parks, including Banff, Jasper and Waterton Lakes, serve primarily to display the grandeur of the Rocky Mountains to non-resident tourists but, by their very existence, they also offer sanctuary to a number of wildlife species and their associated ecosystems. Combining federal and provincial protected areas, most of the contiguous Rocky Mountains are protected, as are the large keystone species like grizzly bears, bighorn sheep, and mountain goats that inhabit them.

In central Alberta, while its small size may preclude a greater value of ecosystem representation, Elk Island National Park is a combination of game preserve for elk and bison and local recreation facility. The more isolated Wood Buffalo National Park serves as a wildlife preserve for bison as well as the summer home and breeding habitat of the endangered whooping crane. At the same time, it is also unique as a boreal forest river delta system. Other at-risk species occurring in protected areas include threatened caribou herds, now protected in the Willmore Wilderness and Caribou Mountains Wildland Provincial Park. Similarly, endangered bull trout that occur in the Kakwa Wildland Provincial Park and the three Wilderness Areas are protected from fishing. Other keystone species protected by the parks include cougar—with the highest density in North America in the Sheep River Provincial Wildlands area of Kananaskis Country—and elk—with up to 1000 wintering elk reported in the Whaleback area (Bob Creek Wildland and Black Creek Heritage Rangeland). From a hunting and fishing perspective, some of the larger parks like Willmore and the northern wildland preserves provide opportunities for hunting and fishing in near wilderness environments, something that is becoming increasingly scarce in the world.

Along with national and provincial parks, and other governmental designations, there is a third level of land protection that has been used in Alberta for many years. This is the use of conservation easements and land trusts most successfully exemplified by the work of The Nature Conservancy of Canada. However, Ducks Unlimited Canada, Rocky Mountain Elk Foundation, Alberta Conservation Association, Southern Alberta Land Trust Society and others are also active in using this as another tool for habitat and biodiversity protection.

"Today, parks protect some very significant wildlife habitats. This will become increasingly important as land use intensifies across the province."
ARCHIE LANDALS, PARKS AND PROTECTED AREAS

THE NATURE CONSERVANCY OF CANADA

The Nature Conservancy of Canada (NCC) is dedicated to preserving ecologically significant areas through outright purchase, donations and conservation easements. Since 1962, NCC has secured a long-term future for more than 1200 properties in Canada, comprising 1.73 million acres of woodlands and seashores, internationally significant wetlands, threatened prairies, and a host of other natural places. The most recent of these secured areas in Alberta includes a 17,000 acre parcel of range lands surrounding Cypress Hills put under easement to ensure it remains as such.

SUFFIELD NATIONAL WILDLIFE AREA
[NYREE SHARP]

The native prairie ecosystem in the southeastern part of the province is the most threatened ecosystem in Alberta, and one of the most human-altered and fragmented landscapes in Canada. Canadian Forces Base (CFB) Suffield is one of the largest remaining areas of intact, fully functioning grassland in the Canadian prairies. It provides habitat for a large number of relatively restricted native plant and animal species. Its history includes ranching, grazing, oil and gas development and military exercises and training, but the disturbance to the area has been relatively low in intensity and extent.

The Suffield area was originally settled by cattlemen in the 1880s and until 1941, the main land use was low-impact agriculture, with only a small percentage of the land ever being broken. The Suffield Block (2690 sq. km) was expropriated by the Dominion Government in 1941 for defence research and experimentation by the British Army. British and Canadian troops occupied it for the next several years. In 1947, the land was transferred to the Canadian Research Board for chemical and biological weapons testing, and in 1972 it was transferred back to the Canadian Armed Forces. Since 1972, the Suffield Block has been used by British and Canadian troops as well as the Defence Research Board for training exercises and weapons training. Some areas, including the Middle Sandhills, have also been used for cattle grazing, managed by the Prairie Farm Rehabilitation Association, and for oil and gas exploration. The Middle Sandhills and Mixed Grasslands areas, along the west side of the South Saskatchewan River, were identified as environmentally critical areas in the early 1970s. On March 11, 1992, a memorandum of understanding (MOU) was signed between the Department of National Defence and Environment Canada to establish these areas as a National Wildlife Area (NWA).

The Suffield area was first recognized as an ecologically important area long before the memorandum of understanding to establish the NWA was signed. Part of the Suffield Block served as a pronghorn antelope sanctuary from 1915 to 1938, and a large pasture in the Middle Sandhills areas was closed to grazing in 1977 to protect this sensitive landscape. Several significant archaeological sites have also been identified within the Suffield Block, and they are protected from military and industrial activity. Around the same time that the MOU was signed, it was recognized that a herd of about 700 feral horses was posing a threat to

native wildlife and the fragile ecosystem of the Middle Sandhills. The herd was removed, and elk (which had been extirpated from the area) were brought in after much debate to fill the ecological role of a large grazing animal in the system.

The Canadian Wildlife Service (CWS) first became involved in the area in 1971, when the British Army proposed using the Suffield Block for potentially destructive training exercises. Dr. Ward Stevens made a preliminary inventory of the area. His recommendation that the ecologically sensitive portions along the eastern boundary of the base be declared out of bounds was accepted. These lands were initially proposed as a National Wildlife Area by Len Shandruk in 1986, and the Department of National Defence agreed to sign a memorandum of understanding (MOU) in 1992. In 1994, Garry Trottier led a multidisciplinary inventory of wildlife in the proposed NWA: a three-year project funded by the Canadian Wildlife Service and the Department of National Defence and supported by specialists from a number of agencies and individuals. The results confirmed that the area was important for a number of rare, threatened and endangered prairie species including Ord's kangaroo rat, burrowing owl and ferruginous hawk.

The area currently provides habitat for over 1100 known species of plants, mammals, birds, reptiles, amphibians and insects, including 14 species listed as species at risk in Canada and/or Alberta. This abundance and variety in wildlife can be attributed to the wide range of undisturbed habitats in the NWA such as grasslands, sand hills, riparian areas and wetlands. The Suffield Block is a significant refuge, providing key habitat for many endemic grassland species. An extensive list of rare vascular plants is found there, some of which are rare at the national level, and the area is important for upland game birds, waterfowl, reptiles and amphibians, arthropods not found elsewhere in the province, small mammals and ungulates, particularly for pronghorn antelope habitat and migration.[13]

The memorandum of understanding between Environment Canada and the Department of National Defence was renewed in 2001, as it was about to expire. The proposed National Wildlife Area, of approximately 458 sq. km, was officially designated under the Canada Wildlife Act in 2003.

A Shift in Policy and Programs Promoting Habitat Management

In the 1970s, along with Public Lands, Forestry, and Parks, the Fish and Wildlife Division recognized the need to become a part of the picture of multiple land-use planning. Unlike its sister divisions, however, the Fish and Wildlife Division's mandate was to manage fish and wildlife populations but it had no legislated ability to designate the protection, maintenance or production of wildlife habitat as a preferred land-use. On crown lands, the Forest Service could designate lands for timber production, Public Lands could designate land for grazing leases, and Parks could designate lands for protected areas. Fish and wildlife management was harvest management, with anything beyond that being a process of persuading others to protect the land for fish and wildlife populations.

To some degree, the Division did have some tools at its disposal to manage some habitat issues. It could acquire by purchase or by land easement small areas considered prime habitat for fish and game or areas required for access for the use and harvest of these resources. It could also use easements to protect areas along stream banks and areas required for access into good fishing streams and lakes. Under the land-use planning system, it could also place "reservations" for land areas considered as prime habitat for fish and game. Given its budget, however, the purchase of either land or easements on any large scale was beyond reach. As early as 1969, Dr. Wood acknowledged the disparity between the various components of multiple land-use management:

In order to properly utilize our renewable resources efficiently and to the fullest extent, it is necessary to bring in the principle of multiple use. The supply of the land is static. The demand is increasing and this requires careful planning and a close cooperation between the different agencies administering the renewable resources. To properly utilize our renewable resources not only requires careful planning within the Department of Lands and Forests but between other departments as well. The biggest challenge that faces us today in the management of our renewable resources is the planning and coordination of the

development and use of these resources into our economic and social system in such a way that they will be used most efficiently with the maximum returns for present and future generations. Many conflicts will arise and solutions should be based on intelligent knowledgeable decisions. The general public is taking an increasing interest in natural resource problems and policies and since the laws governing the use of our natural resources must be passed in the Legislature by Members of the Legislative Assembly, who represent the people, it is of utmost importance that we keep the public well informed of what we are proposing to do and why.

By 1970, fish and wildlife management was increasingly coming up against the problem of competitive users on the landscape with fish and wildlife habitat issues falling behind the pack. In 1970-1971, Gordon R. Kerr became the new Director of Fish and Wildlife, and swiftly marked a fundamental shift in policy from an emphasis on "harvest management" to "habitat management".

To fund this new direction, a new source of support was required. In the Alberta Fish and Game Association newsletter *defending all outdoors*, volume 6, number 2, February 1972, Mr. Jim Heather, Vice-President of Zone 2, reported on his meeting with a new Minister of Lands and Forests to discuss a habitat stamp.

In a meeting with Dr. Warrack, Minister of the Lands and Forests, on December 20, 1971, I had the opportunity to ask him the following questions: "Would you be receptive to the implementation, without delay, of a habitat stamp of no less than a $2.00 value, that such a stamp be levied upon all purchasers of hunting and fishing licences, and that all funds so derived be specifically earmarked for the purpose of improving, retaining, and restoring fish and wildlife habitat in the province of Alberta"? Dr. Warrack expressed a genuine interest on this subject as outlined, and promised he would investigate in the near future.

Gordon Kerr also recalled the program origins: "Close working relationships between the Fish and Wildlife Division and the Alberta Fish and

Game Association allowed for this program to be jointly designed and with active support of the Minister of the day, Dr. Allan Warrack, it was adopted without a single voice of protest."

Legislation enacted under Section 10 of the *Wildlife Act* paved the way for habitat stamps to be sold under regulations. The receipts, together with donations and bequests, would form a "Fish and Wildlife Habitat Enhancement Fund". As well, the "Buck for Wildlife" program was implemented with funding from an increase in fees charged to all licensed hunters and fishermen.

374

With policy and dollars in hand, an earnest effort in habitat management was made. The $2.00 habitat levy of fishing licences was used mostly for reservoir improvements, the building of fish barriers, development of new reservoirs, stocking dugout ponds, stream regulation and improvement projects, stream fencing, lake aeration projects, bank stabilization projects, and beaver management. The $5.00 habitat levy on hunting licences was used for wildlife projects, including shelterbelt maintenance for upland game birds, island stabilization for colonial nesting birds

SHELTERBELTS WERE PLANTED TO PROVIDE HABITAT FOR UPLAND GAME BIRDS AND OTHER WILDLIFE SPECIES.
COURTESY ALBERTA FISH AND WILDLIFE DIVISION

like pelicans and cormorants, clearing or burning to increase range for ungulates, installing hay bales and nest boxes in wetlands and other wetland improvements for waterfowl and installing perforated culverts for problem beaver.

A ROCK ISLAND BUILT IN THE WINTER FOR CANADA GEESE AND OTHER ISLAND NESTERS.
COURTESY DUCKS UNLIMITED CANADA.

GORDON KERR, WORKING FOR HABITAT
[INTERVIEWED BY PAT VALASTIN ON APRIL 10TH, 2003, IN EDMONTON]

"I was born at Coleman, Alberta, April 5, 1939. I spent my early years riding horses, fishing, hunting, trapping, playing hockey, curling and, when required, going to school. My grandfather and grand uncle were active conservationists as well as hunters and fishermen. Our home was a ranch four miles from town and one mile from the Forest Reserve. That gave me a few thousand square miles of Public Land as a back yard. There were few roads in the area, four-wheel drive trucks were a novelty, and it was before seismic became well used in petroleum exploration.

"My father took me to my first Fish and Game meeting when I was only nine, in 1948. George Spargo, Executive Secretary of the Alberta Fish and Game Association was there. My father took him fishing and we all caught a number of cutthroat trout. He was so pleased with his day he gave me his fishing rod. I still have it these 56 plus years later. I also remember meeting my father's friend Jack Morden who was the local forest officer at The Gap on the Old Man River. At the time, he was live-trapping and relocating beaver. We also went with him to make pheasant releases. I was fascinated with the things he and my father were doing.

"I went to the University of Montana from 1958 to 1961 taking zoology with a wildlife management focus. I took my MSc at the University of Alberta. My thesis was on Rocky Mountain goat ecology on Mount Hamell (before the town of Grand Cache was created) when it was still 12 hours from the nearest all-weather road. It was fantastic country with hundreds of caribou, grizzlies, and impressive herds of bighorn sheep. The professor who had the greatest influence for my thesis was Dr. John Holmes, a parasitologist but with a much broader view of things. The person to whom I owe the most was John Stelfox, a regional wildlife

biologist who did as much work on my thesis as I did.

"Following three summers as a student biologist, in 1963 I joined the staff of the Alberta Fish and Wildlife Division as assistant district biologist in Lethbridge. I became regional wildlife biologist at St. Paul in 1965. Then John Stelfox left to join the Canadian Wildlife Service, and I was assigned the Edson region, while retaining responsibility for St. Paul. Recruitment was slow and soon the problems of wolf predation on livestock throughout the north found me assigned to cover the Peace River region as well! While hectic at the time it was in fact an undreamed of opportunity to experience wildlife management throughout the province.

"George Mitchell was Chief Wildlife Biologist but had been away at university. He left the Division to become a professor at the University of Regina. I was then appointed Chief Wildlife Biologist. Shortly thereafter, Bob Webb left the Division to join the Wildlife Branch of Manitoba. We diminished to the point where staff consisted of Bill Wishart, Gaylen Armstrong and me. The task at hand was to rebuild the team. We proceeded to recruit four new regional biologists straight out of university. David Neave was assigned to Red Deer, Milan Novak went

WILDLIFE BIOLOGIST GORDON KERR DURING HIS RESEARCH ON MOUNTAIN GOATS AT MOUNT HAMELL BY BIG SMOKY RIVER, 1961.
CREDIT: J. STELFOX

375

to St. Paul, Gerry Lynch to Edson, and Harold Carr to Calgary. Gaylen Armstrong remained in Lethbridge and Bill Wishart became our first Wildlife Research Biologist.

"When Stu Smith left to join the Alberta Environment Conservation Authority in 1972, I was promoted to Director. In this period, land management and habitat became the clear priority for both fisheries and wildlife management. In a year or two, the department was reorganized again and my position evolved into Assistant Deputy Minister. In spite of the growth of the Division and a focus on habitat, wildlife and fisheries resources continued to lose ground to economy-based resource developments. Fish and wildlife habitat lost every land-use battle. It was clear that until wildlife and environment in general became a basis for income and jobs, nothing was going to change. It is interesting that the 'Father of Conservation', Aldo Leopold, in the 1930s and 1940s, recognized the need for wildlife to compete economically with other resources but even in today's environment, little progress to that end has been made across Canada. In Alberta there are two solitudes, private land and Public Land. On Public Lands decisions are governed by forest acts in the Green Area and by either the Public Lands Act or the Parks Act on all White Area public land. Water is governed by the Water Resources legislation. Fisheries and wildlife legislation has no direct decision-making power in land-use. The thrust of the Fish and Wildlife Division to demand land commitments placed us at odds with the balance of our own department as well as with the departments of Environment and Agriculture.

"This situation of continuing conflict and the fact that I had worked for a long time with the Fish and Wildlife Division, basically doing the same things with little long-term satisfaction and little likelihood of change I decided I couldn't see myself continuing for 20 more years. I decided I wanted to become a consultant. I had co-chaired the Kananaskis Country Planning Committee and had also been directly involved in the Eastern Slopes Resource Management Policy development, working with industry in making the policy work in restricted areas. The concept of multiple land-use was wearing thin and the emerging concept of integrated resource management seemed like a great opportunity to join the private industry world.

"I had just begun the process of departure when the ceiling fell in on the economy in Alberta. It was late in 1980. As a result of the federal National Energy Program, all the petroleum exploration headed for the USA or off-shore. Added to that was a general economic decline across the country. Jobs were disappearing, consulting companies were shutting down, and the future of a guy who had just cut relations with his employer didn't look good. My departure coincided with the cut back of government and the marked decline of the Fish and Wildlife Division. I was fortunate enough to have been there for its best years, and didn't have to deal directly with the undoing of many hard fought gains.

"While opportunity in the consulting field quickly diminished, it turned out that good fortune befell me once again. The Director of the Canadian Wildlife Service (CWS), Western and Northern Region position became available. Getting back to biological science work seemed attractive and the CWS was a first-class research organization. As Regional Director of CWS, it brought me back to Alberta conservation work in two unique and significant ways. A Canada-wide habitat program, funded via a coalition of governments and non-government groups had been briefly explored. By 1984, it was taking on a clear form and on a short secondment to Ottawa I was able to play a part in helping the new *Wildlife Habitat Canada* become a reality. We recruited David Neave, previously Director of Wildlife and then Director of Habitat in Alberta, to become Executive Director of Wildlife Habitat Canada (WHC). WHC became a model federal and provincial non-governmental program partnership across the country.

"The second opportunity was even more rewarding. Since European settlement, over 70% of marshes and other wetlands in the prairie region have been lost to agricultural draining and other developmental activities. That loss of habitat, aggravated by prolonged drought and high bird harvests in the USA, were considered to be the causes of the extreme decline in waterfowl populations throughout the continent. The focussed effort to address these issues brought about the signing of the North American Waterfowl Management Plan between Canada, the USA and Mexico. In the beginning, there was no money committed. Perseverance by a handful of people in Canada (primarily Dr. Jim Patterson of CWS and Stew

Morrison of Ducks Unlimited Canada) and a few USA counterparts prevailed. Money was committed to specific projects, which allowed for processes to be designed and tested. The momentum grew.

"The prairies of Canada was the first significant target area for waterfowl and wetland recovery. The Prairie Habitat Joint Venture (PHJV) was formed as the planning and coordinating group. I had the good fortune to be Chair of this team of two Federal Departments, Ducks Unlimited, the Delta Waterfowl Research Station, Wildlife Habitat Canada and three provincial wildlife agencies. It was a challenge. We spent countless hours over many months, in many meetings. Finally, implementation plans were endorsed and the real ground work began. The work of Dr. A. J. (Sandy) Macaulay, who served as Program Coordinator, was integral in our success. The PHJV became a model for the continent. Implementation was at the provincial level with prairie-wide strategic planning. Ducks Unlimited Canada was selected as the logical on-the-ground primary delivery agent.

"As the strategy and prairie-wide planning phase became routine, I changed jobs to try my hand at pure administration. After two years of that, however, I was happy to accept the position of Executive Director of the Alberta NAWMP office on an inter-governmental secondment. After a year in the Alberta NAWMP office, it was apparent that our structure was top heavy. I suggested, somewhat in jest, I could 'work and get paid for two and a half days a week and I would fish for two and a half days a week'. I guess I convinced them too well. After a structural review it was agreed that my position was not needed at all and Ernie Ewaschuk took over in addition to his other duties.

"Rather than return to CWS, I retired in the spring of 1994 to go consulting, as had been my dream

of fifteen years before. I established 'KERR and Associates'. It was a pleasant change. I finally got back to some science, wildlife biology and applied sustainable land management. It was rewarding to work on the Special Places 2000 program in the Canmore Corridor, elk range delineations and history in the Crowsnest Pass, private land and White Area forest (woodlot) inventory, etc. But what has been even more fun and rewarding has been the volunteer time spent in non-government groups. I joined the Land Stewardship Centre of Canada where I serve on the Board. I was also elected to the Board of the Woodlot Association of Alberta. Representing the Woodlot Association on the Environmental Stewardship Action Team of the Alberta Ag-Summit 2000 and co-chairing that group with Ernie Ewaschuk for two years was a rewarding experience. The ultimate outcome of that effort, to reward land managers for deliberate production of ecological goods and services, will be a major advancement in the future. If sustainable ecosystems, biodiversity and other public goods such as water and clean air were a source of income and the wildlife and land we claim to love were to benefit at the same time, would the land manager not choose to manage for it? As we observe climate change, increasing species at risk, etc. it is clear that we have no choice but to do so.

"There is no greater honour than to be recognized by one's peers and therefore it is gratifying to have received recognition such as the Canada Sustainable Forest Management Recognition Award from Wildlife Habitat Canada in 2002, and the William Rowan Distinguished Service Award from the Alberta Chapter of The Wildlife Society in 2003. There were many people who I worked with who were instrumental in making me look good. The same can be said for conservation in general. All the success stories worthy of mention are the result of teamwork. And so it has been a great journey and one which continues to unfold!"

[Today, Gordon is as busy as ever, but on his own time-table. He also tries to do more fishing than he used to!]

377

ENVIRONMENTAL CONSULTING AND THE ALBERTA SOCIETY OF PROFESSIONAL BIOLOGISTS
[DAVE EALEY AND ROBIN LEECH]

With a growing environmental awareness in the early 1970s, biologists began to play a role alongside engineers and other professionals in the resource development of Alberta. Key to their expertise was the ability to apply science to better planning of and mitigation for the effects of non-renewable oil and gas, coal and limestone, and renewable resource industry activities.

As the number of projects grew, so too did the need for more scientists. While government agencies, like the newly formed Department of Environment, provided some of this expertise, the climate was also right for private entrepreneurs. The first environmental consultants arrived in Alberta in the late 1960s. Experts were needed to assess the environmental impact of megaprojects such as the construction and infilling of the W.A.C. Bennett Dam on the Peace River between 1969 and 1971. Robin Leech recalls: "The study of the impact of the Bennett Dam on the Peace-Athabasca Delta was huge. I have one of the few extant copies of this work. It takes more than a metre of shelf space." Similarly, the Mackenzie Valley Pipeline Inquiry (or Berger Commission, 1974-1977) and the Alberta Oil Sands Environmental Research Project (AOSERP, 1977–1980) were extensive and comprehensive in their efforts to understand the impacts that such large-scale development would have, not only on fish and wildlife but also on the surrounding air, land, and water.

One of the very first of these early environmental consultants was Tom Beak (Beak Consulting). Beak came from Ontario and worked as a water quality specialist conducting analyses on the Athabasca River near Fort McMurray. About the same time, Ron Jakimchuk, later joined by Glen Semenchuk, formed Renewable Resources Consulting Services and worked on a number of major pipeline projects throughout the 1970s. Bill Costerton, a microbiologist from Vernon, BC, formed a consulting company and was involved with AOSERP in the early-to-mid-1970s.

Lu Bayrock and Ted Reimchen (Bayrock and Reimchen), geologists in the early 1970s, focussed much of their work on the surficial geology of the east slopes. Here they produced knowledge about

where roads could and could not go because of slope stability, and where bridges could not go because of siltation problems for fish-spawning beds. Obviously, this had tremendous biological implications. About the same time, the team at Pecan Resources, Louise Horstman and Ted Code, started a company out of Morinville. Beth MacCallum started Bighorn Environmental out of Edson and has been on the leading edge of many strip-mining reclamation techniques for Cardinal Coal. Other consultants of the 1970s included Ron Thomas and Bob Webb (former employees of the Alberta Fish and Wildlife Division); Ryan and Hilchie of LGL Limited 1971; Dave Penner and Associates; and Dave Westworth and Associates. Having acquired an environmental component in 1995, Golder and Associates started environmental work in Alberta shortly thereafter. Gary Ash, R, L&L, a company that started in Alberta in 1977, merged with Golder and Associates in 2001.

Increasingly, traditional fish and wildlife biologists worked alongside reclamation and air and water quality specialists. However, the recognition of biologists as professionals was unheard of. Professional engineers, with their own legislation, and a tradition of professional and public accountability, were recognized as the "responsible" officers for signing off environmental impact assessments. Not surprisingly, this did not sit well with many highly trained biologists. It was apparent that a professional organization and recognized standards for the profession was needed.

Consequently, a small group of biologists founded the Alberta Society of Professional Biologists on March 5, 1975. These founders (Stuart Smith, Raymond Schweinsburg, Dale Alsager, Ron Jakimchuk and Don Dabbs) provided early leadership that helped sustain the association during its formative years. Official registration as a Professional Association was finally achieved on February 28, 1991. Registration of the Society gave its members exclusive use of the title "Professional Biologist" and the abbreviations "P.Biol." and "P Biol".

After 30 years as an organization, ASPB today represents more than 550 biologists in government, industry, consulting, education, and enforcement. The Society's purpose is to regulate the professional practice of biology in the province of Alberta, to protect public interests, and to enhance the professional status of biologists. ASPB held their first symposium in 1977 on the topic of Environmental Impact Assessment, and some 20 symposia/conferences have followed since then. The range of topics has been wide, including Science Policy and the Public, Environmental Monitoring, Fish and Wildlife Management, Native People and Renewable Resource Management, and Cumulative Effects Assessment.

Since 1981, ASPB has promoted academic training in biology through annual scholarships at the University of Alberta, University of Calgary, and University of Lethbridge. In memory of an early member of the Society, the ASPB, along with Professional Biologists of British Columbia, recognize a graduate student in aquatic biology by offering the D. Allan Birdsall Scholarship at the University of Alberta. In addition, the Peggy Thompson Award recognizes

excellence in publishing of biological information. The highest honour of the ASPB is the J. Dewey Soper Award, given periodically to a Canadian biologist who makes significant contributions to the field of biology.[15] Soper Award recipients include Stu Smith, Ian McTaggart-Cowan, Richard Fyfe, Valerius Geist, Stephen Herrero, Charley Bird, Geoff Holroyd, Joe Nelson, and Ian Stirling.

Today, the Alberta Society of Professional Biologists continues to grow and mature as a professional body committed to excellence in the practice of biology benefitting professionals both in government and in private industry. As well, over the past three decades the environmental consulting industry has flourished in Alberta, making major contributions to the management of the fish and wildlife resource and to research, mitigation and remediation work. Today, this industry is a major employer and training ground for many young environmental and fish and wildlife biologists and technicians.

RECLAMATION OF WILDLIFE HABITAT IN ALBERTA'S FOOTHILLS
[BETH MacCALLUM, BIGHORN ENVIRONMENTAL DESIGN LTD.]

Production of diverse wildlife habitat is a key part of the reclamation process associated with coal mining in the subalpine ecoregion of Alberta. A variety of reclamation techniques used on the Luscar and Gregg River mines in west central Alberta has produced the conditions for colonization of these altered habitats by bighorn sheep, elk, mule deer, numerous small mammals, birds, and their predators. Grizzly bears den on the mines, scavenge ram carcasses in the spring, hunt elk calves and forage in the reclaimed grasslands. Coyotes opportunistically hunt the mines and gray wolves systematically travel through the area. Great-horned owls and common ravens nest on highwalls designed into the final landscape. These highwalls and associated talus also provide escape terrain for bighorn sheep, and specialized habitat for hoary marmots, pika and rock wrens.

In Alberta, legislation and direction regarding mining and reclamation plans are found in *Alberta Environmental Protection and Enhancement Act* (1992) and various regulations and guides. Provincial reclamation requirements in Alberta have, as a basic objective, the return of lands disturbed by development to a capability equivalent to pre-disturbance conditions. This implies that the reclaimed lands should be able to support similar, but not necessarily identical, land-uses to the predevelopment conditions.

Reclamation of open pit coal mines is carried out in a progressive fashion meaning that once mining of the first pit developments are completed, they are back-filled and sloped, and the overburden and topsoil are replaced, seeded with a grass/legume mix, and planted to shrubs and trees. This results in a steadily increasing amount of reclaimed land over the life of the mine. Wildlife habitat has been accepted as an end land-use objective for reclamation of open pit coal mines in Alberta since Cardinal River Coals Limited submitted one of the first reclamation plans for wildlife habitat in the late 1970s for the Luscar Mine site.

Mountain mining with truck and shovel techniques results in discontinuous surface disturbance; the working landscape quickly becomes a mosaic of lands being prepared for mining, active mining, blocks of undisturbed mature landscape and various stages of reclamation completion. The maintenance of mature landscape elements within the mining disturbance area is an important feature for wildlife occupation of the mines during the operation phase. Complete

restoration of disturbed areas is not usually possible given the scale of coal mining. So, a pragmatic ecosystem approach is adopted that attempts to integrate procedures that restore pre-mine habitat condition, replace habitat function, and exchange certain components for others of similar benefit. Initial priority is given to re-establishing critical habitat that may have been disturbed by the mining process (e.g., ungulate winter range, raptor nesting habitat). Habitat needs for a broad range of wildlife that existed prior to mining are addressed by the use of "umbrella" species and by the integration of specialized habitat features into the reclaimed landscape.

Ungulates are often used as umbrella species for reclamation to wildlife habitat because they have large home ranges, require a variety of landform features and vegetation types to fulfill their annual life requirements, and are important prey for carnivores and scavengers (both mammalian and avian). These characteristics require the planner to work at the landscape level. As well, certain ungulate species can respond relatively quickly to reclamation even in an early development stage, therefore they provide a useful monitoring tool for reclamation success.

Once reclamation began at the Luscar and Gregg River mines, bighorn sheep from adjacent alpine habitats voluntarily colonized the reclaimed landscapes, and incorporated the reclaimed areas into their annual movement patterns. Mining activity is directed and predictable: bighorn sheep and other wildlife have the capability to learn to habituate to this type of human behaviour. Reclamation of the Luscar and Gregg River mines has provided new habitat for bighorn sheep which has resulted in a significant population increase. These habitat developments take on more significance when put into context with range losses experienced by bighorn sheep in North America during European settlement. The reclaimed landscapes are used primarily as winter range by bighorn sheep, but other activities such as lambing, rutting and summer use also occur.

The rate of population increase for bighorn sheep on the Luscar Mine between 1985 and 2002 was 3.8% per year despite a 12% annual ewe removal by means of non-trophy harvest (1984 to 1996), capture and export to various locations in the western US and Alberta (1989 to 2001), natural mortality, accident, poaching or other causes. The rate of population increase for bighorn sheep on the Gregg River Mine between 1993 and 2002 was 24% with no annual ewe removals other than natural mortality. This is near the theoretical limit for animals bearing young at three years (30%). The 2002 fall population combined for Luscar and Gregg River was 798 bighorn sheep. This is one of the largest bighorn sheep herds in North America.

Use of reclaimed habitat by elk on the Luscar and Gregg River mines was initially limited by low regional population numbers. The first use of the Luscar Mine by elk, recorded during the annual surveys, was by two cows in the winter of 1990/1991, and by the fall of 2002 the elk population at the Luscar Mine was 155. Elk were not observed systematically on the Gregg River Mine until the fall of 2002 when 17 elk were recorded. Elk use the reclaimed landscape primarily for winter range, but in recent years they have expanded their activity to include calving, rutting and summer use. Mule deer are common on both mines and take advantage of the forage/cover interface in a fashion similar to elk. In 2002, 159 mule deer were reported on the Luscar Mine and 54 on the Gregg River Mine.

Gray wolf, coyote and red fox are present on the Luscar and Gregg River mines. The presence of diverse prey (bighorn sheep, mule deer, elk and high concentrations of small mammals) and lack of human harassment contribute to carnivore use of the Luscar and Gregg River mines. Wolves did not systematically use the Luscar Mine until the elk population began to increase. This added a third ungulate species in significant numbers to the prey base in addition to

bighorn sheep and mule deer. Grizzly bears are regular occupants of these mines.

High densities of small mammals associated with reclamation provides a prey base for mammalian carnivores such as coyote and fox and for local and migrating diurnal raptors (northern harrier, American kestrel, red-tailed hawk, and rough-legged hawk), as well as for those owls which prefer to hunt the forest margin (e.g., great horned owl). Other small mammals such as pika, snowshoe hare, least chipmunk, woodchuck, hoary marmot, golden-mantled ground squirrel, red squirrel, beaver, and porcupine are present in appropriate habitat on the mines. Ninety bird species have been identified on the Luscar Mine and 64 on the Gregg River Mine.

The landscape on these two mines in 2004 consists primarily of early succession grasslands interspersed with undisturbed coniferous and riparian habitats, reclaimed highwalls and footwalls, a number of lake developments, barren ground not yet seeded, and inactive mine pits. The progressive nature of reclamation together with the establishment of settling ponds, lakes, specialized habitat features and habitats that allow colonization by ungulates and small mammals has created a bridge for a variety of wildlife to continue to use this landscape during the operational phase of the mines.

AERIAL VIEW OF CARDINAL RIVER COAL MINE OPERATIONS.
CREDIT: B. MacCALLUM

integrated and sustainable land-use and natural-resource management. Similarly, work initiated under the Ag Summit 2000 process to value and develop market mechanisms for

ecological goods and services, such as watershed protection and biodiversity, are also interesting developments to watch in the near future.

It is essential that combinations of resources be compatible or complementary to each other and at no time conflicting to the extent that the productivity of the land is reduced. In some cases this may mean that a combination of uses is not necessarily that combination which will give the greatest dollar return or the greatest unit output over the short run.[16]

JAMES T. NALBACH, DEPARTMENT OF LANDS AND FORESTS, 1970

In Summary

As we look back over the last century, the issues surrounding fish and wildlife habitat are complex, but progress has been made. At one time, fish and wildlife was regarded by some as something to be exploited or, if it stood in the way of development, to be eliminated. Predators were exterminated; bounties were given for wolf pelts, crow feet, and ground squirrel tails; and habitat was ploughed, chopped down, or paved over. Little, if any, thought was given to its preservation, except by fish and game associations, rod and gun clubs and some far-seeing individuals such as Benjamin Lawton, the first Chief Game Guardian of Alberta.

Today, a great deal of time and energy go into fish and wildlife and habitat management. Researchers spend years studying populations and defining limiting factors and critical stress points. Biologists continue to find innovative methods to adequately survey declining populations. Mapping and GIS specialists use satellite imagery to measure remaining habitat. Population modellers and forecasters try to

determine how much habitat can be removed before wildlife populations start to decline and how far populations can decline before reaching a point of no return. Multi-stakeholder committees, a microcosm of Alberta society, are asked to weigh the socio-economic and ecological costs of retaining at-risk and other species on the landscape. But is it enough?

While we've come a long way, there remains much to be done. Certainly, many conservation agencies have achieved a great deal through education and information. The environmental movement has made many aware of the need to preserve habitat and has attracted many followers from the mildly interested to the dogmatic. Non-government organizations like the Canadian Parks and Wilderness Society and the Alberta Wilderness Association fight hard to protect our wildlife and our wild places. All this, however, does not alter the fact that an increase in sheer numbers of people travelling in or near wildland areas has put increasing pressure on wildlife habitat. The problem is not confined to industrial development and urban expansion. Hunters, anglers, hikers and other recreation seekers also take their toll. And issues are not always clear-cut. The building of a highway may disturb habitat, but it also creates jobs. The finished product is a convenience to the traveller, or a matter of safety, or a lifeline to a small community.

Fish and Wildlife—as competitors for Alberta's landscape—rarely come out on top. The habitat required continues to disappear incrementally. Perhaps what is needed is a Wildlife Habitat Conservation Objective that sets in legislation the protection of a minimum amount of wildlife habitat for a given area. This idea is not that far-fetched. John Stelfox concurs:

> This idea could dovetail with a wildlife and forest management initiative of the 1980s that set minimum population objectives for each Wildlife Management Zone, for each of the big game and endangered species. Alberta Forest Service insisted that effective forest-wildlife management was impossible unless the Fish and Wildlife Division determined their minimum population management objectives for each species. That same idea needs to apply to wildlife habitat, acreage requirements, especially for critical winter habitat.

Legislation for water conservation objectives, though not yet widely implemented, does exist for the benefit of protecting aquatic ecosystems. Aquatic ecosystems should, at least in theory, also benefit from the federal Fisheries Act, which has a no-net-loss policy for fisheries habitat. The provincial relationship with the enforcer of this policy, the Department of Fisheries and Oceans, is a tenuous one, and the two jurisdictions tend to tread lightly in each other's presence. Nonetheless, such tools as management objectives, no-net-loss policies, and mitigation techniques are available, but perhaps need to be applied more creatively than they are today. As well, and perhaps most importantly new tools for fish and wildlife habitat management must be developed to meet the challenges of a new century.

Fortunately, while jobs and food on the table are important to Albertans, there are few among us who want to see the loss of our natural capital including our wildlife and our wild spaces. While resource development and industrial growth are positive instruments for long-term economic gain, they must be balanced with social and ecological well-being and we must find new and innovative ways to achieve such balance. This was true one hundred years ago. It is true today. And it will continue to be true in the future.

387

"It is inconceivable to me that an ethical relation to land can exist without love, respect and admiration for land and a high regard for its value."
ALDO LEOPOLD

DFO'S FISH HABITAT MANAGEMENT ROLE IN ALBERTA
[NADINE STILLER]

Under Canada's *Constitution Act* (1867), the federal government has jurisdiction over all seacoast and inland fisheries which it manages through the federal *Fisheries Act* (1868). The *Fisheries Act* applies in all of Canada's freshwater and marine waterbodies, and extends offshore to encompass Canada's exclusive economic zone. However, the administration of freshwater fisheries was delegated to the provinces of Quebec and Ontario at the turn of the 19th century. Delegation to Manitoba, Saskatchewan, Alberta, and British Columbia followed in the 1930s with approval of their respective Natural Resources Transfer Agreements under the *Constitution Act*. The Yukon Territory was also delegated similar authorities under an agreement between the two levels of government in 1989.

Prior to 1999, the Department of Fisheries and Oceans (DFO) focussed its efforts in Alberta on scientific research related to the Northern Rivers Basin Study. They also participated in reviews of environmental impact assessments for large-scale projects such as the Oldman Dam Water Management Project, oil sands projects, and Cheviot Coal Mine Development to ensure that responsibilities under the *Fisheries Act*, the *Navigable Waters Protection Act* and the *Canadian Environmental Assessment Act* were addressed.

The *Fisheries Act* contains provisions for both fish habitat protection and pollution prevention. However, pollution prevention provisions are administered by Environment Canada (EC). The fish habitat protection provisions are administered federally by DFO with provincial government participation. In 1999, the Federal Government announced that it would strengthen its Fish Habitat Protection Program. New operational areas were created: the Prairies Area and the Ontario-Great Lakes Area. The Prairies Area encompasses the provinces of Alberta, Saskatchewan and Manitoba and supports eight District Offices, with four in Alberta (Lethbridge, Calgary, Edmonton and Peace River) and an Area Head Office located in Calgary.

As outlined in DFO's *Policy for the Management of Fish Habitat* (1986), there are three main goals of the Fish Habitat Management Program in Alberta: 1) Fish Habitat Conservation which incorporates a no-net-loss guiding principle; 2) Fish Habitat Restoration; and 3) Fish Habitat Development through promoting enhancement opportunities. The Policy applies to those habitats directly or indirectly supporting existing or potential commercial, recreational or subsistence fisheries. To achieve these goals, DFO works cooperatively with provincial agencies and interest groups to protect fish habitat, participating in watershed management planning, supporting and fostering fish habitat research, public outreach and stewardship activities.

DFO also participates in the review process, where developers proposing to work in or near water submit project proposals to DFO. Under the *Fisheries Act,* projects that alter, disrupt or destroy fish habitat are required to have the Minister of Fisheries and Oceans' authorization to do so. Submitted projects are reviewed to examine whether fish habitat is likely to be affected, if an authorization is warranted, and if mitigation or compensation is required to achieve "no net loss". Where voluntary compliance does not occur, and the fish habitat provisions of the *Act* are violated, the department may take legal action.

More recently, DFO's role has expanded to include responsibilities related to the *Species at Risk Act* promulgated in June 2003. Alberta's fisheries resources are an important aspect of Alberta's socio-economic fabric. DFO's Fish Habitat Protection Program is committed to working to ensure the conservation and protection of healthy fisheries resources.

388

MAJOR EVENTS IN FISH AND WILDLIFE HABITAT MANAGEMENT IN ALBERTA

1935	The *Prairie Farm Rehabilitation Act* (PFRA) receives Royal Assent to secure rehabilitation of drought and soil-drifting areas on the prairies.
1947	The first major oil field discovery is made at Leduc. The Eastern Rockies Conservation Board is formed for watershed protection and, indirectly, fish and wildlife habitat protection.
1956	John Stelfox initiates what becomes a 40-year study on impacts of logging on wildlife in the Hinton area.
1962	The *Agricultural Rehabilitation and Development Act* encourages reversion of submarginal farms to "natural habitat".
1968-1969	The Fish and Wildlife Division makes a major land acquisition near Brooks, to be used for wildlife habitat development.
1970-1971	The Fish and Wildlife Division broadens its emphasis from harvest management to include habitat management.
1971-1972	Several habitat development programs are initiated including shelterbelt plantings for upland game birds.
1974	The Fish and Wildlife Habitat Fund (Buck for Wildlife) is established with the objectives to maintain, create, and enhance wildlife habitat.
1975	The Alberta Society of Professional Biologists is established to represent professional biologists working in Alberta.
1980	A Habitat Protection and Management Branch is created in the Fish and Wildlife Division.
1986	It is generally accepted that 40% of the original wetland habitat in Canada has been lost to drainage.
1999	The federal Department of Fisheries and Oceans opens up four district offices in Alberta in order to strengthen its Fish Habitat Protection Program.
2005	The Alberta Conservation Association takes the lead in creating a provincial Habitat Working Group with the goal of creating a strategic and coordinated framework for fish and wildlife habitat management in Alberta.

389

References • CHAPTER 11

1 Quoted in *Ensuring the Common for the Goose: Implementing Effective Watershed Policies* by Hanna J. Cortner and Margaret A. Moote, USDA Forest Service Proceedings RMRS-P-13. 2000.

2 Hardy, W.G. 1967. *Alberta – A Natural History*. Mismat Corporation, Edmonton.

3 Wood, V.A. 1969. Alberta's Public Lands. 1969. Alberta Lands Forests Parks Wildlife 12(1): 16-23. Department of Lands and Forests, Edmonton.

4 From a photocopy found in the office of Bill Wishart. No publication information provided.

5 The records of the Eastern Rockies Conservation Board Meetings, as well as its work, are preserved at the Provincial Archives of Alberta, Accession 74.169 (hereinafter referred to as PAA 74.169). They are filed under the heading Provincial Parks Board. These papers contain a wealth of material on the work of this body. Most of the records consist of minutes of meetings and some relevant correspondence. The information contained therein concerns the protection of watersheds, which, while intended for human use, nonetheless illustrate implications for wildlife. Much of this material also deals with the engineering aspects of the work of the Board. The Board was officially created by an Act of the Alberta Legislature in 1948.

6 W.R. Hanson. Interview with Eric Holmgren. Calgary, Alberta, October 11, 1985. Mr. Hanson provided much useful information concerning the work of the ERFCB.

7 PAA 74.169. Minute 4-11, June 13-14, 1948.

8 PAA 74.169. Game Winter Range, 1949-1950. This document forwarded to J. Harvie—then Deputy Minister of the Department of Lands and Forests—was found in the files and records of minutes.

9 PAA 74.169. Minute 64-3. This minute noted that elk required a very large range.

[10] PAA 74.169 Annual Report of the Eastern Rockies Forest Conservation Board, 1958. No formal published report was issued; the report was simply typed, mimeographed and copies distributed to members.

[11] Wood, V.A., op cit., p. 22.

[12] Norman A. Willmore in his public address to the Edson community, Feb. 25, 1955. (www.ualberta.ca/ERSC/willmore/right.html).

[13] Patriquin, D.L. and D.L. Skinner. 1992. Review and assessment of the vegetation, wildlife and habitat of CFB Suffield, Alberta. D.A. Westworth and Associates, Ltd, Edmonton.

[14] Kennett, Steven A. 2002. Reinventing Integrated Resource Management in Alberta: Bold new Initiative or 'Déjà vu all over again'? Alberta Wilderness Association, www.AlbertaWilderness.ca Calgary.

[15] Soper's achievements are highlighted in Chapter 8.

[16] Nalbach, James. 1970. Multiple Resource Management Planning. Alberta Lands Forests Parks Wildlife. 13(2): 30-35, Department of Lands and Forests, Edmonton.

LEARNING FROM THE PAST AND LOOKING TO THE FUTURE

Petra Rowell with contributions from Mark Boyce, Dawn Dickinson, Dave Ealey, Ernie Ewaschuk, Lee Foote, Guy L'Heureux, Gordon Kerr, Dennis McDonald, Don Meredith, Dave Moyles, Margo Pybus, Blair Rippin, Kelly Semple, Chris Shank, Bob Stevenson, Michael Sullivan and Bill Wishart

We cannot change our past, but we can choose our future. That future can be better, and wilder, than today. Working together to restore the wild beauty, space, freedom and wildlife that have always shaped our collective dream of Canada, we can heal not just our land but ourselves. Healing, hope, home: in restoring the wild to our native land, we may yet find our way home at last.[1]

KEVIN VAN TIGHEM

Lessons Learned

The primary focus of *Fish, Fur & Feathers* has been to provide an enlightening and entertaining glimpse of the many facets of fish and wildlife management in Alberta during the last one hundred years. But like other historical works of this nature, there are also valuable lessons to be learned from within. While the following is by no means a complete or scholarly attempt to analyze the subject, we provide the reader with just a few last thoughts and reflections on where we have gone with fish and wildlife management throughout the last century and where we may need to go in the future.

To frame this discussion, we informally polled our ranks, gathering responses and lively discourse from a number of fish and wildlife users, biologists, managers and academics, both working and retired. Herein, we review the three eras of fish and wildlife management observed over the past century, discuss some of the most significant advances made, and ruminate on a few of the biggest or most controversial mistakes. We then provide a few collective thoughts on what fish and wildlife management needs in order to be successful in the next century.

Examining the Three Eras of Wildlife Management

It is probably safe to say that in looking toward the future, managers must understand what worked well in the past. They must know the benefits of all the management tools in the basket including the tools used throughout the three eras of wildlife management discussed previously.

For the most part, fish and wildlife management to date has focussed on the needs of consumptive users. At the turn of the century, overexploitation, driven by the demands of the fur trade and the market hunters, resulted in the decline of many ungulate species. As ungulates and other game species were then regarded as a significant natural resource (they made up a large portion of the provincial population's diet), concern was expressed and actions were taken by early managers.

THE ERA OF PRESERVATION

Although little was known about game management at the time, it was believed that creating game preserves free from harvest pressure would allow ungulate populations to expand "through their natural increase" (the surplus of young that reach survival over natural mortality). Thus, the era of preservation was triggered and, even today, continues to provide benefit to Albertans. For example, local overexploitation of elk at the turn of the century, and subsequent public concern for a small remaining herd, led to their protection with the creation of the Island Park Preserve in 1906—a legacy today known as Elk Island National Park. In general, game preserves worked well on a local basis.

Although the effort to preserve wildlands for wildlife has never left us, the preservationist era was perhaps best marked in Alberta by the establishment of the national parks between 1885 (Banff National Park) and 1922 (Wood Buffalo National Park). The mountain parks were protected largely for their scenic beauty and tourism potential, with wildlife a secondary consideration. In contrast, national parks on the prairies, parklands and boreal forest were created specifically to preserve the big game (antelope, elk and bison) that resided within them. Similarly, bird sanctuaries would provide protection for waterfowl and other bird species.

Today, the setting aside of large tracts of land, with complete protection from human expansion and industrial activities, is becoming increasingly difficult. Yet there remains a strong argument that we should continue to use preservation as an active wildlife management tool: that preservation of certain areas or habitats is essential if we are to maintain populations of some species, most notably, grizzly bears and caribou.

Hence, preservation will likely continue to play an important role in this century. Existing national parks and, to a lesser degree, provincial parks will continue to provide protection to wildlife. If tenderly cared for, these sanctuaries will continue to act as a source of wild animals. However, preservation or protectionism does not mean stagnation. Wildlife is in a continual state of flux and population levels cannot be frozen in time. Parks and protected areas today face a number of pressures including increasing development up to and within their borders, an increasing number of visitors, natural and human-caused fire, fragmented habitat and disjointed predator-prey interactions. In some situations, park managers are faced with reconstructing natural systems, as much as preserving them.

THE ERA OF CONSERVATION

Mid-way through the century, the settler population had grown substantially. Land wasn't as readily available for preserves as before and new methods of game management were required. Efforts to protect the last of the bison before the turn of the century had resulted in the first attempts to regulate harvest through hunting restrictions. The early game ordinances subsequently evolved into today's more comprehensive *Wildlife Act*. Legislation came too late for the bison but was in place when a burgeoning settler population drove the need to better regulate the harvest of the remaining game animals for the benefit of all those who depended on them.

The era of conservation is often associated with the early publications of C. Gordon Hewitt and Aldo Leopold. Hired biologists trained in this thinking brought this era to Alberta in the mid-1950s. Inventories were taken, birth rates and death rates calculated, and the harvestable surplus determined and managed. Game management worked well. While today, a decline in consumptive use is evident, the reality is that fishing and hunting will continue to be with us for some time yet, and may even have a resurgence in popularity from time to time. Hence, there is a need to retain Leopold-type game management (conservation) and enforcement. Perhaps there are even lessons to be learned from game management techniques that can be applied to non-game species as well.

THE ERA OF SHARED STEWARDSHIP

Preservation and conservation have both served us well in the past and will continue to do so in the future. But fish and wildlife also require their stake in a continually shrinking habitat base including the air above us, the ground under our feet, and the water in our rivers and lakes. Without securing adequate habitat, there is little use for old or new management techniques.

To some degree, the intensified use of a finite landscape and the natural resources it contains has

FISHING AND HUNTING WILL LIKELY BE A PART OF THE MANAGEMENT SCENARIO FOR SOME TIME TO COME YET.
CREDIT: D. FAIRLESS

393

forced land and natural resource managers, once operating in isolation, to start paying attention to one another. This evolving era of "shared stewardship" is probably best exemplified by the Alberta Environmental Farm Plan and the Cows and Fish programs. Although both are relative newcomers to the Alberta scene, these programs are effective at partnering and providing tools to the agricultural community such that land owners can be effective stewards—managing their land for production, as well as a number of ecological functions like watershed protection and wildlife habitat. Other examples of shared

HEALTHY WATERSHEDS ARE IMPORTANT FOR SUSTAINABLE AGRICULTURE AND FOR DOWNSTREAM MUNICIPAL, INDUSTRIAL, AND OTHER USERS. THEY ALSO PROVIDE EXCELLENT HABITAT FOR A WIDE VARIETY OF FISH AND WILDLIFE. A WIN:WIN SITUATION FOR EVERYONE.
CREDIT: D. FAIRLESS

stewardship can be found in the multi-stakeholder approach to endangered species recovery work in the province. For example, the Blue Flag Recovery Team, a diverse group of land owners, plant enthusiasts and government biologists, all have very different needs. Yet they have pooled their knowledge and resources, finding enough common ground to successfully manage this threatened plant found in the ranching areas of southeastern Alberta.

Shared stewardship is not a new idea. In fact, it is very much in line with what Aldo Leopold wrote about conservation in the 1940s and 1950s. Many conservation agencies have been engaged in this activity for some time. Organizations like the Alberta Fish and Game Association, Ducks Unlimited Canada, Federation of Alberta Naturalists, North American Waterfowl Management Plan, Rocky Mountain Elk Foundation, Trout Unlimited, Alberta Conservation Association, and others have created numerous multi-stakeholder partnerships and conservation initiatives that integrate a variety of users and user needs across sectoral boundaries for

the benefit of the fish and wildlife resource. But is it working? Dawn Dickinson shares her uncertainty: "While the shared stewardship concept has promise and is great in theory, there are many pitfalls; it can become corrupted and there is a tendency for local interests to give too narrow a focus, whereas management of wildlife is a provincial or national issue..." Blair Rippin, a retired wildlife biologist, adds: "I generally agree with the three eras but I think we are barely beginning an era of effective shared stewardship."

Whether they have been successful or not, looking back over the century, one can conclude that yes, all three eras of wildlife management—preservation, conservation and shared stewardship—have occurred and are still occurring in Alberta. More importantly, understanding these eras and the role they played in the past will help us to use the management philosophies behind them more effectively in the future: at a time when we may need as many options in the tool box as possible.

GORDON KERR SUMS UP A CENTURY OF WILDLIFE MANAGEMENT IN ALBERTA

Between 1850 and 1900, we were into commercial fishing, commercial hunting, commercial trapping, living off the land and selling what you could to the point that it caused a major decline in wildlife. So we went into a protective regulations phase. There were laws and enforcement, and hunting seasons were generally closed from about 1915 to 1940. The prediction at the time was the extinction of all sorts of things. My father was born in 1905 and didn't see a moose until about 1935. He said that when he was a teenager in the Crowsnest Pass, "to see an elk track was such an event that you got off your horse to have a look at it"!

Well, then we went into the biological science era about 1955 to 1965. The first biologists came to Alberta. The same thing was happening in other provinces and the United States. We went into harvest liberalization within renewable limits. We got into female deer hunting, non-trophy sheep and so on. But there was a subsequent change in land-use such that habitat declined and became a problem. We lost a lot to agriculture, forestry, and petroleum such that those renewable limits that you could have this liberalized harvest on, got lower and lower.

And so we developed programs like Buck for Wildlife, North American Waterfowl Management Plan, and other habitat-orientated programs from the 1970s to 1995. These programs were good but they had limited effectiveness, as it requires intensive and expensive management. And that management is separate from what is going on in agriculture, petroleum, and forestry. So it's really paying twice. Paying to cut it down and paying to put it back. Better to manage for it in the first place. I think that that is where the future lies, but you'll still have to have the protective regulations, the biological sciences and I think you still have to have the special programs continue. There are places where you will have to manage for wildlife first rather than secondarily.

Most Significant Advances of the Past Century

Continuing our introspection, we asked our colleagues: "What do you think were the most important advances in fish and wildlife management over the past century?" As one might expect, responses were varied:

INTRODUCTION OF SEASONS AND QUOTAS

Many agreed a significant occurrence was the realization by the public that the devastating year-long harvesting of fish and wildlife had to be replaced by controlled harvest of only the surplus. The Game Ordinances of 1892 introduced seasons and quotas and other restrictions to make subsistence, commercial, and recreational fishing, hunting, and trapping sustainable for all. This early legislation set the foundation for a more comprehensive provincial *Wildlife Act*, with parallel development in federal and provincial fisheries legislation.

EFFECTIVE ENFORCEMENT

Of course, rules and regulations would have been meaningless without the Game Guardians to enforce them, which they did voluntarily for many years. Today, the spirit and determination of the early Game Guardians is well reflected in our highly trained and sophisticated conservation law enforcement agencies. Through the century, both federal and provincial fish and wildlife biologists often worked closely with legislators and enforcers. The marriage between them, like many relationships, was full of ups and downs but evolved into an effective process for fine-tuning hunting, trapping, and recreational and commercial fishing regulations. This cooperation also ensured effective implementation and public support for changes such as the use of female big game seasons, the 4/5-curl requirement in bighorn ram hunting regulations, and the catch-and-release fisheries policy. Enforcement officers and biologists also worked together to provide quick and effective responses to problem wildlife and disease outbreaks.

MIGRATORY BIRDS CONVENTION ACT

A piece of legislation outstanding for its time was the Migratory Birds Convention Act. This Act represented a high point of international negotiation and cooperation for the conservation of waterfowl and other migratory birds in North America. Established in 1916, this international agreement has withstood the test of time and has formed the foundation for many subsequent migratory bird initiatives between the United States, Canada and Mexico.

ESTABLISHMENT OF PARKS AND PRESERVES

Where seasons and bag limits failed to sustain wildlife, the establishment of parks and preserves provided protection for game animals to reproduce and for populations to recover. The use of game preserves was significant in the recovery of elk, bison and antelope. The small handful of individuals responsible for the creation of the national parks system, and later, the provincial parks, are gratefully acknowledged for their foresight. Their legacy will benefit Albertans for generations to come.

ALDO LEOPOLD'S GAME MANAGEMENT

Another highpoint of the century was the realization that fish and wildlife management had to be based on scientific knowledge of populations, their trends, limiting factors, and the surplus available for a sustainable harvest. This realization included a gradual incorporation of ecological concepts into the field of wildlife biology and a shift to science-based thinking triggered by the management principles of Aldo Leopold. Much of this early thinking was undertaken at the universities by researchers like Drs. Rowan and Miller who investigated major issues like the ten-year game cycle (the "conundrum of the century"), the "riddle of migration", and the "wormy whitefish" problem.

HIRING TRAINED BIOLOGISTS

At a time when many were sceptical about such methods, the hiring of professional biologists to conduct this scientific enquiry was a bold move by Game Commissioner Eric Huestis. Early biologists Martin Paetz, Ron Thomas, George Mitchell, Bob Webb, John Stelfox, Bill Wishart and others laid down the foundation of scientific enquiry into Alberta's fish and wildlife. They did so with little more than their eyes and ears (and often, on foot, too!)

395

WILDLIFE MANAGEMENT UNITS

Wildlife management methods were refined as zones and wildlife management units came into play. Today, the collection of wildlife information within these units is greatly enhanced by investigative techniques such as animal immobilization, improved aerial survey (including improved aircraft and observational methods), Landsat photography and other remote sensing tools, telemetry (conventional and satellite), geographic positioning systems (GPS), DNA analyses, and digital geographic information systems (GIS), not to mention all-terrain and four-wheel-drive transportation.

ADAPTIVE FISHERIES MANAGEMENT

Concurrent with the progress in wildlife was the advancement of fisheries management. While the century started out with a strong focus on hatcheries and fish stocking, this by itself did not prevent a dramatic downturn in some more heavily harvested populations, like walleye, throughout the second half of the century. Fortunately, fisheries management has a strong foundation in science. Together with habitat improvement programs, more sustainable harvest limits instituted in the late 1990s have contributed to an increase in some fish populations in the last few years. As well, there has been a shift away from stocking introduced exotic fishes and towards the rehabilitation of native fishes (most notably, bull trout). The trend toward more catch-and-release regulations has also been key to fish population recovery, particularly in Alberta's stream trout fisheries.

EFFECTIVE PARTNERSHIPS

As well as forging new techniques, fish and wildlife managers also had to forge new relationships. The close relationship between managers and the users of the fish and game

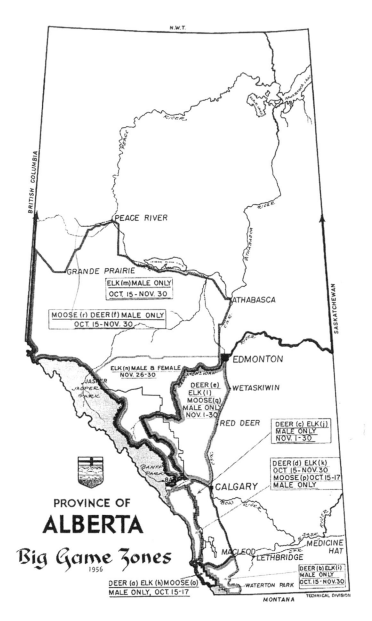

MAP OF ALBERTA'S BIG GAME ZONES IN 1956.

resource, including the fish and game associations, guide and outfitter associations, trapping and fishing groups, led to a number of successes including one of the best hunter education programs in North America, improvements to outfitter guide policies, development of humane trapping methods, and other advancements. Added to this mix were the conservation agencies like Ducks Unlimited Canada, The Nature Conservancy of Canada, Wildlife Habitat Canada and others that often created a bridge between the

WILDLIFE MANAGEMENT UNITS

April 2000

MAP OF ALBERTA'S WILDLIFE MANAGEMENT UNITS IN 2000.

397

and wildlife management textbooks, this type of relationship building was, and will continue to be, instrumental in maintaining wildlife and their habitat on both private and crown landscapes.

A BROADER DEFINITION OF WILDLIFE

The change in philosophy as we moved from the humble beginnings of the *Game Act*, to a broader inclusion of non-game species under the *Wildlife Act* is seen by many as a highpoint of the century. This ideology has expanded to today's recognition of the need to preserve all of Alberta's biodiversity. Actual management of biodiversity is a complex matter. Whether or not we will be successful in this aspect is yet to be determined.

FUNDING MECHANISMS

Although few members of the public would single out fees as a highlight of the century, there is no doubt that the various licensing and game stamp programs in use over the years proved to be an effective method to fund fish and wildlife management. From the first fishing and hunting licence fees, to Rowan's use of game stamps and the eventual creation of the Buck for Wildlife Fund, such programs have been important for acquiring the means to protect and enhance fish and wildlife and their habitat. Today, much of the fish and wildlife research and habitat work is funded from these dollars. However, as the number of anglers and hunters declines, so too will this pot of dollars, hence the need for tomorrow's managers to think up new methods for funding fish and wildlife work. Wildlife management, within the context of ecological goods and services, requires broad public support, not just that of hunters, fishermen, and birdwatchers.

SPECIES REINTRODUCTIONS

Finally, while there are many more highlights of the century that could be mentioned, we close with just one more—introductions. The introduction of exotic species would likely be frowned upon today. Nonetheless, the release of pheasants and gray partridge to south and central Alberta was a successful endeavour as was the early

biologists and the land holders in charge of the habitat on which fish and wildlife depend. And finally, fish and wildlife managers, biologists and technicians in government, industry, academia, and conservation agencies have worked with the oil and gas, agriculture, mining, forestry and other industries to define the area and components that make up wildlife habitat and to develop land-use guidelines and best-management practices to mitigate the human footprint. In general, this has been a cooperative effort with participants looking for win:win scenarios. The woodland caribou research program is an example of such cooperation. Though rarely acknowledged in fish establishment and operation of the Brooks Pheasant Hatchery. Many habitat and shelterbelt programs, not to mention many upland game bird censuses of both native and non-native species, would not have occurred if there had not been this keen interest in hunting a variety of game birds. Similarly, the introductions of endemic big game species including bison into Wainwright Buffalo and Elk Island parks, a free-ranging disease-free herd of wood bison in the Hay-Zama area, and the relocation of elk to many areas around the province, were also successful. Mountain goat management was another significant event where transplanted animals were used to re-stock depleted historic range with considerable success. The introduction of exotic fish such as coho salmon and golden trout and the translocation of rainbow trout and endemics such as whitefish and perch met with varying degrees of success. Nonetheless, these and other introductions provided many valuable experiences and lessons were learned that may not have been learned otherwise.

Biggest Mistakes of the Century

After pondering the many achievements of fish and wildlife management over the century, it only seems fair to include a discussion of the low points. When asked: "What do you see as the biggest mistake, failure or most controversial issue in fish and wildlife management in the past century?" respondents again listed a variety of topics that ranged in scale and perspective.

TRANSFER OF DISEASED BISON

From a biological viewpoint, the federal decision to transfer diseased plains bison from Wainwright Buffalo Park to Wood Buffalo National Park is seen by many as the biggest mistake of the century. The debate about the future of this diseased and genetically mixed species has been with us since their transfer in 1924-28 with no signs of abating in the near future.

GAME FARMING

In the controversial category, most respondents identified the introduction and expansion of game farming with its potential for disease problems to affect wild populations and allowing wildlife to become a marketable, agricultural commodity as issues, but opinions varied as to whether or not these actions have had some merit or not.

TRIALIA, A 3/4 BISON HYBRID AT WAINWRIGHT BUFFALO NATIONAL PARK.
COURTESY B. STEVENSON

"Fish and Wildlife issues are dear to the heart of all people and therefore controversial."

GUY L'HEUREUX

PREDATOR CONTROL

The persistence of a 1920s attitude towards predators by some (witness the change in status of cormorants from "at-risk" to "vermin" almost overnight) is a complex and ongoing problem. The increase in cormorants on Lac La Biche is the result of a change in predator-prey relationships in fish stocks in the lake. Eliminating cormorants will not fix the fisheries problem. Conversely, overly brazen coyotes around the perimeters of urban centres and acreage developments do little to elicit public sympathy for these and other wildlife species.

TOO MANY FISHERMEN

The continued commercial net fishing in waters already stressed by recreational anglers and the continued belief that the reduction of fish populations could be easily overcome by building more fish hatcheries and stocking more fish (or removing more cormorants and other fish-eating

birds) were issues throughout the century. These problems are yet to see their final resolution.

LOSS OF HABITAT

And finally, many respondents pointed out that it has been a failure of society to recognize the value of wildlife habitat and to preserve more land in its natural state in Alberta. This was seen as particularly true in the agricultural area which has seen a steady increase in the number of endangered and threatened species across the prairie and parkland natural regions. However, this issue is not limited to the southern half of the province. In the north, the inability to manage woodland caribou in a manner that allows for a sustainable population, let alone a surplus for harvest, comes as a result of the failure to protect large tracts of old growth boreal forest from human disturbance. Associated with the failure to recognize the value of habitat was the loss of our wetlands, drained and ploughed to grow additional cereal crops. Drainage resulted in not only the loss of the wetlands themselves (and the wildlife associated with them), but also gave rise to new problems such as flooding or the loss of natural water storage potential, vital during periods of drought.

YOUNG DOUBLE-CRESTED CORMORANTS IN THEIR NEST ON LAKE NEWELL, 1951.
CREDIT: REX GARY SCHMIDT COURTESY ALBERTA FISH AND WILDLIFE DIVISION

399

Garnering Public and Political Support through Effective Public Education

Inevitably, when discussing the subject of fish and wildlife management, the failure to secure public and political support, and hence funding and resources, is probably the most frequently discussed issue and source of frustration. Many respondents mentioned the lack of public profile of fish and wildlife policy and public complacency with fish and wildlife issues as major impediments to successfully managing this resource. Dr.

OUTRAGEOUS NOTIONS FROM A CENTURY OF WILDLIFE MANAGEMENT IN ALBERTA

IN THE PAST, WHO WOULD HAVE THOUGHT...

...that game seasons and bag limits, first viewed with disgust by settlers, were needed and would ensure the sustainability of wildlife for future generations?

▪ ▪ ▪

...that anything but older male animals should be harvested? Bill Wishart tells a great story about an early Alberta Fish and Game Association (AFGA) conference where, after great discussion, he finally got Andy Russell to accept the idea of bighorn ewe seasons. Then Russell sold the rest of the crowd on its merits.

▪ ▪ ▪

...that anyone would attempt electrofishing? Think about it. Using electricity while standing in water!

DICK VINCENT OF MONTANA FISH AND GAME (BEHIND BOAT) TRAINING ALBERTA FISHERIES STAFF CARL HUNT, GORD HAUGEN, STAN CLEMENTS, AND MEL KRAFT IN ELECTROFISHING TECHNIQUES ON JUMPING POUND CREEK, 1968.
CREDIT: D. MCDONALD.

▪ ▪ ▪

...that someday there would be a bow season on deer? Alberta's settlers would have thought it outrageous to try to kill a deer with a bow and arrow.

▪ ▪ ▪

...that WIN (wildlife identification number) cards and computerized phone-in draw systems for hunting licences would come into use? That was the sort of thing heard on *Buck Rogers* or the *Jetsons*.

▪ ▪ ▪

...that biologists would be concerned about protection of the little small-flowered sand verbena (a small plant in southern Alberta)?

...that humans would have to build bridges across highways for wildlife?

BIGHORN SHEEP AND HUMANS SEEM TO SHARE THIS FAVOURED PIECE OF HIGHWAY OUTSIDE JASPER.
CREDIT: B. WISHART

▪ ▪ ▪

...that sportsmen would be concerned about the quality of game for consumption because of mercury levels in fish and upland game birds, chronic wasting disease in cervids, and other diseases?

▪ ▪ ▪

...that the once-common bull trout would become a threatened species?

▪ ▪ ▪

...that moose draws would be held in the prairies?

▪ ▪ ▪

...that moose would be considered for use as military draft animals to navigate muskeg areas?

▪ ▪ ▪

...that the commercial fishing industry, promoted as an important part of the economy in the 1930s through the 1950s, would be bought out by the provincial government and consolidated into a record low number of operators in the new millennium?

▪ ▪ ▪

...that firearms, the most important tool to those who settled this land, would become restricted?

LOOKING AT MORE RECENT YEARS, WHO TODAY WOULD THINK...

...Canada geese were once scarce in central Alberta? Efforts at translocating Canada geese in the 1960s seem outrageous now but were obviously very successful!

■ ■ ■

...that the beaver was once scarce? One of Officer John Doonanco's original jobs in the 1940s was to reintroduce beavers into the northeast.

■ ■ ■

...that we would see a 30-bird bag limit on white geese, whose populations have exploded in recent years due to their reduced harvest and the expansion of their wintering habitat?

AND FINALLY, LOOKING TOWARD THE FUTURE, WHO WOULD THINK THAT WE MIGHT SOMEDAY SEE...

...that some fishing lakes will be allotted tags for the allocation of fishing privileges the same way that big game tags are allocated now.

■ ■ ■

...that trappers, the providers of much of the data on furbearers during the last century, might all but disappear in the new millennium?

■ ■ ■

...that game farms would have more elk "behind wire" (in captivity) than there are in the wild?

Mark Boyce, a University of Alberta professor stated:

> "Our biggest failure has been the failure to sustain funding for fish and wildlife management in the province with a gradual erosion of support, the loss of wildlife research programs, insufficient funds for inventory and monitoring, and thereby sound wildlife management."

Kelly Semple, Executive Director of the Hunting for Tomorrow Foundation, concurs:

> The need to make fish and wildlife a part of the value system of every Albertan is essential if we are to be able to effectively manage this resource in the future. The reality is that we do not have sufficient public and political support to devote the necessary manpower and financial resources to the task at hand. This support must be garnered from the general public who in turn will ultimately influence political will.

401

Many attribute this failure to gain public and political support to our lack of effectiveness at public education relative to fish and wildlife and their habitat requirements. Unfortunately, many biologists, although well-versed in their subject area, are ineffective at communicating in a public forum to a non-scientific audience. Perhaps our greatest shortcoming as a profession is not to have recognized this deficiency and to have acted upon it. Retired fisheries biologist Dennis McDonald noted: "It has been a failure of the Fish and Wildlife Division to recognize the need for an effective public education and information program and to put more staff and resources into this program area." Ernie Ewaschuk concurs: "All the strategic planning sessions I have been involved with have always rated education and communications as the number one goal; however when it came to allocating the budget, education ended up at the bottom with little or no funding!"

THE FUTURE OF PUBLIC COMMUNICATION
[DON H. MEREDITH]

If you want to know how people value wildlife, take some mounted specimens or a collection of skulls or furbearer pelts to any elementary school classroom (or a meeting of adults for that matter). Pass the items around and let the kids touch them while you talk about them. It won't be long before hands start flying in the air as students ask a host of questions and answering these will more than fill your allotted time.

Albertans value their wildlife and wild places! Yet over the years, we have failed to adequately fund information and education programs that would have informed them about the important roles these elements of our Alberta heritage play in our environment, culture and well-being.

How the future of fish and wildlife management unfolds in this province will largely depend on how well informed Albertans are about the issues that affect these resources. One thing is for certain: fishing and hunting will have less and less influence on management plans and programs. As we are already seeing, larger slices of the financial "pie" will be given for such things as endangered species and other so-called "non-game" wildlife and habitat programs. This is not to say that hunting and fishing will not be important factors; they just won't be the major factors affecting management as they have in the past. If you wish Albertans to support the conservation of fish and wildlife, you have to serve the needs of the majority of those Albertans who do not hunt or fish. In so doing, you also have to provide a way for this majority to willingly contribute financially to fish and wildlife conservation, as anglers and hunters do through licence fees. A conservation fund solely financed and dictated by hunters and anglers will not survive.

So, how do you inform Albertans about fish and wildlife matters when government budgets are reduced and more and more of the management of the resource is being delegated to non-government organizations and private industry? The present hodgepodge of public communication plans and programs (or lack of them) from a variety of stakeholder groups is often redundant and contradictory. What is needed is a central strategy that takes into account all the ways Albertans value wildlife, not just the concerns of specific interest groups. Government is the logical place for this strategy to be formulated and implemented, but in the present climate, a non-government agency may have to step in to fill the vacuum.

Not only do fish and wildlife professionals have to start "thinking outside the box", they have to understand and respect their audiences which include the public at large. Use of terms like "biodiversity", "ecosystem management", and "sustainable development" only serves to alienate portions of those audiences who will not bother to find out what these words mean. Instead, we need to be more inclusive in our public communications, making every opportunity a "teachable moment" where people can learn, for example, why a large number of different kinds of plants and animals in the woods or fields is preferable to just a few.

The term "non-game" should also be stricken from our lexicon. Its use appears to isolate certain activities and people who are actually working in the mainstream. All wildlife biologists should be non-game as well as game biologists. Likewise, the term "fisheries biologist" implies a biologist who works only with "game" fish. An "aquatic biologist" works with all kinds of fish, invertebrates and their habitats, and not just to support fisheries but also to support whole aquatic ecosystems.

Predicting the future is often a mug's game. However, if we are to provide a proper fish and wildlife heritage for future generations of Albertans, we must make sure that the current generations are well informed about their resources and the issues that affect them. Albertans will always value wildlife and wild places. The question is how much and where?

[DON MEREDITH IS A WRITER, BIOLOGIST AND FORMER COORDINATOR OF INFORMATION AND EDUCATION FOR ALBERTA FISH AND WILDLIFE, 1989-2002.]

I believe that the public needs to be much better informed about wildlife issues and that improved education could go a long way towards fixing other problems. One thing that has been done in Wisconsin is the implementation of an environmental certification requirement for schoolteachers. Before a person can be certified to teach in the public school system, everyone must have at least one three-credit course in environmental science, ecology, or related field. Likewise, environmental education is a mandatory component of all elementary school programs.

MARK BOYCE

The Fish and Wildlife Division— Time for a New Approach?

Whether perceived or real, this lack of public and political support is perhaps most keenly felt by those associated with the Alberta Fish and Wildlife Division. Although many other institutions and organizations have contributed to fish and wildlife management over the century, the Division is recognized as the government authority with the mandate and responsibility to manage and protect Alberta's fish and wildlife resource for the public good, today and in the future. Yet the constant reorganizations and budget reductions this Division has undergone throughout the century, along with a lack of input into land-use decision-making in an increasingly resource-driven economy, led many to question how this mandate could possibly be delivered upon.

The many departmental changes the Division has lived through over the years is a particular sore spot for many, giving rise to the moniker bestowed on the division as the "lost child that nobody wanted". When trying to explain this "lost child" syndrome, a number of reasons were provided. Bill Wishart provides the following: "For one, the division has no direct role in assigning land management activities. Hence, the FATE of wildlife is in the hands of Forestry, Agriculture, Transportation and Energy."

One biologist expresses his frustration: "We are often the only government agency that says 'No. No, you can't shoot that moose out of season or put a net in that stream. No, you can't drill there or put a gravel pit here. We usually are the only ones in government to tell individuals or companies that they can't do what they want because science-based, ecologically sound reasoning tells us that action will have a negative impact on a provincial resource.'"

While the reality is that energy, agriculture, forestry, and even parks bring in more direct revenue than wildlife in a strictly accounting sense, such explanations are oversimplifying the situation. The management of fish and wildlife presents a complex challenge. In addition to understanding the biology and ecological relationships among plants and animals, managers must also consider the influences of diverse issues such as public attitudes; the objectives of agriculture, forestry and mineral extraction sectors; First Nations' attitudes and entitlements; the expectations of hunters, anglers, and conservationists; and even public health issues. Fish and wildlife management does not fit easily into one department but crosses over a number of disciplines. In the past, the movement from department to department was the result of trying to peg fish and wildlife management into one discipline—sometimes more closely aligned with parks and protectionism, sometimes lumped in with other renewable resources. Perhaps what has been missing is a more holistic ecological perspective. Fish and wildlife, or more broadly, biodiversity, is part of the landscape and a healthy environment. Its management requires a government-wide approach; yet even when it is housed within the same departments, it is often isolated and distinct from agencies that manage public land, forests, water, air, health, etc.

As Blair Rippin points out:

Although wildlife played a pivotal role in early European exploration and settlement, the rush to rapidly develop industrial, agricultural, and infrastructural interests

over much of the 20th century resulted in wildlife being taken for granted. In spite of all the shortcomings of the Fish and Wildlife Division, one must give considerable credit to the fact that, through their efforts and the efforts of many other individuals, agencies and organizations, Alberta has a good record in maintaining its fish and wildlife species. We have generally maintained our exploitive regimes (even the illegal ones) within the productive ability of populations. We have recognized when exploitation was excessive and we reduced or stopped it when necessary (e.g., goats, caribou, canvasbacks, etc.).

More importantly, the past is past, and what is needed now is a look at the future. Few would disagree that it is time the Fish and Wildlife Division, and the public that supports it, take a hard look at itself and its

"THE NAME GAME"

In May 2002, an article (originally written for the *Edmonton Journal* by Ed Struzik) appeared in the "That's Outrageous" column of the nationally circulated *Reader's Digest*. The article lamented the fact that despite drastic budget cuts that put an end to all "out-of-province travel, overtime, training and outside contracts", there was still a budget to reorganize and re-dress department staff. Lew Ramstead, a retired Fish and Wildlife Division employee pointed out that since 1962 the department had been reorganized six times, and three of these reorganizations had occurred in the last seven years. "We've got endangered species coming out of our ears, and all the department does is reorganize and order new uniforms. When does it all end so people can get on with their jobs?"

Like most issues, there were two sides to this story and the new uniforms were justified. However, the article, and the debate that ensued, pointed out the deep feelings of frustration that were then present in the Division. These feelings were further intensified for many when the "Fish and Wildlife Division" name was eliminated as an identifiable entity between 1999 and 2001. For many, this further destroyed the "esprit de corps" of the provincial organization along with its well-deserved public image.

We trained hard, but it seemed that every time we were beginning to form up into teams we would be re-organized. I was to learn later in life that we tend to meet any new situations by reorganizing; and a wonderful method it can be for creating the illusion of progress, while producing confusion, inefficiency and demoralization.

ROMAN CENTURION PETRONICUS ARBITER, 210 BC

role in fisheries and wildlife management in Alberta. Where does it want to go? What does it need to get there? And can it successfully overhaul itself to meet the changing needs not only of the fish and wildlife resource but the human population that must coexist along side it?

What, then, is the Future of Fish and Wildlife Management in Alberta?

THE PROBLEM

Today, fisheries and wildlife biologists and technicians from both government and private sector, enforcement staff, academia, and other researchers work diligently with hunters, trappers, naturalists, farmers, ranchers, and industry to maintain our fish and wildlife heritage. Despite the effort, it is evident that this resource is under a growing number of pressures. While many of these pressures have been present throughout the last century, their intensity has increased and is likely to continue to increase in the future. And while many efforts are being made to address them, many fear we are not moving fast enough. Some would say that the traditional mix of programs and approaches to fish and wildlife management isn't enough anymore.

Blair Rippin laments:

Joni Mitchell's words "you don't know what you've got 'til it's gone" is an excellent prophecy for Alberta's fish and wildlife. We were very fortunate to have a great fish and wildlife abundance and diversity heritage by virtue of our geographic/climatic/soils situation. However, our land-use actions will result (if they haven't already done so) in considerable degradation of this bountiful resource before we realize the value of what we had, and it will require major efforts and expense to get it back, if we care to do so. I fear that lack of understanding and failure to act will seriously degrade the standard of living in this province. Wildlife abundance and diversity will be (or already is) the first to suffer irreversible damage.

THE CHALLENGE

The challenge is to channel sufficient resources and effort towards maintaining healthy, functioning ecosystems with the full complement of wildlife species. This is in addition to maintaining a sustainable consumptive and non-consumptive regimen of use that meets the expectations of the public. It also means finding ways of keeping working landscapes healthy, or repairing them where they are not.

THE TIME FOR CHANGE

Ernie Ewaschuk suggests it's time for a paradigm shift:

There is no question that society values wildlife; polls and surveys over the past 25 years have all demonstrated that. Wildlife managers have perhaps failed to win public and political support [and hence funding] because they have focussed too acutely on the species or their habitats. They have failed to come up with "win-win situations" for fish and wildlife as well as farmers, foresters, industry, and society as a whole.

We can no longer be content to settle for maintaining little islands or "postage stamps" of habitat for wildlife; we have to make sure that wildlife are provided for in the major land-use sectors like agriculture, forestry, and energy. To do this we have to come up with economic reasons for these sectors to maintain ecological function (and hence wildlife) on their landscapes. I have a hard time convincing a producer to leave his woodlots intact for deer habitat when he is continually running into them on the road. It is far easier to talk to him about the watershed value of his woodlot in slowing spring runoff, reducing erosion of his soil and recharging his groundwater. As ecologists, we have failed to help society make the connection between healthy wildlife, a healthy environment, and the well-being of humans. We have failed to recognize and make known the value of

405

maintaining ecological functions on the landscape that will provide society with drinkable water, breathable air, productive soils, and yes, biodiversity and all the habitat we will need for harvestable and other species. Far too much effort and funding have been spent treating the 'symptom rather than the disease'.

ALIGNING WITH AN URBAN AUDIENCE

With an increasingly urban population, the connection is no longer visceral between humans and wildlife. Getting public support may become increasingly difficult as we move further and further away from our rural roots and our connection with the land. There is little doubt that the next century of fish and wildlife managers will have to gain support by appealing to a largely "citified" audience. While urban audiences have some sympathy for species at risk and for diminishing biodiversity, few individuals loudly decry current conditions and many wildlife managers and conservationists decry what they perceive as public apathy. Somehow, a new breed of "biodiversity managers" must reconcile the link between urban needs and the needs of wildlife. A connection can be made with urban audiences when wildlife is seen as a barometer of our environmental health: a component of the ecosystems that contribute to the functioning of our air, land, and water systems that we all depend on. Just as resource

development needs to be sustainable to ensure the longevity of our communities, so the ecological functions of the land must also be sustainable to ensure the very health of those communities, be they urban or rural.

NEW PARTNERSHIPS

To rise to this challenge, fish and wildlife managers need to align themselves with a broader group of allies with which to share the mandate of managing fish and wildlife. Only by aligning themselves with other air, land and water managers will fish and wildlife managers be able to give this resource the attention it needs. Fish and wildlife management cannot be carried out in isolation from land and resource management; likewise, fish and wildlife managers must work much more closely with urban planners, forestry, agriculture and energy sectors than they ever have before.

Perhaps it's also time for the Division to reach out, renew and strengthen its bonds within government departments and with its traditional partners, like the Alberta Fish and Game Association, Ducks Unlimited Canada, Rocky Mountain Elk Foundation, rural landowner groups and the Canadian Wildlife Service, etc. It is also time it built new bonds with not-so-traditional partners like Canadian Parks and Wilderness Society and Alberta Wilderness Association.

Perhaps the greatest allies' wildlife managers may have for the salvation of wildlife in the future will come from a group that we might least expect. Economists, who until recently have been treating the environmental costs of doing business as "externalities", are now placing dollar values on ecological goods and services and talking about the value of "natural capital" as part of true-cost accounting.

ERNIE EWASCHUK

Strengthened relationships and an increasing role for the private sector is also a positive change for fish and wildlife resources. The integration of industry, academics and government in entities such as the Cumulative Environmental Management Association in the oil sands area in the northeast, the Alberta Cooperative Conservation Research Unit arising out of the province's universities, and the Foothills Model Forest program are great examples of where fish and wildlife and natural resource management is heading.

In the past, much of the fish and wildlife management was undertaken primarily by the private sector (for example, the early fish and game associations). It gradually became more complex, involving provincial and federal governments more directly, as well as universities, technical schools, museums, various private organizations, and consultants. Each contributed their own piece. Such relationships tend to occur in a cyclic fashion. Today, we are again moving more and more back toward the private sector involvement in fish and wildlife management. Consultants now do the bulk of environmental impact assessment work. Alberta Conservation Association and other conservation organizations carry out the bulk of species inventories and habitat enhancement work.

ACCRU: THE ALBERTA COOPERATIVE CONSERVATION RESEARCH UNIT
[MICHAEL SULLIVAN]

There has been a long and beneficial association in Alberta between fish and wildlife managers and university researchers. At the formation of the University of Alberta Zoology Department [currently the Biological Sciences Department] in the 1940s, Drs. R.B. Miller and William Rowan initiated landmark research to solve questions posed by the first generation of Alberta resource managers. Improving the methods of stocking trout, unravelling the mysteries of an economically devastating fish parasite, investigating the mysterious ten-year cycle in various wildlife populations and solving "the riddle of migration" are examples of early and valuable close collaborations. These collaborations continued over the years through cooperative research projects, training of graduate students, specialized training of provincial staff, and cooperation with the logistics of complex field operations. The value of formalizing and strengthening this relationship often was discussed over campfires or conference room beers. The experiences of Alberta wildlifers collaborating with workers in officially sanctioned Wildlife and Fisheries Cooperative Units in Ontario, Alaska, and Wyoming (to name a few) reinforced the desire to form a similar organization in Alberta.

A fledgling Co-op was finally instituted in 2002, primarily through the hard work of University of Alberta professors Drs. Bob Hudson and Bill Samuel. The Alberta Cooperative Conservation Research Unit (ACCRU) is based at the University of Alberta, but enjoys the collaboration of academic staff from all three Alberta universities (Alberta, Calgary, and Lethbridge). Its goals are three-fold: to produce reliable scientific information that has direct value for stewards of sustainable wildlife and fisheries resources; to train graduate students with both the academic and applied skills needed to be effective resource managers; and to provide cutting-edge training and upgrading to fisheries and wildlife professionals. In its short duration, the Co-op Unit has hosted conferences and courses on topics as diverse as chronic wasting disease, wildlife handling techniques, and the ethics of hunting. Graduate students are able to take advantage of the presence of experienced wildlife staff in getting advice and direction for applied projects. And those same graduate students often reciprocate in teaching the old dogs new tricks about statistics and computers. With the increased urbanization of students and the rapid, complex advances of resource sciences, this type of close collaboration between academics and field managers has become a critical need. Maintaining these strong ties is a valued tradition in Alberta and should serve us well into the future.

However, no central organization oversees these many efforts that are often haphazard and at times, even at odds with one another. Perhaps this is a future role that the provincial authority, through a renewed Fish and Wildlife Division can fulfill. A new government authority could show leadership as the overseer, or systems manager, to set policy and direction for the management of all biodiversity, to ensure that other agencies have the capacity to carry out on-the-ground responsibilities, and to monitor and measure results to ensure success is occurring in an iterative and adaptive management process.

A new way of thinking about fish and wildlife as a part of overall ecosystem health; new and renewed partnerships that garner enthusiasm, knowledge and resources; and effective tools: these are perhaps what is required to manage fish and wildlife in the new millennium. There may even be some new tools, like habitat objectives, no-net-loss of wildlife habitat, and habitat mitigation banks, that we haven't even examined yet. And perhaps that's the biggest reason for a book like this: getting our profession to think about where it's been and where it's going and what it needs to get there. Along the way, we need to celebrate our fish and wildlife resource, our successes with fish and wildlife management, and the individuals who have committed entire lifetimes to achieving such a positive outcome.

In Closing...

In the late 1800s, overexploitation of harvestable game prompted a number of individuals to champion the eras of preservation and later, conservation. One hundred years later, the loss of wildlife habitat and its effect on populations is apparent. Hopefully, as it did a century ago, this realization will again prompt a body of individuals to champion a new era, one that focusses not only on preserving wildlife and wildlife habitat, but also biodiversity, ecological functioning, and all the natural capital that Alberta has been blessed with.

Thinking outside the box will be the challenge for the next generation of fish and wildlife managers who will have to conceive new solutions to maintain this resource as a part of the Alberta Advantage. Fortunately, as Foote and Sullivan point out below, this younger cohort, poised to take us through the next century, are well suited for what will no doubt be a daunting task.

TIME FOR A COOPERATIVE, UNIFIED APPROACH...

A cooperative, unified approach is not a new idea. John Stelfox, talking about the man who hired him, Eric Huestis, recalls the vision of the 1950s. "Huestis believed strongly in a cooperative, unified approach to managing all natural, renewable resources, rather than a number of separate competing agencies, each vying for the top and for budgets. During the 1950s, Forest Officers, Conservation Officers and biologists worked together as a team on wildlife and fisheries matters and shared the use of Government equipment, accommodation, and facilities, etc. This kept Government costs to a minimum and it broadened our knowledge by constantly working with staff from allied government agencies. Everyone worked together, with a broader understanding for the common goal of properly managing all renewable resources."

One would hope that our government that so smartly eliminated the economic debt would then invest resources to repay the "ecological debt" that was run up to pay the former.

ERNIE EWASCHUK.

THE FUTURE OF WILDLIFE AND FISHERIES MANAGEMENT IN ALBERTA: THE PROMISE IN OUR YOUNG BIOLOGISTS

[DRS. A. LEE FOOTE AND MICHAEL G. SULLIVAN[2]]

Who will be in the driver's seat to steer Alberta's wildlife management in the years 2005-2025; what are their credentials and beliefs? A good place to look for those answers is in the offices of the Provincial Fish and Wildlife Division or the Alberta Conservation Association. A recent informal poll of the new wildlife biologists in the coffee room of one Edmonton office showed a surprising profile. Most of the new Provincial Biologist staff had never fired a gun or caught a fish, nor do they ever intend to. Yucca moths and leopard frogs rated higher on priority scales than bighorns. Computer skills far outweigh canoeing and snowshoeing skills. Most new biologists are female and none had heard of Jack O'Connor, Andy Russell, or George Mitchell. Their formative influences were Owl Magazine, David Suzuki, and Dave Schindler. Many got into biology as a profession to try to *stop* hunters and fishermen from killing animals.

Today's biologists grew up in a province with a population three times denser than it was in the 1960s; no unallocated forest; and wilderness entirely confined to parks. Northern Alberta has never been anything but an industrial landscape and Fort McMurray has always been a booming city. Concepts like "developing fisheries", "underexploited resources", and "inaccessible wilderness" are nothing more than fascinating historical anecdotes to be filed away alongside the fur trade and buffalo hunters. Their broad resumes show they are computer fluent, aware of social, political, and economic forces affecting wildlife resources, idealistic and brimming with the belief that they can make a difference.

Within this demographic there is cause for great hope and encouragement but all too often their qualifications are seen as inadequate or even as a threat to many of our 50-plus year-old colleagues. Are these newbies anti-hunting? Can they pull their own weight in field settings? Do they know the difference between a brook and a rainbow trout? There is much more to these questions than meets the eye. Are they *worthy* of being stewards of our precious wildlife resources?

What these questions really represent is a deep professional concern for the future of Alberta wildlife management juxtaposed with a collective fear of change and a sense of helplessness in steering the torrents of redirection taking place around our profession. We have a great dilemma. To whom do we pass the torch? The solution requires understanding, tolerance, patience and adaptation across the generations. Knowing where we came from is essential to knowing where we are going, hence the need for a book such as *Fish, Fur and Feathers*.

Decades of ecological study have demonstrated the intricate complexity of natural systems. Simplistic concepts for manipulating Nature have repeatedly led to resource management failures. Modern wildlife and fisheries management isn't rocket science; it is far more complex (think about it; we put a man on the moon, but we can't keep cod in the ocean). The new generation of biologists has the technology and the knowledge to make sense of the immense complexity of multi-species interactions, economic and social drivers, and global changes. A Leslie matrix seems like a child's arithmetic lesson in comparison to a modern cumulative effects simulation model, but the new generation accepts such tools as a matter of course. In fact, they recognize the impossibility of making intelligent decisions without such complex tools. For them, accessing digital information is second nature, quantitative treatment of data to generate defensible forecasts and management strategies are expectations; multi-ethnic and mixed-gender work settings are the norm, the importance of communication skills is dogma, as are the subtleties of economic tradeoffs, demographic shifts, stakeholder inputs, and human dimensions of wildlife. They are schooled in advanced techniques of creative teamwork, scenario modelling, adaptive management, stakeholder analysis, and Best Management Practices. These concepts did not even exist during the 1970s.

Indeed, our treasured concepts from the 1970s are considered fair game by the new generation. Today's students question paradigms, as should all

409

critical-thinking scientists. "Let sleeping dogmas die" is a basis for scientific advancement. We old guys shouldn't be offended that our cherished institutions (e.g., maximum sustained yield, diversity of edges, sustainable development) are being re-examined to see if they remain valid, should be recycled with new additions, or simply and utterly discarded. As mentors, it is our job to make sure the baby isn't thrown out with the bath water, but we must surely throw out old bath water.

As for pulling their own weight, most of the fresh recruits are in far better physical shape, have healthier diets, and take better care of themselves than the older generation. Emergency trips to the nearest town because the tobacco ran out—is a story from the distant past. Firearms? Most have replaced proficiency using a 30.06 with the knowledge that most bear "problems" can be avoided through simple precautions. For the new generation, today's fieldwork is, above all, governed by the concept of "leaving a lighter footprint". The old-timers' stories of sampling fish with rotenone and detonator cord are listened to with horror, not humour.

What about the traditional bloodsport of public meetings? How will these sensitive and thoughtful young women and men react when confronted with angry, shouting commercial fishermen? Perhaps we should reflect on these too-often disturbing situations and question our own roles in facilitating them. Do these traditional conflicts escalate because of too much testosterone and posturing on both sides? Few, if any, macho gill-netters or angry Fish and Gamers will even begin a raised-voice argument with a polite young woman who obviously knows a heck of a lot about the management of the resource. A change from traditional roles may be precisely what these situations demand, and what the new generation can provide.

Do *they* know the difference between a jackfish and a walleye? Would *we* recognize the difference

between a shorthead and a slimy sculpin or a boreal owl from a northern saw-whet owl? They also are less likely to mistake "good game qualities" for ecological importance. Natural history and local conditions can be learned quickly by either party on an as-needed basis. Working together, the naturalist skills of all are elevated. Even so, critical-thinking skills trump encyclopedic knowledge every time.

Critical thinking and change are essential. Do we have 20-years of wildlife field experience, or one year of experience 20 times?

Finally, an unspoken initiation or "secret handshakes" of acceptance into the culture of wildlifers has traditionally been proficiency with rod or gun. The simple fact that most new biologists come from a non-hunting background does not mean they are anti-hunting. Most are willing to learn the skills or at least to understand and accept that hunting is a passion for some and not for others. We too should accept that the pleasure the new generation takes from seeing a black-throated green warbler may be as real and tangible as our satisfaction in calling a 50-inch moose (though one aspiring biologist quipped "Gosh, that's not a very tall moose!"). Virtually all people can enjoy the health aspects of consuming wild fish and game even if they eschew beef, pork and chicken. If outdated acceptance criteria remain, the new breed of biologist is not likely to measure up—is likely to be passed over for promotion—will ultimately become disenchanted, and inevitably leave the field. This would be a tragedy.

What role does our more senior cadre of seasoned, experienced biologists play in all this? First and foremost, we should welcome and learn from the young reinforcements; secondly, we should impart knowledge gracefully. Despite an amazing list of wildlife success stories we also need to recognize we have a frustrating lack of progress in certain areas (examples include: endangered species protection, special places, fisheries harvest control, non-game wildlife, habitat fragmentation, access

"The definition of insanity is doing the same thing over and over and expecting different results."
JACK WARD THOMAS

management, illegal harvests, integrated resource management). There is no need for new biologists to have to repeat our mistakes, or reinvent our hard-earned wheels. We need to find ways to share our knowledge, expertise, and duties in a mentoring environment of mutual respect. Finally, we should propel the best of our new gladiators into roles of responsibility to represent the resource and us. The teamwork of new and old biologist is likely to earn new respect, garner greater public support, and elevate the status of agencies. This approach may involve continuing to improve ties with policy makers, research scientists, university environments, the media, and, importantly, children. Eventually we should work ourselves out of a job, hand over the reins and know that our best efforts will live on in the work of another generation. In short, incoming biologists are beautifully prepared for what is to come and are wildlife and fishery resources' best assurance of an adaptive and effective future.

"After we've lost a natural place, it's gone for everyone—hikers, campers, boaters, bicyclists, animal watchers, fishers, hunters and wildlife—a complete and absolutely democratic tragedy of emptiness. For this reason, it's vital that we overthrow differences, find common ground in our shared love for the natural world, and work together to defend the wild."
RICHARD K. NELSON

411

"This then, is the story of the management and conservation of fish and wildlife in Alberta over the past century. It is a story whose end has not come; it will never come. Fish and wildlife management is ongoing, not only in Alberta, but elsewhere in Canada, and indeed throughout the world."
ERIC HOLMGREN 1986

References • EPILOGUE

[1] Van Tighem, Kevin. 2000. Home Range: Writings on Conservation and Restoration. Altitude Publishing. Canmore, Alberta pp. 196, 204

[2] ALF, a relative newcomer to Alberta and MGS, a life-long resident of Alberta, bring complementary perspectives to this article.

Index

413